ShaderX^4

Advanced Rendering Techniques

ShaderX⁴

Advanced Rendering Techniques

Edited by Wolfgang Engel

CHARLES RIVER MEDIA, INC.

Hingham, Massachusetts

Cover Design: Tyler Creative
Cover Images: Copyright 2005 Microsoft Corporation. Images from Age of Empires III developed by Ensemble Studios.
Reprinted with permission.

CHARLES RIVER MEDIA, INC.
10 Downer Avenue
Hingham, Massachusetts 02043
781-740-0400
781-740-8816 (FAX)
info@charlesriver.com
www.charlesriver.com

This book is printed on acid-free paper.

Wolfgang Engel. *ShaderX⁴: Advanced Rendering Techniques.*
ISBN: 1-58450-425-0

Library of Congress Cataloging-in-Publication Data

Engel, Wolfgang F.
  ShaderX4 : advanced rendering techniques / [Wolfgang Engel].— 1st ed.
    p. cm.
  Includes index.
  ISBN 1-58450-425-0 (hardcover with cd : alk. paper)
  1. Computer games—Programming. 2. Three-dimensional display systems.
  3. Computer graphics. I. Title.
  QA76.76.C672E64 2005
  794.8'1526—dc22

                    2005032282

Printed in the United States of America
05 7 6 5 4 3 2 First Edition

Contents

Preface

The talented editors and contributors of this book spent eight months writing, selecting, editing, and finalizing the articles for this newest volume of the *ShaderX* series. We hope you find these state-of-the-art graphics-programming articles useful in your own work. As with the other *ShaderX* books, all of the topics cover ready-to-use ideas and procedures that can solve many or (all) of your daily graphics programming challenges.

I would like to thank the section editors for the fantastic job they did. The work of Kenneth Hurley, Sebastien St. Laurent, Natalya Tatarchuk, Eric Haines, Tom Forsyth, and Matthias Wloka ensures that the quality of the series stands up to the expectations of our readers. The volunteer proofreaders, Juan Rufes and Jesper Lehmann Poulson, also did a great job! The great-looking cover image comes from the *Age of Empire III* team. Thanks for allowing us to use it. The team at Charles River Media made the whole project happen: Dave Pallai, Jenifer Niles, and the production team, who took the articles and made them into a book.

Special thanks also goes to our families and friends, who spent many evenings and weekends during the long book production cycle without us.

I hope you have as much fun reading this book as we had creating it.

—Wolfgang Engel

P.S. Plans for an upcoming project named ShaderX^5 are already in progress. Any comments, proposals, and suggestions are highly welcome (*wolf@shaderx.com*).

About the Editors

Dean Calver

Dean Calver figured that out at age 2 that games are fun, and has spent the following years working out how to make better games. Having no real preference for console or PC has produced a mixed career flipping between them for every project. Professionally, he started on a war game, then did three years of a racing game followed by an X-COM style game, then arcade classic updates, and currently working on a 3D graphic adventure. Dean studies various subjects including optics, mathematics, and other geeky things for fun.

Wolfgang Engel

Wolfgang is a senior graphics Programmer in the core technology group at Rockstar San Diego. He is the editor of the *ShaderX* book series and the author of *Programming Vertex and Pixel Shaders*. Wolfgang is a frequent speaker on conferences world-wide and publishes articles on several websites. He writes the X-Gen Column on the XGI developer web-site.

Tom Forsyth

Tom Forsyth has been obsessed by 3D graphics since seeing Elite on his ZX Spectrum. Since then he has always tried to make hardware beg for mercy. Tom has written triangle-drawing routines on the Spectrum, Sinclair QL, Atari ST, Sega 32X, Saturn, Dreamcast, PC, GamePark32 and XBox, and he's getting quite good at them now. Tom's coding past includes writing curved-surface stuff for Sega and graphics drivers for 3Dlabs. Currently he works in Guildford at Muckyfoot Productions, where past projects are *Urban Chaos, StarTopia* and *Blade II*.

Eric Haines

Eric Haines, a graduate of the Cornell Program of Computer Graphics, is currently a lead software engineer at Autodesk, Inc. He coauthored the book *Real-Time Rendering*, now in its second edition. He is also a member of the editorial board for the journal of graphics tools, the archivist for the *Graphics Gems* repository, and the webmaster for *ACM Transactions on Graphics*. He is currently addicted to the game *Battlefield 1942* . His homepage is at *http://www.erichaines.com* .

Kenneth Hurley

Kenneth has worked for notable game and technology companies such as Electronic Arts, Intel, and most recently was a senior engineer at NVIDIA Corporation. While there, he participated in the Xbox hardware and numerous video games including Tiger Woods Golf. Kenneth has been a consultant for several Silicon Valley companies and worked with the United States government on the latest military equipment, including the highly acclaimed Land Warrior. Kenneth's passion and experience for the gaming industry is what brings him to the helm of Signature Devices. With over 20 years of experience, this is Kenneth's second start-up as an independent developer, giving him perspective and a strong understanding of the demands of running an up and coming development company. He has contributed to best selling computer books on 3-D graphics and he is a requested speaker at conventions and workshops around the country. Kenneth received his Bachelor of Science degree in computer science from the University of Maryland.

Sebastien St. Laurent

Sebastien St. Laurent holds a degree in Computer Engineering from Sherbrooke University in Quebec (Canada) where he graduated at top of his class in 1999. Since then, he worked on many video game titles including: *Space Invaders, Dave Mira Freestyle BMX, Dave Mira Freestyle BMX2, Aggressive Inline, BMX XXX*. Sebastien is now currently employed with the Microsoft Corporation where he is a graphics developer for the Microsoft Game Studios. Sebastien St. Laurent is also a published author who has written *Shaders for Game Programmers and Artists* and *The COMPLETE Effect and HLSL Guide*.

Natalya Tatarchuk

Natalya is a Senior Software Engineer in the ATI Research, Inc. 3D Application Research Group where she is investigating innovative graphics techniques in the real-time domain for current and future platforms. In the past she has been the lead for the tools group at the 3D Application Research Group, working on a pioneering real-time shader development environment RenderMonkeyTM IDE. Natalya has been in the graphics industry for many years, previously working on award-winning haptic 3D modeling software, scientific visualization libraries and various other projects. She has published articles in the *ShaderX* books, *Game Programming Gems, Game Developer* magazine and Gamasutra.com, amongst others. She has presented novel techniques at various conferences throughout the world, including SIGGRAPH sketches and presentations, GDC, GDC-Europe, Microsoft Meltdown and Russian GDCs. Natalya graduated with BAs in Computers Science and Mathematics from Boston University and is currently pursuing an SM in Computer Science with concentration in Graphics at Harvard University.

Matthias Wloka

Matthias Wloka works in the technical developer relations group at NVIDIA. There, he gets to collaborate with game developers on, performance-optimizing their game among other work. He is also always tinkering with the latest graphics hardware to explore the limits of interactive real-time rendering. Before joining NVIDIA, Matthias was a game developer himself, working for GameFX/THQ Inc. He received his M.S. in computer science from Brown University in 1990, and his B.S. from Christian Albrechts University in Kiel , Germany in 1987.

About the Contributors

Brief biographies are included here for those contributors who submitted them.

Andrew Aksyonoff

Andrew's FAQ on realtime software rendering, created back in 1998, is still recognized by Russian graphics programmers. This background allowed him to work on KDlab's award-winning "Perimeter" RTS title in 2002. He's currently the technical director at SkyFallen, working on "The Blood Magic" RPG. Andrew manages research and development of the inhouse engine and provides support to the companies licensing it.

Elisabeth André

Elisabeth André is a full professor for Computer Science at Augsburg University, Germany, where she is chairing the laboratory for Multimedia Concepts and Applications. She has been teaching various courses on AI and Computer Games at her university and has been on the program, committee of several games-related events, including ICEC'2004, the academic track of "Computer Science and Magic" in association with Game Convention Developer Conference 2005, Intetain 2005, and Edutainment 2006. Futhermore, she has been conducting various projects on educational game environments for the EU, including Puppet (1998–2001) and eCircus (planned start early in 2006).

Barnabás Aszódi

Barnabás Aszódi is a Ph.D. student of the computer graphics programmer at the Budapest University of Technology and Economics. He works on multimedia systems and GPU algorithms aiming at photo-realistic real-time rendering.

Wessam Bahnassi

Wessam is a hardcore old-time gamer. Games are one thing in life that interests him the most.

Actually, he is interested in everything, ranging from electronics to music to architecture (his current study) to novelty, and ultimately to programming and shaders! Being an experienced C++ programmer for over six years, Wessam has done many real-time 3D projects based on Direct3D. That is when Microsoft rewarded him as a Most Valuable Professional (MVP) in DirectX. Currently, he is a lead programmer at In|Framez, where he is employing his experience in designing and programming the DirectSkeleton 3D engine.

Philippe Beaudoin

Philippe is working on his Ph.D. at the University of Montreal while teaching computer graphics at the Ecole Polytechnique. His research interest is in 3D rendering and animation and focuses mainly on technologies to increase quality and performances of real-time applications and video games. Before he went back to school, Philippe worked as a hardware architect at Matrox Graphics where he developed various vertex and pixel shader technologies. He also developed video games for various consoles while working at Digital Fiction.

Florian Born

After his studies of mathematics and physics, Florian worked as a teacher before he started at Vulpine in 2000. In 2003, he and some collegues from Vulpine founded Trinigy, a German middleware provider for the Vision game engine.

Like many others, Florian started his career in computer programming 20 years ago on a C64. Later, on a PC, he was especially fascinated by 3D graphics and the technology behind it.

Jordi Catà

Jordi is a senior software engineer at the University of Girona (participating in the GameTools European Project) and leader of his own software development company. He works adding new illumination techniques (like Obscurances) in 3D game engines (Crystal Space, Ogre) at Girona Graphics Group. His research interest is in 3D rendering and focuses to increase quality and perfomance of 3D real-time applications, video games, and DCC from a software engineering point of view.

Yung-feng Chi

Yung-feng is a software engineer at XGI Technology Inc. in Taiwan where he works on 3D demos with the newest shader technology. He is interested in GPU algorithms aiming at lifelike real-time rendering and offline photo-realistic rendering.

Martin Christen

Martin started programming on a C16 back in 1985. He developed many shareware games for the Amiga and MacOS. In 1996, he founded Algomedia Software, a game company releasing MacOS titles. Today, he works at GEONOVA *http://www.geonova.ch*, the 3D geoinformation company located in Switzerland.

He is programming the 3D engine for terrain visualization. In his spare time, he writes demos and tutorials for the OpenGL Shading Language at *http://www.clockworkcoders.com*

Carsten Dachsbacher

Carsten Dachsbacher is a Ph.D. student in Computer Graphics at the University of Erlangen-Nuremberg, Germany. His research focuses on interactive, hardware-assisted computer graphics; in particular, he is working on interactive global illumination techniques, procedural models for rendering photo-realistic virtual terrains, and point-based-rendering. He worked as a freelancer for various (game) companies programming mainly real-time 3D graphics and published some of his work at conferences and in books and magazines.

Joachim Diepstraten

Joachim is a Ph.D. Student at the Visualization and Interactive Systems Group at the German University Stuttgart in Computer Science. He was interested in real-time computer graphics at the age of 15 by starting to write his own EGA and VGA graphics and rasterization routines first in PASCAL and later with C/ASM under the now infamous DOS operating system. With the death of DOS, he moved on to Sun's Java to program a real-time software 3D engine in Java and even a simple realtime raytracer. But he soon noticed that hardware graphics accelerators are the key to maximum interactive performance. Now he is doing research on finding solutions for interactive mobile graphics, squeezing the latest out of the programmable features of graphics hardware, non-photorealstic-rendering and rendering of everyday and natural objects using graphics hardware for achieving real-time performance by following his personal slogan: If it cannot be done in real-time, it is impractical!

Bryan Dudash

Graduating Virginia Tech, Bryan made the big move across the country to work in Seattle for the now defunct Sierra Online. After working at Sierra and getting his Master's at the University of Washington, he needed a change. Desiring a smaller company, he joined a startup Xbox game company Escape Factory, working hard on an unreleased Unreal Engine license title. Publisher issues forced the cancellation, and he joined NVIDIA in 2003 as a member of the Developer Technology (devtech) team. In late 2004, he made a slightly larger move to Tokyo, Japan. He spends his days (and nights) educating developers on the black art of GPU programming, studying Japanese, eating sushi, and fighting off ninjas.

Mike Eißele

After graduating in Computer Science, Mike joined the Visualization and Interactive Systems Group as a Ph.D. student at the University of Stuttgart. He started programming on the C64 where he coded real-time graphic demos. For hardware accelerated graphics programming, he started with OpenGL but switched to DirectX since the introduction of the Vertex- and PixelShader paradigms.

Dustin Franklin

Dustin is currently the Lead Graphics Engineer at Mystic Game Development, where he works on next-generation middleware packages. He just started studying (among other things) at Johns Hopkins University this fall as an undergraduate. Dustin is also a Microsoft Most Valuable Professional (MVP) in DirectX. He loves music (the Red Hot Chili Peppers are by far his favorite), playing sports (of any kind), and good old DuckHunt. His Web site is *www.circlesoft.org*.

Sergi Funtané

Sergi is a computer engineering student at the University of Girona, Spain. He developed an OpenGL port for PlayStation®2. He is currently working on GPU algorithms to improve graphics realism in video games and DCC applications for the Girona Graphics Group in the University of Girona. He is participating in the Gametools european project.

Holger Grün

Holger started his love affair with 3D real-time graphics back in the 1993 when it was all about writing perspectively correct software texture mappers. In 1997, he joined a UK-based game middleware developer as a research engineer. After that, he headed the development team of a now defunct German games company and afterwards worked for a simulation company developing CIGs (computer image generator) software. Holger now works for Intel as technical marketing engineer—his love affair with 3D graphics still intact.

Christian Kleinhuis

Since the early 1990s Christian has been addicted to real-time computer animation when he got an Amiga500 at the age of 13. He's played a lot with (realtime-)fractal generation, and after spending years as a web developer is now back on track aspiring a degree in Computer Science at the University of Bonn working as a visualization engineer in fluid dynamics.

Janne Kontkanen

Janne has 15 years of background in computer graphics. It all began as a hobby around 1990 and later grew into a master's degree and a career in industry. His work experience ranges from scientific computing (Finnish IT Center for Science) to developing real-time computer graphics middleware (Hybrid Graphics Ltd.) and giving lectures and training in software development and design (Tieturi). Currently, he is working toward his Ph.D. related to illumination and rendering at the Helsinki University of Technology. His research interest and expertise covers the rendering techniques used in both real-time and offline graphics.

Samuli Laine

Samuli Laine is currently a full-time Ph.D. student at Helsinki University of Technology. He is on study leave from Hybrid Graphics Ltd., where he has worked for several years developing real-time graphics software, offline visibility preprocessing tools, and graphics hardware architecture design. Most of Laine's current research is concentrated on efficient computation of soft shadows in offline renderers.

István Lazányi

István is a Ph.D. student at the Budapest University of Technology and Economics since 2003. His research interests include material models global illumination algorithms, and GPU programming for realistic rendering.

Ping-Man Lam

Ping-Man Lam received the B.Eng. degree in electronics from City University of Hong Kong in 2002. He is currently a Ph.D. student in the Department of Electronic Engineering, City University of Hong Kong. His research interests include global illumination algorithms and GPU programming. He has several years of GPU programming experience.

Chi-Sing Leung

Chi Sing Leung received his Ph.D. in computer science from the Chinese University of Hong Kong. He is currently an Associate Professor in the Department of Electronic Engineering, City University of Hong Kong. His research interests include neural computing, communications, global illumination algorithms, and GPU programming. He has published over 50 international journal papers. From 1995 to 1997, he worked on the bidirectional associative memory model. He proved that the recalling processing of higher order BAM is unstable and proposed a statistical method to analyze the behavior of higher order BAM. In 1997, he proposed a neural-based data protection method for vector quantization data over noisy channels. From 1998 to 2002, he worked on the property of extended Kalman filtering learning in neural networks. From 2001, he has been working on several projects related to compressing image based rendering data. In 2005, he received the 2005 IEEE Transactions on Multimedia Prize Paper Award for his paper titled, "The Plenoptic Illumination Function" published in 2002. His research interests include global illumination algorithms and GPU programming. In addition, from 2001 to 2005, he provided consultancy service for DBS bank (Hong Kong) Limited.

Morgan McGuire

Morgan creates 3D and video technologies at Brown University and commercial game companies like ROBLOX and Blue Axion. He maintains the Open Source G3D Engine and writes for industry and research publications. Morgan is currently advising courses in game development at Brown and Harvard.

Alex Méndez-Feliu

Alex is a Ph.D. student in the Girona Graphics Group at the University of Girona. His work aims to apply global illumination techniques and its simplified forms, like obscurances, in video game and real-time environments. He is participating in the Gametools project of the VI European Framework.

Jason Mitchell

Jason is a software engineer at Valve Software in Bellevue, Washington where he works on cutting-edge graphics techniques. Prior to joining Valve, Jason was the team lead of the 3D Application Research Group at ATI Research where he worked for eight years.

Martin Mittring

Martin started his first experiments early with text-based computers, which led to a passion for computer and graphics in particular. He studied computer science and worked in a German games company. He is currently lead graphics programmer at Crytek where he worked on the Polybump tools and various modules for the game FarCry.

Michael Nischt

Michael is a student researcher in Computer Science and Multimedia at the University of Augsburg, Germany. Since 2001, he has been supervising practical courses on computer games and animated agents. Currently, he is completing his master's thesis on an agent-based interface to graphics engines. From the very beginning of his studies, the animation and rendering of virtual characters has been one of his main research interests. While conducting practical projects in this area, he has achieved a great deal of experience in utilizing both OpenGL and DirectX as well as their shading languages for hardware accelerated graphics programming.

Masahiko Nitanda

Masahiko liked playing a PC game every day when he was a boy—and he is a Japanese game programmer now. Recently, he developed a 3D RPG game for PSP, and previously, he developed an action game for Xbox®. Various troubles will be encountered in game development, but he believes that it can overcome by the love of it, and compassion for others.

Manuel M. Oliveira

Manuel M. Oliveira received his Ph.D. in Computer Science from the University of North Carolina at Chapel Hill. He is currently an Associate Professor at Instituto de Informática, Universidade Federal do Rio Grande do Sul (UFRGS), in Brazil. Before joining the faculty at UFRGS, he worked for two years as an Assistant Professor of Computer Science at the State University of New York at Stony Brook. His interests include image-based modeling and rendering, innovative uses of graphics hardware, real-time rendering, 3D photography, surface reconstruction from point clouds, medical applications of imaging technologies, and building virtual replicas of real environments. His homepage is *http://www.inf.ufrgs.br/~oliveira*.

Eric Paquette

Eric Paquette is a professor at the École de Technologie Supérieure engineering school in the Software & IT Engineering department. His research interests include realistic image synthesis, simulation of natural phenomena, programmable graphics hardware, and visualization. Professor Paquette received his B.Sc. in Computer Science from Université de Sherbrooke, Canada, his M.Sc. degree in Computer Science from Université de Montréal, Canada, and his Ph.D. degree in Computer Science from Université de Montréal, Canada and Université Joseph Fourier, France.

Kurt Pelzer

Kurt Pelzer is a senior software engineer at Piranha Bytes, where he works on the PC game *Gothic 3*. Kurt was involved in the development of *Gothic* and the top-selling *Gothic II* (awarded as "RPG of the Year" in Germany during 2001 and 2002, respectively). In 2003 followed the add-on *Gothic II—The Night of the Raven*. Prior to that, he was a senior programmer at Codecult, developed Codecult's 3D-Engine Codecreatures, and built several real-time simulations and tech-demos on that technology (for example, a simulation of the Shanghai "Transrapid" track for SIEMENS AG, a tech-demo for NVIDIA's GeForce 4 Ti launch, and the well-known Codecreatures Benchmark Pro). Kurt has published in *ShaderX 2, GPU Gems, GPU Gems 2,* and *Game Programming Gems 4.*

Emil Persson

Emil holds a master's degree in Computer Science and Engineering from Luleå University of Technology. After his studies, Emil joined ATI in 2004 where he's working with top game developers to deliver the best performance and latest technology in their games. Emil also works on the ATI SDK, providing technical sample applications and papers. In his spare time, Emil runs the site *www.humus.ca* where he provides demo applications showing various techniques, tricks, or just plain eye-candy.

Pierre Poulin

Pierre Poulin has been a professor since 1994 in the Department of Computer Science (IRO) at the Universite de Montreal. His research interests include realistic and real-time rendering, simulation of natural phenomena, image-based modeling and rendering, visualization, and animation.

Aras Pranckevičius

The same day he got his first ZX Spectrum, Aras wrote some mosaic-drawing program. Apparently, that left him impressed, and since then he's been doing graphics demos, small games and similar stuff on various platforms. Aras has worked in a couple of software companies, with works ranging from databases/Web to motion recognition to videogames. He has a master's degree in Computer Science, has a nice family, and right now works as a senior programmer in an "ordinary software" company. He still devotes all of his spare time to real-time computer graphics and demoscene.

Gilberto Rosado

Gilberto Rosado is a graduate of DigiPen Institute of Technology, where he studied video game programming for four years. His senior year game project at DigiPen, *Kisses,* was a finalist at the 2005 Independent Games Festival. After working at Pipeworks Software on *Godzilla: Save the Earth,* Gil joined Rainbow Studios where he now works as a graphics programmer on killer new games. Gil has also been published in *AI Game Programming Wisdom 2.*

Mateu Sbert

Mateu Sbert is professor and head of the Institute of Informatics and Applications at the University of Girona, and has authored around 100 technical papers. His research interests include the application of Monte Carlo and Integral Geometry techniques to radiosity and global illumination.

Daniel Scherzer

Daniel Scherzer is master student at the Vienna University of Technology with his research interest in the field of real-time rendering. He began his computer life by playing on a C64. What started out as a way to avoid homework ("Mum, I'm working on my computer!") became a serious addiction with his first PC. At some point, he took up programming to boost the capabilities of his computer and still tries to do so.

Thorsten Scheuermann

Thorsten is a software engineer in ATI's 3D Application Research Group where he works on graphics demos and novel rendering techniques as part of ATI's Demo Team. Prior to working at ATI he was a member of the Effective Virtual Environments research group at the University of North Carolina at Chapel Hill, which gave him the opportunity to play with all sorts of expensive VR toys and to create sickness-inducing immersive games. Thorsten received a master's degree in Computer Science from UNC and previously studied at the University of Karlsruhe in Germany.

Christian Schüler

Christian Schüler is a software engineer at Phenomic Game Development in Ingelheim, Germany, where he drives engine development for the upcoming *Spellforce 2*. He has been coding since the C64 age, and actively works in the games industry since 2002.

Tibor Schütz

Tibor Schütz started experimenting with interface devices in the late 1980s and switched his main interest to computer graphics and simulation in the middle 1990s. Studying computer science from 2000–2005, he is now occupied with the integration of CAD functionality into VR environments. His spare time interests also include the artistic use of computers for creating coded animations.

Oles V. Shishkovtsov

At the age of 13, Oles became interested in programming and graphics. In the following years, he won two national competitions on programming along with many regional ones, and became a participant of the Junior Academy of Science of Ukraine at 17. At 19, Oles started to work for a small game-development company White Lynx as a software developer engineer/graphics programmer where he successfully completed three projects. Since 2000, Oles is working for GSC-GameWorld as an engine architect/team leader and is doing R&D in his free time. He spent the last three years on *S.T.A.L.K.E.R.: Shadows Of Chernobyl.* Oles' primary areas of interest are computer graphics, networking, and physics.

Marco Spoerl

Just as everyone else, Marco started programming way back on a C64. After buying a PC (actually just because of his affection to chainsaw-wielding space marines), he got hold of computer graphics. After receiving his diploma in Computer Science, he worked at Codecult Software, contributing to the Codecreatures Engine and the Code-creatures-Benchmark-Pro. After a short walk on the wild side as a freelance software developer, he's currently earning his keep working on driving training simulators for trains, trucks, cars, and tanks. Actually, he's seriously thinking about opening his own game studio.

Vlad Stamate

Vlad became passionate about computer games ever since he discovered them on a Spectrum Sinclair 128+. Games were his road to learning computer programming. After studying in a computer science high school, he graduated with a BSc degree in Graphic Design from Richmond College. After graduation, he started working in the R&D department of PowerVR technologies as a design engineer. Currently, Vlad works for Sony Computer Entertainment Europe as part of their Technology Group and is involved in software development for Sony game related products.

Jean-François St. Amour

Jean-François has worked at both ends of the graphics hardware spectrum. He is currently employed at Gameloft's Montreal studio where he works on OpenGL ES capable mobile platforms. He recently completed his M.Sc. at the University of Montreal where he worked on high-quality soft shadows for games and other real-time applications, as well as general-purpose computation on the GPU. Before starting his graduate studies, Jean-François worked at Matrox in the Imaging group.

Nicolau Sunyer

Nicolau is a Ph.D. student at the University of Girona, Spain. He is now working on GPU accelerated global illumination techniques (radiosity, obscurances,...). He is currently a member of the Girona Graphics Group, whose aim is to improve the graphics realism in video games and DCC applications. He is participating in the Gametools European project.

László Szirmay-Kalos

László is a full professor and head of the Computer Graphics Group at the Budapest University of Technology and Economics. He graduated from this university in 1987 and received his Ph.D. in 1990. He is the author of 150 technical papers and five books. His current research interests include global illumination algorithms, and the application of the GPU to speed up these methods.

Imagire Takashi

Takashi has been a professional game programmer for five years and has mainly done work for PlayStation and PlayStation2. Currently, he is programming real-time 3D graphics in his sparetime, while focusing on the newest shader technology. A big number of articles and demos on shader programming can be found on his Web site *http://www.t-pot.com/* (Japanese). His goal is to publish his demos immediately after the release of new shader technology.

Damian Trebilco

Damian holds a first class honours degree in software engineering from Queensland University of Technology. As a result of his dissertation work into simulating emotion in virtual characters, he joined the games company Auran in late 2001. There, he works on graphics and shader-based systems like the Bridge-IT demo used in the Nvidia NV30 launch. In his spare time, Damian works on the OpenGL debugging tool GLIntercept. (*http://glintercept.nutty.org*).

Michael Wimmer

Dr. Michael Wimmer is an assistant professor at the Institute of Computer Graphics and Algorithms of the Vienna University of Technology, where he received his MSc in 1997 and Ph.D. in 2001. His current research interests are real-time rendering, virtual and augmented reality, computer games, real-time visualization of urban environments and rendering of vegetation, and he has (co)authored several scientific papers in the afore-mentioned fields. He is also teaching courses on 3D computer games and real-time rendering.

Tien-Tsin Wong

Tien-Tsin Wong is an associate professor in the Department of Computer Science & Engineering in the Chinese University of Hong Kong (CUHK). He has been programming for the last 17 years, including writing publicly available codes/libraries/demos/toolkit (check his homepage) and codes for all his graphics research. He works on GPU techniques, rendering, image-based relighting, natural phenomenon modeling, and multimedia data compression. He proposed a method to simulate dust accumulation (IEEE CGA 1995) and other surface imperfections (SIGGRAPH 2005). He also proposed, the apparent BRDF, one of the earliest techniques for relighting (precomputed lighting) in 1997. He is a SIGGRAPH author. Besides academic papers, he has written game development related articles in *Graphics Gems V, Graphics Programming Methods, Shader X^3* and *Shader X^4*. Recently, he has been working on projects for general-purpose usage of GPU, such as evolutionary computing (such as genetic algorithms) on GPU, and discrete wavelet transform on GPU. He received the "IEEE Transaction on Multimedia Prize Paper Award 2005" and the "CUHK Young Researcher Award 2004." His web site is at: *http://www.cse.cuhk.edu.hk/~ttwong*

Cyril Zeller

Cyril Zeller works in the developer technology group at NVIDIA. Before joining NVIDIA, Cyril was a senior software engineer developing games at Electronic Arts, Inc. He received a Ph.D. in Computer Vision from the Ecole Polytechnique, France.

Renaldas Zioma

Renald Zioma has been driven (mad) by computer graphics since he saw *ZX Spectrum*. After learning assembly and writing a Tetris clone for his ZX, he switched to PC, finished school, wrote a couple small noncommercial games, gained experience with object-oriented programming and design while working at the software development company, received BS degree in Computer Science from Kaunas University of Technology, and returned to his roots while working as a professional game programmer for the last 18 months. Recently, he finished a demo of a 3D fighting game based on real-time motion recognition for Interamotion, LLC. In his spare time, he is programming demos, games, and organizing small demo/gamescene related events in Lithuania.

GEOMETRY
MANIPULATION

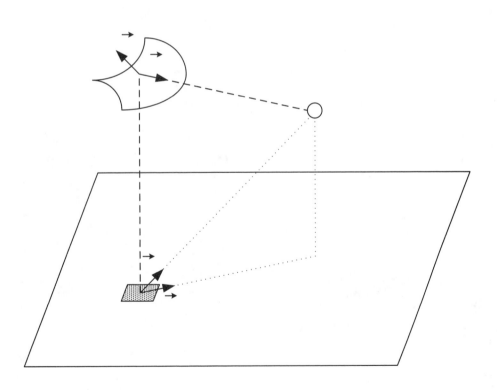

Introduction

Kenneth Hurley

The "Geometry Manipulation" section of the book focuses on the ability of graphic processor units (GPUs) to process and generate geometry in exciting and interesting ways. From "Better Geometry Batching Using Light Buffers" to "Skinning with Anitextures," each author has spent a great deal of time and effort to convey unique ideas to the reader.

"Better Geometry Batching Using Light Buffers" delves into the topic of light buffers and gives details on how to implement them. Light buffers are very similar to but have advantages over traditional deferred shading methods. Renaldas explores the process and shows how his technique can be achieved in real-time applications.

Cyril Zeller is by far one of the smartest people I know. I had the pleasure of working with him at NVIDIA, and I'm sure you see his talent after reading his cloth simulation article. He presents his article with an explanation of the physics involved in cloth simulation and demonstrates how to achieve this on modern GPUs.

Discrete wavelets have found their way into a myriad of applications, from compression to BRDF representation. Tien-Tsin, et al. provide great insight into speed-ups using the GPU versus the CPU on generating a 2D discrete wavelet transformation. His article also explores interesting uses for DWTs by using them for geometric deformation.

Morph target animation is not a new subject, but we wanted to include Christian Kleinhuis' article because it shows how to effectively use the GPU when using morph targets. Because the section was on geometry manipulation, his article pertained very much to this section.

The article "Real-Time Character Animation" takes morph target animation one step further and presents two separate GPU-based vertex modification and rendering methods. These methods avoid recomputation during multiple rendering passes and increase the parallelism of the GPU/CPU interaction, which is tantamount to performance.

"Skinning with AniTextures" is the final article in the section, which describes techniques for using textures for animation. It contains clever tricks to use Shader Model 3.0 texture fetching inside the vertex shader for using in skinning animation. The technique requires Shader Model 3.0 for evaluation of skinning in a vertex shader, but offers other techniques with Shader Model 2.0.

In conclusion, it has been my pleasure to be the section editor for "Geometry Manipulation." I have contributed as much as possible to the ShaderX series and enjoy working with Wolfgang. With the authors contributing great content, I've found myself inspired, and hope to write some articles for the next ShaderX series of books.

1.1

Better Geometry Batching Using Light Buffers

Renaldas Zioma

Introduction

The computational power of a GPU increases at a much higher rate than a CPU [Fernando04]. The GPU alone can process huge amounts of geometry during one frame; however, geometry submission results in a large side cost for the CPU. The importance of feeding the GPU with more geometry in a single call increases every day.

Several techniques, usually called geometry batching, were developed in order to allow a large amount of geometry submission—geometry instancing and atlas textures among them—in one call. However, lighting environments impose great restrictions on the applicability of these techniques in real games. The need for sorting geometry by light and the limited number of lights that can be processed per vertex and per pixel greatly reduce the possibility of batch geometry.

This article discusses an approach for collecting lighting information separately from the scene geometry and storing it in the so-called light buffers. Lighting information is collected before the actual rendering takes place and later is passed in a uniform way to the geometry pixel shaders. The light position, relative direction, color, and attenuation factors are extracted from the light buffers and are used for common per-pixel lighting equations.

Extending existing pixel and vertex shaders with light buffer functionality is a straightforward task. Light buffer implementation, opposite to deferred shading, doesn't impose any additional restrictions on the instance-specific material information.

Common Ways of Lighting the Scene

The following approaches are used to render scenes with large numbers of lights:

- Multi-pass lighting. Several of the most important lights affecting a specific geometry instance are found on the CPU. Light intensity is calculated for each light in a separate rendering pass and is accumulated in the frame buffer using additive blending [Blythe99].
- Several lights are combined in one pass. This is an extension of the multi-pass technique. Several lights affecting specific instances are passed and processed simultaneously in the vertex and pixel shaders.

- Lights for multiple instances are passed to the vertex shader simultaneously. The vertex shader chooses appropriate light according to an index of the instance and passes specific light data to the pixel shader.
- Spherical harmonics for incident lighting. Several lights infinitely distant from the instance can be compressed into a compact representation using spherical harmonics. Lighting information is decompressed in the vertex and pixel shaders during the shading of the instance [Green03].
- Geometry is divided into smaller parts. To reduce the number of lights affecting a single instance, large surfaces, such as terrains, can be subdivided into patches. Relevant lights are then found for each patch separately.

A number of problems can potentially arise when utilizing the previous approaches:

- Large number of render calls. Multi-pass rendering and dividing geometry into smaller parts usually increase the number of render calls substantially. The number of render calls is directly dependent on the complexity of the lighting information (number and types of lights).
- The length of the shaders. The pixel shader length increases substantially when several lights are applied at once. The major drawback is that the number of lights is determined on the whole instance and not on affected pixels, thus making this technique ineffective for large instances lit by many small lights.
- Number of lights passed to the shader is limited by the number of available shader constants. This can be an issue for a geometry-instancing approach because different instances can be affected by different lights, thus requiring N*M lights to be passed to the shader (where N is a number of instances and M is a maximum number of lights affecting one instance).
- Additional CPU cost is required to find the nearest lights for all instances. Such cost is directly dependent on the complexity of potentially visible instances and the number of lights in the scene. CPU cost may be substantial when a very large numbers of instances are used.
- Spherical harmonics are suitable only for infinitely distant lights.

Deferred Shading

Traditionally, geometry is processed along with the actual shading of the primitives. Deferred shading submits the scene geometry only once, storing surface attributes into the additional buffers (G-Buffers). During the scene shading pass, information from the G-Buffers is retrieved at a 1:1 mapping ratio to frame pixels, and each pixel is shaded individually.

Deferred shading has the following advantages over traditional approaches:

- Improves geometry batching. Because geometry and lighting information are processed in separate passes, much better geometry batching is achieved.

- Shader complexity. Very complex shaders might be applied regardless of the length restrictions implied by specific GPUs because shading can be easily divided into several passes.
- Potential pixel shader cost reduction. Only necessary pixels are processed in the shading pass, which can be very important if complex pixel shaders are applied.
- Rendering complexity is reduced. Because geometry and lighting information are processed separately, the resulting complexity is not a combination of both as in the case of traditional rendering.

However, deferred shading has the following drawbacks:

- Huge video memory footprint. All necessary attributes required for the actual shading need to be stored in the G-Buffers. Usually, position, normal, color, glossiness, and material identifiers need to be stored [Hargreaves04]. Although data can be packed, the memory footprint can be significant due to the fact that a 1:1 mapping ratio to frame pixels and high precision in several components are required.
- Huge fill-rate cost. G-Buffers contain large amounts of data; storing and accessing it can be bound by memory bandwidth.
- Introducing additional attributes to the surface requires creation of additional G-Buffers. Because G-Buffers are uniform across the scene, all instances are forced to store these additional attribute values (at least the default values).

Concept of the Light Buffer

Target Games

Several game genres, such as RTS, RPG, and some action games, usually present an almost top-down or bird's-eye view of the world to the player. It is common for such games to have a large number of dynamic units and an especially large amount of static geometry visible to the player. This geometry could be a good target for instancing or batching. However, the same types of games have large numbers of dynamic, arbitrary moving lights as well—for example, missiles, car lights, explosions, and gunfire lights to name a few. Such amounts of dynamic lights prevent geometry batching on a large scale and also require a large amount of CPU processing to determine possibly lit geometry for each light.

Luckily, such games have visual representation that is forgiving for small errors in dynamic lights positioning along the axis perpendicular to the actual game "plane."

Separating Light Information

Deferred shading provides important advantages, compared to traditional rendering, by separating lighting and geometry-specific information. The same idea lies at the heart of the proposed light buffer approach.

Lighting information can be effectively stored in additional off-screen buffers before scene geometry is submitted. This lighting information is provided to the geometry shading pass later. Such processes can be understood as an inverse variant of G-Buffers—instead of storing information about the visible geometry in the buffers, the information about the lights is stored.

Storing lighting information instead of geometry information has an important advantage—much more error can be tolerated in the lighting attributes. Because lighting information usually is smooth, the lighting attributes can be linearly interpolated without a noticeable decrease in final image quality. For example, lower resolution than the target frame buffer can be used for the light buffers, which saves both memory and fill rate.

Light Buffer Information

Light buffers represent a slice of lighting information. A light buffer is represented as a set of two-dimensional textures in the video memory. A set of two-dimensional textures forms a plane of light buffers and is used to capture lighting information during the rendering frame.

Three-dimensional lighting information is projected onto a two-dimensional plane, thus making spatial orientation of the light buffer very important to resulting quality. The light buffer plane must be oriented in world space to minimize potential lighting information losses. The orientation of the plane must stay constant for a duration of one frame, although it may be altered between frames.

Each texel of light buffer needs to contain the following information:

- Origin of light
- Direction toward light
- Color of light
- Light attenuation factor

Information about the volume of the light (in the case of spotlights) can be redundant, because only light-buffer pixels that are affected by the light contain valid information.

Because such an amount of raw lighting information is restrictive, the approach to pack data into 8-bit RGBA textures is required.

Goals

The following goals were considered during development of the light buffers approach:

- Improve geometry batching. Lighting and geometry shading information should be separated to reduce complexity and allow better geometry batching.
- Reduce memory footprint and fill-rate cost. Data stored in the light buffer should be less forgiving for errors, allowing lower per-component precision and lower resolution of the storage textures. Effective data packing is required as well.

- Reduce any additional restrictions for material-specific attributes.
- Reduce modifications required in order to integrate light buffers into already existing shaders.

Implementation

Light information is accumulated in the light buffers at the start of each frame. Lights are rendered into the light buffer using simple geometry primitives—spheres, cones, and quads can be employed for this task. Information about the light is packed and stored using a special pixel shader. This technique can benefit from the usage of multiple render targets.

Once the light buffer is ready, the main geometry can be rendered. Textures containing light buffer information are passed to the pixel shaders. For each pixel of the rendered geometry, information is read from the light buffer, unpacked, and applied to usual lighting calculation formulas (see Figures 1.1.1 and 1.1.2).

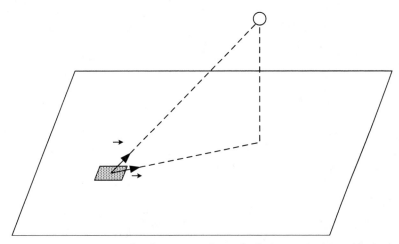

FIGURE 1.1.1   *Spatial information about the light is stored in each texel of the light buffer.*

Notation:

- z—Distance from the light origin to the light buffer plane.
- r—Distance from the light buffer texel center to the light origin projected onto the light buffer plane.
- **L**—Normalized vector pointing from the center of the light buffer texel to the light. Note that this normal is not stored in light buffer explicitly and used here only for clarification.
- **L'**—Normalized projection of **L** onto the light buffer plane.

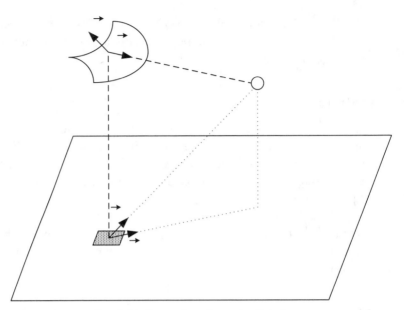

FIGURE 1.1.2   *Spatial information about the light is reconstructed for each pixel of shaded surface.*

Notation:

- d—Distance from the origin of the light to the pixel of the shaded surface.
- $\mathbf{L_s}$—Normalized direction vector from the pixel on the shaded surface to the light.
- $\mathbf{N}$—Normal of the surface.

Packing Data

Storing Lights in the Buffer

The origin and direction to light cannot be stored explicitly in the light buffer. Storing such information in the texture with 8-bit components would lead to significant precision errors and result in unpleasant lighting artifacts. Instead, an approach to store spatial information relative to the center of the light buffers texel form is chosen.

The following algorithm is used to pack and store data:

1. Calculate the vector pointing from the center of the light buffer texel to the light.
2. Project the vector onto the light buffer plane.
3. Store the length of the projected vector in the buffer.
4. Normalize the projected vector and store it in the buffer as a two-dimensional normal.
5. Calculate the distance between the light buffer plane and the origin of the light and store it in the buffer.

Because distance is stored in 8-bit components, the value should be appropriately scaled to retain as much precision as possible. The resulting distance must be in the range [0..1]. Additional operation is required for the signed range of distance—values should be transformed from [−1..1] to [0..1] range. An inverse operation takes place during the shading step when the lighting information is unpacked from the light buffers.

The resulting light buffer holds the following information in the components of its first RGBA texture:

Red: The X component of normalized direction to light is projected onto the light buffer plane (L').

Green: The Y component of normalized direction to light is projected onto the light buffer plane (L').

Blue: The distance from the light origin to the light buffer plane (z) is packed into an 8-bit value.

Alpha: The distance from the light buffer texel center to the light origin is projected onto the light buffer plane (r) packed into an 8-bit value.

The second texture is used to store the color and light attenuation factor of the lights. If color information and attenuation about each specific light is not necessary, a second texture can be omitted altogether, which saves memory and processing power. The light buffer holds the following information in the components of its second RGBA texture:

• **RGB**—light color
• **Alpha**—light attenuation factor

Light Shapes

Lights are rendered into the light buffer using suitable geometry primitives. As with G-Buffers, spatial complexity of the light is orthogonal to the complexity of the geometry shading process.

In some cases, quads can be the preferred choice of geometry for rendering lights into the light buffer. Pixels that are outside of the falloff distance of light or are outside the cone of light can be rejected using the `texkill` instruction (in HLSL, `clip` intrinsic function).

Some specific cases may allow light information to be precalculated and stored in the texture. Only a portion of lighting attributes needs to be calculated in runtime in such a case. For example, if a light's shape remains constant, the packed normal and distance to the light's origin projected on the light buffer plane can be calculated a priori and stored in the separate texture. During rendering to the light buffer, only the distance between the origin of the light and the light buffer plane needs to be calculated.

Light Buffer Spatial Orientation

Light buffer spatial orientation in the world space should be chosen with care. Because two-dimensional textures with low-precision components are favored, precision errors are inevitable. Components storing relative distance to the light are specifically sensitive to errors, especially distance between the light and the plane of the light buffer.

Spatial orientation of the light buffer must be chosen to minimize potential precision errors. Such spatial orientation can be derived from the representation of the game world itself. For example, if game activity takes place on a terrain, it is best to orient the light buffer plane along the terrain.

Intersecting Lights

The number of lights is stored in one light buffer. When several lights intersect on the light buffer's plane, an approach to deal with intersecting lights is required.

The easiest approach is to blend several lights in the light buffer, which sacrifices quality of the resulting shading. Color and attenuation information can be blended directly in the frame buffer using alpha blending functionality. However, a special pixel shader is required to correctly blend spatial information. Intersecting lights are found on the CPU and fed into the pixel shader, which is responsible for blending and storing the appropriate information.

The approach outlined above tends to sacrifice quality in the regions of multiple light intersections. If quality becomes an issue and visible artifacts appear, lights can be distributed into several light buffers. It is important to note that several light buffers can share one texture containing color information of the lights without a big decrease in visual quality.

It's common for games to use only three or four of the most important lights per object and reject the others. It should be sufficient to use three or four light buffer textures to store spatial light information and one additional texture to capture color information. However, the actual number of the light buffers is dependent upon the lighting complexity of the scene and the expected visual quality. The number of the active light buffers can be chosen a priori or adjusted according to the real-time information.

Following, CPU- and GPU-based approaches for distributing lights into several buffers are discussed.

CPU Approach

A simple distribution algorithm can be used on the CPU: If a light intersects the region of another light, which is already stored in a buffer, the new light is moved into the next light buffer or its effect for the current light buffer pixel is rejected.

The algorithm can be improved by taking into account the approximation of the scene geometry—sorting or completely rejecting lights based on the approximately measured effect on the geometry.

GPU Approach

The depth peeling [Everitt99] approach is used to distribute information among several light buffers. Depth peeling strips away intersecting light layers. Each successive pass of algorithm stores light information in the different light buffer.

The number of required light buffers can be reduced by laying the depth of the scene geometry first and taking into account only lights that contribute to the resulting image. Depth of the scene geometry is passed as a texture to the pixel shader responsible for storing information into the light buffer, thus rejecting unnecessary lights based on the distance between light and geometry. It is worth mentioning that rendering geometry in order to lay depth first does not require any material-specific information, minimizing render-call counts using geometry batching and instancing.

Data Unpacking

Information from light buffers must be provided to all visible and lit pixels in the scene. Light buffer textures are applied to geometry using projective texture mapping. The process of projective texture mapping effectively transforms geometry into the light buffer space, thus resolving spatial relation between the light and the geometry.

The following algorithm is used to unpack information about lights from the buffer. This algorithm is applied for each pixel of the lit surface:

1. Unpack direction and distance to the light using information from the first texture.
   a. Unpack distance from light plane to origin of light (z) value stored in **Blue** channel of light buffer.
   b. Unpack distance from light buffer pixel center to light origin projected onto light buffer plane (r) values and **Alpha** channel of light buffer.
   c. Calculate Z component difference between light origin and pixel position of the shaded surface: `z = unpack( lightBuffer.z ) - wPos.z;` variable `wPos` is vertex world position interpolated across the polygon.
   d. Reconstruct $\mathbf{L_s}$ vector from (z), (r) and 2D normal $\mathbf{L'}$, stored in **Red** and **Green** channel: `Ls.xy = unpackNormal( lightBuffer.xy ) * lightBuffer.a; Ls.z = z;`.
   3. Obtain distance to light by measuring $\mathbf{L_s}$ vector and normalize it for further usage in common lighting calculations: `dist = length( Ls ); Ls = Ls / dist;`.
2. Read color and light attenuation information from the second texture.
3. Proceed with common per-pixel lighting calculation using reconstructed distance to light and L normal.
4. Repeat for all active light buffers.

Optimization and Improvements

Masking Unlit Pixels

Complexity of shading pixel shaders tends to increase in the modern games. It is desirable to render only affected pixels. The stencil test may be employed in order to reject pixels that are not affected by the lights. Before the geometry shading pass, an additional quad with a simple pixel shader is rendered. A pixel shader determines if the specific texel of light buffer has no information about the light (not valid texels will contain a zero length vector representing direction to light), rejecting writes to stencil buffer. After this operation, the stencil buffer contains a bit mask for several light buffers. During the geometry shading pass, unnecessary pixels will be rejected based on the stencil values saving the fill rate.

Precision and Memory Footprint Improvements

Various possibilities exist to store lighting information in the light buffer.

Instead of storing the explicit attenuation factor and light color, the representing index can be employed to identify specific light. The index can be stored in the light buffer and can be used as a coordinate for a dependent texture read to access light attributes information during surface shading.

Floating point textures can be employed to store spatial information to reduce precision errors. Alternatively, if higher precision is supported in the pixel shader, the relative distance may be stored and extracted from the pair of 8-bit components.

Combining these techniques, a more compact light buffer representation or more precise version of algorithm may be achieved.

Pixel Shader Versions 1.1–1.4

The light buffer approach is oriented mostly toward newer video cards that support 2.0 version pixel shaders, where batching is especially important to keep the GPU busy. However, this algorithm can be implemented on PS1.x class hardware as well.

The most computationally expensive operation of the described algorithm is per-pixel normalization of the reconstructed light (L_s) vector. Although this operation cannot be mapped directly to PS1.x hardware, it can be calculated using Newton-Raphson approximation [Borse97].

PS1.x implementation can be limited by the number of supported textures, thus requiring multiple passes for full shading algorithm.

Results

Figure 1.1.3 compares the result of the geometry lit using a standard multi-pass approach with a light buffer approach. No visual differences are observed in the results, unless significant numbers of lights are intersecting.

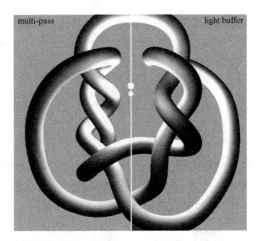

FIGURE 1.1.3   *Comparison of standard multi-pass and light buffer lighting approach.*

Figure 1.1.4 compares lighting results using light buffers with different resolutions. Surprisingly, even a low-resolution light buffer produces visually plausible results.

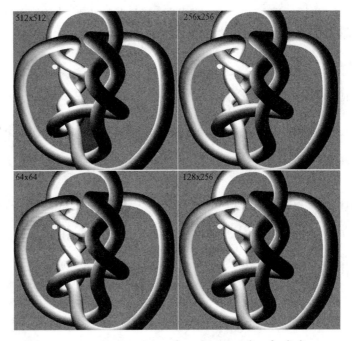

FIGURE 1.1.4   *Comparison of resulting quality for light buffers with different resolution.*

The proposed light buffer approach provides the following advantages:

- Improves potential geometry batching.
- Has an acceptable memory footprint.
- Complex shaders can applied only when necessary because the technique provides a possibility to determine lit pixels before shading.
- Can be trivially integrated into existing vertex/pixel shaders.
- Can be implemented on low-end hardware.

The light buffer approach has the following drawbacks:

- Requires additional care to orient light buffer planes.
- Light intersection problem has no simple solution and requires case-specific hand tuning.
- May require a large number of underlying buffers to capture environments densely populated with large intersecting lights.

Summary

This article presented a technique to separate lighting and scene geometry information to reduce the complexity of the shading and increase geometry batching possibilities. The data required to capture lighting spatial information and additional attributes along with possibilities of its compact representation was discussed. The technique is oriented toward and handles well scenarios with a large number of relatively small lights scattered across the scene.

References

[Blythe99] Blythe, D., et al., "Lighting and Shading Techniques for Interactive Applications," SIGGRAPH, 1999.

[Borse97] Borse, G. J., "Numerical Methods with MATLAB," PWS Publishing Company: pp. 165, 1997.

[Everitt99] Everitt, C., "Interactive order-independent transparency," White paper, *NVidia*, 1999.

[Fernando04] Fernando, R., et al., "Programming Graphics Hardware," Eurographics, 2004.

[Green03] Green, R., "Spherical harmonic lighting: the gritty details," Game Developers Conference, 2003.

[Hargreaves04] Hargreaves, S., "Deferred Shading," Game Developers Conference, 2004.

1.2

Practical Cloth Simulation on Modern GPUs

Cyril Zeller

Introduction

The latest generation of GPU offers enough computation power and flexibility that it can be efficiently used to free the CPU of some other tasks rather than just rendering.

Not every task lends itself well to a GPU implementation, but cloth simulation does. Indeed, a piece of cloth can be modeled as a 2D network of many particles with the same dynamic, thus mapping naturally to a texture processed by the same pixel shader. Such a mapping is also texture-cache friendly because each particle generally interacts only with its neighboring particles.

The implementation described in this article is geared toward performance and visual realism, rather than physical accuracy. As such, it is suitable to applications such as 3D games and virtual reality systems. These applications usually don't need the result of the cloth simulation on the CPU, as it is only used for rendering, making a GPU implementation even more relevant.

The following section describes the general algorithm used to simulate cloth and the section after, its implementation on a GPU supporting Shader Model 3, like the NVIDIA GeForce 6 Series and later.

Algorithm

Overview

The algorithm is based on the simulation technique described in [Jakobsen 2001], which has been successfully used in games (see also [Meggs 2005]).

A cloth object is modeled as a set of particles. Each particle is subject to some external forces—such as gravity, wind, and drag—and a series of constraints to maintain the overall shape of the object and prevent interpenetration with the environment. These concurrent constraints are resolved by relaxation at each simulation step.

Some of the particles in the set may be attached to the environment or interactively dragged around by the user. Such particles are considered "fixed" by the simulation because they aren't subject to any force or constraint, and their positions are computed based on the environment or the user motion instead.

Force

Newton's law tells us how the forces move each particle:

$$\mathbf{A} = \mathbf{F} - c\mathbf{V} \qquad (1.2.1)$$

where $\mathbf{A}$ is the acceleration of the particle and $\mathbf{V}$, its velocity. The drag force is modeled as $-c\mathbf{V}$ where c is a positive number close to 0 and $\mathbf{F}$ regroups all the forces that don't depend on the particle's velocity. Equation 1.2.1 assumes that the mass of the particles has been factored into c and $\mathbf{F}$.

Several schemes exist to derive the position of the particle from its acceleration at each simulation step.

Euler integration stores the position and velocity, $\mathbf{P}_n$ and $\mathbf{V}_n$, at simulation step n, and updates them using the following formula directly derived from Equation 1.2.1 and the definition of velocity and acceleration:

$$\mathbf{A}_n = \mathbf{F} - c\mathbf{V}_n \qquad (1.2.2)$$

$$\mathbf{V}_{n+1} = \mathbf{V}_n + \Delta t_n \mathbf{A}_n \qquad (1.2.3)$$

$$\mathbf{P}_{n+1} = \mathbf{P}_n + \Delta t_n \mathbf{V}_n \qquad (1.2.4)$$

where Δt_n is the time step between step n and step $n+1$.

Another integration scheme that originates from the domain of molecular dynamics is Verlet integration. It doesn't store the velocity, but the positions $\mathbf{P}_n$ at step n and $\mathbf{P}_{n-1}$ at step $n-1$ instead. The position $\mathbf{P}_{n+1}$ at step $n+1$ can then be derived from $\mathbf{P}_n$ and $\mathbf{P}_{n-1}$ by rewriting Equations 1.2.2, 1.2.3, and 1.2.4 for step $n-1$:

$$\mathbf{A}_{n-1} = \mathbf{F} - c\mathbf{V}_{n-1} \qquad (1.2.5)$$

$$\mathbf{V}_n = \mathbf{V}_{n-1} + \Delta t_{n-1} \mathbf{A}_{n-1} \qquad (1.2.6)$$

$$\mathbf{P}_n = \mathbf{P}_{n-1} + \Delta t_{n-1} \mathbf{V}_{n-1} \qquad (1.2.7)$$

Equations 1.2.5 and 1.2.6 give V_n in function of $\mathbf{V}_{n-1}$, and Equation 1.2.7 gives $\mathbf{V}_{n-1}$ in function of $\mathbf{P}_n$ and $\mathbf{P}_{n-1}$. By combining both, we get $\mathbf{V}_n$ in function of $\mathbf{P}_n$ and $\mathbf{P}_{n-1}$, and replacing $\mathbf{V}_n$ in Equation 1.2.4 yields:

$$\mathbf{P}_{n+1} = \mathbf{P}_n + \frac{\Delta t_n}{\Delta t_{n-1}}(1 - \Delta t_{n-1}c)(\mathbf{P}_n - \mathbf{P}_{n-1}) + \Delta t_n \Delta t_{n-1}\mathbf{F} \qquad (1.2.8)$$

Although it is less accurate than Euler integration, we use Verlet integration as it is inexpensive and generally more stable, especially for large time steps.

Spring Constraints

Each particle is linked to its neighboring particles through springs. As in [Jakobsen 2001], we don't simulate these springs as forces, but as distance constraints. This amounts to considering each spring as having an infinite stiffness, generating an infinite force that instantaneously brings back the spring to its length at rest whenever it's compressed or stretched.

In practice, a distance constraint between particles P and Q—at positions **P** and **Q** respectively—connected by a spring is enforced by moving them away or toward each other. More precisely, if the spring's distance at rest is d, the distance constraint between P and Q is enforced by computing:

$$\mathbf{D} = (1 - \frac{d}{\text{dist}(\mathbf{P}, \mathbf{Q})})(\mathbf{Q} - \mathbf{P})$$

and displacing:

$$P \text{ by } r_\mathrm{P}\mathbf{D} \qquad\qquad (1.2.9\text{a})$$

$$Q \text{ by } -r_\mathrm{Q}\mathbf{D} \qquad\qquad (1.2.9\text{b})$$

where $(r_\mathrm{P}, r_\mathrm{Q})$ is equal to:

$$
\begin{array}{ll}
(0.5, 0.5) & \text{if none of the particles is fixed,} \\
(0, 1) & \text{if P is fixed,} \\
(1, 0) & \text{if Q is fixed,} \\
(0, 0) & \text{if both are fixed.}
\end{array}
$$

We call r_P and r_Q the responsivenesses of P and Q with respect to each other. They correspond to the normalized inverses of their masses (see [Jakobsen 2001] for more details). A responsiveness of 0 corresponds to an infinite mass. A value of (0.5, 0.5) for $(r_\mathrm{P}, r_\mathrm{Q})$ means that both particles have the same mass.

The result of enforcing the distant constraint between P and Q is that the distance between the two particles becomes equal to the spring's distance at rest. Now, of course, that will in general no longer be the case after one relaxation iteration, as both particles are subject to other concurrent distance constraints. This is why we still get some elastic behavior, although springs aren't simulated with finite forces.

Collision Constraints

The environment is defined as a set of collision objects of various geometric types: planes, spheres, boxes, or ellipsoids.

A collision constraint between a particle and a collision object is enforced by checking whether the particle is inside the object, and if it is, by moving the particle to the position at the surface of the object that is the closest to the particle's current position.

In the case of the ellipsoid, computing the closest position requires an iterative calculation, so for simplicity and speed, the particle is moved to the intersection of the ellipsoid with the line that goes from the ellipsoid's center to the particle's current position.

Relaxation

Relaxation is an iterative method of solving a system of equations. It doesn't rely on algebra to find a direct solution to the system, but instead starts with a guess solution and repeatedly updates it until some convergence criterion is met.

In our case, the system of equations is made of all the spring constraints and collision constraints, and the guess solution is the positions of the particles after Verlet integration. At every relaxation iteration, the positions are updated by sequentially enforcing each of the constraints. The collision constraints are enforced at the end of each iteration, as they are the most visibly noticeable when not verified.

We don't compute any convergence criterion, but simply stop after a certain number of iterations. One iteration often produces already good results because convergence happens across frames as well.

Here's an outline of one simulation step:

```
Step-Position:
    For each fixed particle
        Set the particle's position
Step-Force:
    For each non-fixed particle
        Apply forces using Equation 1.2.8
Step-Relaxation:
    For each relaxation iteration
        Step-Relaxation-Spring:
            For every spring constraint
                Move the two corresponding particles
                using Equation 1.2.9a and 1.2.9b
        Step-Relaxation-Collision:
            For every particle
                For every collision object
                    If the particle is inside the object
                        Move the particle to the boundary of the object
```

GPU Implementation

Overview

The algorithm described in the previous section is implemented entirely on the GPU, meaning that the positions of the particles are computed by the GPU and stored in video memory. They're never read back to the CPU.

Every step of the time-stepping loop consists, as usual, of a simulation step that computes the positions of the particles and a rendering step that displays the result to the screen. The difference with the usual setting is that, in our case, the vertex buffer used to render a cloth object doesn't contain the positions of the particles, but only the static information required to look up these positions from video memory.

The HLSL code related to the simulation step is in `ClothSim.fx` and the HLSL code related to rendering step is in `Scene.fx`.

Storage

The positions of the particles are stored into floating-point textures. We use a texel format with four components: the r, g, and b components correspond to the particle position in 3D space, and the w component encodes some information about the particle type such as whether it is fixed (see the `IsFree` function). Each component is a 32-bit floating-point number, which is necessary to get correct simulation results.

Since Verlet integration requires both the current and the old position, we need at least two textures to hold the particle positions at these different times. An additional texture to hold the new particle positions is also required because we can't update a texture while reading from it. The three position textures get rotated after each position update.

Many objects, such as curtains, flags, tablecloths, or capes, can be modeled as a rectangular piece of cloth, in which case there is a direct mapping between the mesh representing these objects and the texture holding the positions of the particles. More complex objects that are represented by non-rectangular meshes or meshes with holes are dealt with by remeshing them into a 2D array of quantized points called a geometry image [Gu et al. 2002].

A geometry image is created from a given mesh by cutting it along a network of edge paths such that it becomes topologically equivalent to a disk, then reparametrizing the result over the unit square domain, and finally using this new parametrization to sample the mesh geometry over a grid covering the entire domain. The vertices located along the seam are mapped to the sides of the unit square. Those vertices that belong to the portions of the seam that are not part of the mesh boundary are duplicated and map to two different locations on the sides of the unit square. They are replicated even more when they're at the nodes of the network forming the seam. The particles corresponding to each of the replicates of a given vertex are simulated independently during steps *Step-Force* and *Step-Relaxation-Spring,* and their positions are reconciled during *Step-Relaxation-Collision* by averaging them. Each encodes in its w component the texture coordinates of the next one, thus creating a circular single-linked list of all the particles representing this vertex (see the `IsASeamParticle` and `GetNextTexCoord` functions).

Spring Configuration

To maintain strong data locality when processing the position texture, each particle is only linked to its direct neighbors. There are in general eight of them, as illustrated in

Figure 1.2.1. Structural springs resist stretching and compressing of the cloth, and optional shear springs resist in-plane shearing.

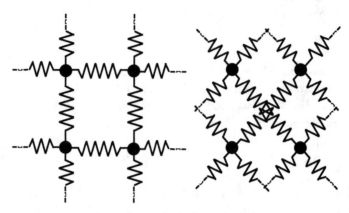

FIGURE 1.2.1   *Particles are linked together by structural springs (left) and shear springs (right).*

Simulation Step

The simulation step consists of repeatedly updating the position texture by setting it as the render target and rendering the appropriate geometry with the appropriate pixel shader. The next paragraphs describe how the steps of the algorithm outlined in the previous section are translated into pixel shaders. For all these steps, *Step-Position* excepted, the positions of all particles are updated. In this case, the appropriate geometry to render is a quad covering the entire render target.

Initialization

The positions of the particles are reset using either the pixel shader ResetPosition for flat rectangular meshes, or the pixel shader ResetPositionFromTexture for generic meshes.

The types of the particles are reset using the pixel shaders SetFree, SetUnfree, and SetSeamValue.

Step-Position

This step updates the positions of the fixed particles only. In this case, the appropriate geometry to render is a list of points of 1-pixel size, each corresponding to a fixed particle. This is assuming that there are far fewer fixed than nonfixed particles.

The pixel shader is either SetPosition if the positions of the fixed particles are just passed as vertex attributes, or TransformPosition if they are calculated by transforming the current positions through some transform matrix. TransformPosition is typically used when the fixed particles are moved around by the user.

Step-Force

For this step, the pixel shader is `ApplyForces`. It updates the position of every non-fixed particle based on Equation 1.2.8. Note that it is executed for every fixed particle as well, but the position of each such particle isn't modified.

The wind is faked as a horizontal force whose direction varies across the surface of the cloth according to a 2D-noise texture. When fetching the noise texture using the position-texture coordinates for every particle, we also add an offset only dependent on time to animate the wind.

Step-Relaxation

It's important that two constraints with one particle in common get enforced sequentially for the relaxation algorithm to converge. In other words, the second constraint needs to be enforced based on the new position of the particle in common that has been computed as a result of enforcing the first constraint. If both constraints only depend on one particle, such as for collision constraints, we achieve this by simply enforcing them one after the other in a single pixel shader execution. However, if both constraints depend on more than one particle, such as for spring constraints, this isn't feasible because enforcing each such constraint requires more than one pixel shader execution to update the position of each corresponding particle. Therefore, in this last case, the result of enforcing the first constraint needs to be saved to a texture so it's available to each of the pixel shader executions necessary to enforce the second constraint. This implies that such dependent constraints have to be handled in two separate rendering passes.

Step-Relaxation-Spring

As a consequence, the spring constraints are split into eight groups, so the constraints inside each group are independent from each other and can be enforced in parallel in one rendering pass. These eight rendering passes simulate the eight springs generally attached to a particle.

Four rendering passes handle the structural spring constraints (see Figure 1.2.2). One pass handles the x-aligned structural spring constraints corresponding to the even columns of the position texture (`SatisfySpringConstraintXSpringEven`); another handles the x-aligned structural spring constraints corresponding to the odd columns (`SatisfySpringConstraintXSpringOdd`); and two other passes handle the y-aligned structural spring constraints in a similar way (`SatisfySpringConstraintYSpringEven` and `SatisfySpringConstraintXSpringOdd`).

Likewise, four other rendering passes handle the shear spring constraints when applicable (see Figure 1.2.3): `SatisfySpringConstraintXYSpringDownEven`, `SatisfySpringConstraintXYSpringDownOdd`, `SatisfySpringConstraintXYSpringUpEven`, and `SatisfySpringConstraintXYSpringUpOdd`.

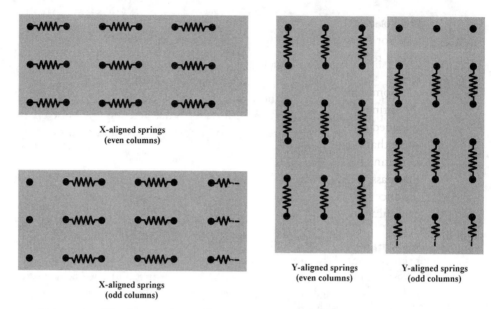

FIGURE 1.2.2   *The four rendering passes used to enforce the structural spring constraints.*

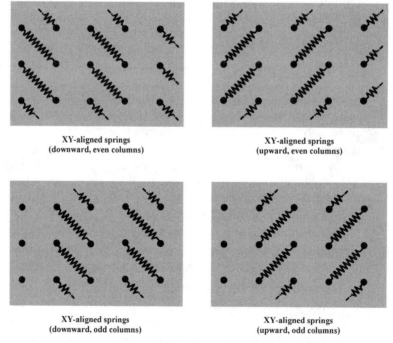

FIGURE 1.2.3   *The four rendering passes used to enforce the shear spring constraints.*

For each of these eight rendering passes, a texture holds the responsiveness to be used for every particle during that pass. Particles located at the boundary of the cloth have a responsiveness of 0 when they're involved in no constraint during a particular pass.

Some simple cloth objects can be modeled with the same distance at rest for all the springs of a certain type (x-aligned or y-aligned), in which case the distance at rest is loaded as a constant before each rendering pass. More complex cloth objects necessitate that every spring has its own distance at rest, in which case, for each of the eight rendering passes, a texture holds the distance at rest to be used for every spring during that pass. The distance at rest of a spring linking two particles is usually taken as the distance between the positions of these two particles when the cloth object is in some canonical posture.

Step-Relaxation-Collision

The pixel shader `SatisfySeamAndCollisionConstraints` first handles the case of the particles that are replicates of the same vertex as explained earlier. It does so by checking the type of the particle, and if it's a seam particle, by looping through all the corresponding replicates to compute the average position. This case only appears when the position texture is a geometry image.

Then it handles the collision constraints: for each particle, it goes through all the collision objects and updates the particle's position each time it happens to be inside the object.

Collision objects are stored into 1D textures, one for each geometric type. Storing them as constants would be faster and the preferred way in the case where the number of objects is known before shader compilation. Here, we assume that this number varies, for example, because the application performs a coarse collision detection to prune it down before every simulation step. In this case, constants can't be used because Shader Model 3 doesn't support constant indexing inside the pixel shader.

Normals

The technique `ComputeNormals` regroups the pixel shaders used to compute the normals for every particle based on their positions. These normals are stored into a 32-bit floating-point texture with four components per texel, the w component being identical to the corresponding w component in the position texture for any given particle. This texture is set as the render target and gets updated by rendering a quad covering the entire render target.

The normal of a particle is calculated by averaging the normals of the triangles the particle belongs to. Determining triangles to which a particle belongs requires distinguishing various cases depending on whether the particle is located in the interior of the texture, at one of its sides, or at one of its corners. The branching needed to handle these cases can be performed either entirely on the GPU inside the pixel shader, or entirely on the CPU with one rendering pass per case, or on both processors; for example, by using one pass for the interior of the texture and another for its boundary.

In the case of a seam particle, the normals of every replicate are averaged together.

Rendering Step

The vertex buffer used to render a cloth object only contains the texture coordinates to look up the position and normal textures using the vertex texture fetch capability of Shader Model 3. These lookups are performed by `SimulatedVS` or `SimulatedBump MappedVS`. `SimulatedBumpMappedVS` only differs from `SimulatedVS` in that it computes for every vertex a tangent vector that gets passed to the pixel shader for bump mapping.

Cuts

When in cut mode, the user cuts cloth by dragging the mouse over a cloth object from one window point to another. To compute the cuts, these two window points are back-projected to their corresponding world space positions to define a 3D triangle together with the camera origin. This triangle then acts as a cutter (see Figure 1.2.4): every cloth triangle it intersects is removed from the cloth mesh and the corresponding springs are suppressed.

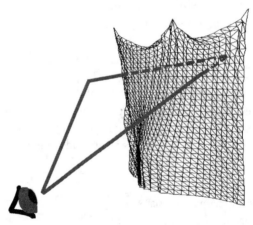

FIGURE 1.2.4   *The triangle defined by the mouse motion acts as a cutter.*

To determine all the cloth triangles that intersect with the cutter, we use a render target that has as many pixels as there are triangles in the cloth mesh. These pixels have a boolean value: 1 if the triangle is cut and 0 otherwise. They're first all set to 0 and then we render a quad covering the entire render target using the pixel shader `Cut` from `ClothSim.fx`. This pixel shader sets to 1 the pixels whose corresponding triangles intersect with the cutter. After the rendering is done, the render target is read back to the CPU and the cloth index buffer and responsiveness textures are modified accordingly. A spring is suppressed by zeroing the responsiveness of the two particles it links.

Summary

In this article, we proposed a method to simulate cloth on modern GPUs. It modeled a piece of cloth as a network of particles whose positions and normals were stored into floating-point textures. These textures got updated by a succession of pixel shaders and looked up by the vertex shader during the rendering pass.

The method proved to be stable, fast, and flexible enough that it can be used in real applications.

References

[Jakobsen 2001] Jakobsen, Thomas, "Advanced character physics." Game Developers Conference, 2001.

[Gu et al. 2002] Gu, Xianfeng, Steven, Gortler, and Hugues, Hoppe, "Geometry Images." *ACM SIGGRAPH 2002, 355–361.*

[Meggs 2005] Meggs, Andrew, "Parachute Pants and Denim Dresses: Taking Real-Time Cloth Beyond Curtains." Game Developers Conference, 2005.

1.3

Shader Implementation of Discrete Wavelet Transform

Tien-Tsin Wong and Chi-Sing Leung

Introduction

Wavelet techniques [Chui92][Daubechies92] have become an important tool in computer graphics. Many wavelet-based applications [Stollnitz96] have been developed in recent years, including global illumination, BRDF representation, wavelet environment matting, and progressive meshes. However, due to the intensive computation nature of a *discrete wavelet transform* (DWT), its software implementation suffers from long execution time when dealing with large-scale data; for example, an image (or data grid) of 1024×1024. In this article, we present a simple method to implement the 2D DWT on a GPU [Wang04]. Although simple, the method can support a variety of wavelets (including Haar, Cohen-Daubechies-Fauraue 9/7, and so on) and various boundary extension schemes.

Wavelets Basics

A one-step 1D forward DWT is illustrated in Figure 1.3.1. Given an input data sequence $d(n)$, it is transformed (decomposed) into two sets of coefficients, low-frequency L and high-frequency H coefficients via convolving $d(n)$ with the low-pass (h) and high-pass (g) filters, respectively. It is this pair of filters that actually defines the wavelet being used. As the filtered data contain redundancy, half of them are enough for reconstruction; therefore, a downsampling process is done after the convolution.

The convolution and downsampling process is recursively applied to the low-frequency coefficients at each level. This produces multiple levels of high-frequency (detail) coefficients and one set of low-frequency (coarse) coefficients.

For the 2D case, one step of forward DWT produces three bands (*LH*, *HL*, *HH*) of detail coefficients and one band (*LL*) of coarse coefficients. Figure 1.3.2 shows one step of 2D forward DWT.

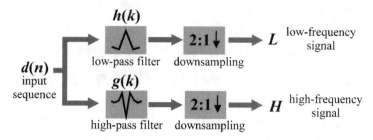

FIGURE 1.3.1   *One step of 1-D forward DWT contains convolution and downsampling.*

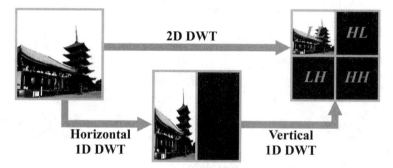

FIGURE 1.3.2   *For separable wavelets, one step of 2D forward DWT can be achieved by applying 1-D DWT once horizontally (for rows) and once vertically (for columns).*

In general, the 2D DWT is computational expensive. Fortunately, for *separable* wavelets, one step of 2D forward DWT can be achieved by applying 1D forward DWT once horizontally and then once vertically. Hence, we will focus our implementation on 1D DWT only. Mathematically, a one-step 1D forward DWT and downsampling for input signal $\{\lambda_j(n)\}$ at level j can be expressed as:

$$\lambda_{j-1}(n) = \sum_k h(k) \cdot \lambda_j(2n-k) \qquad (1.3.1)$$

$$\gamma_{j-1}(n) = \sum_k g(k) \cdot \lambda_j(2n+1-k) \qquad (1.3.2)$$

where $\{\lambda_{j-1}(n)\}$ and $\{\gamma_{j-1}(n)\}$ are coarse and details coefficients at level $j-1$, respectively; $h(k)$ and $g(k)$ are low-pass and high-pass decomposition filters, respectively. The length of filter depends on the wavelet filter selected.

Conversely, given the coarse $\{\lambda_{j-1}(n)\}$ and detail $\{\gamma_{j-1}(n)\}$ coefficients at level $j-1$, the reconstruction of signal $\{\lambda_j(n)\}$ at level j is expressed as:

$$\lambda_j(n) = \sum_k h'(k) \cdot \lambda_{j-1}(n-k) + \sum_k g'(k) \cdot \gamma_{j-1}(n-k) \qquad (1.3.3)$$

where $h'(k)$ and $g'(k)$ are low-pass and high-pass reconstruction filters, respectively. Careful readers should be aware that *both* decomposition and reconstruction processes are in the generic form of convolution:

$$X(n) = \sum_k F(k) \cdot Y(n,k) \qquad (1.3.4)$$

where F is the filter, and X and Y are the output and input data. Such simple convolution can be efficiently achieved in a modern GPU. Hence, this motivates us to implement DWT in the form of fragment shader. At each fragment, we execute Equation 1.3.4 once to perform a step of decomposition/reconstruction. Note that the length of filter kernel, K_o, is normally small; for example, $K_o = 9$ for biorthogonal 9/7 wavelet.

Forward DWT

Concatenation and Filter Selection

Let's illustrate the forward DWT with a running example of a nine-element data sequence at level j (see Figure 1.3.3(a)). Theoretically, for each *base position* (convolution center), we need to perform both high-pass and low-pass filtering centered at this position. In our example, 18 linear sums are needed in total. However, due to the downsampling, we can skip half of them (nine in our example). To do so, low-pass filtering is only performed at even base positions while high-pass filtering is only performed at odd ones. This produces nine outputs (five coarse and four detail coefficients) at level $j-1$. Figure 1.3.3 (a) shows how we concatenate coarse and detail coefficients, and how the base positions at level j are associated with the output coefficients at level $j-1$.

To facilitate the shader implementation of forward DWT and keep the computation in place, we need to unify the computation of coarse and detail coefficients in Equations 1.3.1 and 1.3.2. We first concatenate coarse $\{\lambda_{j-1}(n)\}$ and detail $\{\gamma_{j-1}(n)\}$ coefficients to form $\{z_{j-1}(n)\}$ (Figure 1.3.3(a), bottom). Then, Equations 1.3.1 and 1.3.2 can be rewritten in a single form

$$z_{j-1}(n) = \sum_k f_{j-1}^D(n,k) \cdot d_j(n,k) \qquad (1.3.5)$$

where $d_j(n,k)$ returns the appropriate data in level j for convolution, $f_{j-1}^D(n,k)$ is a position-dependent filter that selects the appropriate filter values for convolution, and superscript D stands for decomposition.

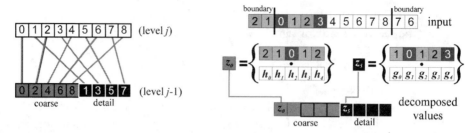

FIGURE 1.3.3 *(a) Downsampling and concatenation. (b) Decomposition is achieved by performing convolution on the input sequence with appropriate low-pass and high-pass filters.*

To implement this forward DWT on GPU, we create a floating-point texture to hold the data grid or image (with size of $W \times H$). At each output pixel (coefficient) $n \in [0, W-1]$, we execute a fragment shader to compute the convolution in Equation 1.3.5. $f_{j-1}^{D}(n,k)$ and $d_j(n,k)$ are looked up from tables (textures) with the help of two variables, α (*filter selector*) and β (*base position*). Filter selector α tells us whether the current pixel belongs to the low-passed or high-passed regions after DWT. If it is a low-passed pixel, the low-pass filter kernel is used for convolution, and vice versa. According to our concatenation scheme in Figure 1.3.3(a), α is given by

$$\alpha = \begin{cases} 1 & \text{(high pass),} \quad \text{if } n > L/2 \\ 0 & \text{(low pass),} \quad \text{otherwise} \end{cases} \qquad (1.3.6)$$

where L is the length of input data sequence at current level j. $L = W$ only when it is at the first level of decomposition. Variable β is the base position of convolution at level j given n. According to Figure 1.3.3(a), β is computed as

$$\beta = 2\left(n - \alpha\left\lceil\frac{L}{2}\right\rceil\right) + \alpha + 0.5 \qquad (1.3.7)$$

where 0.5 is added to address the pixel center during texture fetching. The convolution in Equation 1.3.5 basically fetches K_o neighboring pixels centering at β. In general, low-pass and high-pass filter kernels may have different lengths (K_o). We should keep K_o as the larger one to keep the implementation uniformity.

Boundary Extension

If the fetching of neighbors goes beyond the boundary of the current level (Figure 1.3.3(b)), we need to extend the boundary. Common extension schemes (Figure 1.3.4) include periodic padding, symmetric periodic padding, zero padding, and so on. In our example, we apply symmetrical periodic extension that mirrors pixels across the boundary, with the boundary pixel not mirrored. Note that the following discussion does not restrict to any specific kind of boundary extension.

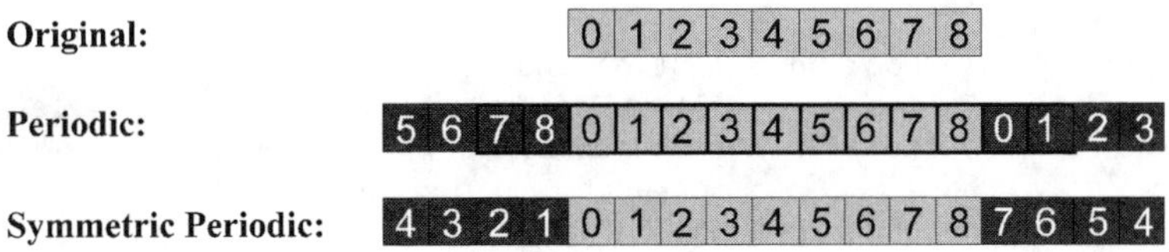

Original: `0 1 2 3 4 5 6 7 8`

Periodic: `5 6 7 8 0 1 2 3 4 5 6 7 8 0 1 2 3`

Symmetric Periodic: `4 3 2 1 0 1 2 3 4 5 6 7 8 7 6 5 4`

FIGURE 1.3.4 *Boundary extension schemes for a nine-element data sequence.*

Instead of computing α, β and boundary extension within the fragment shader, we precompute and store them in a 2D texture (`lut`). This table-lookup approach offers the flexibility in implementing different extension schemes by replacing the addresses in this indirect address table. The texture is organized with each row holding boundary extended addresses, α and β values for one particular level of DWT. Inside each texel, channel r stores the indirect addresses of pixels with boundaries extended. Channels g and b store α and β, respectively. Therefore, the width of a table for an input data sequence with maximum length L is $L + K_o - 1$. Figure 1.3.5 shows two levels of indirect addresses stored in the texture with data sequence of length $W = 14$ and $K_o = 9$. Dark gray indicates the boundary-extended elements, while the light gray indicates elements within the level of the data sequence. This texture is small in size as the number of rows is equal to $\log_2(W)$.

`4 3 2 1 0 1 2 3 4 5 6 7 8 9 10 11 12 13 12 11 10 9`
`4 3 2 1 0 1 2 3 4 5 6 5 4 3 2`

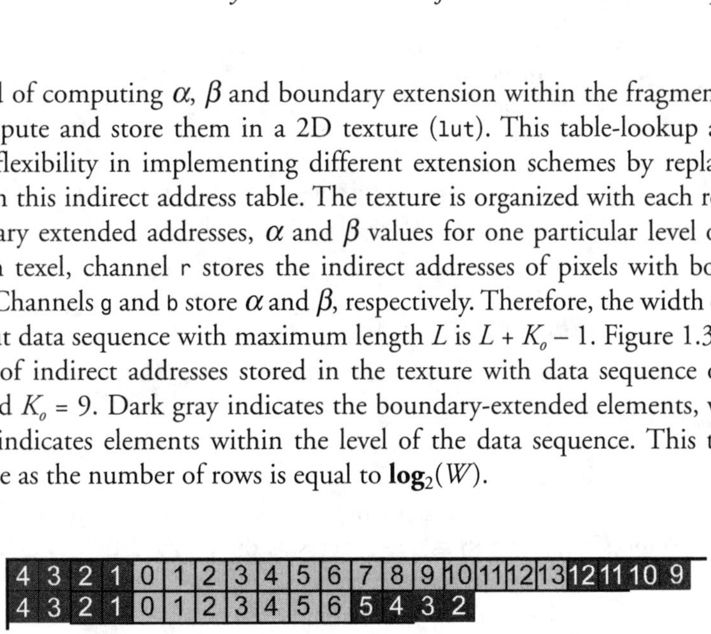

FIGURE 1.3.5 *The precomputed table storing the indirect addresses of boundary extended data.*

With the lookup table, the fragment shader mainly performs look-up and convolution. The following shader code shows an example one-step horizontal 1D forward DWT of biorthogonal 9/7 wavelets ($K_o = 9$). The vertical 1D forward DWT can be implemented similarly. Multiple levels of wavelet decomposition can be achieved by recursively applying these horizontal and vertical 1D DWT shaders on the coarse coefficients at different levels.

```
fragout_float main(vf30 IN,
uniform samplerRECT dwt,     // DWT coefficients
uniform samplerRECT filter,  // low-pass & high-pass filters
uniform samplerRECT lut,     // indirect address table
```

```
uniform float        level)  // current level
{
  float  base, offset;
  float2 neighbor;
  float3 lookup, sum=float3(0,0,0);

  // Look up α (lut.g) and β (lut.b)
  lookup      = f3texRECT(lut, float2(IN.TEX0.x+4,level+0.5));
  offset      = lookup.g*9;    // 0 - low-pass, 1 - high-pass
  base        = lookup.b;
  neighbor.y = IN.TEX0.y;

  for (int i=0; i<9; i++)
  {
    // Look up the indirect addresses stored in lut.r
    neighbor.x = f3texRECT(lut,float2(base+i,level+0.5)).r;
    // Convolve corresponding filter values, f_{j-1}^D (n,k) with data from
    // level j, d_j(n,k)
      sum +=
        f3texRECT (filter,float2(i+offset+0.5,0.5))
        .x*f3texRECT(dwt,neighbor);
  }
  fragout_float OUT;
  OUT.col = float4(sum, 1.0);
  return OUT;
}
```

Inverse DWT

Although the inverse DWT is mathematically different from the forward one (Equation 1.3.3), we show that, by using the indirect address table, the inverse DWT reduces to almost the same process as the forward DWT. During the inverse DWT, both coarse $\{\lambda_{j-1}(n)\}$ and detail $\{\gamma_{j-1}(n)\}$ coefficients at level $j–1$ are used to reconstruct signal $\{\lambda_j(n)\}$ by Equation 1.3.3. Similar to the forward DWT, we need to rewrite the equation as

$$d_j(n) = \sum_k f_{j-1}^R(n,k) \cdot z_{j-1}(n,k) \tag{1.3.8}$$

where $z_{j-1}(n,k)$ returns the appropriate data in level $j–1$ for reconstruction, and $f_{j-1}^R(n,k)$ is a position-dependent filter that selects the appropriate filter values for reconstruction. Superscript R stands for reconstruction.

Upsampling and Interleaving

In the inverse DWT, the indirect addressing of $z_{j-1}(n,k)$ is more complicated than that in the forward DWT, due to the upsampling, zero-padding, and boundary extension. We illustrate this via the same nine-element decomposed data in Figure 1.3.6.

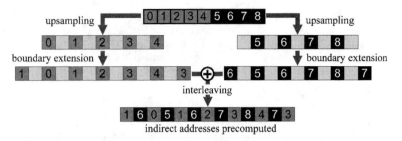

FIGURE 1.3.6 *Virtual upsampling and interleaving for precomputation of indirect addresses.*

Both coarse and detail coefficients at level j–1 are upsampled, padded with zeros and boundary extended. Zero-padding effectively interleaves the upsampled coarse and detail coefficients. Note that we do not actually perform the upsampling or interleaving. Instead, we only precompute the indirect addresses and store them in the indirect address table.

Once the indirect address table is ready, values in the next level can be reconstructed by convolution (Figure 1.3.7), just like the forward DWT. Based on the odd/even status of the position of the reconstructing pixel, we decide the reconstruction filter to convolve. Note that low-frequency elements must be multiplied by the low-pass reconstruction filter, h', while high-frequency elements must be multiplied by a high-pass reconstruction filter, g'. Position-dependent filter $f_{j-1}^{R}(n,k)$ achieves such filter selection by interleaving the filter kernel values of g' and h' as illustrated in Figure 1.3.7. In general, h' and g' may have different lengths.

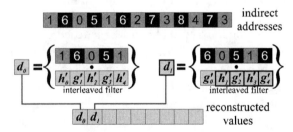

FIGURE 1.3.7 *Reconstruction filtering in inverse DWT.*

Once the lookup table (lut) is constructed with this virtual upsampling and interleaving, the inverse DWT shader mainly performs look-up and convolution, just like the forward one. The following shader code shows an example one-step horizontal 1D inverse DWT of biorthogonal 9/7 wavelets (K_{o} = 9).

```
fragout_float main(vf30 IN,
                   uniform samplerRECT dwt,
                   uniform samplerRECT filter,
                   uniform samplerRECT lut,
                   uniform float       level)
{
  float  lookup;
  float2 st, filter_st;
  float3 sum=float3(0,0,0);
  // Look up the filter selector (lut.g)
  lookup   = f4texRECT(lut,float2(IN.TEX0.x,level+0.5)).g;
  filter_st = float2(lookup*9.0+0.5,0.5);
  st       = float2(0.0,IN.TEX0.y);

  for (int i=0 ; i<9 ; i++)
  {
  // Look up the indirect address stored in lut.r
    st.x        = f4texRECT(lut,float2(IN.TEX0.x+i,level+0.5)).r;
    // Look up filter values (filter.x) and convolve f^R_{j-1}(n,k)·z_{j-1}(n,k)
    sum         += f3texRECT(filter,filter_st).x * f3texRECT(dwt,st);
filter_st.x += 1.0;
    }

fragout_float OUT;
OUT.col = float4(sum, 1.0);
return OUT;
}
```

Geometric Deformation in Wavelet Domain

We have applied our GPU-based DWT engine to geometric deformations in which the designer can modify control points of a NURBS 3D model in the transformed domain. The control points in 3D are organized in a grid structure and stored in memory as three 2D arrays, one for each x-, y-, and z-coordinate. DWT is then applied to these control-point arrays to obtain wavelet coefficients at the desired decomposition level. The designer can arbitrarily scale the wavelet coefficients at different frequency levels to achieve the desired effect. Figure 1.3.8 shows three deformed heads along with the scaling configurations of wavelet coefficients. The coefficients with no scaling are color-coded in gray, while those being scaled up and down are color-coded in dark gray and light gray, respectively. Interesting effects can be achieved in real time.

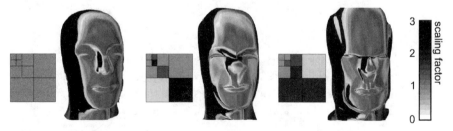

FIGURE 1.3.8   *Real-time geometric modeling in wavelet domain.*

Summary

In this article, we demonstrated how to implement a DWT shader on a GPU. A unified shader implementation for mathematically different forward and inverse DWT was proposed. With the indirect addressing, both shaders for forward and inverse DWTs are basically performing the same three operations: indirect addressing of data, filter selection, and convolution. Different wavelet filter kernels and boundary extension schemes can be easily incorporated by modifying the filter kernel values and indirect address table. The source code (both C++ library interface and JasPer JPEG2000 implementation) and demo are available on the companion CD-ROM and at the home page *http://www.cse.cuhk.edu.hk/~ttwong/software/dwtgpu/dwtgpu.html.*

ON THE CD

Acknowledgments

We would also like to thank Jianqing Wang for the demo implementation. The work is supported by the Research Grants Council of the Hong Kong Special Administrative Region, under RGC Earmarked Grants (Project No. CUHK 4189/03E) and a research grant from City University of Hong Kong (Project No. 7001703).

References

[Chui92] Chui, Charles K, *An Introduction to Wavelets*, Academic Press, 1992.

[Daubechies92] Daubechies, Ingrid, *Ten Lectures on Wavelets*, SIAM, 1996.

[Wang04] Wang, Jianqing, Tien-Tsin Wong, Pheng-Ann Heng, and Chi-Sing Leung, "Discrete Wavelet Transform on GPU," in *Proceedings of ACM Workshop on General Purpose Computing on Graphics Processors*, Los Angeles, USA, August 2004, p. C-41.

[Stollnitz96] Stollnitz, Eric J., Tony D. DeRose, and David H. Salesin, *Wavelets for Computer Graphics, Theory and Applications*, Morgan Kaufmann Publishers, Inc, 1996.

1.4

Morph Target Animation Using DirectX

Christian Kleinhuis

Morph target animation is a method used in 3D-rendering applications, where one base mesh can morph into multiple targets at the same time. Often used for facial animation, it is effective in creating lifelike motion such as the way a fish glides through water.

What Is Morph Target Animation?

Morphing is a technique where one objects transforms into another object. It is a linear *morphing* from one object into another. Consider the following situation: when one object transforms to more than one target—for example—two, each target is given its own weight. Think of a smiling face and a sad face. Ideally, when both targets have the same weight, they will sum to zero, but this is not always the case. When morphing between two objects, morphing is done by linear interpolation of vertices. It is clear that both objects should have the same number of vertices and share one index buffer for connecting these vertices. If we want to use morph targets, we only need to consider that we can have more than one target, which can be reached from our base object. For a 1D value, the process of summing the weighted targets together is as follows:

```
float X;            // Base Value
float T[n];         // Morph Targets
float Z[n];         // Weight for X[n]
float Y=X;          // Transformed Position
for(i=0 ;i<n ;i++){
   Y+= (T[n]-X)*Z[n]
}
```

The term (T[n]-X) can be solved in a preprocessing part when creating the vertex buffers; thus, fewer instructions are used in the shader itself. Figures 1.4.1 through 1.4.5 show various morph aspects, modelled by Jan Peters.

Implementation

First, the number of streams needs to be checked to see if they are supported by the hardware. This can be accomplished by querying the device capabilities after the creation of the base Direct3D9 object. It can be queried in the following way to obtain

FIGURE 1.4.1   *The Base mesh.*

FIGURE 1.4.2   *Mouth closed.*

FIGURE 1.4.3   *Left eye shut.*

FIGURE 1.4.4   *Right eye shut.*

FIGURE 1.4.5   *Three morph targets with different weights.*

Figures 1.4.1–1.4.5 © 2005. Reprinted with permission from Jan Peters.

access to a data structure containing all the information needed to decide if there are enough streams accessible from the vertex shader:

```
LPDIRECT3D9          m_pD3D;
LPDIRECT3DDEVICE9    m_pd3dDevice;
D3DCAPS9             *pCaps;
m_pD3D->GetDeviceCaps(D3DADAPTER_DEFAULT,D3DDEVTYPE_HAL,pCaps);
```

pCaps contains a pointer to the D3DCAPS9 structure, which contains the desired information:

```
typedef struct _D3DCAPS9 {
[…]
    DWORD MaxStreams;
    DWORD MaxStreamStride;
    DWORD VertexShaderVersion;
[…]
} D3DCAPS9;
```

MaxStreams is the value of interest; here it should be at least

```
[Number of Morphtargets ]+1
```

If the graphics card can handle the number of input streams, an appropriate flexible vertex declaration is needed. In DirectX, a Flexible Vertex Declaration consisting of several streams has to be set up, and a vertex shader integrates these streams into one single output. After that, the vertex buffer needs to be prepared. One main buffer with absolute vertex positions is needed. Moreover, to save bandwidth on the graphics card bus, an index buffer for connecting these vertices together should be used.

Loading the Meshes

The meshes need to be loaded into memory. This is done with .X files stored on disk and using D3DXLoadMeshFromX:

```
hr = D3DXLoadMeshFromX(filename, D3DXMESH_MANAGED, m_pd3dDevice,
    NULL, NULL, NULL, NULL, &pBaseMesh);
```

where filename is a valid filename of a file stored on disk. D3DXMESH_MANAGED is a member of the D3DXMESH enumeration. The last parameter is the pointer to a D3DXMESH interface.

Preparing the Vertex Buffers

The vertex declaration must contain the original vertex data like position, color, or texture coordinates, and space for a completely independent stream data, which will be the position data of the individual morph targets.

Example

The base vertex format consists of a position coordinate and a texture coordinate:

```
struct VERTEX
{
    FLOAT x, y, z;
    FLOAT tu, tv;
};
#define D3DFVF_ VERTEX (D3DFVF_XYZ | D3DFVF_TEX0)
```

For the target stream data, a new position coordinate is included:

```
struct TARGETVERTEX
{
    FLOAT x, y, z;
};
#define D3DFVF_TARGETVERTEX (D3DFVF_XYZ)
```

The corresponding vertex stream declaration should look like this:

```
D3DVERTEXELEMENT9 morphDeclaration[] =
{
    { 0, 0,  D3DDECLTYPE_FLOAT3, D3DDECLMETHOD_DEFAULT,
                                 D3DDECLUSAGE_POSITION, 0 },
    { 0, 12, D3DDECLTYPE_ FLOAT2, D3DDECLMETHOD_DEFAULT,
                                 D3DDECLUSAGE_TEXCOORD, 0 ),
```

```
        { 1, 20, D3DDECLTYPE_FLOAT3, D3DDECLMETHOD_DEFAULT,
                                    D3DDECLUSAGE_POSITION, 1 },
.
.
with N as the number of Morph Targets desired, and
N<MaxNumberOfStreams
.
.
        { N, 12+M*12, D3DDECLTYPE_FLOAT3,   D3DDECLMETHOD_DEFAULT,
                                    D3DDECLUSAGE_POSITION, N },
        D3DDECL_END()
};
```

Then, a vertex declaration object has to be made from the preceding declaration:

```
LPDIRECT3DVERTEXDECLARATION9 m_pVertexDeclaration;
m_pd3dDevice ->CreateVertexDeclaration(morphDeclaration,
    &m_pVertexDeclaration );
```

If the vertex declaration is set up as desired, the vertex buffers have to be filled with the appropriate vertex data. In this case, the vertex data consists of the relative positions to the base mesh position of each vertex.

Create a vertex buffer for each of the morph targets and base meshes, respectively.

```
LPDIRECT3DDEVICE9  m_pd3dDevice;
int                NumberOfVertices;
LPDIRECT3DVERTEXBUFFER9 * buffer;
m_pd3dDevice>CreateVertexBuffer(
    sizeof(TARGETVERTEX)*NumberOfVertices,
D3DUSAGE_WRITEONLY, D3DFVF_TARGETVERTEX, D3DPOOL_SYSTEMMEM,
buffer, NULL);
```

Then, lock the main vertex buffer (containing the base mesh vertex data) and lock the morph-target buffer. Now, for each vertex, the distance to the base mesh is calculated. This has to be done for each target mesh desired:

```
pBaseMesh->LockVertexBuffer(0, (LPVOID*)& base) );
pTargetMesh->LockVertexBuffer(0, (LPVOID*)& target) );
buffer ->Lock (0, (LPVOID*)& ne) &transformedtarget);

for (int i =0; i<NumberOfVertices;i++){
    transformedtarget[index].x= target [index].x- base[index].x;
    transformedtarget[index].y= target [index].y- base[index].y;
    transformedtarget[index].z= target [index].z- base[index].z;
    index++;
}
```

Preparing the Rendering Process

Before rendering the morph-target mesh, the vertex declaration has to be set:

```
m_pd3dDevice ->SetVertexDeclaration(m_pVertexDeclaration);
```

In addition, the weight for each morph target has to be set so the shader knows what to do with the stream data. These constants are now set as float-4 values, where each of the four components defines a different weight. Setting these weights can be done in a single step, but remember that you need to set up a weight list divisible by 4, even if you are using six or any other number of targets.

```
float vWeights[numberOfTargets];
m_pd3dDevice->SetVertexShaderConstantF(20, vWeight,numberOfTar-
gets/4 );
```

The constant register used is now c20, but it could be any other constant register. If more than four targets are used the subsequent constant registers are used to load the weight data so they cannot be used for any other purpose.

The Shader

The shader needs to be set up carefully now because when many position streams are used, the shader has to be told how to map the streams to variables. This is done at the beginning of the shader code. Vertex Shader v2.0 is the best for this purpose because at least two operations are needed for each morph target. In the next piece of code, N holds the number of desired morph targets that are used. The space for each weight of these targets is needed. This also has to be done by hand; for example, constant register c20.x holds the weight for target 1 and following c20.y ... c21.x, c20.y the weight for target 2, and so on.

```
;   c20.x  ; weight for target 1
    …. define subsequent weights in following constant registers
;   c20.y  ; weight for target 2
;   c20.z  ; weight for target 3
;   c20.w  ; weight for target 4
;   c21.x  ; weight for target 5

vs.2.0
dcl_position0 v0 ; the base mesh
dcl_position1 v1 ; morph target 1
dcl_position2 v2 ; morph target 2
…
dcl_positionN vN ; morph target N
```

The shader itself reads the position data, and multiplies it with its weight saved in a constant register.

First, load the base mesh data:

```
mov r0,v0
```

Then, the distance stored in v1 is added to the base mesh multiplied by the corresponding weight. Remember that only relative data is saved in the stream data. It won't be preprocessed in this way, and an additional "sub" command must be executed:

```
mad r0, v1, c20.x,r0
```

This has to be done for each target stream defined:

```
mad r0, vN, cXX.x,r0
```

Now r0 contains the morphed vertex position data. It can now be projected and transformed as usual.

To transform the normal correctly, it is crucial to normalize the normal after blending the weights together. This is done with the following code segment, assuming that the vector to be normalized resides in r0:

```
dp3 r11.x,r0.xyz,r0.xyz
rsq r11.xyz,r11.x
mul r3.xyz,r3.xyz,r11.xyz
```

Using a High-Level Shader Language

First, the definition of the vertex shader return structure is shown:

```
struct VS_OUTPUT
{
 float4 Pos    : POSITION;
 float3 Normal: NORMAL;
 float2 Tex    : TEXCOORD0;
};
```

The function header contains space for the normal and position data for each morph target intended to use:

```
VS_OUTPUT VS(
 float3 Pos1   : POSITION0,
 float3 Pos2   : POSITION1,

   ...
 float3 Posn   : POSITIONN,
 float3 Normal1 : NORMAL0,
 float3 Normal2 : NORMAL1,

   ...
 float3 NormalN : NORMALN,
 float2 Tex    : TEXCOORD0)
{
    VS_OUTPUT output;
    float3 normal;
    float3 position;

 position=Pos1;
 position+=(Pos1-Pos2)*weight[1];
 position+=(Pos1-Pos2)*weight[2];

 // up to N times, the term (Pos1-Pos2) simplifies to Pos2
 // when data is precomputed
 position+=(Pos1-PosN)*weight[N];
```

```
normal=Normal1;
normal +=( Normal1- Normal2)*weight[1];
normal +=( Normal1- Normal3)*weight[2];

// up to N times, the term (Pos1-Pos2) simplifies to Pos2
// when data is precomputed
normal+=( Normal1- NormalN)*weight[N];
normal=normalize(normal)
    ...
```

Summary

The linear interpolation of the normal sometimes leads to an incorrectly rendered object. For interpolating the direction of a normal, the use of quaternions and SLERP [Bobick98] interpolation can lead to a better visual appearance of this interpolation. Under Vertex Shader v2.0, with its limited set of instruction slots, the technique is inadequate. Under Vertex Shader v3.0, the interpolation of morph targets, which can represent a linear animation morph sequence, is often called "in-between" objects or "step-objects." Morph target animation on a vertex shader can be a quite useful method when a limited number of targets are used. However it should be noted that the programmer has to take care of many variables, constant registers, and stream data and their correct mapping to the graphics card. Further morph targets can also contain in-between targets as [Burkersroda04] has described in *ShaderX³*. Then, each morph target is a linear morphing, which must be computed accordingly. In the end, morph target animation can consume a great deal of memory, but serves well if different regions of a mesh have to be animated independently.

References

[Burkersroda04] Burkersroda, Ronny, *ShaderX³*, Charles River Media, 2004.
[Bobick98] Bobick, Nick, "Rotating Objects Using Quaternions," available online at *http://www.gamasutra.com/features/19980703/quaternions_01.htm*, July 3, 1998.

1.5

Real-Time Character Animation on the GPU

Michael Nischt and Elisabeth André

In today's computer games, virtual characters are becoming more and more realistic due to a higher polygon count and improved lighting and animation techniques. However, rendering a busy scene with many of them can consume a serious amount of computational power at the burden of other subsystems, such as collision detection, artificial intelligence, or game logic. Since the early days of programmable shaders, developers have been trying to shift the calculation toward the GPU, but it is not yet working to full capacity. In this article, we describe how the capabilities of the newest graphics hardware may be exploited to speed up the animation of characters. We start with a brief description of widely used animation techniques followed by a discussion of an earlier GPU-based implementation approach. Afterward, we explain how to separate vertex modification from rendering, which is advisable if the latter is done in multiple passes. Finally, we provide guidelines to decide whether utilizing the GPU for animation purposes is reasonable and indicate which enhancements may be achievable with the upcoming generation of graphic chips.

Common Animation Techniques

Before stepping into algorithms, we provide a brief overview of the employed animation techniques. We restrict ourselves to the most commonly used techniques. A comprehensive overview of animation techniques may be found in [Lander97], [Lander00], and [Watt03].

Morphing

A still widely used technique is *morphing*, which is nothing more than performing a weighted linear interpolation between the vertices of some meshes. A very popular implementation is so-called *vertex tweening*, where only two key meshes are blended varying by time. A well-known problem of vertex tweening is the occurrence of distortions if a body is rotated (see [Watt03]). A more sophisticated approach, which does not suffer this affliction, is to use the technique for small local displacements only. These are represented by relative vectors from a base mesh to the target meshes and therefore are called *morph targets*. A good collection of those is probably the most intuitive way to perform facial animations, because the interpolation weights often correspond to emotions or modifiers, such as "raise-left-eyebrow." Another common technique is muscular deformation, triggered by joint angles of an underlying skeleton, which is the topic of the next subsection.

Skeletal Animation

Because the interpolation weights of the morph targets are an intuitive parameterization for local displacements, a virtual skeleton provides a natural interface for body motions, and using inverse kinematics enables the generation of new animations on the fly. Furthermore, the skeleton's joint angles can be blended easily if a transition is needed. Older skeleton-based techniques usually rely on simple *hierarchical* animation. To accomplish this, a mesh vertex is attached to exactly one bone by transforming it with the inverse of a bone's world matrix. At any frame, the bone's position or orientation changes, the vertex must be transformed with the bone's current world matrix. The problem with this technique is that either the body has to be composed of several rigid body meshes, or a buckling occurs at regions where two bones are connected. Since this method results in very unnatural animations for humans, *skeletal subspace deformation* is used to achieve a visual enhancement. By employing this technique, a single vertex can be attached to multiple bones and be transformed by them. The transformation process is very similar: just put each vertex into every associated bone space by multiplying the inverse of the initial transformation, and then apply the current world transformation. Afterward, the resulting vertices are blended using the standard morphing technique from the last subsection. Here, a blending weight can be regarded as an influencing factor of a single bone, which usually decreases with the distance from the bone's center of mass.

A Shader Model 2.0 Based Approach

There has been a significant amount of research on making better use of the GPU (for example, see [GPUGems04]).

We start from the work described in [Beeson04], a sophisticated approach that is hard to improve without using the Shader Model 3.0 multiple render targets and four component floating-point texture formats, such as A32B32G32R32F in DirectX 9.0. The approach is of high interest to our work because the referred implementation uses morph targets for facial animation and skeletal subspace deformation for body movements, as introduced in the last section.

One of the first things Beeson emphasizes is the great challenge to fit the animation data into the fixed number of input registers—even for Vertex Shader 3.0 the limit of 16 input registers with four components each still remains. Having four registers already consumed by the position, normal, tangent, and texture-coordinate attributes, there are 12 left for animation data. We agree with the author that four bones influencing a single vertex suffice, and therefore a skeletal animation algorithm should only use one register for blending indices and another for the blending weights. Difficulties arising from a fixed number of registers do not become apparent until using morph targets that quickly fill the remaining 10 registers—in particular, if a morph target also includes normals and tangents. The basic idea behind Beeson's reference implementation is to omit the additional tangents and just reorthonormalize the tangent of the neutral pose with the morphed normal. As a result, up to five morph targets can be used. Another limitation is the number of available constant registers. The morph targets can almost be ignored because only a single scalar is needed for each active vertex weight, but every bone's deformation matrix uses up to four full constant registers. A common solution to both, which allows the processing of complex skeletons, and enables the usage of many morph targets, is to split the mesh into different partitions and use a separate call to a `DrawPrimitives` function for each. Of course, this neither increases the number of active morph targets per vertex nor the number of bone influences per vertex. More precisely, the upper bounds apply even to all vertices of a single triangle, because processing is done upon primitives. Finally, it is possible to use specialized shader variants compiled with the upper bounds for the submesh instead of using the original ones. On the other hand, always keep in mind that every batch consumes a certain amount of communication with the graphics driver.

An even more serious problem than the amount of per-vertex data is that modifications are performed during the rendering process. As a consequence, the geometry is transformed every pass anew. Using multi-pass techniques, such as shadow- or dynamic-cube mapping, an application can soon become vertex-limited. For the same reason, the modified vertices are not available to the application. This information may be required, however, for the accurate detection of collisions or the generation of shadow volumes.

Separation of Vertex Modification and Rendering

Fortunately, the latest graphics hardware makes available a number of new possibilities for character animation. Probably the easiest modification method that can be applied to an existing Shader Model 2.0 algorithm is to use dynamic branching in order to skip the processing of unused bones or morph targets. Likewise, it is now possible to separate the modification and the rendering process if the hardware supports four component floating-point texture formats and multiple render targets. These are needed because each manipulated vertex attribute—in most cases, the position, the normal, and maybe the tangent—are written to a single pixel of a dedicated render target. In the next section, this process is described as well as how the final vertices can be accessed during the rendering passes or by the application afterward.

Storage Procedures

As mentioned, vertex data are written to pixels after the desired modification has been performed. Regarding the vertex array as simple and one-dimensional, and the frame buffer as two-dimensional, the following bijective mapping between both is applied:

```
index2D.x = index % textureWidth;
index2D.y = index / textureWidth;

index = index2D.y * texWidth + index2D.x;
```

Using this convention, a common procedure is to draw a screen-aligned quad with corner points $(0,0),(1,0),(0,1),(1,1)$. A minimal vertex shader, as follows, maps them to the canonical viewing volume. Finally, the Viewport, which is adjusted by the texture's dimension, carries out the rest.

```
float4 VS(float4 index2D : POSITION0, out float4 outIndex2D : TEXCO-
ORD0) : POSITION
{
    outIndex2D = index2D;
    return float4(2 * index2D.x - 1, -2 * index2D.y + 1, 0, 1);
}
```

Furthermore, the two-dimensional index is forwarded, and therefore, the interpolated values almost correspond to the index of the destination pixel. The only thing left is to correct them by the half of a texel in each direction—see [Steed05] for a detailed description on how to map texels to pixels. Retrieving the original vertex data is done by using texture lookups. Taken for granted, these are of the same dimension as the render targets. Now, modification can be performed and the results assigned to the output registers as the following code indicates:

```
float2 halfTexel = float2(0.5/texWidth,0.5/texHeight);

void PS(float4 index2D : TEXCOORD0,
            out float4 position : COLOR0,
        out float4 normal    : COLOR1, ...)
{
    index2D.xy += halfTexel;
    float4 vertAttr0 = tex2Dlod(Sampler0, index2D);
    float4 vertAttr1 = tex2Dlod(Sampler1, index2D);
    ..
    ..
    // perform modification and assign the
    // final vertex attributes to the output registers
}
```

The main advantage of this approach lies in the fact that it keeps the workload for the vertex and the geometry processing units at a minimum. On the other hand, all per-vertex data has to be accessed through texture lookups, and the use of all the 16 sampler stages that the latest pixel shader version provides may result in a slowdown. Furthermore, the number of constant registers is lower for pixel shaders—224 instead of 256 guaranteed for vertex shaders at version 3.0. This fact turns out even more problematic, as it is not possible to divide the modification process into several pieces because only a single quad is drawn. As an unavoidable result, the constant registers must hold all the bone matrices and morph target weights instead of only those used by a group of vertices. Therefore, a straightforward reuse of most existing Shader Model 2.0 algorithms is not feasible. Another point worth mentioning is redundant computation, which may occur if the number of pixels being written to is greater than the number of vertices available to modify. Unfortunately, this problem cannot always be avoided due to constraints on texture size. Nevertheless, the approach is almost ideal for copy operations and simple algorithms like vertex tweening.

Another methodology is to apply the modification in the vertex shader and use only a dummy pixel shader, which maps its inputs to the render targets. In contrast to the previous approach, the destination pixel must be specified explicitly as a Vertex Shader input, which is accomplished by using an additional input stream containing the two-dimensional index. The following code fragment illustrates the setup:

```
for(int i=0; i<numberOfVertices; i++)
{
    // 1d -> 2d
    index2D.x = (float) (i % texWidth);
    index2D.y = (float) (i / texWidth);

    // normalization
    indices2D[i].x = index2D.x / texWidth  + halfTexel.x;
    indices2D[i].y = index2D.y / texHeight + halfTexel.y;
}
```

First, the 1D index is converted into a 2D index, exactly as mentioned previously. Afterward, it is normalized in such way that it can be used for texture lookups. For a better comprehension, Figure 1.5.1 shows all possible indices using an 8 × 8 render target.

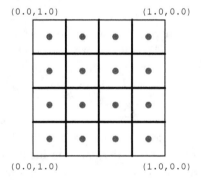

FIGURE 1.5.1 *All indices using an 8 × 8 render target.*

A great benefit of this approach is that existing algorithms, such as those used by [Beeson04], can be adopted with minimal modifications. In this case, we replace the texture coordinate, which is not modified, by the index of the destination pixel.

```
float4 VS(float4 index2D : TEXCOORD0, .. ,
        out float4 pixel     ,
        out float4 position : TEXCOORD0,
        out float4 normal    : TEXCOORD1, ..) : POSITION
{
```

```
        // perform modification and assign the
        // final vertex attributes to the output registers
        ..

        ..
        return float4(2 * index2D.x - 1, -2 * index2D.y + 1, 0, 1);
}
```

An eminent advantage using this technique is that the segmentation into modification groups is easy. The difference compared to procedures, which combine modification and rendering, is that vertices of two disjoint groups can belong to the same triangle. Moreover, it is actually possible to perform additional modifications in the pixel shader and the index may be forwarded in order to use texture lookups. (Note: here, the index can be used with adding an offset.) However, we do not recommend this extension due to our experience with speed issues. Finally, it should be mentioned that with this technique it is also possible to perform even more specific manipulations by explicit declaration of the target pixel. As a result, it can be seen as an *indexed* version of the ProcessVertices function as provided by Direct3D. Thus, we never took advantage of this; the pure ProcessVertices functionality is sufficient. Unfortunately, the Direct3D implementation is always performed on the CPU.

Accessing the Modified Data

Using one of the procedures described earlier, the modified vertex attributes finally are stored in the pixels of the render targets during the last stage of the graphics pipeline. The tricky part now is to get the modified data back into the pipeline. In doing so, a bypass through the system memory must be avoided.

A perfect method would be a "Direct-Render-To-VertexBuffer" by binding a VertexBuffer as a render target during the first rendering pass or by binding the render target as a VertexBuffer within the second. Unfortunately, this is not yet possible, although a similar Direct-Render-To-Texture functionality is available in both Direct3D and OpenGL (EXT_framebuffer_object). Nevertheless, using OpenGL (ARB_pixel_buffer_object), it is possible to perform a fast, asynchronous copy from a render target to a vertex buffer object inside the video memory.

Another approach is to make use of the present Direct-Render-To-Texture capability and to access the modified vertex attributes by using texture lookups within the Vertex Shader. In order to read the final values, the 2D indices, computed during the second modification technique mentioned previously, can be reused as they are. The following code fragment illustrates how to modify an existing vertex shader if vertex positions, normals, and tangents are stored in individual textures:

```
float4 VS(float4 index2D   : TEXCOORD0,
          float2 inTexCoord: TEXCOORD1
          out float2 outTexCoord : TEXCOORD0, ..) : POSITION
{
    float4 position = tex2Dlod(PositionSampler, index2D);
    float4 normal   = tex2Dlod(NormalSampler,   index2D);
    float4 tangent  = tex2Dlod(TangentSampler,  index2D);
```

```
      outTexCoord = inTexCoord;

      // do lighting, ..
      ..
      ..
  }
```

It is important to note that vertex textures have a high latency. Because current available graphics hardware that supports vertex textures cannot execute vertex textures and other instructions in parallel, this latency can't be hidden by the execution time of other instructions.

Moreover, this problem is amplified because coherency of texture access affects performance, and the hardware is usually optimized to operate on square blocks instead of linear data. The problem becomes worse when using multiple rendering passes, which is why we recommend the previous, nondirect method when using OpenGL.

CPU versus GPU

There is no question that performing vertex modification on the GPU, if done wisely, can increase the overall performance. This section provides hints about when to shift the workload toward the GPU and which technique should be used in a particular situation.

First, it is important to note that, if applicable, it is preferable to perform modification and rendering in a single pass. Pushing the data all the way through the graphics pipeline in order to modify some vertex attributes in a separate pass would be an avoidable overhead. On the other hand, using a technique proposed in the last section enables reuse of the modified data during multiple rendering passes. It is also possible to copy the modified positions back into system memory. A practical application is to perform accurate collision detections if bounding tests succeed. At this point it is worth mentioning that according to our experimental results, accessing the modified vertex attributes using vertex texturing is always slower than performing a fast copy within the video memory. At this point, unfortunately, this capability is provided exclusively by OpenGL.

Moreover, we have discovered that the maximum number of active morph targets per vertex can be used as a criterion about when deciding whether the GPU should be utilized at all. We evaluated two different implementations to bypass the problem that only a few morph targets fit into the input registers of a vertex shader. Unfortunately, none of them is practicable. The first one suffers from the texture fetch latency because all morph targets are stored in a texture that is accessed within the vertex shader. In contrast to this approach, the second only requires a single texture lookup, but the additional modification pass, during which the individual morph targets are summed up, adds stress to the hardware.

In addition, some optimizations that can be easily achieved on the CPU may not be possible or may have a contrary effect on the GPU. For example, vertex positions have to be duplicated prior to storing them into a `VertexBuffer` if different vertex normals are used to create a hard edge or if texturing is not continuous. Consequently, applying modification before splitting the vertices can help to prevent unnecessary computations.

Finally, a hybrid approach like the one that follows can be the solution for many of the problems discussed previously:

1. Let the CPU compute the final vertex attributes used during rendering frame n and n + k.
2. Let the GPU perform vertex tweening at frames greater than n and smaller than n + k.

The great benefit of this technique is that vertex tweening is supported by almost all hardware, and there are no restrictions on the other modification algorithms used, because these are executed on the CPU. Likewise, the algorithm is scalable because k can be adjusted, whereby increasing the value may result in a distortion, but computational power is saved. On the other side, the application must be able to preestimate a character's state for k frames, which in particular compromises whether the character is visible during the next k frames. This technique should be used if animations are fairly complex and the virtual scene contains many characters, which allows starting the individual modifications to be *phase shifted* to prevent negative performance peaks at single frames.

Summary

This article presented two separate GPU-based vertex modification and rendering methods that avoid recomputation during multiple rendering passes and therefore increase the application potential of GPU-based character animation. However, to achieve this separation, the vertices have to be sent through all the stages of the graphics pipeline. Furthermore, the direct reuse of a frame buffer's content as a vertex stream is not yet possible. In addition, we showed example scenarios where it is not reasonable to perform the computation on the GPU even though it is in general more optimized on floating-point operations. As a consequence, there is no single answer to the question of whether to perform computations on the GPU or the CPU and which techniques should be used.

References

[Beeson04] Beeson, C., *Animation the "Dawn"* in F. Randima (ed.): GPU Gems, Addison Wesley, pp. 63–72, 2004.

[Calver05] Calver, D., *Accessing and Modifying Topology on the GPU* in W. Engel (ed.): *ShaderX³*, Charles River Media, pp. 5–19, 2005.

[GPUGems04] Randima, F., *GPU Gems*, Addison Wesley, 2004.

[Green05] Green, S., *GeForce 6 Series OpenGL Extensions*, 2005.

[Lander97] Lander, J., *On Creating Cool Real-Time 3D*, 1997, *http://www.gamasutra. com,* 1997

[Lander00] Lander, J., *Using Technology to Create Believable 3D Characters*, Game Developers Conference, 2002.

[Latta04] Latta, L., *Building a Million Particle System*, Game Developers Conference, 2004.

[MollerHaines02] Akenine-Möller, T., and E. Haines, *Real-Time Rendering Second Edition*, AK Peters Ltd, pp. 35–36, 2002.

[Steed05] Steed, J., *Directly Mapping Texels to Pixel*, DirectX 9.0 SDK Update, June 2005.

[Watt03] Watt, A., F. Policarpo, *3D Games: Animation and Advanced Real-Time Rendering, Volume Two*, Pearson Education Limited, 2003.

1.6

AniTextures

Wessam Bahnassi

Of Animation and Texture

In our daily graphics programming life, we are used to using many different techniques to build complex 3D scenes. Among these techniques is texturing, which gives 3D objects a distinct look, and animation, which blows life into the whole scene. The usage of textures has become much more than just decal-rendered polygons. Textures are now being utilized as lookup tables, normal maps, height maps, masks, depth maps, and more. Today, we present a new usage for textures: animation. This article explains how modern hardware can aid in performing common animation calculations by using its advanced capabilities. Since most animations are calculated for display output only, the natural place for doing these calculations is in the GPU.

Colors of Animation

In its simplest form, an animation is defined as a set of values that change over time. There are several different ways to manage animations, each of which is a specific balance between speed and memory consumption. For example, one way is to lay out an array of key values so that each entry in the array is matched to an animation frame (see Figure 1.6.1).

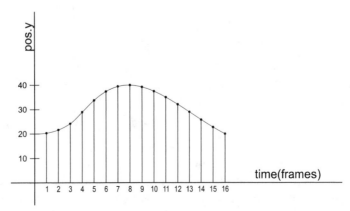

FIGURE 1.6.1 *An animation curve in its plotted form.*

Here, we can easily choose the keys used in the current time of animation by looking up the previous and next keys from the current time. For example:

```
// Get animation value at frame 45.4
float fPrevKey = aAnimKeys[45];
float fNextKey = aAnimKeys[46];
float fCurrentValue = LERP(fPrevKey,fNextKey,0.4);
```

This is usually called "plotted animation" because it has a key at each frame, and this is not the natural way that animators define animations. Plotted animations result naturally from motion capture data, and unnaturally by animators explicitly asking the 3D animation package to convert their animation data to this form (for example, plotting a complex animation mixer).

However, common animations usually have keys laid out to specify what is called a *function curve* (fcurve). This curve, when evaluated with its formula at the required time, returns the correct interpolated value. The keys themselves now hold parameters that are fed to the evaluation function. Common evaluation functions include the linear interpolator (which does not need any additional key data), Hermite spline interpolator, and the Cubic spline interpolator. The last two require additional tangent information at each key to define the slope of the function curve at a specified key.

The most important aspect of this type of animation is that it is not tied directly to time. That is, you can have one key at frame 1 and another key at frame 1000 and use a Hermite interpolator to ease in or ease out animation, whereas in the case of plotted animation this would take 1000 array entries to define *almost* the same animation (see Figure 1.6.2).

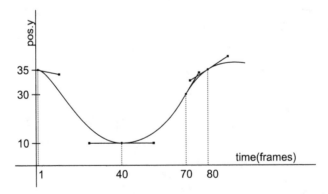

FIGURE 1.6.2   *Function curve defining animation over time.*

This clearly shows how fcurves conserve memory at the expense of additional calculations. The calculations even grow more complex with real-world animations. A single fcurve animation can contain many key frames at different times. This requires advanced management to be able to extract the correct relevant keys of the function before passing them to the interpolator. This operation usually involves a searching algorithm (for example, a binary search). Such an operation is most suited for a CPU and not a GPU. The GPU architecture is not optimized for conditions and breaking loops, while this is what searching algorithms are about! Thus, if we want to do animation quickly on the GPU, we need to use plotted animation. The application can either receive plotted animation directly from art files, or generate them easily by doing an evaluation pass over all animation frames at the start of day.

So, What Are AniTextures?

AniTextures are textures that hold plotted animations, where each texel maps to an animation key at a specified time. Textures are two-dimensional by nature, whereas animations are one-dimensional. This suggests that we can store many animations in the second dimension of the texture, and this is actually one of the benefits of AniTextures: increased batching! Differently animated parameters can refer to different animations in the single texture, so each can behave differently from the other.

Common animation loops are from 1 to 10 seconds long. For 30 fps playback, this means 300 key frames. Textures can be as big as 2048 × 2048; this means we can store 2048 animations each about 1 minute in length (over 30 hours of animation) all in one AniTexture, which is a large amount of data. For a single animation, we store key values consecutively in the x dimension; each different animation is stored in a single full row.

Figure 1.6.3 looks at the overall layout of an AniTexture.

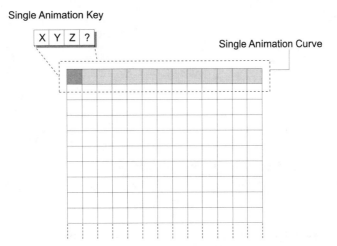

FIGURE 1.6.3   *An overall look at the layout of an AniTexture.*

The actual values stored in AniTextures can be of any suitable type. Values with limited range can fit nicely into normal A8R8G8B8 textures; this includes color animation, angular values, and directional values. Values of higher range need floating-point textures to be able to correctly represent the animation; positional information is a nice example of values that need floating-point textures.

So, based on what we want to animate, we need different capabilities of hardware. In the first case (limited range values), AniTextures can be utilized on any shader-capable hardware. In the latter case, hardware capable of handling floating-point textures is required (as is the case with many of the common Shader Model 2.0 GPUs).

Also, *where* you want to utilize the results will affect the required level of hardware support. AniTextures can be evaluated both at the pixel shader level or the vertex shader level thanks to the advent of Shader Model 3.0 hardware.

How AniTextures Work

It is well known that animations can be evaluated at subframes to achieve smooth animations that play at scenes running in high refresh rates (60 fps or more hopefully). For 30 fps animation playback speed, this means that it is required to find values at subframes like 12.5, 24.75, and so on. The fractional number denotes the mix amount between the previous and next key frames. Now, if we remember how GPUs sample textures, we can see that it does just what we want! Given a texture coordinate, the texture will be sampled such that the output is linearly interpolated between the two texels surrounding the current UV coordinate (see Figure 1.6.4). The amount of mix is directly controlled by how close the UV coordinate is to one texel than the other (the fractional part of the texel position).

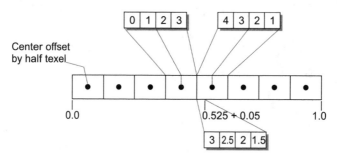

FIGURE 1.6.4   *Interpolating values in an AniTexture is done by normally sampling the texture at the correct UV coordinate.*

One thing we should keep in mind is that texels need to be sampled at their centers in order for us to be able to get discreet values from the texture. This requires a half-texel offset in the UV coordinates we use. So, at time 0, the correct UV for an animation stored at the first row of the AniTexture is:

```
float fU = (1/fAniTexture_Width) * 0.5;
float fV = (1/fAniTexture_Height) * 0.5;
```

Basically we are getting interpolation between two four-channel keys of animation for free! All we have to do is calculate the correct UV coordinate based on the current animation time and use that for accessing the AniTexture.

One thing we did not mention yet are the dimensions of the AniTexture. As we said, many animations should fit in the AniTexture. However, not all animations have the same length. For example, the walk loop might be 2 seconds long, while the run loop might be 1 second long. How should these animations be fit into the AniTexture?

For reasons that will become apparent in the next section, we need all our animations to occupy their full row. Say we have an AniTexture that is 512 texels wide. Here, a 300-frame animation needs to be stretched to fit 512 texels. A 100-frame animation needs to be stretched to fit 512 texels, too. The application should store the amount of stretching done on each animation for correct playback speed later. We name this value the *Keyframe Step*, and it is calculated as:

$$Keyframe\ Step = \frac{AniTexture\ Width}{Original\ Animation\ Length}$$

For a given time, we can calculate the UV coordinates as:

$$U = Keyframe \times Time \times TexelSize$$

where $TexelSize = \dfrac{1}{AniTexture\ Width}$

KeyframeStep values for the different animations are best passed as constants set along with the AniTexture.

The AniTexture Controls

Animations can be run in several modes of playback; also, the interpolation of key frames can have different modes. Interpolation modes include constant and linear interpolation. Playback modes include forward only, loop, and ping-pong. These generally specify how time outside the animation length is interpreted.

Interpolation Modes

Constant Interpolation: Also read "no-interpolation!" This mode of interpolation is useful for animations with sudden jumps (for example, clock arms). Here, the mixing weight is evaluated. If it is less than 0.5, the previous keyframe value is returned; otherwise, the next keyframe is returned. Remembering what texture filtering modes we have available, we find that *nearest point sampling* implements the same idea. So, to use constant interpolation, we just set the AniTexture sampler state to use point filtering, and that is it.

Linear Interpolation: This is the default mode of interpolation. As we mentioned previously, this mode works by taking a weighted average between the previous and next keyframe values based on how close the sampling point is to one key as opposed to the other. This is exactly what *linear filtering* is in terms of texture sampler states.

Spline Interpolation: This mode has no meaning for plotted animations. But just for reference, using a *Gaussian Quad* texture filter will give ease-in/ease-out results between two keyframes. Because our keyframes are so close to each other, the effect of this interpolation type is not noticeable.

Playback Modes

Forward Only: In this mode of playback, time values that exceed the animation length result in the same value as the last keyframe in the animation. The graph in Figure 1.6.5 shows the behavior of this mode.

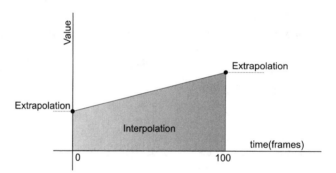

FIGURE 1.6.5   *Forward-only playback clamps the terminal animation keyframes for out-of-range time requests.*

Playback modes for AniTextures are manipulated via controlling *texture addressing mode* in the sampler state. For this kind of playback, using *Clamp* addressing will give us the correct behavior for time values that exceed animation length in both directions (negative and positive). This way, animated parameters "freeze" their last value after their animation time is done.

Loop: A common mode for walking characters and many other animated parameters. In this mode, the net time is calculated as the global time modulus or the animation length. This results in a saw-tooth access pattern as seen in Figure 1.6.6.

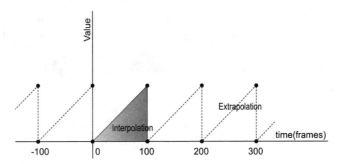

FIGURE 1.6.6 *Loop playback reinterprets out-of-range time requests as repeats within the animation length.*

Loop playback can be achieved by using *Wrap* addressing mode. Easy enough?

Ping-Pong: Although less common than the loop mode, ping-pong still has its uses (for example, certain dance animations). This mode is similar to loop, but the loop is not for a single forward pass over the animation length; rather, each loop covers a full forward run, and then is followed by a backward run. Figure 1.6.7 illustrates this.

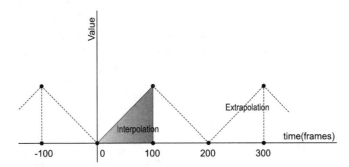

FIGURE 1.6.7 *Ping-pong playback plots as a curve made of repeating triangles. The top peak of each triangle is at the last frame of the original animation.*

Ping-pong playback is set by applying *Mirror* addressing to the AniTexture sampler.

Because AniTextures make heavy use of texture addressing modes, it now becomes apparent why we needed to stretch our animations to cover the full row of texels that an animation resides in. Otherwise, we would need to implement the addressing ourselves, which is far from optimal when compared to the built-in addressing capabilities of the GPU.

Everything seems to work well together, except for one small issue that appears when using a combo of linear interpolation and loop animation. Due to the fact that we are using wrap addressing, when we sample at the end of the texture (0 or 1) we actually make a blend between the first and last texels. Figure 1.6.8 illustrates the problem more clearly.

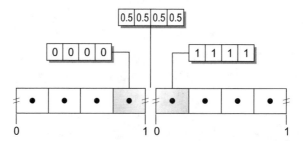

FIGURE 1.6.8   *Sampling at either end of the texture involves a linear blend between the first and last texels.*

Based on what is actually being animated, this might not be much of a problem. One extreme case in which this problem proves to be annoying positional animation. To be specific, when the first and last keyframes are not staged together, we notice a number of frames in which the position is interpolated between the last and first keyframes. Figure 1.6.9 shows a ball that plays an animation that moves it along the Y-axis in looping linear interpolation. The problem is apparent at the end of each loop.

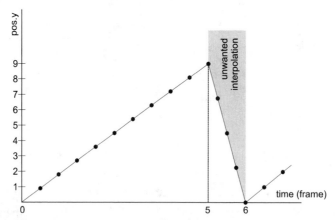

FIGURE 1.6.9   *Based on what is being animated, the problem might not be apparent. In this case, it is very visible and can be annoying.*

This problem can be solved by reverting to constant interpolation, although it results in somewhat choppy motion at high rendering frame rates.

A Couple of Notes

AniTextures open a wide variety of capabilities to the developer, among them animation mixing. This can be very easily and efficiently implemented via AniTextures. One can mix sampled values using different mix weights or just add them together and renormalize them to get that half-running, half-walking character animation all done on the GPU.

AniTextures do not make use of mipmaps. While this would have been a great way of managing LOD for animations, it simply does not work for us here because smaller mipmaps have to shrink in size in both directions, which means we will actually lose a big number of full animations with each smaller mipmap level.

What the Sample Applications Do

ON THE CD

On the companion CD-ROM are two sample applications. One implements AniTextures in a simple way to clearly introduce the technique. The second sample implements an advanced application of AniTextures for animating a skinned character. Both samples include the shader code required to correctly deal with AniTextures, as well as setup code to actually create the AniTextures.

In the case of the skinning sample, the AniTexture contains animations of positional and rotational data of the many bones influencing the character's skin. The application builds bone transformation matrices out of the correct keyframes based on the current animation time. These matrices are stored in another texture that is accessed in the vertex shader to get the influencing bone transforms for each vertex.

Both sample applications are heavily commented with descriptions of implementation details. Have fun!

Conclusion

This article introduced a new method for doing animations fully on the GPU by storing large amounts of animation keyframes into 2D textures. The process involves careful construction of the AniTexture and correct texture coordinate calculations. The article exploited the many combinations of texture addressing and filtering options used with AniTextures to get specific output results (for example, looping and ping-pong). AniTextures can contain integer values or floating-point values, and can be used to animate any parameter like colors, position, and rotation.

AniTextures open a big area for research to developers. Implementing animation mixers with AniTextures is seamless, very simple, and efficient. The importance of AniTextures will increase with the advent of geometry shaders and newer shader models, because these will have less latency when sampling textures at the vertex level.

RENDERING TECHNIQUES

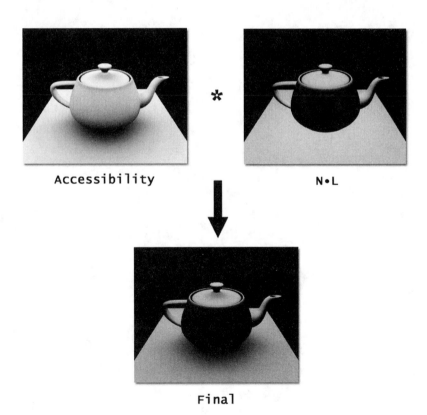

Accessibility   *   N•L

Final

Introduction

Sebastien St. Laurent

Welcome to the "Rendering Techniques" section of *ShaderX⁴*. This section is the meatiest of this book, as it covers what is at the core of rendering with shaders —visual techniques to bring your graphics to a new level of realism. That being said, this edition of *ShaderX* is no exception and brings you the latest techniques, taking advantage of both the latest generation of rendering hardware and techniques that can be used on older hardware, enhancing all graphical experiences. We will be covering a wide variety of topics regarding several aspects of rendering.

The *Interlaced Rendering* article explains how you can take advantage of interlacing, a technique used in television broadcasting technology to reduce your fill rate use while maintaining good visual quality. Following this, *Triangle Mesh Tangent Space Calculation* goes in depth on the generation of tangent space matrices as used in the *FarCry* game.

Hardware-Based Ambient Occlusion, *Ambient Occlusion Fields*, and *Real-Time Obscurances* approach different aspects of the topic of enhancing object lighting by the use of ambient occlusion, which takes into account surface self-shadowing and self-reflectance. The next two articles, *Rendering Surface Details with Relief Mapping* and *Bump my Shiny Metal*, discuss the enhancement of geometric surface details by using various bump mapping and relief mapping techniques. In addition, *Dot-Product for Efficient Detail Texture Mapping* goes over efficient techniques that can be used to implement high-quality detail mapping even on lower-end hardware.

The following article, *Real-Time Rendering and Simulation of the Airbrush Media for Metallic Appearance*, overviews in detail how you can take advantage of the rendering hardware to treat your materials as if they were airbrushed. *Dynamic Global Illuminations Using an Environment Map* covers a technique that can be used to generate quality global illumination of a scene by taking advantage of environment mapping techniques. Speaking of which, *Dynamic Glossy Environment Reflection Using Summed-Area Tables* discusses a technique in which an environment map can be dynamically blurred at any level to handle various levels of surface specularity, and *Real-Time Environment Mapping with Equal Solid-Angle Spherical Quad-Map* approaches an alternative to cube mapping that offers better quality by ensuring an even distribution of samples within the environment map.

The final articles are self-explanatory but cover a wide variety of techniques that can greatly enhance your graphics. *Fog Volumes*, as the title implies, covers a powerful technique that can be used to generate volumetric fog. In addition, *Real-Time Caustics* goes over an approach that can be used to render caustics generated by both reflections and refractions in real time. *Reflective Shadow Maps* covers a radiosity-like approach that follows the idea of shadow maps.

As you can see, there is a lot of material to cover, so let's get to work!

2.1

Interlaced Rendering

Oles V. Shishkovtsov

This article may be thought of as a research in GPU-based deinterlacing. Its primary purpose, however, is to allow computationally or bandwidth-intensive graphics applications to run almost twice as fast with minimal loss of visual quality, or to raise the visual quality bar by means of temporal supersampling without too much of a performance impact. In the context of computer-generated images, this article discusses a form of temporal caching.

Introduction

The idea behind this technique may be familiar to people who are set to deal with television and/or digital video. When the first TV standards were defined around 1930, there wasn't a technology available that could record or display fast enough. In those days, interlaced transmission was used to reduce the bandwidth requirements by half without losing vertical resolution in quiet areas (in motion areas you would not notice much anyway). So, by means of the interlaced scan, frame rate is doubled as compared to that of the progressive scan under the same bandwidth occupation. Thus, the interlaced scan allows still or slow-moving areas to be perceived with high vertical details, while fast-moving areas are perceived with a higher temporal rate (at half vertical resolution). If you replace all the occurrences of the word "bandwidth" with "bandwidth and computation," you will understand the importance of such old technique to CG graphics, assuming adequate image reconstruction can be developed for traditional (now) progressive displays.

Field-based Rendering

For each frame, we have to keep track of the current field (top or bottom) and render only to that field. The whole process is illustrated in Figure 2.1.1. To accomplish this, we modify the current projection transformation to shift the sampling positions one-half pixel up or down depending on the field we are rendering. To make the rendering process efficient, we must either subdivide the rendering target into two parts (upper half for "top" fields and lower half for "bottom" fields) or use two separate rendering targets of half-height each. The first option is easier from an implementation point of view, but the second approach is much more efficient, especially on multi-GPU setups where the driver can easily distinguish what to synchronize among GPUs.

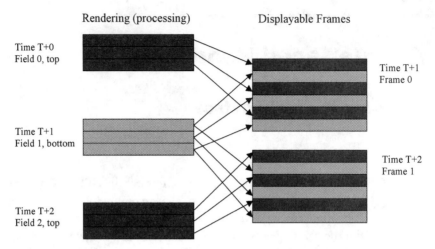

Rendering (processing)   Displayable Frames

Time T+0
Field 0, top

                                                                                Time T+1
                                                                                Frame 0

Time T+1
Field 1, bottom

                                                                                Time T+2
                                                                                Frame 1

Time T+2
Field 2, top

FIGURE 2.1.1   *Field-based rendering illustration.*

Mipmapping Issues

There is one caveat in the basic implementation of field-based rendering. The mipmap level selection used, for a given fragment, is dependent on the instantaneous ratio of variation of the texture coordinate space (u, v) to the variation of the screen coordinates (x, y). By reducing vertical resolution of sampling in field rendering, smaller resolution mipmap levels are selected, which results in blurring of the textures in the final picture. The best solution would be to supply our own calculated partial derivative of texture coordinates with respect to the screen-space *y* coordinate in all texture-sampling instructions. In HLSL, this would look like replacing all `tex2D` `(sampler,tc)` with `tex2Dgrad(sampler,tc,ddx(tc),ddy(tc)/2)`. Although the calculation of the derivatives can be done for any ps20 hardware [Pharr03], sampling with user-supplied gradients cannot be done without explicit hardware support. While this approach is correct, hardware support is limited and can be slow on current generations of hardware.

Fortunately, there is an alternative approach that is much cheaper and well supported—anisotropic texture filtering. Doubling the maximum number of anisotropic samples enhances vertical resolution almost up to the normal level and slightly improves horizontal texture resolution. In other words, if normal rendering is using a maximum anisotropy level of two, setting it to four will do the trick. Note that this is not the 100% correct solution, either, but it is difficult to tell visually.

Overview of Deinterlacing

Because a single frame consists of two fields generated at two different moments in time, we get the artifacts shown in Figure 2.1.2, which are usually called sawtooth-type edge distortion or mice teeth.

FIGURE 2.1.2   *Artifacts arising while moving the camera.*

The deinterlace process attempts to resolve this problem by creating a clean frame from the two fields. There are two basic classes of deinterlacing algorithms: non-motion-compensated and motion-compensated. Non-motion-compensated methods can be further subdivided into linear and nonlinear categories. Both categories contain spatial (or intrafield), temporal (or interfield), and spatio-temporal algorithms.

Let's start with a completely static scene: nothing moves, nothing blinks, and the camera is still. Displaying both fields interleaved (this is usually called "weave") produces exactly the same picture as if we render that picture in the conventional, progressive way. Everything works well until the scene becomes dynamic, by moving the camera, for example. That's because weave is a linear filter that implements pure temporal interpolation.

The most common solution for resolving such artifacts is blending fields together or displaying both fields one after another, filling missing (old) scanlines with averages of the scanline above and below. The later is usually called *bob-filter* or interpolation. Both methods lose the vertical resolution in addition to ghosting effects from blending and half-pixel jumping while the fields are interpolating. Because of these issues, it is not the ready-to-use, complete, and robust solution we are seeking.

The linear vertical-temporal filter is a combination of the linear-spatial and linear-temporal filters. The vertical-temporal deinterlacer is the best-performing of the linear filters. This method gradually reduces the vertical detail as the temporal frequencies increase. The contribution from the neighboring fields is limited to the high vertical frequencies, such that motion artifacts can be minimized.

A more sophisticated approach to deinterlacing uses some form of motion detection and compensation. Motion-compensated deinterlacing measures the interfield motion, and then aligns data between the two video fields, maximizing the vertical resolution of the image.

Motion compensation involves shifting the pixels in the two temporally displaced fields to a common point in time. Determining the amount of shift for each pixel is referred to as motion estimation, in which motion vectors are identified and tracked from one field to another. This is typically implemented as a block-matching process. The GPU-assisted implementation of motion estimation was already developed in

[Kelly04]. We show you how to use a simplified form of motion compensation specifically in the context of CG graphics.

For more interested readers, we recommend an excellent review of deinterlacing techniques by Gerard de Haan [Bellers00].

GPU-based Adaptive Deinterlacing

Our goal is to provide maximum detail in relatively still scenes while hiding the artifacts resulting from movement or subtle color changes such as blinking-light sources. We do this by deinterlacing only the parts of the image where it is needed and keeping other parts untouched. First, note that we can always use the last field rendered "as is" because it is guaranteed to be up to date. Therefore, we have to process only previous (old) fields, deinterlacing them as necessary. Interpolation has proven to be the method for deinterlacing (where needed) because it introduces the least artifacts. This means that we need to do a per-pixel selection between weaving and interpolation based on how much the area looks likely to have interlacing artifacts.

The pattern we are searching for can be formulated as follows: our old field's scanline significantly differs from the recent scanline above it *and* the recent scanline below it. But there is a problem here. Depending on the definition of "significantly differs," some parts of the image can be falsely detected as interlaced even for a totally static picture. This artifact is especially prominent on real object edges that are detected as similar to the interlaced pattern, but in fact they aren't. A simple correction step is to "undo" that decision on real edges if the recent pixel above significantly differs from the recent pixel below. In HLSL, the code to search the patterns and determining weight would look like the following:

```
half    detect_ilace   (half3 prev, half3 c0, half3 c1)
{
    half3    ilace   =    abs    (c0-prev)      *abs(c1-prev);
    half3    edge    =    abs    (c1-c0) *abs(c1-c0);
    half     w_ilace =    dot    (ilace, k1);
    half     w_edge  =    dot    (edge,k2);
        return saturate    (w_ilace - w_edge);
}
```

Here, $c0$ is the pixel above, $c1$ – below, $k1$-strength of interlace-pattern-detection, and $k2$-strength of edge-pattern-detection.

With the appropriate selection of $k1$ and $k2$, the algorithm can perform the interlace pattern detection well. The only problem left is that a few remaining pixels (less than 1% of the image, usually) may be slightly flickering, but only in static or almost static scenes. The solution we choose is pretty straightforward and directly mappable to the GPU. Because blending the fields in a static picture does not show ghosting and provides similar resolution to interpolation, we gradually lerp between two methods based on camera speed. Because camera movement (commonly called dominant motion) is the major factor causing interlacing artifacts, using its linear and angular velocity is a good estimation to determine which method to use.

Image Reprojection as a Form of Motion Compensation

Up to this point, all we get is a relatively good per-pixel adaptive deinterlacer running on any ps_2_0-capable GPU (with some trickery this can be made to run on ps_1_1 shader model hardware):

```
half3  deinterlace(float2 UV: TEXCOORD0, float2 UVC0: TEXCOORD1,
float2 UVC1: TEXCOORD2 ) : COLOR
{
        half3  prev   =     tex2D        (s_previous, UV);
        half3  c0     =     tex2D        (s_current,  UVC0);
        half3  c1     =     tex2D        (s_current,  UVC1);
        half3  r_bob  =     (c0+c1)/2.h;
        half3  r_blend=     (r_bob+prev)/2.h;
        half3  r_mix  =     lerp(r_blend,r_bob,
                            g_dominant_motion_factor);
        half3  r_weave=     prev;
        half   factor =     detect_ilace  (prev,c0,c1));
        return (lerp  (r_weave,r_mix,factor), factor);
}
```

The inherent difference between prerecorded video footage and real-time-generated CG graphics lies in the fact that we know "how the previous frame/field was constructed." That means that with some bookkeeping, we can easily render a frame or two from the past. In other words, we know each screen-space pixel 3D position in several time domains. One note should be made: most games that use a post-processing pipeline should already have position or depth data available at some place.

That is especially true for deferred renderers [Hargreaves04] where the G-buffer already contains more than enough data [Saito90].

In the offline world, many acceleration techniques were developed, and one of them was storing the positions of already rendered points (or micro-polys) of the previous frame and reprojecting them onto the new camera plane [Badt88] [Adelson95]. Those methods can save a considerable amount of computation (usually high-cost ray tracing) by recomputing only the pixels that are potentially incorrect. However, there are some problems: external (missing information outside the old frustum), internal (appearance of previously occluded pixels), exposure errors, and another one particularly important for CG graphics—shading errors—in which a point's color may change when viewed from a different angle or due to an external, loosely controllable influence such as a new light source.

We can use a similar approach in real-time rendering because it doesn't really matter what kind of errors we get—they will be similar to the interlaced patterns and will be discarded in favor of the deinterlaced pixel. So, the only context in which reprojection would be useful for us is when there is a possibility to keep full vertical resolution at the current pixel.

The straightforward implementation on a GPU requires us to walk through the old-pixel positions, reprojecting them onto the new camera plane—and the most troublesome thing for the GPU is to write the pixel colors into that position on the rendering surface. This can be done using Vertex Shader Model 3 by creating a grid consisting of vertices placed in the previous field pixel center and using vertex texturing to get actual positions. There are a few drawbacks: the performance of sampling, the large number of vertices required, the cost of format conversion, and limited hardware support.

But we can cheat again. Instead of processing old fragments and reprojecting them into the new space, we can process new fragments (from a recent field) and use their positions to reproject into the old space and just take the sample from the old field. This is not entirely correct because it only compensates for camera movement, and even then it assumes the continuity in geometric representation because it uses a half-pixel shift inside the field. However, we have to note that this approach hides the problem due to internal exposure errors, which is a good thing.

Conclusion

The technique presented here can be useful for any pixel-shading-heavy application in two ways. The first is an obvious increase in performance, which theoretically may approach nearly a twofold speedup. Second, quality increases by means of temporal super-sampling with a very small performance cost. Of course, the proof is in the implementation. The second usage model was implemented in the commercial PC game *S.T.A.L.K.E.R. Shadow of Chernobyl* (courtesy of THQ® Inc.), which is based on deferred shading architecture, and the results are spectacular. Also, make sure to check the sample implementation on the companion CD-ROM.

ON THE CD

References

[Bellars00] Bellers, E.B., and G. de Haan, De-interlacing. A Key Technology for Scan Rate Conversion, Elsevier, 2000.

[Kelly04] Kelly, F., and A. Kokaram, Fast Image Interpolation for Motion Estimation using Graphics Hardware, 2000.

[Pharr03] Pharr, M., "Fast Filter-Width Estimates with Texture Maps," GPU-Gems, 2003.

[Hargreaves04] Hargreaves, Shawn, and Mark Harris, "Deferred Shading" Presentation. Available online at *http://download.nvidia.com/developer/presentations/2004/6800_Leagues/6800_Leagues_Deferred_Shading.pdf*, 2004.

[Saito90] Saito, T., and T. Takahashi, "Comprehensible Rendering of 3-D Shapes." *Computer Graphics (Proceedings of SIGRAPH 90) 24*(4), (August 2004): pp. 197–206.

[Adelson95] Adelson, S. J., and L. F. Hodges, Generating Exact Ray-Traced Animation Frames by Reprojection. *IEEE Computer Graphics and Applications, 15*(3), (May 1995): pp. 43–52.

[Badt88] Badt, S., "Two Algorithms Taking Advantage of Temporal Coherence in Ray Tracing," *The Visual Computer, 4*(3) (September. 1988): pp. 123–132.

2.2

Triangle Mesh Tangent Space Calculation

Martin Mittring

Introduction

Transforming vectors in a common vector space can greatly simplify per-pixel lighting computations. This is often the key to move instructions from the pixel shader to the vertex shader. Usually, pixel shaders are executed with greater frequency, which means this move can result in faster rendering.

To transform vectors from tangent space to object space, the tangent space matrix is needed (useful for normal mapped cube-map reflections). To transform back, the inverse of the tangent space matrix is needed (useful for half-angle phong lighting).

The tangent space matrix is a 3×3 matrix that is oriented to the object surface. The matrix consists of three vectors where one vector represents the surface normal and is also called normal $\vec{n}$, and the other two vectors that are commonly known as binormal $\vec{b}$ and tangent $\vec{t}$. We believe the terms *binormal* and *tangent* are not descriptive enough, so we try to use more useful names here. We use $\vec{u}$ for the positive x direction on the texture and $\vec{v}$ for the positive y direction on the texture.

In some cases, the tangent space matrix can be defined with an explicit parametric representation (for example, Torus, Plane, Sphere), but that's not possible for arbitrary triangle meshes. A simple and common form of using the tangent space is storing the matrix per vertex from where it can be used either directly in the vertex shader or interpolated and passed to the pixel shader.

This article presents an algorithm to calculate a tangent space matrix for each vertex.

- T, tangent space matrix
- O, object space matrix
- $\vec{u}$, positive x direction on the texture
- $\vec{v}$, positive y direction on the texture
- $\vec{n}$, surface normal

$$T = (\vec{u}, \vec{v}, \vec{n})$$

Normal Maps

Normal vectors are 3D vectors perpendicular to a surface, and as it simplifies processing the vector is often kept in unit length. Normal maps store a 2D array of normal vectors in a texture encoded as a color. Because the encoding is simple, it is real-time friendly. Each vector component is scaled and offset to bring it from the range [−1,1] to the color range [0,1].

To compute normal maps from a 3D model you need a mapping between a surface point and a position on the texture. You can save texture space by mapping 3D model areas with the same normals to the same texture area.

World, Object, and Tangent Space

You can store your normals in world space or transform them into object space; both methods allow you to place several instances of your model mirrored or rotated. However, if you want to reuse your normal map details for rotated or mirrored parts of your model, you run into problems.

If you want to reuse your texture on any arbitrary surface (for example, tiled over a curved surface), you need to introduce a new space that is oriented to the surface. Vectors stored in tangent space allow us to reuse the texture and offer other useful properties for the normal map. As the transformed vectors are all roughly pointing in the (0,0,1) direction, this results in a nice bluish-colored texture and enables easier texture compression.

Normal Maps from Bump Maps

Bump maps are grayscale textures that modify the surface normal to simulate more surface detail. The grayscale value corresponds to the surface height, and to extract the surface normal you need several lookups into the bump texture. As most hand-crafted bitmaps are done in 8 bit, the result suffers from that as well. This problem becomes noticeable most for soft surface variations. The typical solution for this is blurring, which means even more lookups are needed.

As the bump map has no correlation to the object surface, we need to store the normal in a surface independent way, and tangent space serves this purpose.

List of Requirements

- Easy to integrate in existing projects: The implementation should be available in C/C++ source code, independent from input and output data formats through a simple interface.
- Efficient in calculation and memory usage: The computation might be used in a preprocess, but it can also be used during loading in the 3D engine where this requirement is more important.
- As little magic values as possible: Having bias or threshold values in the code can easily lead to problems. In the worst case, you need different values for different parts of your 3D models.
- Mirroring support (even with rotated or stretched UV texturing): Mirroring the mesh or the UV mapping is changing the triangle orientation in UV space. In UV space, a triangle is either clockwise or counterclockwise oriented. The orien-

tation is changed when mirroring the UV mapping or mirroring the mesh. The latter is because the mirroring affects the surface orientation, and to fix that you need to change the triangle indices that also affect the UV orientation. The algorithm needs to support mirroring because it's common practice in asset creation and the tangent space matrix can easily support this. However, the mirror borders create special challenges for the algorithm.

- Minimum amount of vertex splits: Mirroring may require vertex splits, which leads to an increased vertex count. This would increase the memory required and result in decreased performance, since more vertex shader executions are needed and the vertex cache would perform less efficiently.
- Predictable results: The triangle order shouldn't affect the result and vertices should only be affected by their direct neighborhood.
- Tessellation independent result (for example, turning inner edge of a quad should not affect the result): The top image in Figure 2.2.1 shows the correct result, and the bottom image demonstrates an incorrect one.

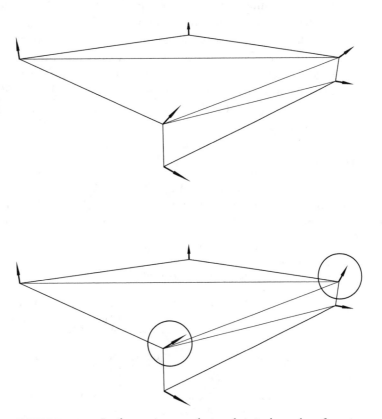

FIGURE 2.2.1 *In the top image, the result is independent from its tessellation. In the bottom image, you can seen the result of simply averaging the triangle normals per vertex (count the number of triangles with the same normal on the critical vertices).*

- Tiling textures: It should be possible to use the UV coordinates not only in the 0..1 range.
- Should work well with the established blue normal map format: This is useful because many tools use this format and there is also hardware decompression support (for example, ATI 3DC, NVidia CxV8U8). In this format, each color defines a normal tilt in the mapping U and V direction. Assuming the stored vector is normalized, the red channel defines the tilt in the $\vec{u}$ direction, the green channel defines the tilt in the $\vec{v}$ direction, and the blue channel is actually redundant.
- Floating point exception free (given proper input): Floating point exceptions often result in significant slowdowns, so it is best to add checks for the critical computations.
- Heavily tested and proven.
- The smooth definition of edges is application independent: An artist using Maya defines angles for smooth interpolation per edge. In 3D Studio, the artist can define the interpolation through smoothing groups. For each triangle a 32-bit mask defines the triangle smoothing group assignment. An edge is interpolated smoothly if the touching triangles share at least one smoothing group (maskA & maskB !=0).
- Smooth/hard edges where defined: No matter how the artist specified the smooth edges, the result should not be affected by using different materials, UV unwrapping, or mirroring. Consider a cylinder unwrapped in multiple ways: no matter how the artist specifies the smooth edges, the result should be the same.
- Documented algorithm.

Implementation

The algorithm is implemented in the TangentSpaceCalculation.h header file. You only need this file because the code was written for easy reuse. The implementation makes use of a proxy class and you only need to implement this proxy class.

```
struct ITriangleInputProxy
{
    unsigned int GetTriangleCount() const;

    void GetTriangleIndices( const unsigned int indwTriNo,
        unsigned int outdwPos[3], unsigned int outdwNorm[3],
        unsigned int outdwUV[3] ) const;

    void GetPos( const unsigned int indwPos,
        float outfPos[3] ) const;

    void GetUV( const unsigned int indwPos,
        float outfUV[2] ) const;
};
```

For performance reasons, we decided not to use virtual functions and used a template implementation instead. Note that you don't need to provide the normal vectors, as they are a byproduct of the tangent space calculation. However, you need to return the normal indices per triangle to define the hard edges. This is our way to define smooth/hard edges application independent. If you only have smoothing groups (for example, 3DStudio) or maximum angles per edge (for example, Maya), you need to convert this information into the normal indices per triangle. Most likely, you don't need to write that code yourself; often you can request this through a function call in your exporter or modeling application.

Executing the computation looks like this (if your proxy is called CTriangle InputProxy):

```
CTangentSpaceCalculation<CTriangleInputProxy> tangents;
CTriangleInputProxy input(inoutData);
tangents.CalculateTangentSpace(input);
```

Getting the data back from the class can look like this:

```
unsigned int dwCnt=tangents.GetBaseCount();
unsigned int dwTriNo;
for(dwTriNo=0;dwTriNo<dwTriCount;++dwTriNo)
{
    unsigned int dwBaseIndex[3];
    tangents.GetTriangleBaseIndices(dwTriNo,dwBaseIndex);
    // ... store the base index for the 3 triangle corners
}
for(unsigned int dwC=0;dwC<dwCnt;++dwC)
{
    float vU,vV,vN;
    tangents.GetBase(dwC,vU,vV,vN);
    // ... store T or invert and store T_inv
}
```

Algorithm in Three Steps

Step 1

First, the tangent space matrix is calculated per triangle separately. The derivation of this is not very difficult but not really needed here. The following code computes $\vec{u}$, $\vec{v}$, and $\vec{n}$ per triangle:

```
CVec3 vA=vPos[1]-vPos[0], vB=vPos[2]-vPos[0];
float fDeltaU1=vUV[1].x-vUV[0].x;
float fDeltaU2=vUV[2].x-vUV[0].x;
float fDeltaV1=vUV[1].y-vUV[0].y;
float fDeltaV2=vUV[2].y-vUV[0].y;
// area(u1*v2-u2*v1)/2
float div=(fDeltaU1*fDeltaV2-fDeltaU2*fDeltaV1);
CVec3 vU,vV,vN=normalize(cross(vA,vB));
if(div!=0.0)
{
```

```
        float fAreaMul2=fabsf(div);
        float a = fDeltaV2/div;
        float b = -fDeltaV1/div;
        float c = -fDeltaU2/div;
        float d = fDeltaU1/div;
        vU=normalize(vA*a+vB*b)*fAreaMul2;
        vV=normalize(vA*c+vB*d)*fAreaMul2;
    }
    else { vU=CVec3(0,0,0);vV=CVec3(0,0,0); }
```

Note that $\vec{u}$ and $\vec{v}$ become weighted by the UV triangle size—this is needed to fix problems with small triangles in UV that dominate the result of their local neighborhood. Bigger UV triangles are usually the more important surfaces.

Unfortunately, the resulting matrix can already be degenerated; this happens if either the triangle in UV or the 3D triangle is degenerated to a line or point. For performance reasons, we don't check for this case, but you might want to extend the implementation or check your input data in an earlier step. Usually, this isn't a problem since artists check their mesh for shading artifacts anyway. Also, in most cases the problem becomes fixed in the following steps with data from the neighbor triangles. The input data might include illegal float values (NaN), and for performance reasons we also decided not to check the full input data. We only check for illegal float values in the UV input data. We assume the position data is okay, as such problems would already show up during asset creation.

Step 2

Now, for all vertices we need to gather the normal vector contribution from the nearby triangles. We need to compute one normal vector for each vertex position and each normal index at this position. In our implementation, the STL multimap is used to store the normal vector in the tangent space matrix (key = position index, normal index).

As there are only a few normals per vertex, the multimap could be replaced by something more specialized and faster, but we chose the multimap for readability. The normals are weighted by their angle to get the tessellation independent result (requirement). For this step, an STL map would have worked, but the following step requires us to store multiple values per key so we used the multimap.

```
// for each triangle corner
for(e=0;e<3;e++)
{
    float fWeight = CalcAngleBetween(
        vPos[(e+2)%3]-vPos[e],vPos[(e+1)%3]-vPos[e] );
    // this method creates a new multimap entry if needed
    // it also sums up the weighted normals
    AddNormal2Base(mBaseMap,dwPos[e],dwNorm[e],TriBase.n*fWeight);
}
```

Step 3

Now all vertices should gather their $\vec{u}$ and $\vec{v}$ contribution from the nearby triangles.

To get the tessellation independent result (requirement), we also weight $\vec{u}$ and $\vec{v}$ by the angle.

```
// for each triangle corner
for(e=0;e<3;e++)
{
    float fWeight=CalcAngleBetween(
        vPos[(e+2)%3]-vPos[e], vPos[(e+1)%3]-vPos[e] );
    // this method creates a new multimap entry if needed
    // it also sums up the weighted vU and vV contributions
    Indx.p[e] = AddUV2Base(mBaseMap,dwPos[e],dwNorm[e],
                    TriBase.u*fWeight,TriBase.v*fWeight,
                    normalize(TriBase.n));
}
```

The gathering is a bit more complicated because they cannot all be summed together. We need to separate the mirrored ones from those that aren't mirrored (to get better mirror borders) that can be checked with the matrix parity.

```
bool bParity = cross(inU,inV)*inNormN>0;
bool bParityRef = dot(cross(refFound.u,refFound.v),refFound.n)>0;
if(bParityRef!=bParity)
    continue;
```

We also need to check for heavy rotations. We use a threshold angle between the half-angle vectors of the matrices we want to compare. There is no all-fitting angle, but to get fewer vertex splits it should not be smaller than 45 degrees, and to avoid severe stretching (for example, on the top part of an unwrapped hemisphere), the angle should not be greater than 90 degrees. We decided to use 90 degrees because it is simple to check and saves vertex splits. It's also better to force the artist to adjust the input (if unsatisfied by the result) than having unpredictable behavior. To measure the angle independently from the normal we project both half-angle vectors into the normal plane:

```
CVec3 vRotHalf = vrefUV - inNormN*dot(inNormN,vrefUV);
bool bHalfAngleCheck = dot((inU+inV),vRotHalf) > 0;
if(!bHalfAngleCheck)
    continue;
```

T and T–1

As mentioned in the introduction, both the tangent space matrix and its inverse are useful. Storing both of them per vertex would be a waste of memory. In most cases, you only need the inverted matrix, but if you limit your engine to this you lose a lot of flexibility. We can construct one from the other but doing it efficiently is crucial.

Math tells us that if the matrix is orthonormal (all vectors unit length and perpendicular to each other), the matrix inversion can be replaced by the much simpler transpose operation. The transpose operation is tempting to use here because we might not lose shader instructions whereas the matrix inversion comes at a much higher cost.

Orthonormalization

We can compute the matrix so all vectors are unit length, and $\vec{u}$ and the $\vec{v}$ are always perpendicular to the normal. But when using sheared texture assignment (unavoidable in real-world cases), $\vec{u}$ and $\vec{v}$ also become sheared, and we lose the orthonormal property of the matrix. Then, the transpose operation becomes an approximation of the inversion, and vectors transformed with the approximated matrix might be reduced in length and become distorted.

Many shading computations are dependent on the dot product between unit vectors, which exposes the length reduction of our vectors. The diffuse shading might appear darker but the effects are amplified in power functions, making the specular even disappearing. Fortunately, the length can be fixed by shader computations (for example, cube map renormalization or the normalize function). These extra computations, and other shading artifacts caused by common techniques like linear interpolation are well worth avoiding.

Although the vector direction might also become distorted, it is usually only noticeable on mirror edges. Keeping the base orthonormal is a very useful property, and math shows various ways to orthonormalize matrices. Here are three ways:

- The Gram-Schmitt Ortho-normalization algorithm is based on the idea of removing contributions of vectors that are assumed valid. The vectors also become renormalized to make them unit length: $\vec{a}' = \vec{a} - (\vec{a} \cdot \vec{n}) * \vec{n}$ where $\vec{n}$ is assumed to be normalized. Assuming the matrix is not degenerated, this always results in an orthonormal base. Unfortunately, the order in which you process the vectors affects the result. In our case, two different results are possible because we don't need the full computation. We know $\vec{n}$ is already valid and $\vec{u}$ and $\vec{v}$ are already perpendicular to $\vec{n}$. We can either assume $\vec{u}$ is valid to reconstruct $\vec{v}$, or assume $\vec{v}$ is valid and to reconstruct $\vec{u}$.

- You can use the cross product to reconstruct the new vector, but to support mirroring you need to keep the matrix orientation (also matrix parity). You need to negate the result or flip the cross product input values depending on triangle orientation in UV space (signed area computation or other method). There is no reason to prefer one vector over the other so we search for an algorithm that treats both equally.

- You can do so by computing the half vector between $\vec{u}$ and $\vec{v}$, and reconstruct the new $\vec{u}$ and $\vec{v}$ by computing two vectors that are 45 degrees to the half vectors and perpendicular to the normal:

```
// (N is dominating, U and V equal weighted)
// Input: vector vUin, vVin, vNin unnormalized
// Output: vUout,vVout,vNout
vHalf = normalize(vUin+vVin);
vNout = normalize(vNin);
f = sqrt(0.5f);                              // for 45 degree rotation
vO = normalize(cross(vHalf,vNout)) * f;
vH = normalize(cross(vNout,vO)) * f;
if(vO*Uin>0)
    { vUout = vH+vO; vVout = vH-vO; }
  else
    { vUout = vH-vO; vVout = vH+vO; }
```

Should We Orthonormalize?

We tried with and without renormalization and realized that the effect is noticeable where we do vertex splits mirroring or extreme rotations. The problem is worse when using extreme texture shearing, but this is something an artist can avoid. We cannot avoid the vertex split, but we might be able to adjust the vertices to reduce the problem. In *FarCry*, we decided to not orthonormalize and told our artist to fix the problem by adjusting the asset UV mapping. Although orthonormalization reduces the problem it also hides the problem for the artist. It would be a good idea to activate the orthonormalization after the UV mapping is adjusted. We also use mirroring only where appropriate (for example, not in the face). We believe the algorithm can be improved there, but so far we haven't found a solution with the required quality. If you want to start your own experiments, search for the code starting with "method #1" in Object3D.cpp.

Checking Our Requirements

- Easy to integrate: Integration requires only one header file to be included and only one class needs to be implemented. Starting the computation and getting the result can be done with a few calls. You might need to do simple preprocessing if your data does not consist of indexed normal, position, and UV data. Internal computations require a small 3D vector class, but this class is included and hidden from the caller to avoid problems with other 3D vector classes. STL is required for the container vector and multimap.
- Efficient in calculation and memory usage: The algorithm execution time scales well with the input data size, and because of using C++ templates the interface avoids costly virtual function calls. However, for readability we left out some optimizations.
- As few magic values as possible: The presented implementation does not have one value to tweak. In cases where the result is not compelling, the UV mapping should be modified.
- Mirroring (even with rotated or stretched UV texturing): On seams between areas of different orientation the vertices need to be split.
- Minimum amount of vertex splits (for best render performance).

- Predictable results: Ignoring the unavoidable floating point computation errors we can say the algorithm is stable with one exception: in the rare case where matrices need to be split for strong rotations, the triangle insertion order can affect the result. As strong rotations should be avoided anyway, we decided to accept this flaw. What that means to you is if you compute a tangent space normal map for a mesh with such strong rotations and you want to apply the normal map to the same mesh but with different triangle order (for example, after strip-fying), you might see a break in the shading.
- Tessellation independent result (for example, turning inner edge of a quad should not affect the result): The problem is solved by weighting the triangle normal contribution per vertex by its angle at the vertex. Weighting by the triangle area might work in some cases, but then a simple triangle split might affect the result although the input mesh looks visually the same.
- Tiling textures: We support tiling textures without additional effort because we ignore UV mapping borders. All computations in UV space are relative, and the scale of the mapping is irrelevant.
- Should work well with the established blue normal map format.
- Floating point exception is free if input is fine.
- Heavily tested and proven: The presented implementation was not only used in the *Polybump* tools and in *CryEngine*. *FarCry* shipped with it but it was only used for animated characters. In the first patch, we activated the computation for all models, which fixed some shading artifacts and reduced vertex splits.
- Independent how smooth edges are defined: Both Maya and the 3DStudio data can be easily transformed into indexed normals (each triangle stores three normal indices). The algorithm does not even need the normal itself, as the normal is a byproduct of the tangent space calculation.
- Smooth/hard edges where defined: The shading cracks between materials were avoided by completely ignoring materials and treating the mesh as one. If your input mesh is already split up by materials, you need to combine the triangles or adjust your proxy class implementation accordingly. This requirement is necessary to keep artist control but it might cause shading artifacts in cases where the UV surface is bent a lot. Some 3D meshes are difficult to unwrap to a 2D surface. Introducing hard edges and smart unwrapping can greatly improve the result. Here is the major challenge for the artist; this is where the tangent space shows its limits. Tools such as the *Polybump* tool can still provide smooth edges through the normal maps.
- Documented algorithm: You currently read the documentation—more details you can find in the source code.

The Mirror Seams Problem

Unfortunately, with our implementation we might see a break in the shading on mirror seams. In most cases, the problem can be fixed by adjusting the UV mapping. You might be tempted to fix the problem by constructing the mirrored tangent space through negating $\vec{u}$ or $\vec{v}$, but that would solve the problem only if the mirror edge in the UV mapping is horizontal or vertical. The problem becomes even more complex when you think about the general case where the mirror edge on the left and the right triangle don't share the same angle in the UV mapping. Even this might be solvable for one edge, but most likely the mirror seam consists of a connected chain of edges with various angles in the UV mapping. So far, we haven't found a solution that does not limit our artists or hides problem from them.

Sample Application

The sample application is a slightly modified version of the Polybump Previewer. Polybump is a Crytek product to compute normal maps for a low-poly object (for example, 2000 faces) from high-poly objects (for example, 4 million polygons). The previewer application was already available to download but the source code wasn't public. In the sample directory you can find the previewer source code cleaned up.

Extensions

In real-time rendering, the tangent space matrix is stored per vertex. The straightforward implementation requires 36 bytes (nine floats) per vertex. As the values are in the defined range –1..1, we can store each component in 2 bytes (very good results) or even 1 byte (in most cases quite good results). This brings us down to 18 or even 12 bytes (three colors but with an unused alpha component). As the normal is always perpendicular to the other two base vectors, we can reconstruct this vector by using a cross product and negate it depending on a parity bit (mirroring). We no longer need to store the normal and come down to 8 bytes (two colors, one alpha component used to store the parity, another alpha component unused). With renormalization you can get the best out of the compressed 8-bit values. Make sure you round the values when quantizing to the 8-bit value, as a simple floor/trunc/cast would offset your data. Using the normalization, you don't need to store a certain vector length, and by carefully selecting the right 8-bit values you can improve the quality further.

```
// HLSL shader code to reconstruct tangent base vector
// from two color values (8 bytes)
half4 vHelp = (Color0-0.5)*2;
half3 vU = normalize(vHelp.xyz);
half3 vV = normalize((Color1.xyz-0.5)*2);
// matrix parity is stored in the alpha channel
half3 vN = normalize(cross(vU,vV)) * vHelp.a;
```

If you want to store high-poly normals in your normal map, you might want to transform your normals into the reconstructed space. This step in the preprocess gives you more accurate shading at runtime.

Tips

- To avoid problems you should always use the same tangent space computation (for example, animated/static object, normal map generation from high-poly mesh). To share tools it's good to stick to established methods (we encourage you to use our computation).
- Some shading artifacts might appear because of the tangent space matrix interpolation within the triangle. This problem can be reduced by renormalization in the pixel shader. Unfortunately, it's not possible to compute a perfect solution, but most artifacts can be avoided by good UV unwrapping. Artists should understand that avoiding stretching and shearing in the input UV is important for good results. Most other problems can be avoided by using a proper tangent space calculation. High-quality lighting often requires shaders with renormalization, but in some cases you can omit the needed instructions (for example, diffuse normal mapping, cube map reflections, low-curvature mesh).
- If you want to check your mesh for shading artifacts, you should check the model in a dark ambient environment lit by few light sources. The material should have a strong homogeneous white specular and a colorful diffuse color. Most artifacts appear in the specular, as this computation is the most sensitive. You can also write a pixel shader to visualize matrix distortions as colors.
- From time to time you might need to check a tangent space texture, and then it's good to keep a reference tangent space texture in a central place. We use a square with a 45-degree chamfer.
- Most shading computations based on dot products to get circular gradients, for diffuse and specular. To avoid elliptical-shaped gradients you need to compute it in an orthogonal space. To do so you can transform the bump normal into world or object space and do the shading there. Be aware that this might add pixel shader instructions and you need more interpolators.
- Notice that storing normal maps in 8 bit textures with the simple *2 and −1 does not allow you to store vectors parallel to the coordinate axis because the scalar 0 cannot be represented. The problem occurs because 255 steps equally distributed over the range −1..1 miss the value 0. Again the problem only becomes noticeable in the specular at mirror edges. You can solve the problem by adjusting the scaling and offset constants. Make sure the most important normal (0,0,1) becomes reconstructed correctly.

Conclusion

The presented method solves the problem of computing the tangent space for an arbitrary triangle mesh. The implementation is easy to integrate, and the results can be seen in shipped products. We don't claim that we solved the problem completely, and we believe improvements are possible. Unfortunately, the idea behind the tangent space matrix is flawed already. Even if all vertices have the perfect matrix stored, the linear interpolation can cause shading artifacts. The tangent space computation is very useful for old and current hardware, but the shading power we now have at pixel level might offer new ways to solve the problem.

Acknowledgments

The method was developed together with Ivo Herzeg at Crytek, with the help of Andrey Khonich and the whole Crytek team. Special thanks to Sergey Nenakhov for reviewing the article.

References

Terathon Software. "Computing tangent space basis vectors for an arbitrary mesh," *http://www.terathon.com/code/tangent.html*

Mathematics for 3D Game Programming & Computer Graphics, "Calculating Tangent Vectors" Section 6.8.3. List of tools that create normal maps from high-poly models.

List of tools that create normal maps from high-poly models. *http://www.fredmoreau. net/cg_resource/techniques/normalmaps.htm.*

Derivation of the Tangent Space Matrix. *http://www.blacksmith-studios.dk/projects/ downloads/tangent_matrix_derivation.php.*

2.3

Hardware-Based Ambient Occlusion

Dustin Franklin

Through the last five years, we have experienced tremendous leaps in both the performance and capability of graphics hardware. In particular, environmental lighting has been pushed to the forefront through numerous technical advances, such as Precomputed Radiance Transfer and other real-time adaptations of spherical harmonics.

An additional global illumination technique, commonly referred to as *ambient occlusion*, has been the topic of many developments. Although it is simpler than many of the other methods, it serves as a satisfying approximation. Likewise, it carries no performance hit at runtime and can be used on all hardware with basic programmable vertex and pixel shaders (even vs_1_1 and ps_1_1 will suffice).

Introduction to Ambient Occlusion

Ambient occlusion simulates how geometry blocks itself from incoming environmental light. In essence, it is an advanced ambient term in the lighting equation that scales the diffuse term. The result is a detailed self-shadowing phenomenon that produces smooth transitions between shaded and lighted areas. In addition, it can be used to cast footprint-like shadows onto ground geometry. Figure 2.3.1 shows the difference between standard $N \bullet L$ lighting and ambient occlusion lighting.

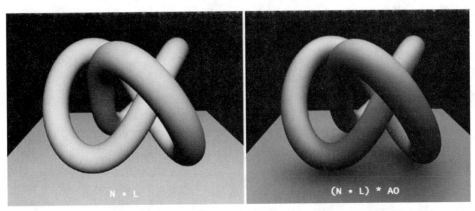

FIGURE 2.3.1 *A comparison between standard $N \bullet L$ and ambient occlusion lighting.*

All of the computations involved are performed in an offline preprocess. The *accessibility*, or the percentage of incoming environmental light that actually reaches the polygon, is calculated for each face. For lowly tessellated geometry, it is acceptable to calculate on a per-vertex basis, where highly tessellated geometry is best suited for per-face. After all calculations are complete, the accessibility values are saved to a texture, a chunk inside of the mesh data, or an outside file. This data is then used in the real-time application.

Consider Figure 2.3.2 for a practical illustration of accessibility. Point *P* lies on a surface and is adjacent to other polygons. In this situation, the other faces block over half of the incoming light, so its accessibility would be around 0.5.

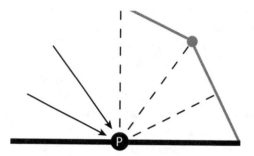

FIGURE 2.3.2   *Accessibility of a face.*

One way to calculate the accessibility of each face is to take a ray-tracer-based approach. For each triangle, a random hemispherical distribution of rays, representing individual rays of environmental light, is tested for intersection with the current polygon. The accessibility is simply the number of rays that intersect only the current face divided by the total number of rays (see Listing 2.3.1).

Listing 2.3.1   Accessibility calculation using ray tracing.

```
For each triangle
{
    Generate random set of rays
    numUnoccluded = 0;

    For each ray
    {
        if( ray only intersects current triangle )
        {
            numUnoccluded++;
        }
    }

    accessibility = numUnoccluded / numRays;
}
```

Hayden Landis and his team at Industrial Light + Magic originally pioneered this process for use on numerous blockbuster films, including *Pearl Harbor* [Landis02]. At the time, ray tracing was a logical approach and provided satisfactory speed and accuracy, considering the final medium. However, with the ever-increasing power and feature set of modern day GPUs, some techniques have been developed to shift the bulk of the processing off the CPU. The aim of this is to decrease the preprocessing time of each model, making asset pipelines shorter and more efficient.

Matt Pharr and Simon Green of NVIDIA have developed a method that utilizes the GPU to calculate ambient occlusion data, primarily through the use of a process similar to shadow mapping [Pharr04]. The object is surrounded with a hemispherical set of shadow-mapped lights. To calculate accessibility, the shadow contributions of each light are averaged in a floating-point accumulation buffer. The scene is rendered from the perspective of each light, accumulating the shadow images to form the final occlusion image. However, this method still represents incoming environmental light through a finite number of sources. Since ambient light does not originate from a particular set of sources, it would be better to sample the environment in its entirety.

Occlusion Queries

Occlusion queries were supported in hardware with the release of DirectX9. They can be used to determine the number of pixels that pass z-testing while the query is active. If the query returns 0, the primitives drawn are not visible from the current camera position. Likewise, if the query returns a number greater than 0, the primitives drawn are visible.

We can use occlusion queries to determine the accessibility of each face. In Figure 2.3.3, an object is placed inside its bounding box (representing the environment) and on top of a plane (representing the ground).

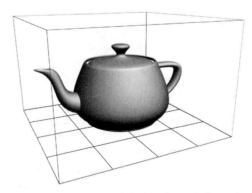

FIGURE 2.3.3 *Model placed inside bounding box and plane.*

For each face, the scene is rendered from the viewpoint of the current triangle. The eye point of the camera is the center of the face (see Figure 2.3.4), while the viewing direction is its normal.

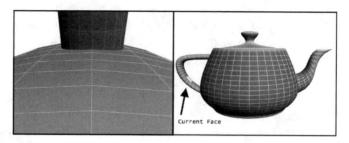

FIGURE 2.3.4   *Model rendered from the perspective of the face.*

After the model and ground plane are drawn, a query is issued during the rendering of the bounding box, allowing us to determine the number of pixels of the environment that are visible. The ground plane is rendered separate and not included in the occlusion count because incoming environmental light does not originate from the ground. The accessibility is then simply the percentage of the pixels that are visible:

$$accessibility = \frac{numPixelsVisible}{totalPixels}$$

In essence, we are calculating the percentage of the environment that can be seen from each face. However, one render per face is usually not enough to capture the full environment. The field of view could be increased to 180°, but distortion heavily skews the final image to the point where the accessibility values are completely inaccurate. Instead, we can create an additional set of viewpoint rays, render from each new viewpoint, and average the results. The number of additional viewpoints, not including the normal, is known as the *detail level*. The higher the detail level, the higher the quality of the ambient occlusion data. However, with increased detail level comes increased rendering: the number of passes for each face is *detailLevel + 1*. Remember, we need to make a pass from the normal viewpoint, too.

These additional rays are derived from the normal of each face. Instead of randomly distributing the viewpoints, the same orientations are used for each face (see Figure 2.3.5). First, each ray is rotated toward the triangle itself. They are then rotated evenly to form a circle, depending on detail level.

Due to the asynchronous nature of occlusion queries, it can take up to two to three frames for the query to become ready to retrieve. Instead of stalling the CPU, we can create a query for each pass. After all the rendering is complete, each query is retrieved. At this point, if the queries are not ready, the CPU must be stalled. How-

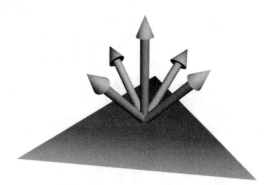

FIGURE 2.3.5   *Distribution of viewpoints.*

ever, if the model is highly tessellated and there is a moderate detail level, then many, if not all, of the queries will be ready immediately.

Algorithm Outline

Listing 2.3.2 is a pseudocode outline of the preprocessing algorithm introduced in the previous section.

Listing 2.3.2   Pseudocode of the preprocessing algorithm.

```
// Initialization
Set Render States
    ShadeMode  = Flat
    ColorWrite = Disabled
    Lighting   = Off
    AlphaBlend = Off

Create vertex declaration

Create bounding box mesh for model
Create lower plane mesh for model

// Create an occlusion query for each render pass
// Num Queries = Num Passes = Detail Level + 1
Create occlusion queries

// Build a set of base viewing rays
// Num Rays = Num Passes = Detail Level + 1
// Titled rays are angled 45° towards the Z-axis
// Titled rays are rotated around the X-axis in a circle
Initialize and transform rays

// Calculate the accessibility for each face
For each face
{
    Lock vertex and index buffers
```

```
Find center of the face  // Average position of the 3 vertices
Find normal of the face  // Average normal of the 3 vertices

Unlock vertex and index buffers

// Transform set of base rays to this face's orientation
Axis of rotation  = Cross( face normal, base normal )
Angle of rotation = Dot( face normal, base normal )
Rotate each ray on the defined axis by the angle

// Rendering pass for each viewing ray
For each ray
{
    // Create view matrix
    // Eyepoint  = center of face
    // Direction = current ray
    Build viewing matrix

    // Create perspective matrix
    // Very low near-plane value (.01) — need geometry that
    // is very close to be visible — requires 24-bit buffer
    Build perspective matrix

    Clear Scene


    // Render ground and model before the query is issued
    Render lower plane
    Render model

    Issue query
        Render bounding box
    End Query
}

// Retrieve all the queries and find the average accessibility
accessibility = 0.0
numPixels     = screenWidth * screenHeight

For each query
{
   Retrieve results   // Loop until it becomes available
   accessibility += actualPixelsVisible / numPixels
}

// Average by the number of passes
accessibility /= Detail Level + 1
}
```

After the processing is complete, the data is saved to some type of file.

Rendering

Integrating the generated ambient occlusion data into the rendering pipeline is trivial, since it serves as a scaling factor for the final diffuse term. In Figure 2.3.6, the $N \bullet L$ term is combined with the ambient occlusion term. However, in most practical applications, it would be combined with a diffuse texture term, among others.

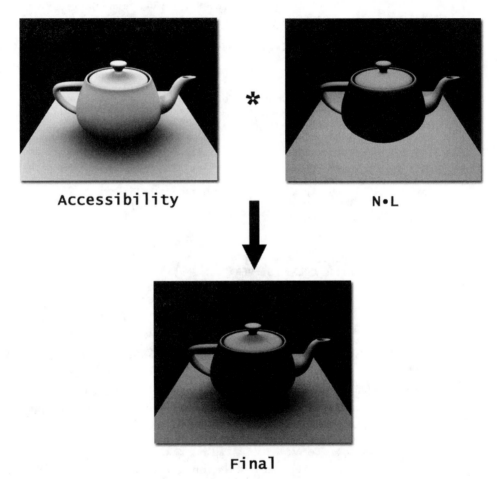

FIGURE 2.3.6 $N \bullet L$ *combined with ambient occlusion.*

The simplicity of this operation allows for this technique to be utilized on the lowest shader profiles, vs_1_1 and ps_1_1. Vertex and pixel shader fragments are shown in Listing 2.3.3.

Listing 2.3.3   Vertex and pixel shader

```
// Vertex Shader
VERT_OUT AO_VS( VERT_IN IN )
{
    VERT_OUT OUT;

    // Transform coordinates
    float4 objPos   = float4( IN.Position, 1.0 );
    float4 worldPos = mul( objPos, g_mWorld );
    float4 lightVec = normalize( LightPos - worldPos );
    float4 objLight = normalize( mul( lightVec, g_mWorldInverse ));

    // Standard N·L Lighting
    float4 Nn  = normalize( IN.Normal );
    float  ldn = dot( objLight, Nn );

    // Fill struct
    OUT.diffCol      = ldn * float4( BaseColor, 1.0 );
    OUT.diffCol.w    = 1.0;
    OUT.HPosition    = mul( objPos, g_mWorldViewProjection );
    OUT.UV           = IN.UV.xy;
    OUT.access       = IN.accessibility;

    return OUT;
}

// Pixel Shader
float4 AO_LIT_PS( VERT_OUT IN ) : COLOR
{
    return IN.diffCol * float4( BaseColor, 1.0 ) *
      float4( IN.access, IN.access, In.access, 1.0 );
}
```

If the data was generated on a per-face basis, it must first be converted to per-vertex. This can be done by averaging the accessibility values of each face to which the current vertex belongs. If the mesh is highly tessellated, take this approach instead of calculating the data on a per-vertex basis initially. Otherwise, visible artifacts will appear.

Results

Naturally, as detail level increases, the time it takes to process a model also increases. However, many other factors also contribute to the overall performance of the algorithm. The amount of faces in the model is important, because of the additional accessibility calculations, the increased rendering time per pass. Additionally, the detail level is linked to the amount of time the CPU is stalled waiting for the occlusion queries to become ready. This is because that more passes per face give the asynchronous mechanisms more time to process before we attempt to retrieve them. For this reason, the change in time between detail level is not linear (for example, it doesn't take twice as long to process a model with detail level 8 as it does with detail level 4). Of course, the speed of the GPU is the most noticeable and influential factor.

Table 2.3.1 shows a comparison of performance at different detail levels. A standard teapot model, composed of 13,843 vertices and 27,400 faces, was used for benchmarking (see Figure 2.3.7). It was tested on an AMD 2600+ (2.08GHz) with an ATI 9600XT.

Table 2.3.1 Comparison of Algorithm Performance Across Detail Levels

Detail Level	Avg. Accessibility	Std. Deviation	Time
2	.5658	.3458	35.175s
4	.5691	.3406	63.002s
8	.5718	.3408	104.988s
16	.5732	.3421	312.443s

The visual difference between detail levels greatly depends on the model being processed. Relatively simple geometry, such as the teapot and knot meshes, generally maintains the same visual quality across detail levels. However, complex geometry, composed of many concave sections, is more susceptible to differing visual quality.

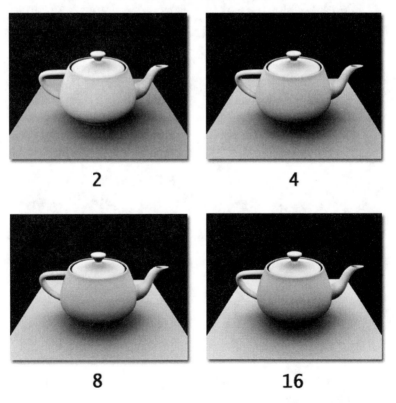

FIGURE 2.3.7   *Teapot shaded with accessibility values, generated from multiple detail levels.*

Conclusion

Using occlusion queries, we have established and analyzed a new algorithm for generating ambient occlusion data. This algorithm is adjustable in detail, allowing for scalable computation time. Because all of the data is calculated in an offline process, there is virtually no performance hit at runtime.

Where other algorithms simulate incoming ambient light from the perspective of the outside environment, this technique does the opposite and assumes the perspective of the model itself. Other methods, such as PRT, may provide more detailed and accurate results but at the expense of processing time. However, this approach yields visually appealing results and does so with minimal precomputation time.

References

[Landis02] H. Landis, "Production-Ready Global Illumination," Course 16 notes, *SIGGRAPH 2002, http://www.renderman.org/RMR/Books/sig02.course16.pdf.gz*, 2002.

[Pharr04] Pharr, M., and S. Green, *Ambient Occlusion. GPU Gems.* Fernando, Randima, Editors. New York: Addison Wesley, 2004.

2.4

Ambient Occlusion Fields

Janne Kontkanen and Samuli Laine

Introduction

Ambient occlusion refers to the strength of the shadow for ambient illumination that arrives from all directions with constant brightness. The resulting ambient shadow is typically soft except near the contact points between the caster and the receiver. A car casting a shadow on the ground on a cloudy day is a typical real-life example.

Ambient occlusion was invented by Zhukov et al under the name *obscurances* [Zhukov98]. Later, the method became popular in production rendering [Landis02] [Christensen02], and is currently supported by many commercial rendering packages.

Computing the ambient occlusion requires evaluating expensive hemispherical integrals on the surface being shadowed. Because of this, real-time computation of ambient occlusion is generally not feasible. However, the self-shadows of rigid objects do not change over time, so they can be precomputed once and reused in multiple animation frames. Unfortunately, this approach leads to serious lack of realism because mutual shadowing between objects cannot be supported. The most obvious deficiency is the absence of contact shadows between close-by surfaces. This article describes a technique called *ambient occlusion fields* [Kontkanen05] for approximating the ambient shadows cast by rigid bodies in real time. See the results in Figure 2.4.1.

FIGURE 2.4.1   *A coffee mug casts a shadow to the ground. This application runs 100–125 frames per second on an ATI Radeon 9800XT with 1024×768 resolution and six-sample FSAA. Precomputation time was 15 minutes, and the mug consists of 21,384 triangles. Cube-map resolution is 64^2 per face.*

Ambient Occlusion Fields

The basic idea of ambient occlusion fields is that the ambient shadow cast by a rigid object can be precomputed at points outside the object, and fetched from this precomputed data during rendering.

The spherical cap approximation is one of the key ideas of ambient occlusion fields. Instead of evaluating the ambient occlusion using accurate geometry, the shadow caster is approximated by a spherical cap (see Figure 2.4.2). A spherical cap is defined by its size (solid angle) and central direction. Thus, for each location on the receiving surface it suffices to determine the size and direction for the cap that best represent the shadow caster as seen from that location.

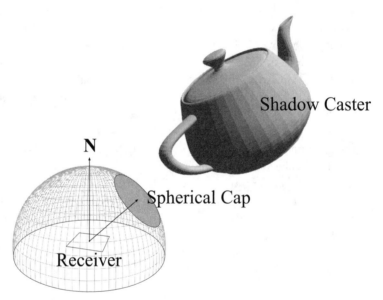

FIGURE 2.4.2 *The spherical cap approximation. The shadow caster is approximated by a spherical cap when rendering the shadow on the receiver.*

In the local coordinate frame of the shadow caster, both the size and the direction of the spherical cap are functions of the 3D location of the receiver point. Assuming that the shadow caster is rigid, these functions do not change over time and can be precomputed.

This data is precomputed for each shadow caster, and used at runtime to evaluate the ambient occlusion on the receiving surfaces. At runtime, the receiver point is first transformed into the local coordinate frame of the shadow caster. Then, the cap parameters are fetched from the precomputed data. Finally, ambient occlusion is computed according to both the cap and the normal of the receiving surface.

For compactness, the precomputed volumetric data is stored in a cube map where each texel describes an analytic function of radial distance. Thus, when determining the cap parameters during rendering, these analytic functions are read from the cube maps and evaluated in the fragment shader.

Precomputation

The precomputation is done for each shadow caster separately. However, if multiple shadow casters have the same shape, the data can be reused, reducing both memory consumption and precomputation time.

Given a point in space, first consider the problem of converting the shadow caster into a spherical cap so that it approximates the occlusion as seen from that point. This operation is executed for many points outside the shadow caster during the precomputation stage.

For a single point, the size of the cap is determined so that it subtends the same solid angle as does the object. The direction of the cap is computed by taking the average of the directions occluded by the object. In practice, the easiest solution is to sample the occlusion caused by the object over all directions. The sampling can be performed using ray tracing or rasterization.

An obvious way to store the spherical cap parameters would be to sample them at the nodes of a regular 3D grid surrounding the shadow caster and store the results into a volumetric texture. The main drawback of this approach is its high memory consumption. To save storage space and concentrate more resolution to the close neighborhood of the shadow caster, the information is flattened into a cube-map in the local coordinate frame of the shadow caster. Thus, the direction defines the texel, and each texel stores a function of radial distance from the center of the shadow caster. For determining the functions, the cap size and direction are measured in multiple locations along the radial lines defined by the cube-map texels (see Figure 2.4.3).

For nice contact shadows, the sampling locations are distributed with increasing density toward the object, but no samples should be taken inside the convex hull. For shadows inside the convex hull, a simple approximation needs to be used (see the next section). For simplicity, all of the following code fragments assume that the object is scaled so that its bounding radius is approximately one. C++ code for distributing the sampling locations for a single direction is given here:

```
float r0 = getDistanceToConvexHull(direction);
const int NUM_SAMPLES = 24;
Vector3 locations[NUM_SAMPLES];

// generate the sampling locations
for (int j=0; j < NUM_SAMPLES; j++)
{
    float t = (float)j/(float)NUM_SAMPLES;
    float d = r0+3.0*t*t;
    locations[j] = d*direction;
}
```

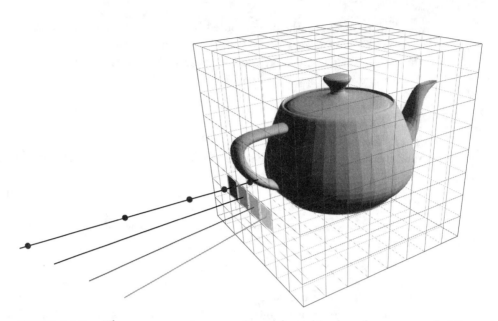

FIGURE 2.4.3 *The precomputation stage: For each texel in the cube map, a radial line that passes through the texel and the center of the object is identified. Then, occlusion characteristics of the object are measured in several locations along the line. Finally, suitable analytic models are fitted into the data, yielding a small number of scalar parameters that are stored into the cube-map texel.*

For each cube-map texel, heuristic models are fitted for both the size and the direction of the cap. Consider a single texel with index i. The model for the cap size is $\Omega(i,r) = (a_i r^2 + b_i r + c_i)^{-1}$, where i refers to a cube-map texel and thus identifies the direction. Parameter r is the radial distance from the center of the occluder. For each texel i, coefficients a_i, b_i, and c_i must be found. This is done by measuring the actual solid angle along the radial line identified by the texel and fitting the model into the data by minimizing a weighted squared error of the denominator polynomial. In C++ code, this looks like:

```
// locations = array of sampling locations along the radial line
// occlusion = measured solid angle at the sampling locations
// n         = number of sampling locations
Matrix3x3 X(0,0,0, 0,0,0, 0,0,0);
Vector3   Y(0,0,0);
for (int i=0; i < n; i++)
{
    float x = locations[i].length(); // distance from center
    float y = 1.0/occlusion[i];
    float w = occlusion[i]*occlusion[i];
    Matrix3x3 A;
    for (int j=0; j < 3; j++)
```

```
        for (int k=0; k < 3; k++)
            A[j][k] = powf(x, j+k);
    X += w*A;
    Y += w*Vector3(y, x*y, x*x*y);
}
Vector3 abc = invert(X)*Y; //the resulting coefficients a, b and c
```

The heuristic model for the direction of the cap is $Y(i,r) = \text{normalize}(C_i - r\,\omega_i)$, where ω_i is the unit vector pointing at the direction of texel i. Thus, the model forces the central direction of the cap toward a fixed point C_i when the receiver point lies on the radial line associated with texel i. Here, the challenge of fitting is to find location C_i for each i. In our implementation, C_i is found by choosing the point in space that has the smallest approximate mean square angular deviation from the measured cap directions. In addition, a user-specified weight, w_c, is used for favoring points C_i that are located close to the object. This correction term also guarantees that a single optimal value for C_i exists. In code, this is:

```
// locations = array of sampling locations along the radial line
// direction = measured average direction of occlusion
// n         = number of sampling locations
float wc = 16;                             // favor close-by points weight
Matrix3 A(-wc,0,0, 0,-wc,0, 0,0,-wc); // set -wc on diagonal
Vector3 B(0,0,0);

for (int i=0; i < n; i++)
{
    Vector3 d = direction[i];
    Vector3 p = locations[i];
    float   w = 1.0/dot(p,p);

    Matrix3 M;
    M[0][0] = d.x*d.x-1; M[0][1] = d.x*d.y;   M[0][2] = d.x*d.z;
    M[1][0] = d.y*d.x;   M[1][1] = d.y*d.y-1; M[1][2] = d.y*d.z;
    M[2][0] = d.z*d.x;   M[2][1] = d.z*d.y;   M[2][2] = d.z*d.z-1;

    A += w * M;
    B += w * (d * dot(d, p) - p);
}
Vector3 C = invert(A)*B; // the result
```

Since models Ω and Y are inherently smooth, they can only model the characteristics of the spherical cap outside the convex hull of the caster. Inside the convex hull, any kind of discontinuities may appear due to concavities of the shadow caster. For this reason, the described fitting procedure should only be done for measurements outside the convex hull.

In total, seven scalar values have to be stored for each direction:

- a, b, c for the size of the cap
- C for the direction of the cap (three scalars)
- r_0, the distance from the center to the convex hull along the radial line

Since a conventional cube map can only store up to four scalar values per texel, two cube maps are required to store this data.

During rendering, a spherical cap must be converted into ambient occlusion value. This is given by a cosine-weighted hemispherical integral of the cap. An analytic solution for the integral exists, but it is too complicated to be evaluated in the fragment shader. However, the result depends only on the size of the cap and the angle between the cap direction and surface normal. Thus, an efficient solution is to precompute the integrals into a 2D lookup table parameterized by the size of the cap and the cosine of the angle between cap direction and surface normal. The values in the table can be easily computed using Monte Carlo integration. Because of the smooth nature of the data, relatively low resolution is sufficient for the table.

Rendering

When rendering a fragment on the receiving surface, the coefficients for Ω and $\mathbf{Y}$ are fetched from the cube map corresponding to the shadow caster and evaluated to determine the size and direction of the spherical cap. Then, the spherical cap is integrated against the surface normal of the fragment by using a lookup table (see the previous section). Full Cg code of the fragment shader is given here.

```
pixel_out main(const in float3       pos        : TEXCOORD0,
               const in float3       normal     : TEXCOORD1,
               uniform samplerCUBE   poly       : TEXUNIT0,
               uniform samplerCUBE   c          : TEXUNIT1,
               uniform sampler2D     capTable   : TEXUNIT2,
               uniform const float4  polyScale  : C0,
               uniform const float4  polyBias   : C1,
               uniform const float3  cScale     : C2,
               uniform const float3  cBias      : C3)
{
    const float falloff0 = 3.0f;    // falloff radius 1
    const float falloff1 = 6.0f;    // falloff radius 2
    float r = length(pos);
    if (r > falloff1)
        discard;

    float3 dir    = normalize(pos);
    float4 abcr0  = texCUBE(poly, pos) * polyScale + polyBias;
    float  rclamp = max(r, abcr0.w);
    float  om     = 1.0 / (abcr0.x + abcr0.y*rclamp +
                        abcr0.z*rclamp*rclamp);
    float3 c0     = (float3)texCUBE(c, pos) * cScale + cBias;
    float3 capdir = normalize(c0 - rclamp * dir);
    float  cosang = dot(normalize(normal), capdir) * 0.5 + 0.5;
    float  ao     = (float)tex2D(capTable, float2(om, cosang)); // LUT

    if (r < abcr0.w)                // inside the convex hull?
    {
```

```
        float t = r/abcr0.w;
        ao = lerp(0.5f, ao, t*t);    // constant shadow 0.5
    }

    ao *= smoothstep(falloff1, falloff0, r);
    pixel_out OUT;
    OUT.color.w = 1-ao;
    return OUT;
}
```

The input parameters `pos` and `normal` are the position and the normal of the receiver point in the object space of the shadow caster. Cube map `poly` contains the polynomial coefficients *a*, *b*, *c* and the distance to the convex hull r_0 for each texel. Cube map c contains points **C** for each texel. In practice, more than 8-bit precision is required for both of these cube maps. Since most current hardware does not support bilinear interpolation from floating-point textures, 16-bit integer textures are used. Scale and bias terms `polyScale`, `polyBias`, `cScale`, and `cBias` are used to scale the 16-bit integer range to the actual range of the data. Finally, `capTable` is the 2D lookup table that contains the hemispherical cosine-weighted cap integrals. In this texture, 8-bit resolution is sufficient.

Outside the convex hull of the shadow caster the spherical cap approximation gives convincing shadows, but in the concavities of the caster the limitations of the approximation become apparent. For this reason, the spherical cap approximation is used only outside the convex hull of the object. Inside the hull, the ambient occlusion is simply ramped toward a value representing a strong shadow (a user-defined constant, 0.5 in the preceding shader). In a similar manner, to limit the region of influence of the shadow caster, the shadow can be ramped smoothly to zero between two falloff distances (3.0 and 6.0 in the preceding shader). This allows early exit from the shader in case the fragment is outside the region of influence of the shadow caster.

To render shadows from multiple casters, the shadows are blended together multiplicatively, and the receiving geometry is rerendered for each caster. Although this sounds inefficient, early depth test of graphics hardware helps to speed up all but the first pass. Thus a simple algorithm goes as follows:

1. Render the scene with ambient light only.
2. Render the scene for each shadow caster and multiplicatively blend in the shadows.

Numerous optimizations are possible. For example, it makes no sense to rerender objects that are clearly outside the region of influence of a certain shadow caster. This can be detected by using bounding boxes or spheres. In addition, deferred shading [Deering88] can be used to avoid rendering the scene multiple times.

For Further Reading

- "Dynamic Ambient Occlusion and Indirect Lighting," *Game Programming Gems 2,* Charles River Media, 2002.
- "Precomputed Shadow Fields for Dynamic Scenes," Proceedings of ACM Siggraph 2005.
- "Precomputed Radiance Transfer for Real-Time Rendering in Dynamic Low-Frequency Lighting Environments," in particular the section on "Neighborhood Transfer," Proceedings of ACM Siggraph 2002.

References

[Christensen02] Christensen, P. H., "Note #35: Ambient Occlusion, Image-Based Illumination and Global Illumination," Photorealistic Renderman Application Notes, 2002.

[Deering88] Deering, M. et al., "The Triangle Processor and Normal Vector Shader: A VLSI System for High Performance Graphics," Computer Graphics (Proceedings of ACM SIGGRAPH 88): pp. 21–30.

[Kontkanen05] Kontkanen, J. and S. Laine, "Ambient Occlusion Fields," ACM SIGGRAPH Symposium on Interactive 3D Graphics and Games, 2005: pp. 41–48.

[Landis02] Landis, H., Renderman in Production, ACM SIGGRAPH 2002, Course 16.

[Zhukov98] Zhukov, S. et al., "An Ambient Light Illumination Model," Rendering Techniques '98 (Proceedings of the Eurographics Workshop of Rendering): pp. 45–55.

2.5

Rendering Surface Details in Games with Relief Mapping Using a Minimally Invasive Approach

Fábio Policarpo and Manuel M. Oliveira

Introduction

The presence of geometric details on object surfaces dramatically changes the way light interacts with these surfaces. While synthesizing realistic pictures requires simulating this interaction as faithfully as possible, explicitly modeling all the small details on a surface tends to be impractical. Recognizing the importance of surface details for shading, computer graphics researchers have devised techniques to simulate the appearance of small surface details [Blinn78] and to modify the underlying geometry using a mesh of micropolygons [Cook84].

By applying a perturbation to the surface normals, bump mapping [Blinn78] can achieve some impressive shading effects while keeping a low polygonal count for the scene. As a result, normal mapping has become a very popular choice among game developers. Unfortunately, normal mapping only deals with the variation of the surface normal caused by the small details and hence does not handle self-occlusions, shadows, and silhouettes. By changing the actual geometry, displacement mapping [Cook84] offers these features, but requires the transformation and rasterization of a large number of extra polygons, significantly impacting an application's frame rate. A recently introduced technique called *relief mapping* [Policarpo05] [Oliveira00] provides a good balance between the visual quality of displacement mapping and the speed of normal mapping. Figure 2.5.1 shows a scene exhibiting a teapot rendered with our relief-mapping shader, where one can observe self-occlusions and self-shadowing effects.

Several popular games, such as *DOOM 3*™, make intensive use of normal mapping for rendering. As a result, most surfaces within the game lack parallax, self-occlusions, self-shadowing, and correct projected shadows. In this article, we present a minimally invasive approach to add relief mapping to existing games (and to graphics applications in general) with the goal of improving their rendering quality. To accomplish this, one only needs to compute a set of depth maps from the set of available normal maps, and to edit and recompile the vertex and pixel shaders to make use of relief mapping. No

FIGURE 2.5.1   *A teapot rendered with our relief-mapping shader.*

access to the source code of the main application is necessary. We demonstrate this concept by adding relief mapping rendering capabilities to *DOOM 3* and to a game prototype. In addition, we show a complete implementation of a relief-mapping shader written in Cg, which can be used as a reference.

Relief Mapping—A Brief Review

Relief mapping [Policarpo05] is a technique for simulating the appearance of geometric surface details on polygonal models. The surface details are represented by a depth map and by a normal map, both stored into a single 32-bit-per-texel RGBA texture, called a relief texture [Oliveira00]. The mapping of a relief texture to a geometric model is done in the conventional way, assigning to each vertex a pair of texture coordinates.

The depth data is normalized to the [0,1] range and can be appropriately scaled to match the intended depth for each surface in the scene. This can be achieved by storing scaling factors on a per-vertex basis. If no scaling factors are provided, a global factor can be used instead. Relief mapping assumes that the geometric details are below the polygonal surface. Thus, a sample with zero depth represents a point on the polygonal surface itself, whereas a sample with depth equal to $d \in [0,1]$ will be $d \times scaling\ factor$ units below the surface. Figure 2.5.2 shows a cross section of a height-field surface reconstructed from a depth map with a scaling factor equal to 1.0.

Relief rendering is done on the GPU by performing a ray-height-field intersection in texture space. Let f be a fragment of a relief texture-mapped polygon and let (s,t) be its associated relief-texture coordinates. The process of computing f's shading can be divided into three steps. The first step is to transform the viewing direction into f's tangent space. Then, P, the closest intersection between the transformed viewing direction V and the height-field surface is computed (Figure 2.5.2). Finally,

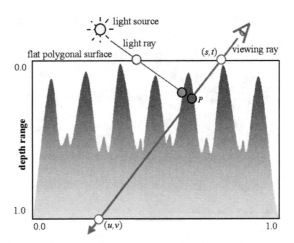

FIGURE 2.5.2   *A cross section of a height-field surface reconstructed from a depth map.*

P's associated normal (sampled from the normal map component of the relief texture) and its 3D coordinates are used to shade *f* using some illumination model.

The intersection between the viewing ray and the height field is performed in 2D texture space, searching along a segment ranging from coordinates *(s,t)* to *(u,v)*. The *(u,v)* coordinates are computed from three elements: the entry point *(s,t)* of the viewing ray, the transformed viewing direction *V*, and the depth scaling factor. This is illustrated in Figure 2.5.2. Note that although the cross-section representation shown in Figure 2.5.2 seems to suggest the need of a 3D representation, the actual intersection can be computed in 2D. The search for an intersection involves sampling the depth map starting at *(s,t)* and stepping toward *(u,v)* until one finds a stored depth value that is smaller than the corresponding depth of the *V* vector at this point, or until *(u,v)* is reached. Note that reaching *(u,v)* means that we have hit the bottom of the height-field surface and, therefore, have found an intersection point there.

The search for the intersection point starts with a linear search along the segment from *(s,t)* to *(u,v)*, looking for a first point where *V* would be under the height-field surface. Figure 2.5.3 (left) illustrates this situation. There, the number inside the circles indicates the steps of the linear search. Once a point under the surface is found, the actual intersection point is obtained using a binary search to refine the result (see Figure 2.5.3, right). Note that the binary search is an important component of the relief-rendering algorithm, since it finds precise intersections taking advantage of the bilinear filtering capabilities of the texture subsystem. This allows for extreme close-ups of relief-mapped surfaces without noticeable texture artifacts.

Given the intersection point *P* (see Figure 2.5.2), its *Z* coordinate expressed in the camera coordinate system is used to update the Z-buffer (after projection and division

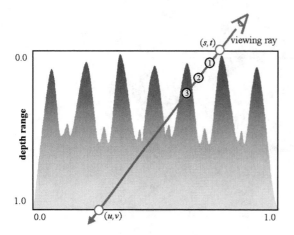
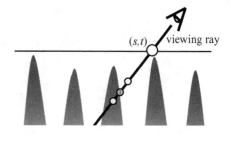

FIGURE 2.5.3　*The search for the intersection point starts with a linear search along the segment from (s,t) to (u,v), looking for a first point where V would be under the height-field surface.*

by w). This allows for proper occlusion between relief-mapped surfaces and other objects in the scene, as well as for the use of shadow mapping [Williams78] for casting shadows among the various scene objects. Lighting and self-shadowing are computed by checking whether a light ray (also expressed in f's tangent space) reaches any other surface before reaching the point to be shaded (see Figure 2.5.2). Since one just needs to check if the light ray is blocked, only the linear search is sufficient. Note that the linear search may miss some thin structures depending on the lighting (viewing) ray direction and on the linear step size. This aliasing problem can be reduced by using a smaller step size or by making the search adaptive using precomputed information about the location of the fine structures.

Generating Relief Textures from Normal Maps

A depth map can be obtained from a normal map by assigning a depth value for a given texel and computing the depth for the remaining texels relative to the first one. Note that this procedure assumes that the underlying surface is continuous. This is, in fact, a reasonable assumption, as normal maps cannot represent depth discontinuities. For games that make use of the textures' alpha channels, such as the case of *DOOM 3*, the depth can be stored, for example, in the alpha channel of the specular maps.

Minimally Invasive Relief-Mapping Rendering for Games

It is possible to add relief-mapping capabilities to existing games in a minimally invasive way. Once the normal maps have been converted to relief maps, all that needs to be done is to modify the game's vertex and pixel shaders to perform relief-mapping rendering. The following section explains how this can be achieved.

Adding Relief Mapping to *DOOM 3*

DOOM 3 is a popular game developed by id Software, Inc. Its shaders make extensive use of normal mapping to reduce the amount of geometry that needs to be rendered. As such, *DOOM 3* is an ideal application for demonstrating how easy it is to add relief mapping to an existing application. Doing so only requires adding a few lines of code to its shaders, which are written in assembly language. Due to space constraints, we limit ourselves to show the additional lines and to indicate where these lines should be inserted in the original shaders.

The vertex shader has to be modified to compute the viewing direction in tangent space, as discussed in the brief review about relief mapping. To do that, only three new lines of code need to be inserted after the first instruction used to calculate and store the normalized vector from the vertex to the viewer.

```
...
# attrib[9]   TEX1      tangent[0]
# attrib[10]  TEX2      tangent[1]
# attrib[11]  TEX3      normal
...
# calculate normalized ... in R1
SUB             R1, ...        # part of the original code

# view vector in tangent space. Next 3 lines are the new code
DP3             result.texcoord[7].x, vertex.attrib[9], -R1;
DP3             result.texcoord[7].y, vertex.attrib[10], -R1;
DP3             result.texcoord[7].z, vertex.attrib[11], -R1;

DP3     R2, ...  # original code resumes here
```

Modifying the fragment shader requires adding several lines of code, as shown next. Fortunately, everything can be inserted before the first line of the original shader. Note that the code for the linear and binary searches is shown with a single iteration each, and needs to be replicated a certain number of times to perform the complete search. We have omitted the repetitions to save space.

```
!!ARBfp1.0
OPTION ARB_precision_hint_nicest;

# relief mapping: view vector with depth factor
OPTION NV_fragment_program;
PARAM const = { 0, 1, 0.075, 0.1 };
PARAM const2 = { 0.5, 2.0, 0, 0 };
TEMP view, RT, RA, RB;

DP3 view, fragment.texcoord[7], fragment.texcoord[7];
RSQ view, view.x;
MUL view, view.x, fragment.texcoord[7];
```

```
RCP RA.x, view.z;                    # RA=1.0/view.z
MUL view.xy, view, const.z;          # view.xy*=depth
MUL view, view, -RA.x;               # view*=-RA
MUL view, view, const.w;             # view/=10
MOV RT, fragment.texcoord[1];        # RT=texcoord
MOV RT.z, const.y;                   # RT.z=1

# linear search (LS) - repeat this 9x in your code for 9 steps of LS
TEX RA, RT, texture[5], 2D;          # RA=tex(RT)
SGTC RB.w, RT.z, RA.w;               # if (RT.z>RA.w)
ADD RT(GT.w), RT, view;              #       RT+=view;

# binary search (BS) - repeat this 5x in your code for 5 steps of BS
TEX RA, RT, texture[5], 2D;          # RA=tex(RT)
MUL view, view, const2.x;            # view*=0.5
SGTC RB.w, RT.z, RA.w;               # if (RT.z>RA.w)
MAD RT(GT.w), view, const2.y, RT;    #       RT+=view*2;
SUB RT, RT, view;                    # RT-=view;

# original code starts here …
```

Besides adding the preceding code fragment, one needs to replace, in the original shader, all following occurrences of `fragment.texcoord[1]`, `fragment.texcoord[4]`, and `fragment.texcoord[5]` (which represent the texture coordinates for the normal, diffuse, and specular maps, respectively) with the register `RT`. Such a register stores the computed relief-texture coordinates of the intersection point P (see Figure 2.5.2), which are needed to access the normal, diffuse, and depth maps required for shading. Note that the depth maps are stored in the specular map's alpha channel, since the original normal maps are compressed, not supporting alpha channel modification.

Figure 2.5.4 shows a side-by-side comparison of two screenshots taken from *DOOM 3*. On the left, one sees an image rendered by the original shaders using normal mapping. Notice how the surfaces look flat, with no self-occlusions. The image on the right was rendered using the modified shaders to support relief mapping. The depth maps for all textures of the game were computed directly from the normal maps. The modified shaders do not handle self-shadowing or update the Z-buffer for projecting correct shadows on the displaced surface. The intention was to keep the example as simple and clear as possible, as *DOOM 3* shaders are written in assembly code. Because the original shaders do not produce self-shadowing or proper interpenetration, we managed to keep the example simple while providing a reasonable comparison. The image rendered using relief mapping clearly highlights some surface details (see Figure 2.5.4, right). For example, note the disks sticking out of the panel and the slanted surface between the panel and the pathway. The lighting difference on the back, where a man is standing, is due to a light flashing while the images were acquired.

To evaluate the performance of both implementations, we run a time demo (DOOM 3 demo1) using a resolution of 640 × 480 pixels, with 4× anti-aliasing. The average frame rate when using the original shaders based on normal mapping was 83.2 fps. The average frame rate obtained with the modified shaders using relief mapping

FIGURE 2.5.4 *A side-by-side comparison of two screenshots taken from* DOOM 3. *Image from DOOM 3 © 2004 id Software, Inc. Used with permission.*

was 39.5 fps when using ten steps of linear search and five steps of binary search. The measurements were made on an Athlon64 3000+ (2 GHz), with 1 GB of memory (2×512 DDR400), AGP 8X, and a GeForce6800 GT card with 256 MB of memory.

For relief rendering, the frame rate varied with the number of active lights. As the modified code calculates ray intersection and performs lighting calculations in the same shader, having multiple lights illuminating the same polygon means recomputing the ray intersection for that polygon once per light source. A more efficient solution would be to calculate the ray intersection only once per frame and apply lighting as a separate shader (deferred shading). Such an approach, although efficient, would require modifying the application code, which may not be available as it was in the case for *DOOM 3*.

Adding Relief Mapping to a Game Prototype

Using the minimally invasive strategy described earlier, we added relief-mapping capabilities to a game prototype whose shaders were written in HLSL. Figure 2.5.5 shows a screenshot taken from it, where the ground and the wall details are rendered using relief mapping. Note the self-occlusions and self-shadowing on these surfaces.

Relief Mapping in Cg

The previous sections discussed how to add relief-mapping capabilities to existing games by performing minor changes to their vertex and fragment shaders. In order to provide more complete implementation details, this section presents a complete version of a relief-mapping fragment shader written in the Cg shader language. This shader is part of a demo that compares the renderings produced by normal, parallax, and relief mapping. You should be able to easily translate it to other shading languages

FIGURE 2.5.5   *A screenshot of a game prototype, where the ground and the wall details are rendered using relief mapping. Note the self-occlusions and self-shadowing on these surfaces.*
© 2005. *Reprinted with permission from Master Creating Gmbh.*

ON THE CD

and to adapt it to your own applications. The images shown in Figure 2.5.6 were rendered using this demo, whose source and executable codes can be can found on the accompanying CD-ROM.

FIGURE 2.5.6   *Images generated using the demo provided on the companion CD-ROM.*

The shader takes, among its parameters, the fragment 3D position (vpos) and the light position (lightpos), both in camera space. The view vector is then mapped to the fragment's tangent space and scaled according to the relief texture dimensions.

This scaling is necessary to correctly render the depth in the same units as the scene objects that the relief texture will be mapped to. This is achieved by dividing the view vector X, Y, and Z components by the dimensions of the texture tile and the depth-scaling factor, respectively. The dimensions of a tile are stored on a per-vertex basis in the *W* coordinates of the tangent (`IN.tangent.w`) and binormal (`IN.binormal.w`) vectors, respectively.

Once the view vector has been appropriately scaled, the linear and binary searches are performed. This is followed by a depth-buffer update and self-shadowing computation. Note that once the depth buffer has been updated, relief-mapped objects can be integrated with other objects, allowing both categories to cast and to receive shadows using, for example, shadow mapping [Williams78].

```
struct v2f {
        float4 hpos      : POSITION;   float4 color    : COLOR0;
        float3 vpos      : TEXCOORD0;  float2 texcoord : TEXCOORD1;
        float3 normal    : TEXCOORD2;  float4 tangent  : TEXCOORD3;
        float4 binormal  : TEXCOORD4;
};

struct f2s { float4 color : COLOR; };

void ray_intersect_rm_linear(in sampler2D reliefmap,
  inout float3 p, inout float3 v) {
        const int linear_search_steps=10;
        v/=linear_search_steps;
        for( int i=0;i<linear_search_steps-1;i++ ){
                float4 t=tex2D(reliefmap,p.xy);
                if (p.z<t.w)
                        p+=v;
        }
}

void ray_intersect_rm_binary(in sampler2D reliefmap,
        inout float3 p, inout float3 v) {
        const int binary_search_steps=6;
        for( int i=0;i<binary_search_steps;i++ ){
                v*=0.5;
                float4 t=tex2D(reliefmap,p.xy);
                if (p.z<t.w)
                        p+=2*v;
                p-=v;
        }
}

f2s main_frag_relief(v2f IN,
        uniform sampler2D rmtex:TEXUNIT0,      // rm texture map
        uniform sampler2D colortex:TEXUNIT1,   // color texture map
        uniform float4 lightpos,               // light position
        uniform float4 ambient,                // ambient color
        uniform float4 diffuse,                // diffuse color
        uniform float4 specular,               // specular color
```

```
        uniform float2 planes,                // near/far plane info
        uniform float  tile,                  // tile factor
        uniform float  depth)                 // depth factor
{

        f2s OUT;

        float3 view = normalize(IN.vpos);     // normalized view vector
        float vz = dot(-view,IN.normal);
        float3 v = normalize( float3( dot(view,IN.tangent.xyz),
                    dot(view,IN.binormal.xyz), vz)); // view in tangent space
        // scale depth.
        float3 scale = float3(IN.tangent.w,IN.binormal.w,depth)/tile;
        v *= scale.z/(scale*v.z);

        float3 p = float3(IN.texcoord*tile,0);

        ray_intersect_rm_linear(rmtex,p,v);   // linear search
        ray_intersect_rm_binary(rmtex,p,v);   // binary search

        float4 t = tex2D(rmtex,p.xy);         // fetch normal
        float4 c = tex2D(colortex,p.xy);      // fetch color

        // expand normal from normal map in local polygon space
        t.xyz -= 0.5;
        t.xyz = normalize(t.x*IN.tangent.xyz + t.y*IN.binormal.xyz +
                    t.z*IN.normal);
        float3 pos = IN.vpos+view*p.z*depth/vz;
        float3 light = normalize(pos-lightpos.xyz); // normalize it

#ifdef RM_DEPTHCORRECT
        // a=-far/(far-near); b=-far*near/(far-near); Z=(a*z+b)/-z;
        OUT.depth = ((planes.x*pos.z+planes.y)/-pos.z);
#endif

        float att  = saturate(dot(-light,IN.normal));
        float diff = saturate(dot(-light,t.xyz));
        float spec = saturate(dot(normalize(-light-view),t.xyz));
        float4 finalcolor = ambient*c;
#ifdef RM_SHADOWS
        // compute light ray vector in tangent space
        v = normalize( float3( dot(light,IN.tangent.xyz),
            dot(light,IN.binormal.xyz), dot(-light,IN.normal)));
        v *= scale.z/(scale*v.z);
        // compute light ray entry point in texture space
        float3 lp = p-v*p.z;
        ray_intersect_rm_linear(rmtex,lp,v);

        if (lp.z<p.z-0.05) { // if pixel in shadow
          diff *= 0.3;
          spec = 0;
        }
```

```
#endif
        // compute final color
    finalcolor.xyz += att*(c.xyz*diffuse.xyz*diff +
      specular.xyz*pow(spec, specular.w));
        finalcolor.w = 1.0;
        OUT.color = finalcolor;
        return OUT;
}
```

Conclusion

In this article, we described how to add relief-mapping capabilities to modern games using a minimally invasive approach. Relief-mapping visual benefits can be achieved by performing small changes to the vertex and fragment shaders of the applications. We also presented a fully functional implementation of relief mapping in Cg, which should allow you to add relief-mapping functionality to your own applications. Although effective when the only source code available is the shaders, the minimally invasive approach described here does not guarantee an efficient integration of relief-mapping capabilities. Faster implementations should split the intersection and shading steps of the algorithm into separate fragment programs. This way, the intersection procedure can be performed only once per fragment, while lighting computation is performed by a separate fragment program. In this case, all lights can be handled in a single pass, or multiple passes can be performed without incurring in unnecessary work.

Acknowledgments

We want to thank id Software, Inc. for kindly granting permission to use the *DOOM 3* image shown in Figure 2.5.4. Master Creating GmbH provided the screenshot shown in Figure 2.5.5. The conversion of normal maps to depth maps was performed with a multigrid Poisson solver written by Carlos Scheidegger and Gustavo Neto.

References

[Blinn78] Blinn, J., "Simulation of Wrinkled Surfaces," Proceedings of SIGGRAPH 1978, pp. 286–292.

[Cook84] Cook, R., "Shade Tress", Proceedings of SIGGRAPH 1984, pp. 223–231.

[Oliveira00] Oliveira, M. M., Bishop, G., and McAllister, D., "Relief Texture Mapping," Proceedings of SIGGRAPH 2000, pp. 359–368.

[Policarpo05] Policarpo, F., Oliveira, M. M., and Comba, J., "Real-Time Relief Mapping on Arbitrary Polygonal Surfaces," ACM SIGGRAPH 2005 Symposium on Interactive 3D Graphics and Games, pp. 155–162.

[Williams78] Williams, L., "Casting Curved Shadows on Curved Surfaces". SIGGRAPH 1978, pp. 270–274.

2.6

Real-Time Obscurances with Color Bleeding

Alex Méndez-Feliu, Mateu Sbert, Jordi Catà, Nicolau Sunyer, and Sergi Funtané

Introduction

The obscurance method is a powerful technique that simulates the effect of diffuse interreflections, that is, radiosity, on an object at a much lower performance cost. Its main advantage lies in the fact that this technique considers only neighboring interactions instead of attempting to solve all the global ones. Another advantage of this technique is that it is decoupled from direct illumination computation. In this article, we show how obscurances can be used in a video-game environment, allowing realistic and fast illumination of the scene.

Radiosity techniques [Goral84] are commonly used to simulate diffuse global illumination—although very powerful and increasingly faster [Bekaert98], they do not yet fulfill the requirements for fast and efficient real-time scene editing or rendering. With radiosity, the interaction of each surface in the scene with each of the other surfaces has to be (at least potentially) considered; the obscurance method [Zhukov98] [Iones03] being designed to offer a fast alternative to radiosity.

This technique can deal with any number of moving light sources with no added cost since the indirect illumination and direct illumination are effectively decoupled. The obscurance technique also allows the addition of color bleeding [Mendez03] to your lighting.

Obscurances have already been used in 3D computer games and animations in a simplified form commonly called ambient occlusions [Christensen03], [Pharr04], [Bunnel05]. In this article, a new algorithm to compute obscurances using depth peeling [Everitt01] is presented. In addition, we discuss the real-time update of obscurances for moving objects within a scene.

Obscurances

The obscurance illumination model ([Zhukov98] [Iones03]) has been defined to take account of the indirect (diffuse) illumination while being totally decoupled from direct illumination. Within the obscurance model, the indirect illumination for a point P is defined as:

$$I(P) = \frac{1}{\pi} \times R(P) \times I_A \times \int\limits_{\omega \in \Omega} \rho(d(P, \omega)) \cos\theta d\omega \qquad (2.6.1)$$

where

- $d(P, \omega)$ is the distance between P and the next surface at direction ω.
- $\rho(d)$ is a function that determines the magnitude of ambient light incoming from neighborhood d, and taking values between 0 and 1.
- θ is the angle between direction ω and the normal at P.
- I_A is the ambient light intensity.
- $R(P)$ is the reflectivity at the point P.
- $\frac{1}{\pi}$ is a normalization factor such that if $\rho() = 1$ over the whole hemisphere Ω, then $I(P)$ is $R.I_A$.

Direct illumination can then be added to Equation 2.6.1 to obtain the final illumination of the point.

As you can see in Figure 2.6.1, the function $\rho()$ increases with the distance d.

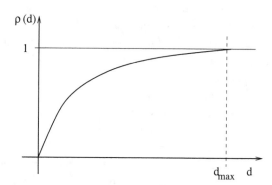

FIGURE 2.6.1   *Function $\rho(d)$.*

Function $\rho(d)$ will be equal to 1 for $d \geq d_{max}$. This means that we are not taking into account occlusions farther than d_{max}; we only take the "neighboring" ones. The function we used is $\sqrt{d/d_{max}}$ if $d < d_{max}$, and 1 otherwise.

The obscurance of the point P is then defined as:

$$W(P) = \frac{1}{\pi} \times \int\limits_{\omega \in \Omega} \rho(d(P, \omega)) \cos\theta d\omega \qquad (2.6.2)$$

Since $0 \leq \rho(d) \leq 1$, we can assume that $0 \leq W(P) \leq 1$. The obscurance for a patch (in radiosity terms, a polygon from a subdivided mesh) is the average of the obscurances for all points within the patch. An obscurance value of 1 means that the patch is totally open (or not occluded by neighboring polygons), while a value of 0 means that it is totally closed (or occluded by neighboring polygons).

For a closed environment, the ambient light in Equation 2.6.1 can be computed as the average light intensity in the scene using the following formula:

$$I_A = \frac{R_{ave}}{(1 - R_{ave})} \cdot \frac{\sum_{i=1}^{n} A_i . E_i}{A_{total}}, \quad \text{where} \quad R_{ave} = \frac{\sum_{i=1}^{n} A_i . R_i}{A_{total}} \quad (2.6.3)$$

where A_i, E_i, and R_i are the area, emissivity, and reflectivity of patch i, respectively, A_{total} is the sum of the areas, and n is the number of patches in the scene. The ambient term considered here corresponds to the indirect illumination only, as direct illumination is computed separately.

Since the obscurance computation only takes into account the neighborhood of a patch (that is, near than d_{max}), the computation can be done very efficiently. For further details see [Zhukov98] [Iones03].

Color Bleeding

The obscurance approach presented in the previous section lacks one of the features that comes from radiosity lighting—color bleeding. Because the light reflected from a patch acquires some of its color, the surrounding patches receive colored indirect lighting. Here, we present a straightforward technique to account for this color bleeding, with no added computational cost.

The obscurances formula (Equation 2.6.4) is modified slightly to include the reflectivity term of the patches:

$$W(P) = \frac{1}{\pi} \times \int_{\omega \in \Omega} R(Q) \rho(d(P, \omega)) \cos \theta d\omega \quad (2.6.4)$$

where $R(Q)$ is the reflectivity of point Q as seen from P in direction ω. When no surface is seen at a distance less than d_{max} in direction ω, the obscurance takes the value of R_{ave}.

For coherency, the ambient light equation (Equation 2.6.5) also has to be modified, yielding the following:

$$I_A = \frac{1}{(1 - R_{ave})} \cdot \frac{\sum_{i=1}^{n} A_i . E_i}{A_{total}} \quad (2.6.5)$$

The improved obscurance model can be computed in several ways. The usual option is to compute the obscurance equation (Equation 2.6.4) using the Monte Carlo (or quasi Monte Carlo) ray-casting technique, which casts several rays from a patch distributed along $cos\theta$. The obscurance for the patch i will then be the average of the values gathered by the rays cast from this patch:

$$W(i) = \frac{1}{N_i}\sum_{j=1}^{N_i}\rho_j R_{int}$$

(2.6.6)

where N_i is the number of rays cast from patch i, R_{int} is the reflectance at the intersected patch (if no patch is intersected, then we take R_{ave}), and ρ_j is the value of the function $\rho()$ for line j. Several Monte Carlo and quasi-Monte Carlo sampling techniques have been tested for obscurance computation in [Mendez04a], and the Halton quasi-Monte Carlo sequence gave the best performance.

But this quasi-Monte Carlo approach is not our only option. Sbert [Sbert97] demonstrated that casting cosine distributed rays from all patches in the scene is equivalent to casting global lines joining random points of the bounding sphere of the scene. Furthermore, it is also equivalent to casting bundles or parallel rays of random directions (see Figure 2.6.2). Bundles of parallel rays can be efficiently cast on the graphics hardware using the depth-peeling algorithm as shown in the next section.

Rays from every patch   Global lines   Bundles of parallel rays

FIGURE 2.6.2   *Different ray-tracing techniques for computing obscurances.*

Figure 2.6.3a shows the Cornell box scene computed with the obscurances but without color bleeding, while in Figure 2.6.3b we have used our improved algorithm. Color bleeding is clearly visible, adding a lot of realism to the image. Compare these images with the one obtained with a more complete radiosity algorithm (see Figure 2.6.3c) and you see that the improved obscurance method represents a step forward toward simulating a radiosity image, with no added cost. See color versions on the companion CD-ROM.

ON THE CD

FIGURE 2.6.3 *a) Obscurances without color bleeding. b) Obscurances with color bleeding. c) A radiosity solution.*

GPU Obscurances Using Depth Peeling

The basic idea behind the depth-peeling technique is to extract visibility layers from the scene in order to do some computation between them. In [Everitt01], the technique is used to achieve order-independent transparency. Global illumination [Szirmay98] [Hachisuka05] has been done also with depth peeling.

We can see the pixel image resulting from depth peeling as being equivalent to tracing a bundle of parallel rays through the scene where each pixel corresponds to a ray in the bundle. Each of these rays may intersect several surfaces in the scene, and through depth peeling we can discover all of the intersections in the form of image layers and not only the closest one obtained by the z-buffer algorithm.

Once we have chosen a random direction for the bundle, the computation of obscurances with depth peeling is divided into two phases. In the first phase, layers are obtained using depth peeling. In the second phase, the obscurances between each pair of layers are computed and the result is added and averaged in the corresponding obscurance map position.

Depth Peeling

We assume that in a preprocessing step the scene completely is mapped to a single texture atlas. A texel of the texture atlas corresponds to a small surface area, thus texels obscurance patches. When a patch is referenced, we simply use the texture address of the corresponding texel.

The obscurance computation picks a random direction and carries out the depth-peeling process in this direction. When we let the GPU do it for us, we use an orthogonal projection, and from the sampled direction we render the scene setting the model-view transform to rotate the sample direction to the z axis.

We use the *pixel* (RGBA) of an image layer to store the patch identification; a flag indicates whether the patch is front-facing or back-facing to the camera and the camera to patch distance. Our pixel buffer is initialized with $(-1.0,-1.0,1.0,1.0)$, giving us reasonable default values.

The facing direction of a pixel can be determined by using the cosine of the angle between the camera's -z vector and the normal vector of the patch. If the result is greater than 0, it is front-facing; otherwise, it is back-facing. The cosine can be determined by using the z component of the dot product between the inverse transpose model-view matrix and the normalized normal vector of the patch.

As we store the pixels in a four-component float array (or the RGBA color), we use the first two components to store the patch ID (RG $\leftarrow$ (u,v)), the third to store the cosine (B $\leftarrow \cos\alpha$), and the fourth component to store the distance between the camera and the patch (A $\leftarrow$ z).

The vertex shader receives the vertex coordinates, the texture coordinates (in (u,v), identifying the texel), and the normal, and generates the cosine and the transformed vertex position:

```
void main( float4 position : POSITION,
           float2 texCoord : TEXCOORD0,   //Patch ID
           float4 Norm     : NORMAL,      //Patch Normal

           out float4 oposition : POSITION,
           out float2 otexCoord : TEXCOORD0,
           out float  cosine    : TEXCOORD1,

           uniform float4x4 modelView,
           uniform float4x4 modelViewInvTrans)
{
      oposition = mul(modelView,position);
      otexCoord = texCoord;

      cosine = mul(modelViewInvTrans,Norm).z;
                        //sample direction is rotated to (0,0,1)
}
```

The fragment shader receives the interpolated texture coordinates of the fragment, the position (where z is the depth), the cosine, and the interpolated texture coordinates of the patch. For the first layer, the depth does not need to be compared with the previous one. However, for all subsequent layers, we sample the previous layer using the texture coordinates and discard it if the previous layer's depth (the sample's fourth component) is closer to the camera than the actual fragment, thus getting the peeling effect (see Figure 2.6.4).

This rendering step is repeated until all pixels are discarded. The images of all the rendered layers define all of the ray-surface intersections (see Figure 2.6.5).

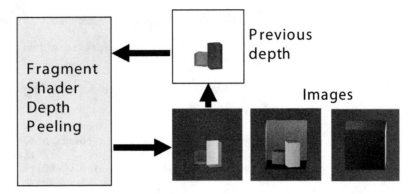

FIGURE 2.6.4   *Schema of the depth peeling with GPU.*

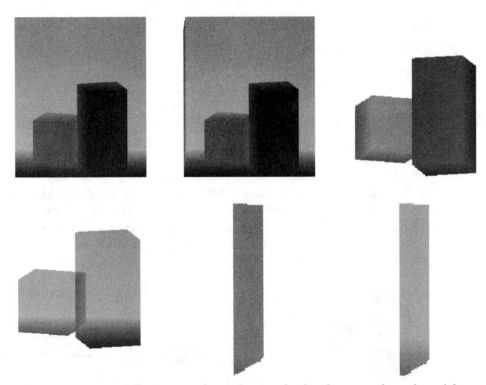

FIGURE 2.6.5   *Six different image layers showing depth information for each pixel for the Cornell Box scene.*

```
void main(float4 position : WPOS,
          float2 texCoord : TEXCOORD0,        //Patch ID
          float  cosine   : TEXCOORD1,        //Patch Orientation
```

```
                    out float4 color : COLOR,    //Patch ID + Orientation + Depth

                    uniform sampler2D ztex,      //previous depth image
                    uniform float res,           //resolution of projection win-
        dow
                    uniform float first)         //is first layer?
        {
            if( first == 0.0 )                   // not first -> peel
            {
                    float depth = tex2D(ztex,position.xy/res).a;
                                                 //last depth
                    if (position.z < (depth + 0.000001)) discard;
                                                 //ignore previous
        // layers
            }
            color.rg = texCoord;
            color.b = cosine;
            color.a = position.z; //new depth
        }
```

Obscurances

For each pair of consecutive layers, the obscurance formula is computed.

We configure the camera to obtain a one-to-one mapping between pixels and texels. The size of the view port is set to the same resolution as the obscurance map, starting from (0,0), with an orthogonal projection from −1 to +1 in both dimensions.

Each pair of consecutive images is taken from the texture memory and sent to the graphic pipeline as a stream of points of size 1.0 (render to vertex array). This way, we can update a single position in the target buffer for each element of the image. This generates a pair of point streams—A and B—that are merged and sent to the vertex shader. Stream A is sent as vertex positions and stream B as texture coordinates. As we generate the streams in both images in the same way, points at the same position in streams A and B are at the same position in consecutive images, thus they may see each other in the sampling direction and consequently transfer energy (see Figure 2.6.6).

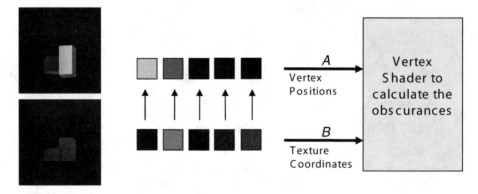

FIGURE 2.6.6   *Two consecutive layers (left) generate two streams of points carrying patch IDs (middle) that are merged together and processed by the vertex shader (right).*

The obscurance computation needs to be done bidirectionally, but we cannot generate two values in different positions of the target buffer in a single pass and thus we have to do a two-pass transfer. In the first pass, we update the patches in the projection that generated stream A using the information in pixels of stream B (see Figure 2.6.6). In the second pass, the streams are exchanged, thus the same set of shaders is used in both directions.

If a patch in stream A cannot see the corresponding patch in stream B, the vertex carrying this patch is eliminated by moving it out of the view frustum. If patches see each other and the difference between their distances to the camera is less than d_{max}, the transfer is done. If the distance is greater or transfers with the background, the patch gets the ambient reflectivity. If the patches do not see each other, the vertex is discarded. When the transfer process is done, we generate vertex coordinates to update the position in the obscurance map that corresponds to the patch identified by the two first components of the current pixel element in stream A.

The vertex shader needs to generate vertex coordinates in homogeneous clip space. The desired position is encoded as the patch ID but is in a normalized form (as 2D texture coordinates are in the range $[0..1]$). Equation 2.6.7 computes which homogeneous clip coordinates we need to generate to obtain the desired normalized window coordinates given a camera and a view port set, as explained earlier.

$$\begin{pmatrix} x_c \\ y_c \\ z_c \\ w_c \end{pmatrix} = \begin{pmatrix} 2x_w - 1 \\ 2y_w - 1 \\ 2z_w - 1 \\ 1 \end{pmatrix} \tag{2.6.7}$$

Note that the clipping process only keeps the fragment if $-w_c \leq z_c \leq w_c$. As we define a w_c of 1, the clipping process will only keep the fragment when $-1 \leq z_c \leq 1$. If $z_c = 2.0$ then $z_w = 1.5$ and the fragment is out of the view frustum and is discarded. If we set $z_c = 0.0$ then $z_w = 0.5$, the vertex is kept by the clipping process. Therefore we can use the z_c value as a way to accept or discard vertices.

The vertex shader for the obscurance transfer process is:

```
void main( float4 A : POSITION,           //x,y = ID; z = Orientation;
                                          //w = Depth;
           float4 B : TEXCOORD0,          //x,y = ID; z = Orientation;
                                          //w = Depth;

       out float4 oposition : POSITION,
       out float2 pA        : TEXCOORD0, //Texture coordinates of A.
       out float2 pB        : TEXCOORD1, //Texture coordinates of B.
       out float distance   : TEXCOORD2, //Distance.
```

```
                        uniform float direction) //Switch of direction
    {
      //If patches see each other, i.e. both exist and one is front
      //facing and the other is back facing.
      //Direction tells if we are transferring in the camera -z direction
      //or +z.
      //A.r contains the patch ID. If it contains -1.0 means that it does
      //not belong to the scene.
      //A.b contains the cosine.
      if(((direction == 0) && (A.r != -1.0) && (A.b < 0.0)
            && ((B.b > 0.0) || (B.r == -1.0)))
         || ((direction == 1) && (A.r != -1.0) && (A.b > 0.0)
            && ((B.b < 0.0) || (B.r == -1.0)))))
      {
          pA = float2(A.r, A.g); //Set the texture coordinates for A.
          pB = float2(B.r, B.g); //Set the texture coordinates for B.
          //Create vertex to update desired position. z = 0.0 =>
          //kept by clipping
          oposition = float4((pA * 2.0) - float2(1.0, 1.0), 0.0, 1.0);
          //Calculate distance. If patch in stream B not in scene =>
          //distance = 1.0
          distance = (texCoord.b != 1.0)? abs(B.a – A.a) : 1.0;
      }
      else //If there's no transfer move out from the view frustum.
      {
          // z = 2.0 to get the id ignored by clipping.
          oposition = float4( 0.0, 0.0, 2.0, 1.0 );
          p1 = p2 = float2(1.0, 1.0);
          distance = 0.5;
      }
    }
```

The fragment shader just applies the obscurance formula $\rho = \sqrt{d/d_{max}}$ if $d < d_{max}$ and 1 otherwise.

```
void main( float2 pA : TEXCOORD0,      //Texture coordinates of A.
           float2 pB : TEXCOORD1,      //Texture coordinates of B.
           float  distance  : TEXCOORD2,

           out float4 ocolor : COLOR,

           uniform sampler2D reflectivity,
           uniform float dmax,
           uniform float3 ambient)
{
    if(d>=dmax) ocolor.rgb = ambient; //If distance > dmax, add ambient
    //else we apply the obscurances formula
    else ocolor.rgb = tex2D(reflectivity,pB).rgb *
sqrt(distance/dmax);
    ocolor.a = 1.0;
}
```

Figures 2.6.7, 2.6.8, and 2.6.9 show the results of applying our algorithm to models of the De Espona library. We show, respectively, the obscurances map, obscurances with direct illumination, and direct illumination with constant ambient term. Observe the quality of the illumination obtained with obscurances.

FIGURE 2.6.7 *Cathedral model, 193,180 polygons, obscurances computed in 38 seconds. Left: obscurances map; middle: obscurances with direct illumination; right: constant ambient term with direct illumination.*

FIGURE 2.6.8 *Tank model, 225,280 polygons, obscurances computed in 38 seconds. Left: obscurances map; middle: obscurances with direct illumination; right: constant ambient term with direct illumination.*

FIGURE 2.6.9 *Car model, 97,473 polygons, obscurances computed in 32 seconds. Left: obscurances map; middle: obscurances with direct illumination; right: constant ambient term with direct illumination.*

Real-Time Update for Moving Objects

Although the computation of the initial obscurance value is not done in real time, we can update them in real time efficiently for a moderate number of polygons.

We store the patches initially influenced by the dynamic objects, that is, the patches that have been used in the computation of the obscurances for a dynamic object. When the object moves to a new position, the obscurances from this list have to be recalculated. Obviously, you also have to recalculate the obscurances of the patches of the moving object, and this causes an update of the list of influenced patches. Lastly, the obscurances of these new patches have to be recalculated, completing the whole update process.

The depth-peeling algorithm, as explained earlier, is not the ideal algorithm to recompute the obscurances for a small part of the scene or moving objects, since by its nature it processes the whole scene at a time. More practical candidates are the computation by ray tracing or hemi-cube projection.

For this article, we consider the ray-tracing approach. The algorithm starts by creating a list of influenced patches. For each patch we compute the initial obscurance. If a ray from a patch hits a moving object, we store the patch in the list of influenced patches. The patches of the moving objects are also stored in this list.

When an object moves to a new position, the obscurances are recomputed for each patch in the list of influenced patches, creating a new list of influenced patches.

Figure 2.6.10 shows the results of recomputing in real time the obscurances for a moving object using the ray-tracing technique.

 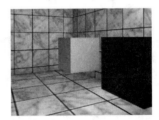 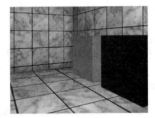

FIGURE 2.6.10   *Three positions of a moving object showing the dynamic recomputation of obscurances.*

Conclusion

In this article, we showed how the obscurances method, a simple way to simulate diffuse global illumination, can be implemented in an efficient way in the GPU using the depth-peeling technique.

We also saw that, as we query just a limited space around an object, obscurances can be updated in real time for moving objects in the scene and the surfaces around, using a ray-casting technique.

As future work, we plan to improve the efficiency of the depth-peeling technique by reading back in the CPU the textures to be analyzed using the symmetric PCI Express buffer. We will also study the efficiency of the hemi-cube projection method for the real-time update for moving objects.

The extension of obscurances to nondiffuse environments is also considered.

References

[Bekaert98] Bekaert, P., L, Neumann, A., Neumann, M., Sbert., Y., Willems, "Hierarchical Monte Carlo Radiosity," Springer-Wien, NewYork (Proc. of Eurographics Rendering Workshop'98, Vienna, Austria), pp. 259–268.

[Bunnel05] Bunnel, M., "Dynamic Ambient Occlusion and Indirect Lighting," *GPU Gems 2* Editors Matt Pharr and Randima Fernando, Addison Wesley Professional, 2005.

[Christensen03] Christensen, P. H., "Global Illumination and All That," SIG-GRAPH 2003 course notes #9 (RenderMan: Theory and Practice) (July 2003): pp 31–72, ACM.

[Everitt01] Everitt, C., "Interactive Order-Independent Transparency," Technical report, NVIDIA Corporation, 2001.

[Goral84] Goral C., et al.: "Modeling the Interaction of Light Between Diffuse Sources," ACM SIGGRAPH'84 Conf. Proc.

[Cohen85] Cohen, M. F., Greenberg, D. P., "The Hemi-Cube: A Radiosity Solution for Complex Environments" Computer Graphics (SIGGRAPH '85 Proceedings), 19(3) (July 1985): pp 31–40.

[Hachisuka05] Hachisuka, T., "High-Quality Global Illumination Rendering Using Rasterization," *GPU Gems 2*, Editors Matt Pharr and Randima Fernando, Addison-Wesley Professional, 2005.

[Iones03] Iones, A., Krupkin, A., Sbert, M, Zhukov, S. "Fast Realistic Lighting for Video Games," to appear in *IEEE Computer Graphics & Applications*, May–June 2003.

[Mendez03] Méndez-Feliu, À., Sbert, M., Catà, J., "Real-time Obscurances with Color Bleeding," *Proceedings of the Spring Conference on Computer Graphics 2003*, Budmerice, Slovak Republic, pp. 171–176, ACM Press, New York, NY, USA, 2003.

[Mendez04a] Méndez-Feliu, À., Sbert, M., "Comparing Hemisphere Sampling Techniques for Obscurance Computation," International Conference on Computer Graphics and Artificial Intelligence 3IA 2004, Limoges, France, May 2004.

[Nagy03] Nagy, Z., and R., Klein, "Depth-Peeling for Texture-Based Volume Rendering" in proceedings of Pacific Graphics 2003, October 2003.

[Pharr04] Pharr, M., and S., Green, "Ambient Occlusion," *GPU Gems* by Addison Wesley Professional, 2004.

[Sbert97] Sbert, M., The Use of Global Random Directions to Compute Radiosity. Global Monte Carlo Techniques, PhD dissertation, Technical University of Catalonia, 1997.

[Szirmay98] Szirmay-Kalos, L., and Purgathofer, W., "Global Ray-Bundle Tracing with Hardware Acceleration," in Proc. of 9th Eurographics Rendering Workshop.

[Zhukov98] Zhukov, S., Iones, A., and Kronin, G.: "An Ambient Light Illumination Model," Rendering Techniques '98, Springer-Wien, NewYork (Proc. of Eurographics Rendering Workshop '98—Vienna, Austria), pp. 45–55.

2.7

Bump My Shiny Metal

Andrew Aksyonoff

It's 2005. The shader revolution, introduced by GeForce 3, occured about four years ago—or in other words, two hardware generations ago. The Shader Model 3.0 has everyone talking about it. Next-generation consoles are on their way. Nobody should probably care about Shaders version 1.x these days.

However, looking at the Valve's Steam survey reveals that such hardware is still present on about 15% of PCs. Then there are an additional 15% of users with GeForce FX 5200s and 5600s hardware—which is especially slow if running Shaders version 2.0. And last but not least, there are 20 million Xbox® consoles installed, and these consoles are not going away any time soon, even after the Xbox-360 is launched.

So we still want to have some support for older PC hardware and Xbox (which is a little special, but very close to Vertex Shaders 1.1 and Pixel Shaders 1.3). The pixel shader portion is pretty limited as it only has four texture slots and eight arithmetic instruction slots. We will probably need to make many passes—and revert to simpler scenes—to achieve nice lighting effects.

Choose one of the currently used 3D rendering engines and ask yourself the question: What kind of shading does it apply on most surfaces? Of course, there is a basic diffuse texture that is improved with the help of normal-mapped diffuse lighting, and there are specular highlights (which in turn need to be modulated with a specular map). Normal mapping needs to be done in tangent space, so don't forget to throw in a normalizing cube map. There also should be some shadows; at least a single shadow from a directional light source. Or maybe a light map. Or both a light map and a shadow combined. Combining all these maps alone requires two or three passes because we can only use four textures at a time, right?

Not necessarily. It turns out that we can fit a whole lot of lighting work inside a single pass even when using Pixel Shader 1.1.

This article explains how this can be accomplished.

Every Other Hardware Is Doing This, So Why Can't We?

Consider this classic Blinn lighting equation (Equation 2.7.1) that we would like to implement:

$$Pixel = Texture_{Diffuse} \times (Color_{Diffuse} \times (N \cdot L) \times K_{Shadow} + Color_{Ambien}) + \quad (2.7.1)$$

$$+ \; Texture_{Specular} \times Color_{Specular} \times (N \cdot H)^{SpecularPower} \times K_{Shadow},$$

where K_{Shadow} is shadow map value (0 for shadowed pixels, 1 for unshadowed), L is the light direction vector, and H is a half-vector (Equation 2.7.2).

$$H = normalize\ (L + normalize\ (Camera - Position)). \qquad (2.7.2)$$

Recalling that N should be read from the normal map and H should be linearly interpolated and normalized, we end up with the following maps to combine:

1. Diffuse map ($Texture_{Diffuse}$)
2. Normal map (N)
3. Specular map ($Texture_{Specular}$)
4. Normalizer cube map (H)
5. Shadow map (K_{Shadow})

They do not directly fit in four texture samplers available on Pixel Shader 1.1 hardware. This is where we have to switch to multi-pass rendering—or do some tricks.

We will assume that we're using hardware that has built-in shadow map support for all the example code in this article—just to keep it simple. The NVidia hardware has had support for this since GeForce-3. Older ATI hardware, on the other hand, is mostly Pixel Shader 1.4 capable, which gives us enough additional pixel shader instruction slots to implement shadow mapping manually.

Trick 1: Mixing a Bump/Specular Cocktail

Let us use a grayscale specular map, using $Color_{Specular}$ to partially compensate for the loss of the full color. It can then be baked into a normal map's alpha channel—note that this doesn't introduce any problems as long as normal and specular maps share the same mapping, which is the usual case. With this mixed normal/specular map, everything fits into four texture samplers. Now the problem is that we only have eight instruction slots available, and Equation 2.7.1 would take about 10 slots to implement (using MAD wherever possible and implementing pow() as only two MULs).

Trick 2: Parallelizing Pixel Shader

Pixel Shader 1.1 can execute two instructions in parallel, one in vector (color) and one in scalar (alpha) pipe. This is called co-issuing and by carefully using it, we can make those eight instruction slots turn to almost 16. Most diffuse lighting operations are on three component colors (utilizing the vector pipe), but a significant part of specular lighting can actually be calculated in scalar pipe, as demonstrated in Listing 2.7.1. Note that specular lighting generally takes more slots to complete, so we need to start computing it as early as possible.

Listing 2.7.1 Calculated specular lighting in scalar pipe

```
ps_1_1

// v0 = ambient color + material luminosity color + ...
// v1 = directional light in tangent space

#define SPEC c6 // c6 = material specular color
#define DIFF c7 // c7 = material diffuse color

tex t0 // shadow map
tex t1 // normal/specular mixed map
tex t2 // cubemap normalizer for half angle vector H
tex t3 // diffuse map

dp3_sat r1.rgb, t1_bx2, t2_bx2 // (1) (N.H)

dp3_sat r0.rgb, t1_bx2, v1_bx2 // (2) (N.L)
+mul_sat r0.a, r1.b, r1.b      // (2) (N.H)^2

mul r0.rgb, r0, t0             // (3) (N.L)*shadow
+mul r0.a, r0.a, t0.b          // (3) ((N.H)^2)*shadow

mad_sat r0.rgb, r0, DIFF, v0   // (4) (N.L)*shadow*diffcol+ambi
+mul_sat r0.a, r0.a, r0.a      // (4) ((N.H)^4)*shadow

mul_sat r0.rgb, r0, t3         // (5) diffmap*difflighting
+mul_sat r0.a, r0.a, t1.a      // (5) ((N.H)^4)*shadow*specmap

mad_sat r0.rgb, r0.a, SPEC, r0 // (6) result
+mov r0.a, t3.a                // (6) diffuse map alpha
```

This shader now only takes six slots, so we have two extra slots available for additional tricks and features. For example, we are not limited to using a specular power of four (explained in more detail in the following section).

Trick 3: Unflattening Shadows

The image produced with the shader from Listing 2.7.1 suffers greatly in the shadowed areas. This is because the only lighting equation term that is not zero is diffuse texture modulated with ambient color, making the shadows appear dull and flat.

To fix that, we propose a pair of so-called *shadow transparency* coefficients that are inserted into Equation 2.7.3 as follows:

$$Pixel = Texture_{Diffuse} \times (Color_{Diffuse} \times (N \cdot L) \times DiffK_{Shadow} + Color_{Ambien}) + \quad (2.7.3)$$

$$+ \ Texture_{Specular} \times Color_{Specular} \times (N \cdot H)^{SpecularPower} \times SpecK_{Shadow},$$

where

$$DiffK_{Shadow} = K_{Shadow} \times (1 - DiffTransp) + DiffTransp, \qquad (2.7.4)$$

$$SpecK_{Shadow} = K_{Shadow} \times (1 - SpecTransp) + SpecTransp,$$

$$DiffK_{Shadow}, SpecTransp_{Shadow} \in [0,1].$$

These coefficients are directly controlled by artists. Shadow transparency controls how much of the diffuse and specular lighting terms will be added to the ambient light when in the shadow, which enables artists to remove that flat look from shadowed regions, while still preserving clearly recognizable shadows. The shader only changes slightly and now looks like Listing 2.7.2.

Listing 2.7.2   Shadow Transperancy

```
#define SPECK c4 // c4.rgb=1-DiffTransp, c4.a=DiffTransp
#define DIFFK c5 // c5.b=1-SpecTransp, c5.a=SpecTransp

dp3_sat r1.rgb, t1_bx2, t2_bx2    // (1) (N.H)

dp3_sat r0.rgb, t1_bx2, v1_bx2    // (2) (N.L)
+mul_sat r0.a, r1.b, r1.b         // (2) (N.H)^2

mad r1.rgb, t0, DIFFK, DIFFK.a    // (3) diff_shadow
+mad r1.a, t0.b, SPECK.b, SPECK.a // (3) spec_shadow

mul r0, r0, r1                    // (4) (N.L)*diff_shadow
                                  // (4) ((N.H)^2)*spec_shadow

// slots 5-7 are identical to slots 4-6 in Listing 2.7.1
```

In our experimentation, adding as much as half of the specular term in the shadowed areas almost never looks bad, while adding diffuse is more subtle and therefore not significant enough to be able to control directly (although significant enough to apply it). We ended up changing the range for SpecK$_{Shadow}$ to [0.5, 1] and calculating DiffK$_{Shadow}$ as

$$DiffK_{Shadow} = 2 \times SpecK_{Shadow} - 1, \qquad (2.7.5)$$

using _bx2 the pixel shader modifier instead of directly specifying and calculating it.

Trick 4: Let There Be More Light!

What we have just obtained is a pixel shader that does a complete bump + specular + shadow per-pixel lighting in one pass. But wait, there also is the vertex shader, which we can use to add some more per-vertex lighting instead of simple scene ambient lighting and material luminosity.

Let's add as many diffuse omnidirectional lights as possible (spotlights, which only require one additional angle attenuation coefficient compared to omnidirectional lights, are left as an excercise to the reader). The formula to compute lighting from single omnidirectional light is:

$$Lighting = OmniColor \times Diffuse \times Attenuation,$$

$$Diffuse = Clamp\Big(N \cdot normalize\big(OmniPos - Pos\big), 0, 1\Big),$$

$$Attenuation = Clamp\left(1 - \frac{\big(OmniPos - Pos\big)^2}{OmniRange^2}, 0, 1\right).$$

(2.7.6)

Naïve implementations of this formula would take about 10 to 13 instruction slots per light. However, processing the lights in specially arranged groups of four allows us to compute lighting from four omnidirectional lights in only 25 vertex shader slots (see Listing 2.7.3).

Listing 2.7.3 Processing Omnidirectional Lights

```
// OMNIRANGES = ( 1.0f / (omni[i].range^2) )
add r3, -v0, OMNIPOS[0]      // L0 = center0-point
add r4, -v0, OMNIPOS[1]      // L1 = center1-point
add r5, -v0, OMNIPOS[2]      // L2 = center2-point
add r6, -v0, OMNIPOS[3]      // L3 = center3-point
dp3 r7.x, r3, r3             // dist0^2
dp3 r7.y, r4, r4             // dist1^2
dp3 r7.z, r5, r5             // dist2^2
dp3 r7.w, r6, r6             // dist3^2
rsq r8.x, r7.x               // 1/dist0
rsq r8.y, r7.y               // 1/dist1
rsq r8.z, r7.z               // 1/dist2
rsq r8.w, r7.w               // 1/dist3
mul r7, r7, -OMNIRANGES      // -dist_i^2/range_i^2
max r7, r7, -ONE             // clamp(-dist_i^2/range_i^2,-1,0)
dp3 r2.x, v1, r3             // N dot L0
dp3 r2.y, v1, r4             // N dot L1
dp3 r2.z, v1, r5             // N dot L2
dp3 r2.w, v1, r6             // N dot L3
mul r8, r8, r2               // N dot normalize(L_i)
max r8, r8, ZERO             // clamp N dot L
mad r8, r8, r7, r8           // clamp(N dot L_i)*attn_i
mul r9, r8.x, OMNICOLOR[0]       // r9 = omni0.diffuse
mad r9, r8.y, OMNICOLOR[1], r9 // r9 += omni1.diffuse
mad r9, r8.z, OMNICOLOR[2], r9 // r9 += omni2.diffuse
mad r9, r8.w, OMNICOLOR[3], r9 // r9 += omni3.diffuse
```

The key idea here is vectorizing every single scalar calculation that can be vectorized—almost every MUL or MAX instruction in this shader fragment is an example.

Note, for example, how inverse square ranges are packed together into single OMNI-RANGES constant for this vectorization purpose.

The omnidirectional lighting is then combined with the ambient lighting and material luminosity and then written to oD0 in the vertex shader. The pixel shader does not require any changes.

Even though we need to have positions, texcoords, fog, and tangent space all computed in the vertex shader, this vectorization is efficient enough to process up to 12 omnidirectional lights without hitting the 128-instruction-slot limit of Vertex Shader 1.1. The complete vertex shader listing is too long (and boring) to be provided here, so it is on the accompanying CD-ROM.

ON THE CD

Trick 5: Recalling Spec-tac-ular Power Trick

This is not a new trick, but rather a reminder. Our pixel shader yields a fixed specular power equal to 4, but, thanks to excellent research by Philippe Beaudoin published in [Beaudoin02], we can actually implement variable specular power in the very same number of instruction slots.

The key idea is that instead of trying to compute power function in the shader directly, we approximate it with a function that easily maps to pixel shader instructions. One of the good approximations, which we demonstrate here, would be:

$$x^n \approx 16 \times \left(Ax + B\right)^2, A, B \in \left[0,1\right],\qquad(2.7.7)$$

where A and B coefficients are specially computed to minimize the approximation error. With a power of 2 in the approximation function we use here, maximum error is about 0.04–0.06, so you may want to use higher powers to reduce the error. See [Beaudoin02] for more details, functions, and the source code.

Applying this trick to our shader gives the following final shader in Listing 2.7.4.

Listing 2.7.4   Specular Power Shader

```
#define POW c3 // c3.b=B, c3.a=A, for m=2. see [Beaudoin02]

dp3_sat r1.rgb, t1_bx2, t2_bx2        // (1) (N.H)

dp3_sat r0.rgb, t1_bx2, v1_bx2        // (2) (N.L)
+mad_x4_sat r0.a, r1.b, POW.a, POW.b  // (2) (N.H)*A+B

mul_x4_sat r1.rgb, r0.a, r0.a         // (3) (N.H)^n
+mad r1.a, t0.b, SPECK.b, SPECK.a     // (3) specshadow

mul_sat r0.rgb, r0, r1_bx2.a     // (4) (N.L)*diffshadow
+mul_sat r0.a, r1.b, r1.a         // (4) ((N.H)^n)*specshadow

mad_sat r0.rgb, r0, DIFF, v0      // (5) (N.L)*shadow*diffcol+ambi
+mul_sat r0.a, r0.a, t1.a         // (5) ((N.H)^n)*shadow*specmap
```

```
mul_sat r0.rgb, r0, t3          // (6) diffmap*difflighting

mad_sat r0.rgb, r0.a, SPEC, r0  // (7) result
+mov r0.a, t3.a                 // (7) diffuse map alpha
```

The only thing we will add here is that we can pass the A and B specular power constants directly to the UI available to artists, instead of only giving the specular power slider and calculating A/B internally. These constants behave intuitively enough to be manually edited.

Do You Wanna Go Higher?

By higher, we mean a higher Pixel Shader version, as techniques shown are not at all tightly coupled to Pixel Shader 1.1-capable hardware with hardware shadow map support.

Porting to Pixel Shader 1.4 should be pretty straightforward—you could either pack depth information in the pixel shader or use a lookup texture when rendering the shadow map, and then unpack when applying the map. Having two extra texture stages and support for dependent reads, we could add simple environment mapping with a mask, or maybe true per-pixel environment bump mapping, or some other effect—while still fitting in one pixel shader and one rendering pass.

The tricks shown could also be applied to DX9 hardware. This is obvious when we talk about vertex shaders, but careful pixel shader scheduling could also be used with Pixel Shader 2.0 for fillrate optimization purposes. It is known that (at least) the R300 supports both scaler and vector pipes internally, so properly scheduled pixel shader 2.0 will execute faster.

In fact, we still have a few free instructions left in our shader, so there are more possibilities even on Pixel Shader 1.1 hardware. Take, for example, the specular map that we grayscaled. We could modulate it not only with a plain constant color, but with a diffuse texture as well. Or we could pass two colors and then use map value to lerp between them. Or we could pack another scalar into diffuse map alpha and try to use it for reconstructing more specular map detail.

And hey . . . there always is an option to make two passes.

Conclusion

In this article, we showed you how to implement a shader that combines dynamic normal-mapped diffuse and specular lighting (with a specular power that can be varied in runtime), shadow mapping (with shadow transparency coefficients to make shadowed areas more vivid), and up to 12 per-vertex omnidirectional light sources all in one pass using Pixel Shader 1.1 hardware. A number of optimization tricks demonstrated, were shadow transparency coefficients, aiming to improve final image quality, were introduced.

The techniques described were mainly developed by the author back in 2003, while working at Skyfallen entertainment on the *Blood Magic* RPG game. Minor shader optimizations, however, have been happening ever since.

Special thanks go to Boris Batkin, who currently is a lead programmer at Midway Games, for his invaluable advice on graphics and shader programming and optimization.

References

[Steam05] Valve's Steam survey, available online at *http://www.steampowered.com/ status/survey.html*, May 29, 2005.

[Beaudoin02] Beaudoin, P., J., Guardado, "A Non-Integer Power Function on the Pixel Shader," available online at *http://www.gamasutra.com/features/20020801/ beaudoin_01.htm*, May 29, 2005.

2.8

Ray-Traced Fog Volumes

Holger Grün and Marco Spoerl

Introduction

This article introduces a new way to render volumetric fog. Volume entry and exit points are ray traced on a per-vertex or per-pixel basis. We do not need render-to-texture operations per fog volume and can therefore efficiently render several fog volumes. Our method analytically handles simple shapes. Arbitrary and even animated volumes can be rendered using an approximation based on spherical harmonics.

The technique described in this article has been developed for an application that was performance limited by complex fragment operations. We therefore tried to find a way to realize volume fog that shifts the processing load from the fragment to the vertex processing units of the GPU. Furthermore, we needed a method that can efficiently draw a potentially big number of overlapping fog volumes. Other methods perform at least one render-to-texture operation per fog volume. Since render-to-texture operations can have a serious impact on performance, we needed to find a different approach to the problem. We describe ray intersection computations on a per-vertex basis, but these could also be moved to the fragment level as this fits the needs of your application.

Related Work

Basically, all methods used to render fog volumes follow the same order of operations. First, all opaque scene objects are rendered as usual. The fog volume's back and front faces are rendered afterward in two separate phases. Finally, the volume depth is determined and blended with the scene.

[Měch01] describes the algorithm used in SGI's Performer, version 2.4, to render fog, clouds, and other gaseous phenomena. Due to the lack of programmable graphics hardware at the time of writing of that article, the method uses a six-pass technique utilizing the color buffer and stencil buffer to store and manipulate the depth information.

In [Boyd03], the method used in the Microsoft® DirectX 8.1 SDK volume fog sample is explained. The original version, which appeared in the 2001 Game Developers Conference proceedings, describes a technique with at least four passes (one additional pass is required when the camera is inside the fog volume), using each pixel's alpha value to store its depth value w. The supplement to [Boyd03] introduced handling of concave fog volumes and an improvement to the precision of the depth values by encoding it in the pixel's remaining color channels.

The idea of using the RGB triplet to store depth values is used extensively in [James04]. In that paper, an algorithm is described that renders the depth of all opaque objects and the depths of the fog volume's front and back faces to three separate textures. These are used afterward to calculate the volume's thickness, which is converted to color via a simple 1D-texture lookup.

Our Technique

Basic Idea

As with all the former techniques described previously, we compute what part of a viewing ray lies inside a given fog volume. More accurately, we compute the ray's entry and its exit point as it passes through a volume (see Figure 2.8.1).

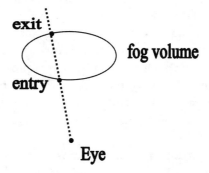

FIGURE 2.8.1   *Elliptical 2D fog volume with ray entry and exit points.*

What sets our method apart from all other methods is that we do not compute the entry and exit per-pixel, but per-vertex. This can save up to two render-to-texture operations.

We will first describe how to we deal with simple cases of analytic fog volumes like cylinders or ellipsoids and start by decomposing the problem of determining the amount of fog a volume applies to an output image into four steps.

1. Render a texture that contains the depth values of scene geometry as seen from the current camera position and orientation.
2. Determine the portion of the screen that is affected by the fog volume.
3. After all other geometry, render the back faces of a convex mesh that encloses the volume fog region. For each vertex, set up a ray from the eye through the vertex. In the vertex program, determine the intersections of the ray with the volume thus computing the entry and the exit point.
4. In the fragment program, use entry and exit depth along with the scene depth to compute how much fog needs to be applied to a fragment.

Step 1

All scene geometry is rendered and a buffer that contains linearly distributed z values that range from 0 to 1 is generated. This can be achieved by an additional render pass that color-codes linear depth (see [James04]). One may want to draw color-coded depth first and draw the normal color image next using a z-compare mode that only draws pixels that are equal in depth with the ones in the z-buffer. This helps to get speedups on early z rejection hardware if present. Since the additional depth pass doubles the amount of transformed vertices, utilizing multiple render targets and only using one draw and transformation pass may be taken into consideration. Depth will be output to the second buffer that could be a floating-point buffer to get around color-coding depth values. Finally, a depth-replacing fragment program that writes linear z to the z-buffer could be used. Without any doubt there are other ways to generate a texture with a linear z distribution. Our implementation needed to draw depth anyway—we do a limited form of deferred lighting that needs depth information. The resulting depth needs to be transferred to or bound as a texture that will be used in Step 4.

Step 2

We construct a convex polyhedral two-manifold container object around the volume fog object. Drawing the container will conservatively cover all pixels covered by the fog (see Figure 2.8.2).

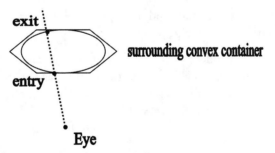

FIGURE 2.8.2   *2D example of a convex container placed around a fog volume.*

To properly handle the case of an eye point that is inside the container we choose to draw the back faces of the container. Drawing back faces will still cover the same amount of the screen pixels that the front faces would cover. We draw the container after all other geometry and blend the output RGB color with the screen color using the fragment program's output alpha as the blend factor.

Step 3

In the vertex program for the container object, a ray from the eye through the vertex is set up. Remember that this vertex is on the back of the polyhedral container object. The entry and exit intersection points of the ray with the volume are computed, and the linear z of the entry and exit points are passed to the fragment program. Of course, this means that the entry and exit points will be linearly interpolated within screen portions covered by the back faces of the container mesh. This introduces an error because the container mesh will have faces that cover more than one pixel. Choosing a moderate to high degree of tessellation will provide sufficient quality, though.

Step 4

In the fragment program, the scene depth texture at the current fragment is sampled. The scene depth is checked for being smaller than volume entry depth. If so, the output fog color RGB and an alpha of 0 is written. A value *MaxDepth* is set to the maximum of scene depth and exit depth. The corresponding value *DeltaDepth* is computed as the difference between entry depth and *MaxDepth*. Output the fog RGB color and *DeltaDepth* as the alpha value. One may actually want to scale *DeltaDepth* with some density modifier of the volume fog before writing it to alpha.

To give a real hands-on example, we proceed to an actual implementation for a simple analytic volume fog object: an elliptical cylinder.

Ray Tracing an Elliptical Cylinder

We first define what kind of elliptical cylinder we want to draw and what parameters can be used to change its appearance:

- The cylinder has a vertical axis that is parallel to the world space up-axis—we will from now on assume that the world space up-axis is the z-axis.
- The cylinder has a height that extends along the positive and the negative up-axis.
- The cylinder has two radii.
- The cylinder can be rotated around the up-axis.

Now, as a container mesh, we choose a moderately to highly tessellated approximation of the standard cylinder—this means the cylinder ranges from –1 to 1 z-wise and has a radius of 1 (see Figure 2.8.3).

To transform the standard cylinder into the elliptical cylinder described previously, we set up a matrix that scales and rotates the standard cylinder. This matrix represents a transform from standard cylinder space to cylinder model space. Inside the vertex program we transform the camera point into standard cylinder space by applying the inverse of the aforementioned matrix. Given the eye point in standard cylinder space, we can now carry on and perform our intersection calculations with the standard cylinder. This is much easier than intersection calculations with a more general cylinder.

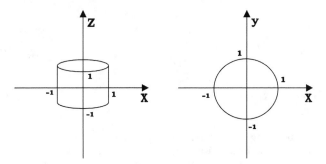

FIGURE 2.8.3 *The unit cylinder.*

We furthermore know that the vertex that is passed to the vertex program is the exit point of the ray because it lies on the back of the cylinder. This means we only need to compute the entry point—which simplifies the code even more. Of course, the entry point is assumed to be at the eye point if the eye turns out to be inside the cylinder.

The following vertex and fragment programs show in detail how it all comes together.

Vertex Program

```
// define inputs from application
struct VpInput
{
    float4 position : POSITION;
};

// define outputs from vertex shader
struct VpOutput
{
    float4 position     : POSITION;     // clip space position
    float2 linEntryExit : TEXCOORD0;    // x carries entry z,
                                        // y carries exit z
    float4 stq          : TEXCOORD1;    // stq for projective
                                        // depth texture
                                        // access
    float  fogCoord     : TEXCOORD2;    // fogCoord used to access a
                                        // fog texture for global fog
};

// function that checks if a point is inside the standard cylinder
float isInsideCylinder( float3 p )
  {
  float res = 0.0; // initialize result that indicates outside point

  // if inside vertical range
  if( p.z >= -1.0 && p.z <= 1.0 )
```

```
    {
    // if 2d position is inside or on unit circle
    if( dot( p.xy, p.xy ) <= 1.0 )
      res = 1.0; // yes this point is inside the standard cylinder
    }

  return res;
  }

// function that returns a ray parameter
// ( for a ray = localEye + parameter * vd )
// that is clipped by the vertical cylinder bounds and is not closer
// to eye than the point defined by input ray parameter k
float clipMax( float3 localEye, float k, float3 vd )
  {
  float res;
  float isz = localEye.z + k * vd.z; // compute current distance from eye

  // if current max k is outside the vertical range of the cylinder
  if( isz > 1.0 || isz < -1.0 )
    {
    float c   = isz > 1.0 ? 1.0 : -1.0; // compute verticalLimit

    // intersect ray localEye + k * vd with plane z = verticalLimit
    // localEye.z + k * vd.z - verticalLimit = 0
    // k = ( 1 - localEye.z ) / vd.z
    res = max( ( c - localEye.z ) / vd.z, k ); // return max
    }
  else
    res = k; // return old k — no need to clip

  return res;
  }

// vertex program
VpOutput main
  (
          VpInput   input,
    uniform float4x4 modelViewProj,
    uniform float4x4 modelView,
    uniform float4x4 modelViewIT,        // inverse transposed of
                                         // model view matrix
    uniform float    near,
    uniform float    inv_range,          // 1 / ( far − near )
    uniform float2   fogRange,           // carries range of global fog
    uniform float    halfTexDepthWidth,  // 0.5 * width of rectangular
                                         // texture that contains
                                         // linear depth
    uniform float    halfTexDepthHeight  // 0.5 * height of rectangular
                                         // texture that contains
                                         // linear depth

  )
  {
```

```
const float EPS     = 0.0001;
VpOutput    output;

// transform vertex position into homogenous clip-space
output.position = mul( modelViewProj, input.position );

// compute fog coord
output.fogCoord = fogRange.y * (output.position.w - fogRange.x );

// get eye point in local standard cylinder space
// this is equivalent to modelViewI * ( 0,0,0,1 )
float3 localEye = modelViewIT._m30_m31_m32;

// init null fog result - this will be overridden if there
// is a proper result => exit is set to the proper depth value
// for the vertex
output.linEntryExit = output.position.ww;

// if the local eye point is inside the cylinder => trivial result
if( isInsideCylinder( localEye ) > 0.0 )
  {
  // entry point is near
  output.linEntryExit.x = near;
  }
else // we have to find the nontrivial entry point
  {
  // now compute vector from local eyepoint to vertex
  float3 vd = input.position.xyz - localEye;

  // if vd too small
  if( dot( vd, vd ) < EPS )
    {
    // replace it with local lookAt vector
    // compute lookat in cylinder space => we want to compute
    // modelViewIIT * ( 0,0,-1,0 ) this is modelViewT * ( 0,0,-1,0 )
    vd = -modelView._m20_m21_m22;
    }

  // normalize vector from eye to exit point
  normalize( vd );

  // compute intersection of ray = localEye + k * vd with infinite
  // cylinder do a 2d to check if in the xy plane
  // the 2d ray intersects the unit circle around the origin
  // ( ep2d + k * vd2d - ( 0,0 ) ) ^2 == 1
  // ( ep2d * ep2d - 1 ) + 2 k ( vd2d * ep2d ) + k^2 * ( vd2d*vd2d ) == 0
  // k^2 * a + k * b + c == 0
  float a = dot( vd.xy, vd.xy );
  float b = 2.0 * dot( vd.xy, localEye.xy );
  float c = dot( localEye.xy, localEye.xy ) - 1.0;
  float p = ( b / a );
  float q = ( c / a );
  float D = 0.25 * ( p * p ) - q;
```

```
        // we have two real solutions or one double solution
        if( D >= EPS )
          {
          float sqrtD = sqrt( D );
          float l1    = -0.5 * p + sqrtD;
          float l2    = -0.5 * p - sqrtD;
          float k     = min( l1, l2 );

          // clip to upper/lower vertical limit planes
          k = clipMax( localEye, k, vd );

          // if entry intersection in front of us
          if( k > 0 )
            {
            // compute view space position of cylinder entry point is
            output.linEntryExit.x = -dot( modelView._m20_m21_m22_m23,
                                    float4( localEye + k * vd, 1 )
);
            }
          }
        else // D <= 0 => check for lookat parallel to cylinder axis
          {
          // if inside infinite cylinder
          if( dot( localEye.xy, localEye.xy ) <= 1.0 )
            {
            // clip for first intersection away from eye
            float k = clipMax( localEye, 0, vd );

            // compute view space position of cylinder exit point is
            output.linEntryExit.x = -dot( modelView._m20_m21_m22_m23,
                                    float4( localEye + k * vd, 1 )
);
            }
          }
        }

    // normalize z-values
    output.linEntryExit = ( output.linEntryExit - near.xx ) * inv_range;

    // output position for projective depth texture lookup
    output.stq.x = halfTexDepthWidth  * ( output.position.x +
                                          output.position.w );
    output.stq.y = halfTexDepthHeight * ( output.position.y +
                                          output.position.w );
    output.stq.z =                        output.position.w;

    return output;
    }
```

Fragment Program

```
// define interpolated inputs from vertex program
struct FpInput
{
    float2 linEntryExit : TEXCOORD0; // x carries entry z, y carries exit z
    float4 stq          : TEXCOORD1; // stq for projective depth texture
                                     // access
    float  fogCoord     : TEXCOORD2; // fogCoord used to access a fog
                                     // texture for global fog
};

// define outputs
struct FpOutput
{
    float4 color        : COLOR;
};

// fragment program
FpOutput main
(
        FpInput    input,
    uniform samplerRECT depthTexture, // texture that contains linearly
                                      // distributed scene depth
    uniform sampler1D   fogTable,     // texture that contains fog density
    uniform float       fogDensity,   // alpha for the full max diameter
                                      // of the fog ellipse
    uniform float3      fogColor,     // color of global fog
    uniform float3      volumeFogColor// color of fog volume
)
  {
  FpOutput   output;

  // sample depth texture for current pixel
  float3    sceneRGB   = texRECTproj( depthTexture, input.stq.xyz ).rgb;

  // decode depth — we assume a color coded depth here
  float     sceneDepth = saturate( dot( sceneRGB.rgb,
                                   float3(1,1.0/256.0,1.0/65536.0)));

  // if the scene does not completely cover the fog volume
  if( sceneDepth > input.linEntryExit.x )
    {
    // sample fog table
    float fogFactor = tex1D( fogTable, input.fogCoord ).r;

    // compute output fog in alpha channel
    output.color.a = saturate( fogDensity * ( min( input.linEntryExit.y,
                                              sceneDepth ) —
                                              input.linEntryExit.x));
```

```
// color is blend of fog color and volume color based on fog
output.color.rgb = lerp( fogColor, volumeFogColor, fogFactor );
}
else // no output
  {
  output.color = float4( 0,0,0,0 );
  }

return output;
}
```

Ray Tracing Other Analytic Shapes

Other analytic shapes like spheres and ellipsoids can be handled in a similar manner. Just choose an appropriate bounding volume. We have implemented an extension to these methods to render volumetric dust or smoke that is represented by a set of spheres. The vertex program we have written loops through an array of spheres and tracks minimum depth entry and maximum depth exit points.

You will have noticed that this algorithm is not correct because we do not properly account for un-fogged space between spheres, it assumes that the gap is also filled with fog (see Figure 2.8.4 for details). One way around this is, of course, to pass several entry- and exit-depth values to the fragment program. We chose to ignore this problem because nobody was able to observe these errors.

The beauty of this approach was that we could render volumetric smoke and dust that would result in high depth complexity with just one pass and depth complexity of one.

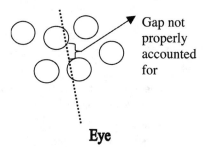

FIGURE 2.8.4   *Set of spheres with a gap not accounted for.*

Since analytic shaped fog volumes are somewhat limiting, we will now describe how to handle arbitrarily shaped volumes and even concave volumes.

Ray Tracing Arbitrary Polyhedrons

The first thing that comes to mind when considering arbitrarily shaped polyhedrons is that computing ray intersections is certainly harder than for analytic shapes. It is, of course, possible to ray trace polygonal scenes on the GPU as all the work on ray tracing scenes on the GPU shows (see [Purcell02].) Further, it would be possible to describe a simple polyhedron via uniform fragment or vertex program parameters. Finally, packing polyhedron geometry into a vertex texture would also be an option.

We did not want to apply any of these approaches, but found a way to approximate the distance a ray passes through a fog volume. Let us assume that we have a good enough and densely enough tessellated polygonal approximation of the polyhedron we want to ray trace. We wanted to—given the direction from the eye to a vertex on a back face—precompute for this vertex the distance a ray travels through the polyhedron.

All viewing directions from an eye point to a specific vertex form a sphere around this vertex. We choose to approximate the distance traveled through the volume, which is a function on this sphere, via spherical harmonics.

For brevity, we do not describe the theory behind spherical harmonics here, but there are many good introductions to this topic (see [Green03]).

The following pseudocode explains the preprocessing algorithm that we perform per vertex and what additional data we have to also store in the vertex buffer describing the polyhedron.

```
for every vertex V on the tessellated polyhedron
  {
  float CV[ number of spherical harmonics basis function ]

  set array CV to 0.0

  for all directions D from a set of directional samples that cover the
  unit sphere
    {
    float3 I = nearest Intersect( ray from V with direction D,
polyhedron )
    float  L = distance( P, I )

    Scale L so that it maps to 1.0 for the maximum distance that can be
    Traveled through the volume

    For all functions F of the spherical harmonics basis you use
      {
      float C = evaluate F( D );

      CV[ F ] += L * C * ( 4.0 * PI / number of directional samples)
      }

    //Save array of sums CV to store them along with the vertex position
    //into the vertex buffer to have them available in the vertex program
    }
  }
```

Given the precomputed data in the vertex buffer, the vertex program performs the following steps:

1. Determines the vector V from the eye to the vertex.
2. Evaluates all basis functions at the normalized vector.
3. Sums up the product of basis function and coefficient stored per vertex.
4. Rescales the sum to recover approximate distance traveled through the volume.
5. Adds distance times V to the input vertex to compute the entry point.
6. Passes depth of entry point and depth of vertex to the fragment program.

The fragment program is the same are we used to ray trace our cylinder.

Since we choose to record the earliest intersection with the polyhedron, the algorithm outlined previously also works for concave polyhedrons (see Figure 2.8.5).

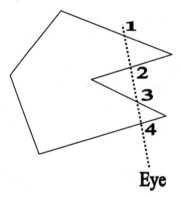

FIGURE 2.8.5   *Handling of concave objects.*

Again, we draw the back faces. If we assume that a face that contains exit point 1 is drawn first, our vertex program will approximately return point 2 as the appropriate exit point and the appropriate amount of fog is added to the scene for the fog segment between 1 and 2. Next, a face that contains exit point 3 is drawn and our vertex program will approximately return point 4 as the appropriate exit point. Again, the appropriate amount of fog is added to the scene for the segment between 3 and 4.

We have chosen an approximation with nine basis functions, and the results were good enough for the shapes we wanted to approximate. If you want to animate a polyhedron, something we did not implement, we suggest that you present the animated polyhedron as a set of key frames and linearly interpolate spherical harmonic (SH) coefficients.

To conclude our text on volumetric fog, we will present some ideas on how to extend the technique.

Future Directions

It would be interesting to work on the following extensions.

Volumetric Texturing of the Volumes

If we assume a repeating low-frequency 3D texture, then for every voxel we could approximate the integrated fog along a viewing direction by a set of precomputed 3D SH coefficient textures. The approximated density could be added to or multiplied with the ray-traced distance through the volume. Animation of the texture could be done via texture coordinate animation or a set of 3D textures—which is very memory intensive.

Scattering of Light Inside the Volume

Given a directional light with variable direction and a varying viewing direction, the precomputed amount of light that reaches the eye is a 4D function. Reduction techniques like SVD and similar to the ones used to approximate BRDFs (see, for example, [Kautz99]), could be used to approximate this 4D function.

References

[Boyd03] Boyd, Charles, and Dan Baker, "Volumetric Rendering in Realtime," available online at *http://www.gamasutra.com/20011003/boyd_01.htm*, 2001.

[Green03] Green, Robin, "Spherical Harmonic Lighting: The Gritty Details," available online at *http://www.research.scea.com/gdc2003/spherical-harmonic-lighting.html*, 2003.

[James04] James, Greg, and Simon Green, "Real-Time Animated Transluency," available online at *http://download.nvidia.com/developer/presentations/GDC_2004/GDC_2004_TranslucentAnimatedObjects.pdf*, 2004.

[Kautz99] Kautz, Jan, and Michael D. McCool, "Interactive Rendering with Arbitrary BRDFs Using Separable Approximations," 10th Eurographics Rendering Workshop, 1999.

[Měch01] Měch, Radomír, "Hardware-Accelerated Real-Time Rendering of Gaseous Phenomena," *Journal of Graphics Tools,* vol. 6.

[Purcell02] Purcell, Timothy J., Ian Buck, William R. Mark, and Pat Hanrahan, "Ray Tracing on Programmable Graphics Hardware," ACM Transactions on Graphics 21 (3) 2002: pp. 703–712.

2.9

Dynamic Global Illumination Using Tetrahedron Environment Mapping

Imagire Takashi

Introduction

Precomputed Radiance Transfer (PRT) [Sloan02] is a well-known technique for calculating global illumination in real time, and it is a good candidate as a standard method of lighting calculation for next-generation games. PRT precomputes the approximated reflectance of a surface to be lit by a suitable polynomial. The application calculates the lighting from the incoming radiance and the precomputed reflectivity. The PRT method using spherical harmonics as base functions is especially well known. In [Sloan02], the light transfer equation is discussed under the given lighting environment, and the method of efficiently reproducing shading using several approximations (for example, not taking into account self-shadowing or taking it into account) is also discussed. How to model incoming radiance is not discussed and is considered a different problem. Information of incoming radiance is usually taken from a physical base or from the information contained in an image used as a base. For example, photographs of the scenery seen from a certain place are taken, and the realistic lighting is achieved by using them as a source when calculating the coefficients for the expanding basis.

The method of using these photographs is basically a calculation based on static information (and might not be suitable for interactive applications, although a peer-rendered movie can be used to compute the expanding coefficients in such cases). In games where the characters keep moving around fast in 3D space, the object receiving the influence and the environment responsible for the global illumination are changing. The method to precompute based on the photograph cannot be used in such cases. Irradiance volume is designed as a method for the partial correspondence to the movement of the character in the space [Gene88]. Irradiance volume is a method of computing radiance at each point by dividing the space into a grid, preparing the expanding coefficients of each grid point, and interpolating expanding coefficients in a peripheral grid at each point of the space. The situations in which irradiance volume can be used are limited. As the degree of division of the grid increases, given a certain degree of spatial detail, memory quickly becomes insufficient as the increment in the amount of data is proportional to $O(n^3)$. Moreover, there is a difficulty due to the dynamic change of the environment.

Some games have information about dynamic incoming radiance: they use an environment map. In genres such as third person shooter (TPS), racing, and so on, it is usual to calculate information of incoming radiance from all azimuths; that is, to use an environment map in real time (even though not every game creates an environment map each frame, nearly all racing games use dynamic environment mapping). If the 2D integration calculations can be done, the data needed for PRT can be obtained from an environment map, and this can be done in real time. These operations will be described in detail shortly. First, we will describe tetrahedron environment mapping.

Tetrahedron Environment Mapping

Introduction

Alhough cubic environment mapping [Greene86] is well known as a dynamic environment mapping technique, it is necessary to render the scene six times to make a dynamic cube map, which increases the vertex processing and the number of drawing batches. On the other hand, sphere mapping and paraboloid mapping do a nonlinear geometric transformation and need a special shader. Moreover, because the polygon is misinterpreted when the ridgeline of the polygon does not face to the center of the screen and the rendering is done, it is also difficult to make an accurate image. An idea that combines the low rendering costs of sphere maps and the simplicity of the geometric transformation of cube maps exists. It is called a tetrahedron map. It is enough to cover all solid angles, and arranging the texture as a cube map covering the object can be achieved using only the four textures of a tetrahedron map.

Let's imagine the molecular structure of a diamond. In a diamond, the atoms are arranged as the vertices of tetrahedrons. For example, we have the tetrahedron defined by the four vertices $(-1, -1, -1)$, $(1, 1, -1)$, $(1, -1, 1)$, and $(-1, 1, 1)$ (the distance between the diamond atoms in a tetrahedron is 1.54 angstrom). When three arbitrary points are chosen from these four points, a plane is made. Objects located in the origin (center of the tetrahedron) can be completely covered by the four planes defining the tetrahedron. The set of textures created by rendering each plane as the screen is called a tetrahedron map. A tetrahedron environment map with which all solid angles are covered can be made by placing the camera at the origin and then rendering with the camera facing each of the four planes.

Implementation

Let's devise a concrete method of rendering. Rendering to a tetrahedron map needs a special setting for the view and the projection matrices. Think about the rendering to the plane defined by the points $v0 = (1, 1, -1)$, $v1 = (1, -1, 1)$, and $v2 = (-1, 1, 1)$. The position of the camera is considered to be at the origin. The straight line passing through the origin and perpendicular to this plane intersects the plane at the point $(1/3, 1/3, 1/3)$. This point is the center of the three vertices, and a positional vector is

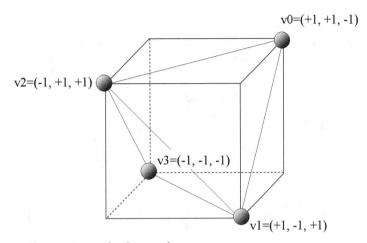

FIGURE 2.9.1   *The diamond structure.*

a vector that is facing the opposite way of v3 = (–1,–1,–1), which is another vertex of the tetrahedron (see Figure 2.9.1). This feature is an important property because in order to calculate the view matrix, the look vector just goes in the opposite direction as the vertex not contained in the plane we are considering in the rendering. The up vector is just one of the vertices defining the plane (v0, v1, or v2 in this case). Figure 2.9.2 shows the rendered scene.

FIGURE 2.9.2   *Render the scene as usual.*

The calculation of the projection matrix is explained now. The field of view is necessary to calculate the projection matrix. Think about the vertical field of view. The distance of the midpoint (0,0,1) of the triangle v0, v2, v1, to v0 is sqrt(6). On the other hand, because the perpendicular passes through ($\frac{1}{3}$, $\frac{1}{3}$, $\frac{1}{3}$), the distance between the plane and the origin (camera position) is $\frac{1}{sqrt(3)}$. Therefore, the vertical field of view is $fovy = 2 * \arctan\left(\left(\frac{sqrt(6)}{2} / \frac{1}{sqrt(3)}\right)\right) = 2 * \arctan\left(\frac{3}{sqrt(2)}\right)$. Now we need to calculate the aspect ratio. We have the height of the triangle, which is sqrt(6), and the length of the base, which is 2*sqrt(2). Then, the aspect ratio is width/height, and that is 2*sqrt(2)/sqrt(6) = $\frac{2}{sqrt(3)}$.

Although you may treat a tetrahedron environment map as a group of four textures, they can be brought together as one texture. The areas with unique information of the four textures are sets of the isosceles triangles inside areas made at a base and upper center (see Figure 2.9.3).

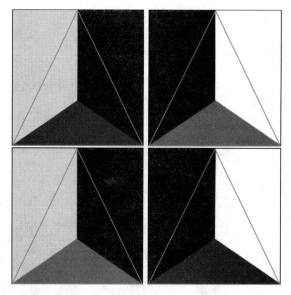

FIGURE 2.9.3 *Tetrahedron map with four textures.*

Other areas are included in other textures and can be considered extra information. Therefore, the size of a tetrahedron map can be cut in half by extracting only a triangular part and combining it with other textures. To combine textures, the vertex that is the center of the upper part of the triangle is moved to the left, as shown in Figure 2.9.4. Next, to keep the textures from overlapping, two of the textures are flipped vertically (see Figure 2.9.5). To move the drawing area we only have to apply the following matrix on the projection matrix:

$$
Bias_{Tetrahedron} = \begin{bmatrix} 1 & 0 & 0 & 0 \\ 0 & 1 & 0 & 0 \\ 0 & 0 & 1 & 0 \\ 0 & 1 & 0 & 1 \end{bmatrix} \begin{bmatrix} 1 & 0 & 0 & 0 \\ -0.5 & 1 & 0 & 0 \\ 0 & 0 & 1 & 0 \\ 0 & 0 & 0 & 1 \end{bmatrix} \begin{bmatrix} 1 & 0 & 0 & 0 \\ 0 & 1 & 0 & 0 \\ 0 & 0 & 1 & 0 \\ 0 & -1 & 0 & 1 \end{bmatrix}
$$

This matrix moves 1.0 in the direction of y and clamps the y value of the projection coordinates of the viewport to the range from 0.0 to 2.0. Next, x is moved in a negative direction in proportion to the value of y. The isosceles triangle of each of the unique areas is shifted to a right-angled triangle by this operation. Finally, it moves −1.0 in the direction of y to undo the first translation. This is not a necessary operation to generate the right-angled triangle. It only has to be set up to draw on the upper-right half or the lower-left half using a user-defined clipping plane when an environment map is made. It is necessary to reverse the up-vector when rendering in the upper-right part, and to reverse the shift direction. By dividing the view port up while rendering we can produce a tetrahedron map as one texture (see Figure 2.9.6).

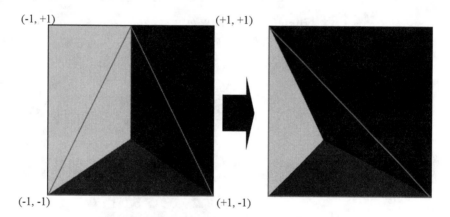

FIGURE 2.9.4 *Before the transformation to pack the map in a texture and after the transformation.*

Because sampling is not supported in hardware when a tetrahedron map is read, it is necessary to calculate the texture coordinates. Because the interpolation is not beautifully done with sampling that steps over the texture boundary, it is not a good method. A better way of reading the tetrahedron map is to project the tetrahedron map to a cube map beforehand and adopt the method of reading it as a cube map when sampling it. Because sampling a cube map can be done in hardware getting the texture coordinate just from a direction vector, the texture mapping can be done very easily. Projection from a tetrahedron map to a cube map is done by simply pointing the camera in six directions like dynamically making a cube map, and drawing each of the faces in the tetrahedron map.

FIGURE 2.9.5   *Transformed tetrahedron textures. Textures on the right side are flipped vertically.*

FIGURE 2.9.6   *Tetrahedron map brought together in one texture.*

Special conversion is unnecessary to draw a tetrahedron map. The tetrahedron map is put on the polygon model of a pyramid (tetrahedron) and the rendering is done. Because projection to a cube map can be achieved using one triangle strip, if the tetrahedron map is brought together in one texture, it is possible to create a cube map faster this way than creating the cube map directly.

All Solid-Angle Integration Using Environment Mapping

It is possible to calculate the integral of a function using 2D information stored in textures just by doing texture mapping with the textures in a certain way to obtain the results we want. The technique—mipmapping—is widely used for rendering textured-mapped polygons. To generate each of the levels of a mipmap, the original texture is reduced to another texture half its size, and the pixels of the original texture are averaged to calculate the pixels for the next texture. The resulting rendering is much better and more natural when, depending on the area of the screen occupied by the polygon to be rendered (and depending on the distance of the polygon to the camera), a texture of the mipmap is chosen in a way that for rendering farther polygons smaller textures are used. Mipmap textures can be made in real time. All we have to do is render the original texture to a rendering target half the size of the texture and use bilinear interpolation. This technique is useful for the integration calculation. Let's assume that the size of the original texture is a power of two. At this time, information can be consolidated up to the size of 1×1 by recursively building the mipmap. This consolidated information (color value) is a value in which the entire original texture is averaged (see Figure 2.9.7). When we consider the value of the texture to be a function value and do this calculation, we discretize the two-dimensional integral calculation. This operation

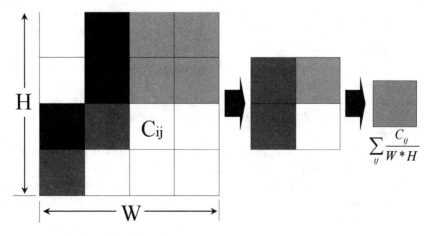

FIGURE 2.9.7 *Mipmap creation.*

can be done again using the resulting texture from the last calculation. It is possible to consolidate it in information that is smaller than half by writing a complex shader because there is no need to make the half-size mipmaps when the image reduces as an integration calculation is made.

Wide processing becomes possible if you think about this calculation as a general integral, although the calculation done by mipmaps is only an averaging operation. After two textures of equal size are multiplied, let's reduce up to one texel using mipmapping. The result is an average of the result of multiplying each element of two 2D arrays. This result can be considered to have made $S^{-1} \iint f(x,y)g(x,y)dxdy$ proportional to the value in which two functions f(x, y) and g(x, y) with the 2D domain are integrated in a limited discrete area of two dimensions. Here, if S is $\iint dxdy$ the area of the area integration and this area is known beforehand, it is possible to extract it out of the area integral as a constant coefficient. When the integrated function can give a negative value, it is necessary to use a signed texture format such as a floating-point format. In environments where signed textures cannot be used, it is necessary to take into account the calculation of a certain bias so the value does not become negative. Moreover, when the format of the texture is decided, it is necessary to consider the accuracy of the numerical value.

When the average operation previously mentioned is applied to an environment map, the result of integrating the incoming radiance from all azimuths with some functions is obtained because the domain of the function of an environment map covers all the solid angles. For example, when the texture that stores the direction in 3D space—where the red, green, and blue components of the texels in an environment map are used to store the x, y, and z coordinates—is prepared and the color of the environment map is reduced to one texel, the average direction of the incident light is obtained. Because this reduced texture becomes the average strength of the incoming radiance without any more calculations, a pseudo source of light can be made based on this information and can be used for lighting. However, when integrating in the solid angle, it is necessary to take the Jacobian into consideration. Because a part of the solid angle is projected to the plane when a tetrahedron map or a cube map is made, the ratio of the density of a solid corner and the density on an environment map is different at each position. Therefore, it is necessary to use the coefficient of the Jacobian in the function that is going to be used when the solid angle is integrated. Concretely, the density of the solid angle at the position where only θ is taken into account from the point of view is proportional to $\cos^2 \theta$ for the tetrahedron map. After the texture containing the Jacobian is multiplied with the function to be requested later, it is necessary to average the result because the Jacobian becomes a pattern (see Figure 2.9.8) in a tetrahedron map brought together in one texture.

FIGURE 2.9.8 *Jacobian texture.*

Calculation of the PRT Coefficients

PRT is a method that decomposes the reflectance computation of light into terms that can be and terms cannot be precomputed, thereby decreasing the required computing power greatly by only computing the terms that cannot be precalculated while rendering. In an actual computation, a real-time calculation is possible by doing an approximated calculation in order to break the calculation into the low-level terms of the series expansion (the elements containing information about the low-frequency components).

PRT solves the transport equation of light that describes radiance reflection. Radiance reflects from the surface of the object $L(x;\omega_o)$ as follows:

$$L(x;\omega_o) = \sum_i M^i(x;\omega_o)L_i$$

$$M^i(x;\omega_o) = \int fr(\omega_o,\omega)y^i(\omega)V(x;\omega)\max(0,(\mathbf{N}\cdot\omega))d\omega$$

$$L_i = \int y_i(\omega)L(\omega)d\omega$$

The term $M^i(x;\omega_o)$ can be precomputed. L_i is obtained from the environment of the lighting resulting from the expansion of the incoming radiance expanded by the basis $\{y_i(\omega)\}$. The set $\{y^i(\omega)\}$ is dual basis of $\{y_i(\omega)\}$. It is equal to 1 when i and j are equal if $y^i(\omega)$ and $y_j(\omega)$ are multiplied and integrated in all solid angles, and when i and j are not equal it is equal to 0. Spherical Harmonics functions are often used for this pair of base functions.

$fr(\omega_o,\omega)$ is a BRDF (Bidirectional Reflectance Distribution Function). $V(x;\omega)$ is a visibility function that describes whether the light is occluded by other parts of the object. N is a normal vector, and the domain of integration is all solid angles.

Although L_i changes if the environment of the incoming radiance changes, this quantity can be derived from an environment map. Because L_i can be derived by multiplying the base function $y_i(\omega)$ with the incoming radiance and integrating it in all solid angles, it becomes a coefficient in which $y_i(\omega)$ is stored as a texture. Obtained as a function in texel to which an environment map corresponds, the result of the reduction after the texture is multiplied to an environment map and is averaged using mipmapping down to one texel.

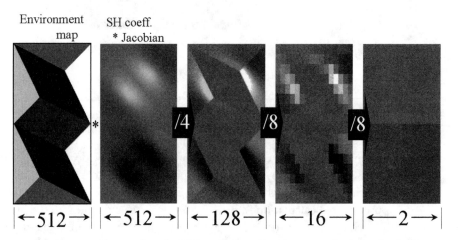

FIGURE 2.9.9 *Computing the SH coefficient (l = 1, m = –1). A final value is obtained by sampling the center of the texture of 2 × 2. Just two values are multiplied for easiness of calculations excluding the values in the left.*

When we treat the BRDF of the diffuse reflection, because the term $M^i(x;\omega_o)$ of the precomputation becomes a function of the position and of the degree of the expanding basis without depending on the direction of the reflection, $M^i(x;\omega_o)$ can be maintained by storing one texture as each degree of the basis or only adding the data of the dimension of the basis to the vertex data.

Because integration using a tetrahedron map is not done in the hemisphere but at all solid angles, it is possible to use it to calculate a translucent material. As a simple method of expressing a translucent medium, the amount of attenuation of light is estimated from the thickness of the medium from the point to the light source [Simon04]. It is possible to combine this with PRT by decomposing an environment map for each amount of attenuation considered, being this environment map the result of the source light from all surroundings, by a suitable functional base of spherical harmonics functions. In the method described in this article, a point light or a parallel light were considered. The transport equation becomes:

$$L(x;\omega_o) = \sum_i M^i(x;\omega_o)L_i$$

$$M^i(x;\omega_o) = \int fr(\omega_o,\omega)y^i(\omega)d(x;\omega)|(\omega,N)|d\omega$$

$$L_i = \int y_i(\omega)L(\omega)d\omega$$

Here, $d(x;\omega)$ expresses the amount of light that will be attenuated by the influence of the medium by the time incident light reaches x from an infinite distance in the direction ω. As an easy approximation, the exponential of the thickness of the direction ω of the medium can be used. The computation performed at rendering can use the same one as the calculation of the diffuse reflection.

Because the coefficients in all directions of the reflection are needed for arbitrary BRDF, a large amount of data is needed for the calculation just as described. As a good approximation, the matrix assumes each to be a column and a row by making BRDF of incoming direction and outgoing direction a quantum. This matrix calculates only a big element of the absolute value of the diagonalized element after it makes it to be diagonal and is advocated to the method of expressing a gorgeous reflection characteristic using few coefficients [Xinguo04].

In this method, BRDF is resolved to the function only in the incoming direction and the function only in the outgoing direction as

$$fr(\omega_o,\omega) = \sum_k G_k(\omega_o)\sigma_k F_k(\omega)$$

If resolved BRDF is substituted for the radiance transfer equation, it becomes

$$L(x;\omega_o) = \sum_k \sum_i G_k(\omega_o)M^{ki}(x)L_i$$

$$M^{ki}(x) = \int \sigma_k F_k(\omega)y^i(\omega)V(x;\omega)\max(0,(\omega,N))d\omega$$

$$L_i = \int y_i(\omega)L(\omega)d\omega$$

$M^{ki}(x)$ is a precomputed value and it is possible to prepare it as a texture and the corresponding vertex data. $G_k(\omega_o)$ can be prepared as a texture. Because $G_k(\omega_o)$ doesn't depend on the position of the vertex if the material is the same, it only has to prepare the number of sheets of the number of degrees of k necessary as a texture. The texture coordinates for this texture are not prepared vertex data but are ω_o. This method can use the expanding method of the basis that uses an environment map for diffuse PRT almost as originally devised.

FIGURE 2.9.10   *Diffuse PRT.*

FIGURE 2.9.11   *Subsurface PRT.*

FIGURE 2.9.12   *Glossary PRT.*

Conclusion

This article introduced the method of using an environment map as a computational method of calculating the expanding coefficients of the incoming radiance of PRT. Tetrahedron environment mapping was used as the environment mapping technique. The computing load is not too high even though tetrahedron mapping needs a special projection matrix. Tetrahedron mapping is promising as the standard method of making environment maps in the future. Regretfully, current hardware does not yet support sampling a tetrahedron map, making it necessary to project it to a cube map or compute the texture coordinates manually. The implementation of the calculation of these texture coordinates in hardware is our wish for GPU manufacturers; it is not difficult to implement, and we would like their cooperation on this issue. In this article, the compression of the PRT data introduced only the factorization expression to arbitrary PRT. In the future, the need to compress data will surely disappear due to the capability of next-generation GPUs to transfer data at high rates. However, it is our assumption that the method described in this article will be useful in the future just changing the part related to data compression.

References

[Sloan02] Sloan, Peter-Pike, Jan Kautz, and John Snyder, "Precomputed Radiance Transfer for Real-Time Rendering in Dynamic, Low-Frequency Lighting Environments," ACM Transactions on Graphics, 21, 3, (July 2002): pp. 527–536.

[Gene98] Greger, Gene, Peter Shirley, Philip M. Hubbard, and Donald P. Greenberg, "The Irradiance Volume," *IEEE Computer Graphics and Applications,* 18(2) (March 1998): pp. 32–43.

[Greene86] Greene, Ned, "Environment Mapping and Other Applications of World Projections," *IEEE Computer Graphics and Applications,* 6(11) (November 1986): pp. 21–29.

[Simon04] Green, Simon, "Real-Time Approximations to Subsurface Scattering," *GPU Gems*, Chapter 16: pp. 263–278.

[Xinguo04] Liu, Xinguo, Peter-Pike Sloan, Heung-Yeung Shum, and John Snyder. "All-Frequency Precomputed Radiance Transfer for Glossy Objects," Eurographics Symposium on Rendering 2004, June 2004.

2.10

Real-Time Rendering and Simulation of the Airbrush Medium for Metallic Appearance

Joachim Diepstraten and Tibor Schütz

Introduction

The goal of computer graphics—especially in rendering algorithms for three-dimensional objects—has always been to generate the most realistic images possible. This is called *photorealism*. To achieve this goal, a tremendous amount of effort has been spent to make images appear more realistic. Lately, this has been true for real-time or interactive generated images. Another area of interest in computer graphics is concentrated on the generation of meaningful images. Often, images produced by artists have a more pleasant or meaningful appearance to an observer than a realistic-looking counterpart. This fact has been taken up by interactive media in computer and video games. Popular examples include [WindWaker03] [XIII03] [AutoModellista03]. Among the benefits realized when using this approach are that these techniques often are less difficult to implement, need fewer resources, produce interesting or "cool looking" images, and draw the audience to the product.

However, there is an artistic medium that has been mostly neglected so far in academia and commercial products that combines the best of both worlds—realism with abstraction. This medium is called *airbrush*.

The goal of this article is to present a simple method that allows the reproduction of semirealistic images using a simulated airbrushing method. The special focus of this article lies in the reproduction of metallic surfaces with all its different characteristics. Metallic surfaces are often found in airbrushed images because they are one of its specialties and highlights. It has been shown that the airbrush medium has many attributes that correspond quite well to features found in programmable rasterization hardware.

Airbrush as an Artistic Medium

To understand some of the later techniques, it is first necessary to understand the medium itself, as well as its complexity and appearance. Therefore, some general characteristics are provided to serve as background information that should be kept in mind for the later sections.

Application Areas

Airbrushing is used in many different areas. The most popular applications include the coating of commercial plates, retouching of photos, and creation of realistic imageries as well as free artistic design. Airbrushing is able to produce perfect-looking color shades and clear images by leaving out unnecessary and disturbing details. It is a popular tool for the creation of illustrations and graphics for commercials, and also can be used for extending pen-and-ink line drawings in construction plans or for the colorization of cartoon images.

Color Application

Colors are an important aspect in airbrushing and basically its main appeal and advantage compared to all other artistic media. In airbrush, the term *pigment* is often used instead of color to distinguish between color as material and color as an attribute. The same convention is followed throughout this article.

In airbrushing, basically two different types of pigments are used: the first group consists of glazes and tusches that use subtractive color mixture and have a low opacity; the second group consists of opacity pigments with a mixture that corresponds directly to the amount of pigments found on the underlying surface. In rare cases, glimmering pigments with additive color mixture are used because they have a strong metallic glimmering that is mostly found in effect coating .

Glazes are always sprayed in a bright to dark tone because they have a very low opacity; in contrast, opacity pigments allow a spraying in an arbitrary order.

Airbrush images often consist of a few basic colors because cleaning the airbrush when changing the pigments requires a lot of effort. With the help of color mixture that is achieved through differences in the strength of the pigments, the final color palette of the image is created. The strength, shade, and width of a pigment can be smoothly influenced through variations in the air-to-pigment ratio, the angle of spraying, and the distance to the surface.

Picture Design

Airbrushing can handle very smooth and organic shadings, but requires different types of aids for hard shading gradients and edges. For this reason, masks are the second-most important tool in the toolset of an airbrush artist. They help to limit the direction of spraying and can consist of several different materials like cardboard, paper, or foliage. By varying the distance to the underlying image surface and the sharpness of the mask, it is possible to generate different shadings and structures. Masks can also be used to simulate shades and hard shadows by moving the mask over the image.

Lightning effects are created either by using a reference image or through imagined light sources. Often, an infinitely faraway light source (directional light) is used.

Surface reflections in airbrush are mostly only illustrated in an idealistic form. For example, in an indoor scenario only the key features of the room, such as the appearance of one or more windows, are reflected on the surface-reflective objects.

In outdoor scenarios, a single color for both the sky horizon and the ground are used, and these two colors are disjointed through a regular or an irregular color-shading pattern.

Self-shadowing is often exaggerated in airbrush images to make it appear livelier. Furthermore, shadows are only very sparsely used; for example, at very narrow neighboring parts of an object, at places where a missing shadow would be obvious, or to engender the location of an object in the scenery.

Special Artistic Effects

This section describes different artistic styles that can be used in airbrush to create different artistic effects often found in airbrush images. This is not a complete list; it only focuses on the most popular ones.

Splattering

Sometimes, homogeny color shading is not desired; for example, for rough surfaces like sand, stone, or impure and oxidized metal. For these kinds of surfaces, a spattering pigmentation works far better. This effect can easily be achieved by changing the amount of air in the air-to-pigment ratio.

Scratching Techniques

By using a knife or sandpaper, it is possible to scratch off a layer of pigments on the image to make the background surface color visible again. This can be helpful in the creation of brushed and milled surfaces effects.

Highlights

Nearly every painting technique suffers from the problem of a limited dynamic range of pigments that are required to simulate high-reflective surfaces like water or metals. To still be able to re-create such surfaces, the brightest regions are oversprayed in a cloud-like pattern with white pigments. This creates the effect that bright light overshines neighboring areas in an image. When used correctly, this effect re-creates the effect of overilluminated areas of a picture as they appear in a real camera (see Figure 2.10.1).

Star Effects

Optical systems often show star shapes with four, six, or eight branches around very bright light sources and reflections. Compared to the area-like appearance of highlights, they are used to simulate point highlights at a high-quality polished surface. However, star effects can often be combined with highlights. Figure 2.10.2 shows how star effects can be used.

Simulation of Airbrush Coloring

For the final image, only the appearance of the pigments is relevant—not how it was created. The appearance of pigments depends on the ratio between the area covered with pigments and the uncovered area, which give it the advantage of being able to be simulated through a dithering process. The in- and output data for the dithering are not color information but the local and average intensity of a pigment. The method

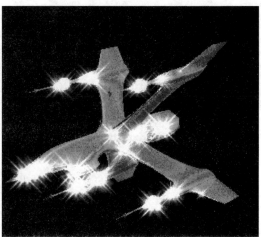

FIGURE 2.10.1   *An example picture that demonstrates the use of overexposed highlights.*

FIGURE 2.10.2   *An example picture that demonstrates the use of star effects.*

described in this article uses an image-space dithering to ensure a stable and object-independent spreading of pigments as it is guaranteed on paper. It relates to a method described in [Freudenberg02] that corresponds more or less to an ordered dithering method.

The basis of the dithering method is to assign random values to the corresponding pigments in image space. The random values range equally between zero and one with an expected value of 0.5. Afterward, these values are subtracted from the local intensity that also lies in a range between zero and one. The difference x between both values will be translated into the resulting local intensity value through a stepping function $S(x)$ (see Figure 2.10.3).

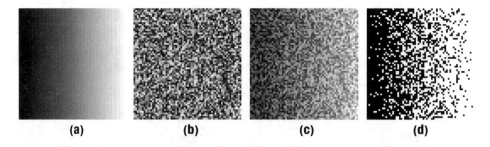

| (a) | (b) | (c) | (d) |

FIGURE 2.10.3   *(a) Original intensity of the image; (b) 1:1 texel mapping of random values; (c) pixel-wise difference x between intensity and random value; and (d) after using stepping function S(x).*

For assigning random values to the pixels it is easiest to use a random texture that maps 1:1 from texel to pixel. This texture should contain equally distributed random values in the range of [0..1]. How these random numbers are generated is insignificant, so standard modulo pseudo random generators can be used. It should be ensured that there is an equal distribution of numbers; otherwise, an equilibrium of the middle intensity after the dithering cannot be assured. Such a texture can be created with an arbitrary texture that has N random values calculated as $I = \frac{i-1}{N-1}$, where *i* is in the range *[1,N]*.

Improving the Distribution of Pigments

With this current stepping function, all pigments will have the same size and the achieved shadings will appear a little rough. If you look again at the pigment coating but this time under a stochastic view, you notice that the pigment sizes correspond to a random density *D(x)* with the selected random stepping function *S(x)*.

A realistic assumption is that every sprayed drop underlies an equal distribution. Under the assumption that the pigments are still in a liquid form and the covering area is the sum of all these drop sizes, the random density will form a bell-shaped curve [Wolfram05] after intensive spraying. A nearly equal result can be achieved by assuming a normal distribution. In this case, the random function can be seen as a general stepping function (see Figure 2.10.4).

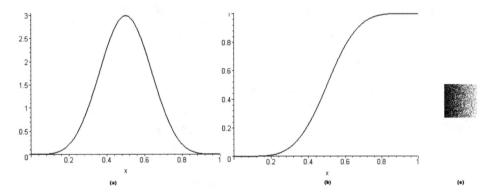

FIGURE 2.10.4   *(a) Density of the stepping function; (b) stepping function* S(x); *(c) new image after using stepping function* S(x).

Unfortunately, there is a little problem when using a smoother stepping function, because the intensity on the boundary of the interval [0..1] after saturation in the pixel processing no longer linearly corresponds to the value *I = average(S(x))*. Most notable, the average values of zero and one are no longer possible. To compensate for this problem, the intensity interval of [0..1] can be projected to a new intensity interval [−σ/2 .. 1 + σ/2]. This ensures that the average values of zero and one are possible again, however, it no longer provides linear mapping between the original intensity and the resulting average value. An adaptive correction that restricts the width of the stepping function to $\frac{2*\min(I,1-I)}{\max(S(x))-\min(S(x))}$ assures a linear mapping again by sacrificing the constant distribution of pigments.

This is only a disadvantage when dealing with very wide distributions. Today's displays have a resolution that is significantly lower than the minimal pigment size of an airbrush drop on paper. Therefore, it is useful to assume a partial homogeny pigment distribution of a pixel. This corresponds to random values that have an equal expectation value but low variance in its difference x. Additionally, it is possible to modulate the variance according to the distance and simulate the effect of decreasing level of detail for distant object surfaces.

The HLSL code looks like the following. (We present the vertex shader code, which basically does all the precomputation and stores them in texture coordinates for access in the pixel shader. We show the vertex shader only once because it already does everything we require later.)

```
struct PixelVertex
{
    float4 Position       : POSITION;
    float4 ScreenPosition : TEXCOORD0;
    float3 Normal         : TEXCOORD1;
    float3 Tangent        : TEXCOORD2;
    float3 BiNormal       : TEXCOORD3;
    float4 Texture2x      : TEXCOORD4;
    float3 CameraVec      : TEXCOORD5;
    float3 WorldPosition  : TEXCOORD6;
};

PixelVertex Airbrushshader_main(
    float4 VertexPosition : POSITION,
    float3 VertexNormal   : NORMAL,
    float3 VertexTangent  : TANGENT,
    float2 VertexTex      : TEXCOORD0)
{
    PixelVertex Res;

    //transform position into projection space
    Res.Position = mul( g_mWorldViewProjection, VertexPosition );
    Res.ScreenPosition=    float4((g_screenSizeVector.x/2.)/g_texSize,
                                  (g_screenSizeVector.y/2.)/g_texSize,
                                  1.,1.)*Res.Position;

    Res.Texture2x.xy = VertexTex;
    Res.Texture2x.zw = VertexTex;

    //transform Normal into Worldcoordinates
    Res.Normal = normalize(mul(g_matWorldInvTrans,VertexNormal));
```

```
                    //transform tangent into world space and compute binormal
                    Res.Tangente = normalize(mul(g_mWorld,float4(VertexTangent.xyz,
                                                                  0.)));
                    Res.BiNormal = cross(Res.Normal,Res.Tangente);

                    //compute Position in Worldcoordinates (for pointLight sources)
                    Res.WorldPosition = mul(g_mWorld,VertexPosition);
                    Res.CameraVec = normalize(mul(g_mWorld,VertexPosition).xyz
                                              - g_cameraVec);
                    return Res;
}

float4 Airbrushshader_main(float4 screenPosition : TEXCOORD0,
                           float3 IntNormal       : TEXCOORD1,
                           float3 IntTangente     : TEXCOORD2,
                           float3 IntBiNormal     : TEXCOORD3,
                           float4 Texture2x       : TEXCOORD4,
                           float3 IntCameraVect   : TEXCOORD5,
                           float3 WorldPosition   : TEXCOORD6) : COLOR
    {


//Store parameters related to the object
   float2 Texture = Textur2x.xy;
   float2 TextureMod = Textur2x.zw;

   //compute sprayParameter
   float Localscattering = g_distribution;
   if(g_DepthDamping_On) Localscattering*= (1.-(screenPosition.z/
                                                screenPosition.w)*
                                                g_depthDamping);

   //scale modulationTexture according to the viewing range
   float2 texCoord = (screenPosition.xy/
                      screenPosition.w)+0.5f/TexSize;

   float4 randomValue = tex2D(RandomValues,texCoord);

   // transform random values to [-0.5, 0.5] which is more convenient
   // to use within the spray() function

   float4 SprayParameter =  Localscattering*
                            (0.5-randomValue);

   [Shading computation, store result in intensity]
   .
   .

   .
   float color = Spray(intensity,SprayParameter.x);
   .
   .

   .
```

The Spray function as follows looks for the simple pigment distribution model:

```
float Spray(float Intensity, float Sprayparam)
{
  float localIntensity = Intensity-Sprayparam;
  float correction= 1. - g_distribution;
  return saturate((localIntensity - 0.5) / g_shade *
                                    correction + 0.5);
}
```

g_distribution and g_shade are two global float parameters. For the improved pigment distribution model, the code looks like

```
float Spray(float Intensity, float Sprayparam)
{
    //adaptive correction, Hermite-Interpolation
    float localintensity = Intensity-Sprayparam;
    float correction = 2.*saturate(min(intensity,1.-intensity))*
                              (1-g_scattering);
    return smoothstep(-g_gradient*correction,g_gradient*
                      correction,localintensity-0.5);
}
```

g_gradient and g_scattering are two global float parameters, and smoothstep is the HLSL build-in function.

Adding Animation Support

All image space dithering algorithms have one big disadvantage when it comes to moving objects because the dependency on the position in the image space becomes obvious. This effect is often referred to as the *shower door* effect. To avoid this effect, an additional modulation texture is attached to the object. This texture produces stepless and directional independent shadings between zero and one. It is possible to produce this sort of texture by using filtered Perlin noise textures or overlaid summations of sinus functions. The value read from this texture is simply added to the random value of the pixel modulo one.

By using this trick, the pigmentation level of a pixel is changed. The amount of change is determined directly from the movement of the object and produces the appearance as the picture would be repainted in each frame. As an additional side effect, it decreases the repetition pattern of the image space random texture.

For animation support, only a few lines in the previous code have to be changed. Add

```
float Modulation = tex2D(Modulater,TexturMod);
```

and change

```
float4 SprayParameter =  Localscattering*
                          (0.5 - randomValue);
```

to

```
float4 SprayParameter =  Localscattering*
                         (0.5-frac(randomValue+Modulation));
```

Recreation of Scratching Patterns

In airbrushing, polished and brushed surfaces are often simulated by using fine lines that correspond to the brushing direction. The direction of the lines can be seen as 2D vectors that are projected on the surface of the object, which is then again projected onto the paper. In total, it represents quite well the visualization of a 2D vector field.

A well-known method to represent 2D vector fields in image space is called line integral convolution (LIC). In LIC, a one-dimensional filter kernel is used on a 2D random texture (see also [Cabral93]). The orientation of this one-dimensional filter kernel depends on the direction of the 2D vector stored in the vector field [Cabral93].

In our case, the same random texture can be used as for determining the previous spraying parameter. For an efficient filtering, each sampling point should have a different random number. On the other hand, the kernel of the filter should be used on the smallest area around a sampling point. The greatest distance between two pixels can be found along its diagonal and corresponds to $\sqrt{2} * pixelsize$.

Unfortunately, the sum of several equally distributed random values I does not result in an equally distributed random value. Instead, for the weighted sum from n equally distributed random values in the range of zero to one, the following random density is achieved [Wolfram05]:

$$D(I) = \frac{1}{2(n-1)!} * \sum_{k=0}^{n} n * -1^{k} * \binom{n}{k} * (I-k)^{n-1} * \mathrm{sgn}(I-k)$$

It is possible to get equally distributed random values i by taking the corresponding random function $S(x)$ into account $(i = S(I))$. For a fixed number of sampling points, this function can be precomputed and stored inside a texture map. For the simulation of scratch patterns in the shader, add the following lines of HLSL code:

```
float2 Rotation = normalize(tex2D(AnisoMap,Textur.xy));
float3 AnisoAxis = Rotation.x * Tangent + Rotation.y * Binormale;

//Project and scale anisotropic tangent
float3 AnisoTangent = mul(matViewProjection,float4(AnisoAxis.xyz,0));
float2 AnisoTangentInScreen = 1. / (TexSize/sqrt(2.))
                             * normalize(AnisoTangent.xy
                             - AnisoAxis.z *
                             normalize(screenPosition.xy));
float2 TexPosP = screenPosition.xy / screenPosition.w;
float2 TexPosN = screenPosition.xy / screenPosition.w;
//compute filtered values
float4 RandomAniso = randomValue;
```

```
for(int i = 0;i < ((SamplePoints - 1) / 2);i++)
{
  TexPosP-= AnisoTangentInScreen;
  TexPosN+= AnisoTangentInScreen;
  RandomAniso+= tex2D(RandomValues,TexPosP);
  RandomAniso+= tex2D(RandomValues,TexPosN);
}

//create equal distributed values:
RandomAniso = tex2D(Relinearize,RandomAniso / SamplePoints);
randomValue = lerp(RandomAniso,randomValue,Isotropy);
```

`Isotropy` is a global float parameter and corresponds to the isotropy of the surface. `SamplePoints` is a global integer parameter and determines how many sampling points should be used. Satisfying results can already be achieved with a value of four or five.

Lighting Model for Simulating Metallic Appearance

Because we now know how to re-create arbitrary simulation of airbrush shading patterns, it is now the right time to look at a corresponding lighting model for computing the shading patterns we want to airbrush. In theory, every lighting model should be practical for reproducing airbrush effects as long as it contains an ambient-diffuse and a specular term. Because this article is basically interested in reproducing the effects seen on metallic surfaces, a model was chosen that takes into account most of the properties seen in metals.

A slightly modified version of the Ashikhmin and Shirley model [Ashikhmin00] seems to be a suitable candidate in our case. It is a good compromise between quality, performance, complexity, and adjustability. It supports an angle-dependent fresnel term as well as anisotropic features. In addition to this model, an environment map is used to enhance the specular term.

Diffuse and Specular Lighting Terms

The diffuse term of our lighting model simply confirms to the classic Lambert model, leading to:

$$I_D = Color_D * \sum_{i=1}^{n} \max(N \bullet L_i, 0) * I_i + Color_a.$$

In some cases, however, it is more suitable to, instead of ignoring the negative angles, use a counterlight such as in cool and warm shading [Gooch98].

The specular term of our lighting model more or less follows the cosine lobe model, which is the BRDF form of the well-known Blinn-Phong model but ensures reciprocity and energy conversion.

$I_S = Color_S \sum_{i=1}^{n} sat((N \cdot H)^n * c * I_i)$, where c contains $\frac{n+1}{2*\pi}$ and in our case also $\frac{1}{\max(N \cdot H, N \cdot L)}$ as described by Ashikhmin and Shirley [Ashikhmin00].

Environment Map

To simulate highly glossy materials like metals, an additional environment map is used to include reflections. To simulate the roughness of different surfaces, the reflection vector is perturbed by random vectors. The final reflection vector follows the same distribution as a specular light reflection coming from the same direction. Luckily, one sample from the environment per pixel is enough because the generated pattern is visibly indistinguishable from the distribution of the airbrush itself. However, the environment map needs to be low-pass filtered because small changes in the angle of the size of the distribution cone of the modulated reflection vector could lead to a moving picture.

For reflection maps, it is currently most common to use cube maps, but in the case of airbrushing an even more basic approach can be used. Additionally, it has the advantage that the reflection maps can be created more easily compared to cube environment maps. What we do is take a normal 2D texture—for example, a panorama image—and use it as a cylinder. The mantel surface corresponds to the texture and the top and bottom surfaces are an arbitrary horizon and ground color. The texture, coordinates for the texture can be computed as (see Figure 2.10.5):

$$u = 0.5 + \frac{\arctan(x/z)}{2*\pi} \text{ and } v = 0.5 * \frac{y}{\sqrt{1-y^2}} * \frac{1}{h} \text{ for a reflection vector } \mathbf{R}(x,y,z).$$

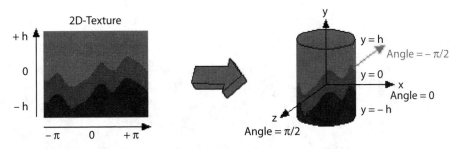

FIGURE 2.10.5   *Texture coordinate computation.*

Anisotropic

Certain metallic surfaces show an anisotropic behavior either naturally or after a processing step like brushing. Simple anisotropy of a surface can be modeled as the direction of maximal roughness with a minimal roughness direction lying vertical to it. The corresponding specular exponent is the result of a linear interpolation between the minimal and maximum specular exponent depending on the angle between the projected halfway vector on the surface and the anisotropic direction of the surface.

*Specular*_exp = *Spec*_*min* * O + *Spec*_*max* * $(1 - O$, where $O = \frac{(\mathbf{H} \cdot \mathbf{A})^2}{1 - (\mathbf{H} \cdot \mathbf{N})^2}$ and the normalization factor c is, in this case, $\sqrt{\frac{(Spec\_min+1)*(Spec\_max+1)}{2*\pi}}$.

Additional Effects

At the beginning of this article, several special effects were mentioned that airbrush artists often use to enhance the appearance of the image or to achieve a special appearance that supports the realism or surrealism of an image. This section describes in more detail a relatively easy method to simulate two of these effects.

Highlights

Reflections that are brighter than the chosen dynamic range tend to brighten up their surrounding neighborhood. To simulate this effect, a two-pass solution is used that is quite similar to HDR techniques [Shastry04]. In the first phase, the specular intensity of the image is rendered into a separate render target that can later be bound as a texture. In the second pass, the image-space filtered values are read from the texture and added to the normal rendered image using a white color. For simulating highlights, a basic version of the distribution of an airbrush, it is only necessary—depending on the position in image space—to use a few values of the filter kernel. This allows you to avoid a complete and complex filter kernel. The reading position X_t in the specular texture can also be shifted by the value b in the direction of the image space-projected light vector L if desired. This leads to the final texel position after the i-th iteration:

$$X_t = X_p + R(i, X_p) + b * L$$

Figure 2.10.6 demonstrates the visual effect of adding a highlight to the image.

(a)   (b)   (c)   (d)

FIGURE 2.10.6   *(a) Intensity map of specular shading; (b) intensity map after using airbrush filtering; (c) airbrush image without using extra highlight pass; (d) airbrush image after applying extra highlight pass.*

The HLSL code for rendering the highlights follows:

```
float4 AddHilight_Pixel_Shader(float4 Textur2x    : TEXCOORD0,
                               float2 lightVec    : TEXCOORD1) : COLOR
{
 //compute effect parameters
 float4 sprayParameter=frac(tex2D(RandomValues,Textur2x.zw)+
                        tex2D(RandomValues,Textur2x.xy).aaaa)-0.5;
```

```
float4 Sprayoffset=sprayParameter*g_highlightdistance;
float2 Lightoffset=g_highlightoffset*lightVec;

//compute effect
float2 Readposition=Textur2x.xy+Lightoffset;
float4 HighLightColor=0;
HighLightColor+=tex2D(SpecularTex,Readposition+Sprayoffset.xy)*
                    (1.-2.*length(sprayParameter.xy));
HighLightColor+=tex2D(SpecularTex,Readposition+Sprayoffset.zw)*
                    (1.-2.*length(sprayParameter.zw));
HighLightColor+=tex2D(SpecularTex,Readposition+Sprayoffset.yw)*
                    (1.-2.*length(sprayParameter.yw));
HighLightColor+=tex2D(SpecularTex,Readposition+Sprayoffset.xz)*
                    (1.-2.*length(sprayParameter.xz));
return HighLightColor;
}
```

Star Effects

Star-shaped reflections can also be added in a second rendering pass through filtering
of the specular texture, but this leads to an incredibly large computation effort. It is
more reasonable to evaluate the specular texture on certain points, and depending on
the resulting intensity at these points, to add a star-shaped reflection or not. Corresponding testing points can either be added manually to the drawn objects or chosen
randomly from the already existing vertices. The star reflections are then rendered as
billboard or point sprites. Figure 2.10.7 demonstrates the resulting effect when adding
star effects to a rendered image.

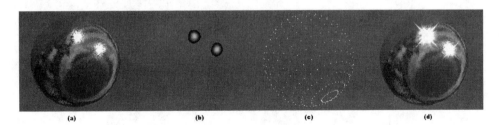

FIGURE 2.10.7   *(a) Airbrush image without star effects; (b) intensity map of specular
shading; (c) visible vertices of the sphere; (d) airbrush image after applying star effects.*

The HLSL code for rendering the star highlights follows:

```
struct Hilight_Star_pass_PixelVertex
{
    float4 Position       : POSITION;
    float2 ScreenPosition : COLOR0;
    float  Starsize       : PSIZE;
};
```

```
Hilight_pass_PixelVertex  Star_Vertex_Shader_main(
    float4 VertexPosition : POSITION,
    float3 VertexNormal   : NORMAL,
    float2 VertexTex      : TEXCOORD0)
{

    Hilight_Star_pass_PixelVertex Res;


    Res.Position = mul( g_mWorldViewProjection, VertexPosition );

    //compute random and specular texture coordinates
    Res.ScreenPosition.x = (1.0f + Res.Position.x/Res.Position.w)*0.5;
    Res.ScreenPosition.y = (1.0f - Res.Position.y/Res.Position.w)*0.5;

    float3 Normal = normalize(mul(g_matWorldInvTrans,
                                  VertexNormal.xyz));

    //global lighting parameters
    float intensitySpecular = 0;
    float3 WorldPosition = mul(g_mWorld,VertexPosition);

    //compute view direction in world coordinates
    float3 CameraVec = normalize(mul(g_mWorld,VertexPosition).xyz -
                                 g_cameraVec);

    float3 specularOrientation;
    float cos_specularAngle;
    specularOrientation = normalize(-CameraVec+g_lightVec);
    cos_specularAngle = dot(specularOrientation,Normal);
    intensitySpecular+=pow(saturate(cos_specularAngle),
                                    specularColor.w);

    Res.StarSize = intensitySpecular*g_spriteSize;

    return Res;
}

float4 Star_Pixel_Shader(float2 TexEffekt: TEXCOORD0,
                         float4 TexPos: COLOR0) : COLOR0
{
  return spriteBrightness*tex2D(EffektSprite,TexEffekt)*
                          tex2D(SpecularTex,TexPos.xy);
}
```

g_spriteSize is a global float parameter and represents the size of the star-shaped pixelsprite.

References

[Ashikhmin00] Ashikhmin, M. and P. Shirley, "An Anisotropic Phong Light Reflection Model," University of Utah, 2000.

[AutoModellista03] Capcom "Auto Modellista" Sony PlayStation 2 game, 2003.

[Cabral93] Cabral, B. and L. Leedom, "Imaging vector fields using line integral convolution," Proceedings of the 20th annual conference on computer graphics and interactive techniques (SIGGRAPH 1993): pp. 263–272.

[Freudenberg02] Freudenberg, B., Masuch, M., et al., "Real-Time Halftoning: A Primitive for Non-Photorealistic Shading," 13th Workshop on Rendering, 2002: pp. 227–231.

[Gooch98] Gooch, A., B. Gooch, et al. "A non-photorealistic lighting model for automatic technical illustration," Proceedings of the 25th annual conference on computer graphics and interactive techniques (SIGGRAPH 1998): pp 447–452.

[Shastry04] Shastry, A. S., "High Dynamic Range Rendering," Available online at *http://www.gamedev.net/reference/articles/article2108.asp*, July 19, 2004.

[WindWaker03] Nintendo, *The Legend of Zelda: The Wind Waker*, Nintendo® GameCube game, 2003.

[Wolfram05] Wolfram Research Inc., "Mathematics: Probability and Statistics: Statistical Distributions: Continuous Distributions: Uniform Sum Distribution" available online at *http://mathworld.wolfram.com/UniformSumDistribution.html*, June 12, 2005.

2.11

Dynamic Glossy Environment Reflections Using Summed-Area Tables

Justin Hensley and
Thorsten Scheuermann

Introduction

In this article, we introduce a technique to rapidly generate summed-area tables using graphics hardware and apply them to rendering glossy environment reflections. Summed-area tables, originally introduced by [Crow84], provide a way to determine the average color of arbitrarily large rectangular regions of an image in a constant amount of time, which is useful for convolving an image with a box filter kernel. The algorithm used for generating summed-area tables is similar to the recursive doubling technique used in scientific computing and allows the generation of a summed-area table in O(log n) render passes.

Figure 2.11.1 shows an example of the environment reflection shader. The advantage over other techniques for rendering environment reflections is that everything is dynamic: the environment map does not need to be prefiltered in an offline process, and instead can be updated each frame. Moreover, the reflection glossiness (the apparent blurriness of the reflection) can vary per pixel.

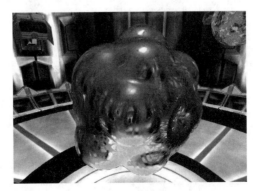

FIGURE 2.11.1 *An example object using summed-area tables to display dynamic glossy environment reflections. The glossiness (or blurriness) of the surface is controlled using a scrolling texture map. © 2005.*
Reprinted with permission from ATI Technologies, Inc.

187

Summed-Area Tables

Originally introduced by [Crow84] as an alternative to mipmaps, a summed-area table S is an array in which each entry s_{ij} holds the sum of the pixel values between the sample location and the top-left corner of the corresponding input image T (see Figure 2.11.2).

$$s_{mn} = \sum_{j=1}^{m}\sum_{i=1}^{n} t_{ij}$$

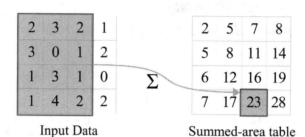

Input Data　　　　　　　　　　　　Summed-area table

FIGURE 2.11.2　*Example input texture and corresponding summed-area table.*

Summed-area tables enable the fast summation of the pixel values in an arbitrarily sized, axis-aligned rectangle at a fixed computational cost. Figure 2.11.3 illustrates how a summed-area table is used to compute the sum of pixel values spanning a rectangular region. To find the integral of the values in the dark rectangle, we begin with the precomputed integral from $(0, 0)$ to (x_R, y_B), which is the value stored at (x_R, y_B) in the summed-area table. The integrals of the rectangles $(0, 0)$ to (x_R, y_T) and $(0, 0)$ to (x_L, y_B) are subtracted. The integral of the hatched box, $(0, 0)$ to (x_L, y_T), is then added to compensate for having been subtracted twice.

The average value of a group of pixels can be calculated by dividing the sum by the area. This technique allows the convolution of an input image with a box filter to be computed. The advantage of using summed-area tables for this task is that the filter support can be varied on a per-pixel level without increasing the computation cost.

The following HLSL function returns a box-filtered texture sample from a summed-area table:

```
float4 tex2D_SAT_blur(sampler tSAT, float2 uv, float2 size)
{
  float4 result = tex2D(tSAT, uv + 0.5 * size);             // LR
  result -= tex2D(tSAT, uv + float2(0.5, -0.5) * size);  // UR
  result -= tex2D(tSAT, uv + float2(-0.5, 0.5) * size);  // LL
  result += tex2D(tSAT, uv - 0.5 * size);                   // UL
  result /= size.x * size.y;

  return result;
}
```

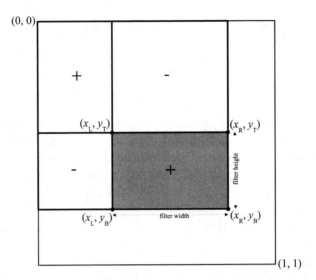

FIGURE 2.11.3 *Using the summed-area table representation to average over a rectangular area of the input image.*

Due to the high-precision requirements of summed-area tables—the sum of all texels of the input image can be quite large—they are stored in 32-bit per-channel floating-point textures. On graphics hardware that does not support bilinear texture filtering for 32-bit float textures, it is important to be careful about rounding issues. Texture samples from the summed-area table will use nearest sampling, which amounts to rounding the texture coordinate to a multiple of 1/*texture size*. This means that the filter kernel size has to be rounded accordingly to a multiple of 1/*texture size* in the shader. Otherwise, the computed pixel average will not be correct.

Figure 2.11.4 shows an example image blurred using the summed-area table approach and a visualization of the summed-area table.

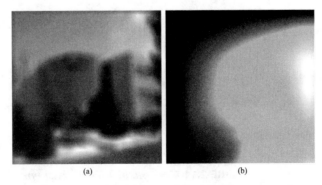

(a)   (b)

FIGURE 2.11.4 *(a) An image blurred using summed-area tables. (b) A visualization of the summed-area table itself.*
© *2005. Reprinted with permission from ATI Technologies, Inc.*

Summed-Area Table Creation Using GPUs

To efficiently convert a texture to a summed-area table on the GPU, we use a technique called recursive doubling [Dubois77] that is often used in high-performance and parallel computing. Using recursive doubling, a parallel gather operation among n processors can be performed in only $\log_2(n)$ steps, where a single step consists of each processor passing its accumulated result to another processor. In a similar manner, our method uses the GPU to accumulate results so that only $O(\log n)$ render passes are needed for constructing summed-area tables.

Our algorithm proceeds in two phases: first, a horizontal phase, and then a vertical phase. During the horizontal phase, results are accumulated along pixel rows; during the vertical phase, results are accumulated along columns of pixels. For an image of width w and height h, the horizontal phase consists of n passes, where $n =$ ceil($\log_2 w$), and the vertical phase consists of m passes, where $m =$ ceil($\log_2 h$).

The render passes for each phase use two render targets: one that stores the output of the previous pass and is used as the input to the current pass, and one that stores the output of the current pass. After each pass, the role of the two render targets switches. During the first pass of the horizontal phase, the input texture is bound as the source texture.

Horizontal Phase

In each pass, we render a quad covering the whole render target using a pixel shader that simply sums two texels P_{i-1} from the results of the previous pass, which are bound as the input texture. For each render pass i, the distance between the two texels doubles: $P_i(x, y) = P_{i-1}(x, y) + P_{i-1}(x - 2^i, y)$.

Figure 2.11.5 shows an example of how the horizontal phase works on one texture row.

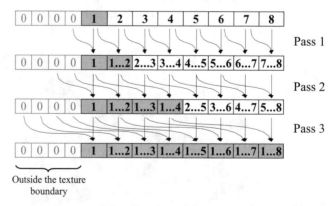

FIGURE 2.11.5   *Visualization of the summed-area table creation algorithm on one row. The x...y notation indicates the sum of which input texels are stored in each cell. The gray cells hold their final sum for the horizontal pass.*

The texture coordinates to sample from are computed in the vertex shader and passed down to the pixel shader. Here is an example vertex shader for the horizontal phase:

```
float fPassIndex;      // pass index starting at 0
float2 vPixelSize;     // pixel size is 1/resolution
float4x4 mVP;          // view-projection matrix

struct VsOutput
{
  float4 pos        : POSITION0;
  float2 uv[2]      : TEXCOORD0; // texture coordinates
};

VsOutput main(float4 inPos: POSITION,
              float2 inUV : TEXCOORD0)
{
  VsOutput o;

  // transform vertex (we are assuming that the application has set
  // up screen-aligned quad drawing and is sending the necessary
  // view-projection matrix and vertex positions)
  o.pos = mul (inPos, mVP);

  // compute offset between the two texels to be added
  float passOffset = pow(2.0, fPassIndex) * vPixelSize.x;

  // output texture coordinates for horizontal phase
  o.uv[0] = inUV;
  o.uv[1] = inUV - float2(passOffset, 0);

  return o;
}
```

The pixel shader code for processing each render pass is very simple and can be used for both the horizontal and vertical phase passes. Here is the HLSL function that computes the pixel shader output:

```
float4 SATPass2Tap(sampler tSrc, float2 uv[2])
{
  float4 t[2];

  // add two neighboring texture samples
  t[0] = tex2D(tSrc, uv[0]);
  t[1] = tex2D(tSrc, uv[1]);

  return t[0] + t[1];
}
```

Vertical Phase

The vertical phase works almost the same as the horizontal phase, except that the results of the vertical phase are accumulated along pixel columns, not rows. The only necessary change is the section of the vertex shader that computes the texture coordinates:

```
[...]
float passOffset = pow(2.0, fPassIndex) * vPixelSize.y;

// output texture coordinates for horizontal phase
o.uv[0] = inUV;
o.uv[1] = inUV - float2(0, passOffset);
[...]
```

Note that the shader constant fPassIndex must be reset to 0 at the beginning of the vertical phase.

Boundary Conditions

As indicated in Figure 2.11.5, some of the texture samples to be accumulated will be fetched from outside our texture. To ensure that the sum is not incorrectly changed by these texture samples, the appropriate texture clamping behavior needs to be set up.

The easiest way to accomplish this is by enabling the "clamp to border color" texture clamping state (D3DTADDRESS_BORDER in Direct3D) and setting the border color to (0, 0, 0, 0). Alternatively, it is possible to use "clamp to edge" mode (D3DTADDRESS_CLAMP), but then all border texels of the input texture must be set to (0, 0, 0, 0) by rendering a one-texel border into it.

Optimizing Summed-Area Table Creation Performance

The basic summed-area table creation algorithm outlined in the previous section can be optimized in several ways.

Performing More Work per Render Pass

Modern GPUs can easily perform more operations per pass than just adding two texture samples as explained in the previous section. Accumulating a higher number of samples s per pass (4, 8, or even 16) allows trading off per-pass complexity with the overall number of required render passes. Doing so can significantly increase summed-area table creation performance. The generic formula to determine the required number of passes is $\text{ceil}(\log_2 w) \times \text{ceil}(\log_s h)$.

Here is a set of example shaders for accumulating 16 samples per pass. Changing these shaders to accumulate fewer samples per pass should be straightforward.

Here is the vertex shader for the horizontal phase:

```
float fPassIndex;
float2 vPixelSize;
float4x4 mVP;

struct VsOutput
{
    float4 pos        : POSITION0;
    float4 uv[8]      : TEXCOORD0; // 16 UVs stuffed in 8 float4
};
```

```
VsOutput main(float4 inPos: POSITION,
              float2 inUV : TEXCOORD0)
{
  VsOutput o;

  // transform vertex (assuming app has set up screen-aligned
  // quad drawing)
  o.pos = mul (inPos, mVP);

  float passOffset = pow(16.0, fPassIndex) * vPixelSize.x;

  // output first two texcoords
  o.uv[0].xy = inUV;
  // Use wz swizzle because this is a native swizzle in PS2.0.
  // This helps save some instructions in the pixel shader.
  o.uv[0].wz = o.uv[0].xy - float2(passOffset, 0);

  // compute remaining 14 texcoords for neighboring pixels
  for (int i=1; i<8; i++)
  {
    o.uv[i].xy = o.uv[0].xy - float2((2.0 * i) * passOffset, 0);
    o.uv[i].wz = o.uv[0].xy -
                  float2((2.0 * i + 1.0) * passOffset, 0);
  }

  return o;
}
```

Here is the pixel shader:

```
float4 SATPass16Tap(sampler tSrc, float4 uv[8])
{
  float4 t[8];

// add 16 texture samples with pyramidal scheme to
// maintain precision
  for (int i=0; i<8; i++)
  {
    // .wz is a native swizzle in PS2.0 that doesn't generate
    // additional MOV instructions
    t[i] = tex2D(tSrc, uv[i].xy) + tex2D(tSrc, uv[i].wz);
  }

  t[0] += t[1]; t[2] += t[3];
  t[4] += t[5]; t[6] += t[7];

  t[0] += t[2]; t[4] += t[6];

  return t[0] + t[4];
}
```

We found in our experiments that depending on the texture size, four or eight samples per pass resulted in the best overall summed-area table generation performance. We believe the optimal number of samples per pass depends largely on the overhead of render target switches and the design of the texture cache on the target platform.

Avoiding Unnecessary Work

As was seen in Figure 2.11.5, after n passes, the first s^n pixels of each texture row (or column for the horizontal phase) already hold their final sum. Therefore, it is wasteful to keep performing computations on these pixels by rendering full-screen quads that cover all pixels for each pass. Instead, for the horizontal phase we use our summed-area table creation shader only on a quad with the corner coordinates $(s^n, 0)$-(w, h). The already completed pixels still have to be copied from the source to the destination render target by rendering a quad with the coordinates $(0, 0)$-(s^n-1, h) using a shader that just returns the input texels. The vertical phase proceeds accordingly with the quad coordinates $(0, s^n)$-(w, h) and $(0, 0)$-(w, s^n-1), respectively.

Precision Considerations

A key challenge to using summed-area tables in a production environment is the numerical loss of precision. The summed-area table approach can exhibit significant noise because several of the steps involve taking the difference between two relatively large numbers whose values are very close. Using signed offsets from a constant value instead of using absolute values as input to summed-area table creation can mitigate the precision loss.

This approach improves precision in two ways:

- There is a 1-bit gain in precision because the sign bit now becomes useful.
- The summed-area function is no longer monotonic; therefore, the maximum value reached has a relatively lower magnitude.

To reconstruct a sample from a summed-area table created in this manner, all we need to do is add the offset amount back to the final result before returning it from `tex2D_SAT_blur(…)`.

We have found that biasing the input values by -0.5 can improve precision significantly when reconstructing unblurred samples from the summed-area table. Depending on the image data, even better results can be achieved when the input values are biased by the average image color, but then additional work to determine the average color is necessary.

To properly implement the precision improvement trick, it is necessary to take rounding issues into account. For 8-bit input textures, it is important to choose a bias value that can be represented exactly as an 8-bit integer value. When dealing with 8-bit texture data, the GPU maps 0 to 0.0 and 255 to 1.0. With this mapping, 0.5 cannot be represented as an integer because it lies between 127 and 128. This is why we choose a bias value of 127/255 in practice. This value must be set as the border color so that texture samples from outside the texture are properly biased back to 0 (see the section "Boundary Conditions"). In the summed-area table creation pixel shader, all texture lookups are offset by this value. For example:

```
float4 SATPass2TapBias(sampler tSrc, float2 uv[2])
{
  float4 t[2];

  // add two neighboring texture samples, applying
  // a bias to improve overall precision
  t[0] = tex2D(tSrc, uv[0]) - 127.0/255.0;
  t[1] = tex2D(tSrc, uv[1]) - 127.0/255.0;

  return t[0] + t[1];
}
```

Fortunately, the precision error introduced when computing and storing summed-area tables with insufficient numerical precision is unbiased, which means that the error averages out to 0 as we reconstruct blurrier samples from the summed-area table. This means that despite precision problems, blurry summed-area table samples still return a fairly accurate averaged value.

Dynamic Glossy Reflections

Using dynamically generated summed-area tables, we can render objects that reflect their environment using a dynamic environment map with per-pixel control over the blurriness of the reflection (see Figure 2.11.1). The rendering steps for this effect are:

1. Render a dynamic cube map from the center of the reflective object.
2. Convert the cube map into a dual-paraboloid map.
3. Convert the dual-paraboloid map faces into summed-area tables.
4. Render the object using a summed-area dual-paraboloid map to enable per-pixel blurring.

The reason we convert the cube map to a dual-paraboloid map is twofold. First, the summed-area table concept does not map well to cube maps, which are defined on a spherical domain. Second, filtering the reflections using a box filter in dual-paraboloid map space introduces less distortion.

Dual-Paraboloid Environment Mapping

A dual-paraboloid (DP) environment mapping—introduced by [Heidrich98]—consists of two textures, each of which stores half of the environment as projected by a parabolic mirror (see Figure 2.11.6). The alpha channel of each dual-paraboloid map face stores a circular mask that indicates whether a pixel contains relevant data. Note that for our technique, the color channels must be 0 where alpha is 0.

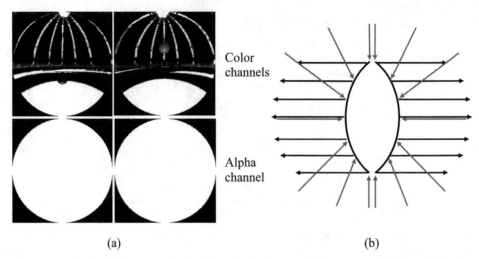

Color
channels

Alpha
channel

(a)   (b)

FIGURE 2.11.6   *(a) An example dual-paraboloid map. (b) Diagram of the paraboloid projection. © 2005. Reprinted with permission from ATI Technologies, Inc.*

Here is an HLSL function that returns an environment sample from a set of DP map faces:

```
float3 texDP (sampler tFront, sampler tBack, float3 dir)
{
  // convert 3D lookup vector into 2D texture coordinates
float2 frontUV = float2(0.5, -0.5) * dir.xy / (1.0 - dir.z) +
                 0.5;
  float2 backUV  = float2(0.5, -0.5) * dir.xy / (1.0 + dir.z) +
                 0.5;

  // sample DP map faces and blend together
  float4 cFront = tex2D (tFront, frontUV);
  float4 cBack  = tex2D (tBack, backUV);

  return cFront.rgb + cBack.rgb;
}
```

Note that an alternative to the explicit texture coordinate computation in the pixel shader is to use projective texture lookups [Blythe99].

Converting Cube Maps to Dual-Paraboloid Maps

To convert a cube map into a DP map, we can use the formulas found in [Blythe99], which allow us to convert a texel coordinate on the front or back face of a DP map to a 3D direction. We render to each face of the DP map using a pixel shader that converts the current position into the 3D direction, samples from the cube map using the direction, and outputs the sample into the DP map. This example shader performs the necessary conversion for the front DP map face:

```
samplerCube tCube;     // the cubemap to convert to a DP map

float4 main (float2 inUV :TEXCOORD0 /* quad texcoord from 0..1 */)
      : COLOR
{
  float2 uv = 2.0 * inUV - 1.0; // scale and bias into -1..1 range
  float3 dir;                   // lookup direction for cubemap

  // convert front DP face texture coordinate to 3D direction
  dir.x = 2.0 * uv.x;
  dir.y = 2.0 * uv.y;
  dir.z = -1.0 + dot (uv, uv);
  dir /= (dot (uv, uv) + 1.0);

  // compute circular mask for alpha channel
  float alpha = (dot(uv, uv) < 1.0) ? 1.0 : 0.0;

  // look up cubemap texture sample and multiply with alpha mask
  return float4(texCUBE(tCube, dir).rgb, 1.0) * alpha;
}
```

Only a few lines need to change to perform the conversion for the back DP map face:

```
[...]
// convert backDP face texture coordinate to 3D direction
dir.x = -2.0 * uv.x;
dir.y = -2.0 * uv.y;
dir.z = 1.0 - dot (uv, uv);
dir /= (dot (uv, uv) + 1.0);
[...]
```

Instead of converting from 2D texture coordinates to 3D directions in the shader, the conversion can be precomputed and stored in a lookup texture.

Putting the Full Effect Together

Figure 2.11.7 shows a diagram of the steps necessary to render objects using dynamic glossy reflections. After converting the cube map to a DP map, we convert each DP map face to a summed-area table as explained in the first half of the article. To compute a blurred environment map sample for the summed-area DP map, we can use the following HLSL function:

```
float3 texDP_SAT (sampler tFront,     // texture samplers
                  sampler tBack,      // for the SAT DP map
                  float3 dir,         // lookup direction
                  float2 filterSize)  // dimensions of box
                                      // filter kernel
{
```

```
// convert 3D lookup vector into 2D texture coordinates
float2 frontUV = float2(0.5, -0.5) * dir.xy / (1.0 - dir.z) +
                 0.5;
float2 backUV  =  float2(0.5, -0.5) * dir.xy / (1.0 + dir.z) +
                 0.5;

// sample DP map faces and blend together
float4 cFront = tex2D_SAT_blur (tFront, frontUV, filterSize);
float4 cBack = tex2D_SAT_blur (tBack, backUV, filterSize);
float4 cRefl = cFront + cBack;

// normalize result
return cRefl.rgb / cRefl.a;
}
```

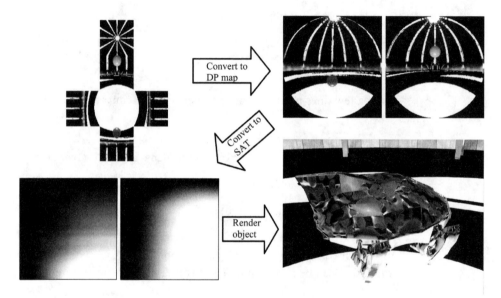

FIGURE 2.11.7 *Overview of the rendering steps necessary for the dynamic glossy reflections technique: dynamic cube map, conversion to dual-paraboloid maps, conversion to summed-area tables, rendering the reflective object. © 2005. Reprinted with permission from ATI Technologies, Inc.*

The function computes the 2D texture coordinates the same way as a regular DP map lookup and then uses the tex2D_SAT_blur(...) HLSL function introduced earlier to perform the actual texture lookup. The result needs to be normalized by the filtered alpha value, which contains the ratio of valid and unused pixels covered by the box filter kernel on each of the DP map faces. This ensures that the black unused pixels in the DP map faces do not contribute to the filtered result and incorrectly darken it.

The advantage of this rendering technique is that the filterSize parameter of the texDP_SAT(...) function can vary per pixel and be animated over time. In our example, we read it from a scrolling texture (see Figure 2.11.1).

Using More Complex Reflection Filter Kernels

It is possible to approximate more complex filter functions than a box filter by averaging several box-filtered texture samples. Figure 2.11.8a shows an example rendering using four concentric box-filtered lookups averaged together to form a pyramidal filter kernel shape. Note that the blur appears smoother than in the simple box-filtered case.

Figure 2.11.8b shows an example of approximating a Phong BRDF using two box-filtered environment lookups. The first environment map lookup uses a large filter kernel size and is in the normal direction to approximate the contribution of the Lambertian term in the Phong model. The second environment map lookup uses a smaller filter kernel and is centered on the reflection vector to approximate the contribution of the specular phong lobe.

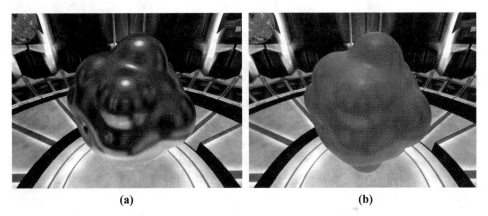

(a) (b)

FIGURE 2.11.8 *(a) Glossy reflections using four concentric summed-area table samples forming a pyramidal filter kernel. (b) A Phong BRDF approximation using two summed-area table lookups. © 2005. Reprinted with permission from ATI Technologies, Inc.*

Conclusion

Summed-area tables are a useful image representation tool because they allow blurring the image using an axis-aligned box filter kernel of arbitrary sizes that can vary from pixel to pixel. We presented an algorithm to efficiently create summed-area tables on a GPU. We also introduced a technique for rendering dynamic glossy environment reflections that takes advantage of the summed-area table representation of a dynamic dual-paraboloid map in order to support arbitrarily blurry reflections.

References

[Blythe99] Blythe, D., "Advanced Graphics Programming Techniques Using OpenGL," SIGGRAPH 1999 course notes. Available online at *http://www.opengl.org/resources/tutorials/sig99/advanced99/notes/node184.html*.

[Crow84] Crow, F. C., "Summed-area tables for texture mapping," Proceedings of the 11th Annual Conference on Computer Graphics and Interactive Techniques, ACM Press, 1984: pp. 207–212.

[Dubois77] Dubois, P., G. Rodrigue, "An analysis of the recursive doubling algorithm," High Speed Computer and Algorithm Organization, 1977: pp. 299–305.

[Heidrich98] Heidrich, W. and H. P. Seidel, "View-independent environment maps," Proceedings of the SIGGRAPH/Eurographics Workshop on Graphics Hardware, 1998.

2.12

Real-Time Caustics by GPU

Masahiko Nitanda

Introduction

As a result of reflecting or refracting a countless number of times, light on metal, glass, or water surfaces condenses and a fantastic visual pattern is created. This pattern is called caustics. Currently, real-time caustics rendering is a difficult problem because it requires many rays to be traced from the light source that will be reflected or refracted.

Because the computation of reflection and refraction is simple, real-time caustics rendering is possible with little ingenuity. This article illustrates how to compute and render caustics in real time on the GPU without any precomputations. This technique is an approximation method because it only treats the first specular reflection or refraction. However, it is enough to render the heart-shaped caustics as shown in color plates 1 and 2.

Feature

Our technique is based on the following assumptions:

- It is required that the object be built with many vertices.
- It assumes that the caustics are caused only by the first specular reflection or refraction.
- The caustics will be generated on a plane.

The light emitted from the light source is reflected and refracted on the object surface, eventually reaching a "floor" plane. This technique calculates that point's position for several reflected and refracted rays of light through the object's surface to determine the density of the light that falls on a plane. Through this process, you will notice portions of the floor plane where the light points are concentrated, thus becoming the area where the light density is high. This is where caustics appear. Our technique performs this calculation per vertex, so many vertices are needed as shown in Figure 2.12.1.

In the real world, caustics are formed by the accumulation of several reflections and refractions. However, our technique deals with caustics generated only by a single reflection and refraction. If the object's form is simple enough, a single reflection or refraction will give good caustics results. In regard to refraction, light enters the inside of an object meaning that two refractions occur, one when the light enters the object

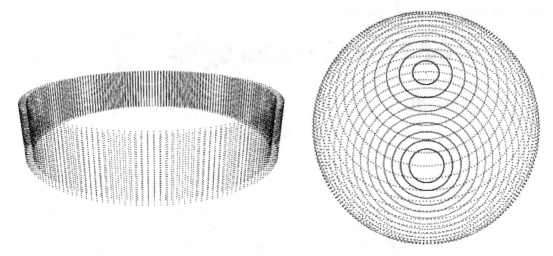

FIGURE 2.12.1   *These objects were built by many vertices to compute the path of the photon per vertex.*

and the second when the light exits the object and reaches the plane, as shown in Figure 2.12.2. In this case, we only treat the first refraction. However, it can be considered that the caustics that appear at the bottom of a water surface are caused by a one-time refraction.

We assume that the caustics appear on a single plane to simplify the calculations. However, you can handle more complex surfaces by considering them as a collection of planes and repeating the process for each of them.

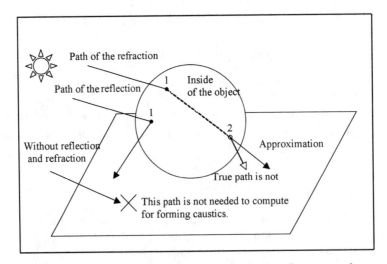

FIGURE 2.12.2   *Caustics are formed by multiple reflections and refractions, but this technique only considers the first specular reflection or refraction.*

Procedure

You can consider every vertex of the object causing caustics as one photon. The photon discharged from the light source is reflected and refracted on the surface of an object and then collides with a plane, as shown in Figure 2.12.3. Each colliding point, or photon, is then rendered additively into a texture. The pattern generated by all the points of light appears as shown in Figure 2.12.4. This texture is considered to be a texture showing the density of light and can be used as the origin of our caustics texture.

As you can see from Figure 2.12.4, the reason why many object vertices are needed is to ensure that the process can generate a sufficient point density to approximate a reasonable caustics texture.

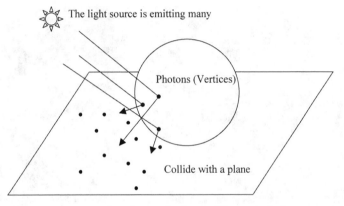

FIGURE 2.12.3 *The photon discharged from the light source is reflected and refracted on the surface of an object and then collides with a plane.*

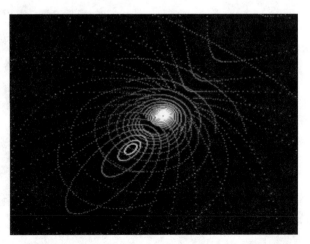

FIGURE 2.12.4 *This is the density texture of the light on the plane caused by the refraction on the ball surface.*

However, even if it is created by sufficient vertices, a density texture still exhibits a scattered pattern. For our technique, you can simply blur the texture and then use it directly as a caustics texture.

To complete the process, a base (diffuse) texture, a shadow texture, and the caustics texture are blended together, as shown in Figures 2.12.5, 2.12.6, 2.12.7, and 2.12.8. You can then render a plane using this composite texture and environment map the object using this texture.

Although a shadow texture may be created by the technique of your choice, such as a shadow map or volume shadow, you have to be cautious of artifacts such as "jaggies." Because the shadow now blends with the caustics, any portion of the shadow that shows artifacts may make the caustics look conspicuous.

FIGURE 2.12.5 *Base (diffuse) texture of the object.*

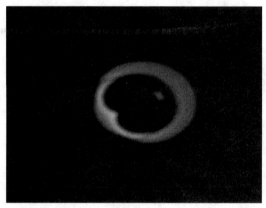

FIGURE 2.12.6 *Caustics texture.*

FIGURE 2.12.7 *Shadow texture.*

FIGURE 2.12.8 *Blend texture of base and caustics and shadow texture.*

Implementation

You can implement this technique using an HLSL shader, and, of course, this technique can also be applied to OpenGL.

Creation of a Density Texture

To create the density texture, calculations that determine the position at which the photon emitted from the light source is reflected and refracted by the object, and collides with arbitrary planes are performed by the vertex shader. To use the collision points to shade the plane and as an environment map, the position coordinates the vertex shader outputs that must be transformed to the plane's texture space.

Following are the standard formulas respectively used for the calculation of reflection and refraction.

$$\text{Reflection} = 2\left(\mathbf{E'} \cdot \mathbf{N}\right)\mathbf{N} + \mathbf{E}$$

$$\text{Refraction} = \left(\frac{n1}{n2}\right)\left[\mathbf{E} - \mathbf{N}\left\{\sqrt{\left(\frac{n2}{n1}\right)^2 - 1 + \left(\mathbf{E'} \cdot \mathbf{N}\right)^2} - \mathbf{E'} \cdot \mathbf{N}\right\}\right]$$

E: Direction of incidence of a photon
E': Reverse vector of the **E** (= −**E**)
N: Normal vector
$n1$: Refractive index of the air (≈ 1)
$n2$: Refractive index of the object (*water* ≈ 1.33, *glass* ≈ 1.5, etc.)

To simplify the implementation, ($n1/n2$) and ($n2/n1$) are constants and can be calculated ahead of time. Following are the HLSL functions used to calculate both the reflection and refraction.

```
float3 GetReflection(float3 incidentLDir, float3 normal){
    float3 tmp = dot(normal, -incidentLDir);
    tmp    = tmp * normal;
    tmp    += tmp;
    return tmp + incidentLDir;
} // GetReflection

// g_RefractiveIndex (n2/n1, (n2/n1)^2, n1/n2, 0)
float3 GetRefraction(float3 incidentLDir, float3 normal){
    float3 tmp  = dot(-incidentLDir, normal);
    float3 tmp2 = tmp * tmp;         // (E'.N)^2
    tmp2 += g_RefractiveIndex.y;     // (n2/n1)^2     + (E'.N)^2
    tmp2 -= 1;                       // (n2/n1)^2 - 1 + (E'.N)^2
    tmp2  = sqrt(tmp2);              // √{(n2/n1)^2 - 1 + (E'.N)^2}
    tmp2 -= tmp;                     // √{(n2/n1)^2 - 1 + (E'.N)^2} -
E'.N
```

```
// E - N x [√{(n2/n1)^2 - 1 + (E'.N)^2} - E'.N]
tmp2  = incidentLDir - normal * tmp2;

    return g_RefractiveIndex.z * tmp2;
} // GetRefraction
```

You can compute the position at which the reflected and refracted photons inter-sect with the plane by using the easy formula, as shown in Figure 2.12.9. This formula essentially determines the intersection of a straight line with a plane.

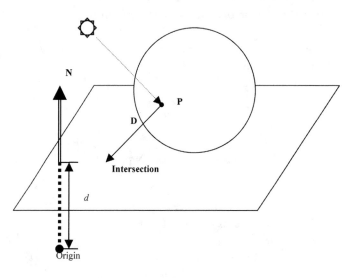

$$I(\text{Intersection}) = P + D\left\{ \frac{(P \cdot N) - d}{(D \cdot -N)} \right\}$$

P: The position in the world coordinates of the object's vertex
D: The normalized direction vector originating from the reflection or refraction.
N: Normal vector of the plane
d: Distance from the world coordinate origin to the plane

FIGURE 2.12.9   *The intersection can be calculated with an easy formula.*

Because the coordinates to output are the coordinates of the plane's texture space, **I** is changed as follows:

$$I'x = (T \cdot I) \times TextureScaleX$$
$$I'y = (B \cdot I) \times TextureScaleY$$

T: Tangent vector of a plane
B: Binormal vector of a plane

This process requires two separate shaders for both reflection and refraction. To simplify the implementation, the shader can include both reflection and refraction by using preprocessor directives as follows:

```
VS_OUTPUT main(const VS_INPUT i){
    VS_OUTPUT o;
#if REFRACTION
    float3 dir = GetRefraction(g_LDir, i.Normal);
#else
    float3 dir = GetReflection(g_LDir, i.Normal/*world*/);
#endif

    dir = normalize(dir);

    // Compute intersection of the photon and the plane
    float dist = dot(i.Pos.xyz, g_Plane.xyz) - g_Plane.w;
    float cos  = dot(dir       , -g_Plane.xyz);
    float t    = dist / cos;

    float4 causticsPos = float4(i.Pos.xyz + dir * t, 1);

    // Transform to plane's texture space
    o.Pos.x  = dot(causticsPos.xyz, g_PlaneTangent .xyz) * g_Plane-
TexScale.x;
    o.Pos.y  = dot(causticsPos.xyz, g_PlaneBinormal.xyz) * g_Plane-
TexScale.y;
    o.Pos.zw = 1;

    o.Color = dot(-g_LDir, i.Normal) > 0 ? float4(1, 1, 1, 1) : 0;
    return o;
}// main
```

Points are drawn by using D3DPT_POINTLIST with their color multiplied by the suitable scale for a specular lighting.

```
c[0] = mesh->Specular.r * scale;
c[1] = mesh->Specular.g * scale;
c[2] = mesh->Specular.b * scale;
c[3] = mesh->Specular.a;
iDev->SetPixelShaderConstantF(PSI_SPECULAR, c, 1);
```

The Blending of a Base Texture, a Shadow Texture, and a Caustics Texture

The three textures are blended as follows:

$$BaseTexture \times ShadowTexture + CausticsTexture$$

The shadow texture is multiplied with the base texture by using the following render states:

```
iDev->SetRenderState(D3DRS_SRCBLEND , D3DBLEND_DESTCOLOR);
iDev->SetRenderState(D3DRS_DESTBLEND, D3DBLEND_ZERO      );
```

The caustics texture is then added using the following render states:

```
iDev->SetRenderState(D3DRS_SRCBLEND , D3DBLEND_ONE);
iDev->SetRenderState(D3DRS_DESTBLEND, D3DBLEND_ONE);
```

Finally, generate mipmaps for this composite texture to obtain the best shading results. If you are using DirectX, this is easily accomplished by calling `GenerateMip-SubLevels`.

Applying the Texture as an Environment Map for Your Object

Common environment mapping techniques, such as a cube maps and sphere maps, are generated from a single point in space. Because there is volume in an object, to obtain proper results we create an environment map for all the points of the surface of an object (see Figure 2.12.10). If not done this way, the position of nearby reflected objects shifts from their original space. In the case of an object and a plane, if they both touch, it is even more apparent. Moreover, it turns out that such environment mapping techniques cannot deal with the reflections in the inside of a ring. Although reflections appear to be easy to implement, it is difficult to it draw correctly in real-time rendering.

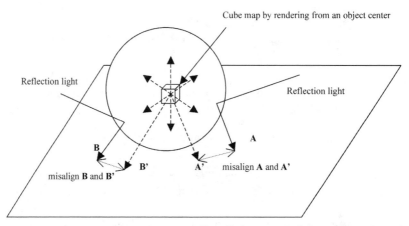

FIGURE 2.12.10   *Environment map for all the points of the surface of an object.*

For this article, the texture used to shade the floor plane (*Base × Shadow + Caustics*) is used directly as an environment map. Consequently, you are getting the proper reflection of the shadows and caustics on the object because reflection of the object on the object is not included. The UV coordinates for the environment map can be obtained by calculating the intersection of reflected light and the floor plane, which, in fact, is similar to the approach used to generate the caustic's density texture.

```
VS_OUTPUT main(const VS_INPUT i)
{
    VS_OUTPUT o;

    float3 camDir   = getCameraDir(i.Pos.xyz/*world*/);
    float4 scPos    = mul(i.Pos, g_TMat);
    o.Pos           = scPos;

    float  fresnel  = getFresnel(camDir, i.Normal);
    o.Fresnel       = fresnel;

    //----------------------------------------------------------------
    // Reflect
#if !_R
    float3 reflectDir   = getReflection(camDir, i.Normal/*world*/);
    if (reflectDir.y >= -.1f) o.Fresnel.w = 0; // mask

    reflectDir = normalize(reflectDir);

    float dist = dot(i.Pos.xyz ,  g_Plane.xyz) - g_Plane.w;
    float cos  = dot(reflectDir, -g_Plane.xyz);
    float t    = dist / cos;

    float3 intersection = i.Pos.xyz + reflectDir * t;

// Transform to plane's texture space
    o.ReflectTexCoord.x = dot(intersection.xyz, g_PlaneTangent .xyz)
*
                                g_PlaneTexScale.x + g_PlaneTexScale.z;
    o.ReflectTexCoord.y = dot(intersection.xyz, g_PlaneBinormal.xyz)
*
                                g_PlaneTexScale.y + g_PlaneTexScale.w;
    o.ReflectTexCoord.x = dot(intersection.xyz, g_PlaneTangent .xyz) *
                                g_PlaneTexScale.x + g_PlaneTexScale.z;
#endif

#if _R
    //----------------------------------------------------------------
    // Refract
    float3 refractDir   = getRefraction(camDir, i.Normal);
    if (refractDir.y >= -.1f) o.Fresnel.w = 0; // mask
    else o.Fresnel.w = 1.f;

    refractDir = normalize(refractDir);

    float dist = dot(i.Pos.xyz ,  g_Plane.xyz) - g_Plane.w;
    float cos  = dot(refractDir, -g_Plane.xyz);
    float t    = dist / cos;

    float3 intersection = i.Pos.xyz + refractDir * t;

    // Transform to plane's texture space
  o.RefractTexCoord.x = dot(intersection.xyz, g_PlaneTangent .xyz) *
                                g_PlaneTexScale.x + g_PlaneTexScale.z;
```

```
        o.RefractTexCoord.y = dot(intersection.xyz, g_PlaneBinormal.xyz) *
                              g_PlaneTexScale.y + g_PlaneTexScale.w;
#endif

    return o;
}// main
```

Demo

ON THE CD

The demo program (from which the color plates were generated) using this technique is included on the companion CD-ROM.

All the HLSL shaders were compiled by versions VS_1_1 and PS_1_1 or PS_1_4. Caustics rendering can be done without Shader 2.0 and does not require a cutting-edge PC.

The object is changed by the left-clicking the mouse and the state of each render target can be viewed by a right-click of the mouse.

Conclusion

When this demo program was executed on a notebook PC that has the NVIDIA GeForceFx Go 5200 chipset, it was running at about 30 FPS. This was using only Shader versions VS_1_1 and PS_1_1 or PS_1_4.

One especially a difficult task is dealing with the refraction of an object with a complex shape. For this demo, refraction was only treated in the case of a sphere and water surface. But because these were simple shapes, it generated an appropriate result. However, with a cognac glass, for example, it is difficult to draw the caustics generated by two or more refractions.

2.13

Dot-Product for Efficient Detail Texture Mapping

Renaldas Zioma

Introduction

Large open environments can be easily rendered in real-time using modern graphics hardware. However, a vast amount of texture memory is required to capture visual details for such scenes.

While lack of the texture memory is a crucial factor for the current generation game consoles, even memory-rich PC systems can significantly suffer due to limited memory and bus bandwidth. Simple brute-force solutions, even employing texture compression (DXT, S3TC) to decrease texture memory footprint, are not viable to capture specific details for large and spatially varying surfaces such as terrain or large constructions.

This article discusses an approach allowing you to store information about the detailed surface in a memory efficient form. The proposed approach relies on source image decomposition into color and frequency domains and efficient runtime reconstruction at runtime in a pixel shader. The data decomposition benefits from ideas widely used in lossy compression algorithms. The runtime reconstruction of the detail data is based on the multi-texturing practices developed earlier by [Bloom00] [Vlachos02]. The balance between quality and performance was a key factor in developing this particular approach.

Implementation tips will be discussed in order to achieve a practical reconstruction pixel shader on PS1.1 class hardware.

Standard Surface Reconstruction Techniques

Since there is no room to store all the required texture details in the memory, the surface texture can be synthesized at runtime. Multi-texturing—a method when several textures are blended together to create desired surface image—has proven itself as a viable solution for reducing texture memory footprint.

Widely used cases of multi-texturing include:

- Detail texture mapping—applying additional texture containing repeating micro-material specific patterns
- Texture splatting—compositing several materials to create heterogeneous surface

Proposed Approach for Detail Texture Mapping

The proposed approach is based on the following concepts:

- Image data of the surface can be represented as a set of different layers.
- Ideas from lossy compression theory can be applied to reduce the amount of data contained in different layers.
- Some layers may contain color and some may contain only grayscale details.
- Several grayscale details can be combined into one texture.
- The implementation combining layers should be written with efficiency as a primary goal, because it is executed for each pixel of the surface.

The data required for image reconstruction can be either extracted from the existing surface image (satellite scan data, photos) using frequency domain analysis, or be directly created by artists. In most cases, the information is visually intuitive, thus it can be easily understood and directly manipulated by the artists.

Image reconstruction data is stored in layers and contains the following information:

- Low-frequency color map
- High-frequency grayscale details
- Middle-frequency grayscale details
- High-frequency color details that have considerably high spatial locality
- Proportions of the details to be applied at each point of the surface

The dot product operation is used to blend several layers together at once, effectively reconstructing surface image data at runtime. Such an approach dramatically decreases the number of required texture units and allows implementation of considerably shorter pixel shaders, thus making detailed surface rendering possible on PS1.1-class hardware in a single pass.

Goals

The main goals considered during the development of this approach include:

Reduce tiling artifacts: Low-frequency components of the detail textures will incur tiling artifacts. However, it is hard to completely remove low-frequency information from the detail texture because it will make details too repetitive and visually uninteresting. Instead, several material-specific details could be applied to minimize visual tiling and add unique features to the surface.

Reduce memory bandwidth: Detail texture mapping reduces the memory bandwidth dramatically; however, in case of grayscale details only one channel of the usual RGBA texture is used. Instead, four grayscale detail textures could be combined into one RGBA texture occupying different channels (Red, Green, Blue, and Alpha).

Reduce the length of pixel shader: Combining several detail materials may lead to a prohibitively expensive pixel shader. This is especially true for the PS1.1–PS1.3 hardware that has a very limited texture access functionality.

Single-pass reconstruction: Rendering of surfaces with large numbers of vertices (such as terrain) or surfaces requiring complex vertex shaders (such as skinned meshes) can become a serious performance bottleneck. The number of passes required for image data reconstruction should be kept to a minimum.

Main Concepts of Detail Texture Mapping

Textured surfaces, when observed closely, can look unrealistically smooth and blurry. This happens when a single texel covers multiple screen pixels where the linear magnification filter produces a smooth look. To avoid such unpleasant effects, the source texture must contain enough high-frequency details.

High-Frequency Details

Many real-world surfaces contain high-frequency details; however, these details usually form repetitive patterns. For example, a plank of wood has a distinguishable pattern of details that repeats itself across the entire surface.

A portion of a high-resolution image thus can be stored in a smaller texture. Such textures are usually called detail textures. Because the detail texture represents a small portion of surface detail, it should be repeated over the entire surface. During rendering, when higher frequencies than what are stored in base surface texture are required, the detail texture is combined to obtain a better result.

Detail textures should not contain low-frequency information in order to reduce the tiling artifacts. High-frequency details can be extracted from the high-resolution surface image by applying a standard high-pass filter (see Figure 2.13.1).

FIGURE 2.13.1   *Texture details can be extracted by applying a high-pass filter.*

Multiple Detail Materials

On the other hand, large heterogeneous surfaces will contain significantly varying medium-frequency details. Such information can be represented using separate detail textures with information about specific underlying materials such as sand, rock, grass, gravel, cloth, or human skin.

During the reconstruction process, several materials are mixed together in proportion to the local properties of the surface.

In general, the quality of surface depends on the maximum number of the layers applied. However, graphics cards can apply only a limited number of layers, which is especially important for PS1.1 hardware. Due to such limitations, a PS1.1 implementation requires multiple passes to combine the appropriate number of different materials (see Figure 2.13.2).

FIGURE 2.13.2   *Different surface materials.*

Luminance and Chrominance Information

The color information can be omitted from the high-frequency detail maps. This assumption is based on the observation that the human eye is more sensitive to changes in brightness than color [Blinn98]. Because brightness contains more perceptual information, the high-frequency grayscale information should be preserved, while more error can be tolerated in the color components of the source image.

The source surface image can be transformed into the luminance/chrominance color space. The luminance (grayscale component) can be analyzed for repeating patterns and stored as a set of grayscale detail textures. The chrominance (color component) can be significantly downsampled, leaving only low-frequency information and stored at a much lower resolution than the source surface image. Usually, texture containing color components is applied to the surface without tiling.

This process is somewhat similar to JPEG lossy compression: image chrominance (color information) is downsampled, while the image is analyzed in frequency domain to omit some frequencies and quantize the data [Wallace91].

Leaving only the grayscale information of the details allows packing up to four different layers into one RGBA texture, and the number of required texture samplers and the complexity of the pixel shader are reduced.

Data Unpacking

According to the premises discussed in the previous paragraph, the data is stored with separate low-frequency color and details packed as four grayscale layers in one RGBA texture. To reconstruct the surface image, the detail layers are mixed together in proportion to properties of the surface at the given pixel and are then modulated with the downsampled color information.

Attempt to Read Packed Data

PS1.1–PS1.3-class hardware has limited swizzling and component access capabilities —only the alpha and the blue channels can be accessed directly. A common way to overcome this limitation is to use dot-product operations in order to gain access to specific components of the texture. Using this approach, the data unpacking process can be presented as a series of multiplications and dot-products:

```
float4 layers = tex2D( PackedDetailSampler, uv );
float r = dot( layers, float3(1,0,0) );
float g = dot( layers, float3(0,1,0) );
float result = r*mask0 + g*mask1 + layers.b*mask2 + layers.a*mask3;
```

Note that the variables mask0 .. mask3 contain the various material properties of the surface.

Although such an approach is programmatically valid, it produces long pixel shaders. However, there is a way to unpack the data more efficiently.

Four Layers in a Single Instruction

The detail layers are mixed together in proportion to properties of the surface using the following equation:

$$I = \sum layer_i * mask_i$$

Such an operation is actually the dot-product of two n-dimensional vectors. If properties of the surface are combined into four-dimensional vectors, the blending boils down to a simple dot-product of two four-dimensional vectors:

```
float result = dot( layers, mask );
```

The information about the surface properties can be stored per vertex using a four-dimensional vector or even per pixel with an additional RGBA texture (see Figure 2.13.3).

FIGURE 2.13.3   *Blending grayscale detail layers using dot-product.*

dp4 Instruction Caveat

The dp4 instruction became available with the 1.2 pixel shader model. However, it counts as two arithmetic instructions (for both PS1.2 and PS1.3). Practice shows that a detail texture mapping shader tends to be shorter if the dp4 instruction is avoided. It is, in fact, better to expand the operations into a combination of a three-dimensional dot-product, addition, and multiplication. Doing so gives more freedom for the HLSL compiler to reorder operations in a more optimal way.

Simplified Shader

Once the grayscale information of the surface has been reconstructed, you can then apply the color information. The following HLSL code is a simple implementation of the surface reconstruction pixel shader:

```
float4 colors = tex2D( colorMapSampler, lowFreqUV );
float4 layers = tex2D( packedDetailSampler, highFreqUV );
float4 mask = tex2D( packedMaskSampler, highFreqUV );
float  details = dot( layers, mask );
return float4( colors.rgb * details, 1 );
```

Restrictions

The described approach imposes some restrictions on the source data:

*   All grayscale detail layers stored in a single RGBA texture must be of the same size.
*   Because several detail layers are actually sampled at the same time, they have the same repeat rate over the entire surface.
*   RGBA textures containing several detail texture layers should not be compressed using DXT compression. The detail texture containing high-frequency information is a poor candidate for compression. However, the texture containing surface properties is a good candidate for DXT compression.

Detail layers usually contain less information in lower frequencies and thus can be easily modified to meet the first and second criteria.

Improvements

Signed Detail Textures

It is common to modulate low-frequency color information with the grayscale details. However, such an approach has one disadvantage—the surface tends to be darker as more materials are applied to it (no matter how bright the colors are, multiplying them by details will only make them darker). The darkening of the surface can be compensated by increasing brightness of the color texture. However, this eventually leads to washed-out colors on the reconstructed surface, and in practice it can be hard for artists to predict brightness of the resulting surface.

Signed intensity textures can be used to overcome the darkening issue. The detail layer then is interpreted as containing intensity values in the range [−1, 1]. The sampled values are converted from the range [0, 1] to a signed range of [−1, 1] and are summed with color information during the final surface-color combination process [Blythe99].

Several Frequency Bands for Details

Usually, detail textures are used in the very close proximity of surface. However, in the case of very large surfaces, it could be reasonable to capture more than one frequency band worth of detail. For example, a surface covered with gravel has repetitive pattern of pebbles when observed from a distance. At the same time, each pebble has a repetitive pattern of cracks and dots when examined closely (see Figure 2.13.4). All these details can be extracted and captured in separate detail textures.

It is obvious that the surface must have more than one set of texture coordinates if details are applied at different frequencies. Such texture coordinates can be trivially calculated in the vertex shader given the frequency, or repeat rate of the details. Different

FIGURE 2.13.4   *Surface patterns observed from different distances.*

texture coordinate sets imply that different frequencies should be placed in separate RGBA detail textures.

It is worth mentioning that the same surface property information can be reused when different detail layers represent the same materials but at different frequencies. This helps to reduce the number of reconstruction passes needed for 1.1–1.3 pixel shaders.

Using Color for Details

The color information of the surface is downsampled, sacrificing the visual quality in order to reduce memory footprint. Adding small colorful details later can improve the visual quality of reconstructed surfaces. Such detail could be flowers and autumn leaves on the terrain or veins on the skin.

Small color details are a local property of the surface. This fact is especially useful for the surfaces that are subdivided into smaller segments (patches). It is beneficial because different detail textures containing color can then be applied to different parts of the surface.

The alpha channel of the texture containing low-frequency color information can be used to store the blending factor to use when blending the detail texture with the surface.

Putting It All Together

The final pixel shader is improved according to the techniques described in the previous section. Support for signed texture details in two frequency bands, additional high-frequency detail colors, simple per-vertex lighting, and optimization considerations are introduced to the pixel shader. The surface properties information can be stored per vertex and passed to the pixel shader through the COLOR1 interpolator in order to save one texture slot. The resulting pixel shader can be compiled for the PS1.1 target.

HLSL code for the final shader:

```
half4 lowColor = tex2D( ColorMapSampler, IN.lowFreqUV );
half4 midDetailLayers = unpackSigned( tex2D( PackedDetail0Sam-
pler, IN.midFreqUV ) );
half4 highDetailLayers = unpackSigned( tex2D( PackedDetail1Sam-
pler, IN.highFreqUV ) );
half4 highColor = tex2D( ColorDetailSampler, IN.midFreqUV );
// unpack and calculate detail intensities
half midDetails = dotOp( midDetailLayers, IN.mask );
half highDetails = dotOp( highDetailLayers, IN.mask );
// add medium frequency details
half3 diffuse = lowColor + midDetails;
// calculate combined opacity for color details
half colorMask = lowColor.a * highColor.a;
// apply color details
half3 o = lerpOp( diffuse, c.rgb, colorMask );
// add high frequency details
o = o + highDetails;
return half4( IN.diffuseColor * o + lightAmbient, 1 );
```

The unpackSigned function is used to convert value from range [0, 1] to signed range [-1, 1].

```
half4 unpackSigned( half4 value ) {
    return value * 2 - 1;
}
```

The following functions are used instead of the HLSL intrinsic functions to allow better instruction reordering possibilities for the HLSL compiler. This step is important for the pixel shader to be compiled under the PS1.1 target.

```
half dotOp( half4 a, half4 b ) {
    return dot( a.rgb, b.rgb ) + a.a * b.a;
}
half4 lerpOp( half4 a, half4 b, half t ) {
    return a + t * ( b - a );
}
```

Applicability

The described technique for detail texture mapping is suitable for large surfaces when the considerable amount of texture details and several different surface materials are required while needing good rendering speed. The following types of surfaces can benefit from the application of such a technique:

- Terrain
- In-game characters (skin and clothes)
- Large buildings

The described technique was used for the terrain rendering in the upcoming real-time strategy title *PSI: Syberian Conflict* developed by Wireframe Dreams Studios.

Conclusion

This article presented a technique for rendering large surfaces with unique visual details. The technique helped to reduce the texture memory footprint required by the surface texture and improved rendering speed. The proposed approach can be extended for high-end graphics hardware by introducing more materials, utilizing more frequency bands for detail information, and adding more color details. Dependent texture functionality may be employed for the future quality improvements as well.

References

[Blinn98] Blinn, J., "The Wonderful World of Video," *Jim Blinn's Corner: Dirty Pixels*, 1998.

[Bloom00] Bloom, C., "Terrain Texture Compositing by Blending in the Frame-Buffer," available online at *http://www.cbloom.com/3d/techdocs/splatting.txt*, November 2, 2000.

[Blythe99] Blythe, D., et al, "Lighting and Shading Techniques for Interactive Applications," SIGGRAPH, 1999.

[Vlachos02] Vlachos, A., "Texturing Terrain Using Pixel Shaders," *ShaderX: Vertex and Pixel Shader Tips and Tricks*, 2002.

[Wallace91] Wallace, G. K., "The JPEG still picture compression standard," Commun. ACM 34 (4), 1991.

2.14

Real-Time Environment Mapping with Equal Solid-Angle Spherical Quad-Map

Tien-Tsin Wong, Liang Wan, Chi-Sing Leung, and Ping-Man Lam

Introduction

Cube maps have long been used for environment mapping in many video game applications. The mirror reflection on a racing car is a typical example of their use. The quadrilateral shape of a cube map facilitates its storage, and its computational simplicity popularizes its usage. However, cube maps partition and sample the reflection sphere *unevenly* (see Figure 2.14.1, left), as the face centers have a lower sample density than the edge and corner areas. In other words, each pixel in the cube map has a different solid angle, and hence the cube map does not uniformly represent the 360° environment.

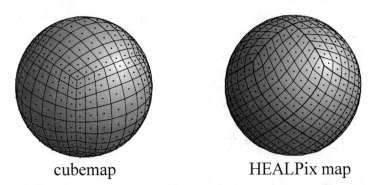

cubemap   HEALPix map

FIGURE 2.14.1 *Comparison of a traditional cube map (left) and a HEALPix map (right).*

In this article, we describe a sphere-to-rectangle mapping that partitions the spherical surface, or 360° environment, evenly (see Figure 2.14.1, right). This mapping is known as *HEALPix* (Hierarchical Equal Area, iso-Latitude Pixelisation [Górski99]), a sphere-partitioning scheme borrowed from the field of astrophysics. Using simple curvilinear equations, HEALPix partitions the spherical surface into 12 base spherical quadrilaterals of equal area (see Figure 2.14.2, left). Each quadrilateral (quad for short) can be further subdivided as needed. With this approach, subdivided quads at the same level are guaranteed to have the same spherical area.

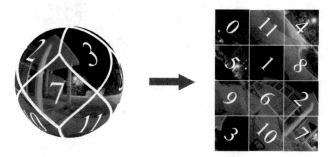

FIGURE 2.14.2   *HEALPix partitions the sphere into 12 base quads. The rectilinear structure of a HEALPix map (which consists of 12 base quads) fits efficiently in memory.*

In this article, we apply this partitioning scheme to environment mapping. The goal is to map a 360° environment to a rectangular HEALPix map that fits nicely into memory (see Figure 2.14.2). More importantly, all of the texels in this map span the same solid angle; that is, they are equally important. Furthermore, the generated HEALPix map copes properly with modern texture compression techniques like S3TC or DXTC.

Due to the millions of texture lookup operations in practical game applications, the key is to efficiently fetch the texels of a HEALPix map (see Figure 2.14.2, right) given a lookup direction (3D vector) in real time. This article demonstrates that the computation of HEALPix mapping can be efficiently implemented using approximately 20 lines of shader code. We then show that, when the same amount of storage is used, a HEALPix map can preserve better visual details than a cube map can (see Figure 2.14.7). Finally, we describe in detail how to perform mipmapping on the HEALPix map.

Sphere-to-Rectangle Mapping

Sphere Partitioning and Subdivision

Before continuing, let us review the construction of a traditional cube map. It starts from a base polyhedron (cube). Subdivision is first done on this base polyhedron and then projected onto the spherical surface. Note that area may not be preserved after this projection. Texels with an equal area on the cube map may not have the same solid angle on the spherical surface.

Unlike the cube map, HEALPix partitioning is performed directly on the spherical surface without any projections. First, the sphere is partitioned into 12 base quads by a set of simple curvilinear equations, indicated as the solid curves on the left in Figure

2.14.3. At the next level, each base quad is further subdivided into four subquads (see Figure 2.14.3, center), again with the same set of curvilinear equations. This subdivision continues until the desired level of resolution is reached (see Figure 2.14.3, right), that is, where each subquad corresponds to a texel in the HEALPix map.

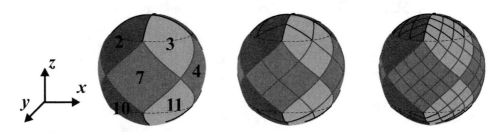

FIGURE 2.14.3 *Three levels of HEALPix partitioning.*

To perform the partitioning, the sphere is first divided into equatorial and polar zones. The zone enclosed within the "arctic" and "antarctic" circles at $z = \pm 2/3$ (dotted lines in Figures 2.14.3 and 2.14.4) is called the equatorial zone; the remaining areas are the polar zones. We employ different sets of curvilinear equations for these two different zones. Within the equatorial zone, the first-level subdivision curves are defined as

$$-\frac{1}{2}+t\pm\frac{3}{4}z = K, \quad K = 0,1,2,3 \tag{2.14.1}$$

where $z = \cos\theta$ and $t = 2\phi/\pi$ (see Figure 2.14.4 for the meaning of notations). Within the polar zones, the boundaries of the *first-level* base quads are defined as

$$\phi = K \cdot \frac{\pi}{2}, \quad K = 0,1,2,3 \tag{2.14.2}$$

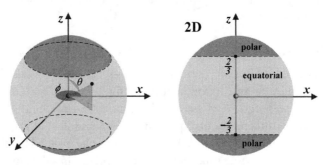

FIGURE 2.14.4 *Equatorial and polar zones.*

The sets of equations result in 12 equal-area base quads (see Figure 2.14.3, left).

To generate the next level of partitioning, we again employ a different set of curvilinear equations for the equatorial and polar zones. For the equatorial zone, the partitioning curves have a similar form as that for the first-level boundaries (see Figure 2.14.3, equatorial zone). Let N_s be the number of intervals along each side of the base quad. The partition curves have the following form:

$$-\frac{1}{2}+t+\frac{3}{4}z=\frac{k}{N_s}, \quad k=0,1,\cdots,\left(4N_s-1\right) \qquad (2.14.3)$$

and

$$-\frac{1}{2}+t-\frac{3}{4}z=\frac{l}{N_s}, \quad l=0,1,\cdots,\left(4N_s-1\right) \qquad (2.14.4)$$

Note that Equations 2.14.3 (k-curves) and 2.14.4 (l-curves) are the generalization of Equation 2.14.1. Both of them are used during the subdivision. On the other hand, the polar zones are further partitioned by using another set of curve equations. In addition to Equation 2.14.2 we have

$$\sqrt{3\left(1-|z|\right)}\cdot t=\frac{k}{N_s}, \quad k=1,\cdots,\left(N_s-1\right) \qquad (2.14.5)$$

and

$$\sqrt{3\left(1-|z|\right)}\cdot\left(1-t\right)=\frac{l}{N_s}, \quad l=1,\cdots,\left(N_s-1\right) \qquad (2.14.6)$$

where the pair of indices (k,l) forms the local coordinates of a subquad within a base quad. Again, both of them (k-curves and l-curves) have to be used during subdivision. Note that Equations 2.14.5 and 2.14.6 only define the curves in one quadrant, $0 \le t \le 1$. These curves can be easily extended to cover the other three quadrants of the polar caps by adding the appropriate offsets. Figure 2.14.3 shows how these curves look in the polar zones.

Properties

The HEALPix partitioning scheme has several nice geometric properties that facilitate its application in environment mapping.

First, subquads at the same level have the same solid angle. This can be proved by spherical integration of Equations 2.14.3 and 2.14.4 for equatorial zone and Equations 2.14.2, 2.14.5, and 2.14.6 for the polar zone. Therefore, texels in a HEALPix map have the same importance when representing the environment.

Second, the associated sampling pattern of the HEALPix partitioning scheme is uniformly distributed over the sphere. The sampling pattern is formed by putting a sample point at the center of each subquad. Note that the solid-angle equality does not necessarily guarantee uniform distribution. We have formally analyzed this uniform distribution property using a mathematical measurement of generalized discrepancy. Our analysis [Wan05] shows that the associated sampling pattern has a very low discrepancy (lower value means the sampling pattern is more uniformly distributed). In other words, the HEALPix map evenly samples the 360° environment.

Although the shape of subquads may vary a little, they are more or less the same shape. Both the texels in the HEALPix map and the subquads on the spherical surface have a quadrilateral shape. This allows us to naturally store the content of subquads in rectilinear texture memory, and is important for achieving reasonable bilinear interpolation or mipmapping during rendering.

Environment Mapping with HEALPix

Because of its advantageous properties, the adoption of HEALPix for environment mapping can be justified. Figure 2.14.5 shows the results of two HEALPix-based environment-mapped objects. Both of them are rendered with bilinear interpolation only.

(a) Torus   (b) Teapot

FIGURE 2.14.5   *Rendering results of HEALPix-based environment-mapped objects. All of the results are generated using bilinear interpolation only. (For (b): © Panorama reprinted with permission from Laurent Thion / www.ecliptique.com)*

Layout of Base Tiles

Because the HEALPix partitioning starts from 12 base quads (or tiles), we need to define how to pack the 12 tiles in a 2D texture. Figure 2.14.6(a) shows the 4×3 layout and the orientation of each tile. The number of the tiles in the figure corresponds to the numbering in Figure 2.14.3 (left). The tiles are packed in an effort to maximize the number of seamless boundaries, which facilitates image compression of the HEALPix maps. This arrangement also let us visualize the 360° environment on a plane. However, no matter how the tiles are packed, discontinuities continue to exist, as shown in Figure 2.14.6(b).

FIGURE 2.14.6   *(a) The layout of the 12 base tiles. (b) The HEALPix map of The Statue of Liberty in Paris. (For (b): © Panorama reprinted with permission from Laurent Thion / www.ecliptique.com).*

The Mapping Shader

The key to a practical environment mapping technique is its computational efficiency as there may be millions of texture lookups within a second. We now demonstrate how to implement the HEALPix mapping shader with real-time performance.

Environment mapping is a simple technique used to simulate reflective surfaces by assuming that illumination is from a distant environment, ignoring self-reflections and only accounting for the contribution from the direction of the surface reflection. Consider a screen pixel: environment mapping fills its color with a texel value from the environment map. The texel being looked up is determined by the ray reflected from the intersection point (corresponding to the screen pixel) of the object in the scene. In other words, the basic operation is to map a reflection ray, or a normalized 3D direction (x,y,z), to a texture coordinate (fn,u,v) in the HEALPix map, where integer $f_n \in [0,11]$ is an index for base tiles in Figure 2.14.6(a), and (u,v) is the *local* coordinate within a base tile, such that u, v are real numbers within $[0,1]$.

The mapping operation consists of two parts—equatorial and polar. First detected is whether the input (x,y,z) falls into the equatorial or polar zone. For the equatorial zone, Equations 2.14.3 and 2.14.4 are used while Equations 2.14.2, 2.14.5, and 2.14.6 are used for the polar zone. The basic idea is to locate which base quad the input (x,y,z) falls onto, and then determine the offset (u,v) within the base quad. The approach effectively "quantizes" (x,y,z) according to the curve equations we presented earlier. The following Cg shader shows our implementation of this mapping. Because we use a left-handed system in these equations, some conversion is needed if you use a right-handed system.

```
00   float3 hpmap(float3 dir)
01   {
02     float  fn, u, v, iu, iv, x, y, z;
03     float  t, tt, tn, tf;
04     float  za, tmp, zone, south;
05     float3 res;
06
07     // Right-hand and left-hand conversion, skip if consistent
08     x = dir.x;    y = dir.z;    z = dir.y;
09
10     // Compute t = 2ϕ/π
11     t      = atan2(-y, x)/1.5707963;
12     t     += step(t, 0.f) * 4.0;
13
14     // Check it falls into equatorial or polar zone, z = ±2/3
15     za     = 3.0 * abs(z);
16     tf     = modf(t, tn);
17     // zone = step(2.0, za);
18
19     if (za < 2.0) {                 // Equatorial zone (Eqn. 3 & 4)
20        tt    = t + 0.5;
21        tmp   = z * 0.75;            // 3z/4
22        u     = modf(tt + tmp, iu);
23        v     = modf(tt - tmp, iv); // u,v are the local coordinates
24        fn    = min(iu, iv);
25        fn   += 4 + (sign(iv-iu)-floor(fn/4))*4; // base tile index
26        res   = float3(fn, u, v);
27     } else {                        // Polar zone (Eqn. 2, 5 & 6)
28        tmp   = sqrt(3.0f - za);     // √(3(1-|z|))
29        south = (z<0);               // check south or north pole
30        tt    = tmp * tf;
31        tmp   = 1.0 - tmp;
32        tf    = tmp * south;
33        // Compute face index and local coordinates in the polar zone
34        res   = float3(tn+8*south, tmp-tf+tt, tf+tt);
35     }
36     // res = lerp(float3(fn,u,v), res, zone);
37     return res;
38   }
```

For educational purposes, the preceding Cg code uses an `if` statement. On GPUs with dynamic branching, there is a slight performance improvement of 10 to 15 fps.

On a GPU without dynamic branching, the `if` statement can be taken away and the code should be slightly modified as follows: lines 19, 26, 27, and 35 should be removed while lines 17 and 36 should be uncommented.

Bilinear Interpolation and Boundary Extension

So far, nothing has been said about filtering such as bilinear interpolation. This can be easily done by defining the HEALPix map as a rectangle texture object. Both GL_NV_TEXTURE_RECTANGLE and GL_ARB_texture_non_power_of_two support hardware-based bilinear interpolation by enabling GL_BIILNEAR. Careful readers should already be asking about the seam problem at the discontinuous boundaries of the base tiles and the texture boundaries. To fix this problem, the dimension of each base tile can be extended by two pixels in each direction, and these pixels are filled by

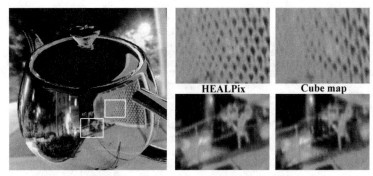

(a) Environment map: Chung Chi Chapel

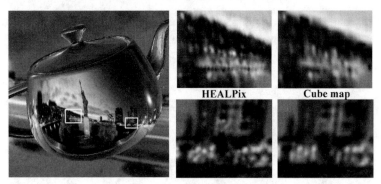

(b) Environment map: The Statue of Liberty

FIGURE 2.14.7   *Visual comparison of environment mapping with HEALPix maps (middle column) and cube maps (right column). The resolution of both HEALPix maps is 90 × 90 × 12 = 97,200 pixels, while that of both cube maps is 128 × 128 × 6 = 98,304 pixels. More image details are preserved by the HEALPix map. ((b):*
© *Panorama reprinted with permission from Laurent Thion/www.ecliptique.com)*

copying the corresponding values from neighboring tiles. This boundary extension process is done on the fly during the loading of the HEALPix map from disk. The local coordinate (u, v) for the tiles should also be modified to (u',v'), where $u' = u + 1$ and $v' = v + 1$, to account for the extension.

An environment mapping program is implemented using the previous shader and tested on a Pentium 4 1.5 GHz CPU configured with nVidia GeforceFX 6800 Ultra. The application achieves a very high frame rate of 206 fps (for the "`if`" version) with a screen size of 512×512. We now do a side-by-side comparison of the results using the HEALPix map to that of the cube map. To make a fair comparison, similar storage sizes are used for both maps. The resolution of the HEALPix map is $90 \times 90 \times 12 = 97{,}200$ pixels, while the resolution of the cube map is $128 \times 128 \times 6 = 98{,}304$ pixels. Note that more pixels were intentionally used for the cube map. Figure 2.14.7 shows the results, both with bilinear interpolation enabled. It can be seen that the HEALPix map preserves more visual detail than the cube map does.

Mipmapping

Obviously, bilinear interpolation alone is not sufficient for today's high-quality rendering. A naïve approach to mipmapping [Williams83] with a HEALPix map is to enable the hardware-based mipmapping directly on the HEALPix map. This results in apparent visual artifacts due to the discontinuous boundary among base tiles.

In common mipmapping, we maintain a pyramid of textures with decreasing resolution from bottom to top levels. By selecting the texels from the appropriate level, prefiltering is achieved, helping to reduce aliasing artifacts. The selection of the proper level is based on a level-of-detail parameter λ computed for each screen pixel (fragment). A popular definition of λ [Heckbert83] is

$$\lambda = \log_2 \left[\max \left\{ \sqrt{\left(\partial u / \partial x\right)^2 + \left(\partial v / \partial x\right)^2}, \ \sqrt{\left(\partial u / \partial y\right)^2 + \left(\partial v / \partial y\right)^2} \right\} \right]. \quad (2.14.7)$$

Hence, the estimation of λ depends on the computation of four partial derivatives $\partial u/\partial x$, $\partial v/\partial x$, $\partial u/\partial y$, and $\partial v/\partial y$. For discrete images, the derivatives can be computed by simple forward differencing

$$\begin{aligned} \partial u / \partial x &= u_{10} - u_{00}, & \partial v / \partial x &= v_{10} - v_{00}, \\ \partial u / \partial y &= u_{01} - u_{00}, & \partial v / \partial y &= v_{01} - v_{00}. \end{aligned} \quad (2.14.8)$$

where (f_{00}, u_{00}, v_{00}) is the corresponding texture coordinate for the current fragment (x, y); (f_{10}, u_{10}, v_{10}) corresponds to the horizontal neighboring fragment $(x + 1, y)$; and (f_{01}, u_{01}, v_{01}) corresponds to the vertical neighbor $(x, y + 1)$. Note that the (u, v) obtained is *local* to the tile. If (f_{10}, u_{10}, v_{10}) or (f_{01}, u_{01}, v_{01}) falls onto a different tile as the current fragment (that is, $f_{00} \neq f_{10}$ or $f_{00} \neq f_{01}$), the partial derivatives may be wrongly computed, especially at the discontinuous tile boundaries.

Local Tile Space

To overcome this problem, we compute the partial derivatives in the local tile space of the current tile f_{00}. In this space, the range of coordinate is [0,0] to [1,1], while the ranges of neighboring tiles are the logical extension (example in Figure 2.14.8(b)). In general, we want to transform (f_{01}, u_{01}, v_{01}) and (f_{10}, u_{10}, v_{10}) to the local tile space of f_{00} if they are not in the same tile. Such transformation is expressed as

$$\begin{bmatrix} u'_{01} \\ v'_{01} \end{bmatrix} = \mathbf{M}_{01 \to 00} \begin{bmatrix} u_{01} \\ v_{01} \\ 1 \end{bmatrix} \tag{2.14.9}$$

where $\mathbf{M}_{01 \to 00}$ is a 2×3 transformation matrix that transforms a (u_{01}, v_{01}) in tile f_{01} to f_{00} and has the following form

$$\mathbf{M}_{01 \to 00} = \begin{bmatrix} \mathbf{R} & | & \mathbf{T} \end{bmatrix} \tag{2.14.10}$$

where $\mathbf{R}$ and $\mathbf{T}$ are the 2×2 rotation and 2×1 translation matrices, respectively. Moreover, the element of $\mathbf{R}$ must be either 0, 1, or −1. We can construct two 12×12 tables, one for rotation matrices, rot, and one for translation matrix, tran. Each element in table rot contains four values, and hence rot fits into an RGBA texture. On the other hand, each element in table tran contains two values. Using these two tables, $\mathbf{M}_{01 \to 00}$ can be looked up by $\text{rot}[f_{01}, f_{00}]$ and $\text{tran}[f_{01}, f_{00}]$. Once the texture coordinates are transformed, the level-of-detail parameter λ can be computed according to Equations 2.14.7 and 2.14.8. The following shader computes λ.

```
float hplod(in float2 uv : TEXCOORD0,
            uniform float        ns,    // N_s
            uniform samplerRECT hptex, // texture coordinates
                                       // generated by hpmap
            uniform samplerRECT rot,
            uniform samplerRECT tran)
{
    float4 r;
    float3 params00, params01, params10;
    float2 tile01, tile10;
    float  mip;
    // Locate (x,y) in the local tile space
    params00 = f3texRECT(tex, uv);

    // Locate (x,y+1) in the local tile space
    params01  = f3texRECT(tex, uv+float2(0,1));
    tile      = float2(params01.x, params00.x);
    r         = f4texRECT(rot,  tile);    // look up rotation
    tile01    = f2texRECT(tran, tile);    // look up translation
    tile01.x += dot(params01.yz, r.xy);
    tile01.y += dot(params01.yz, r.zw);
```

```
// Locate (x+1,y) in the local tile space
params10   = f3texRECT(tex, uv+float2(1,0));
tile       = float2(params10.x, params00.x);
r          = f4texRECT(rot,  tile);      // look up rotation
tile10     = f2texRECT(tran, tile);      // look up translation
tile10.x += dot(params10.yz, r.xy);
tile10.y += dot(params10.yz, r.zw);

// Compute the level-of-detail
tile10 -= params00.yz;
tile01 -= params00.yz;
mip      = log2(max(length(tile10),length(tile01))) +
           MAXLODLEVEL;
mip      = clamp(mip, 0, MAXLODLEVEL-1);
return mip;
    }
```

To derive the transformation, first visualize the HEALPix map in a more natural way called *fish view* (see Figure 2.14.8(a)). As an example, consider the logical extension of local tile space of tile 0; that is, with tile 0 at the center. With the fish view, the local tile space of tile 0 is extended to cover all other tiles as shown in Figure 2.14.8(b). Note the change of local-frame orientation in each tile. Because the tiles are on a sphere, a neighboring tile can be laid on the east as well as on the west. The neighbor tiles are laid in order to minimize the geodesic distance from tile 0.

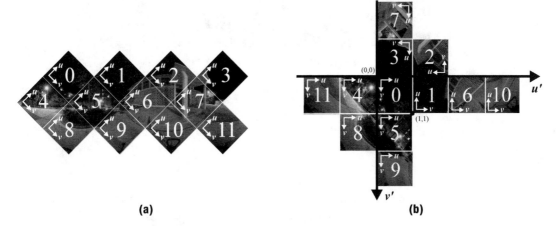

(a)   (b)

FIGURE 2.14.8   *(a) The natural visualization layout—fish view. (b) The logical extension of the local coordinate system with quad 0 at the center.*

Results

The proposed mipmapping technique is implemented using two rendering passes. The first pass computes the texture coordinate (fn,u,v) for each fragment. The second pass computes λ and fetches the texels from the appropriate mipmap level. Figure 2.14.9 shows the mipmapped results and the one with bilinear interpolation alone.

Even though mipmapping introduces more computation, we still achieve a real-time frame rate of 121 fps.

(a) Environment map: The Statue of Liberty

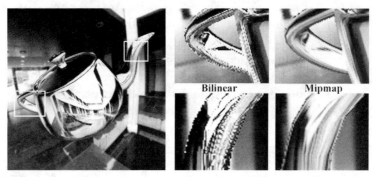

(b) Environment map: Institute of Chinese Studies

FIGURE 2.14.9   *Visual comparison of bilinear-interpolated (middle column) and mipmapped (right column) results. ((a): © Panorama reprinted with permission from Laurent Thion/www.ecliptique.com)*

Conclusion

In this article, we introduced the HEALPix-based environment mapping where all texels in the map are of equal visual importance. We then proposed an efficient shader implementation for texture lookup in order to apply the technique to practical applications. To achieve sophisticated anti-aliasing, we also described how to implement mipmapping on the HEALPix map while dealing with its discontinuous boundaries. Real-time performance is achieved even when mipmapping is enabled. The complete source code and demo programs are available on the companion CD-ROM and at *http://www.cse.cuhk. edu.hk/~ttwong/software/hpmap/hpmap.html.*

ON THE CD

Acknowledgments

We would like to thank Sebastian St. Laurent for careful and constructive review. Thanks to Laurent Thion (*www.ecliptique.com*) for permission to demonstrate our technique with the panorama *The Statue of Liberty in Paris*. The work is supported by The Chinese University of Hong Kong Young Researcher Award (Project No. 4411110) and a research grant from City University of Hong Kong (Project No. 7001819).

References

[Górski99] Górski, Krzysztof M., Eric Hivon, and Benjamin D. Wandelt, "Analysis Issues for Large CMB Data Sets," in Proceedings of the MPA/ESO Cosmology Conference, Evolution of Large-Scale Structure, edited by A. J. Banday, R. S. Sheth, and L. Da Costa, PrintPartners Ipskamp, NL (1999): pp. 37–42 (also astro-ph/9812350).

[Heckbert83] Heckbert, Paul, "Texture mapping polygons in perspective," Computer Graphics Lab., New York Inst. of Technology, Technical Memo no. 13, 1983.

[Wan05] Wan, Liang, Tien-Tsin Wong, and Chi-Sing Leung, "Spherical Q^2-tree for Sampling Dynamic Environment Sequences," in Proceedings of Eurographics Symposium on Rendering 2005 (EGSR 2005), June 2005: pp. 21–30.

[Williams83] Williams, Lance, "Pyramidal Parametrics," in SIGGRAPH '83: Proceedings of the 10th annual conference on computer graphics and interactive techniques, 1983: pp. 1–11.

2.15

I³: Interactive Indirect Illumination

Carsten Dachsbacher and Marc Stamminger

Introduction

The advance of graphics acceleration hardware over the last several years has greatly improved the realism in interactive computer graphics by pushing triangle counts and fill-rate further and further. Programmability allows the rendering of sophisticated lighting effects in real time. But most of these effects—for example, environment maps for reflecting distant objects—are only a part of the whole global illumination. Real global illumination generates many more—sometimes subtle but also important— effects that are mandatory to achieve realism.

Unfortunately, due to their global nature, full global illumination and interactivity are usually incompatible for ordinary scenes. Although there has been remarkable effort in speeding up ray tracing, it still takes several seconds, minutes, or even longer to generate a single image with full global illumination. Dynamic scenes are always difficult to handle with ray tracing, because they require updates for the ray-casting acceleration structures for every frame. Radiosity algorithms are even further from interactive frame rates, but at least a once-computed solution can be rendered from arbitrary view points as long as the scene is static. Instant Radiosity [Keller97] is a hardware-friendly method for fast approximation of a radiosity solution using a random walk and many accumulated render passes with standard shadow maps.

For many purposes, especially for games, global illumination does not need to be absolutely correct—a plausible approximation is often sufficient. The *reflective shadow maps* are a GPU-friendly approach to compute a rough approximation for the one-bounce indirect light within a scene. They are an extension to classic shadow maps and store additional attributes per pixel, namely the light reflected off the hit surface and the spatial emission characteristics. Each pixel is then regarded as a small area light source illuminating the scene. In this article, we describe how this indirect illumination can be computed efficiently and coherently using pixel shaders (version 2.0 and later), resulting in approximate, yet plausible, indirect light.

Reflective Shadow Maps

Reflective shadow maps (RSMs) are based on the work of [Tabellion04] and ideas of the translucent shadow maps [Dachbacher03]: all pixels of a shadow map are considered as indirect light sources that generate the one-bounce indirect illumination in a scene. The starting point is a simple observation: If we have a single-point light source, all one-bounce indirect illumination is caused by surfaces visible in its shadow map. In this case, an extended shadow map is able to capture all information about the indirect lighting in such a scene and no radiosity texture atlas as in [Tabellion04] is needed. Thus, RSMs are more similar to translucent shadow maps, where the pixels of a shadow map are also considered as point lights. Because the indirect light computation is expensive, we can apply a screen-space interpolation method that reduces the number of evaluations and leads to interactive frame rates. If a sufficient tessellation of the scene is provided, a computation per vertex is also possible, making the screen-space interpolation superfluous.

Data

To narrow the computation down, we assume that all surfaces in the scene are diffuse reflectors. As any common shadow map, an RSM stores for each pixel **p** its depth value d_p, but also its world space position x_p, its normal n_p, and the reflected radiant flux Φ_p (wavelength dependent) of the visible surface point (see Figure 2.15.1). Every pixel of the RSM is regarded as a *pixel light* that illuminates the scene indirectly. Of course, the world-space position could be recomputed from the pixel coordinates and the depth values; however, we can save valuable pixel shader instructions by having the world space positions directly available. This is a trade-off between memory bandwidth and computation time, and timings may vary depending on the application.

The additional information completely defines the pixel lights: the flux Φ_p defines its brightness and color, and the normal n_p its spatial emission characteristics (see Figures 2.15.1 and 2.15.2). Assuming that the pixel light is infinitely small, the radiant intensity emitted into direction ω can be described as

$$I_p(\omega) = \Phi_p \max\left\{0, \langle n_p \mid \omega \rangle\right\}, \text{ where } \langle \mid \rangle \text{ is the dot product.}$$

Thus, the irradiance at a surface point **x** with normal **n** due to pixel light **p** is

$$E_p(x,n) = \Phi_p \frac{\max\left\{0, \langle n_p \mid x - x_p \rangle\right\} \max\left\{0, \langle n \mid x_p - x \rangle\right\}}{\left\| x - x_p \right\|^4}$$

By storing the radiant flux instead of radiosity or radiance, we don't have to care about the area of a pixel light, which simplifies the generation and the evaluation of the RSM.

Generation

An RSM is generated like a standard shadow map by rendering the scene from the light's view—but with multiple render targets to store the additional attributes, namely depth, normals, world space position, and the reflected flux. All these components are packed into three textures. The computation of the flux is simple. First, we compute

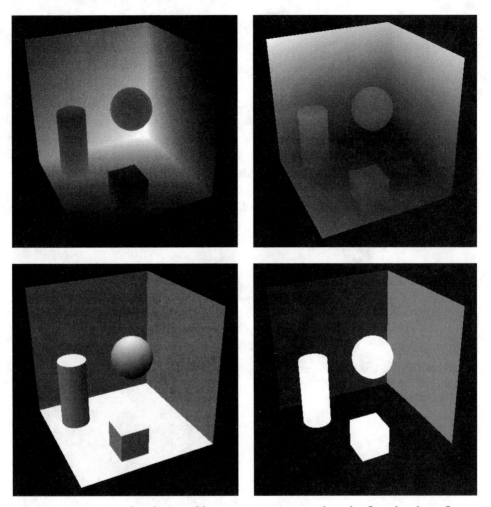

FIGURE 2.15.1 *Depth value, world-space position, normal, and reflected radiant flux value.*

the flux emitted through every pixel. For a uniform parallel light, this is a constant value. For a uniform spot light, the flux decreases with the cosine to the spot direction due to the decreasing solid angle. The reflected flux is then the reflection coefficient of the surface times the flux through the pixel. By storing the flux, we don't need a computation of distance attenuation or receiver cosine. As a result, the flux buffer looks more or less like an unshaded image of the light view (see Figure 2.15.1).

Theory

To compute an approximation for the indirect irradiance at a surface point $\mathbf{x}$ with normal $\mathbf{n}$, we need to sum up the illumination due to all pixel lights $\mathbf{p}$:

$$E(x,n) = \sum_p E_p(x,n) \qquad\qquad (2.15.1)$$

Figure 2.15.2 shows an example of a room with a box illuminated by a spotlight. For a particular pixel **p** of the RSM, we have a corresponding pixel light at position $\mathbf{x_p}$. This light source illuminates the scene with spatial emission characteristics defined by its normal $\mathbf{n_p}$, and thus, the surface at location **x** receives light from it. Because an RSM cannot capture occlusion for indirect lighting, the floor is also lit on the opposite side of the box (e.g. at location **y**). This is, of course, a severe approximation—but in most cases it is better to generate some indirect lighting effects and accept imprecise results. Furthermore, light attenuation with distance alleviates these artifacts. The emission direction of the pixel light corresponding to pixel **q** prevents it from illuminating the floor.

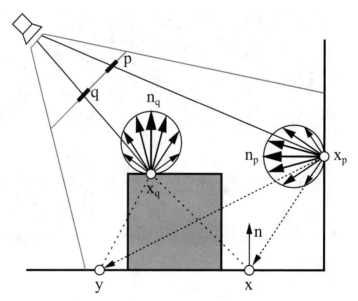

FIGURE 2.15.2   *Example of a room with a box illuminated by a spot light.*

Typical for many global illumination algorithms are problems appearing on an edge between two walls. In this case, the illumination integral has a singularity, which is difficult to integrate numerically. As we do not consider occlusion for the indirect illumination, we can move the pixel lights in negative normal direction by some constant offset and by this partly eliminate these artifacts.

For typical shadow map sizes (512^2 and above), the number of pixels is, of course, way too large to evaluate the above sum for all pixel lights if we target interactive speeds. Thus, we need to reduce the sum to a smaller number of light sources that on the one hand provide a sufficient approximation of the indirect lighting, but on the other hand can be computed fast enough. By using an importance-driven approach, we can reduce the number of pixel lights. This can be about 128 up to a few hundred samples—depending on scene complexity and rendering quality.

The underlying idea can be best described for a situation as shown in Figure 2.15.3. The surface point $\mathbf{x}$ is not directly illuminated and thus not contained in the RSM. If we project $\mathbf{x}$ into the shadow map, the pixel lights that are closest in world space are also close in the shadow map. In general, the distance (measured in the shadow map) between $\mathbf{x}$ and a pixel light $\mathbf{x_p}$ is a reasonable approximation for their distance in world space, as long as their depth values with respect to the light source do not differ significantly. But the most important conclusion is that important indirect lights will always be close in world space and must also be close in the shadow map.

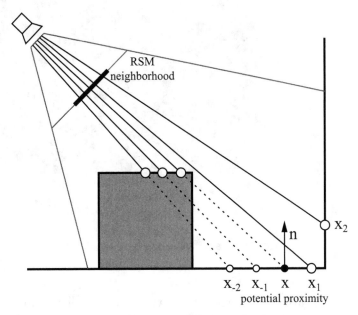

FIGURE 2.15.3   *Indirect lights will always be close.*

In Figure 2.15.3, candidate surface locations (important pixel lights) due to spatial proximity are $\mathbf{x_{-2}}$, $\mathbf{x_{-1}}$, $\mathbf{x_1}$, and $\mathbf{x_2}$. All of them are close to $\mathbf{x}$, but only the emission of the pixel light (belonging to the ray intersecting) $\mathbf{x_2}$ is directed accordingly to contribute to the lighting of $\mathbf{x}$.

Now that we know where to look for potentially important pixel lights, we project the surface point to be lit ($\mathbf{x}$) into the shadow map. Afterward, we select pixel lights around its shadow map coordinate (s,t), where the sample density decreases with the squared distance to (s,t). Such a sampling pattern can be computed using polar coordinates and two uniformly distributed random numbers ξ_1 and ξ_2 with:

$$\left(s + r_{max}\xi_1 \sin(2\pi\xi_2), t + r_{max}\xi_1 \cos(2\pi\xi_2)\right)$$

To compensate for the varying sampling density, we multiply the achieved samples with ξ_1^2 (and perform a final normalization), as shown in Figure 2.15.4 by different disc radii.

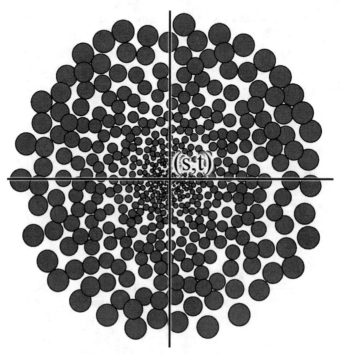

FIGURE 2.15.4   *A final normalization.*

We just need a single sampling pattern that will be used for all indirect light computations. By this, we can precompute such a pattern using Poisson sampling to obtain a more even sample distribution. The temporal coherency prevents flickering in dynamic scenes, but we have to make sure that the number of samples used for evaluation is large enough. Otherwise, the spatial coherency may result in banding artifacts.

Per-Pixel Computation

For rendering the final image, the direct illumination is computed using per-pixel lighting, where the RSM can be used as a standard shadow map. The computation of the indirect lighting is easiest, if we assume for now that we perform the evaluation for each pixel. To decouple scene complexity from rendering performance (as far as possible) and to prevent the execution of complex shaders for hidden surfaces, we apply all lighting computations as a deferred shading process. Especially for GPUs supporting only Pixel Shader 2.0 this is very important. An implementation for these GPUs consists of multiple render passes for indirect lighting: a part of the sampling pattern is provided as shader constants (set by the application), and only a few terms of Equation 2.15.1 can be evaluated at a time. As no floating-point blending is supported natively, the intermediate results have to be blended using shaders. Pixel Shader 3.0 hardware makes things much easier: The sampling pattern is stored in a lookup texture, and the contribution due to all pixel lights can be summed up in a single shader loop. In this case, deferred shading also pays off, as this expensive shader is not executed for hidden surfaces. In this section, we restrict ourselves to the Pixel Shader 3.0 version. The intermediate buffers and generation of the final image is depicted in the pipeline shown in Figure 2.15.5. At first, the RSM and the deferred shading buffers are generated. The latter stores the required information per pixel: world space normal and location, and its corresponding coordinates in light space and the material parameters. These buffers are view-dependent and only need to be updated if the light source or the camera moves.

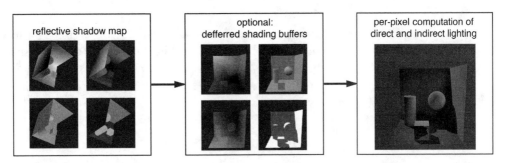

FIGURE 2.15.5 *Intermediate buffers and generation of the final image.*

The following shaders demonstrate the computation of the indirect lighting by gathering the contributions of the pixel lights. The deferred shading textures for the camera view are provided in def0..3 (world-space position, normal, diffuse material color, and shadow map coordinates). For performance reasons, each sample position is used for four evaluations by rotating it 90 degrees at a time. The SAMPLE texture contains the sampling positions, and their weights (stored in its z-component).

```
const int filterTaps = …;
const int SAMPLE_TEX_SIZE = …;

half4 psIndirectLighting( FRAGMENT_DEFERRED fragment ) : COLOR
{
    half4 texCoord = fragment.texture0;
```

```
half3 wsPos    = tex2D( def0, fragment.texture0 ).xyz;
half3 nrml     = tex2D( def1, fragment.texture0 ) * 2 - 1;
half4 material = tex2D( def2, fragment.texture0 );
half4 smPos    = tex2D( def3, fragment.texture0 );

half4 tc = half4( 0.5, 0.5, 0, 0 ) / SAMPLE_TEX_SIZE;
half4 E = 0;

for ( int i = 0; i < filterTaps / 4; i++ )
{
    // get sampling position
    half4 tap1 = tex2D( SAMPLE, tc );
    half4 tap2 = half4( -tap1.y, tap1.x, 0.0, 0.0 );

    E += bounce( wsPos, nrml, smPos + tap1 ) * tap1.z;
    E += bounce( wsPos, nrml, smPos + tap2 ) * tap1.z;
    E += bounce( wsPos, nrml, smPos - tap1 ) * tap1.z;
    E += bounce( wsPos, nrml, smPos - tap2 ) * tap1.z;

    tc.x += 1.0 / SAMPLE_TEX_SIZE;
}

return E * material;
}
```

The bounce function computes the contribution of a single pixel light to a surface location given by its position and normal. The third parameter is the RSM/shadow map texture coordinate. In principle, the form factor between two surface points is computed. As seen often in this context, we use a small distance bias to reduce the impact of common singularities.

```
half4 bounce( half3 surfacePos, half3 normal,
              half4 texcoord )
{
    // pixel light data:
    half3 flux       = tex2D( rsm0, texcoord ).xyz;
    half3 worldSpace = tex2D( rsm1, texcoord ).xyz;
    half3 wsNrml     = tex2D( rsm2, texcoord ).xyz*2-1;

    // light transport computation
    // => R  = normalized vector surface->pixel light
    //    l2 = squared distance
    half3 R  = worldSpace - surfacePos.xyz;
    half  l2 = dot( R, R );
    R        *= rsqrt( l2 );

    // form factor
    half  lR = 1.0 / ( distBias + l2 * PI );
    half  cosThetaI = max( 0, dot( wsNrml, -R ) );
    half  cosThetaJ = max( 0, dot( normal,  R ) );
    half  Fij = cosThetaI * cosThetaJ * lR;

    // return incoming flux and the form factor
    return half4( flux * Fij, Fij );
}
```

World-Space Interpolation

Even by reducing the number of samples to a few hundred, the indirect lighting computation as described previously is still too expensive to be performed for each pixel when targeting interactive frame rates. Fortunately, the indirect lighting of typical scenes is predominantly low frequency. We can exploit this and evaluate the indirect lighting only at fewer locations (in world or screen space), and an interpolation of the color values still provides good results.

When using a world space interpolation, we need a computation of the indirect lighting for the scene vertices—assuming, of course, a sufficient tessellation to capture the low-frequency color signal. Then, the graphics hardware takes care of the interpolation during rasterization without any additional cost. The feasibility of this approach mainly depends on the features of the GPU: we need to compute vertex data (the color values) using pixel shaders whenever the lighting situation changes. For best performance, we need support of render-to-texture functionality and vertex shaders 3.0 to sample these textures, or render-to-vertex-array extensions. Otherwise, the vertex colors have to be read back from the graphics hardware memory to be submitted as vertex data.

Screen-Space Interpolation

The second option does not make great demands on scene geometry or GPU features: an interpolation scheme in screen-space is applied to reduce the number of evaluations for the indirect lighting.

In a first pass, we compute the indirect illumination only for a low-resolution image of the camera view as it would be done for a full per-pixel computation (see Figure 2.15.6). In the next pass, we render the full resolution camera view and check for every pixel if the indirect lighting can be interpolated from the four surrounding low-resolution samples. Samples are suitable for interpolation if their world-space position is nearby the pixels' position (verified by comparing camera space depth values) and if their normals are similar. The contributions of these samples are weighted by the same factors used for a bilinear interpolation. A satisfactory interpolation can also be performed if only three of the neighbors are suitable. Then, a normalization of the interpolation weights is done afterward. If no interpolation is possible, the pixel is discarded in this render pass and its indirect lighting is computed later with a complete light gathering step.

At this point, the image is largely finished, but still contains some pixels for which we have to compute the indirect illumination (marked in red in color plate 5 and shown in Figure 2.15.6). For this, we use the same pixel shaders as for the full per-pixel evaluation. To avoid the recomputation of all pixels, "early z-culling" techniques can be used where available. Another possibility is to render the two final passes as a grid of quadrilaterals on the screen and to use an occlusion query for each quad. If all pixels of a quad have been rendered, the indirect illumination can be interpolated for all pixels. Otherwise, the quadrilateral contains pixels that have been discarded in the first pass and need an accurate computation of the indirect illumination in a second pass.

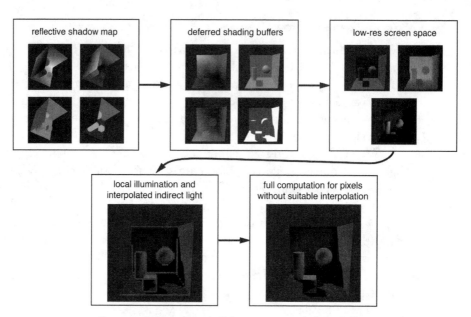

FIGURE 2.15.6   *Low-resolution image of the camera view for a full per-pixel computation. Color plate 5 shows color version.*

The effectiveness of the screen space interpolation scheme, of course, depends on the scene. For planar or smooth surfaces the interpolation works very well and only a few samples are required (see Figure 2.15.7). For complex or unconnected geometry—for example, a tree—the scheme will not be applicable and falls back to a near full evaluation.

FIGURE 2.15.7   *Screen-space interpolation.*

Things to Know...

RSMs are well suited for combination with scenes with a precomputed static lighting stored as lightmaps or vertex colors. The contribution of dynamic lights and the indirect illumination caused by them can be simply blended additively to the prelit scene. As RSMs do not handle self-shadowing for the indirect light, we found that ambient occlusion [Landis02], which can be precomputed and stored within textures, provides a simple method to compensate for this. RSMs can be combined with any soft-shadow algorithm designed for direct illumination. Not capturing the penumbra regions has no great impact, as rough approximations are used anyway. Also imaginable is to use low-resolution RSMs for computing the indirect lighting only and use hardware-supported shadow maps or shadow volumes for rendering of the shadows themselves—but, of course, the resolution of the RSM must be high enough to capture geometry causing significant indirect lighting.

In principle, an RSM can be extended to handle nondiffuse reflectors: instead of the flux, we would store a material ID buffer, and whenever the flux of a pixel light is to be computed the material BRDF must be evaluated to compute the flux reflected toward the current receiver. The main problem is that nondiffuse surfaces require significantly higher sample numbers or dynamic importance sampling to avoid strong artifacts, and interactive frame rates would not be achievable any longer. RSMs for other types of light sources such as omnidirectional lights (with shadow maps stored as cube maps) can be implemented by adapting sampling patters.

Because we consider only a few samples of an RSM for computing the indirect lighting, textured surfaces should be rendered using filtered versions of the texture map; otherwise, strongly varying pixel light brightness may lead to flickering.

When using the screen-space interpolation, it's obvious that the application of deferred shading buffers does not completely decouple scene complexity from rendering time: The adaptive refinement of the initial subsampling depends on the variation of depth and normal values and thus from scene complexity.

FIGURE 2.15.8   *The test scene without indirect lighting (left); 128 samples for indirect lighting (middle); and 512 samples for indirect lighting (right).*

References

[Dachsbacher03] Dachsbacher, Carsten, and Marc, Stamminger, "Translucent Shadow Maps," Proceedings of the 14th Eurographics workshop on Rendering (2003): pp. 197–201.

[Dachsbacher05] Dachsbacher, Carsten, and Marc, Stamminger, "Reflective Shadow Maps," ACM SIGGRAPH Symposium on Interactive 3D Graphics and Games (2005): pp. 203–231.

[Keller97] Keller, Alexander, "Instant Radiosity," Computer Graphics (SIGGRAPH '97 Proceedings) (1997): pp. 49–55.

[Landis02] Landis, H., "Production-ready global illumination," SIGGRAPH Course Notes #16, 2002.

[Tabellion04] Tabellion, Eric, and Arnauld Lamorlette, "An Approximate Global Illumination System for Computer Generated Films," ACM Transactions on Graphics (Proceedings of SIGGRAPH 2004): pp. 469–476.

IMAGE SPACE

Introduction

Natalya Tatarchuk

This section covers all techniques that happen in image space. Because of the increasing pixel shader power of current graphics cards, techniques that were done on the CPU or just avoided due to their expensiveness are now possible.

The article "Texture Compression with Coefficient Domain Shaders" by Chi-Sing Leung, Tien-Tsin Wong, and Ping Man Lam presents a texture compression technique based on transform coding. It achieves real-time decompression by using a shader that works on the coefficient domain.

Motion blur is an important visual cue that is fundamental to creating a sense of speed in a computer-generated image. It can be prohibitively expensive to apply motion blur to a full scene, particularly when rendering an omnidirectional view of the scene to a cube map for subsequent use as a dynamic environment map. Jason Mitchell describes in his article "Motion Blurring Environment Maps" a method for performing an inexpensive postprocessing effect on cube maps to give the impression of motion blur in the resulting reflections. Additionally, this basic framework can be applied to other types of real-time cube-map processing.

Joachim Diepstraten describes in his article "Simulating the Visual Effects of a Video Recording System" how to mimic certain characteristics of a video home system on the graphics card. The characteristics covered here occur either at normal playback or while running the tape at fast-forward and backward during playback.

3.1

Texture Compression with Coefficient Domain Shaders

Chi-Sing Leung, Ping-Man Lam, and Tien-Tsin Wong

Introduction

Texture mapping is an important technique for increasing visual richness of rendered images. High-resolution textures are frequently required to generate realistic images. Due to the memory limit on graphics hardware, textures are usually stored in a compressed format. S3TC [Domine00] is a common texture compression method used in graphics processor units (GPU). Although we can randomly access a texel from an S3TC-compressed texture, the compression ratio of S3TC is rather rigid. For example, the compression ratio of RGB textures is fixed at 6:1.

Transform coding techniques, such as discrete cosine transform (DCT) [Wallace92] and discrete wavelet transform (DWT) [Joshi97], are common compression techniques in image compression. By controlling the number of transformed coefficients used or the quantization step sizes, the compression ratio can be dynamically modified in the transform coding techniques. However, in the conventional transform coding approach [Wong03], the compressed textures are first decompressed and then loaded into the GPU memory before rendering.

This article presents a texture compression technique based on *transform coding*. It achieves real-time decompression by using a shader that works on the coefficient domain. In our approach, the shader directly interpolates a texel value from transformed coefficients without reconstructing the whole block of texels. Figure 3.1.1 illustrates the whole process graphically. First, a texture is compressed by a transform coding technique. Then, the quantized transform coefficients are held in the GPU memory. During the rendering, a texel value can be randomly accessed from the transformed coefficients.

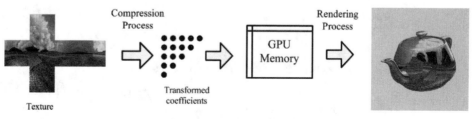

FIGURE 3.1.1 *Transform coding texture compression method algorithm.*

Preparing Transformed Coefficient Textures

Before introducing the coefficient shader, we first describe our compression method and the organization of the transformed coefficients in GPU memory.

Block-Based Partition

In transform coding, the first step is to divide a texture into a number of nonoverlapped image blocks (shown in Figure 3.1.2). For example, given a texture with resolution equal to $N_x \times N_y$, we can partition it into a number of blocks with a size equal to 8×8, just like JPEG. Hence, after partition, a texture contains $(N_x \times N_y)/64$ blocks and each of them is indicated by two indices, b_x and b_y, which define the block position, given by

$$b_x = \text{floor}\left(\frac{x}{8}\right) \quad \text{and} \quad b_y = \text{floor}\left(\frac{y}{8}\right)$$

In other words, a texel, denoted as $\text{Im}(x,y)$, can also be expressed as

$$\text{Im}(x, y) = \text{Im}\left[(b_x \cdot 8 + s), (b_y \cdot 8 + t)\right] = h_{b_x, b_y}(s, t) \tag{3.1.1}$$

where s and t are the local coordinates along horizontal and vertical directions, respectively, given by $s = x \mod 8$ and $t = y \mod 8$. A data block at block position (b_x, b_y) is denoted as h_{b_x, b_y}.

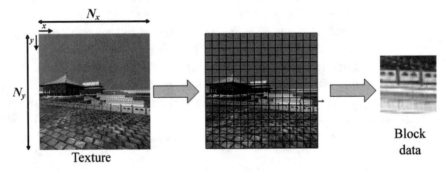

FIGURE 3.1.2   *A texture is partitioned into a number of overlapped data blocks.*

Transform Coding: Discrete Cosine Transform

After the partition process, those data blocks are then transformed from the spatial domain to the frequency domain based on DCT. The transformed coefficients $h_{b_x, b_y}(w,z)$'s of a data block h_{b_x, b_y} is given by

$$H_{b_x,b_y}(w,z)=c_w c_z \sum_{s=0}^{7}\sum_{t=0}^{7}\cos\frac{(2s+1)w\pi}{16}\cos\frac{(2t+1)z\pi}{16}h_{b_x,b_y}(s,t) \qquad (3.1.2)$$

for $w = 0,...,7$ and $z = 0,...,7$, where

$$c_w, c_z = \begin{cases} \dfrac{1}{2\sqrt{2}}, & \text{for } w,z=0 \\ \dfrac{1}{2}, & \text{otherwise} \end{cases}$$

The indices w and z are used for indicating the frequencies of transformed coefficients along horizontal and vertical direction (see Figure 3.1.3), respectively. As shown in Figure 3.1.3, for each data block, after the DCT process, the number of transformed coefficients is the same as the number of data in a data block. For example, if the data block size is 8 × 8, the number of transformed coefficients acquired in a block is equal to 64.

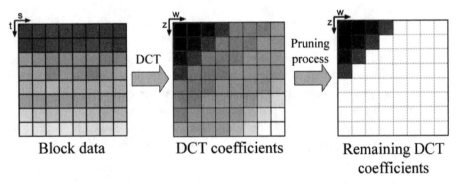

FIGURE 3.1.3 *The transform process and remaining DCT coefficients.*

As the spatial property of a texture is similar to a natural image, the energy of the low-frequency transformed coefficients is usually much greater than that of the high-frequency ones. Hence, even when we delete some high-frequency transformed coefficients, the reconstructed data block from the remaining low-frequency coefficients will not contain serious artifacts. Therefore, in our implementation, we keep only the DCT coefficients in the upper-left corner (low-frequency ones) (see Figure 3.1.3). As an example, 10 transformed coefficients are kept in the upper-left corner.

Transformed Coefficient Texture

After DCT and the pruning processes, a data block is represented by k transformed coefficients. As shown in Figure 3.1.4, these k coefficients can be considered as a coefficient vector. Since there are $B_x \times B_y$ data blocks in a texture, where $B_x = \frac{N_x}{8}$ and $B_y = \frac{N_y}{8}$, there are totally $B_x \times B_y$ coefficients vectors in a texture. These vectors can form a 2D array of vectors (shown in Figure 3.1.5).

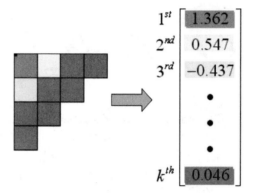

FIGURE 3.1.4   *Formation of a coefficient vector.*

To achieve the rendering process in the coefficient domain, we restructure the array of k-dimensional coefficients to form *k coefficient textures,* as in Figure 3.1.5. They are sorted into bins in the following manner: The first coefficients (lowest-frequency DCT coefficients) of all coefficient vectors are grouped to form the first coefficient texture. This process is repeatedly applied to form other coefficient textures. Each coefficient texture is an image of real values (can be positive or negative). With this rebinning process, there are form k coefficient textures. The size of each texture is $B_x \times B_y$. Each represents a particular frequency component of the original texture.

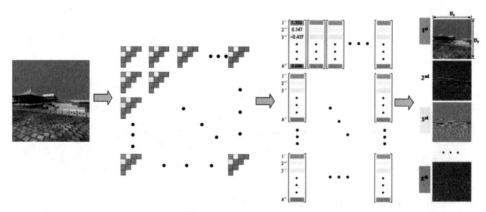

FIGURE 3.1.5   *Formation of coefficient textures.*

Compression and Coefficient Texture Format

The proposed approach is a two-level compression method. In the first level, we control the number of transformed coefficients used for compression. In the second level, we quantize the transformed coefficient textures. This gives us a flexible model for controlling the compression ratio.

Number of Coefficient Textures

In the first level of compression we need to be able to modify the number of transformed coefficients used. If we look back at the transform process (see Figure 3.1.3), we notice that the shape of remaining DCT coefficients is similar to a triangle. We can control the first-level compression ratio by adjusting the size of this triangle. Figure 3.1.6 shows three examples of preserving coefficients, each with a different number of DCT coefficients.

An index m, which depends on (w,z), is assigned to each transformed coefficient. These indices are used to indicate the coefficient textures.

Mapping from (w,z) to m
(a) $k = 21$
(b) $k = 15$
(c) $k = 10$

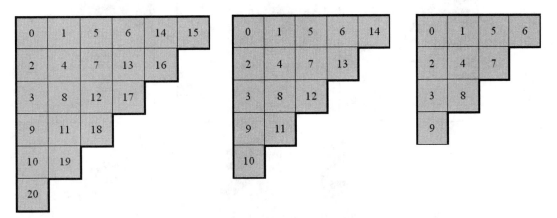

FIGURE 3.1.6   *Three schemes to preserve coefficients.*

Second-Level Compression

Before we can load the coefficient textures into GPU memory, we need to quantize them to a precision that is supported by OpenGL. For each coefficient texture, *texel* values α_i are first bounded within $[a, b]$, where $a = \bar{\alpha} - 6\sigma$ and $b = \bar{\alpha} + 6\sigma$. The parameters $\bar{\alpha}$ and σ are the mean and the standard derivation of texel values, respectively.

Each texture has its own a and b. Afterward, each texture is rescaled to the range of [0, 1] by

$$\alpha_i' = \frac{\alpha_i - a}{b - a} \qquad (3.1.3)$$

where α_i' is the rescaled value of α_i. After rescaling, there are k rescaled coefficient textures. With this mean shift and rescaling, we can make a better use of bits allocated.

Each texture is then quantized to an OpenGL-supported texture format. In OpenGL, there are several supported texture formats, like GL_RGB8, GL_RGB4, GL_R3_G3_B2, and so on, each with different precision. As low-frequency coefficients contain more energy than the high-frequency ones, we should quantize low-frequency coefficient textures with a *high precision* and high-frequency coefficient textures with a low precision. With this approach, we can achieve a variety of compression ratios via different combinations of OpenGL texture formats. Figure 3.1.7 shows three different combinations of texture formats supported by OpenGL and provides us the overall compression ratios of 6:1, 12:1, and 16:1.

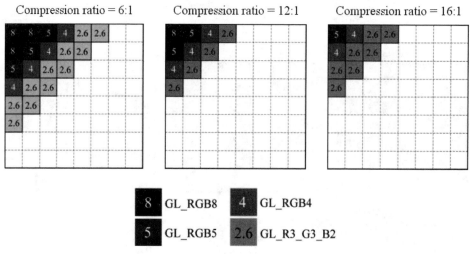

FIGURE 3.1.7 *Three different quantization schemes.*

In the left scheme in Figure 3.1.7, the *overall* compression ratio is equal to 6:1. There are three low-frequency coefficient textures (the left-upper DCT coefficients) that are quantized with the format GL_RGB8. Some high-frequency coefficient textures are quantized with the format GL_R3_G3_B2. Since the number of elements in a data block is 64, the number of bits needed to represent the original data (without any compression) is equal to $64 \times 8 \times 3 = 1536$. In the 6:1 compression scheme, the number of bits actually used for representing a rescaled coefficient vector is 251.

Thus, the compression ratio is $\frac{1536}{251} \approx \frac{6}{1}$. The following C code fragment defines different compression schemes.

```
// max_bind: number of coefficients used (k)
GLuint QDCT_LEVEL_LIST[][max_bind] = {
  {
    // compression ratio = 16:1
    GL_RGB5,
    GL_RGB4, GL_RGB4,
    GL_R3_G3_B2, GL_R3_G3_B2, GL_R3_G3_B2,
    GL_R3_G3_B2, GL_R3_G3_B2, GL_R3_G3_B2, GL_R3_G3_B2
  },
  {
    // compression ratio = 12:1
    GL_RGB8,
    GL_RGB5, GL_RGB5,
    GL_RGB4, GL_RGB4, GL_RGB4,
    GL_R3_G3_B2, GL_R3_G3_B2, GL_R3_G3_B2, GL_R3_G3_B2
  }
};
```

The following C code loads the rescaled coefficient textures into GPU memory. Note that the quantization is automatically done by OpenGL.

```
// max_bind: number of coefficient textures used
// dctmap[j]: coefficient texture
// dctw: coefficient texture width (Bx)
// dcth: coefficient texture height (By)
glGenTextures( max_bind, GL_coef );
  for( j=0; j<max_bind; j++ )
  {
    glBindTexture( GL_TEXTURE_2D, GL_coef[j] );
    glTexParameterf( GL_TEXTURE_2D, GL_TEXTURE_MIN_FILTER, GL_NEAREST
);
    glTexParameterf( GL_TEXTURE_2D, GL_TEXTURE_MAG_FILTER, GL_NEAREST
);
    glTexParameterf( GL_TEXTURE_2D, GL_TEXTURE_WRAP_S,
GL_CLAMP_TO_EDGE );
    glTexParameterf( GL_TEXTURE_2D, GL_TEXTURE_WRAP_T,
GL_CLAMP_TO_EDGE );
    glTexImage2D( GL_TEXTURE_2D, 0, QDCT_LEVEL_LIST[QDCT_LEVEL][j],
                  dctw, dcth, 0, GL_RGB, GL_FLOAT,
&dctmap[j].pm[0][0] );
  }
```

Real-Time Decompression and Rendering

Given a texel coordinate (x, y), the texel value can be *directly* obtained, given by

$$\text{texel value at } (x, y) = c_w c_z \sum_{w=0}^{\Delta} \sum_{z=0}^{\Delta-w} \cos\frac{(2s'+1)w\pi}{16} \cos\frac{(2t'+1)z\pi}{16} H_{b_x, b_y}(w, z) \quad (3.1.4)$$

where $b_x = floor\left(\frac{x}{8}\right)$, $b_y = floor\left(\frac{y}{8}\right)$, $s' = x - 8b_x$, $t' = y - 8b_y$, and $\Delta + 1$ is the maximum length of remaining transformed coefficients in either w or z direction (Figure 3.1.3). Note that the coefficient texture values $H_{b_x,b_y}(w,z)$'s are obtained from the quantized coefficient texture. To accelerate the rendering process, the basis function value

$$R_m(s',t') = \cos\frac{(2s'+1)w\pi}{16}\cos\frac{(2t'+1)z\pi}{16} \qquad (3.1.5)$$

can be obtained by looking up multiple precomputed cosine tables. In Equation 3.1.5, m is the basis index obtained from w and z (see Figure 3.1.6).

In rendering Equation 3.1.4, the values of x and y are not limited to integers. This is because the interpolation process for noninteger values of x and y could be automatically done by the cosine lookup tables. The following C code precomputes the cosine values and loads the cosine lookup tables into the GPU memory.

```
// basis_res: cosine table resolution
// dat: variable to store the sampled cosine value
void prepare_cosmap()
{
  int    basis_res = 1024;
  int    i, j, idx;
  float  theta;
  FLOAT4 *dat = (FLOAT4*) malloc( 2 * basis_res * sizeof(FLOAT4) );

  // prepare cosine map: cos_nx, where n=1 to 8
  for( j=0; j<2; j++ )
  {
    for( i=0; i<basis_res; i++ )
    {
      idx = j*basis_res + i;
      theta = PI * (i+.5)/basis_res ;
      dat[idx].x = cos( (j*4+1) * theta );
      dat[idx].y = cos( (j*4+2) * theta );
      dat[idx].z = cos( (j*4+3) * theta );
      dat[idx].w = cos( (j*4+4) * theta );

      // map the cosine map values lie between 0 and 1
      dat[idx] = dat[idx] + 1;
      dat[idx] = dat[idx] / 2;
    }
  }

  // load the cosine maps to GPU memory
  glGenTextures( 2, GL_cosmap );
  for( j=0; j<2; j++ )
  {
    glBindTexture( GL_TEXTURE_1D, GL_cosmap[j] );
      glTexParameterf( GL_TEXTURE_1D, GL_TEXTURE_MIN_FILTER, GL_LIN-
EAR );
```

```
        glTexParameterf( GL_TEXTURE_1D, GL_TEXTURE_MAG_FILTER, GL_LIN-
    EAR );
        glTexParameterf( GL_TEXTURE_1D, GL_TEXTURE_WRAP_S,
    GL_CLAMP_TO_EDGE );
        glTexParameterf( GL_TEXTURE_1D, GL_TEXTURE_WRAP_T,
    GL_CLAMP_TO_EDGE );
        glTexImage1D( GL_TEXTURE_1D, 0, GL_RGBA, basis_res, 0, GL_RGBA,
    GL_FLOAT,
                          &dat[j*basis_res] );
    }
    free(dat);
}
```

After determining those basis values $R_m(s',t')$'s, every quantized texture is de-quantized with its own a and b parameter value. With the de-quantized *transformed coefficient textures*, we can reconstruct any texel in the texture randomly by a texel-wise combination of them. Figure 3.1.8 illustrates the reconstruction process (Equation 3.1.4) graphically.

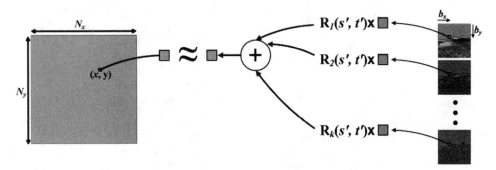

FIGURE 3.1.8 *Reconstructing a texel value by linear combination of coefficient texel values and $R_m(s, t)$'s.*

The following code shows the reconstruction process. In this example, the resolution of the textures equals to 128×128.

```
#define max_bind 10
#define n_blk 128
float3 main(
  float2 tex_cord : TEXCOORD0,
  uniform sampler1D cosmap[2],     // cosine function lookup texture
  uniform sampler2D coef[max_bind], // transformed coefficient texture
  uniform float3    sf[max_bind],  // scale parameter
  uniform float3    of[max_bind]   // offset parameter
):COLOR0
{
  float  R[max_bind];
  float2 b;                        // block index (bx, by)
  float2 st;                       // local block coordinate (s, t)
```

```
  float vx[8], vy[8];                   // vx, vy: cosine value in x and
y directions
  float4 dctx0, dcty0, dctx1, dcty1;
  float3 acc;
  int zz[64] =                          // (u, v) coordinate maps to
basis index m
  {
     0,  1,   8, 16,  9,  2,   3, 10,
    17, 24, 32, 25, 18, 11,  4,  5,
    12, 19, 26, 33, 40, 48, 41, 34,
    27, 20, 13,  6,  7,  14, 21, 28,
    35, 42, 49, 56, 57, 50, 43, 36,
    29, 22, 15, 23, 30, 37, 44, 51,
    58, 59, 52, 45, 38, 31, 39, 46,
    53, 60, 61, 54, 47, 55, 62, 63
  };
  b  = (floor(tex_cord*n_blk)+0.5)/n_blk;
  st = frac(tex_cord*n_blk);

  dctx0 = 2*f4tex1D(cosmap[0],st.x)-1;  dcty0 =
2*f4tex1D(cosmap[0],st.y )-1;
  dctx1 = 2*f4tex1D(cosmap[1],st.x)-1;  dcty1 =
2*f4tex1D(cosmap[1],st.y)-1;

  dctx0 *= 1.41421356;      dcty0 *= 1.41421356;
  dctx1 *= 1.41421356;      dcty1 *= 1.41421356;

  vx[0] = 1;                 vy[0] = 1;
  vx[1] = dctx0.x;           vy[1] = dcty0.x;
  vx[2] = dctx0.y;           vy[2] = dcty0.y;
  vx[3] = dctx0.z;           vy[3] = dcty0.z;
  vx[4] = dctx0.w;           vy[4] = dcty0.w;
  vx[5] = dctx1.x;           vy[5] = dcty1.x;
  vx[6] = dctx1.y;           vy[6] = dcty1.y;
  vx[7] = dctx1.z;           vy[7] = dcty1.z;

  for( int i=0; i<max_bind; i++ )
    R[i] = vx[zz[i]%8] * vy[zz[i]/8];
  for( int i=0; i<max_bind ; i++ )     // linear combination
    acc += R[i] * ( f3tex2D( coef[i], b ) * sf[i] + of[i] );
  return acc;
}
```

Figure 3.1.9 shows the rendering results of an environment mapping example. The environment cube map in this example is compressed with various methods. The resolution of each cube face is 1024 × 1024. Figures 3.1.9(a) and 3.1.9(b) show rendered results of the original cube map and the S3TC-compressed cube map, respectively. Figures 3.1.9(c) and 3.1.9(d) show rendered results of our proposed method with compression ratios of 12:1 and 16:1. The visual quality of our approach is comparable to that of the S3TC approach while ours achieves higher and flexible compression ratio. Interested readers are referred to the companion CD-ROM for demos and source code of this example.

ON THE CD

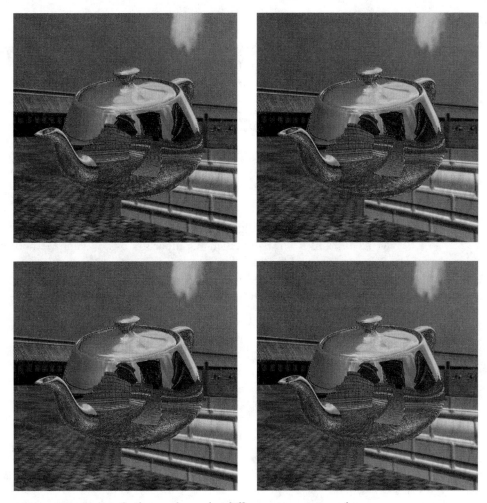

FIGURE 3.1.9 *Rendering results under different compression schemes.*

Conclusion

In this article, we presented a transform coding-based texture compression technique. The transformed coefficients are stored on GPU memory. Moreover, the corresponding shader from transformed coefficients is presented. The advantage of our technique is that the texel value can be randomly accessed without reconstructing any unwanted texel values. Our proposed method offers a flexible compression ratio and can achieve real-time decompression and rendering capability. Interested readers are referred to the companion CD-ROM for demos as well as the following homepage:

ON THE CD

http://www.ee.cityu.edu.hk/~csleung/

Acknowledgments

We would also like to thank Gray Ho for the demo implementation. The work is supported by a research grant from City University of Hong Kong (Project No. 7001819) and CUHK Direct Grant for Research (Project ID: 2050319).

References

[Domine00] Domine, S., "Using Texture Compression in OpenGL," available online at *http://www.nvidia.com*.

[Wallace92] Wallace, G. K., "The JPEG Still Picture Compression Standard," *IEEE Transactions on Consumer Electronics*," vol. 38, no. 1 (February 1992): pp. xviii–xxxiv.

[Joshi97] Joshi, R. L., H. Jafarkhani, J. H. Kasner, T. R. Fischer, N. Farvardin, M. W. Marcellin, and R. H. Bamberger, "Comparison of Different Methods of Classification in Subband Coding of Images," *IEEE Transactions on Image Processing*, vol. 6, no. 11 (November 1997): pp. 1473–1486.

[Wong03] Wong, T. T., and C. S. Leung, "Compression of Illumination Adjustable Image," *IEEE Trans. Circuit Systems: Video Technology*, vol. 13 (November 2003): pp. 1107–1118.

3.2

Motion Blurring Environment Maps

Jason Mitchell

Introduction

Motion blur is an important visual cue that is fundamental to creating a sense of speed in a computer-generated image. It can be prohibitively expensive to apply motion blur to a full scene, particularly when rendering an omnidirectional view of the scene to a cube map for subsequent use as a dynamic environment map. In this chapter, we describe a method for using graphics hardware to perform an inexpensive postprocessing effect on cube maps to give the impression of motion blur in the resulting reflections in real time. Additionally, this basic framework can be applied to other types of real-time cube map processing. Though the motion blurred reflections were not used in the final demo, this work was developed while working at ATI for RADEON X850 demo *Ruby: Dangerous Curves*.

Motion Blur

Motion blur is an artifact of the photographic process that we have all become accustomed to during a lifetime of viewing still and moving pictures of the real world. In a real physical camera, a shutter opens and film or digital sensors are exposed to light for a finite amount of time. During this time, parts of the scene and the camera itself can be in motion, generating a blurring effect that we refer to as motion blur. In offline computer graphics for feature films, motion blur is a fundamental visual cue that is required to give the proper sense of realism. The cost of rendering such motion blur is often quite high, however, which is one reason it is generally completely absent from real-time video games. In some games, motion blur is approximated by re-using some small contribution from previously-rendered frames or by drawing geometric trails or "speed lines" behind specific fast-moving objects. With ever-increasing graphics hardware power, it may eventually be possible to achieve even higher quality motion blur on full scenes using techniques such as screen space vector motion blur or even a brute-force accumulation buffer [Haeberli90].

In this article, however, we focus specifically on motion blur in reflections when we are in the frame of reference of the moving object. This scenario is quite common in racing games where the viewer is constantly trailing behind a shiny vehicle. Before discussing the details of this technique, we outline a method for using graphics hardware to perform image-processing operations on cube maps in general.

Processing Cube Maps

When performing image processing, we typically think of sampling data from one or more 2D rectangular input images and writing into a 2D rectangular output image. When considering omnidirectional maps, however, it is convenient to think about distributing the data on the unit sphere or unit cube, rather than in a 2D plane [Greene86]. In 2D, we draw a quadrilateral in order to invoke a filter kernel—implemented as a pixel shader—for each pixel in the output image [Mitchell02]. Similarly, in order to invoke a pixel shader for each texel in an output cube map, we draw a series of six quadrilaterals, one into each face. The vertices defining these quads contain 3D texture coordinates that correspond to the position of the output texel on the unit cube. Naturally, these quads must be oriented according to the conventions of the API used, such as the Direct3D cube map addressing convention shown in Figure 3.2.1. In the sample application on the companion CD-ROM, the routine FillScreenAlignedQuads() is used to correctly initialize these six quads for cube map processing.

ON THE CD

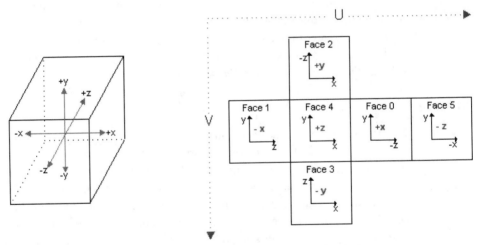

FIGURE 3.2.1   *Direct3D cube map orientation in UV/Render Target space.*

To process a cube map, we merely cycle through the six faces of the output cube map, setting the render target to the face and drawing the appropriate quadrilateral.

Shading

Now that we know how to invoke a pixel shader at each cube map texel, what kind of processing can we do on a cube or sphere? How do we sample input? In this article, we wish to perform a directional blurring operation on an input cube map in order to approximate motion blurred reflections. To achieve this visual effect, we would like to integrate, preferably in high dynamic range space, along some direction of motion projected onto the unit sphere, for every point on the unblurred input texture. Our cube face-aligned quadrilaterals have been initialized so that the interpolated 3D texture coordinate input is equivalent to the location on the unit cube of the texel that is being written to by a given invocation of the pixel shader. We can normalize this 3D vector to obtain as a point on the unit sphere around which we can build a filter kernel to sample the input cube map.

Filter Kernels on a Unit Sphere

There are many ways to build a filter kernel relative to a reference point on a unit sphere. One could pre-generate a set of filter tap offsets relative to the center point, derive the sample locations in the shader or some combination of the two. In any case, sampling from the input cube map is very natural because of the way that cube map sampling hardware is built. That is, the pixel shader does not have to be written to account for messy details such as cube face selection or sample location normalization since the cube map addressing hardware handles these operations automatically [Voorhies94]. Really, all we have to do is compute some vectors as a function of the input vector, use them to sample the input map and combine the resulting samples to get a single final result. In the case of motion blur, we want to sample along an arc on the unit sphere.

Motion Blurring a Cube Map

In Figure 3.2.2, we show a cube map of the tunnel in ATI's demo *Ruby: Dangerous Curves* mapped onto a sphere (using the sphere's normal, not a reflection vector, for illustration). In this case, the object onto which this cube map would be textured is moving quickly down the hallway (roughly part (a) of the Figure) and is in the same frame of reference as the camera (i.e. the camera is chasing the object, as is common in racing games). For illustration, the amount of blur is increased from Figure 3.2.2(a) through Figure 3.2.2(d). You can think of this as increasing the velocity of the object or increasing the exposure time. An interesting note about this filtering operation is that both the magnitude and direction of the blur varies across the sphere. That is, there is very little blur when the sphere's normal aligns with the direction of motion, while blur is at its maximum when the sphere's normal is perpendicular to the direction of motion.

To achieve this effect, we use the cube map processing technique described previously and derive a different filter kernel at every texel in the output map by evenly distributing 11 samples along a line segment that lies in the plane containing both the sphere's normal and the motion vector. The length of the arc is also varied at every texel so that more blur happens perpendicular to the direction of motion, and almost

FIGURE 3.2.2   *Increasing amounts of motion blur in the cube map.*

no blur occurs along the direction of motion. Looking at the pixel shader in Listing 3.2.1, you can see that there is only one `float3` input called up. This value is a point on the unit cube, so we must first normalize it if any of our later dot products are to be meaningful. We then compute a blur magnitude using an arbitrary function of the angle between the motion vector and the current point on the unit sphere which has the property that it is maximal perpendicular to the motion vector and falls off to zero parallel to the motion vector. We next project the motion vector into the tangent plane of the current unit vector to determine the alignment of our arc. We then take 11 samples from the input cube map along a line segment in the tangent plane and equally weight the samples to get our final result.

Listing 3.2.1   Pixel Shader for Motion Blur Technique

```
float4 ps_process_cubemap( float3 up : TEXCOORD0 ) : COLOR0
{
   // Normalize
   float3 vNormal = normalize(up);

   // Magnitude of blur
   float fBlurMagnitude = sqrt(1.0f - abs(dot(g_vMotionVector,
vNormal)));

   // Project motion vector into tangent plane
   float3 vTangent = normalize(g_vMotionVector -
                           dot(g_vMotionVector, vNormal) *
vNormal);

   // Accumulate along motion vector projected into tangent plane
   float4 sum = texCUBE( cSampler, vNormal);
   sum += texCUBE( cSampler, vNormal + vTangent *  1.0f * g_fEpsilon
                * fBlurMagnitude );
   sum += texCUBE( cSampler, vNormal + vTangent *  2.0f * g_fEpsilon
                * fBlurMagnitude );
   sum += texCUBE( cSampler, vNormal + vTangent *  3.0f * g_fEpsilon
                * fBlurMagnitude );
   sum += texCUBE( cSampler, vNormal + vTangent *  4.0f * g_fEpsilon
                * fBlurMagnitude );
   sum += texCUBE( cSampler, vNormal + vTangent *  5.0f * g_fEpsilon
                * fBlurMagnitude );
   sum += texCUBE( cSampler, vNormal + vTangent * -1.0f * g_fEpsilon
                * fBlurMagnitude );
   sum += texCUBE( cSampler, vNormal + vTangent * -2.0f * g_fEpsilon
                * fBlurMagnitude );
   sum += texCUBE( cSampler, vNormal + vTangent * -3.0f * g_fEpsilon
                * fBlurMagnitude );
   sum += texCUBE( cSampler, vNormal + vTangent * -4.0f * g_fEpsilon
                * fBlurMagnitude );
   sum += texCUBE( cSampler, vNormal + vTangent * -5.0f * g_fEpsilon
                * fBlurMagnitude );

   // Normalize and return
   return sum / 11.0f;
}
```

There is no need to renormalize the perturbed vectors, which will not be unit length, since the cube map hardware will still sample in the appropriate direction from the input cube map. Additionally, there is no need to worry about how our filter kernel may span several faces of the input cube map, since the hardware does face selection for us for each tap. It's worth mentioning that this simple filter kernel is meant to be quick to code and easy to explain. It may have some undesirable properties for some applications, such as the fact that the samples aren't evenly spaced on the unit sphere, but rather are spaced in the tangent plane of the center tap. Additionally, the samples are all equally weighted, which may not be desirable for some situations. Both of these properties of this kernel are straightforward to correct, however.

While this motion blur technique is a fairly simple effect targeted at a specific application, it points to the larger idea of using graphics hardware to process cube maps. One could easily imagine using much larger kernels to produce dynamic glossy or even diffuse reflections based upon environment maps. This kind of technique could also potentially be used in a hardware-accelerated offline radiosity solver. Another attractive aspect of this technique is the ability to easily turn the feature on or off in an engine, based on the capabilities or performance of the graphics card used in the system.

Conclusion

Here we have developed a straightforward framework for cube map processing that is applicable when the camera is chasing a reflective object. This basic framework can be used to accelerate other forms of integration on the unit sphere in order to compute glossy or even diffuse reflections. Such as technique was used to compute a dynamic ambient lighting term in NVIDIA's *Mad Mod Mike* demo [NVIDIA05].

As mentioned, the filter kernel used in this chapter is a simple one, which does not evenly distribute its samples on the unit sphere or account for the warping that occurs near the corners of the unit cube. For more precise applications, it may be desirable to do a more even distribution or to account for the warping of the cube map data toward the corners of the unit cube, as is done by ATI's CubeMapGen [Isidoro05].

References

[Greene86] Greene, Ned, "Environment mapping and other applications of world projections," *IEEE Computer Graphics and Applications*, v.6 n.11, p.21-29, November 1986.

[Haeberli90] Haeberli, Paul and Kurt Akeley, "The Accumulation Buffer: Hardware Support for High-Quality Rendering," SIGGRAPH 1990.

[Isidoro05] Isidoro, John R. and Jason L. Mitchell, "Angular Extent Filtering with Edge Fixup for Seamless Cubemap Filtering," SIGGRAPH 2005 Technical Sketch. Los Angeles, August 2005. Available online at *http://www.ati.com/ developer/cubemapgen/*

[Mitchell02] Mitchell, Jason L. "Image Processing with Direct3D Pixel Shaders" in *ShaderX: Vertex and Pixel Shaders Tips and Tricks*, Wolfgang Engel editor, Wordware, May 2002.

[NVIDIA05] "GPU Programming Exposed: The Naked Truth Behind NVIDIA's Demos." Available online at *http://download.nvidia.com/developer/presentations/ 2005/SIGGRAPH/Truth_About_NVIDIA_Demos.pdf*

[Voorhies94] Voorhies, Douglas and James Foran, "Reflection Vector Shading Hardware," SIGGRAPH 1994.

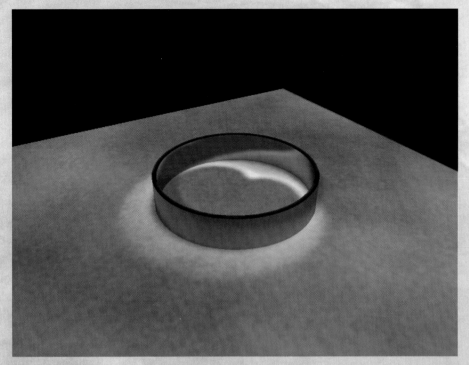

COLOR PLATE 1   *Heart-shaped caustics using real-time rendering technique.*

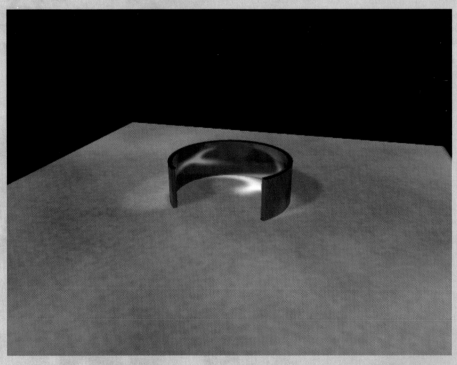

COLOR PLATE 2   *Another view of heart-shaped caustics using real-time rendering technique.*

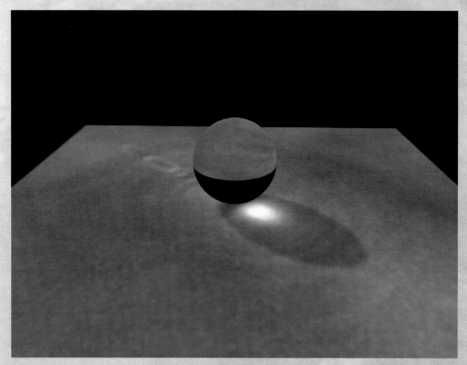

COLOR PLATE 3 *Application of real-time caustics rendering demo.*

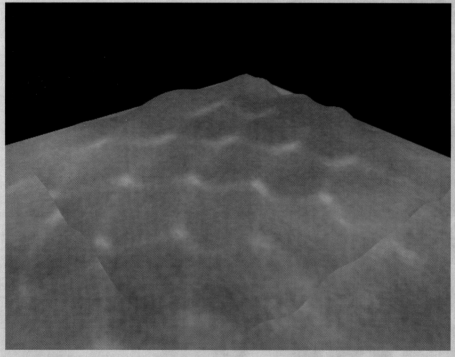

COLOR PLATE 4 *Image from real-time caustics rendering demo.*

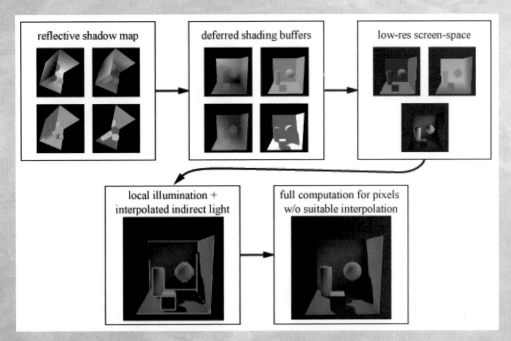

COLOR PLATE 5 *Computing indirect per-pixel illumination.*

COLOR PLATE 6 *Scene from* Spellforce 2 *demonstrating the technique from article 4.2.*

COLOR PLATE 7 *Real-time soft shadows using the PDSM technique.*

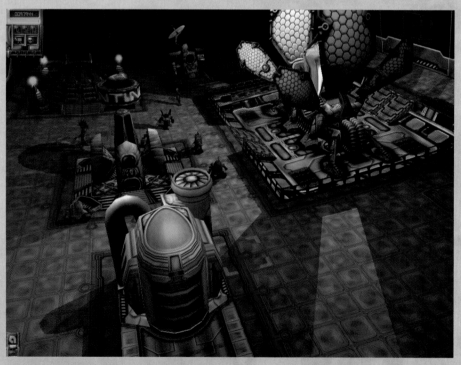

COLOR PLATE 8 *Scene from* Startopia *demo showing shadow-buffer partitioning.*

COLOR PLATE 9   *Scene from* Startopia *demo showing shadow-buffer partitioning.*

COLOR PLATE 10   *Winter wonderland effects.*

COLOR PLATE 11 *Rendered snow cover.*

COLOR PLATE 12 *Shallow water animation using the real-time technique.*

COLOR PLATE 13   *Terrain rendered with cached procedural texture technique.*

COLOR PLATE 14   *Diffuse, specular, and emissive maps for the Earth from article 8.1.*

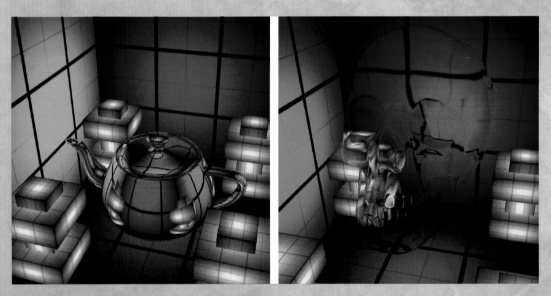

3.3

Simulating the Visual Effects of a Video Recording System

Joachim Diepstraten

Introduction

In 1972, Philips introduced a machine that changed the world significantly, the home videocassette recorder (VCR). More than 30 years later, the well-known technique of recording analog video and audio signals for playback later is on the brink of extinction. Digital recording and playback devices are driving the VCR's market share down. In a decade or more, VCRs might be long forgotten. On the one hand, it is likely that no one will really miss the analog video recording technology because of its degrading image quality compared to its source material. On the other hand, previous efforts like [DigiEffects05] have been spent on image filtering and image-manipulation filters to let images or video sequences appear as they were projected by an old film projector—a technique that no longer exists. Adding brownish or black-and-white filters and film grain to a picture gives it a more old-fashioned, charming look.

Videocassette recorders also have certain characteristics making them unique to other playback media. These occur either at normal playback or while fast–forwarding the tape or rewinding it during playback. In this article, some of these characteristics are analyzed, and a real-time image-filtering algorithm is developed by using programmable graphics hardware to reproduce those effects. The observations described in this article relate only to VHS (video home system), which still is the most common system on the market.

Characteristics of a VHS Video Recording System

During the normal playback of a previously recorded image on a VHS VCR the following properties can be observed. The most unique is loss of resolution. Resolution relates to the number of distinguishable adjacent vertical picture lines. Increased resolution means enhances detail, and results in brighter, clearer images, and smooth image fields. A VHS recorder has only 240 lines compared to 300 lines of a conventional TV signal. This relates to the limited recording and playback frequency of a standard VHS VCR. It allows only 3.2 MHz for audio, synchronization, luminance, and chromaticity signal; a TV set, in contrast, normally has 7 MHz, and a TV broadcast usually uses approximately 5 MHz for the same amount of information.

Another characteristic that can be observed is picture noise. Playbacks from VCRs seldom produce crystal-clear pictures; instead, the images tend to have noisy areas. This noise is an artifact related to the magnetic storage medium. The quality of the videotape microstructure and the recording/playback heads of the VCR have the biggest influence on this value. Using playback during fast-forwarding or rewinding of the tape introduces additional artifacts, because the VCR has to keep the image synchronization stable. For a great part of the picture this can be ensured, leading to a relatively stable image while spinning. But in certain image regions the synchronization is lost. These regions mostly consist of horizontal scanlines shifting between frames, and mixtures of chromaticity between frames. It is likely that the position, number, and size of these regions are related to differences found in video heads. Surprisingly, the overall position of a region is quite stable, but very often it differs between forward and backward spinning. The number and position of unstable regions can differ between different VCR models as well.

When pausing the VCR—especially those models that do not have a digital correction feature built in—it often is unable to produce a fully still image. Often, the video head is positioned between the two potential frames, which causes a visual image that appears to slightly jump back and forth between the two frames.

Implementation

As with most image-filtering implementations using the GPU, the input geometry is simply a textured screen-filled quad. This texture can either come from a series of bitmap images loaded from the hard drive or an already rendered scene. The loss of lines or resolution can be simulated in a straightforward way—we apply a lower resolution mipmap level from the mipmap chain of the source textures. If we are lacking the mip chain for the source images, it can generated on the fly with the `Direct3D StretchRect()` functionality (part of the Direct3D API).

The image noise characteristics seen when playing back a recorded image can be simulated by adding random values to each texel that is read from the input texture. These random values can be precomputed and stored in an arbitrary texture. Since VCRs do not operate in RGB color space as computer graphics devices do, it is recommended for authenticity to convert the incoming colors from the source texture to the corresponding color space. For PAL devices, that would be YUV; for NTSC devices it is YIC. This color space transformation could be done by using the `D3DXLoadSurfaceFromSurface` routine (found in the Direct3D Extension library, it is a wrapper around different surface-to-surface copy routines). Select either YUY2 or UYVY as the destination surface format, and the method converts the source texture accordingly. The downside of this approach is the slowness of this method's execution since it runs on the CPU and also requires reading the texture data back into system memory. This can cause a problem if we want to apply this technique for previously rendered scenes on the fly. Instead, you can use a pixel shader to do the conversion, add the noise, and convert back the result to RGB space before outputting the final pixel color. RGB-to-YUV conversion is a basic operation and can be expressed through this formula:

$$Y = 0.299*R + 0.587*G + 0.114*B$$
$$U = (Y - B)*0.565$$
$$U = (Y - R)*0.713$$

An implementation in a pixel shader is quite efficient. The final pixel shader for simulating VCR playback looks like this:

```
ps.2.0
dcl t0
dcl_2d s0
dcl_2d s1
def c5, 0.299, 0.587, 0.114, 0.0
def c6, 0.0, 0.565, 0.713, 0.0
def c7, 1.403, 0.344, 0.714, 1.770
texld r1, t0,s0
// convert to YUV
dp3 r2, r1, c5
sub r2.y, r1.z, r2.x
sub r2.z, r1.x, r2.x
mul r2.yz, r2, c6
// add well-known yittering to YUV
texld r4, t0, s1 // load white noise
mul r4, r4, c29.x // multiply by noise scale factor
add r2, r2, r4 // add white noise to YUV signal

// convert back to RGB
mad r1.x, r2.z, c7.x, r2.x
mad r1.y, r2.y, -c7.y, r2.x
mad r1.y, r2.z, -c7.z, r1.y
mad r1.z, r2.y, c7.w, r2.x
mov oC0, r1
```

Figure 3.3.1 compares the difference between adding noise to an RGB image and noise to a previously converted YUV image.

FIGURE 3.3.1   *Comparison between adding noise to an RGB image (left) and noise to an RGB-to-YUV-converted image that is converted back to RGB (right).*

While the tape is fast-forwarded or rewound during playback additional distortions as previously mentioned come into effect. These are the loss of chromaticity in certain regions of the image, additional noise patterns, and scanline distortions. All of these "defect" areas tend to jump or flicker slightly over time. This jumping can easily be emulated by storing the areas that should be affected in a binary format texture. The fragment regions that should be influenced by the distortion effects are marked with a value that otherwise is set to zero. Inside the pixel shader, the marked area texture is loaded twice with different offsets in the v coordinate of the original texture coordinates of the quad. These offsets can be stored in pixel-shader constants. Values derived from the sinus function are a good source for using as an offset. For the final marking area the minimum of the two values loaded from the texture is taken.

A second texture contains the scanline shifting values for the distortion. In this texture, the magnitude of the shifting is stored, because while winding it is very unlikely that all scanlines are shifted by the same magnitude. In addition, an offset to the v texture coordinate of the quad is added, which may cause the distortion lines to appear to be jumping. To test if a distortion line is outside of the previous marking area, multiply the value by the previously determined area mark value. If it is not outside, the loaded value from this texture is used to add an offset to the u texture coordinate of the quad. Afterward, this new texture coordinate is used to look up the actual color value in the input source texture. But be careful, because the texture coordinate of this texture could actually be greater (less) than one (zero), and that would mean that it should load a part of the next (previous) frame. In an accurate simulation of the effect, the following operation should be done: if the u texture coordinate is greater than one (less than zero) it is subtracted (added) by one, and a texel from the next (previous) frame is loaded, which has been assigned to an additional sampler.

The only effect missing is the chromaticity change. Again, this can be stored in a third texture. Sometimes, there also tend to be a few spots that are extremely bright while winding the tape and they seem to wander from left to right or right to left depending on the winding direction. These spots can also be added in the same texture and the wandering is simulated by adding an offset to the v texture coordinate to its u coordinate. Unfortunately, some graphics cards do not seem to support the wrapping texture address mode for nonpower of two textures; therefore, this wrapping has to be done in the pixel shader itself. The final pixel-shader version 2.0 codes for fast-forward and backward spinning can be found as supplementary material on the companion CD-ROM. The final results look like Figure 3.3.2.

ON THE CD

When pausing the playback of a VCR, often the video heads do not pause exactly at one frame but between two frames. Sometimes, the image jumps between these two images or results in some sort of motion-blurred version between the two frames.

This effect is not difficult to simulate, and it is basically an extension to the normal playback mode. Instead of loading only the current frame, the next frame is loaded as well. Both frames are weighted by a factor that is set as a shader constant and added together before transforming to YUV and adding the picture noise. Figure 3.3.3 demonstrates the received effect.

FIGURE 3.3.2 *Example image of a frame during playback while backward winding.*

FIGURE 3.3.3 *Example image of a frame during pause playback.*

Conclusion

This article described how to implement some of the effects seen with the VCR playback using the programmable hardware. These effects were just a small subset of the variety of all possible image effects due to VCR playback. Some improvements can be made for the described effects as well. For example, picture degrading after making several generation of copies has not been studied, as well as frame dropouts that sometimes occur when there is a fast luminance change between two frames and certain other effects that appear in NTSC or PAL recordings. Additionally, the image noise could be emulated more accurately by studying the signal noise in real VCR playbacks.

References

[DigiEffects05], DigiEffects Euphoria Photoshop PlugIn including aged filmfilter. Available online at *http://www.digieffects.com/frames/euphoria/fx_main.html*, June 12, 2005.

SHADOWS

(a)

(b)

(c)

(d)

Introduction

Eric Haines

Creating shadows at interactive rates continues to be an active area of exploration. In a few decades, we all may simply turn on our RPUs (ray-tracing processing units) and shoot a million shadow rays per pixel, and so perfectly solve the problem. In the meantime, the number of algorithms increases, as each approach has trade-offs among factors such as speed, quality, generality, precomputation time, scalability, resource allocation, and programming effort. One technique casts soft shadows, another performs self-shadowing, and a third uses new GPU capabilities for additional speed and quality. Ultimately it is the designer who must decide what method best fits the minimum hardware requirements, scheduling constraints, and the application's data and presentation style. This section offers a few new tools for improving how shadows are generated and displayed.

In "Soft Projected Shadows," Aras Pranckevičius improves upon a method presented in *ShaderX³* by Jason Mitchell. Drop shadows are generated with penumbrae that properly increase with the distance from the occluding object. This process is done rapidly by using some blurring filters on the occluder distance texture, and then performing width-varying stochastic sampling of the hard-edged drop shadow to create the soft shadow texture. This technique improves on Mitchell's idea in that it is applicable to a wider range of occluding objects than just upright humanoid characters. Christian Schüler's article, "Eliminate Surface Acne with Gradient Shadow Mapping," discusses a problem common to most users of shadow depth-mapping algorithms: self-shadowing. He presents the problem, surveys popular solutions, and then gives a number of relatively easy-to-implement extensions that avoid self-shadowing and floating problems in nearly every case. His illustrations are noteworthy, as they make the problem and the effect of various solutions extremely clear. (Incidentally, my claim to fame is that I coined the phrase "surface acne" around 1988. An awful term, but it stuck.)

In "Real-Time Soft Shadows Using the PDSM Technique," Jean-Francois St. Amour et al. give implementation details for their algorithm for computing the effect of true area lights. The effect of an area light and occluders can be visualized as a set of radiance values in 3D space. This space can be filled with a set of rays from the center of the light, just as a traditional shadow depth buffer works. However, instead of a single occluder distance, along each ray is a function that decreases or increases in its overall radiance value. Because shadows tend to sweep out coherent volumes of space, the set of samples along each ray form a function with distance along the ray that can usually be compressed to just a few values. Because of this simplicity, evaluation of each function can be performed by the GPU at interactive rates. This technique yields highly realistic soft shadows for a static set of occluders and lights at a cost not considerably higher than a shadow depth map. In addition, volumetric fog effects can be produced.

Michael Wimmer and Daniel Scherzer give detailed instructions on how to compute a modified shadow depth buffer projection in "Robust Shadow Mapping with Light-Space Perspective Shadow Maps." This new algorithm optimizes the projection matrix for directional and point lights, with the goal of balancing the shadow quality for all objects in the camera's view frustum. Robust methods for dealing with various situations and potential problems are presented throughout. While the approach appears somewhat involved, its advantage is clear: in many situations this algorithm can improve shadow depth mapping at essentially no cost by simply using a different projection matrix.

Finally, Tom Forsyth ends this section with "Making Shadowbuffers Robust Using Multiple Dynamic Frustums." While Wimmer and Scherzer's technique can improve shadows in some situations, there are times when it can fail to help. Forsyth gives a simple way of attacking the problem: to keep quality high for all objects receiving shadows, create a shadow buffer at the necessary resolution for each object. Now each shadow buffer is guaranteed to have sufficient resolution to capture each shadow. Read his article for many different ways to optimize and improve on this clever idea.

4.1

Soft Projected Shadows

Aras Pranckevičius

Introduction

This article describes a method for simulating a natural shadow penumbra for grayscale projected shadow textures. The use of simple projected shadows is quite common in games that do not require a sophisticated shadowing solution such as a shadow depth map. However, standard projected shadows often result in blocky shadow edges. This problem can be fixed with higher resolution textures, but the shadow boundary still remains hard. Simply blurring the shadow texture does not produce a good-looking penumbra region, as the width of the penumbra should depend on the distance between the shadow caster and receiver.

The method presented here treats shadow receivers as nearly planar surfaces, so distances between casters and receivers can be evaluated efficiently. The penumbra region is computed by applying several smoothing filters to the shadow map. All computations are performed entirely in image space and map well to Pixel Shader 2.0 hardware.

Previous Work

A simple algorithm for soft projected shadows was presented by Jason Mitchell [Mitchell04]: render the character model into a texture, and then use a variable-size filter with a Poisson disk sampling pattern to blur this texture. The size of the blurring kernel is larger at the top of the texture and gradually smaller toward the bottom. The character is rendered in such a way that the feet, which are near the ground, appear at the bottom of the shadow texture, while the head, which is farther from the ground, appears near the top.

General-purpose soft shadow-mapping algorithms have recently been introduced [Valient04, deBoer04]. While they produce good results and have all associated shadow-mapping features (such as self-shadowing), their computational cost is high.

Our algorithm builds upon Mitchell's method and improves it in several ways. It allows rendering multiple shadow casters into a single shadow texture and uses an improved shadow-blurring metric. It can also be viewed as a simplification of general-purpose soft shadow-mapping algorithms: By not allowing self-shadowing, we can replace shadow map dilation operations with efficient separable blurring. In existing algorithms, dilation is required to create outer shadow penumbra regions; that is, penumbrae that are outside the hard shadow boundary. As shadow casters in the shadow texture occupy only the hard shadow portion, dilation effectively "spreads out" caster information. Additionally, our algorithm treats shadow receivers as planar objects, allowing efficient computation of distances to them.

The Algorithm

First, the shadow casters are rendered into a texture with a vertex shader that evaluates the distance from caster to receiver. This distance is stored in a single-channel texture. The shader also calculates the resulting intensity of the light. This is usually zero (that is, full shadowing), although it may be modified according to distance or caster translucency for special effects. This intensity is stored in another single-channel texture. For practical convenience and speed, these two notionally separate textures are actually stored in two channels of a single RGB texture.

Next, the distance texture is uniformly blurred with a separable Gaussian filter, creating outer penumbra regions. A more physically correct method would be to apply a dilation filter to the texture; in fact, some soft shadow depth mapping algorithms actually do this [Valient04, deBoer 04]. However, dilation would require many texture-processing passes (in existing implementations, one pass for each one-texel dilation), whereas a separable Gaussian requires just two passes for even large filter radii.

The last step samples the light intensity texture using a Poisson disk filter and uses the blurred distance channel to vary the filter radius. This way, the filter samples over a larger area as the distance from shadow caster to receiver increases. The resulting shadow texture can be projected onto receivers.

The following sections describe each step of the algorithm in detail.

Rendering the Shadow Texture

One renderable texture and associated depth buffer is required for rendering. The texture should contain at least two color channels with 8-bit precision each (for example, A8R8G8B8 format is acceptable). Here, the R and G channels are used and are cleared to 0 and 1, respectively, while the B and A channels are unused. Reversing the depth compare mode (setting it to "greater") and clearing the depth buffer to zero often produces better results, as doing so ensures that the surfaces that are nearest to the receiver are drawn to the shadow texture (standard depth compare mode would draw surfaces that are nearest to the light).

Shadow casters are rendered to the shadow texture using a vertex shader that outputs the following vertex colors (see Figure 4.1.1):

- R is the approximate distance to the shadow receiver, scaled into the range 0..1. Later, the distance will control the size of the blurring filter, so zeros in this channel will result in sharp shadows, and ones will result in the widest possible penumbra. This approximate distance can be efficiently evaluated when the shadow receiver is a nearly planar surface (for example, by taking the difference between receiver altitude and the caster's vertex altitude). The distance channel is initially cleared to zero to prevent unshadowed regions from using large blurring filters and possibly fetching the false shadow texels. Clearing the distance to zero ensures that unshadowed regions will use the minimal filter size.

- G contains the light intensity; it will be sampled by a spatially varying blur filter. This intensity is usually set to full shadowing (zero) or a small ambient value. It can also be used for special effects (for example, less severe shadows from translucent objects) or can depend on the red channel, so that shadows farther away from the receiver will contain both larger penumbrae and a lighter color, as shown here. Note that making shadows "fade out" in this way only works in some cases and may produce shadow artifacts; for example, if the shadows of two distant occluders overlap.

FIGURE 4.1.1 *Individual channels (RG) of the shadow texture—distance to receiver in the R channel on the left, light intensity in the G channel on the right.*

The vertex shader for rendering casters is as follows (HLSL, vs_1_1 profile):

```
float evalDistance( float3 p ) {
    // simplest case: receiver is a ground plane at y=0
    // just use vertex y value as distance
    return p.y;
}

SPosCol vsMain11( SPos i ) {
    // assume vertices arrive in world space
    SPosCol o;
    o.pos = mul( i.pos, mViewProj );

    // evaluate distance from vertex to receiver
    float dist = evalDistance( i.pos );
```

```
// output colors
o.color.ba = 0; // unused
o.color.r = dist * 0.25; // largest penumbra at 4 units
o.color.g = dist * 0.15; // light intensity
return o;
}
```

The distance to the shadow receiver (the `evalDistance` function in the preceding example) could be more complex. For example, if the terrain receives shadows, the terrain altitude under characters can be passed as a per-instance value.

The pixel shader just passes through the interpolated vertex color.

Shadow Texture Preprocessing

The distance rendered into the R channel of the shadow texture could be used directly to scale the blurring filter, but doing so does not produce good results (see Figure 4.1.2). The problem is that the rendered distance does not provide enough information for the outer penumbra regions; they are considered fully lit as far as the algorithm is concerned. Therefore, a preprocessing step is performed where the distance channel is "spread out" to cover the outer penumbra regions.

FIGURE 4.1.2   *Soft shadows from using the distance directly (left) versus using a spread-out distance (right).*

The correct way to do so would be to repeatedly apply a dilation filter. The number of passes would depend on the largest allowed penumbra radius in texels (usually 10–20). However, we can get good-looking penumbrae by replacing dilation with a simple uniform blurring. Blurring the distance channel spreads it out a bit, so outer penumbra regions obtain similar distance values as inner penumbra regions (see Figure 4.1.3).

A separable Gaussian filter can be used to efficiently blur the shadow texture [Riguer03]. One additional render target is required for intermediate results and the algorithm proceeds as follows:

1. Horizontally blur the R (distance) channel of the shadow texture and output the results into the intermediate texture. Output original (not blurred) values for other color channels.
2. Vertically blur the R channel of the intermediate texture and output the results into the original shadow texture. Again, output the original values for the other three color channels.

FIGURE 4.1.3 *Uniformly blurred distance channel.*

Computing the Soft Shadow Texture

After rendering and preprocessing the shadow texture, it is filtered using a spatially varying filter kernel. We chose to use a Poisson disk filter kernel, a low-pass filter that can shrink and grow based on some criteria. In our case, the criterion will be the blurred distance to shadow receiver.

In our implementation, the filter takes 13 texture samples within a circular area whose radius depends on the blurred distance to the shadow receiver (see Figure 4.1.4). Where the shadow caster and receiver are close together, the filter will sample over a small area, resulting in sharp shadows. As the distance increases, the filter samples over a larger area, resulting in more blurred shadows.

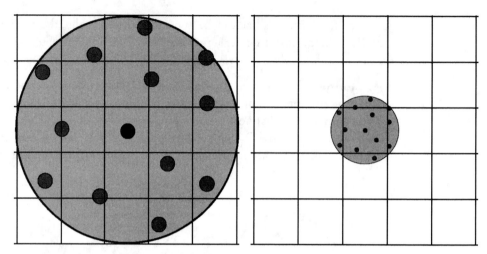

FIGURE 4.1.4   *13-tap Poisson disk filter kernel.*

This spatially varying filter is implemented with the following pixel shader (HLSL, ps_2_0 profile):

```
#define NUM_TAPS 12
half2 filterTaps[NUM_TAPS] = {
    {-0.326212f, -0.405805f},
    {-0.840144f, -0.073580f},
    {-0.695914f,  0.457137f},
    {-0.203345f,  0.620716f},
    { 0.962340f, -0.194983f},
    { 0.473434f, -0.480026f},
    { 0.519456f,  0.767022f},
    { 0.185461f, -0.893124f},
    { 0.507431f,  0.064425f},
    { 0.896420f,  0.412458f},
    {-0.321940f, -0.932615f},
    {-0.791559f, -0.597705f}
};

half4 psMain20( float2 tc0 : TEXCOORD0 ) : COLOR
{
    // sample shadow texture
    half4 col = tex2D( smpBase, tc0 );

    // filter size in texels based on red channel
    const float MAX_PENUMBRA_R = 12.0;
    half scaling = col.r + 0.02;
    half scale = MAX_PENUMBRA_R/SHADOW_MAP_SIZE * scaling;

    // accumulate light intensity (green channel)
    half intensitySum = col.g;
    for( int k = 0; k < NUM_TAPS; ++k ) {
```

```
        float2 tapCoord = tc0 + filterTaps[k] * scale;
        intensitySum += tex2D( smpBase, tapCoord ).g;
    }

    // return averaged light intensity
    return intensitySum / (NUM_TAPS+1);
}
```

The code contains an array of 2D offsets from the center of the filter kernel. These offsets are scaled to vary filter size and added to interpolated texture coordinates. The loop executes for all 13 samples, accumulating scalar light intensity into `intensitySum`. Finally, the averaged intensity is returned.

The filter size is biased (in this shader, by adding 0.02)—this makes shadows just a bit softer and helps to hide shadow map pixellation in hard shadow areas. The maximum penumbra radius is 12 texels in this shader (so the Poisson filter can touch a 24-texel width circle). Recall that a 25-texel blur was used during a preprocessing step; it is this preprocess blur that limits the maximum penumbra size. In other words, the Poisson filter width should not exceed the Gaussian filter width.

The resulting shadow texture can be projected onto shadow receivers and so modulate the lighting using the values from the texture.

Results

Figure 4.1.5 shows this technique in action. The image on the left shows traditional projected shadow textures; the image on the right shows the same scene with soft projected shadows. Notice that the shadow of the character is sharper near the point where the character's feet touch the ground and blurrier as the distance from the ground increases.

FIGURE 4.1.5   *Left: standard projected shadow textures; right: soft projected shadow textures.*

Figure 4.1.6 shows multiple shadow casters using a single shadow texture. Figure 4.1.7 compares Mitchell's algorithm [Mitchell04] (left) with our algorithm (right). Mitchell's algorithm uses the v texture coordinate of the shadow texture as the blurring metric, hence shadows are hard on the left side and soft on the right side of the image. Our algorithm uses approximate distance to the planar receiver as the blurring metric so the resulting penumbrae are more realistic. A more correct approach to calculate penumbra size would involve both the distance from the caster to receiver and the distance from the light to the caster; this could be calculated in the vertex shader as well.

FIGURE 4.1.6   *Multiple shadow casters using a single shadow texture.*

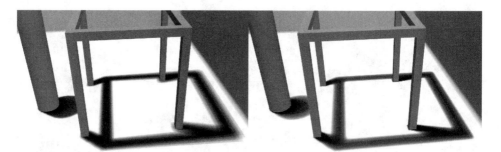

FIGURE 4.1.7   *Left: Mitchell's algorithm; right: our algorithm.*

Scenes in the figures used a 256 × 256 (see Figure 4.1.5) and 1024 × 1024 (see Figures 4.1.6 and 4.1.7) shadow map resolution, a 25-texel width separable Gaussian filter, and a 13-tap Poisson filter. Soft shadow texture computation (that is, overhead, compared to traditional projected shadows) takes just under 1 millisecond on a GeForce 6800GT when using a 256 × 256 shadow texture.

Artifacts and Limitations

Although our algorithm produces aesthetically pleasing results in most cases, it can also produce artifacts in the penumbra regions (see Figure 4.1.8). Because the Poisson disk filter used takes only a finite number of samples (13 in our implementation), sampling artifacts are possible and the resulting light intensity can contain only a finite number of discrete values. This explains the banding visible in Figure 4.1.8. However, in typical game situations this artifact can be masked by the use of high-frequency diffuse or bump map textures.

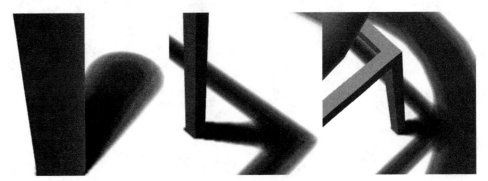

FIGURE 4.1.8 *Possible artifacts: banding in penumbrae (left), stochastic sampling artifacts where penumbrae overlap (middle and right).*

Sample Application

ON THE CD

The sample Xplodar on the companion CD-ROM illustrates soft projected shadows technique. In particular, D3DX effect files caster.fx, filterGaussX.fx, filterGaussY.fx, and filterPoisson.fx contain the shaders used for rendering soft shadows. The same technique is also used in a demoscene application called *in.out.side: the shell*. The demo can be found on the companion CD-ROM or downloaded from its Web page: *http://www.nesnausk.org/inoutside*.

References

[deBoer04] de Boer, Willem H., "Smooth Penumbra Transitions with Shadow Maps," submitted to Journal of Graphics Tools, 2004. Available online at *http://whdeboer. com/papers/smooth_penumbra_trans.pdf*.

[Mitchell04] Mitchell, Jason L., "Poisson Shadow Blur," *ShaderX³*, edited by Wolfgang Engel, Charles River Media, 2004: pp. 403–409.

[Riguer03] Riguer, Guennadi, Natalya Tatarchuk, and John Isidoro, "Real-Time Depth of Field Simulation," *ShaderX²*, edited by Wolfgang Engel, Wordware, 2003: pp. 529–556.

[Valient04] Valient, Michal, and Willem H., de Boer, "Fractional-Disk Soft Shadows," *ShaderX³*, edited by Wolfgang Engel, Charles River Media, 2004: pp. 411–424.

4.2

Eliminating Surface Acne with Gradient Shadow Mapping

Christian Schüler

Introduction

Since its original inception in 1978 [Williams78], shadow mapping has suffered from two major drawbacks, *aliasing* and *surface acne*. Aliasing is a general sampling problem and must be dealt with by better sampling or higher order filtering. "Surface acne" is the nickname for the false self-shadowing artifacts on surfaces that should be lit, and exists independently of resolution or sample precision. This article investigates the surface acne phenomenon and develops techniques to combat the effect.

The Phenomenon of Surface Acne

Figure 4.2.1 shows a scene rendered using the most naïve shadow-mapping algorithm. In the first pass, a view of the scene from the perspective of the light is rendered into a depth map, giving depth values sampled at discrete points. In the second pass, the camera view of the scene is rendered, and each pixel is compared with the nearest corresponding sample from the depth map. If the depth of the pixel is greater than that of the sample, the pixel is considered in shadow.

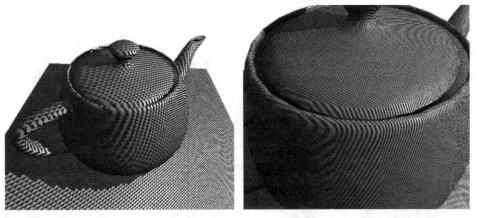

FIGURE 4.2.1 *False shadowing (surface acne) with different depth map resolutions.*

The results show that 50% of the surface appears to be covered with false shadows, scattered around as bands or triangles. This is called "surface acne." Increasing the resolution of the depth map (in the right picture of Figure 4.2.1) doesn't seem to help; again, 50% of the surface is covered with false shadows, albeit smaller in structure.

The reason behind these artifacts becomes clear when looking at Figure 4.2.2. The depth map contains a sampled representation of the closest surfaces facing the light, but due to the sampled nature, it is stair-stepped. The continuous surface is then compared against the sampled surface. If the point in question happens to be at a sample center, the depths will be equal (we assume "infinite" precision). Otherwise, there is a 50% chance that a random point on the original surface is behind the sampled surface, which gives rise to false shadowing.

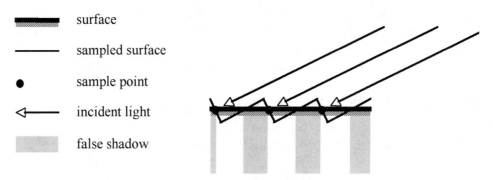

FIGURE 4.2.2   *Surface and sampled surface in comparison. The sample points are taken at the centers of depth map pixels.*

It is worth pointing out that surface acne is not a problem of limited precision, contrary to common belief.

Depth Bias to the Rescue

Numerous approaches have been published that try to tackle the surface acne problem. Originally, Williams [Williams78] introduced a constant *depth bias*, which is added to the samples before they are compared with the true surface, thus moving them away from the light source. This has the effect that the portion that is "popping out" becomes smaller as the depth bias increases. See the left picture in Figure 4.2.3 where a moderate amount of bias has been applied, which is clearly insufficient for high angles of incidence. With increasing bias, eventually the sampled surface can be moved completely behind the true surface (Figure 4.2.3, middle), but this creates a new problem—the false nonshadowing of geometry at the backside of a shadow caster. See the right picture in Figure 4.2.3, where the plane has been moved so that it slices through the teapot, but the pot handle seems to float above the plane due to the large gap caused by the depth bias.

FIGURE 4.2.3 *Low constant depth bias (left); high constant depth bias and gaps caused by a high depth bias (right).*

Despite its limitations, setting a constant depth bias is the most commonly used algorithm. It is a classic "tweak" solution, in the sense that trade-offs must be made and no ideal value really exists.

It is worth noting some of the other approaches that have been proposed to improve the situation. For example, if a scene consists of closed objects with a minimum thickness, it is possible to render back faces into the depth map [Wang94] or the average depth of the front and the back faces [Woo92]. Since the artifacts now occur in the unlit part of the scene, they cannot be seen. However, this type of approach still fails for thin objects or two-sided polygons.

Another way is known as the *ID-buffer*, which instead of numerical depth values, stores object names (or polygon names) [Hourcade85]. Depth comparison is then replaced by name comparison, on the grounds that since the map contains all objects closest to the light, any different object at the same sample position must be in shadow. This approach certainly avoids numerical problems, but at the same time potentially introduces surface acne at object ID boundaries.

Depth Gradient

As the previous section has shown, to avoid false shadows the bias must shift the sampled surface far enough so none of it appears above the true surface (see Figure 4.2.4). In case of a planar surface, this can be accomplished with a single constant bias, but obviously this is not the case for a curved surface. Higher biases are needed for increasing angles of incidence.

We define the term *depth gradient* as the difference between neighboring samples in the depth map, as shown in Figure 4.2.4. The depth gradient is proportional to the tangent of the angle of incidence and can directly be used to scale the bias—a concept that is already known as "slope scale bias" for offsetting co-planar polygons in rendering. Figure 4.2.5 illustrates the idea further as it shows the difference between a surface with constant offset and one with a gradient-scaled offset over the full course of a hemisphere. While the former has the problem of false shadows at grazing angles, the latter is in danger of pushing the offset beyond all limits if the gradient is allowed to grow unbounded. Clamping the gradient to some maximum value is therefore a good idea.

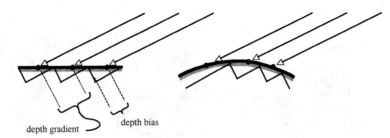

FIGURE 4.2.4   *Depth gradient and bias over a planar surface and a curved surface.*

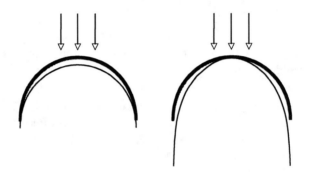

FIGURE 4.2.5   *A surface with constant offset (left) versus gradient-scaled offset (right).*

This idea of a slope-scaled offset for shadow mapping is briefly touched on by Kozlov [Kozlov04], where the author proposes the hardware polygon offset feature in combination with hardware depth buffers to apply the bias while rendering into the depth map. When using shaders with floating point maps, we have two possibilities to compute the depth gradient. On Shader 2.0 hardware, we would need to estimate the gradient on the fly in the second pass (when reading the shadow buffer), by taking the difference of neighboring samples. On Shader 3.0 hardware, we can use shader derivatives in the first pass (when writing the shadow buffer) to ask for the gradient of rendered depth value, and store it in a second channel of the depth map.

Figure 4.2.6 has a grayscale image of gradient values computed in a 2.0 shader. They were computed as the maximum of the horizontal and vertical differences from neighboring samples of the depth map. You can observe that the highest values (white) make up a silhouette with respect to the light source. When this gradient is used to scale the depth bias, the shadowed surfaces already become much less prone to artifacts and "gaps" (Figure 4.2.6, right). A very small constant has been added on top of the gradient-scaled bias so that an offset is maintained even when the gradient becomes zero.

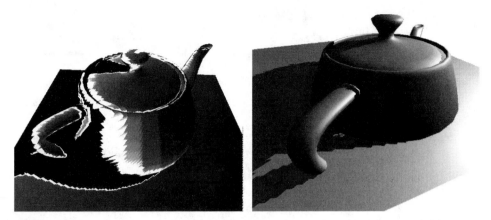

FIGURE 4.2.6   *Depth gradient visualized (left) and a scene with gradient-scaled bias (right).*

A more thorough investigation reveals that some problematic cases remain, mostly because the gradient becomes very large at grazing angles. Clamping the gradient helps this, but clamping too heavily defeats the purpose of gradient scaling, making surface acne reappear.

To improve the quality further we need to employ techniques that allow for a reduced bias at equally perceived quality. Two such techniques are described in the following sections.

Depth Comparison as a Fuzzy Function

With sufficient distance between the occluder and the rendered surface, the decision "to shadow" or "not to shadow" can be seen as binary. However, close to the surface, within one or two multiples of the gradient distance, there is not enough information to justify a yes-or-no decision. Looking again at Figure 4.2.1, every pixel where the sampled surface pops out of the true surface becomes a fully shadowed region, no matter if the sampled surface leaked out only a "little bit." One can imagine that it would be advantageous to have a fuzzy depth comparison instead of a hard-edged one.

We replace the depth comparison with a light visibility function $f(\Delta z)$ that returns 0 for shadowed, 1 for lit, and where $\Delta z = z_s - z$ is the difference between the depth of the sampled surface z_s and the true surface z. Fig 4.2.7 shows different kinds of such visibility functions. The function shown in Figure 4.2.7(A) corresponds to the case of Figure 4.2.1—an unbiased, hard-edged depth comparison. The function shown in Figure 4.2.7(B) corresponds to a fuzzy depth comparison that returns a probability inside an uncertainty region. At the far end of the region, the probability of seeing the light is low, while at the near end, the probability of seeing the light is high.

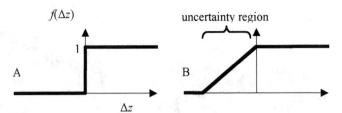

FIGURE 4.2.7   *Light visibility as a function of depth. A: unbiased depth comparison. B: Fuzzy depth comparison.*

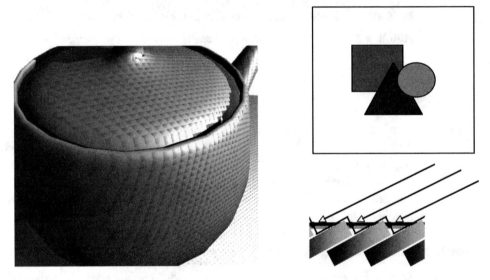

FIGURE 4.2.8   *The fuzzy depth comparison in action. No depth bias is used, but a fuzzy width two times the local gradient.*

The overall effect of a fuzzy depth comparison is more graceful behavior in case of self-shadowing artifacts. It is not by itself sufficient to eliminate surface acne, but in combination with biasing it allows for more aggressive reduction of the depth bias without totally disrupting the image in case of an occasional failure. Compare Figure 4.2.8 to Figure 4.2.1, which is identical to Figure 4.2.8 except the addition of a fuzzy depth comparison. Without any form of depth bias, the self-shadowing artifacts are still there, but much less pronounced.

Going to Interpolated Depth

Traditionally, depth maps have not been interpolated. As long as the depth comparison is discrete and not quantitative, this is the correct thing to do. An interpolated depth is only meaningful over a continuous surface, not across discontinuities like an object boundary.

Nevertheless, in the course of this article we have now introduced two functions that are linear in the depth value, the gradient and the visibility function. So far, both have been computed from taking point samples from the depth map, which is not optimal. Looking at the schematic provided with Figure 4.2.8, you can see how a box-shaped fuzzy region spans underneath each depth sample. One can imagine that a significant increase in quality could be obtained by making the fuzzy region run parallel to the true surface.

A little analysis will discover what we have to expect at discontinuities if we switch to interpolated depth.

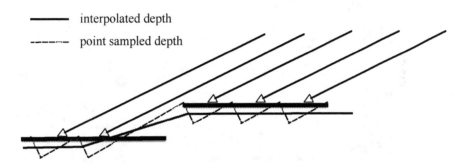

FIGURE 4.2.9 *Interpolated depth in comparison with sampled depth.*

A surface formed from the interpolated depth samples faithfully follows the true surface as long as it is planar (Figure 4.2.9). It does not exhibit the stair-step effect known from the previous figures, which solves many problems we had to begin with (a much smaller depth bias would be sufficient to keep this surface from self-shadowing). Looking at the discontinuity, the interpolation seems to create a "false continuity," which may widen the footprint cast from the upper surface onto the lower. This effect is, however, limited to the width of a single sample, so it seems a small price to pay in exchange for a huge possible benefit.

The main obstacle to switching to interpolated depth is the graphics hardware itself. Filtered, high-precision texture formats are not abundant. Since we also need it to be renderable, there are only a few we can choose from. On a GeForce 6 series, there is half-float RGBA, but it seems wasteful to use only 16 out of 64 bits. On the GeForce FX, the only option is G16R16, which is an integer format, so the depth values must be appropriately scaled. However, it turns out that G16R16 gives more fidelity under filtering than the half-float format, since the 16-bit integer has more precision than the 16-bit float.

Putting It All Together

If we were to combine all three techniques that have been described so far, we would end up with something similar to what is shown in Figure 4.2.10. Both the depth bias and the fuzzy width are scaled by the depth gradient, and the gradient in turn is calculated from neighboring samples taken from an interpolated depth map. The result is a "fuzzy band" that closely follows the contour of a shadow-casting surface and acts as a buffer between the unshadowed and the shadowed regions. This buffer prevents the occasional self-shadowing from being visually disruptive. You can see a downward spike under the lower surface, which happens whenever there is a gradient discontinuity. This spike could reveal the contour of a shadow caster through a wall, for instance. As suggested, the gradient should be clamped to a maximum value to limit the extent of such spikes and prevent gaps.

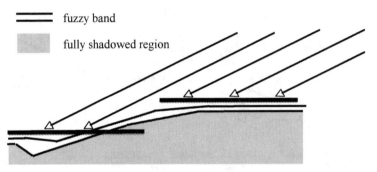

FIGURE 4.2.10   *The fuzzy band created by the combination of gradient-scaled bias, fuzzy comparison, and interpolated depth samples.*

Color plate 6 shows a scene from *Spellforce 2*, courtesy of JoWooD Productions/ Phenomic Game Development. It has been shadow mapped using the techniques discussed in the article, using a single shadow map that extends up to half the view distance. The sun has been positioned deliberately to hit the gate in the foreground at a grazing angle. Traditionally such a scene would be prone to both self-shadowing artifacts on the surfaces, which are hit at grazing angles and gaps behind the wooden beams. These problems have been avoided despite the fact that a single shadow map was used for the whole scene.

Alternative shadow map projections such as PSM [Stamminger02] or TSM [Wimmer04] can be used with gradient-based techniques, as has been done in case of the picture shown in the color plate. When doing so, care must be taken to preserve the linearity of the depth value.

Conclusion

This article discussed techniques to eliminate surface acne in shadow mapping. It introduced the concepts of a depth gradient together with a gradient-scaled bias, a gradient-scaled fuzzy depth comparison, and sampling from an interpolated depth map. It turns out that the combination of these techniques is very powerful, as each amplifies the effectiveness of the other two.

References

[Hourcade85] Hourcade, J. C., and A. Nicolas, "Algorithms for antialiased cast shadows," Computers and Graphics, vol. 9 no. 3, 1985: pp. 259–265.

[Kozlov04] Kozlov, Simon, "Perspective Shadow Maps: Care and Feeding," *GPU Gems*, edited by R. Fernando, Addison Wesley, 2004: pp. 217–244.

[Martin04] Martin, Tobias, and Tiow-Seng Tan, "Anti-Aliasing and Continuity with Trapezoidal Shadow Maps," Proceedings of Eurographics Symposium on Rendering, 2004: pp. 153–160.

[Reeves87] Reeves, W. T., D. H. Salesin, and R. L. Cook, "Rendering antialiased shadows with depth maps," Computer Graphics (SIGGRAPH 87), vol. 21 no. 4, (July 1987): pp. 283–291.

[Stamminger02] Stamminger, Marc, and George Drettakis, "Perspective Shadow Maps," ACM Transactions on Graphics (SIGGRAPH), (July 2002): pp. 557–562.

[Wang94] Wang, Yulan, and Steven Molnar, "Second depth shadow mapping," UNC-CS Technical Report TR94-019, University of North Carolina, 1994.

[Williams78] Williams, Lance, "Casting curved shadows on curved surfaces," Computer Graphics, vol. 23, no. 3, 1978: pp. 270–274.

[Wimmer04] Wimmer, Michael, Daniel Scherzer, and Werner Purgathofer, "Light Space Perspective Shadow Maps," Proceedings of Eurographics Symposium on Rendering, June 2004: pp. 143–151.

[Woo92] Woo, Andrew, "The shadow depth map revisited," in D. Kirk (editor), Graphics Gems III, AB Professional, Boston, 1992.

4.3

Real-Time Soft Shadows Using the PDSM Technique

Jean-François St. Amour, Eric Paquette, Pierre Poulin, and Philippe Beaudoin

Introduction

Shadows provide important cues to understand spatial relationships between lights and objects. Soft shadows are even more desirable because they add a great deal of realism to synthetic images (see Figure 4.3.1). However, because generating soft shadows can be computationally intensive, creating them has traditionally been an off-line and noninteractive process. Recent advances in computer graphics hardware, however, have made possible a new generation of shadow algorithms [Assarsson02, Chan03, Wyman03]. These new techniques allow real-time soft-shadow generation for dynamic scenes at the expense of trading quality for speed. While these methods produce good results for dynamic objects, they lack the high quality that can be achieved with off-line methods.

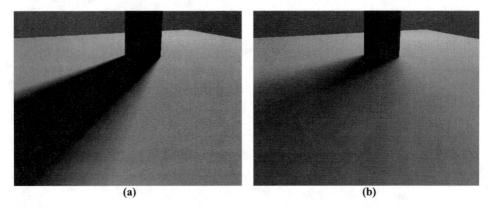

(a)   (b)

FIGURE 4.3.1 *Soft shadows can greatly enhance the realism of a scene. The same cylinder is lit with (a) a small light source or (b) a larger one.*

This article presents a method of generating soft shadows to bridge the gap between off-line and real-time methods. We first introduced this method, Penumbra Deep Shadow Maps (PDSM), in a technical paper [StAmour05] where you can find more details regarding memory usage and performance analysis. The goal of this article is to concentrate on implementation details. The method allows for the precomputation of high-quality soft shadows that can be rendered in real time using modern graphics hardware (see Figure 4.3.1). Moreover, the technique does not require any specific scene representation and can therefore be easily integrated into any graphics engine.

PDSM allows for shadow queries to occur at any location in 3D space. That makes it possible to cast the precomputed shadows on dynamic objects as well as through a participating medium such as mist or fog.

Shadow Maps and the Transmittance Function

Shadow maps are well known for computing hard shadows cast by point light sources. The basic idea is to limit the light source field of view to a pyramidal frustum defined by the point light source and a rectangle placed some distance from it. A 2D texture is embedded in this rectangle and the depth of the first object encountered is stored in each texel.

As an alternative, consider a *binary transmittance function* that associates to each 3D point the value 1 if it lies in the light source frustum and has a clear line of sight of the point light source; otherwise, the value is 0.

A naïve way to add shadows to a scene would therefore be to compute this transmittance function for a voxel grid and store the results in a 3D texture. This texture could then be used in a pixel shader to decide whether a surface point should be lit. This approach fails for numerous reasons, one of which being the large amount of memory required to store the 3D texture at a sufficient resolution. Fortunately, a quick look at the transmittance function shows that it is highly coherent and can be efficiently compressed.

In fact, if we consider the transmittance function along an emission ray from the light source, we notice that it simplifies dramatically. At the light source the function equals 1. As we move along the ray, the function is 1 up to the point where we reach the first scene object. At that point, the function goes to 0 and remains that way for all other points along the ray. This type of function is called a *step function* and can be characterized by a single value d: the depth at which the function goes from 1 to 0 (see Figure 4.3.2). This simple compression of the transmittance function is exactly what a shadow map performs.

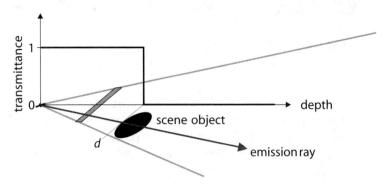

FIGURE 4.3.2   *The transmittance function reduces to a simple step function along an emission ray.*

Soft Shadows

Things get more complicated with area light sources. A simple binary transmittance function is not sufficient to quantify the fraction of the area light source visible from any point in the scene. We therefore need a real-valued transmittance function that associates a number between 0 (fully in shadow) and 1 (fully lit) to any 3D point. Intermediate values indicate that the point is in the penumbra and quantify the partial transmittance.

The naïve strategy of encoding this function in a 3D texture again fails due to prohibitive memory requirements. Moreover, we cannot rely on the simple compression developed for point light sources because step functions cannot suitably approximate the slowly varying transmittance in penumbra regions.

However, the transmittance function is still somewhat coherent and is efficiently compressible. For typical scenes the transmittance function becomes quite simple when studied along emission rays of the area light source. As in the shadow map algorithm, we encode the entire function along rays emitted from a single point—the center of the area light source (see Figure 4.3.3).

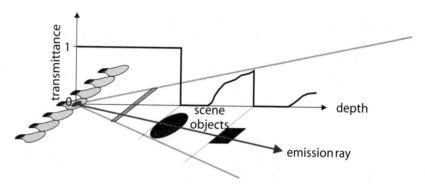

FIGURE 4.3.3 *The transmittance function along emission rays starting from the center of the area light source.*

We again place a 2D texture on the rectangle specifying the light source frustum. Each pixel of the 2D texture is associated with a ray starting at the center of the light source and going through the pixel. The transmittance function along each such ray is simple: it equals 1 at the light source and changes as the ray travels through shadow and penumbra regions. Finding how to compress this function and expressing it in a texture are key ideas behind PDSM.

Penumbra Deep Shadow Maps

Although it was not designed to handle area light sources and soft shadows, the Deep Shadow Map (DSM) algorithm [Lokovic00] bears a number of similarities with PDSM. The goal of DSM is to capture partial occlusion due to the cumulative occlusion of tiny or semitransparent objects. An example of an application of such a technique would be to evaluate the shadow cast by hair illuminated with a point light source. The result is a nonuniform shadow that is darker where numerous strands of hair block the light.

In DSM, as in standard shadow mapping, a 2D texture is placed on the rectangle describing the point light source frustum. However, the function stored in each pixel of the texture is no longer a step function, but rather a real-valued function that decreases from 1 to 0, indicating light transmittance as a function of depth.

Once constructed, the DSM function for each pixel is compressed in order to maintain a reasonably sized structure. We use the same compression technique from DSM for our PDSM. Thus, the technique described in this article can also be used to produce hardware-accelerated DSM.

Constructing the PDSM Function

PDSMs were developed to handle soft shadows from area light sources. As mentioned earlier, such light sources require the use of a real-valued transmittance function that indicates the fraction of light visible from all 3D points. This function is generated in a precomputation stage and is computed mostly in software. We now describe a technique to generate this function in the context of PDSM.

Recall that we want to consider the transmittance function along emission rays starting at the center of the area light source. To compute this function, a 2D texture called the *PDSM texture* is placed on the rectangle defining the area light source frustum.

We need a way to precompute and store the fraction of the light source visible from any 3D point along PDSM rays. As shown in Algorithm 4.3.1, we do so by approximating the area light source using k sample point light sources randomly placed on the emission region (Step 1 and Figure 4.3.4). Instead of using a completely random distribution of the sample points on the area light source, we place the points on a regular grid and jitter their positions. This corresponds to stratified sampling and reduces variance.

Algorithm 4.3.1   PDSM Construction

```
        Initialize each PDSM pixel to a value of k at depth 0
    1   Generate k random sample points on the area light source
        foreach ( sample point )
    2       Compute a shadow map (SM) from the current sample point
            // Merge the SM information to the PDSM
            foreach ( pixel in the PDSM texture )
    3           Compute the associated 3D PDSM ray
    4           Project this PDSM ray in the SM
                foreach ( SM pixel traversed by the ray )
    5               if ( visibility changed from visible to hidden )
    6                   Insert a decrease event into the PDSM
    7               if ( visibility changed from hidden to visible )
    8                   Insert an increase event into the PDSM
```

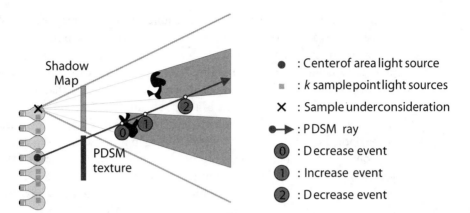

FIGURE 4.3.4   *The PDSM texture, a sample shadow map, and a PDSM ray corresponding to a single PDSM pixel. An event is added to the PDSM ray when visibility changes.*

For each sample point light source, we compute a standard shadow map (Step 2). We then merge the information of all the shadow maps in the PDSM texture. Step 2 uses graphics hardware, but all of the other steps of the precomputation are done in software.

The algorithm walks along each ray of the PDSM (Step 3) and identifies points where changes of visibility occur in the shadow map (Steps 5 and 7). If the visibility changes from visible to hidden (that is, from lit to shadowed), a *decrease event* is added at the depth where the change occurred (Step 6). If it changes from hidden to visible, an *increase event* is added to the ray (Step 8). The events occurring along a ray are stored in the associated pixel of the PDSM texture.

The decrease and increase events are used to track exactly how many sample point light sources are visible from each point along the ray. This number, when divided by k, is an approximation of the fraction of the area light source visible. The result, when all rays are taken together, is a valid approximation of the transmittance function over the entire 3D space. The transmittance function along each ray is rather simple: it equals 1 at the light source and decreases, slowly or abruptly, depending on whether the ray entered a shadow or penumbra region. Along the ray, the light from a sample shadow map becomes invisible as the ray goes behind an object (event 0 in Figure 4.3.4) and becomes visible further along the ray (event 1). Thus, the function can become more complex as its value can decrease and increase, especially for scenes with many small objects. However, as the entire visibility is captured in the preprocessing stage, it reduces the complexity of the real-time rendering stage. In practice, the function usually remains simple as it varies smoothly in penumbra regions and most pixels of the PDSM do not correspond to highly complex visibility situations. The function can thus be easily compressed, as will be presented in the next section.

The inner loop in Algorithm 4.3.1 requires us to trace a ray into the shadow map associated with a sample point light source (Step 4). This is done by scan-converting the ray into the shadow map and traversing it pixel by pixel. For each traversed pixel, a standard shadow map test is used to determine whether the ray is visible or hidden from the sample point light source. When two consecutive shadow map tests yield different results, a visibility event is added (Figure 4.3.5). We know that this event occurred somewhere between the two pixels, but it is difficult to determine its precise depth. Both the depth stored in the shadow map and the depth interpolated during scan-conversion can help solve this problem. Figure 4.3.6 illustrates (a) when to use the shadow map depth information, (b) when to use the ray scan-conversion depth information, and (c) how to compute the depth of increase events. Particular care must be taken during this step, because while the shadow map is usually the most accurate source of depth information, it can also provide erroneous data and as such, must always be validated with the scan-conversion information. Rays that project in a single pixel are handled as a special case and add a single decrease event using the depth from the shadow map.

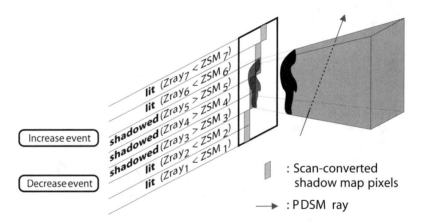

FIGURE 4.3.5 *The 3D PDSM ray is projected in the shadow map and the pixels used to determine the visibility of the ray are identified by software scan-converting the ray using the midpoint algorithm [Foley89].*

When the shadow map depth information is used, it must be transformed to depths in the PDSM for insertion. This computation can be optimized if the light source is planar and if the PDSM and the shadow maps are parallel to each other and parallel to the light source plane [Agrawala00]. In this context, a depth in the shadow map is exactly the same depth in the PDSM, thus requiring no transformation.

Because of the finite depth resolution of the shadow maps, a single ray can contain many events at the same depth or very close to one another. This happens, for example, when the same polygon is viewed by different shadow maps; the shadow map pixels do

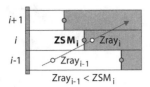 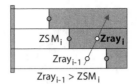 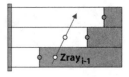

(a) Decrease event depth = ZSM_i (b) Decrease event depth = $Zray_i$ (c) Increase event depth = $Zray_{i-1}$

FIGURE 4.3.6 *Shadow map pixels extend as horizontal regions $i - 1$, i, $i + 1$. Pixel i is under examination. ZSM is the depth information at the center of a shadow map pixel. Zray is the depth information obtained by scan-converting a PDSM ray. The selection between the PDSM ray depth and the shadow map depth depends on the comparison between these two depths: (a) shadow map depth is appropriate, (b) shadow map depth is wrong thus Zray must be used, and (c) an increase event uses the depth of the previous pixel.*

not see the exact same 3D point, but rather points in the same neighborhood. Therefore, events occurring in a depth range close to the resolution of the shadow map are simply merged together. This merge is performed as soon as a new event is added during Steps 6 or 8 of the construction algorithm.

The result is a 2D PDSM texture where each pixel contains a series of events with depths and transmittance values. This texture is a sampled representation of the 3D transmittance function. However, the size of the structures kept in each pixel can still be prohibitive and requires extra compression.

Compressing Ray Functions

As mentioned earlier, the transmittance function along a ray is compressed using the DSM compression technique [Lokovic00]. This compression makes sure that the depths of important events are well preserved in order to prevent the most visible artifacts, such as incorrect self-shadowing. It proceeds first by specifying an error bound ε on the visibility value. For a specific depth, the transmittance obtained with the resulting compressed function is always guaranteed to fall within ε of the uncompressed function at the same depth.

The compression is performed using a greedy algorithm (see Figure 4.3.7 and Algorithm 4.3.2) that starts at the first event along each ray, which is stored precisely. It then tries to find the longest possible linear function that satisfies the error bound. This is done by keeping track of an interval of valid slopes. Each newly encountered event further limits this interval, up to the point where an empty interval is obtained. The algorithm uses the last event that does not cause an empty interval and adjusts the transmittance value of this event such that the resulting line fits in the error bounds of all the events. All events between the starting event and this last valid one are deleted. The algorithm then restarts at this last valid event.

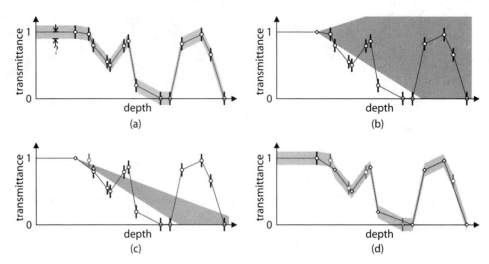

FIGURE 4.3.7   *(a) Compression of a PDSM function with an error bound ε. (b) The first two events define an interval of valid slopes. (c) This interval is further restricted by the third event, which is moved upward to fit within the interval. The fourth event produces an empty interval, so the algorithm restarts at the third event. (d) The result is a function with fewer events that remains within the desired error bounds.*

Algorithm 4.3.2   PDSM Compression

```
StartingEvent = FirstEvent
while ( StartingEvent != LastEvent )
    CurrentEvent = Successor of StartingEvent
    Initialize valid slopes interval
            using StartingEvent and CurrentEvent
    while ( CurrentEvent != LastEvent and
            Adding the successor does not cause an empty interval )
        NextEvent = Successor of CurrentEvent
        Update the interval of valid slopes using NextEvent
        Delete CurrentEvent
        CurrentEvent = NextEvent
    Adjust transmittance of CurrentEvent to fit in valid slopes interval
    StartingEvent = CurrentEvent
```

The PDSM compression gives different results depending on the complexity of the visibility in the scene. From data of scenes with medium to high complexity, an ε value of 2% gives good visual results and allows compression factors around 3 when using 64 sample shadow maps. Furthermore, if more samples are used, the memory needed to store the PDSM remains roughly the same, giving higher compression factors (around 6 with 256 samples).

Rendering

Now that we have precomputed a PDSM, it can be used to quickly evaluate the transmittance anywhere in a scene using a two-step operation. First, we find the PDSM pixel (and thus function) that corresponds to the 3D point we are trying to shade. Second, we evaluate where that particular point lies along the PDSM function, which gives the transmittance factor. Rendering with the PDSM is described in Listing 4.3.3. This algorithm can be used in software-rendering engines, but can also be used in real time on programmable graphics hardware (see the next section).

Algorithm 4.3.3   Rendering With The PDSM Texture

```
1    foreach ( 3D point to shade )
         // 3D point (x,y,z)_world → (x,y,z)_PDSM
2        Project in the PDSM
         // (x,y)_PDSM → f( )
3        Retrieve the appropriate transmittance function
         // f((z)_PDSM) → transmittance
4        Retrieve the transmittance value
         // transmittance → pixel color
5        Modulate the shading by this transmittance
```

In any renderer, creating an image eventually comes down to computing the color of the 3D points in the scene that correspond to the pixels of the image (Step 1). The PDSM algorithm adds some extra steps for transmittance evaluation. We project the 3D point to shade into the PDSM structure to determine the PDSM pixel that contains the relevant transmittance function (Steps 2 and 3). To evaluate the transmittance function, the algorithm searches for the two consecutive events between which the 3D point to shade is located. The list of events is sequentially visited and the transmittance values are linearly interpolated to obtain the transmittance value at the depth of the 3D point to shade (Step 4).

As in many other image-based approaches, instead of evaluating the transmittance value from a single PDSM pixel, the PDSM pixels around the projected 3D point can be considered and the computed transmittance values filtered. Filters of various widths can be applied by evaluating the transmittance functions and weighting the results. The examples presented in this article consider four PDSM pixels with bilinear filtering because it provides a nice balance between quality and cost.

Hardware Rendering

To take advantage of the processing power of programmable graphics hardware, the PDSM rendering can be implemented using a fragment shader. Because the PDSM structure is usually sparse, encoding it efficiently in graphics hardware texture memory is important. The PDSM structure is nothing more than a 2D array of pointers to 1D transmittance functions. The 2D array of pointers can easily be mapped to a 2D texture, which we call the *index texture*. While each PDSM pixel could theoretically be encoded in its own 1D texture, this would be extremely inefficient. We thus choose to encode all the PDSM functions in a single 2D texture—the *data texture*. The data texture contains all the PDSM functions encoded sequentially (see Figure 4.3.8(b)). The index texture simply provides information on where a specific PDSM function is located in the data texture and how many texels it contains (see Figure 4.3.8(a)).

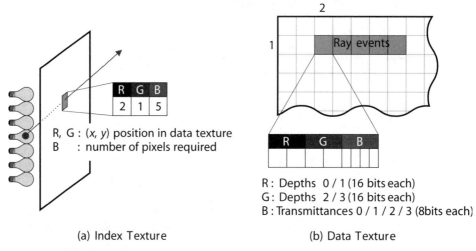

(a) Index Texture   (b) Data Texture

FIGURE 4.3.8   *Texture encoding on the graphics hardware.*

The texture format chosen to encode the index and data textures can vary greatly depending on the application. Available texture memory space, maximum texture sizes, precision requirements, and GPU capabilities dictate the choice of encoding, especially for the data texture. In our examples, we use RGB 16-bit integer format for the index texture (see Figure 4.3.8(a)). Figure 4.3.8(b) gives an example of data texture encoding. It uses RGB 32-bit floating-point textures to efficiently encode four events per pixel. It provides 16-bit precision for the depth component and 8-bit precision for the transmittance value, which we found to be more than sufficient for most applications. This kind of compact format limits texture memory requirements and reduces the number of texture fetches required during the PDSM function evaluation. However, it is important to note that this encoding depends on graphics hardware that supports *packing* instructions.

In our rendering algorithm (Algorithm 4.3.3), we map each step to a regular fragment shader. Step 1 basically describes all the fragments on which the shader runs. Because the fragment shader is considerably more complex with the PDSM technique, extra care should be taken in reducing to the minimum the number of fragments being processed. This can be accomplished in numerous ways (for example, Z-only pass, aggressive culling, and so on.).

Step 2 can be efficiently accomplished using regular projective texturing, which is set up in exactly the same way as for regular shadow mapping, yielding the (x, y, z)PDSM coordinates in PDSM space of the point to shade. The (x, y)PDSM portion is used as the texture coordinate to sample the index texture. The result from this texture lookup is used to access the data texture and thus obtain the correct PDSM function (Step 3).

To evaluate the PDSM function and get the transmittance factor for the current fragment (Step 4), we walk along the events until we find the interval that brackets z_{PDSM}. Using the "address" obtained from the index texture, a dependent texture lookup fetches the first event from the data texture. Getting all subsequent events is then only a matter of incrementing the data texture coordinate until the interval is found or the number of texels indicated in the index texture are traversed. Once the correct interval is found, the fragment transmittance factor is linearly interpolated from the two event transmittance values. Because PDSM compression greatly reduces both average and maximum function lengths, this evaluation can be done very efficiently, allowing the rendering of high-quality soft shadows in real time.

Results

Figure 4.3.9 presents results of scenes rendered in real time with the GPU implementation of the PDSM. Typical resolutions for sample shadow maps and the PDSM texture range from 512^2 to 1024^2, while the typical number of sample shadow maps ranges from 64 to 144. On an AMD Athlon 64 3500+ and a GeForce 6800GT, typical timings for construction range from 30 to 160 seconds while rendering is achieved from 40 to hundreds of FPS.

As previously mentioned, PDSM allows for shadow queries to occur at any 3D location in space. It is therefore possible to seamlessly integrate dynamic objects in the scene after the high-quality shadow has been precomputed (see Figure 4.3.9(c)). Because the precomputation does not include shadow information for the dynamic objects, the shadow cast by these objects must be computed with a standard shadow map or with any other real-time approximate shadowing method. This approach is justified since research [Wanger92] has shown that lower-quality shadows can be appropriate for moving objects.

Finally, the nature of PDSM makes it is possible to generate soft shadows through a participating medium such as mist or fog, yielding realistic light beam effects. In Figure 4.3.9(d), the fog was obtained by placing several alpha-blended polygons at different depths. Each of these polygons is aligned with the projection plane and is shaded using the PDSM transmittance function.

There are some typical problems with shadow mapping techniques that we also inherit. The three major ones are aliasing, possible insufficient Z precision, and bias value choice. As mentioned earlier, aliasing can be greatly reduced by using filtering when evaluating the PDSM. Depth precision problems will usually be caused by poor placement of the near and far clipping planes. The near clipping plane is of particular importance, and placing it as far as possible from the camera greatly improves depth

FIGURE 4.3.9 *Examples of soft shadows computed with the PDSM. From top to bottom, left to right: (a) Complex self-shadowing effects on a dragon model. (b) Park scene with complex geometry and shadows. (c) Complex shadows cast in real time on a car inserted in the precomputed shadows; the shadows cast by the car are computed with percentage closer filtering [Reeves87]. (d) Fog lighted with the PDSM, showing how the transmittance can be evaluated everywhere in the scene. No special treatment is needed; the PDSM shader is simply added to the regular fog shader. See color plate 7 for color version.*

precision. Choosing the perfect bias value is always problematic with shadow mapping algorithms (see "Eliminating surface acne with gradient shadow mapping" [Schüler05]); scene organization, camera and light positions, graphics API and hardware will all affect how you set up your bias. We recommend not using bias during the construction phase; instead, use typical shadow mapping bias techniques (such as polygon offsetting) during the rendering phase.

Conclusion

In this article, we presented how to implement the penumbra deep shadow maps, an efficient way to render soft shadows by precomputing and compressing the transmittance function over the 3D space. This function is encoded in PDSM rays, each of which is tested by scan-conversion in a number of shadow maps to accumulate the distribution of total incoming light along the ray. The resulting structure captures quality hard and soft shadows for light sources ranging from point light to large extended light sources. With this compressed transmittance function, modern graphics hardware can be exploited for the real-time display of static shadows. The PDSM structure is well adapted to real-time interactive applications where complex shadows can be cast over animated characters or through fog.

Additional Resources

The original research paper and accompanying video can be found at *http://www.iro. umontreal.ca/labs/infographie/papers/St-Amour-2005-PDSM/index.html*.

Acknowledgments

The dragon model appears courtesy of the Stanford Computer Graphics Laboratory. The original version of this method appears in the Proceedings of Graphics Interface 2005 [StAmour05].

References

[Agrawala00] Agrawala, M., R. Ramamoorthi, A. Heirich, and L. Moll, "Efficient Image-Based Methods for Rendering Soft Shadows," SIGGRAPH 2000: pp. 375–384.

[Assarsson02] Assarsson, U., and T. Akenine-Möller, "A Geometry-Based Soft Shadow Volume Algorithm Using Graphics Hardware," ACM Trans. on Graphics, 22(3), July 2003: pp. 511–520.

[Chan03] Chan, E., and F. Durand, "Rendering Fake Soft Shadows with Smoothies," Eurographics Symposium on Rendering 2003: pp. 208–218.

[Foley89] Foley, J., A. van Dam, S. Feiner, and J. Hughes, Computer Graphics: Principles and Practice, 2nd edition, Addison Wesley, 1989.

[Lokovic00] Lokovic, T., and E. Veach, "Deep Shadow Maps," SIGGRAPH 2000: pp. 385–392.

[Reeves87] Reeves, W. T., D. Salesin, and R. Cook, "Rendering Antialiased Shadows with Depth Maps," SIGGRAPH 1987: pp. 283–291.

[Schüler05] Schüler, C., "Eliminating Surface Acne with Gradient Shadow Mapping," *Shader X^4*, edited by Wolfgang Engel, Charles River Media, 2005.

[StAmour05] St-Amour, J. F., E. Paquette, and P. Poulin, "Soft Shadows from Extended Light Sources with Penumbra Deep Shadow Maps," Graphics Interface 2005: pp. 105–112.

[Wanger92] Wanger, L., "The Effect of Shadow Quality on the Perception of Spatial Relationships in Computer Generated Imagery," Symposium on Interactive 3D Graphics 1992: pp. 39–42.

[Wyman03] Wyman, C., and C. Hansen, "Penumbra Maps: Approximate Soft Shadows in Real-Time," Eurographics Symposium on Rendering 2003: pp. 202–207.

4.4

Robust Shadow Mapping with Light-Space Perspective Shadow Maps

Michael Wimmer and Daniel Scherzer

Introduction

Shadow mapping is the preferred method for generating realistic shadowing effects both in the film industry and for many computer games. Its popularity is due to the fact that it is both fast and versatile. Shadow mapping requires only one additional rendering pass, independent of the scene complexity. Furthermore, anything that can be rendered can also cast a shadow.

The basic shadow-mapping algorithm is simple: in an initial rendering pass, render the scene from the point of view of the light and save the z-buffer as the so-called shadow map. In the subsequent main rendering pass, render the scene from the eye and transform every fragment into the coordinate system of the shadow map (the so-called light space). If the stored depth is nearer to the light, the fragment is considered to be in shadow and the shading of the fragment is altered to reflect this.

In current graphics hardware, the transformation into light space is done using projective texture mapping, and the required texture comparison operator has been supported natively since the NVIDIA GeForce 3. Another requirement is a high-precision texture format for storing depth values, which is supported either natively or via floating-point textures common in current graphics accelerators.

The main problem with the shadow-mapping algorithm is that, as an image-space algorithm, it is prone to various kinds of aliasing artifacts (see the section "Shadow Mapping Problems"), leading to situations with low image quality. Alternatives to shadow mapping exist mainly in the geometric shadow volume approach, which always produces pixel-correct shadows. However, shadow volumes are restricted to watertight, polygonal occluders and consume large amounts of fill rate for the rasterization of shadow volumes. They also create significant computational overhead for silhouette generation, especially for highly tessellated objects, which makes the shadow volume algorithm greatly dependent on scene complexity.

Recently, several methods have been introduced to overcome the aliasing problems of shadow mapping. Most of them are based on an additional perspective transformation of the shadow map. This transformation redistributes the shadow map resolution so that shadows near the eye have higher resolution than shadows far from the eye. However, the original "Perspective Shadow Maps" [Stamminger02] were difficult to implement correctly due to the intricacies of perspective projections. They also led to poor shadow quality for medium and far objects.

In this article, we describe Light Space Perspective Shadow Maps (LiSPSM) [Wimmer04] as a robust alternative to (perspective) shadow mapping. While LiSPSM also relies on a perspective transformation to redistribute shadow quality, the LiSPSM is applied directly in light space, thus avoiding the problems normally associated with post-perspective space. Furthermore, in LiSPSM, the strength of the perspective effect is calculated so as to equalize shadow quality for near and far objects in the view frustum (see Figure 4.4.1). In the following sections, we first discuss the shadow-mapping aliasing problems in more detail, and then show how to robustly deal with all these problems both for directional and point lights, giving ample implementation detail to avoid many common pitfalls.

FIGURE 4.4.1 *High-quality shadows for near and distant objects using LiSPSM.*

Shadow Mapping Problems

In this section, we briefly discuss the aliasing problems that arise due to the fact that conventional shadow mapping works in image space. We can distinguish three errors.

First, due to the laws of perspective, nearby objects appear larger than distant objects in perspective camera views. However, a standard shadow map for a distant light source has a fixed resolution for all objects, leading to a shadow resolution that is too low for nearby objects. Figure 4.4.2 shows this so-called *perspective aliasing error*.

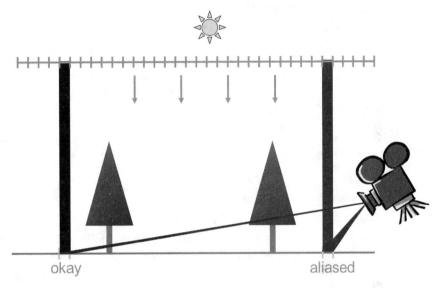

okay   aliased

FIGURE 4.4.2   *Perspective aliasing for standard shadow maps.*

Second, surfaces that are roughly parallel to the light direction are sampled sparsely in the shadow map (see Figure 4.4.3, left). A single shadow texel therefore projects to many pixels on-screen, leading to the *projection aliasing error*. Methods to globally redistribute shadow resolution (like LiSPSM) cannot reduce this effect because it varies with respect to the scene geometry.

Third, differences in sampling from the light and from the eye lead to incorrect *self-shadowing* (see Figure 4.4.3, right), which typically manifests itself in Moiré-like patterns, and needs to be taken into account through some form of biasing [Schüler05].

Finally, since shadow maps require a view frustum for rendering, they cannot easily deal with omnidirectional point lights [Forsyth05]. In this article, we therefore discuss only directional lights and point lights with a direction and validity cone (also known as spot lights).

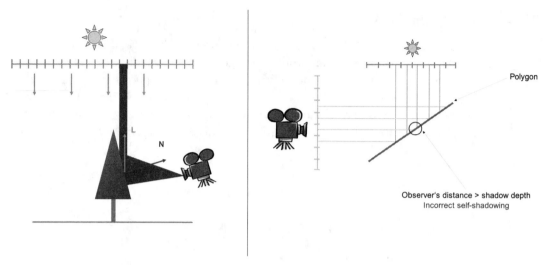

FIGURE 4.4.3   *Projection aliasing (left); incorrect self-shadowing (right).*

Light Space Perspective Shadow Maps—A Recipe

Introduction

In this section, we give a recipe to robustly enhance the shadow-mapping algorithm with LiSPSM. The main idea of LiSPSM is to warp the shadow map by introducing a perspective transform into the shadow-mapping process (see Figure 4.4.4). In the transformed shadow map, near objects have higher resolution, so that shadow quality is equally good for near and distant objects (see Figure 4.4.5).

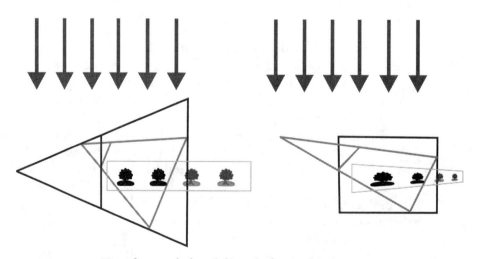

FIGURE 4.4.4   *View frustum before (left) and after (right) the perspective transformation of LiSPSM.*

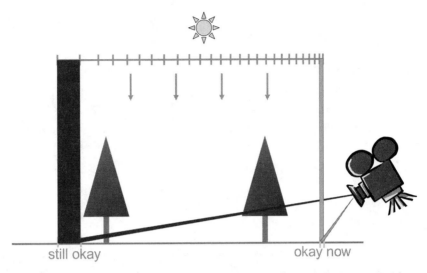

FIGURE 4.4.5 *Redistribution of shadow map samples in LiSPSM to avoid aliasing.*

This perspective transform (hereafter called *LiSPSM projection*) is applied after transforming the geometry into the local (post-perspective) coordinate space of the light, which we call *light space*. For directional lights, transforming to light space involves a rotation and translation, whereas for point lights, we also need to include the perspective projection of the light.

The goal of the LiSPSM projection is to redistribute the resolution in the shadow map. The main advantage of applying the projection in light space is that light rays do not change their order or direction (as long as the LiSPSM projection plane is perpendicular to the shadow map), and therefore lights need not be transformed into post-perspective space (light rays get mapped to light rays, see Figure 4.4.4). This avoids many subtleties that normally arise when dealing with post-perspective space [Stamminger02], such as singularities, missing shadow casters, or changing light-source types and directions (in LiSPSM, all light sources are mapped to directional ones).

The strength of the warping effect (given by the distance of the center of projection from the LiSPSM projection plane) determines how much emphasis is given to near objects compared to distant objects, and needs to be carefully adjusted. Perspective shadow maps [Stamminger04] lead to unsatisfactory results for distant objects because the warp is generally too strong. We therefore show a formula that leads to better results over the whole visual range by equalizing perspective aliasing for near and far objects (Figure 4.4.10 shows how the error is distributed).

Note that with LiSPSM, the shadow map has to be regenerated every frame, which is usually done anyway in a dynamic environment. LiSPSMs are as fast as standard shadow maps, since the perspective transformation is applied by the graphics hardware during shadow generation and therefore incurs no additional cost.

This recipe gives special attention to point lights, which have some peculiarities that need to be addressed.

Algorithm Overview

The main steps of the algorithm are to focus the shadow map on the relevant parts of the scene and to find the perspective matrix and its parameters for LiSPSM (note that the focusing step is a good idea even for standard shadow maps) (see Figure 4.4.6).

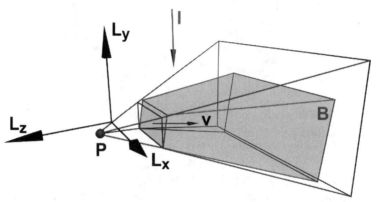

FIGURE 4.4.6   *Construction of the perspective frustum P in 3D.*

1. Focus shadow map on the *focus region* **B**.
2. Find light space matrix **L** (which is a conventional shadow mapping matrix).
    2.1 Set **L** to be the frame $\mathbf{L}_v^{-1}$ created from the view direction **v** and the light direction 1, rooted at the eye point (directional lights) or the light position (point lights).
    2.2. For point lights, append the point light projection $\mathbf{L}_p$, so that $\mathbf{L} = \mathbf{L}_p\mathbf{L}_v^{-1}$.
    2.3. Rotate **L** so that the view frustum points "upward" (in the shadow map), making $\mathbf{L} = \mathbf{L}_r\mathbf{L}_p\mathbf{L}_v^{-1}$.
3. Find LiSPSM projection matrix **P**.
    3.1. Calculate n, the near plane distance of the LiSPSM projection.
    3.2. Find projection center **C** for **P** and generate its translation $\mathbf{P}_t$.
    3.3 Find frustum planes for **P**, giving the LiSPSM matrix as $\mathbf{P} = \mathbf{P}_p\mathbf{P}_t$.
4. Apply shadow mapping using the joint matrix **PL** instead of just **L**.

Focusing the Shadow Map

In standard shadow maps, the view frustum often covers only a small area while the remainder of the shadow map is wasted (no visible information is stored there). It is therefore natural to focus the shadow map on the region in space that can cast a shadow into the view frustum. We extend here the brief discussion from [Wimmer04] with a more efficient method.

The focus region can be calculated as the convex hull of the view frustum **V** and the light position **l** (for directional lights, this position is at infinity), clipped by the scene bounding volume **S** and the light frustum **L**. We call the resulting intersection body **B** and write the calculation as $\mathbf{B} = (\mathbf{V} + \mathbf{l}) \cap \mathbf{S} \cap \mathbf{L}$. Clipping to **S** cuts back large frusta **V** (quite common nowadays) that extend beyond the scene borders.

As an extension to [Wimmer04], we also clip V by S before calculating the convex hull, since this leads to even smaller intersection bodies (the final calculation is then $\mathbf{B} = \big((\mathbf{V} \cap \mathbf{S}) + \mathbf{l}\big) \cap \mathbf{S} \cap \mathbf{L}$). Furthermore, for practically infinite scene extents and view frusta with a far plane near or at infinity, the resulting focus region needs to be bounded by basing the focus region computations on a frustum with a smaller, more practical far plane distance (outside of this frustum, no shadows will appear). This would have to be done for standard shadow maps, as well.

The resulting body **B** defines the focus region that will be used in the following sections (see Figure 4.4.7).

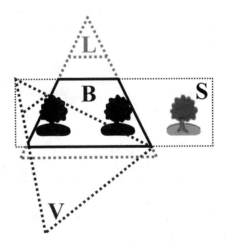

FIGURE 4.4.7 *The view frustum V, a point light frustum L, the scene bounding volume S, and the corresponding focus region B.*

Since all involved bodies are simple convex polyhedra, it is easier to implement the required operations directly instead of using general-purpose convex hull and polyhedra intersection algorithms. We also distinguish between point and directional lights:

```
Object temp;    // temporary intersection object

calcFrustum(temp, invEyeProjView);    // eye frustum
clip(temp, sceneBV);

if (pointLight) {
      convexHullWithPoint(temp, lightPos);
clip(temp, sceneBV);
      calcFrustum(lightFrustum, invLightProjView); // light frustum
      clip(temp, lightFrustum);
}
else {
      convexHullWithDirection(temp, -lightDir, sceneBV);
}

return temp;
```

Some notable operations are:

calcFrustum(): creates a solid view frustum representation (for example, a b-rep) in world space by feeding the eight points of a centered two-unit cube into the inverse of the combined view and projection matrix (**PV**) of the desired frustum.

clip(): intersection of two convex objects. The first object is simply clipped by each plane of the second object and the created holes are filled with new polygons.

The convex hull operation depends on whether the light is a point or directional light:

convexHullWithPoint(): calculates the 3D convex hull of a convex body and a point. It removes all polygons of the body that are front-facing with respect to the point, leaving a hole in the form of a closed edge loop. The hole is closed by connecting the line loop to the point with a triangle fan.

convexHullWithDirection(): The directional case is best handled separately. We extrude the given convex body *temp* along the inverted light direction *–l*. This is done by moving the light-facing polygons of *temp* along *–l* up to the given scene bounding volume. The resulting holes are then filled with quads (see Figure 4.4.8).

Finding the Light Space Matrix L

The light space matrix **L** transforms from world space into light space, the local coordinate frame of the light. This is a space spanned by the plane in which the conventional shadow map is defined, and its normal. For point lights, light space also includes the point light projection. The LiSPSM projection **P** will be defined in light space. Therefore, light space needs to be rotated so that the view vector coincides with the projection direction of **P**.

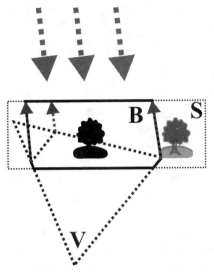

FIGURE 4.4.8   *The directional case of calculating the intersection body B.*

Initial Light Space Definition

The coordinate frame $\mathbf{L}_\nu$ is basically the transformation matrix used in conventional shadow mapping, but with the axes exchanged so that the LiSPSM projection is easier to define (more specifically, the z-axis of light space will also be the z-axis of the LiSPSM projection, which makes the mathematical formalism to find the optimal LiSPSM parameters more natural). It is created from the inverted light direction −1 and the view direction $\mathbf{v}$ in the same way as a look-at matrix (but with y and z changed), using −1 as view direction and $\mathbf{v}$ as up-vector (see Figure 4.4.6).

$$L_{\nu y} = -1$$
$$L_{\nu x} = v \times L_{\nu y}$$
$$L_{\nu z} = L_{\nu x} \times L_{\nu y}$$

This choice makes the shadow projection plane parallel to the *x/z*-plane (as opposed to the *x/y*-plane as in conventional shadow mapping), so the light is actually looking down the *y*-axis. For the frame's origin, we use the eye position for directional lights and the light position for point lights. The required matrix is the inverse of the matrix L_ν, which is constructed from the normalized versions of the above vectors.

For directional lights, we set the light space matrix $\mathbf{L} = \mathbf{L}_v^{-1}$. For point lights, we set $\mathbf{L} = \mathbf{L}_p \mathbf{L}_v^{-1}$, where $\mathbf{L}_p$ is the point light projection matrix associated with the light (a standard projection matrix as defined for example by an OpenGL Frustum-call).

Light Space Rotation

One degree of freedom in determining light space is the rotation on the shadow map plane. The initial frame defined previously rotates the shadow map so that the view vector, projected into the shadow map, points "upward" in the shadow map before perspective projection. For point lights, however, the projection can cause the frustum orientation to flip for views that are tilted with respect to the shadow map.

The aim is to rotate the shadow map (after projection!) so that the redistribution of shadow map samples occurs in the correct direction. We assume that the transformed view vector $\mathbf{v}_{ls}$ (after the point light perspective projection $\mathbf{L}_p$) indicates this "correct" direction. However, we cannot simply transform the *vector* $\mathbf{v}$ by $\mathbf{L}_p$, since parallel directions are not maintained by perspective projection. Instead, we transform a *ray* corresponding to $\mathbf{v}$. A natural choice for the starting point of this ray would be the eye position. However, there is no guarantee that the eye position is in front of the shadow plane or even anywhere near the body $\mathbf{B}$. We therefore employ the following simple algorithm to find a "safe" starting point for the orientation ray:

1. Create the body $\mathbf{LVS} = \mathbf{L} \cap \mathbf{V} \cap \mathbf{S}$ (using the same clipping operations as before).
2. Transform $\mathbf{LVS}$ into eye space.
3. Find a vertex $\mathbf{e}_{eye}$ of $\mathbf{LVS}$ nearest to the eye; that is, with maximum z-coordinate (note that $\mathbf{LVS}$ is by construction always in front of the eye). In order to find a more robust solution, we take the average of all vertices that are within a small distance to the vertex with the maximum z-coordinate.
4. Transform $\mathbf{e}_{eye}$ back into world space $\mathbf{e}_{world}$.

In most cases, $\mathbf{e}_{world}$ will be a point on the near clipping plane of the view frustum. To define the orientation ray, we also find another point $\mathbf{b}_{world}$, which is sufficiently far along $\mathbf{v}$ from $\mathbf{e}_{world}$.

The ray is then transformed to light space by transforming $\mathbf{e}_{world}$ and $\mathbf{b}_{world}$ using $\mathbf{L}$, and homogenizing the points, giving $\mathbf{e}_{ls}$ and $\mathbf{b}_{ls}$.

The rotation $\mathbf{L}_r$ is now created with the light space vectors $[0,1,0]$ as view vector and $\mathbf{b}_{ls} - \mathbf{e}_{ls}$ as up-vector in exactly the same way as in the previous section (look-at). Finally, we include this rotation into our light space matrix by setting $[\mathbf{L} = \mathbf{L}_r \mathbf{L}_p \mathbf{L}_v^{-1}]$.

Finding the LiSPSM Projection Matrix P

The LiSPSM projection matrix $\mathbf{P}$ creates a perspective transformation in light space such that the projection plane of $\mathbf{P}$ is perpendicular to the shadow map plane. As discussed earlier, this ensures that light rays are mapped to light rays so that light direction and type remain unchanged. In order to completely define $\mathbf{P}$, we need to find a projection center $\mathbf{C}$ and the frustum planes.

Finding the LiSPSM Projection Center C

We transform the focus body $\mathbf{B}$ into light space using $\mathbf{L}$ and calculate its bounding box in light space. The near and far planes of the LiSPSM projection are then defined to be at $z = B_{z_{near}}$ and $z = B_{z_{far}}$ (we work along the $-\mathbf{z}$-axis, so $B_{z_{near}} = B_{z_{max}}$ and $B_{z_{far}} = B_{z_{min}}$), respectively, for z-coordinates in light space. To find $\mathbf{C}$, we proceed in two steps. First, select an appropriate point $\mathbf{C}_{start}$ on the near plane of the LiSPSM projection, and then move distance n back from the near plane. The distance n of $\mathbf{C}$ to the near plane is the main parameter of the LiSPSM method and is discussed in a following section; here, we assume it is given.

$\mathbf{C}_{start}$ is defined as $\left\lfloor e_{ls_x}, e_{ls_y}, B_{z_{near}} \right\rfloor^{T}$, that is, the projection of $\mathbf{e}_{ls}$ (see the section "Light space rotation") onto the near plane. $\mathbf{e}_{ls}$ is a good starting point, as it is the best approximation to the original viewpoint we have available in light space (if $\mathbf{C}_{start}$ is close to the original viewpoint, this will help self-shadowing problems later) (see Figure 4.4.9)).

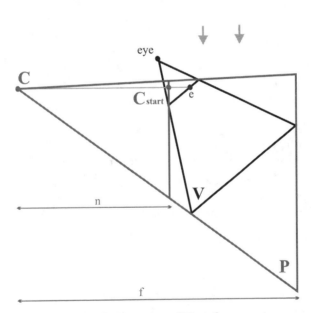

FIGURE 4.4.9   *Construction of $\mathbf{C}_{start}$ from a point $\mathbf{e}_{ls}$ on the camera near plane in light space (for simplicity, V is shown instead of B).*

After calculating $\mathbf{C}$ from $\mathbf{C}_{start}$ and n, $\mathbf{P}$ can be initialized with a translation $\mathbf{P}_t$ that centers light space at $\mathbf{C}$.

LiSPSM Frustum Planes

To find the frustum planes of $\mathbf{P}$, we project $\mathbf{B}$ onto the LiSPSM projection near plane and find its extents. This can be done using a temporary projection matrix $\mathbf{P}_{temp}$ with the frustum parameters $[l,r,b,t] = [-1,+1,-1,+1]$, while from the previous section it already follows that the near plane distance should be set to n, and the far plane distance to $n + |B_{z_{far}} - B_{z_{near}}|$. The bounding rectangle of the projected vertices of $\mathbf{B}$ gives the final frustum parameters l,r,b,t, so that $\mathbf{P}$ can be set up as $\mathbf{P}_p\mathbf{P}_t$. In a last step, $\mathbf{P}$ is also multiplied with the view-port matrix that is usually used to fit the result of the projection, which lies between -1 and 1 in all coordinates, into the range of $[0,1]$ for texture mapping.

Setting the Parameter n

The parameter n encodes the near plane distance of the LiSPSM projection and thus controls the strength of the perspective warping effect. As previously discussed, a smaller n gives a stronger warping effect, causing near shadows to gain quality and far shadows to lose quality. In [Wimmer04], we derived a formula for equalizing shadow quality at the near and far end of the LiSPSM frustum:

$$n_{opt} = \frac{1}{\sin(\gamma)}\left(z_n + \sqrt{z_n\left(z_n + d\sin(\gamma)\right)}\right)$$

In this formula, z_n is the near plane distance of the camera, d is the extent of the frustum of $\mathbf{P}$ in the light space z direction ($d = |B_{z_{far}} - B_{z_{near}}|$), and γ is the absolute value of the angle between view direction and light direction.

A New Formula

This formula works fine for directional lights. For point lights, however, we need to generalize the formula to take into account the change in scale induced by the perspective projection $\mathbf{L}_p$. We also need to take into account that the view frustum may be clipped by the scene bounding box or the light frustum. We have therefore derived a new formula that is applicable to all cases:

$$n_{opt} = \frac{d}{\sqrt{z_1/z_0} - 1}$$

The values z_0 and z_1 (signed!) represent the range of eye-space z-coordinates for which the perspective error should be equalized. Note that for a directional light and a view frustum is contained in the scene bounding box, $z_0 = -z_n$ and $z_1 = -(z_n + d\sin(\gamma))$, and the old formula results.

The Relevant z-values

The values z_0 and z_1 can be said to represent the eye-space z-range for which the LiSPSM projection is optimized. Mathematically, the formula given in the previous section is derived by choosing two points at the near and far plane of the LiSPSM frustum $\mathbf{P}$ and setting n, such that the perspective error is identical for these two points. We choose the points on a line perpendicular to the near plane of **P** (and therefore to the light direction).

As shown in Figure 4.4.10, the idea is to pick z_0 at the intersection of the camera and the LiSPSM frustum near planes. If the camera near plane does not intersect **B**, we translate it along the view Vector until it does, giving a new camera plane (as shown in a previous section, this plane goes through $\mathbf{e}_{world}$).

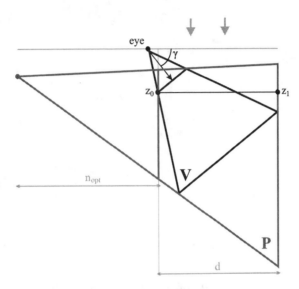

FIGURE 4.4.10 *Construction of z_0 and z_1 (for simplicity, V is shown instead of B).*

To find the intersection point $z_{0_{ls}}$ in light space, we transform the plane equation of the resulting camera plane into light space by multiplying it with the inverse transpose of **L**. Then, we intersect the transformed plane with the planes $z = B_{z_{near}}$ and $x = e_{ls_x}$ to give $z_{0_{ls}}$. The second point, at the LiSPSM far plane, is $z_{1_{ls}} = \lfloor z_{0_{ls_x}}, z_{0_{ls_y}}, B_{z_{far}} \rfloor^T$. The values z_0 and z_1 in eye space are calculated by transforming $z_{0_{ls}}$ and $z_{1_{ls}}$ using $\mathbf{L}^{-1}$ and the camera view matrix.

Note that due to construction, z_0 will usually be fixed at z_n if the camera near plane is at least partly visible in the light frustum. For directional lights, z_1 will give the same (but signed) result as in the original formula. For point lights, z_1 varies due to the perspective projection of the light. Also, both values can vary when **B** differs significantly from **V**.

Considerations for z_n and z_f

For many situations, z_0 and z_1 will—through the construction given in the section "The Relevant z-values"—largely depend on the near and far camera frustum planes

z_n and z_f, so we look at how these values influence shadow quality. Note first that the perspective aliasing error has two maxima at the (LiSPSM) near and far plane, and a minimum near the viewer (see Figure 4.4.11 for $z_f = 100$). When using the formula given previously, the maxima at the near and far plane are equalized. The value of these maxima can be shown to depend on the ratio z_1/z_0. This means that larger frusta (smaller z_n and/or larger z_f) lead to larger errors. However, this is not necessarily visible, because the location of the minimum can accidentally shift to a location where shadow quality is more apparent.

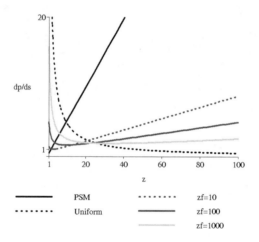

———	PSM	········	zf=10
········	Uniform	———	zf=100
		———	zf=1000

FIGURE 4.4.11   *Error distribution from near plane to z = 100 for LiSPSM (different values of z_f), uniform shadow maps ($z_f = 100$) and PSM ($z_f = 100$).*

Let us then analyze the simple case that the view direction is perpendicular to the light direction, with a directional light source and a view frustum contained in the scene bounding box. The parameter n then evaluates to

$$n_{opt} = z_n + \sqrt{z_n z_f}$$

Enlarging the frustum (bigger z_f) will lead to a smaller warping effect (larger n), because more accuracy needs to go into the distant regions, which can only be achieved by making the mapping more like a uniform shadow map. This can be undesirable for two reasons:

- The total maximum error increases for larger frusta.
- The location of minimum error moves away from the viewer, so the apparent shadow quality can be even lower even although the maximum error is not so strong (see Figure 4.4.10 for error plots with different z_f).

It is therefore advisable to choose z_f as small as possible. Sometimes, however, the far plane is determined through other application concerns. An interesting option is therefore to construct a "virtual" view frustum V_v for the calculation of n. In this virtual frustum, z_f can be used as a tuning parameter by which the user can determine up to which point in the actual view frustum shadows should have acceptable quality. V_v is applied by basing the calculations in the section "Setting the Parameter n" (that is, the values d, z_0, and z_1), not on the intersection body B, but on an intersection body calculated using V_v.

If occlusion culling is used before the main render pass (for example, in a preprocess or in a depth-only pass [Bittner04]), this can be used to adjust z_f automatically: just set z_f to the farthest vertex of the farthest encountered object. Note, however, that this may introduce shadow continuity problems if objects become visible or disappear, because the area of minimum error suddenly moves. Also note that occlusion culling may not be used to reduce the size of the shadow map, because occluded objects can cast shadows into visible areas.

Another effect is that sometimes a smaller value z_n can lead to better apparent shadow quality. A smaller z_n causes a stronger warping effect (smaller n), because more accuracy is needed at the near plane, which in turn moves the area of minimum error nearer to the viewer. The main reason for the apparent better quality is that this area of minimum error is more conspicuous to the viewer than distant shadows, which will deteriorate in the process. If the reduction of shadow quality in distant regions is not visible, then z_f was chosen to be too large in the first place.

B&B: Bias and Blur with LiSPSM

This section deals with the other two problems that occur with shadow mapping—self-shadowing and projection aliasing.

Correct Biasing

The self-shadowing problem, due to the different sampling patterns of the two different projections, is typically handled using biasing; that is, adding a small value to the shadow map value in the comparison so that the fragment always lies in front of the shadow map value if both come from the same object.

The amount of biasing needed actually depends on the slope of the shadow caster polygon; therefore, a *constant bias* does not work in general. Shadow mapping typically uses *slope-scale biasing*, where the graphics hardware generates a bias that correctly depends on the polygon slope (see Figure 4.4.12). Unfortunately, the perspective transform P also influences the shadow map depth value, creating a nonlinear (hyperbolic) distribution of z-values.

Two possible solutions to this problem require the use of fragment shading hardware: The first solution [Martin04] bypasses the matrix P for the shadow map depth values and generates linear depth values separately. The other solution [Kozlov04] calculates the bias in world space and transforms it into post-perspective space as well.

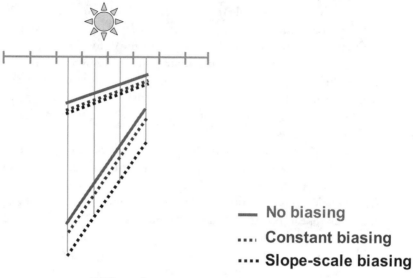

FIGURE 4.4.12   *Different biasing options.*

While both of these solutions can work, we have noticed that with LiSPSM, simple slope-scale biasing works fairly well. This is probably due to the choice of the projection center **C**, which is as close as possible to the original eye direction, and due to the fact that the required perspective warp is often not very strong.

The best results, however, were obtained using a technique called *backside mapping*. This simple trick reverses back-face culling for the shadow map rendering pass, thus only rendering the back sides of objects into the shadow map [Wang94]. This can only be used for closed objects, of course.

A Word on Projection Aliasing

Lighting Equation Effects

Although projection aliasing cannot be avoided using LiSPSM, the Phong lighting model actually comes to our rescue in cases of potential extreme aliasing. The diffuse term, $I = I_L \max(\mathbf{L} \bullet \mathbf{N}, 0)$, is small for receivers that are roughly parallel to the light direction (see Figure 4.4.3, left). Therefore, the shadow and thus the projection aliasing artifacts are barely set off against the remaining illumination. Equally, the specular term can only grow large if the viewer has roughly the same viewing angle as the light. However, in this case, there is no resolution mismatch (the cause for projection aliasing in the first place).

What should be avoided, though, is a strong per-light ambient term, which can lead to strong illumination regardless of the incoming angle. Since the ambient term is meant to simulate global interreflections, a hard shadow due to an ambient term would be unrealistic anyway.

Blurring

Should projection aliasing still be objectionable, the effect can be hidden using a simple image-space blur effect. Instead of rendering the shadow in the main rendering pass, we start with an initial pass where, in addition to the depth buffer, we write the shadow attenuation term (subject to percentage-closer filtering) to the color channel. The shadow term is then copied into a texture using a shader that executes a simple blur. It might be advisable to decrease the blur filter kernel with increasing depth value, so that small shadows in the distance don't get overly blurred. For multiple light sources, this has to be carried out for each light separately, either using multiple passes or the multiple render target functionality in newer cards. During the main rendering pass, the blurred shadow texture(s) is used to attenuate the diffuse color. No shadow calculations are necessary, and depth writes can be disabled.

Conclusion

Shadow mapping is a very popular shadow algorithm especially for computer games. While traditional shadow maps have been prone to aliasing errors, the techniques shown in this article help to improve the quality of shadow mapping in most common situations without increasing the cost of the basic algorithm. Light Space Perspective Shadow Maps redistribute shadow quality so that near objects receive more resolution, but also maintain sufficient resolution for far objects. Here, we showed how to deal robustly with perspective aliasing and biasing, and proposed a method to deal with the problem of projective aliasing.

LiSPSM works for both directional lights and point lights, but have a greater effect for lights that are directional or close to directional. This makes LiSPSM an ideal choice for outdoor lighting of huge scenes (see Figure 4.4.13).

Acknowledgments

We would like to than Stefan Reinalter for writing the DirectX version of the demo.

References

[Bittner04] Bittner, Jiří, Michael Wimmer, Harald Piringer, and Werner Purgathofer, "Coherent Hierarchical Culling: Hardware Occlusion Queries Made Useful," Computer Graphics Forum, vol. 23, no. 3 (EUROGRAPHICS 2004), pp. 615–624.

[Forsyth05] Forsyth, Tom, "Shadowbuffer Frustum Partitioning," *ShaderX⁴*, edited by Wolfgang Engel, Charles River Media, 2005.

[Kozlov04] Kozlov, Simon, "Perspective Shadow Maps: Care and Feeding," *GPU Gems*, edited by R. Fernando, Addison Wesley, 2004: pp. 217–244.

[Martin04] Martin, Tobias, and Tiow-Seng Tan, "Anti-aliasing and continuity with trapezoidal shadow maps," Rendering Techniques 2004 (Proceedings of the Eurographics Symposium on Rendering 2004), pp. 153–160.

FIGURE 4.4.13   *Illustrates the effect of the LiSPSM perspective warp (right) in comparison to standard shadow mapping (left). The lower images show the corresponding light views.*

[Schüler05] Schüler, Christian, "Eliminating Surface Acne with Gradient Shadow Mapping," *ShaderX⁴*, edited by Wolfgang Engel, Charles River Media, 2005.

[Stamminger02] Stamminger, Marc, and Georges Drettakis, "Perspective shadow maps," Computer Graphics, vol. 21, no. 3 (SIGGRAPH 2002), pp. 557–562.

[Wang94] Wang, Yulan, and Steven Molnar, "Second depth shadow mapping," UNC-CS Technical Report TR94-019, University of North Carolina, 1994.

[Wimmer04] Wimmer, Michael, Daniel Scherzer, Werner Purgathofer. "Light Space Perspective Shadow Maps," Rendering Techniques 2004 (Proceedings of the Eurographics Symposium on Rendering 2004), pp. 143–151.

4.5

Making Shadow Buffers Robust Using Multiple Dynamic Frustums

Tom Forsyth

Introduction

Creating shadows using shadow buffers is becoming more and more popular over time. It has lower fill-rate requirements than the main alternative of shadow volumes, can be used on a wider range of geometric objects, and techniques exist or are being developed to add advanced effects such as partial shadowing and penumbrae.

However, while significant progress is being made in the area of the algorithms used to render each pixel affected by a shadow buffer, there are still considerable problems when deciding which parts of the scene should go in a particular shadow buffer, and what frustum to use when rendering that shadow buffer. These high-level questions are fairly simple to solve for constrained scenes, or cases where the lighting environment is fixed ahead of time (for example, *Splinter Cell* [SplinterCell02]). For more general scenes with unconstrained lighting and geometry environments, there are still considerable problems.

Standard Projection

The most obvious sort of projection is the standard perspective projection used by most rendering systems. This type of projection is well supported and simple to calculate, and it works fine in many situations. However, it has some problems.

The major drawback is the distribution of texel density. When the scene is rendered to the shadow buffer using the standard perspective projection, the size of an object in the shadow buffer is inversely proportional to the distance of the object from the light. Put another way, if we take a single texel of the shadow buffer and project it back out into the world and measure its size in meters, we find it is directly proportional to the distance from the light. Thus, at double the distance from the light, texels are twice as large as measured in meters.

In fact, this size is a minimum size only. The texels may in fact be much larger because they are being projected on an object whose surface is not perpendicular to the projection. However, there is little that can be done about this, and according to the angle the size may grow arbitrarily large, so all we can really talk about is the minimum size of the texels. In practice this is a reasonable guide to visual quality.

Thus, the precision of the shadow cast by the light drops off linearly as the distance from the light increases and aliasing artifacts increase. The big problem comes when we examine what precision we require for a particular scene that is being rendered. Now we find that for a consistent visual quality, the highest precision is required closest to the camera. There, objects occupy more screen pixels, and so a particular amount of precision (measured in meters) is far more noticeable. As objects go farther away from the camera, the precision requirements drop, as a texel 1 meter in size covers a smaller number of screen pixels.

It is clear that the amount of precision delivered by the shadow buffer's choice of perspective projection and the precision level required by the camera are independent; one does not affect the other. The ratio between the two precision values determines how much visual aliasing occurs in the scene. This causes the amount of aliasing in the scene to vary widely according to which part of the scene is being looked at.

In particular, consider the standard pathological "dueling frustums" case. This occurs when the camera is looking almost directly at the light source and there is a series of objects in between the two being both lit and viewed. An example of this is a camera looking down a long hallway with a light at the far end, and a series of objects distributed on the floor between the camera and the light.

The crucial measurement for aliasing quality is the texel/pixel ratio. As the size of projected shadow buffer texels goes above 1 pixel in the camera's view, aliasing problems arise. For any given size of shadow buffer and any chosen field of view for the shadow buffer's perspective projection, the size of the texels projected on the walls increases as the walls get further from the light source. But that is happening as the walls get closer to the camera—exactly the wrong behavior for good anti-aliasing. Ideally, the texel size should drop as the walls get closer to the camera. This is why this case is called "dueling frustums" (see Figure 4.5.1), because the requirements for good precision in one frustum (the camera's) are exactly opposite to the behavior caused by the other frustum (the light/shadow buffer's).

FIGURE 4.5.1   *(a) through (c)—dueling frustums.*

Figure 4.5.1 shows an example of dueling frustums. Image 4.5.1(a) shows an overhead view with a light on the left and the camera on the right. The shadow buffer here is rendered with a 16-pixel checkerboard pattern to show the relative texel sizes in the scene. Figure 4.5.1(b) shows the view from the light looking toward the camera, in which all the texels are similar sizes, because this is roughly the view rendered to the shadow buffer. Figure 4.5.1(c) shows the view from the camera. Instead of an even texel size, the size varies from being too small near the light to being too large near the camera.

This problem could be alleviated by increasing the overall texel density in the shadow buffer by giving it more texels; for example, using a 1024×1024 texture instead of a 512×512 texture. The problem is that this merely halves the width of the texels and halves the aliasing problem, but it costs four times the rendering time. And for many of the objects in the scene, such as those close to the light, it is pointless. They already have a lot of texels devoted to them, and they are far away from the camera, so their texel-to-pixel ratio is well below 1 already. It does not need to drop any further, as that is a waste of fill rate and memory.

It is clear from this discussion that using a single perspective projection for each light does not work very well. Doing so can easily put texel precision where it is least necessary, and in a pathological way. Fortunately, the standard rendering pipeline is capable of a more generalized set of projections than the regular ones, and these variants have some useful properties.

Perspective Shadow Mapping and Relations

Perspective Shadow Mapping (PSM) is a cunning trick that uses more of the flexibility of the 4×4 projection matrix in most rendering pipelines [Stamminger02].

The idea is to artificially enlarge objects near the camera. The scene is still rendered from the point of view of the light, but because objects near the camera are enlarged, they get more of the available texel resolution in many cases.

This is somewhat difficult to visualize in practice, and I advise many readers not to try too hard; it breaks all rules of perspective and hurts the brain somewhat. However, the technique is effective in many cases.

There are three major problems with PSM. First, it is tricky to implement. The mathematics are complex, and when rendering the scene, parallel lights need to actually change into point lights, and some point lights need to change into parallel lights or even "anti-point" lights, where the light converges to a point rather than emerging from one.

Second, although it greatly improves the case where the light is shining roughly at right angles to the direction of view, it still does not solve the pathological "dueling frustums" case; in fact, it has no effect on it at all. In that situation, PSM reduces to the same projection as the standard one.

Finally, this technique does not help us much in the case of a point light that shines in all directions. No single projection can span more than 180 degrees of view, so multiple frustums and shadow buffers are still required.

There are further refinements and variants of PSM that help solve or alleviate some of the problems, most notably Trapezoidal Shadow Mapping [Martin04] and Light-Space Perspective Shadow Maps (LiSPSM) [Wimmer04] (see also Article 4.4 in this section on efficient implementation of LiSPSM). However, these still suffer from the fact that they are simply different versions of the existing pipeline's 4 × 4 projection matrix.

Why a Single Projection Is Not Sufficient

The summary of the preceding discussion is that while you can refine the mechanism for mapping a scene into a single shadow buffer with considerable flexibility, it is impossible to get away from the fundamental problem that the projection must be performed such that objects closer to the light must occupy more texels. And yet in some scenes such as the "dueling frustums" case, for effective distribution of rendering power and quality, we require things closer to the light (further from the camera) to occupy fewer texels. There is no single mapping that allows this.

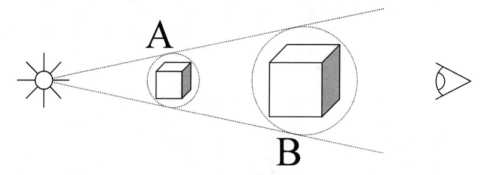

FIGURE 4.5.2   *Size and distance from the camera affect texel resolution, so object B needs a much higher resolution that object A.*

A simple proof of this can be seen in Figure 4.5.2. Object A is exactly big enough to fully shadow object B. They must therefore be rendered at the same size in the shadow buffer and cover the same number of texels. But object B is both closer to the camera and physically bigger, so ideally it would have many more shadow buffer texels devoted to it than object A. No single projection can accommodate both these requirements.

Additionally, all useful mappings must work within the confines of the existing rendering pipeline, which renders triangles with straight edges. Therefore, all mappings must also preserve straight lines. No mappings of this type are able to map the full 360-degree area of influence of a point light source onto a single rendering target. Although other mappings such as paraboloid or spherical mapping can help, they are not compatible with the existing rendering pipeline without large amounts of triangle tessellation. And they still do not solve the problem of distributing precision only where it is needed.

We therefore need to discard the notion of finding the "perfect mapping"—there is no such thing!

Biting the Bullet

Having accepted that no single projection can work in all cases, we face the prospect of having to deal with multiple projections and multiple shadow buffers for each light. That is, we will have multiple, possibly overlapping, shadow buffers, each being used for different shadows in different places in the scene. A simple existing example of this is to use a cube map composed of six different projections to cast shadows in all directions from a point light source.

Although this is more complex than a single shadow buffer, once we have done this and dealt with the complexity of using multiple projections and shadow buffers, we will see that many of the hardest problems faced previously are solved fairly elegantly. We can use different shadow buffers with different sizes and fields of view for shadows in different parts of the scene, and by choosing their fields of view and sizes in texels appropriately, we can concentrate precision and rendering power only where it is needed.

However, using this technique raises a host of questions, such as:

- How do we decide how many shadow buffers to use?
- How do we decide how big they are?
- How do we find what their frustums should be?
- How do we find what their *optimal* frustums should be?
- How do we deal with the areas where two shadow buffers meet?

These are all tough questions, and to answer them all at once is difficult. Fortunately, we can shrink these down to a much simpler pair of questions:

- Given a camera and a light source, which projection and size of shadow buffer should we use to optimally render a single object?
- Given multiple projections and shadow buffer sizes (presumably, one for each object in the scene), can we merge any two of them into one with acceptable efficiency?

These are much easier to answer, and doing so solves many of the problems listed before. But first, let us examine some assumptions and simplifications.

Visible Texel Density Across an Object Is Uniform

Rather than consider all the different parts of an object individually, it is far easier to consider just one point on an object, and consider it lit by a parallel light source. This is a common approximation for many rendering algorithms. The assumption is that a single object is relatively small compared to the distance from it to either the light or the camera, and thus we can consider the lighting solution for one part of the object to apply equally well (within some tolerance) to all other parts of the object.

The other part of the assumption is that we are going to ignore (or fudge) the fact that we are going to calculate only the texel size for surfaces that directly face the light and hope that this is a suitable approximation. As the actual surface of the object faces less toward the light and is lit more obliquely, the size of texels grows rapidly. Fortunately, the lighting in these areas is dim; the perceived shape of the shadows cast upon the surface also becomes distorted, and the eye is less able to tell whether the shadows are strictly "correct" or not, so the perceived error is small. In practice, a global texel-size multiplication factor chosen by experimentation accounts for this effect tolerably well.

The major types of objects that do not obey this assumption are large objects such as terrain, floor tiles, ceilings, walls, entire buildings, objects very close to the camera or a light source, or objects which themselves contain sources of light. Some of these can be handled by special-case code and will be discussed later.

The nice thing about this assumption is that it is true for the vast majority of objects in any given scene. Additionally, in general the more complex the scene, the higher the proportion of objects for which it is true, since as a scene becomes more complex, the average size of objects in the scene tends to decrease. There is a limit to how many walls and desks an indoor office scene can contain, but there is no practical limit to the number of mugs, books, and pens that can occupy those desks. This means that any special-case code is not usually a significant hit to performance.

Each Object Has Exactly One Shadow Buffer for Each Light

This partly follows on from the previous assumption, but it is worth restating. Since the visible texel density (the rendered texel/pixel ratio) is approximated to be constant across an object, it follows that there needs to be only a single shadow buffer that holds the shadowing information for any single object from any single light. This simplifies the algorithm, as once you know the object and the light in question, you need to worry about only a single shadow buffer, and you have all the information needed for rendering.

Additionally, this approach almost manages to solve one of the first questions raised, "how do we deal with the areas where two shadow buffers meet?" by adopting the Zen tactic of "un-asking" the question. We simply assume that there is only ever one shadow buffer per object per light, and thus two shadow buffers can never meet. In fact, this is overly optimistic, but it is remarkably effective, and we will try to deal with the exceptions later.

Note that when talking about a single shadow buffer for a single object, we need to consider how we render only the shadows that *fall* on that object, the shadow receiver. We can ignore how we deal with the *casters* of the shadows. The only thing that determines the visible quality of shadows is how the shadow buffer is mapped onto the receivers. It does not matter how many, how large, or how complex the shadow casters are, or where exactly they are positioned relative to the camera, receiver, or light; the quality of shadows cast is the same.

The Basic Algorithm

The first step is to solve the problem "given a camera, a light source, and an object, choose which projection and size of shadow buffer to use." With the previous assumption, and by making a few more simple ones, this is actually fairly easy.

We have a specified ratio of shadow-buffer texels to screen pixels that we wish to achieve for the entire scene, which determines the visual quality of the shadows. This can be set by a variety of methods, but fundamentally it is a combination of memory limits, rendering speed, and user preference.

With the camera field of view and the screen size and the desired number of texels per screen pixel, a global measure of desired texels per radian for the entire scene is found.

Next, for each object in the scene, the positions of the camera and the object define a desired "texels per meter" on the object that meet the desired quality of shadows.

Now we take each light in the scene and test each object the light can hit that is in the visible frustum. Objects may be culled early on by portal or PVS tests reporting either that the object is not visible to the camera or that the current light cannot illuminate the object.

For each object, we find the conical frustum that has the light as its apex and snugly encloses the object's bounding sphere. The object has a desired number of texels per meter for any shadow buffers being used by it, and we know how large the object is and what the apex angle of the frustum is, so we can calculate the number of texels per radian (somewhat inaccurately called a "texel density" here) required for this frustum. We can also determine the resolution a shadow buffer must be to cover this frustum with that density.

Next, allocate a shadow buffer of that size, set the rendering view to be at the light's position, pointing at the object with exactly the field of view of the frustum, such that the object is perfectly framed, and render the shadow buffer. The objects that are rendered to the shadow buffer include all those between the target object and the light that intersect the frustum, no matter what their size. As mentioned previously, the quality of a shadow buffer's shadows is entirely dependent on what it *casts* its shadow on (the shadow's receiver), not on what is actually causing the shadow (the shadow caster).

Finally, the object is rendered on the screen using the shadow buffer, using standard shadow-buffer methods.

Refinements

The algorithm given so far is extremely inefficient. The number of shadow buffers and rendering passes required is roughly equal to the number of objects in the scene multiplied by the number of lights in the scene, and each shadow buffer must render a large fraction of the objects in the scene. Although it is inefficient, it shows the principles at work. There are a few minor techniques that make this algorithm more efficient, and one very major refinement.

Instead of rendering a shadow buffer, and then rendering the object with the lighting pass that uses that shadow buffer, it is more efficient to render all of the shadow buffers for a single light at once. This way, the rendering view does not need updating as much; it simply turns but does not move, because it is always at the light's position. This means any scene traversal and visibility culling of objects can be performed just once, and then used for all the shadow buffers that the light uses.

Once all the shadow buffers for a single light are rendered, the view can be returned to the standard camera and we can perform the lighting pass for all the objects in the scene. This is more efficient because the lighting context needs to be set up only once.

Merging Frustums

The greatest optimization for the algorithm comes from realizing that two objects that are close together use similar (and overlapping) shadow-buffer frustums and sizes, and will have a similar set of shadow casters in each. The efficient thing to do is to merge them into a single frustum that satisfies the requirements of both objects.

The requirements for the new combined frustum are simple: it must enclose the bounding spheres of both objects, and its texel per radian density must be greater than or equal to both the required texel densities. It does not matter for most shadow-buffering algorithms if there is a higher texel density than required; there is only a loss in quality when there is a lower texel density. However, it can be inefficient to merge two frustums of very different densities. Consider the case shown in Figure 4.5.3. Objects A and B have light frustums that are good candidates for merging, but A is close to the light and far from the camera, while B is the reverse. This is the classic "dueling frustum" case.

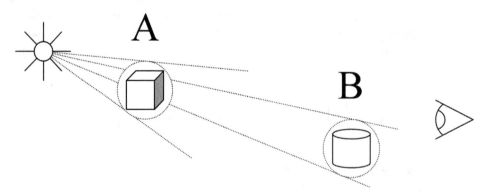

FIGURE 4.5.3   *Merging rules.*

Object B requires a high texels-per-meter ratio because it is close to the camera, but its light frustum is small, so it has a very high texel-per-radian density. Object A is far from the camera and so has a low texel-per-meter ratio, and being close to the light, its frustum covers a lot of radians, and so has a very low texels-per-radian density. If we try to merge these two, we must use the higher of the two texel-per-radian densities (B's), but also the larger frustum of A. This results in a large shadow buffer, meaning that we burn a lot of time drawing a lot of texels. Sadly, most of these texels are wasted, being used for the shadows on A, which are not particularly significant in the scene.

Conversely, merging the two frustums does have a positive benefit: it reduces the number of objects that must be sent down the rendering pipeline. As well as objects A and B, imagine there is an object C that casts shadows on both of them. Using a single frustum, we need to render all three objects to the single shadow buffer. But using two different frustums, the number rises. Object B's shadow buffer still needs to have all three objects rendered into it, but object A's shadow buffer also needs to have objects A and C rendered into it (it does not need object B, because we can use a bounding sphere test to check that object B is too far from the light to cast shadows onto object A). This is an increase from three rendered objects to five.

One way to resolve this is a cutoff ratio between the two texel density values. If the difference is beyond this ratio, the merging is not attempted, and the two are left as separate frustums. Exactly what this ratio is set to depends on the specific rendering architecture. By merging the frustums, we increase the fill rate and memory demands of the shadow buffers. By not merging, we increase the number of objects that must be rendered. In practice, a 4:1 maximum ratio seems to work acceptably for current PC graphics cards, but for different systems there may be different trade-offs.

There is also a second, much simpler cutoff value: the maximum size of a shadow buffer. This is a hard limit for most graphics architectures, often around 2048×2048 texels. If the required texels per radian for the combined frustum needs a shadow buffer larger than this, it simply cannot be done, and the two cannot be merged. In practice, this is rarely a limitation on the PC, and this cutoff is more commonly used to quickly reject extremely inefficient cases such as trying to merge two small objects that are widely separated by empty space. On a console, where video memory is precious, this limit may be more important.

Merging the two frustums is mathematically fiddly, but is shown in the included cone library code. Note the variety of results the merging can produce. The result may be the same as one of the input cones if the other lies entirely inside it, a merging of the two cones, or may not be meaningful because the result cone has an apex angle of greater than 180 degrees. Although it is still a well-formed cone (it is a cone facing in the opposite direction), it is not a frustum that can actually be rendered in existing graphics pipelines. In practice, we also place a stricter limit on the apex angle of the frustum of around 120 degrees. Beyond this angle, the edges of the rendering are distorted so much that texels are used inefficiently, and it is usually better to use two separate frustums instead of one distorted one.

By successively combining frustums and shadow buffers together in this way, the number of shadow buffers and rendering passes required is minimized, while still retaining the flexibility of the original algorithm. Texels are used where they are most effective at producing visible quality, and the distribution automatically copes with any relative positions of camera, object, and light. This includes the dueling frustums case, and the case of an omnidirectional light surrounded by objects, without requiring any special projections or cube-map hardware. In addition, the algorithm is fully dynamic and automatically copes with uneven distributions of objects. If no objects are visible on one side of a light source (for example, the very common case when the light source itself is off one side of the screen), no shadow buffers are used for that area, and no texture memory is wasted.

Merging Order

Note that we have not yet described in what order frustum merges are attempted. This is an area ripe for future research, but the good news is that even a fairly basic greedy algorithm yields acceptable results.

For each light source, a list of the current shadow-buffer frustums and their texels-per-radian values are kept. The world database is traversed in whatever order it happens to be, and each object is considered in turn. First, the object is rejected as a shadow receiver for a variety of reasons: it is invisible to the camera, it is out of range of the light source, and so on.

Then, the object tests all existing frustums for the light to see if any are already suitable for it, both geometrically and for texel density. If so, it adds itself to the list of receivers using that shadow buffer for their shadows. This is a simple greedy search. It does not attempt to find a "best" frustum, it simply picks the first one. In our test application, retrofitting shadows to the *StarTopia* engine, finding the best frustum did not seem to give any useful improvement in quality or rendering time—it simply increased search time.

If no existing frustum is suitable, the object then attempts to find the best existing frustum that it can enlarge (merge with) or refine (increase the texel density) to make it suitable. Many heuristics could be used to measure which is the "best" to modify, but one that seems to work well is to find the frustum whose merged result has the smallest apex angle.

Sometimes, there is no frustum that can be enlarged. In this case, the object creates a new frustum that covers just itself and has the texel density it requires.

Once all frustums for a particular light have been found, the shadow buffer memory is actually allocated, the shadow buffers rendered, and the lighting pass then uses them.

There are many ways to perform the final rendering steps, sorting by light or shadow-buffer texture or object or front-to-back or by shader, according to which methods are optimal for the chosen hardware platform. For a typical DX9-style graphics card, rendering the "ambient" pass front to back, followed by rendering the lighting passes sorted by light, seems to give the best results.

Limits and Enhancements to the Algorithm

The algorithm as given has some weaknesses and cases it does not work well for. Some have already been mentioned in passing, and others are more fundamental. Some solutions are suggested here, although none has been investigated in detail.

Objects Close to the Camera

When an object is close to the camera, or the camera goes inside the object's bounding sphere, the approximation of using the bounding sphere of the object no longer works well.

One option may be to break the object into multiple subobjects and treat each individually. This may mean fragmentation into convex hulls, or single triangles, or even tessellating the individual triangles. Another option may be to try to use the techniques from Perspective Shadow Maps (or TSM or LiSPSM) and the like to distribute the precision across these objects better before having to break them into multiple parts.

The current demo simply clamps the texels-per-meter value to a tweakable minimum, so as the camera gets closer, the shadow buffer texels cease getting smaller in physical size and start getting larger in pixels. This causes more aliasing to be visible.

Objects Close to the Light

Objects close to light sources pose similar problems, again because the approximation of using a bounding sphere breaks down. They cause additional problems because an object with a light source inside it can never be rendered to a single 2D shadow buffer because its frustum covers more than 180 degrees. One option is to fragment the object as with the case of an object close to the camera. However, there may be many lights in a scene, and this fragmentation is expensive, so splitting may be required for many objects.

Another possible option is to use a cube-map shadow buffer. The sides of the cube map are rendered as six individual shadow-buffer frustums; when rendering the object, the hardware joins the edges together seamlessly.

Note that the only shadows that are tricky in this case are those cast *onto* the large object. The large object can cast shadows onto *other* objects just fine. Those other objects are farther from the light, they have perfectly normal (non-cube-map) shadow buffers, and the large object is rendered to them with a standard projection. The fact that most of the large object is clipped during this rendering does not matter, as the shadows are still of a consistent quality.

With this in mind, it is worth mentioning a surprisingly good hack for large, close objects: simply don't create shadows for them at all! If the light source is close to the object, the chance of another object actually getting in the way to cast shadows is slim. This is the approach the demo takes, and it works very well. Of course, the large object does not self-shadow either, which can be a problem.

Objects Close to Both Camera and Light

The worst cases are objects large enough to be close to both a camera and a light, such as walls, buildings, and landscape floor tiles. Although a cube-map shadow buffer can be used, this case suffers badly from the dueling frustum problem. At least three of the cube-map faces will be pointing away from the viewer, and most known hardware requires that all six faces of a cube map be the same texel size, so these faces will be far larger than is actually required for a given texel density.

Clipping, fragmentation, and tessellation can be used, as with objects close to the viewer. With luck or planning, there will be few of these in a frame.

Objects that Are Not Spheres

This problem is more an efficiency concern. Objects such as flat floor tiles or wall tiles obviously break the bounding sphere approximation. In most cases, they display worse aliasing than a sphere; unless they are face-on to the light, the shadow-buffer texels will be stretched across their surface, and thus have fewer texels in one direction than another. To compensate, the required texel density must be raised appropriately. For floor tiles, this can be calculated algorithmically, but in practice, floor tiles are also distorted along the view axis (unless the camera is looking straight down), and while this can also be corrected for algorithmically, in general it is usually easier and just as effective to apply a tweak factor specific to each type of object that multiplies the results of the spherical approximation by a fixed number. Sadly, there are always cases where either the camera or the light looks along the plane at such an angle that no simple mapping can produce sufficient quality.

Frame-to-Frame Coherency

A slightly unexpected problem is that of frame-to-frame coherence. Because the size and projections of shadow buffers are dynamic, it depends on the precise arrangement of the lights and the camera in the scene, and also the exact positions of objects. Because the frustum-merging algorithm is greedy with no memory of the previous frame, as any of these factors change, the arrangement of shadow buffers can change dramatically. This causes discontinuous jumps in image quality from frame to frame.

The human eye is surprisingly tolerant of discontinuities when either the camera or the light source is moving. Although the jumps are visible, they are not particularly objectionable in most cases.

The largest problem occurs if neither camera nor lights move. Here, the eye expects the scene to be static, with no changing pixels except where an object is actually moving. However, because of the greedy algorithm, a single moving object in the corner of the screen may cause changes in shadowing across the entire scene.

There may be ways to solve this by using the shadow buffers found in the previous frame as "seeds" to the algorithm used for the next frame, ensuring that particular objects use the same frustums and shadow buffers as much as possible.

Hiding Seams

The previous section mentioned abrupt temporal changes as objects transition from one shadow buffer to another, but there is a related problem of abrupt spatial changes. Frequently, a large object such as terrain will be broken up into multiple pieces, and adjacent pieces may be given different shadow buffers. The pieces usually share normals, texture coordinates, and textures, and are both meant to be the same object, such as a field of grass. However, because each shadow buffer shows slightly different aliasing artifacts (each of which may not be objectionable in isolation), the seam between them becomes visible as a sharp line of discontinuity. An example of this is shown in Figure 4.5.4, where the texels to the left of the line (added for illustration) are from a different shadow buffer to those on the right of the line, with a significant difference in size and aliasing quality.

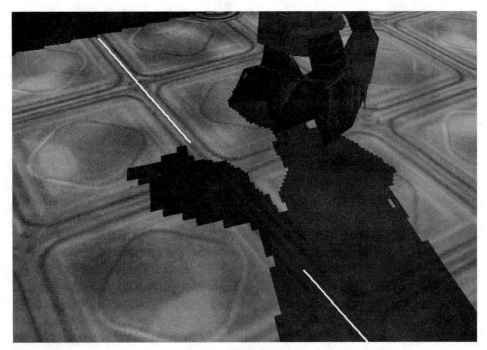

FIGURE 4.5.4 *Varying shadow-buffer resolution artifact at a seam between tiles.*

One possibility tried by others is to perform a screen-space blur of the shadowed/ not shadowed value for each light. This removes the aliasing within each shadow buffer, and smoothes over these boundary discontinuities. While effective, this blur may be expensive on certain hardware.

Another possible alternative is to store or generate connectivity information for each piece of a conceptually whole object and use this to cross-fade between two adjacent shadow buffers at the seam.

Using More Complex Projections

So far, we have assumed that all shadow-buffer frustums use standard perspective projections. However, there is nothing to prevent us using the more advanced projections such as PSM, TSM, and LiSPSM to improve efficiency further. Normally, these algorithms can be difficult to use, have annoying pathological cases, and in many cases provide no benefit over a standard projection.

Fortunately, this frustum-allocation algorithm allows them to be used despite these limitations. Where an advanced projection method does not work well or hits a case that is difficult to implement, the system can try a different projection method, or it can always fall back to a conventional frustum and standard projection system.

This allows different projection methods to be used together for different frustums, even using multiple techniques on the same light source, taking advantage of each technique's particular strengths, but none of its weaknesses.

The Demo

ON THE CD

The demo is a modification of a commercial game called *StarTopia* [StarTopia]. Developing these algorithms made it painfully aware of how well some shadow-buffering algorithms can work in a simple constrained demo, and how badly they can fail in a real, working game. Fortunately, a real game with an engine that was understood well was available, and the shadow-buffer algorithms were retrofitted into *StarTopia*. What is more, the environment is deliberately unconstrained, as a major part of the game is constructing your own architecture, complete with lighting. If ever there was a challenge for a shadowing algorithm, this is surely it!

Within the limitations of the *StarTopia* engine, the algorithm worked even better than expected, with good speed (see caveats below), and requiring minimal changes to art resources. One modification involved marking very small light sources as being so small that there was no point in trying to render them with shadows—they were there simply for spot effects, not illumination. The other modification was moving some light sources that sat on the floor (because it was easy to author them that way) to a small height above the floor. Leaving them sitting level with the floor caused various problems, as the floor sometimes occluded and sometimes didn't, depending on floating-point accuracy epsilons.

The limitations of the engine are:

- It uses a DirectX7 engine, so no pixel shaders are available.
- It uses an ID-based shadow buffer (also called a "priority buffer") with 8-bit values, and performs shadowed rendering by doing an 8-bit equality-comparison using the alpha-test circuitry.
- The floor tiles always get assigned ID 0 (because they cannot self-shadow), but all other objects are assigned their ID semirandomly. Ideally, they should be allocated so that no two objects that overlap in a light frustum are assigned the same ID, but this is a lot of work to add. Therefore, there is a slight chance that two objects may share the same ID, preventing one from casting shadows onto the other.

- Because there is no percentage-closer filtering or similar cleverness, objects have dark "halos" around their edges where the shadow-buffer sampling picks up the ID of the floor instead of the object, and thus thinks the object is in shadow. There are ways to fix this (although it is difficult without pixel shaders), but that wasn't the point of the exercise, so I left it.
- Similarly, the shadow-buffer texels are clearly visible, with no rounding or blurring possible under DirectX7. Again, this is not the point of the exercise—indeed the idea is to achieve a consistent quality despite this obvious aliasing.
- *StarTopia*'s engine does not natively have the concept of multiple render targets or rendering a single object multiple times in a frame. Thus, without extensive rewriting, certain things are hardwired into the rendering engine. When it renders an object, it also does animation sampling, deformation, mouse hit-detection, transformation, and lighting on the CPU—every time. Since objects can be rendered many times (one ambient pass, plus at least two passes for every light that hits the object, and often more), this is an absurd waste of CPU effort. However, because *StarTopia* was designed to run on a 300 MHz Pentium 2, and the demo code was written on a 2.8 GHz Pentium 4, the speed is still fairly acceptable even on complex scenes!

Naturally, any game even considering having real-time shadows in it will have planned for the features ahead of time, as they are integral to any shadowing technique and will not suffer from most of these problems.

More details about *StarTopia* and the shadow-buffer modification (including pictures) can be found at *http://www.eelpi.gotdns.org/startopia/startopia.html*. Figure 4.5.5 shows an image from the demo.

FIGURE 4.5.5 StarTopia, *with shadows using shadow-buffer partitioning. See color plates 8 and 9.*

Conclusion

This algorithm is simple and lacks many refinements mentioned previously. However, despite these it still shows itself to be robust, high quality, and efficient. Fitted with a modern, low-level shadow-buffering renderer using techniques such as percentage-closer filtering, high-quality pixel shaders, cube maps, and many of the other techniques from this book, it should be possible to produce an extremely effective, fast, and versatile engine with ubiquitous shadows.

References

[SplinterCell02] "Tom Clancy's Splinter Cell," developed and published by Ubi Soft, 2002.

[StarTopia00] "StarTopia," developed by Mucky Foot Productions, published by Eidos Interactive, 2000.

[Martin04] Martin, Tobias, and Tiow-Seng Tan, "Anti-aliasing and continuity with trapezoidal shadow maps," Rendering Techniques 2004 (Proceedings of the Eurographics Symposium on Rendering 2004): pp. 153–160.

[Stamminger02] Stamminger, Marc, and Georges Drettakis, "Perspective shadow maps," Computer Graphics, vol. 21, no. 3 (SIGGRAPH 2002): pp. 557–562.

[Wimmer04] Wimmer, Michael, Daniel Scherzer, and Werner Purgathofer, "Light Space Perspective Shadow Maps," Rendering Techniques 2004 (Proceedings of the Eurographics Symposium on Rendering 2004): pp. 143–151.

3D ENGINE DESIGN

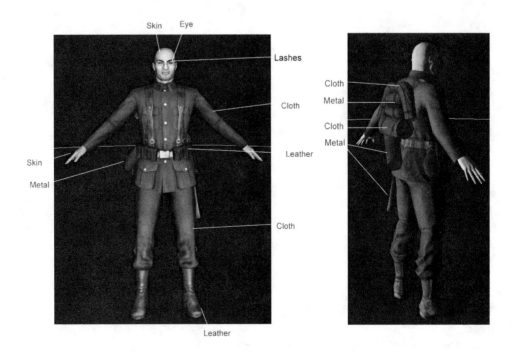

Introduction

Tom Forsyth

As hardware capabilities increase, the simple act of rendering a mesh becomes increasingly complex. A basic low-level interface of setting rendering states, textures, shaders, constants, vertices, and indices is far too fine-grained to deal with directly in modern projects, and there is a need for ever more abstraction layers to wrap up this complexity.

The current favorite for this high-level interface is the D3DXEffects framework that comes with the D3D SDK. This incorporates a huge amount of robust compiling, interface, and scripting code that no application writer would relish rewriting. However, its very flexibility can be intimidating, and finding the optimal path can involve experimentation. The three articles in this section show the results of the authors' experience, and all deal with various aspects of using the effects framework efficiently.

Aras Pranckevičius presents some good low-level interface tips for working with the D3DXEffects framework. The framework has a lot of great timesaving functionality, but getting optimal performance is still somewhat of an art. This article shows how to achieve most of the gains using a few simple rules and wrappers.

Using post-processing effects is still a tricky business as it does not fit the existing one-mesh-at-a-time rendering model. Existing techniques tend to be hard-coded, limiting artistic freedom and increasing iteration time. Gilberto Rosado shows how to integrate post-processing into the D3DXEffect framework, putting a friendlier face on an awkward subject.

Wolfgang Engel presents a high-level overview and shows the entire modern rendering pipeline. This starts with the art tool interface and goes down through multiple exporters, source/data repositories, level editing and material tweaking, runtime resource management, and finally to the renderer. In particular, he highlights the difference between a particular shader used for a particular object and the general class of similar shaders, and shows how the distinction can be used to reduce artist workload and increase speed.

5.1

Tips and Tricks for D3DX Effects-Based Renderers

Aras Pranckevičius

Introduction

This article describes some tips and tricks for implementing a simple D3DX effects-based renderer. The renderer discussed does not provide any particular techniques (such as shadow maps, HDR, or bump-mapping); it is only a system to manage effects, effect parameters, and ensure somewhat efficient render call batching and render state management. Any higher-level rendering tasks (such as shadow mapping, occlusion culling, and so on) can be implemented on top of this base renderer.

There are three key goals when using D3DX effects:

- Achieving good performance
- Conveniently managing effect parameters
- Integrating with content creation tools

This article focuses on the first two points: how to achieve good performance and how to manage effect parameters in a convenient way.

The presented techniques were used on several small games and in my hobby 3D demo/game engine [Dingus05].

Good Performance with D3DX Effects

Device State Management

For quick prototyping, D3DX effects are great because they do lots of work behind the scenes [Aronson03] [DXSDK]. The most notable example is that all Direct3D device states are restored to previous values after the effect ends. However, this hurts the performance because often there is no need to save and restore *all* device states.

Simply turning off state saving/restoring and relying on the effects to set up all state is not a good solution either—each effect would then need to set almost every render state every time. For example, if just a single effect sets some exotic state like ShadeMode to Flat, then all other effects would need to set it back to Gouraud.

The solution described here allows effects to manually restore only the *needed* state (more on that later). In it, each technique in each effect has an extra last pass that restores the changed state, but the pass does not actually draw anything. An example effect could look like this:

```
technique tec20 {
  pass POpaque {
    VertexShader = compile vs_1_1 vsMainOpaque();
    PixelShader = compile ps_1_1 psMainOpaque();
    AlphaTestEnable = True;
    AlphaFunc = Greater;
    AlphaRef = 250;
  }
  pass PAlpha {
    VertexShader = compile vs_1_1 vsMainAlpha();
    PixelShader = compile ps_1_1 psMainAlpha();
    AlphaTestEnable = False;
    ZWriteEnable = False;
    AlphaBlendEnable = True;
    SrcBlend = SrcAlpha;
    DestBlend = InvSrcAlpha;
  }
  pass PRestore {
    AlphaBlendEnable = False;
    ZWriteEnable = True;
  }
}
```

This effect consists of two rendering passes—POpaque renders alpha-tested opaque geometry; PAlpha renders the remaining alpha blended parts. The last pass PRestore is only applied to restore state, but nothing is actually rendered using it. As can be seen, the effect restores AlphaBlendEnable and ZWriteEnable states to "standard" (but not necessarily previous) values; that is, it turns alpha blending off and turns depth writing on. None of the other states (shaders, alpha test parameters, blend factors) is restored.

Which states need to be restored and which do not? That is completely up to the engine and its definition of "standard." For example, if all effects set VertexShader, there is no point in restoring it to previous value—the next effect will set the right vertex shader anyway. Likewise, if all effects that enable alpha blending also set SrcBlend and DestBlend to needed values, there is no point in restoring them. In general, all render states fall into three engine-defined categories:

- Those that need to have "standard" values when beginning any effect. These states need to be restored to the standard values after any effect that modifies them.
- Those that must be set by every technique in each effect. These states do not need to be restored because the next effect will set them anyway.
- Those that do not need to be restored because they do not affect rendering in "standard" situations (that is, render states from the first category, while in "standard" values, turn off render states in this category). When used, these render states must be set; this usually coincides with setting first-category states to non-default values.

Over several projects, I have found it is most convenient to restore (that is, the first category) these states:

- **Most "enable" states:** `AlphaBlendEnable`, `AlphaTestEnable`, `ClipPlaneEnable[n]`, `ColorWriteEnable`, `FogEnable`, `PointSpriteEnable`, `StencilEnable`, `ZEnable`, `ZWriteEnable`.
- **Rarely modified states:** `BlendOp`, `Clipping`, `CullMode`, `DepthBias`, `DitherEnable`, `FillMode`, `LastPixel`, `MultiSampleAntiAlias`, `MultiSampleMask`, `PatchSegments`, `ShadeMode`, `SlopeScaleDepthBias`, `ZFunc`.
- **Rarely modified pixel pipeline states:** `TexCoordIndex[n]`, `TextureTransform-Flags[n]`, `Wrap[n]`.

I usually do not restore these states because they change for every effect (the second category):

- `VertexShader`, `PixelShader`, and any of the shader constants
- Textures and sampler states
- Transforms (world/view/projection) when using the fixed-function vertex pipeline
- TextureStageState operations and arguments when using the fixed-function pixel pipeline (except for the rarely used ones like `TexCoordIndex[n]` and `Texture-TransformFlags[n]`)

The following states are also not restored because they are not enabled under normal situations (that is, the third category). When used, the pass will set them explicitly (this usually coincides with setting some "enable" state to nonstandard value):

- **Alpha blending and alpha testing parameters:** `AlphaFunc`, `AlphaRef`, `Dest-Blend`, `SrcBlend`
- **Stencil parameters:** `StencilFail`, `StencilFunc`, `StencilMask`, `StencilPass`, `StencilWriteMask`, `StencilZFail`

As you can see, most states controlling the fixed-function vertex pipeline (lights, materials, and so on) are missing from these category lists. Controlling the fixed-function transform and lighting pipeline via D3DX effect parameters is a tricky task, and it is probably better to manage it within the engine itself, without using the effect framework. In practice, use of the fixed-function transform and lighting pipe is now rare. Even when hardware support for vertex shaders is unavailable, the software pipeline is usually considered sufficiently fast.

It is a good idea to carefully decide which states go into which of the three categories, because if you change your mind later, many effect files need to be changed!

While using this approach—manually restoring the needed state in a dummy last pass—helps to achieve much better rendering performance, it is quite error-prone. It is easy to forget to restore some needed state, and it can result in hard-to-debug consequences on the later effects.

The debug build of an engine can check that all states from the first category still have the default values after each technique and complain loudly if this is not the case. The last state-restoring pass can also be automatically generated by the engine, but that would require writing a rudimentary parser to see which states are modified by the technique (currently there is no way to get that information via the API). In this case, the effect file could look like this:

```
technique tec20 {
  pass POpaque {
    // ...
  }
  pass PAlpha {
    // ...
  }
  RESTORE_PASS
}
```

The engine would read and parse the effect, construct the restore pass text, and supply it as a value for `RESTORE_PASS` macro when creating the effect.

Redundant State Filtering

D3DX effects can use an "effect state manager"—an object that implements the `ID3DXEffectStateManager` interface. This object receives all state changes that occur inside effects and forwards them to the Direct3D device. Note that if an effect manager is used, it is the manager that actually sets the device states; effects just notify it of needed state changes. The state manager can filter out redundant state changes, thus saving some calls. For example, the manager's `SetTexture` method might be similar to this:

```
HRESULT CEffectStateMgr::SetTexture(
    DWORD stage, IDirect3DBaseTexture9* texture )
{
  // check for redundant set
  if( texture == mCurrTextures[stage] ) {
    ++gStats.redundant.textures; // gather stats
    return S_OK;
  }
  // not redundant — set it
  mTextures[stage] = texture;
  ++gStats.set.textures; // gather stats
  return gD3DDevice.SetTexture( stage, texture );
}
```

What, if any, performance benefit using a state manager brings is highly dependent on the application and the effects themselves. I have seen only small improvements on both pure and non-pure Direct3D device types.

As well as the effect state manager, you can also filter other redundant changes such as render target, depth/stencil, vertex buffer, vertex declaration, and similar changes. Direct3D supposedly does this filtering for you internally, but experience shows some real performance improvements if this is done externally by the application. To do this, just make a simple D3D device wrapper class that has methods like these:

```
void setIndexBuffer( IDirect3DIndexBuffer9* ib );
void setVertexBuffer( int stream,
    IDirect3DVertexBuffer9* vb,
    DWORD offset, DWORD stride );
void setDeclaration( IDirect3DVertexDeclaration9* decl );
void setDeclarationFVF( DWORD fvf );
void setRenderTarget( IDirect3DSurface9* rt, int mrtIndex = 0 );
void setZStencil( IDirect3DSurface9* zs );
```

The implementations of these methods first check if the change is redundant, and exit if it is. If it is not, the new state is remembered and the corresponding D3D device method is called.

Rendering Order

To minimize effects overhead, renderable objects should be sorted by effect. This way, the renderer can issue Begin() and End() on the effect just once for all objects using this effect. Similar methods can be used to render each effect's passes: for each pass, render all objects using it. Rendering loop pseudocode:

```
for each effect {
  effect->Begin( do not save any state )
  for each pass except last one {
    effect->BeginPass()
    for each object using this effect {
      apply per-object effect parameters
      effect->CommitChanges()
      render object
    }
    effect->EndPass()
  }
  // apply restoring pass
  effect->BeginPass( last pass )
  effect->EndPass()
  effect->End()
}
```

As discussed previously, the preceding code treats the last pass of the effect as a "state restore" pass and does not actually render anything with it.

There are situations where it is impossible to sort everything by effect. There can be external order restrictions (transparent objects render after opaque ones, GUI after everything else, and so on), some effects need back-to-front sorting, and so on. For this, a user-defined "priority" (or "layer") value can be added to renderable objects. Additionally, some effects may have annotations that determine order—for example, an instruction to sort all objects using an effect from back to front. The renderer will sort objects by these restrictions first, and only then sort according to effect. Inside the same effect group, objects can be further sorted by distance, textures used, or some other criteria.

Managing Effect Parameters

D3DX Effects allow easy annotation using effect parameters—typed values that are applied by name [Aronson03]. The parameters can influence shaders or be used inside technique descriptions. However, manually setting each parameter for each effect is tedious and does not produce easily maintainable code. It is helpful to have a small system for easy management of the effect parameters.

From the application's point of view, parameters either do not change (for example, an object usually uses the same texture during its lifetime), change rarely (for example, change of texture or material parameters), or change often (for example, object's transformation matrices).

The parameters that do not change are usually set up during object initialization and the most convenient way would be to set them up once and forget them. For parameters that do change, one convenient method is to set up a pointer to the parameter's value, and any changes to the value are automatically applied to the effect.

This article describes a simple class CEffectParams that contains and manages effect parameters—typed name-value or name-pointer pairs. Using this class, most cases can be handled by setting up parameters for each renderable object just once at initialization time. The class's public interface is this:

```
class CEffectParams {
public:
  // name-value parameters
  // used for parameters that do not change
  void addInt( const char* name, int val );
  void addFloat( const char* name, float val );
  void addVec3( const char* name, const Vec3& val );
  void addMatrix( const char* name, const Matrix& val );
  // other parameter types...

  // name-pointer parameters
  // used for parameters that will change
  void addIntRef( const char* name, const int* ptr );
  void addFloatRef( const char* name, const float* ptr );
  void addVec3Ref( const char* name, const Vec3* ptr );
  void addMatrixRef( const char* name, const Matrix* ptr );
  // other parameter types...

  // name-resource parameters
  void addTexture( const char* name, Texture* res );
  void addCubeTexture( const char* name, CubeTexture* res );
  // other parameter types...

  void remove( const char* name );
  void clear();

  void setEffect( ID3DXEffect* fx );
  ID3DXEffect* getEffect() const;
  void applyToEffect();
};
```

Most of the public interface consists of methods to add various typed parameters. Additionally, there are methods to remove a parameter and clear all parameters, as well as methods to set or get an effect, and apply the parameters to the currently set effect.

ID3DXEffect methods to access parameters work much faster if the parameter's handle is supplied, rather than the name as a string [DXSDK]. For this reason, the implementation caches parameter handles where possible using the ID3DXEffect method GetParameterByName(), which returns a handle to the parameter, given its name. The handles are retrieved when a parameter is added or when a new effect is set for an existing CEffectParams object.

The D3DX effects framework has a "parameter block" concept—multiple effect parameters can be captured into a single "parameter block" (similar to D3D device state blocks). Starting with the DX9 June 2005 SDK, there is complete functionality required to make this system work—parameter blocks can be created, applied, and deleted at runtime (previous SDK versions do not have DeleteParameterBlock() functionality). Some parameters in the CEffectParams class could be transparently turned into parameter blocks; the best candidates are name-value and name-resource parameters. Name-pointer parameters are usually used for values that change often, making them less suitable for implementation using parameter blocks. The parameter block would need to be destroyed and re-created each time the value would change, which is not fast.

Implementation

ON THE CD

Source code using these concepts is on the companion CD-ROM and also available online [Dingus05]. Parts of the source code implement separate portions:

- **Renderer:** renderer/RenderContext (.cpp and .h files)
- **Redundant state filtering:** kernel/D3DDevice and kernel/EffectStateManager
- **Described CEffectParams class:** renderer/EffectParams

Conclusion

By combining the described methods, the D3DX effects framework makes editing and rendering effects simple, robust, and efficient. While this does add a small execution-time overhead compared to a low-level D3D renderer, the increased ease of use allows far more iteration and experimentation, and less time implementing housekeeping functions.

References

[Aronson03] Aronson, Dave, and Kris Gray, "Using the Effects Framework." Available online at DirectX Developer Center: *http://msdn.microsoft.com/directx*.
[Dingus05] Dingus 3D Engine and Tools. Available online at *http://dingus.berlios.de*.
[DXSDK] DirectX 9.0 Programmer's Reference, "Effects" section.

5.2

Post-Processing Effects Scripting

Gilberto Rosado

One of the simplest ways to enhance the quality of rendered scenes is to apply post-processing effects to the final image. Effects such as depth of field, bloom, color grading, and blurring are a few of the effects that are possible through post-processing.

Many post-processing effects require intermediate textures to hold the results of previous passes in order to be used in subsequent rendering passes. Unfortunately, there is no intrinsic way a shader can communicate with the graphics engine about the shader's need for different render targets to be set for specific passes, or even whether the shader needs the currently rendered scene as an input texture. This often leads to a coupling of code and data, as code ends up being written for each possible post-processing stage. This increases iteration time when experimenting with post-processing effects and limits artists' ability to add interesting post-processing effects without major help from engine programmers.

This article presents techniques that automate the steps required to render a large number of post-processing effects. This is done by annotating shaders with script-like commands that are sent to the underlying graphics engine. To implement post-processing effects using a scripting syntax, the engine will need to:

- Allocate any intermediate texture render targets needed by the effect
- Know how to feed intermediate render targets to subsequent passes
- Be capable of rendering to multiple render targets at once
- Be capable of properly updating render targets from frame to frame

Overview

Post-processing effects are achieved by supplying the rendered scene as a texture input into a pixel shader program. The application then typically renders a full-screen quad and the pixel shader uses the input textures to render a modified version of the original scene.

Using the D3DX Effects framework [DXSDK], a scripting syntax can be created using a mixture of annotations and semantics in textures and technique passes. In the D3DX Effects format, a parameter, pass, or technique may have any number of annotations. Annotations are defined exactly like any other parameter—a data type, a variable name, an equals sign, and then a value followed by a semicolon. Following is an example of how we might annotate a shader parameter representing a global light position. The `Space` annotation lets the engine know that `LightDirection` should be in world space as opposed to object Space.

```
float3 LightPosition
<
    string Space = "World";
> = {1.0f, -1.0f, 1.0f};
```

Semantics are yet another way to tag metadata to Effect parameters. A parameter is allowed a single semantic, and semantics are case insensitive. A semantic is attached to a parameter by using a colon between the parameter declaration and its default value. For example:

```
float4 LightDirection : Direction
<
    string Space = "World";
> = {0.0f, 10.0f, 0.0f, 1.0f};
```

The preceding `Direction` semantic could be used to tell an engine that it should treat `LightDirection` as a unit vector; therefore, it should normalize the direction vector when setting the variable at runtime.

Once a set of shader annotations and semantics is chosen to tell the graphics engine about any special input textures and render targets that a specific effect will need, a data-driven effect solution can be achieved. With a data-driven shader solution, turnaround time when tweaking a shader's behavior is cut dramatically, and can even be done in real time while running an application that uses the graphics engine.

Scripting Syntax

In this article, we loosely base our scripting syntax around the DXSAS 0.8 spec. Although, at the time of writing, DXSAS no longer defines a scripting format, DXSAS 0.8 is still a good foundation to build our own language around.

The way to attach a script to a pass in our effect is to use a string annotation with the name "Script." A script for a given pass consists of a set of commands to the graphics engine. A command is represented as a simple C-style variable assignment statement, such as variable = value. Here is a list of statements we might implement in the scripting engine:

- **RenderColorTarget[0 − N]:** Set the specified texture as a render target. Some hardware supports multiple render targets, so we can specify up to the maximum amount that the hardware exposes. Setting a render target to an empty string indicates that the render target should be reset to the render target that was present at slot N when we began executing the current effect.
- **ClearSetColor:** Clear the current render target to this color.
- **ClearSetDepth:** Clear the current depth buffer to this value.
- **ClearSetStencil:** Clear the current stencil buffer to this value.

Using these script commands, we can implement an effect that can tell the graphics engine to set a render-target texture, clear it to a particular color, and then render to it. Here is a code snippet on how this would be done:

```
texture RenderTargetTexture;

float4 clearColor = float4(0,0,0,1);

technique RenderToTextureEffect
{
    pass Pass0
    <
        string Script =
            "RenderColorTarget0 = RenderTargetTexture;"
            "ClearSetColor = clearColor;"
            ;
    >
    {
    }
}
```

When specifying a render-target texture in the shader code, we may need to specify its dimensions and format, which can be achieved by using the following annotations used when allocating the render-target texture.

- **Format:** A string annotation that specifies the format for the texture. If not present, we default to a texture format such as A8R8G8B8.
- **Dimensions:** An annotation of type `float2` that explicitly specifies the dimensions of the texture.
- **ViewportRatio:** An annotation of type `float2` that specifies that dimensions of the texture relative to the current viewport.

Following is an example of how you would annotate a render-target texture to indicate that it should be allocated using a single-channel 32-bit floating-point format and dimensions that are half the size of the viewport.

```
texture RenderTargetTexture
<
    string Format = "R32F";
    float2 ViewportRatio = float2(0.5f, 0.5f);
>;
```

Reading Back the Results of a Previous Pass

Some multi-pass, post-processing effects require reading back intermediate data from a previous pass. For example, separable Gaussian filters work by first performing a filter in the horizontal direction and then performing a filter on the results in the vertical direction.

Sampling from render-target textures used in previous passes is easy when using the D3DX Effects framework, as all the engine has to do is associate a render-target texture with a texture defined in an .fx file. To read the texture back in, the shader simply uses a sampler associated with that texture.

Using the Current Scene as Input

Most post-processing effects operate on the currently rendered scene. In this article, we use a semantic SCENE_TEXTURE to specify that the current contents of the back buffer should be copied over to the texture before rendering the effect. Alternatively, if we already have rendered the contents into a render-target texture, we may just pass that texture as an input into our effect.

Following is a code snippet from an effect that implements a separable Gaussian blur. The first pass of the effect requests a render target that is one quarter the size in each dimension of the current viewport and uses a simple pass-through shader to down-sample the current scene to a sixteenth of its original size. The second pass performs a horizontal blur on the downsampled image, and finally, the third pass performs a vertical filter on the results of the second pass while rendering back to the full-screen back buffer.

```
// copy the current scene to this texture before beginning the effect
texture SceneTexture : SCENE_TEXTURE
<float2 Dimensions = float2(1024,1024);>;
sampler SceneSampler = sampler_state
{texture = < SceneTexture >;};

// this texture will hold a down-sampled image of the scene
// since it has smaller dimensions than the scene texture
texture DownSampledTexture
<float2 Dimensions = float2(256, 256);>;
sampler DownSampledSampler = sampler_state
{texture = < DownSampledTexture >;};

// texture that will store the intermediate results of the Gaussian
blur
texture HorizontalBlurTexture;
<float2 Dimensions = float2(256, 256);>;
sampler HorizontalBlurSampler = sampler_state
{texture = < HorizontalBlurTexture >;};

// simple pass through pixel shader
float4 DownSamplePS(float2 texCoord:TEXCOORD0):COLOR
{
    return tex2D(SceneSampler, texCoord).rgb;
}

// pixel kernels for the Gaussian blur
static const int g_KernelSize = 13;
float2 HPixelOffsets[g_KernelSize];
float2 VPixelOffsets[g_KernelSize];
static const float BlurWeights[g_KernelSize];
```

```
// Separable Gaussian blur shader
float4 Blur(
    float2 Tex : TEXCOORD0,
    uniform float2 PixelOffsets[g_KernelSize],
    uniform sampler PassSampler,
    uniform float OneOverSourceWidth
    ): COLOR0
{
    float4 Color = 0;
    for (int i = 0; i < g_KernelSize; i++)
    {
        Color += tex2D(PassSampler, Tex +
            PixelOffsets[i].xy * OneOverSourceWidth ) * BlurWeights[i];
    }
    return Color;
}

#define OneOverDownsampledTextureWidth 1/256

technique SimpleGaussianBlur
{
    pass DownSamplePass
    <
        // set render-target 0 to a texture that is 1/4 the size of the
        // input texture
        string Script = "RenderColorTarget0 = DownSampledTexture;";
    >
    {
        PixelShader = compile ps_2_0 DownSamplePS();
    }

    pass HorizontalBlurPass
    <
        // store the results of the horizontal blur in an intermediate
        // texture
        string Script =  "RenderColorTarget0 = HorizontalBlurTexture;" ;
    >
    {
        PixelShader = compile ps_2_0 Blur(HPixelKernel,
            DownSampledSampler, OneOverDownsampledTextureWidth);
    }

    pass VerticalBlurPass
    <
        // set render-target 0 to the standard backbuffer
        string Script = "RenderColorTarget0 = ;";
    >
    {
        PixelShader = compile ps_2_0 Blur(VPixelKernel,
            HorizontalBlurSampler, OneOverDownsampledTextureWidth);
    }
}
```

Supporting Global Effects

Some post-processing effects cannot be implemented as self-contained techniques, as they might need data from every single object rendered in the scene. For example, a distortion effect may be implemented by having proxy objects in the scene render into a separate distortion buffer, which is later used to distort the currently rendered scene [Forsyth04]. To support such global effects, we need to be able to specify the render targets that need to be unique to these effects. We can again use semantics and annotations to provide a means of expressing this to the engine. In this article, we use the semantic GLOBAL_RENDERTARGET. When the engine sees that the texture being used as either a source or a target has this semantic, it can fetch the texture from a pool of uniquely named global render targets.

The allocation of global render targets is a data-driven process, so at compile time the application may not know what global render targets may be created at runtime. We must therefore develop a mechanism for clearing the global render targets as needed. An annotation with the name "clear" can be used to indicate whether the render-target texture should cleared after each frame it is used, and the clearColor annotation can be used to specify what color to use when clearing the render target. Here is how you would declare a global render target that should be cleared to opaque black after every frame in which it has been used:

```
texture DistortionRenderTarget : GLOBAL_RENDERTARGET
<
    bool clear = true;
    float4 clearColor = float4(0, 0, 0, 1);
>;
```

Implementing the Script Framework

Parsing the Scripts

To get the best possible runtime performance, the script should be parsed in a preprocessing stage or at load time. For every pass in a technique, all the commands need to be parsed and stored in a container that can be iterated at runtime. The parsing of the script is a straightforward process, as the syntax consists entirely of "command = parameter;" pairs. Most of the values will represent parameter handles in the .fx file, while some values, such as the clear color, will usually be constants. The general algorithm for parsing the script becomes:

1. Find all valid "command = parameter;" pairs.
2. Look up the handle to and/or value of input parameter by using the ID3DXEffect functions GetParameterByName() and GetValue(). If the command is a RenderColorTargetN, look at the texture annotations to determine the format and dimensions of the render target.
3. For every pass, store the commands in separate collections, and store all of the pass collections in a technique collection.

Executing the Script

At runtime, as we render each pass of the effect, we can check if there is a script associated with this pass and iterate through executing its commands.

For the `RenderColorTargetN` command, we set the appropriate device render target to a texture that matches the description in the script, as well as a matching depth buffer. We also associate this render target with the texture variable in the Effects interface by using the `ID3DXEffect::SetTexture()` function. Later, when other shaders sample from this texture in the ID3DXEffect interface, it will already refer to the appropriate image.

When encountering the `ClearSetColor`, `ClearSetDepth`, and `ClearSetStencil` commands, we perform a clear with the specified values. As an optimization, we can detect if two or more of these commands happen consecutively and make only one clear call.

Render Target Allocation Strategies

To achieve good runtime performance, we want to keep the number of runtime allocations to a minimum while keeping the amount of memory needed for all of the application's effects as small as possible. When choosing a render target allocation scheme, it is important to analyze the actual needs of the full-screen effects. There are three basic types of full-screen effects in terms of memory needs:

- Self-contained effects that need temporary render-target buffers to use in subsequent passes. These are the simplest kinds of effects from an allocation standpoint; as once they are finished rendering, any render targets can be reused with other effects.
- Global effects that require unique render targets for the duration of a frame. The application will need to provide a semipersistent render target for each of these effects.
- Effects that require feedback from previous frames. These require a persistent render target.

Render-target allocation is an area that is very engine-specific, but a good general solution is to have a global render-target texture pool that allocates the render targets and gives references out as needed. It can keep data about each render target that is requested, such as the dimensions and format. Clients request render targets and give them back when finished, returning them to the pool. The next time the render-target manager is asked for a texture of the same dimensions and format, it already has one allocated and can hand it out to its client.

For global render targets, we can have the render-target pool allocate the specific render targets as they are encountered when parsing the effects, storing them in a separate container that can be quickly looked up by name and passed back to its clients at runtime upon request. To make the best use of memory, different effects that are not active at the same time may use the same render-target textures. If the engine can determine which global effects are going to be active on a particular frame, it can determine the render-target/name associations per frame to make the best use of memory.

Runtime Interaction

To get dynamic behavior from the post-processing effects, a framework that allows for modification of shader parameters is needed. The application should be able to change the look and behavior of the effect at runtime, and optimizations may be achieved by pre-computing data on the CPU and storing the results in shader parameters.

While parameter modification is a feature of the D3DX Effects framework, many wrapper implementations struggle to support this in the context of a particular engine. It is important to think about how to handle arbitrary parameter modification at runtime when starting to integrate D3DXEffects-style interfaces into an existing engine. Ensuring that the application can change effect parameters at runtime can help keep the effects as data-driven as possible, minimizing the number of new C++ classes required when adding new post-processing effects to the game engine.

Enhancements

The script commands discussed here only scratch the surface of the possibilities that shader scripting offers. As an engine's development progresses, more expressive commands such as arbitrary pass looping for accumulation effects may be implemented as needed.

While this article discusses post-processing scripting in the context of D3DX's Effects framework, it is possible to add scripting to most shader solutions in similar ways through the use of custom metadata.

Conclusion

In this article, we discussed a data-driven, full-screen effect framework that can allocate render targets for multi-pass techniques, function with any number of passes using arbitrary viewport dimensions, and is able to perform global full-screen effects such as selective blurs or blooms. We also discussed possible render-target allocation strategies and techniques for parsing the scripts and executing them at runtime.

Acknowledgments

Thanks to Pipeworks Software, in particular Rich Rayl and Dan White, for giving me the opportunity to experiment with post-processing scripting.

References

[DXSDK] Microsoft Corporation, DirectX 9.0 Programmer's Reference.
[Forsyth04] Forsyth, Tom, "Post-Process Fun with Effects Buffers," *ShaderX²*, edited by Wolfgang Engel, Wordware, 2004.

5.3

Case Study: Designing a Shader Subsystem for a Next-Gen Graphics Engine

Wolfgang Engel

Creating a graphics engine for a next-generation title is an extensive task. This article focuses on art pipeline integration of shaders, and the design of the subsystem that deals with materials and meta-materials; in other words, everything associated with shaders.

Background

Following the transition from the DirectX7-based fixed-function pipeline games to the current shader-only titles, production costs increased two to eight times. This was partly because of the increased investment in graphics assets required to satisfy the raised expectations of the end user. The most complex part of these assets is the shaders.

Today's games use up to 2,000 different pixel shaders, according to Gary McTaggart at GDC 2004 for *Half-Life 2* [McTaggart04]. This large volume of data needs to be created (at least partially) by a shader programmer, applied to geometry by the artists and handled by a game engine. The amount of work required is a major contribution to the costs of a game, and handling this many shaders has a large impact on the performance of the graphics engine and therefore the whole game engine.

This article examines the material and shader part of a typical game production workflow, as used at Wings Simulations for an unannounced next-gen game that was scheduled for release at the end of 2006. This will help determine the amount of work needed to create a next-gen, shader-driven game and give a few rules on organizing this workflow efficiently.

Art Pipeline Integration

To manage the art pipeline in an efficient way, it helps to build up a simple workflow diagram as shown in Figure 5.3.1.

The shader programmer uses NVIDIA's FX Composer [FXComposer] together with a plug-in to import geometry files from RAD Game Tools' Granny 3D middleware [Granny]. The shaders are developed there and written to *.fx files in a Perforce repository. These files use the syntax defined by Microsoft's DirectX Standard Semantics and Annotations (DXSAS [DXSAS]). Using DXSAS as a standard throughout

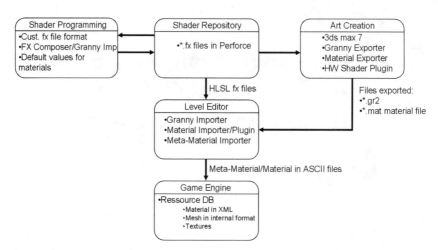

FIGURE 5.3.1 *Shader workflow in a game development team.*

the whole workflow allows the use of standard tools like FX Composer and the 3ds Max 7 hardware plug-in without needing to develop custom tools.

The artists get the *.fx shader effect files from Perforce and use them in the hardware shader plug-in of 3ds Max 7. Figure 5.3.2 shows a screenshot of the hardware shader plug-in.

Using the Material Editor of the hardware shader plug-in, the artists provide values for the parameters in the *.fx file. These are later stored in a *.mat material file that follows an XML syntax. The *.fx file is now called a meta-material, because it just holds the shaders—the parameter data (such as shinyness, material color, roughness, and so on) is stored in the material file.

The level editor imports the *.gr2 Granny file containing the geometry data, the *.mat material file generated by the artists, and the *.fx meta-material file containing the shaders. All these files are stored in the resource database of the game engine. At all stages, the material and meta-material files are human-editable, because they are stored as ASCII files. This means that even if one tool does not work, or has limited functionality, changes can always be made with a simple ASCII editor.

3ds Max 7 Hardware Plug-in

Each meta-material holds a separate code path for 3ds Max's hardware shader plug-in that allows the preview of the shaders with one sky light and one directional light. More light sources are supported in the general shader code path for the engine's in-game lighting. The hardware shader plug-in is poorly documented, and there does not seem to be a way to implement post-processing effects in a generic way. In addition, no kind of shadowing effect is available, so the material preview in 3ds Max can only give a rough impression of how surfaces look in the game. Nevertheless, it is usually good enough to allow artists to edit most of the shader parameters with an interactive preview.

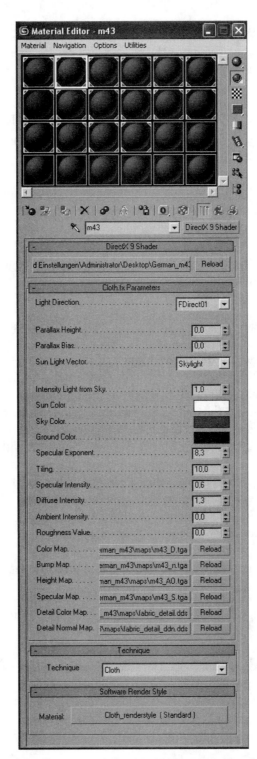

FIGURE 5.3.2 *3ds Max hardware shader plug-in.*

Level Editor

The workflow diagram in Figure 5.3.1 shows the level editor as the most important tool to edit materials. As well as editing level layouts and scripts, the level editor uses the same rendering engine as the final game. Because it renders the complete game scene including lighting, tweaking material parameters can be done while seeing all the post-processing and shadowing effects, whereas the 3ds Max hardware shader plug-in only allows viewing of single materials applied to the models in simple lighting without any post-processing effects applied to them. The level editor offers a bunch of controls to tweak all parameters. There are sliders for numerical parameters, color controls, and drop-down menus. Compared to having a level editor in Maya, this approach is pretty fast and does not have to share resources with a complex environment.

Summary

The workflow shown in Figure 5.3.1 is a simple and low-cost approach. Other advantages of this approach are:

ASCII-based file formats: These allow the shader creation/modification process to continue even if one of the tools in the chain does not work or has incomplete functionality.

Use of industry standards: Using existing tools like ATI's RenderMonkey [RenderMonkey] or NVIDIA's FX Composer should be considered. They only be used in prototyping shaders, and can also be integrated into the production flow shown previously. These tools are getting more and more customizable and are able to import standards like Microsoft's *.fx file format or NVIDIA's Cgfx file format. Staying compatible with the DXSAS syntax reduces the time required to train people with the proper tools and reduces development costs of tools, because they are frequently updated for free.

Data-driven: Storing meta-materials and materials in ASCII files allows shader creation and editing without any source code compilation throughout the entire production workflow.

Integrating a Meta-Material/Material System into a Graphics Engine

Optimizing the graphics engine design for a heavy shader workload needs to be considered in the design stage. Figure 5.3.3 shows a typical modern graphics engine from a bird's-eye view.

The scene graph organizes scene objects (meshes, particle system, everything that can be positioned in the world) in a hierarchical way. Each object can be accessed via a pointer. After the world is constructed from the scene objects, it is processed by the visibility determination system. This system removes hidden objects and culls on the pixel level with occlusion culling, creating databases containing only the visible objects for

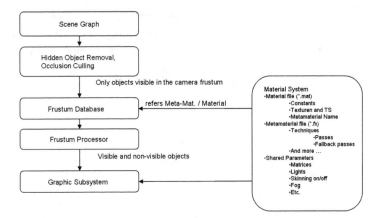

FIGURE 5.3.3 *Graphics engine overview.*

any number of arbitrary frustums. This is crucial for multi-pass rendering or shadowing, because multiple rendering passes should use the smallest possible number of vertices. The frustum database stores all visible objects that should be drawn, and thus references textures, meta-materials, and materials. The frustum processor sorts all drawable objects with the interface IDrawable. Flags are used to tell the renderer how it should deal with objects. Geometry may be stored in one large vertex buffer, which is the most efficient case, or in several vertex buffers, depending on mesh type and size.

The resource system consists of a material system, which manages the meta-materials, materials, shared parameters and the textures for meshes. Similar approaches are described in [Hoeller03] and [Frick02].

The meta-material is a DirectX *.fx effect file following the DXSAS format, containing shaders and data. When combined with textures and rendered on the graphics card, it reproduces the surface properties of a class of real-world materials, such as all shades of human skin or wood grain with a variety of different grain sizes. Textures and data for a specific instance of a material can be stored in a material file and loaded during runtime to change the default values in the meta-material. Each material can be used with only one meta-material; for example, the "mahogany" material settings can only be used with the "wood grain" meta-material.

Meta-Material

Meta-materials describe surface properties of classes of objects in the game world together with the data from the material that is applied to this object. They hold the lighting algorithm, shadow algorithm, and any other algorithms used to describe surface properties. They can even hold algorithms describing light types or other kinds of effects.

Material files hold object-specific parameters like texture filenames, ambient, diffuse and specular intensity, roughness values, all the data necessary for a lighting model, and so on.

It is useful to be able to identify certain surface properties in the engine just by look-ing at the name of the meta-material. Among the examples of possible meta-material names could be default, metallic, water, river, ocean, ocean shore, skin, terrain, cloth, plastic, leather, grass, vegetation, eyes, godrays, post-processing, and so on.

Figures 5.3.4 and 5.3.5 show how some of these meta-materials are applied to a model.

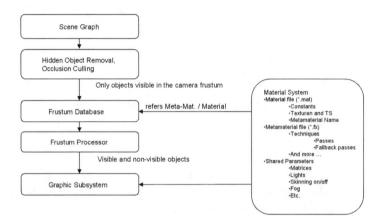

FIGURE 5.3.4   *Applying meta-materials to a face.*

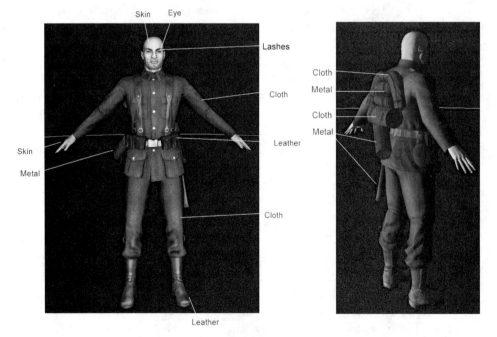

FIGURE 5.3.5   *Applying meta-materials to a model.*

The names are chosen to describe a class of surface properties. For example, "skin" is always used for the skin of humans. Different races and skin colors of humans would just use a different material, but the same meta-material.

If an alien race has a very different kind of skin—for example, a snake-like skin—the artist would create a different meta-material called "alienskin." The idea is that all the main properties of one kind of surface are described in one meta-material *.fx file.

In a game environment with a minimum requirement of ps_2_0, a good number of meta-materials is 15 to 20. This number depends on a number of facts like the underlying graphics hardware, the complexity of the effects, and so on (see the section "Meta-Material/Material-Friendly Object-Sorting in the Graphics Engine" for more information).

As long as the game has a minimum graphics hardware specification of vs_2_0, it makes sense to use just one vertex shader for each meta-material that can switch features on and off via static branches (if-else statements) for different materials. Features might include:

- Number of bones for skinning
- Fog on/off
- Number of per-vertex lights
- Texture coordinate animation

On current vs_2_0 hardware, it seems faster to use static if-else statements than to keep switching between multiple vertex shaders.

With pixel shaders, a "keep it simple and slim" approach is used. Because ps_2_0 offers a huge number of instructions, all pixel shaders should be one-pass shaders by default. In other words, rendering several shader passes to execute one effect should be avoided, because it should be possible to create all necessary effects in one pass with ps_2_0. In other words, one effect gets only one pass to render (== shader pass), whereas there might be several render passes, in which the same shader is used several times (several render passes) to achieve, for example, a shadow effect from several light sources.

If there is an effect that needs a higher number of instructions, a target platform like ps_2_b or ps_3_0 needs to be chosen.

Post-processing effects that need several shader passes need to be written in a way that the passes can be executed one after the other without needing to feed pass-related data "from outside" to the meta-material. To distinguish between techniques in the meta-material that need one pass or several passes, a flag is used in an annotation.

```
bool Multipass = 0;
```

ps_2_0 pixel shaders do not support static or dynamic branches, so a specialized pixel shader needs to be written for each feature. For example, one meta-material might have a default pixel shader, a pixel shader that adds cube environment map support to this default pixel shader, and another that adds parallax instead of regular bump mapping.

Therefore, a meta-material (or, in DirectX-speak, an effect file) holds a collection of pixel shaders and one vertex shader. The number of pixel shaders might reach 20 to 30 shaders. To switch among these pixel shaders, the "pass" statement of the effect file framework is used. This is preferred over the "technique" statement, as switching between techniques causes a reload of the entire effect state. The properties of each pass are read during startup into a pass data structure.

The data provided by the material to the meta-material must always have the same layout, whichever pixel shader is actually used.

Following the concept of the effect file framework, different techniques are chosen during startup depending on the annotations appended to the technique keyword, to account for the capabilities of the underlying hardware. For example, a specific effect might have implementations for several compiler target profiles like ps_2_0, ps_2_a, ps_2_b, and ps_3_0. In this case, the technique with the suitable target profile is chosen during startup.

Handling a Meta-Material in the Graphics Engine

Using the DirectX effect file framework, the meta-material is loaded as an *.fx file by the graphics engine.

It should also be noted that the graphics engine creates all the lookup textures of all meta-materials with pixel shaders that are devoted to this task. The handles of these lookup textures are stored in a list and all the data structures are filled up from the data available in self-defined annotations in the effect file.

Handling Materials in the Graphics Engine

A default material is created for each meta-material found during startup of the engine and filled with the default values supplied by the meta-material. This is the template for all materials that use this meta-material.

A material is an ASCII XML file, exported by the 3ds Max 7 script. A typical material file might have the following content:

```
<?xml version='1.0' encoding='utf-8'?>
<XML>
<m43
AmbientInt="0.000000"
Bias="0.000000"
BlendMode="Overwrite"
BumpMap="Test/m43_n"
ClassName="CFFDX9ResourceMaterial"
ColorMap="Test/m43_D"
DetailColorMap="Test/fabric_detail"
DetailNormalMap="Test/fabric_detail_ddn"
DiffInt="1.300000"
Effect="Cloth"
GroundColor="(0.000000,0.000000,0.000000,1.000000)"
HeightMap="Test/m43_AO"
HeightScale="0.000000"
```

```
HemiIntensity="1.000000"
InterfaceID="{49915438-A4BC-4DFA-86AF-7B12D2F0E161}"
LightPos="(0.000000,0.000000,5.000000,0.000000)"
MaskValue="0"
ModelColor="(0.466667,0.466667,0.466667,1.000000)"
Roughness="0.000000"
SpecExponent="8.300000"
SpecularInt="0.600000"
SpecularMap="Test/m43_S"
Technique="Cloth"
Tiling="10.000000"
TwoSided="False"
WireFrame="False"
/>
</XML>
```

The name of this material file is "m43," which is the name of a specific kind of equipment worn by soldiers in World War II. The material file holds all parameters that are not shared with other materials (see the following list). Parameters are added to the material data structure only where they differ from the defaults set up by the meta-material. Typically, this includes the following kind of data:

- Constant parameters for lighting/reflectance models
- Fog, Fog enable
- Names of textures, texture states, u/v addressing, texture paths
- Cull mode and other culling data if needed
- Name of parent meta-material (held in the "Effect" parameter)

For easier handling, the kind of texture in each texture stage is defined by a convention. That means that, for example, the DetailColorMap is always in sampler s5. A list that outlines such a convention might look like this:

- s0 color map (XML: ColorMap)
- s1 normal or bump map (XML: BumpMap)
- s2 height map (XML: HeightMap)
- s3 camouflage map (XML: CamouFlageMap)
- s4 shadow map (XML: ShadowMap)
- s5 detail map
- s6 environment map
- s7 dirt mask
- s8 look-up table
- s9 look-up table
- ...
- s15

Each mesh references a material. Several meshes can reference the same material. The names used in the mesh file consist of the name of the meta-material, an underscore, and then the name of the material. For example:

```
eyes_blue
eyes_brown
eyes_black
leather_boots
leather_boots_dirty
vegetation_oak
ocean_stormy
ocean_calm
skin_white
skin_brown
skin_black
metallic_brush
metallic_smooth
metallic_matt
```

Shared Parameters

Some parameters can be shared between multiple meta-materials. These include data such as object and camera matrices and lighting environment data.

All these parameters are kept in a single "shared parameters" file. These parameters can be handled by the shared parameter interface provided by the effect file or set globally via `SetVertexShaderConstant*()` or `SetPixelShaderConstant*()` calls by the engine.

The effect file framework interface should only be used for shared parameters that do not change frequently and as little as possible. Otherwise, performance can drop substantially. Furthermore, it might make sense to administrate your render states and texture stages outside of the framework as well. Performance of these components should be regularly measured, as certain parameters may move in or out of the shared parameters file as the engine and game evolve.

The following list shows a number of candidates for shared parameters.

```
shared float4x4 matWorld : World;
shared float4x4 matView : View;
shared float4x4 matProj : Projection;
shared float4x4 matWorldViewProj : WorldViewProjection;
shared float4 vecEye : CameraPosition;
shared float4 vecSunDirection : SunDirection;
shared float3 vecSunColor : SunColor;
shared bool bSkinning : Skinning;
shared bool bInstanced : Instanced;
shared float fFogStarting : FogStarting;
shared float fFogEnding : FogEnding;
shared int EnableFog;
shared int EnableZ;
shared int EnableZWrite;
shared int FogColor;
shared int AmbientColor;
shared int CullMode;
```

```
shared int FillMode;
shared float4x4 arrBlendMatrix[40];
struct SShaderLight
{
float3 vecPosition;
float3 vecDirection;
float4 vecAttenuation;
float4 vecColor;
float3 vecSpot;
};
shared SShaderLight arrShaderLight[3];
```

Meta-Material/Material-Friendly Object-Sorting in the Graphics Engine

Changing a graphics card state can be expensive, and to avoid excessive changes, the rendering order of meta-materials and materials is usually sorted according to various criteria to reduce the number of changes required and thus increase rendering speed. Judging the cost of changing particular states can only be based on measurement and varies from card to card. Nevertheless, rules of thumb can be created based on the following observations.

Changing a Meta-Material

Switching meta-material involves changing the current shaders. It can be one of the most expensive changes because all the data for the new shader needs to be sent to the graphics card. Changing shaders also invalidates nearly all the graphics card's caches.

Changing Constant Shader Data

Changing only the constant data is less expensive because the majority of assets are still cached by the graphics card. However, it is still not free. In one game tested, changing constants on a DirectX 9 graphics card used 4% of the whole CPU performance. Changing constants on an older DirectX 8 graphics card in the same game required an even higher cost—up to 8%.

Changing Textures

The cost of changing textures via SetTexture() depends on the size and format of the texture, but in most cases is one of the cheaper state changes listed here.

Changing the Vertex Buffer Layout

Vertex structures and their declarations should ideally be rounded to the next 32-byte boundary to assist internal graphics hardware caches, although this does depend on the target hardware. Although the DirectX API allows a single vertex shader to be used with multiple different vertex layouts, ideally each vertex shader should always use the same vertex buffer layout; otherwise, the driver must modify the shader each time. To lay out these buffers optimally, compression techniques can be used as described in [Calver02] and [Calver04].

Enabling Early Z-reject

The automatic early z-reject or occlusion-culling mechanism in current graphics hardware tries to cull pixels before they reach the pixel shader stage. In other words, early z-rejects save valuable pixel shader performance. This mechanism works only if objects are sorted roughly front to back. However, correct alpha blending requires a back-to-front sort and therefore conflicts with good z-rejection. One way to deal with alpha blending is to categorize objects as good or bad occluders instead of sorting front to back and run the z-reject against the good occluders. One might also avoid it by emulating its functionality as much as possible in the pixel shader [Caruzzi04].

Rules of Thumb

The following list gives some rules of thumb for changing states in a graphics engine. It covers the most expensive changes first, and gives several strategies to reduce the frequency of changes.

1. Reduce or eliminate shader changes.
   Options:
   - Sort
   - Use fewer shaders
   - Use longer and more general-purpose shaders
2. Reduce or eliminate constant and texture changes.
   Options:
   - Sort
   - Change fewer constants
   - Use more specialized shaders that don't require constant changes (should not be faster then)
3. Reduce or eliminate vertex declaration changes.
   Options:
   - Sort
   - Use fewer vertex declarations, padding vertex buffers if necessary
4. Increase early z-rejection.
   Options:
   - Full front-to-back sort
   - Generally categorize geometry (entities, architectural occluders, portals, and so on) and render good occluders first

It is important to note that the order of rules is not necessarily set in stone and varies between specific drivers and hardware. Having a system that can change this order and measure the results is a good investment, as it allows the engine to account for different hardware environments. As usual, measuring the results is more crucial than a nice-looking theory. These rules just reflect the average behavior of most graphics hardware.

In the particular graphics engine described throughout this article, the following techniques were used to optimize shader state changes:

- The engine sorts objects according to their meta-material (following the state change costs in the preceding list). This engine typically has between 15 and 20 meta-materials, each with around 20 different techniques (each a different pixel shader).
- The engine then sorts objects with the same meta-material according to their materials (constant and texture changes in the preceding list). Sorting objects according to their materials reduces the number of constant and texture switches. States are only set if the parameter data in the material is different from the previously set data in the meta-material. Because objects are already sorted according to their meta-materials, all the materials that are loaded for one meta-material have the same data layout. This means that a minimal number of textures and constants need to be changed when switching materials. A typical engine has around five materials for each meta-material, and up to 256 constants for each material.
- The engine then sorts objects with the same material (and therefore the same meta-material) according to their technique, because each technique has a different pixel shader (note that techniques are actually encoded in the *.fx files using the "pass" keyword for speed, as mentioned previously). Using the same technique several times means reducing pixel-shader switching. Vertex-shader switching is not necessary, because there is only one big vertex shader for all materials in the meta-material.

Conclusion

When writing a next-gen engine with a high shader workload, the following list of rules may help from a business and technical point of view:

- Organize the workflow as efficiently as possible by creating an overview chart and discussing this chart with everyone in the team.
- Use standard tools available from hardware vendors as much as possible. This reduces the effort of updating these tools with every new shader feature.
- Use standards such as DXSAS to administer your shaders, and choose data-driven approaches as much as possible for shaders.
- Classify meta-materials according to their surface structure. A clear naming convention will help when modifying them during the development of the game.
- Create a material system that is optimized for parameter changes.
- Sort in a hardware-friendly way using these rules:
  a. Sort objects according to their meta-material.
  b. Then sort objects according to their material.
  c. Then, sort objects according to their technique.

Acknowledgments

The author wishes to thank his former colleagues at Wings Simulations, where the graphics engine described was developed by a team of highly talented progammers and artists—in particular, Markus Kark, Roman Keskenti, Philipp Krause, Markus Oberrauter, Markus Pietrowski, Cyrus Preuss, and Chris Schmitz.

References

[Calver02] Calver, Dean, "Vertex Decompression in a Shader," Direct3D ShaderX—Vertex and Pixel Shader Programming Tips and Tricks, Wordware, 2002: pp 172–187.

[Calver04] Calver, Dean, "Using Vertex Shaders for Geometry Compression," *ShaderX²: Shader Programming Tips and Tricks with DirectX 9*, edited by Wolfgang Engel, Wordware, 2004: pp 3–13.

[Caruzzi04] Caruzzi, Francesco, "Simulating Blending Operations on Floating-Point Render Targets," *ShaderX²: Shader Programming Tips and Tricks with DirectX 9*, edited by Wolfgang Engel, Wordware, 2004: pp 172–176.

[DXSAS] Available online at *http://msdn.microsoft.com/directx* (search there for DXSAS).

[Frick02] Ingo Frick, "Visualization with the Krass Game Engine," *Direct3D ShaderX—Vertex and Pixel Shader Programming Tips and Tricks,* Wordware Inc., pp. 453–461, 2002, ISBN 1-55622-988-7

[FXComposer] Available online at *http://developer.nvidia.com/object/fx_composer_home.html*.

[Granny03] Available online at *http://www.radgametools.com/*.

[Hoeller03] Oliver Hoeller, "Shaders under Control (Codecreatures Engine)," *ShaderX²—Shader Programming Tips and Tricks with DirectX 0,* Wordware Inc., pp. 107–122, ISBN 1-55622-988-7

[McTaggart04] McTaggart, Gary, "Half-Life 2/Valve Source Shading," GDC 2004. Available online at *http://www2.ati.com/developer/gdc/D3DTutorial10_Half-Life2_Shading.pdf*.

[RenderMonkey] Available online at *http://www.ati.com/developer/rendermonkey/index.html*.

BEYOND PIXELS
AND TRIANGLES

Introduction

Dean Calver

Today's graphics cards are capable of handling a vast variety of algorithms. This section includes articles that use the computational power of graphics cards for tasks not typically used in game graphics.

Vlad Stamate's article "Real-Time Damage Deformation Methods" uses an impact texture to render impact deformation data and deform a mesh accordingly. He also provides a quick performance summary, along with ideas for optimizations.

The article "Ray-Tracing Effects without Tracing Rays" by László Szirmay-Kalos, Barnabás Aszódi, and István Lazányi alters the environment map lookup to provide different local illumination information for every point, based on the relative location from the reference point. This way, at a given time, the authors have just a single environment map for a reflective object, but make localized illumination lookups.

In his article "Implementing Raytracing on the GPU," Martin Christen covers two ways to implement Whitted-style (classic) ray tracing on current-generation consumer-level GPUs. One approach is to put everything into one pixel shader, and the other is to divide the program into smaller kernels and execute the kernels one behind the other (multi-passing).

The article "GPU-powered Path-Finding Using Preprocessed Navigation Mesh Approach" by Renaldas Zioma shows how to improve the path-finding process by taking the benefits from a modern GPU to save CPU processing power for more challenging high-level AI behavior. He chooses the navigation mesh—a popular environment's spatial representation suitable for navigations in 3D computer games—as a target for implementation.

6.1

Real-Time Damage Deformation Methods

Vlad Stamate

Introduction

This article describes techniques for obtaining damage deformation effects. Many of today's games use either decals or other lighting-based effects to give the user damage feedback. Instead, I propose using the new Shader Model 3 (SM3) capabilities to temporarily (and/or permanently) render impact deformation (caused by a projectile or a sizeable object hitting a mesh). The algorithm presented has two parts: the first shows how to use information obtained from a physics engine (like force, direction, and so on) to generate an "impact map" using a blend of noise and heuristics (which will be explained in the article both from a shader and an algorithmical point of view) and render it to a texture. The second part shows how to make use of this "impact map" texture and the Shader Model 3 GPU capability to sample from textures in the vertex shader, to deform a mesh. The article will also explain how multiple passes of deformation can be rendered such that deformations accumulate. Because this is a computationally intensive technique, it provides a quick performance summary and ideas for optimizations.

Current State of Damage Deformation

Most games today use decals to simulate (impact) damage. The decal technique works by applying a damage texture to the "damaged" mesh. The damage texture is usually rendered using a z-offset from the mesh geometry. There is a time decay applied as well such that the alpha value of the texture decreases with time, which makes the decal less and less visible up until the point when the texture is not visible and is no longer drawn. Decal techniques are quite cost effective in terms of performance, and a lot of research has been done in this field to bring in these improvements (see [Lengyel01]).

A different method that produces slightly better visual results employs the use of bump-mapping techniques. In this case, the damage texture can be represented by a heightmap, then transformed into a normal map, and with the help of a fragment program the bump-mapping effect can be displayed. The drawbacks of this technique are usually due to the length of the fragment programs required for proper bump-mapping effects and the fact that in effect it is just a lighting technique open to visual errors.

The Basics

This technique is best applied if we want to simulate the damage done by a small object hitting a large mesh (imagine a bullet from a gun hitting a wall). Small objects can be approximated analytically by representing their movement with a vector that also defines the *collision axis* (the term that will be used from here on) and hence their collision information can be easily calculated.

However, the technique works even if the projectile cannot be approximated analytically. In this case, more information is required, like, for example, the area of the impact and the depth of the impact. More information will be presented about this later.

Obtain the Collision Plane

The "collision plane" is the plane that is defined by the collision axis and the collision point. Figure 6.1.1 illustrates the concept.

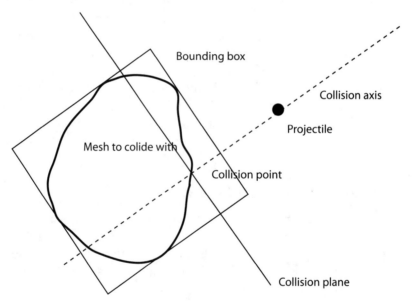

FIGURE 6.1.1   *2D analogy of the deformation model.*

Generate the Deformation Impact Map

The "impact map" (or the deformation map) is the texture that is applied to the mesh in the vertex program and contains information about the deformation.

There are two ways we can generate the deformation map: analytically or with a physical approximation. Creating it using an analytical method works for projectile or small-object situations. Physical approximation needs to be employed for objects whose sizes we can no longer approximate with a "point."

Given the coordinate of the impact at x and y, any point $P(x', y')$ will have a displacement of:

$$displacement = \frac{1}{D^2} * F + noise \qquad (6.1.1)$$

where *displacement* is a three-dimensional vector representing the displacement values, D is the distance from the point of intersection to the current point, in the 2D space of the damage texture, and F represents the impact force. To make the deformation look more realistic we have added some random (or even better—noise-based) values as expressed by a *noise* component (again a three-dimensional vector). The noise values can be loaded from a texture, encoded in a stream, or just calculated at runtime (in the vertex program) by doing some mathematical operations on any of the inputs available. The inverse square root of the distance function gives a nice quadratic curve; however, any linear function works relatively well if computation speed is an issue.

Generate the Impact Triangle List

The problem we need to solve is to find out which triangles of our given mesh—the one that we have previously computed that is going to be subject to deformation—intersect the projectile's path of movement (expressed analytically as a position/axis). Depending on how the mesh is organized (index triangle strips, triangle arrays, and so on), this problem is usually reduced to the following steps: solve a ray-triangle intersection, obtain the triangle that is directly impacted, and then heuristically decide which adjacent triangles will be impacted as well. There are quite a few algorithms out there that quickly solve the ray-triangle intersection, such as [Trumbore97].

Obtain Texture Coordinates

At this point, we know which triangles we need to deform, but how do we do so? Because the deformation takes place inside the vertex program by using lookups into an impact map, we need texture coordinates. These are obtained by projecting vertices onto the collision plane. Projecting a point onto a plane is a relatively cheap operation (from a performance point of view) involving a dot product, a multiply, and a subtract, all applied to vectors. Given a point (x_p, y_p, z_p) and a plane (which equation we already have) $ax + by + cz + d = 0$, the projected point (x', y', z') onto the plane is calculated as shown in Equation 6.1.2.

$$(x', y', z') = (x_p, y_p, z_p) - ((a,b,c,d) \bullet (x_p, y_p, z_p, 1)) * (a,b,c) \qquad (6.1.2)$$

Once onto the collision plane space (2D space), the *x* and *y* coordinates of the projected vertices are actually *uv*s (texture coordinates) in the impact map. This work can be done either in the vertex program or on the CPU. Because the projection requires vector operations, performing it in the vertex program has the speed advantage, and we gain from the fact that another stream of texture coordinates will not have to be transferred to the graphics hardware. Figure 6.1.2 displays the four steps to obtain a deformation mesh.

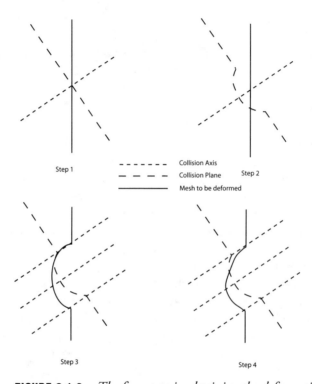

FIGURE 6.1.2   *The four steps in obtaining the deformation map. Step 1—Obtain the intersection point and the collision plane; Step 2—Build the impact map; Step 3—Project the relevant geometry from the mesh onto the collision plane (notice how the deformed geometry looks wrong because it is performed in the wrong space); Step 4—Apply the vertex program and displace the geometry based on the deformation map and the collision axis vector.*

First, we need to find the space to transform into. This is the space where the deformation map lives. This base plane is defined by the normalized direction of the deformation axis and the intersection point with the mesh. The plane equation therefore is:

$$F_x x + F_y y + F_z z + D = 0 \qquad\qquad (6.1.3)$$

where F_x, F_y, and F_z are normalized direction components of the deformation axis, and D is the distance between the (0,0,0) point and the intersection point (projected distance).

After projection, we are now virtually in 2D space. We just need to build a 2D bounding box around the projected triangle values. To build 2D coordinates out of the 3D coordinates we do a bit of cube-map-like technique magic. Looking at the normal of the collision plane we ignore the component that is the largest. This leaves us with three (for the three corners of the triangle), each having only two components. Logically mapping one coordinate to be u and the other remaining coordinate to be v, we can easily set (1,1) to the maximum corner and (0,0) to the minimum corner and interpolate to find out each u and v for the three corners of the triangle. Figure 6.1.3 shows the mapping.

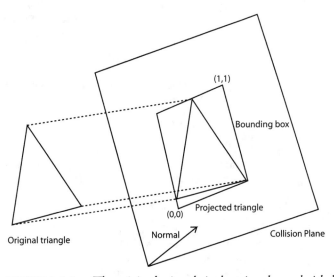

FIGURE 6.1.3   *The original triangle is the triangle we decided to deform, and this shows its projection onto the collision plane and mapping of the texture coordinates.*

The following code showcases the computation required to obtain the texture coordinates. Incoming data to the function is composed by the collision plane equation (represented by the plane normal and distance (D), the number of vertices we need to project, and the vertex data itself. The output is represented by the normalized texture coordinates.

```
void calculateTextureCoords(Point3 planeNormal, float D, float num-
berVertices, Point3 *vertexData, TexCoord2 *normalizedTextureCoord)
{
    unsigned int i;
    TexCoord2 max, min;
    TexCoord2 textureCoord[MAX_VERTICES];

    // For all the vertices of the triangles that are going to be
deformed
    for(i=0; i<numberVertices; i++)
    {
        // Project the vertex onto the collision plane
        Point3 projectedPoint = projectVertex(vertexData[i],
planeNormal, D);

        // Perform the cube-map like simplification
        if(planeNormal.x > planeNormal.y)
        {
            if(planeNormal.x > planeNormal.z)
            {
                textureCoord[i].u = projectedPoint.y;
                textureCoord[i].v = projectedPoint.z;
            }
            else
            {
                textureCoord[i].u = projectedPoint.x;
                textureCoord[i].v = projectedPoint.y;
            }
        }
        else
        {
            textureCoord[i].u = projectedPoint.x;
            textureCoord[i].v = projectedPoint.z;
        }

        // Compute the 2D bounding box of the texture coordinates
        if(max.u < textureCoord[i].u)
            max.u = textureCoord[i].u;
        if(max.v < textureCoord[i].v)
            max.v = textureCoord[i].v;
        if(min.u > textureCoord[i].u)
            min.u = textureCoord[i].u;
        if(min.v > textureCoord[i].v)
            min.v = textureCoord[i].v;
    }

    // A second run through all the vertices is required to calculate
normalized texture coordinates within the bounding box created above
    for(i=0; i<numberVertices; i++)
    {
        normalizedTextureCoord[i] = interpolate(textureCoord[i], min,
max);
    }
}
```

Generate Geometry Tessellation

Because this algorithm is applied in a vertex program (hence at vertex level), the tessellation level of the geometry on which we are applying the deformation is important. The higher the tessellation, the better the visual effect (hence this algorithm step is optional).

The problem we need to solve is simple: given a mesh, we need to increase the tessellation such that when we apply the deformation vertex program the amount of aliasing (due to poor vertex resolution) is acceptable. One simple and quite computational effective method to develop for this technique is a recursive tessellation. This way, we only generate more triangles where we need to because we already have a list of triangles that need to be tessellated as explained previously by either solving triangle-line or sphere-triangle intersection equations. Figure 6.1.4 explains this technique.

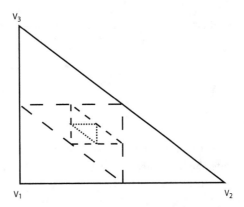

FIGURE 6.1.4   *Recursive tessellation of a triangle. For clarity, only the middle subtriangle has been recursively tessellated, but the algorithm should perform the steps on the adjacent ones as well.*

One of the complications introduced by breaking triangles is the appearance of the t-junctions. A t-junction appears when an edge that is shared by two triangles is broken in two and the new vertex that is created is displaced. The neighboring triangle (which we would not want to touch in this case) has to be touched and broken into two separate triangles. Solving t-junctions is a long-standing issue in terrain rendering algorithms that might perform any kind of adaptive tessellation (see [Boer00]).

And Finally—the Deformation

So, now the stage has been set for us, all the information we need is available, and it remains only to render. The deformed mesh is drawn using our special vertex program. The following inputs are needed for the vertex program: the displacement texture, the collision axis vector (in four floats format), the projected calculated texture coordinates, or the matrix to allow us do the projection.

Here is the implementation using an ARB vertex program:

```
!!ARBvp1.0
# This program requires support for GL_NV_vertex_program3 extension
OPTION NV_vertex_program3;

[...]

# Perform look-up into the impact texture
TXL displace, texcoord, texture[1], 2D;

# Perform look-up into noise texture
TXL noiseValues, texcoord, texture[2], 2D;

# Sample already encodes 1/D^2
# Displacement = (1/D^2) * F + noise
MAD displace, displace, impactForce, noiseValues;

MOV pos.w, 1.0;
SUB pos.xyz, vertex.position, displace;

[...]

END
```

For clarity, in the previous code only the actual displacement code has been kept to illustrate the hardware instructions needed to perform it.

Here is the implementation using a Cg vertex program (a more complete program this time):

```
struct IN
{
    float4 position      : POSITION;
    float3 normal        : NORMAL;
    float2 texUV         : TEXCOORD0;
    float3 diffuse       : TEXCOORD1;
    float3 specular      : TEXCOORD2;
};

struct OUT
{
    float4 clipSpace     : POSITION;
    float3 diffuseCoeff  : COLOR0;
    float3 specularCoeff : COLOR1;
    float3 eyePosition   : TEXCOORD0;
    float3 eyeNormal     : TEXCOORD1;
    float2 uv            : TEXCOORD2;
};
```

```
OUT    main(   IN    input,
               uniform float3 impactForce,
               uniform float4x4 ModelViewProj,
               uniform float4x4 ModelView,
               uniform float4x4 ModelViewIT,
               uniform sampler2D colorMap,
               uniform sampler2D displaceMap)
{
    OUT output;
    float3 displacement;
    float4 newPosition;
    float3 noiseValues;

    // Perform the texture look-up in the damage texture
    float3 sample = tex2D(displaceMap, input.texUV).xyz;

    // Get noise values, for this we use the imapct force
    noiseValues = noise(impactForce);

    // Sample already encodes 1/D^2
    // Displacement = (1/D^2) * F + noise
    displacement = sample.xyz * impactForce + noiseValues;
    // Displace along the normal
    displacement = displacement * input.normal.xyz;
    newPosition = input.position - float4(displacement, 0);

    output.eyePosition = mul(ModelView, input.position).xyz;
    output.eyeNormal = mul(ModelViewIT, float4(input.normal, 1)).xyz;

    output.clipSpace = mul(ModelViewProj, newPosition);

    output.uv = input.texUV;
    output.diffuseCoeff = input.diffuse;
    output.specularCoeff = input.specular;

    return output;
}
```

To compile this program, the Cg compiler needs to use the *vp40* profile (due to the texture lookup).

One of the drawbacks of this technique in the current phase is that the normals of each vertex do not change after deformation even though the triangles that generate the normals have obviously been moved in space due to the deformation being applied to them. Because of this, the per-pixel lighting step looks slightly wrong because it doesn't take into account the deformations we have currently applied.

There are two solutions to this problem. The problem can be solved at the pixel level. We make the normal map (built from the impact map) available to the fragment program together with the Tangent Normal Binormal (TNB) matrix. This path follows closely the typical bump mapping algorithms. For more information on this, read [Dreijer04].

The second solution is to calculate the new vertex normals and send those to the fragment program. In this case, applying any lighting model (be it Phong, Gouraud, and so on) at the fragment level produces correct results with respect to the deformed geometry. One way to produce new normals is to modify the current normal based on the impact map values around the point where sampling is occurring. We do not have access to the position of the vertices that build the triangle we are currently transforming because vertex programming is just a basic form of stream processing. However, we do know the current position, the current normal, the current deformation, and the deformation of the adjacent vertices (by sampling neighboring texels in the impact map). By calculating a "fake" normal based on the impact map values, we can add it to the current real vertex normal and normalize the result, thus obtaining a more correct normal with the respect to the deformed vertex.

This technique fits well with the problem of having to apply different deformations multiple times to the same geometry. This is because the deformation information is kept in a texture. Multiple deformations can either be stored in separate textures (in which case we are limited to four deformation layers per pass, because this is the current graphics hardware limitation on the number of texture layers lookup in a vertex program), or we can precalculate and store as many deformation layers into one texture on the CPU side.

Non-Point Impact Situation

Most of my examples use the projectile-hits-mesh idiom; however, few other cases can be represented relatively well by the technique described previously (for example, terrain deformation from small objects, and so on). Sometimes the impacting mesh cannot be represented anymore by a point, but by real geometry (think of a car hitting a wall, for example). However, the algorithms presented until now still work provided we use different techniques for obtaining the damaged triangle list and building the impact map.

Obtaining the Damaged Triangle List

To do any kind of damage deformation, we need some information from the physics simulation part of the engine, game, application, and so on. The information we need is some kind of sphere of damage (where the damage happens in world coordinates), depth of damage, and maybe a central damage point. The impact map can be constructed now by "projecting" the damage sphere onto the collision plane or using either a Poisson or a Gaussian distribution (knowing the center of damage).

Building the Impact Map

Volumetric collision can often be expressed as a sphere of collision or even an ellipsoidal shape. In this case, the problem can be reduced to a sphere-triangle intersection. We can be quite generous and add any triangle that has at least one vertex inside the collision sphere to our list of triangles to suffer deformation.

Performance Issues

Like the decal technique mentioned in the beginning of this article, we want to limit the time the deformation is visible. This is because during that time, an extra piece of geometry is being drawn to the screen using a relatively complex vertex program. Time decaying is a good addition to this technique because we might not want to display the damage for a very long time because this slows the rendering. If, for example, hardware frustum clipping is performed, the vertex program(s) are executed for all the deformed geometry. That means even if the mesh we are deforming does not appear on the screen (because it will be clipped for being outside the view frustum), the vertex programs will do the texture lookups anyway.

There is a certain latency related to performing texture lookups inside a vertex program. They are, unfortunately, not as fast as texture lookups performed in the fragment program. However, the good news is that the latencies can be hidden by performing other operations after the texture lookup that do not directly depend on the texture lookup result. Even though current shader compilers will probably try to optimize the shader code, arranging the program logic in the way just described can only increase efficiency.

The format of the "impact map" texture must be a float texture: first, because it is used to displace vertices that have coordinates in float format and sometimes the displacement can have a value bigger than 1.0; and second, limitations on current hardware force all textures made available to a vertex program to be in floating-point format. Even though the second restriction might be lifted in the future, using floating-point textures will enable the deformation algorithm to be as flexible as it needs to be. However, floating-point textures are costly in terms of bandwidth. Two things we can do to improve efficiency are to use half-float format and smaller textures (256×256 is most of the time reasonable enough).

Conclusion

This article presented a method of storing deformation data obtained from mesh collision and taking advantage of the new Shader Model 3 capabilities to perform texture lookups in vertex programs to displace vertices in order to model deformations. Current graphics hardware still has some limitations with respect to vertex texturing (four layers of texturing in vertex programs and relatively large latencies caused by texture lookups), but in the future this should be resolved.

CD-ROM Demo Description

ON THE CD

The demo included on the accompanying CD-ROM contains a simple implementation of the algorithm described here. A GPU with support for Shader Model 3 is required to run the application.

References

[Boer00] de Boer, Willem H., "Fast Terrain Rendering Using Geometrical MipMapping," available online at *http://www.flipcode.com/articles/article_geomipmaps.pdf*, 2000.

[Calver04] Calver, Dean, "Accesing and Modifying Topology On the GPU," *ShaderX³ Advanced Rendering with DirectX and OpenGL*, edited by Wolfgang Engel, Charles River Media, 2004.

[Dreijer04] Dreijer, Søren, "Bump Mapping Using CG," available online at *http://www.blacksmith-studios.dk/projects/downloads/bumpmapping_using_cg.php*, 2004.

[Lengyel01] Lengyel, Eric, "Applying Decals To Arbitrary Surfaces," *Game Programming Gems 2*, Charles River Media, 2001.

[Trumbore97] Trumbore, Ben, Tomas Moller, "Fast, Minimum Storage Ray/Triangle Intersection," 1997, Journal of Graphics Tools, 2(1):21–28.

6.2

Ray Tracing Effects without Tracing Rays

László Szirmay-Kalos, Barnabás Aszódi, and István Lazányi

Introduction

The basic operation of rendering is tracing a ray from its origin point at a direction to find that point, which is the source of illumination. The identification of the points visible from the camera requires rays that have the same origin. However, in reflection, refraction, and caustic computation rays are not so coherent, but we need to trace just a single ray from each of many origins. GPU trace rays of the same origin very efficiently by taking a "photo" from the common origin point, but they are far slower to process incoherent rays.

A GPU-friendly approximation technique to compute reflection is *environment mapping* [Blinn76], which assumes that the hit point of the ray is very far, and thus it becomes independent of the ray origin. In this case, reflection rays can be supposed to share the same *reference point*, so we get that case back for which the GPU is an optimal tool. To render a reflective or refractive object, environment mapping takes images about the environment from the center of the object, and then the environment of the object is replaced by a cube textured by these images (see Figure 6.2.1). When the incoming illumination from a direction is needed, instead of sending a ray, the result is looked up in the images constituting the environment map.

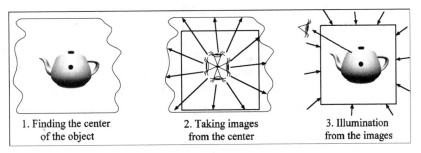

1. Finding the center of the object
2. Taking images from the center
3. Illumination from the images

FIGURE 6.2.1 *Steps of environment mapping.*

A fundamental problem found in environment mapping is that the environment map is the correct representation of the direction-dependent illumination at a single point, which is the reference point of the object. For other points, accurate results can only be expected if the distance of the point of interest from the reference point is negligible, compared to the distance from the surrounding geometry. However, when the object size and the scale of its movements are comparable with the distance from the surrounding surface, errors occur, which create the impression that the object is independent of its illuminating environment.

To attack this problem, we alter the environment map lookup to provide different local illumination information for every point, based on the relative location from the reference point. At a given time, we have just a single environment map for a reflective object, but make localized illumination lookups. Localized image-based lighting has also been proposed by Bjorke [Bjorke04], where a proxy geometry (for example, a sphere or a cube) of the environment is intersected by the reflection ray to obtain the visible point. Unlike Bjorke's approach, we rely solely on environment map lookups. All the geometric information required by the localization process is stored in the environment map. This information is the distance of the source of the illumination from the reference point where the environment map was taken. The algorithm is simple and can be executed by current vertex and pixel shaders at very high frame rates. In the following sections, we present the basic idea and the DirectX/HLSL implementation. Finally, we apply the method for caustics generation.

Localization of the Environment Map

The idea to localize environment maps is discussed using the notations of Figure 6.2.2. Let us assume that the center of our coordinate system is the reference point of the environment map, and we are interested in the illumination of point $\vec{x}$ from direction $\vec{R}$. We suppose that direction vector $\vec{R}$ has unit length.

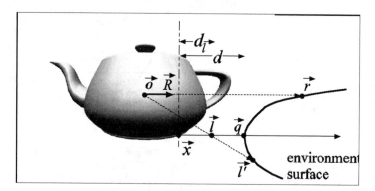

FIGURE 6.2.2 *Notations of environment map localization. The reference point of the environment map is $\vec{o}$. We need the illumination of point $\vec{q}$ being at direction $\vec{R}$ and distance d from shaded point $\vec{x}$. The approximation method finds ray parameter d_l, and consequently point $\vec{l}$ on the ray and point $\vec{l}'$ on the surface.*

When shading point $\vec{x}$, classical environment mapping would look up the illumination selected by direction $\vec{R}$; that is, it would use the radiance of point $\vec{r}$. However, $\vec{r}$ is usually not equal to point $\vec{q}$, which is in direction $\vec{R}$ from $\vec{x}$, and thus satisfies the following ray equation for some distance d:

$$\vec{q} = \vec{x} + \vec{R} \cdot d. \tag{6.2.1}$$

Our localization method finds an approximation of d using an iterative process working with distances between the environment and reference point $\vec{o}$. The required distance information can be computed during the generation of the environment map. While a normal environment map stores the illumination for each direction in the R, G, and B channels, now we also obtain the distance of the visible point for these directions and store it, for example, in the alpha channel. We call these extended environment maps *distance impostors*.

Suppose we have two initial guesses of the ray parameter d_p and d_l, and consequently two points $\vec{p}$ and $\vec{l}$ that are on the ray, but are not necessarily on the surface, and their projections $\vec{p}'$ and $\vec{l}'$ onto the surface from the reference point (see Figure 6.2.3). The accuracy of this approximation can also be checked by reading the distance stored with the direction of $\vec{l}$ in the environment map ($|\vec{l}'|$) and comparing it with $|\vec{l}|$. If point $\vec{l}$ were on the surface, the two distances would be equal. If visible point approximation $\vec{l}$ is in front of the surface, that is $|\vec{l}| < |\vec{l}'|$, the current approximation is an *undershooting* of distance parameter d. On the other hand, the case when point $\vec{l}$ is behind the surface ($|\vec{l}| > |\vec{l}'|$) is called *overshooting*.

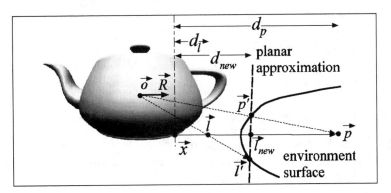

FIGURE 6.2.3 *Iterative refinement of the ray parameter assuming that the environment is planar between points $\vec{p}'$ and $\vec{l}'$ corresponding to overshooting point $\vec{p}$ and undershooting point $\vec{l}$, respectively.*

If the two guesses were of different type (that is, one is an undershooting while the other is an overshooting), the environment surface should intersect the ray between these two points. To find a better approximation, we assume that the environment surface is a plane between the two guesses and compute the intersection $\vec{l}_{neu}$ between the planar surface and the ray. Then, the iteration can proceed replacing either $\vec{p}$ or $\vec{l}$ and by $\vec{l}_{neu}$ depending on whether $\vec{l}_{neu}$ is an overshooting or undershooting.

To compute the intersection point, we have to consider the cases separately when projected point $\vec{l}'$ is equal to $\vec{r}$ because in this case, the ray parameter becomes infinite. In this case, the new ray parameter approximation is

$$d_l = d_p + |\vec{r}| \cdot \left(1 - \frac{|\vec{p}|}{|\vec{p}'|}\right). \qquad (6.2.2)$$

If none of the two points is equal to $\vec{r}$, the ray parameter corresponding to the hit point is:

$$d_{new} = d_l + (d_l - d_p) \cdot \frac{1 - |\vec{l}|/|\vec{l}'|}{|\vec{l}|/|\vec{l}'| - |\vec{p}|/|\vec{p}'|}. \qquad (6.2.3)$$

Having found the new ray parameter, we can obtain the point on the ray, and then looking up the environment map, the point projected onto the environment surface.

To start the iteration process, we need an undershooting approximation and an overshooting approximation. Note that point $\vec{r}$ corresponds to the infinite ray parameter, thus it is the projected point of a sure overshooting. On the other hand, if the object does not intersect the environment, then shaded point $\vec{x}$ is an undershooting.

From a mathematical point of view, the proposed iteration method solves the ray equation with the *false position root finding method* [Weissten03], which converges surely. Note that even with guaranteed convergence, the proposed method is not necessarily equivalent to exact ray tracing in the limiting case. Errors may be due to the discrete surface approximation, or to view dependent occlusions. For example, should the ray hit a point that is not visible from the reference point of the environment map, the presented approximation scheme would obviously be unable to find that. However, when the object is curved and moving, these errors can hardly be recognized visually.

Environment Mapping with Distance Impostors

The computation of distance impostors is very similar to that of classical environment maps. The only difference is that the distance from the reference point is also calculated, which can be stored in a separate texture or in the alpha channel of the environment map. Since the distance is a nonlinear function of the homogeneous coordinates of the points, correct results can be obtained only by letting the pixel shader compute the distance values.

Having the distance impostor, we can place an arbitrary object in the scene and illuminate it with its environment map using custom vertex and pixel-shader programs. The vertex shader transforms object vertices (pos) to normalized screen space by the model-view-projection transformation (TMVP), and also to the coordinate system of the environment map first applying the modeling transform (TM), then translating to the reference point (refpos). View vector V and normal N are also obtained in world coordinates. Note that the normal vector is transformed with the inverse transpose of the modeling transform (TMIT).

```
OUT.hpos = mul(TMVP, IN.pos);          // to normalized screen space
float3 xw = mul(TM, IN.pos).xyz;       // to model space
OUT.x = xw - refpos;                   // to space of environment map
OUT.N = mul(TMIT, IN.norm).xyz;        // normal vector
OUT.V = xw - eyepos;                   // view vector
```

Having the graphics hardware compute the homogeneous division and fill the triangle with linearly interpolating all vertex data, the pixel shader is called to find ray hit $\vec{l}$ and to look up the cube map in this direction. The HLSL code of function Hit computing hit point approximation $\vec{l}$ with the false position method is shown here:

```
float3 Hit(float3 x, float3 R, sampler mp) {
    float rl = texCUBE(mp, R).a;                   // |r|
    float pun = length(x)/texCUBE(mp, x).a;        // |p|/|p'|
    float dun = 0, dov = 0, pov;
    float dl = rl * (1 - pun);                     // eq. 2
    float3 l = x + R * dl;                         // ray equation

    for(int i = 0; i < NITER; i++) {               // iteration
        float llp = length(l)/texCUBE(mp,l).a;     // |l|/|l'|
        if (llp < 0.999) {                         // undershooting
            dun = dl; pun = llp;                   // last undershooting
            dl += (dov == 0) ? rl * (1 - llp) :    // eq. 2
                (dl-dov) * (1-llp)/(llp-pov);      // eq. 3
        } else if (llp > 1.001) {                  // overshooting
            dov = dl; pov = llp;                   // last overshooting
            dl += (dl-dun) * (1-llp)/(llp-pun);    // eq. 3
        }
        l = x + R * dl;                            // ray equation
    }
    return l;                                       // computed hit point
}
```

This function gets ray origin x and direction R, as well as cube map mp, and returns hit point approximation l. We suppose that the distance values are stored in the alpha channel of the environment map. Note that variables dun and dov store the last undershooting and overshooting ray parameters. If there has been no overshooting approximation, point $\vec{r}$ takes the role of the overshooting point.

The pixel shader calls function Hit and looks up the cube map again to find illumination I of the visible point, and computes the reflection by multiplying with the Fresnel function:

```
N = normalize(N); V = normalize(V);
R = reflect(V, N);                     // reflection dir.
float3 l = Hit(x, R, envmap);          // ray hit
float3 I = texCUBE(envmap, l).rgb;     // radiance of the hit point
return I * Fresnel(N, R);              // reflected radiance
```

We applied an approximation of the `Fresnel` function, which is similar to the Schlick's approximation [Schlick94] in terms of computational cost, but can take into account not only *refraction index n* but also *extinction coefficient k*, which is essential for realistic metals [Lazanyi05]:

$$F(\vec{N},\vec{R}) = \frac{(n-1)^2 + k^2 + 4n(1 - \vec{N} \cdot \vec{R})^5}{(n+1)^2 + k^2}.$$

Figure 6.2.4 compares the images rendered by the proposed method with standard environment mapping and ray tracing. Note that for such scenes where the environment is convex from the reference point of the environment map, and there are larger planar surfaces, the new algorithm converges very quickly. The FPS values are measured with 1024×1024 resolution on an NV6800GT.

Classical environment map 260 FPS.

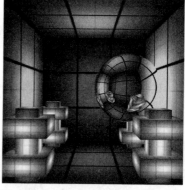
Distance imposter with 1 iteration 202 FPS.

Distance imposter with 3 iterations 140 FPS.

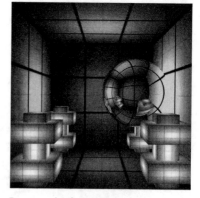
Ray-traced reference.

FIGURE 6.2.4   *Comparison of classical and localized environment map reflections with ray-traced reflections placing the reference point at the center of the room and moving a reflective sphere to different locations.*

Figure 6.2.5 shows a more difficult case where the columns are bigger. Note that the convergence is still pretty fast, but the reflection of the top of the columns is not exactly what we expect. We can observe that the edge of the column is blurred, because the top of the column is not visible from the reference point of the environment map, but is expected to show up in the reflection. In such cases, the algorithm can go only to the edge of the column and substitutes the reflection of the occluded points by the blurred image of the edge.

FIGURE 6.2.5 *A more difficult case when the tops of the columns are not visible from the reference point of the environment map. The images have been rendered using 2, 3, 4, and 10 iterations at 166, 144, 126, and 74 FPS respectively.*

The proposed method can be used not only for reflection but also for refraction calculations if the `reflect` operation is replaced by the `refract` function in the pixel shader (see Figure 6.2.6).

Application to Caustics Generation

The method presented so far can compute the hit point after the reflection, or refraction of the visibility ray. If we replace the eye by a light source, the same method can also be used to determine the ideal bounce of the light ray, which is the cause of caustic effects [Szirmay05].

When rendering the scene from the point of view of the light source, the view plane is placed between the light and the refractor (see Figure 6.2.7). The image on this view plane is called a *caustic map*. Note that this step is very similar to the generation of depth images for shadow maps.

Supposing that the surface is an ideal reflector or refractor, point $\bar{l}$ that receives the illumination of a light source after a reflection or refraction can be obtained by the

FIGURE 6.2.6   *Reflective and refractive objects.*

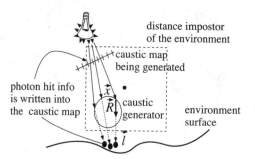

FIGURE 6.2.7   *Caustics generation with environment maps.*

proposed approximate ray tracing, and particularly by calling the Hit function. The photon hit parameters are stored in that caustic map pixel through which the primary light ray arrived at the caustic generator object. There are several alternatives to represent a photon hit. Considering that the reflected radiance caused by a photon hit is the product of the BRDF and the power of the photon, the representation of the photon hit should identify the surface point and its BRDF. A natural identification is the texture coordinates of that surface point, which is hit by the ray. A caustic map pixel stores the identification of the texture map, u and v texture coordinates, and the luminance of the power of the photon. The photon power is computed from the power of the light source and the solid angle subtended by the caustic map pixel.

   The identification of u and v texture coordinates from the direction of the photon hit requires another texture lookup. Suppose that together with the environment map, we also render another map, called uvmap, which has the same structure but stores the u,v coordinates and the texture ID in its pixels. Having found the direction of the photon hit, this map is read to obtain the texture coordinates, which are finally written into the caustic map.

The vertex shader of caustic map generation transforms the points and illumination direction L to the coordinate system of the environment map:

```
OUT.hpos = mul(TMVP, IN.pos);        // to normalized screen space
float3 xw = mul(TM, IN.pos).xyz;     // to model space
OUT.x = xw - refpos;                 // to space of environment map
OUT.N = mul(TMIT, IN.norm);          // normal vector
OUT.L = xw - lightpos;               // light vector
```

Then, the pixel shader computes the location of the photon hit and puts it into the target pixel.

```
N = normalize(N); L = normalize(L);
R = refract(L, N, 1/n);              // or reflect ...
float3 l = Hit(x, R, envmap);        // hit point of the photon
float3 hituv = texCUBE(uvmap, l).xyz; // uv of the hit point
return float4(hituv, power);         // store into caustmap
```

In order to recognize those texels of the caustic map where the refractor is not visible, we initialize the caustic map with –1 alpha values. Checking the sign of the alpha later, we can decide whether it is a photon hit.

The generated caustic map is used to project caustic textures onto surfaces or to modify their light map in the next rendering pass. Every photon hit should be multiplied by the BRDF, and the product is used to modulate a small filter texture that is added to the texture of the surface. The filter texture corresponds to Gaussian filtering in texture space. In this pass, we render as many small quadrilaterals (two adjacent triangles in DirectX) or point sprites as texels the caustic map has. The caustic map texels are addressed one by one with variable caustcoord in the vertex shader shown next. The center of these quadrilaterals is the origin, and their size depends on the support of the Gaussian filter. The vertex shader changes the coordinates of the quadrilateral vertices and centers the quadrilateral at the u,v coordinates of the photon hit in texture space if the alpha value of the caustic map texel addressed by caustcoord is positive, and moves the quadrilateral out of the clipping region if the alpha is negative. This approach requires the texture memory storing the caustic map to be fed back to the vertex shader, which is possible on 3.0-compatible vertex shaders. The vertex shader of projecting caustic textures onto surfaces is as follows:

```
float4 ph = tex2Dlod(caustmap, IN.caustcoord);  // photon hit uv
OUT.filtcoord = IN.pos.xy;                       // filter coords
OUT.texcoord.x = ph.x + IN.pos.x / 2;            // billboard uv
OUT.texcoord.y = ph.y - IN.pos.y / 2;
OUT.hpos.x = ph.x * 2 - 1 + IN.pos.x;            // billboard address
OUT.hpos.y = 1 - ph.y * 2 + IN.pos.y;
OUT.hpos.w = 1;
if (ph.a < 0) OUT.hpos.z = 2;                    // not a hit: ignore
else          OUT.hpos.z = 0;                    // valid hit:
OUT.power = ph.a;                                // photon power
```

Note that the original x,y coordinates of quadrilateral vertices are copied as filter texture coordinates and are also moved to the position of the photon hit in the texture space of the surface. The output position register (hpos) also stores the texture coordinates converted from $[0,1]^2$ to $[-1,1]^2$, which corresponds to rendering to this space. The w and z coordinates of the position register are used to ignore those caustic map elements that have no associated photon hit.

The pixel shader computes the color contribution as the product of the photon power, filter value, and the BRDF.

```
float3 brdf = tex2d(textureid, texcoord);
float  w    = tex2d(filter, filtcoord);
return power * w * brdf;
```

The target of this rendering is the light map or the modified texture map. Note that the contribution of different photons should be added, thus we should set the blending mode to "add" before executing this phase.

Figure 6.2.8 shows the implementation of the caustics generation when a 64×64 resolution caustic map is obtained in each frame, which is fed back to the vertex shader. Note that even with shadow, reflection, and refraction computation, the method executing 10 iterations runs with 50 fps.

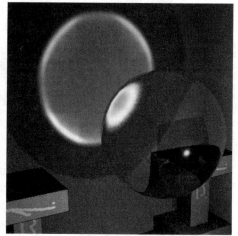

FIGURE 6.2.8   *Real-time caustics caused by a glass sphere ($n=1.3$), rendered by the proposed method at 50 fps.*

Conclusions

In this article, we proposed a localization method for environment maps, which uses the distance values stored in environment map texels. The localization method is equivalent to approximate ray tracing, which solves the ray equation by numerical root finding. The proposed solution can introduce effects in games that are usually simulated by ray tracing, such as reflections and refractions on curved surfaces and caustics.

References

[Blinn76] Blinn, J. F., and M. E. Newell, Texture and reflection in computer generated images. Communications of the ACM 19, 10 (1976): pp. 542–547.

[Bjorke04] Bjorke, K., Image-based lighting. In *GPU Gems*, edited by R. Fernando, NVidia, (2004): pp. 307–322.

[Weisstein03] Weisstein, E. W., Method of False Position. MathWorld—A Wolfram Web Resource. *http://mathworld.wolfram.com/MethodofFalsePosition.html*.

[Schlick94] Schlick, C., A customizable reflectance model for everyday rendering. In Fourth Eurographics Workshop on Rendering, (1993): pp. 73–83.

[Lazanyi05] Lazányi, I., Szirmay-Kalos, L. Fresnel term approximations for metals. In WSCG 2005. Short papers, (2005): pp 77–80.

[Szirmay05] Szirmay-Kalos, L., I. Lazányi, B. Aszódi, and M. Premecz, Approximate ray-tracing on the GPU with distance impostors. Computer Graphics Forum 24, 3 (Eurographics 2005 Proceedings).

6.3

Implementing Ray Tracing on the GPU

Martin Christen

Introduction

This article presents two ways to implement Whitted style ("classic") ray tracing on current-generation consumer-level GPUs. One approach is to put everything into one pixel shader, and the other is to divide the program into smaller kernels via multi-passing. Both approaches have advantages and drawbacks.

The multi-pass approach is programmed using HLSL, and the single shader approach is programmed using GLSL.

What Is Ray Tracing?

Ray tracing is a method of generating realistic images in which the paths of individual rays of light are followed from the viewer to their points of origin.

The core concept of all ray-tracing implementations is to find intersections of a ray with a scene consisting of a set of geometric primitives. The scene to be rendered, therefore, consists of a list of geometric primitives, which are usually simple geometric shapes such as polygons, spheres, cones, and so on. Any kind of object can be used in ray tracing if it is possible to compute an intersection between a ray and the primitive.

Supporting triangles only makes it easier to write, maintain, and optimize the ray tracer and simplifies both design and optimized implementation [Wald04]. Most scenes usually contain few "perfect spheres" or other high-level primitives.

Simple Recursive Ray-Tracing Implementation

Turner Whitted [Whitted80] introduced a simple way to ray trace recursively. Rays of light are traced from the eye through the image plane (screen) to the light source. When a ray hits an object, two new rays are spawned: one for reflection and one for refraction. This can be implemented recursively. The initial ray from the eye is called "primary ray" (see Figure 6.3.1), and all other rays are "secondary rays" (see Figures 6.3.2 and 6.3.3). The main algorithm is easy to implement in C, C++. A pseudocode example is show in Listing 6.3.1.

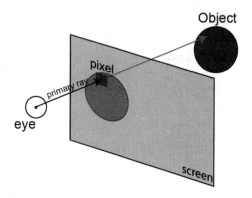

FIGURE 6.3.1   *Primary rays.*

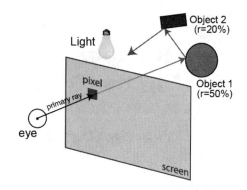

FIGURE 6.3.2   *Primary and secondary rays.*

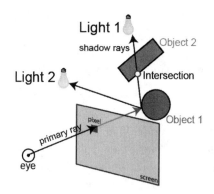

FIGURE 6.3.3   *Multiple light sources.*

Listing 6.3.1   Simple Pseudocode for Recursive Ray Tracer

```
RayRender
{
   for all pixel (x,y)
   {
      calculatePrimaryRay(x,y,ray);   // Ray originating from the
camera/eye
      color = RayTrace(ray);          // Start recursion for this
pixel
      writePixel(x,y,color);          // write pixel to output
buffer
   }
}

Color RayTrace(Ray& ray)
{
   color = BackgroundColor;
   RayIntersect(ray);
```

```
        if (ray.length < INFINITY)
        {
            color = RayShade(ray);
            if (ray.depth < maxDepth && contribution > minContrib)
            {
                if (ObjectIsReflective()) color += kr *
RayTrace(reflected_ray);
                if (ObjectIsTransparent()) color += kt * RayTrace(transmit-
ted_ray);
            }
        }
        return color;
}

Color RayShade(Ray &ray)
{
    for all light sources
    {
        shadowRay=GenerateShadowRay(ray, light[i]);
        if (shadowRay.length > light_distance) localColor += CalcLocal-
Color();
    }
    return localColor;
}
```

Acceleration Techniques

Ray tracing is time consuming because of the high number of intersection tests. Each ray must be checked against all objects in a scene; therefore, the primary approach to accelerate ray tracing is to reduce the total number of hit tests.

Finding the closest object hit by a ray requires the ray to be intersected with the primitives in the scene. A "brute force" approach of simply intersecting the ray with each geometric primitive is too expensive. Accelerating this process usually involves traversing some form of an acceleration structure. A good approach is to use a spatial data structure to find objects nearby the ray. Some examples of spatial data structures include bounding volume hierarchies, BSP trees, kD trees, octrees, uniform grids, adaptive grids, hierarchical grids, and so on [Arvo89].

Mapping Ray Tracing to the GPU

Removing Recursion

Ray tracing is usually implemented in a recursive way. In order to compute the color of primary rays, a recursive ray-tracing algorithm casts additional, secondary rays creating indirect effects like shadows, reflection, or refraction. Figure 6.3.4 illustrates how the path of a ray might be reflected by objects. However, shader hardware doesn't currently support recursion, but because a ray tracer can be rewritten in an iterative way, it can still be implemented on the GPU.

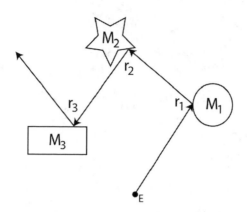

Table 6.3.1 Variables

r_i	Reflection coefficient of material i
M_i	Color of material i
N	Maximal number of iterations

FIGURE 6.3.4 *Path of a ray reflected by three objects.*

The equation to calculate the color at iteration i can be obtained by simply removing the recursion. Calculate the color for one ray, then for two rays, then for three rays, and so on, and then prove the resulting equation by complete induction. The result for n iterations is (see Equation 6.3.1):

$$c(n) = \sum_{j=1}^{n} M_j (\prod_{i-1}^{j-1} r_i)(1 - r_j)$$

(6.3.1)

Choosing the Acceleration Structure

The uniform grid (see Figure 6.3.5) is the easiest spatial data structure to implement on current-generation GPUs because there is minimal data access when traversing it and traversal is linear.

In a uniform grid, the scene is uniformly divided into voxels and those voxels containing triangles or part of a triangle obtain a reference to this triangle (see Figure 6.3.6).

Creating the Uniform Grid

A simple approach can be used to create the uniform grid (see Figure 6.3.7).

For all triangles T_i in the scene:

1. Calculate the bounding cells (b_1, b_2) of Triangle T_i.
2. Test triangle-box intersection: T_i with every cell $C_j \in (b_1, b_2)$.
3. If triangle-box intersection returned true, add a reference of T_i to C_j.

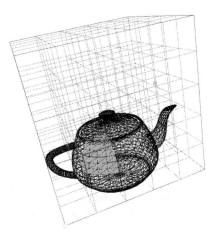

FIGURE 6.3.5 *Spatial data structure— uniform grid.*

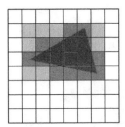

FIGURE 6.3.6 *The triangle is referenced in every cell containing a part of the triangle.*

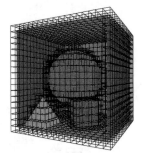

FIGURE 6.3.7 *Scene converted to uniform grid.*

The uniform grid is generated on the CPU and stored in textures. This restricts the current implementation to rendering static scenes only. However, dynamic objects could be stored separately.

Ray-Box Intersection

To further accelerate ray tracing, primary rays should be tested if they actually hit the uniform grid. If they do, the point of intersection is required for further processing. If there is no hit, the ray hits the "sky" and no further processing is necessary for the current pixel (see Listing 6.3.2).

Listing 6.3.2 Ray-Box Intersection in GLSL

```
bool hitbox(Ray r, vec3 m1, vec3 m2, out float tmin, out float tmax)
{
  float tymin, tymax, tzmin, tzmax;
  float flag = 1.0;

  if (r.direction.x >= 0.0)
  {
     tmin = (m1.x - r.startpoint.x) / r.direction.x;
     tmax = (m2.x - r.startpoint.x) / r.direction.x;
  }
  else
  {
     tmin = (m2.x - r.startpoint.x) / r.direction.x;
     tmax = (m1.x - r.startpoint.x) / r.direction.x;
  }

  if (r.direction.y >= 0.0)
  {
     tymin = (m1.y - r.startpoint.y) / r.direction.y;
     tymax = (m2.y - r.startpoint.y) / r.direction.y;
  }
  else
  {
     tymin = (m2.y - r.startpoint.y) / r.direction.y;
     tymax = (m1.y - r.startpoint.y) / r.direction.y;
  }

  if ((tmin > tymax) || (tymin > tmax)) flag = -1.0;
  if (tymin > tmin) tmin = tymin;
  if (tymax < tmax) tmax = tymax;

  if (r.direction.z >= 0.0)
  {
     tzmin = (m1.z - r.startpoint.z) / r.direction.z;
     tzmax = (m2.z - r.startpoint.z) / r.direction.z;
  }
  else
  {
     tzmin = (m2.z - r.startpoint.z) / r.direction.z;
     tzmax = (m1.z - r.startpoint.z) / r.direction.z;
  }

  if ((tmin > tzmax) || (tzmin > tmax)) flag = -1.0;
  if (tzmin > tmin) tmin = tzmin;
  if (tzmax < tmax) tmax = tzmax;

  return (flag > 0.0);
}
```

Smits [Smits96] introduced a way to exploit IEEE floating-point standard to avoid tests for rays that have slopes near zero along an axis. This algorithm is ideal for the GPU because it reduces the total number of expensive conditionals. NVidia implemented the division by zero after the IEEE standard: if a positive number is divided by zero, the result is +INF (max float). If a negative number is divided by zero, the result is –INF (min float). The OpenGL Shading Language standard doesn't specify the behavior of division by zero, so this code may fail on other hardware. This can be prevented by adding additional comparisons to zero.

Traversing the Uniform Grid

John Amanatides and Andrew Woo [Amanatides87] presented a way to traverse the grid fast using a 3D-DDA (digital differential) algorithm (see Figure 6.3.8). With slight modifications, this algorithm can be mapped to the GPU.

FIGURE 6.3.8 *Traversing the uniform grid using a 3D-DDA algorithm.*

The algorithm consists of two steps: initialization and incremental traversal.

Initialization

During the initialization, the voxel position of the origin of the ray is calculated. This can be done with the function world2voxel, which transforms world coordinates (x,y,z) to voxel coordinates (i,j,k) (see Listing 6.3.3).

Listing 6.3.3 GLSL Source: Transforming Coordinates

```
vec3 world2voxel(vec3 world)
{
    vec3 ijk = (world - g1) / _len; // component-wise division
    ijk = INTEGER(ijk);
    return ijk;
}
```

The next step is to calculate the positions at which the ray crosses the voxel boundaries in the x-, y-, and z-direction (see Listing 6.3.4). The positions are stored in variables tMaxX, tMaxY, and tMaxZ. Table 6.3.2 shows the variables used for traversal.

Table 6.3.2   Variables Used for Traversal

G1	Start point (in world coordinates) of the grid.
_len	Vector containing voxel size in x,y, and z direction
curpos	Current position of ray (world coordinates)
_r	Size of grid (r,r,r) (number of voxels)
raydir	Direction of the ray
voxel	Current voxel position

Listing 6.3.4   Voxel Boundaries Calculation

```
float voxel2worldX(float x) { return x * _len.x + g1.x; }
float voxel2worldY(float y) { return y * _len.y + g1.y; }
float voxel2worldZ(float z) { return z * _len.z + g1.z; }

if (raydir.x < 0.0) tMax.x=(voxel2worldX(voxel.x) - curpos.x) / ray-
dir.x;
if (raydir.x > 0.0) tMax.x=(voxel2worldX((voxel.x+1.0)) - curpos.x) /
raydir.x;
if (raydir.y < 0.0) tMax.y=(voxel2worldY(voxel.y) - curpos.y) / ray-
dir.y;
if (raydir.y > 0.0) tMax.y=(voxel2worldY((voxel.y+1.0)) - curpos.y) /
raydir.y;
if (raydir.z < 0.0) tMax.z=(voxel2worldZ(voxel.z) - curpos.z) / ray-
dir.z;
if (raydir.z > 0.0) tMax.z=(voxel2worldZ((voxel.z+1.0)) - curpos.z) /
raydir.z;
```

Incremental Traversal

tDeltaX, tDeltaY, and tDeltaZ indicate how far along the ray must move to equal the corresponding length (in x,y,z direction) of the voxel (length stored in _len).

Another set of variables to calculate is stepX, stepY, and stepZ, which are either −1 or 1 depending on whether the voxel in the direction of the ray is incremented or decremented. To reduce the number of instructions, it is possible to define variables outX, outY, and outZ that specify the first value that is outside the grid; if negative −1, or if positive _r (see Listing 6.3.5).

Listing 6.3.5   Initializing the Traversal

```
stepX = 1.0; stepY = 1.0; stepZ = 1.0;
outX = _r; outY = _r; outZ = _r;
if (raydir.x <  0.0) {stepX = -1.0; outX = -1.0;}
if (raydir.y <  0.0) {stepY = -1.0; outY = -1.0;}
if (raydir.z <  0.0) {stepZ = -1.0; outZ = -1.0;}
```

Now, the actual traversal can start. It is looped until a voxel with a non-empty "Voxel Index" is found or if traversal falls out of the grid (see Listing 6.3.6).

Listing 6.3.6   Uniform Grid Traversal

```
bool c1 = bool(tMax.x < tMax.y);
bool c2 = bool(tMax.x < tMax.z);
bool c3 = bool(tMax.y < tMax.z);

if (c1 && c2)
{
  voxel.x += stepX;
  if (voxel.x==outX) voxel.w=-30.0; // out of voxel space
  tMax.x += tDelta.x;
}
else if (((c1 && !c2) || (!c1 && !c3 )))
{
  voxel.z += stepZ;
  if (voxel.z==outZ) voxel.w=-30.0; // out of voxel space
  tMax.z += tDelta.z;
}
else if (!c1 && c3)
{
  voxel.y += stepY;
  if (voxel.y==outY) voxel.w=-30.0; // out of voxel space
  tMax.y += tDelta.y;
}

//check if (voxel.x, voxel.y, voxel.z) contains data
test(voxel);
```

Storing the 3D Scene

The whole scene, stored in a uniform grid structure (see Figure 6.3.9), has to be mapped to texture memory. The layout is similar to that of Purcell, et al. [Purcell02]. Each cell in the Voxel Index structure contains a pointer to an element list. The element list points to the actual element data—the triangles. As mentioned earlier, to have optimal performance the ray tracer should only use triangles as element data, but it would be possible to support other shapes like perfect spheres here. For now, however, only triangles are used.

The approach presented here uses 2D textures to store the scene. Voxel Index and Grid Element are 32-bit floating-point textures with a one-color component. Element data is a 32-bit floating-point texture with four components. Element data has to be aligned, so access in a 2D texture is optimal; one triangle must always be on the same "line" in the 2D texture.

For bigger scenes, it would be possible to split the scene uniformly and store it in different textures. NVidia-based GPUs support a 32-bit single-precision floating-point format that is very close to the IEEE 754 standard.

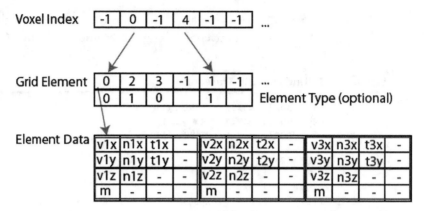

FIGURE 6.3.9   *Storing the 3D scene in a uniform grid.*

Theoretically, it would be possible to address 2^{24}, over 16 million triangles, in a scene, but current-generation consumer graphics hardware has limited memory of 256 MB (512 MB cards exist but are still rare). The maximum number of triangles would be around 1 to 2 million triangles.

Data Structures in Floating-Point Textures

A common problem in general-purpose GPU programming is that our data is stored in 2D floating-point structures, but our data is stored in a one-dimensional array. Even worse, the uniform grid structure is a 3D structure but stored in a 2D array.

Converting this is a bit tricky because we only have floating-point values and no integer division. To convert a floating-point value to an integer value, the GLSL `fract(x)` function can be used (see Listings 6.3.7 through 6.3.9). (Note: In HLSL it is `frac(x)`. Fract returns the fractional part of a floating-point value.)

Listing 6.3.7   Retrieve Texture Coordinate for Grid Element Specified by `listnumber`

```
#define INTEGER(x) (x-fract(x))
vec2 GridElementCoord2D(float listnumber)
{
   vec2 res;
   res.y = listnumber/GEsize;
   res.y = INTEGER(res.y);
   res.x = listnumber-GEsize*res.y;
   return res/GEsize;
}
```

Listing 6.3.8   Voxel Index Structure—Retrieve Texture Coordinate for Voxel (i,j,k)

```
vec2 gridTexCoord(vec3 voxel)
{
   vec2 res;
   float gridnum = voxel.z*_r*_r + voxel.y*_r + voxel.x;
   res.y = gridnum/VIsize;
   res.y = INTEGER(res.y);
   res.x = gridnum-VIsize*res.y;
   return (res/VIsize);
}
```

Listing 6.3.9   Retrieve Texture Coordinate for "Element Data" Structure

```
vec2 ElementCoord2D(float listnumber, float texturesize, float align)
{
   vec2 res;
   float align_size = texturesize / align;
   res.y = listnumber/align_size;
   res.y = INTEGER(res.y);
   res.x = listnumber-align_size*res.y;
   res.x /= align_size;    // scale to [0,1]
   res.y /= texturesize;   // scale to [0,1]
   return res;
}
```

Rendering Small Scenes: Single-Pass GPU Ray Tracer

The fastest way to ray trace on the GPU is writing one shader that reads data from the textures that store the scene and starts the iterative ray-tracing algorithm. This can be done on NVidia GeForce 6800 cards using GLSL.

ON THE CD

The most important parts of the ray tracer source code are presented here. The full source is available on the companion CD-ROM.

Uniform Variables

```
uniform vec3    g1,g2;       // Grid size (min/max of AABB)
uniform vec3    camera_pos;  // Camera position
[cam.camera2shader()]
uniform vec3    _upvec;      // base upvector [cam.camera2shader()]
uniform vec3    _up;         // current up-vector
[cam.camera2shader()]
uniform vec3    _right;      // rightvector [cam.camera2shader()]
uniform vec3    _tl;         // vector to top left
[cam.camera2shader()]
uniform float   _pixelsize;  // pixel size in world coordinates
[cam.camera2shader()]
uniform vec3    _len;        // size of a voxel (length in x-,y-
and z)
```

```
uniform float   _r;              // grid dimension (_r x _r x _r)
uniform vec2    psizeXY;         // size of output area (arbitrary rec-
tangle)
uniform float   VIsize;          // texture size
uniform float   GEsize;          // texture size
uniform float   EDsize;          // texture size
// Textures
// The whole scene (triangles) is stored in these 3 floating point
textures:
uniform sampler2D VI;            // Voxel Index Data
uniform sampler2D GE;            // Grid Element Data (currently trian-
gles only)
uniform sampler2D ED;            // Element Data (currently triangle
data only)
```

Structures

Two structs were added: a triangle structure and a ray structure. They were just added to make the source code a bit more readable.

```
struct Ray
{
    vec3 startpoint;
    vec3 direction;
};

struct Triangle
{
    vec3 A;
    vec3 B;
    vec3 C;
};
```

Creating Primary Rays and Hit Points with the Uniform Grid

Primary rays start from the eye and hit the screen plane. There are three cases:

- If the camera is inside the grid, the initial hit point is simply the current camera position. Continue processing with this point.
- If the primary ray is not hitting the grid, processing of the current pixel can be stopped.
- If the primary ray is hitting the grid, store the hit point and continue processing

   Listing 6.3.10 shows the code for creating primary rays

Listing 6.3.10 Create Primary Rays

```
bool create_primary_ray(out Ray primaryray)
{
    bool state = true;
    vec3 hit = vec3(0,0,0);
```

```
        float tmin, tmax;
        primaryray.startpoint = camera_pos;
        vec2 rd;
        rd.x = gl_TexCoord[0].x * psizeXY.x;
        rd.y = gl_TexCoord[0].y * psizeXY.y;
        primaryray.direction = raydir(rd);

        // if the camera is INSIDE the AAAB, set start to camera position
        if (inbox(primaryray.startpoint, g1,g2))   {
           hit = primaryray.startpoint;
        }
        else
        {
           if (hitbox(primaryray, g1,g2, tmin, tmax))    // check if ray
hits AABB
           {
              if (tmin <= 0.0)                     // tmin must be > 0,
otherwise we're on wrong side
              {
                 state = false;
              }
              else
              {
                 primaryray.startpoint = primaryray.startpoint +
(_EPS_+tmin)*primaryray.direction;
              }
           }
           else  // Ray doesn't hit AABB
           {
              state = false;
           }
        }

        return state;
}
```

Triangle Intersection

When a ray hits a triangle, the resulting hit point must be calculated. There are many approaches to this problem. A fast solution that can be implemented in GLSL is the Möller-Trumbore approach [Möller97] (see Listing 6.3.11).

Listing 6.3.11   One-sided Triangle Intersection

```
float intersect_1(Ray r, Triangle tri, out vec4 ret)
{
   vec3 edge1, edge2, tvec, pvec, qvec;
   float det;
   float res = -1.0;
   ret.w = 0.0;
   edge1 = tri.B-tri.A;
   edge2 = tri.C-tri.A;
   pvec = cross(r.direction, edge2);
```

```
    det = dot(edge1, pvec);
    res = 1.0;
    tvec = r.startpoint - tri.A;
    ret.x = dot(tvec, pvec);
    if (ret.x < 0.0 || ret.x > det) res = -1.0;
    qvec = cross(tvec, edge1);
    ret.y = dot(r.direction, qvec);
    if ((ret.y < 0.0) || ((ret.x + ret.y) > det)) res = -1.0;
    ret.z = dot(edge2, qvec);
    ret /= det;
    if (ret.z<_EPSILON_) res = -1.0;
    return res;
}
```

Main Loop

Listing 6.3.12 Main Loop of the Ray Tracer

```
void main (void)
{
    Triangle norm;
    norm.A = vec3(0.0,0.0,0.0);
    norm.B = vec3(0.0,0.0,0.0);
    norm.C = vec3(0.0,0.0,0.0);          // triangle normals
    Ray primary_ray;                     // primary ray
    vec3 hitpoint;                        // the actual hitpoint
    vec4 uvt = vec4(0.0,0.0,0.0,0.0);    // barycentric coordinates
(hitpoint), w: triangle number
    vec4 color = vec4(0.0,0.0,0.0,0.0); // color buffer value. Ini-
tialize with black!
    bool hashitpoint = false;             // is true if hitpoint was
found
    vec3 tMax, voxel;
    float vival;
    float tribuf = -1.0;                  // to make sure same triangle
isn't tested twice
    bool finish;

    gl_FragColor = vec4(0.0,0.0,0.0,0.0);

    if (create_primary_ray(primary_ray))
    {
        // i=0..N: Number of Iterations
        for (int i=0;i<MAX_ITERATIONS;i++)
        {
            voxelPrecalc(primary_ray, tMax, voxel); // calculate tMax
and voxel
            hashitpoint = false;
            finish = false;
            vival = -1.0;
            while (!finish)
            {
                voxelWalk(primary_ray, tMax, voxel, vival);
                if (vival >= 0.0)
```

```
              {
                  if (triangleTest(voxel, primary_ray, vival, hitpoint,
          uvt, norm, tribuf))
                  {
                      hashitpoint = true;
                      finish = true;
                  }
              }
              else
              {
                  finish = true;
              }
          } // endwhile [!finish loop]

          if (hashitpoint)
          {
              rayshade(primary_ray, norm, hitpoint, uvt, color);
              gl_FragColor += color;
          }
          else
          {
              i=1000;
          }
      }
   }
}
```

First, primary rays are created. Then, the loop over all iterations starts. A "for" loop is used. The higher the maximum number of iterations is, the longer is the resulting fragment program. In the next step, voxels are traversed and all triangles per voxel are tested. To loop through all triangles per voxel, a "while" is used. If a hit point was found during the voxel walk, the color of the pixel is calculated; otherwise, the program terminates for this pixel.

This single-pixel shader approach only works for small scenes because of the limited number of instructions. NVidia GeForce 6800 has a maximum number of 1024 instructions. However, when using loops, the theoretical total number of instructions can be up to 65,535, but this still isn't enough for large scenes.

The NVidia GeForce 7800 doesn't have this limitation. Tests have shown that over 1000 iterations can be made using this single-pass approach.

Rendering Large Scenes: Multi-Pass GPU Ray Tracer

For larger scenes, it is necessary to split the program into small kernels that store intermediate results in textures (see Figure 6.3.10). The program flow control is done in C++. Choosing which shader program has to be executed can be done using occlusion queries.

While this method can be used for larger scenes, it is slower than the single-pass version. Using multiple render targets (MRT), it is possible to store intermediate results in up to four floating-point textures.

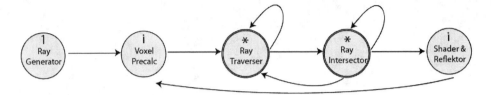

FIGURE 6.3.10   *Kernels for multi-pass ray tracing on GPU.*

Ray Generator

The primary ray generator (see Figure 6.3.11) receives camera data and generates rays for each pixel. Rays are tested for intersection, and if the bounding box of the grid is not hit, the rays are rejected. If the bounding box is hit, the start point of the ray is set to the hit point.

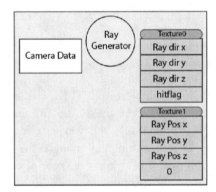

FIGURE 6.3.11   *Ray generator kernel.*

Voxel Precalculation

The voxel precalculation kernel (see Figure 6.3.12) takes a ray as input and calculates the starting voxel (in voxel coordinates) and tMax, which was described in the section "Traversing the Uniform Grid."

Ray Traverser

The traverser (see Figure 6.3.13) checks if the current voxel contains elements (triangles). If triangles are found, the ray is set to a "wait-state"; those triangles are ready to be checked for intersection, but during ray traversal there is nothing more to do, and they are rejected for further traversal operations. If the current voxel is empty, the next voxel will be calculated using a GPU port of the voxel traversal algorithm, described earlier. The information, if triangles are in voxels, is stored in the "Voxel Index" tex-

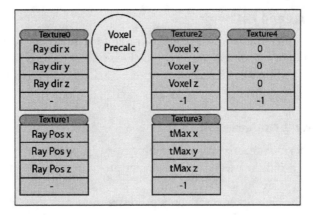

FIGURE 6.3.12 *Voxel precalculation kernel.*

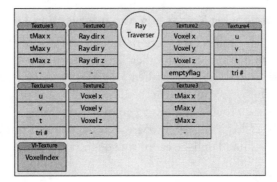

FIGURE 6.3.13 *Ray traverser kernel.*

ture. A value of −1 means there are no triangles to check; otherwise, it contains a value pointing to a "Grid Element" texture containing the list of triangles for that voxel. If the end of the grid is reached, the ray is set to an "overflow- state" and is not processed anymore. Table 6.3.3 shows the ray traversing states.

Table 6.3.3 Ray Traversing States

Active	traverse grid
Wait	ready to check intersections
Dead	ray doesn't hit grid (already rejected in voxel precalculation)
Inactive	a valid hit point was found
Overflow	out of valid voxel space

Shader and Reflector

The shader and reflector fragment program actually calculates the color of the material. A lighting equation is used and the resulting color is added to the buffer. The final ray-traced image is calculated in this kernel. The resulting texture can be directly displayed on-screen.

Early-Z Optimization

NVidia GeForce 6x00/7x00 graphics cards support Early-Z optimization. It is possible to avoid the execution of a shader program if the z-buffer value is already set to a certain value.

The "Ray Intersector" only processes those rays that are in "wait" state. Using the Early-Z technique rays that are in different states can be masked out by adding an additional pass that sets the depth-values of those rays that don't need processing to 1.0. The same can be done for traversal: only rays that are in "active" state require updates.

Load Balancing Traversing and Intersection Loop

One major problem is that both the intersector and the traverser kernel require loops and both depend on each other. The easiest way would be to loop the traverser until no rays are in active state, then loop the intersector kernel until no rays are in wait state. This is very inefficient, because the number of kernel calls has to be minimal to prevent z-culling operations to dominate the calculations. The ray intersector should only be called if enough rays are in wait state and ready for intersection, and the ray traverser should only be called if enough rays are ready for traversal.

Conclusion

Experiments with many different scenes showed that ray tracing on a GPU is an alternative to CPU-based ray tracing. However, ray tracing is not yet much faster than an equal CPU implementation. There is also a possible instability with certain hardware configurations, and the user requires hardware with Pixel Shader 3.0 support. Today, ray tracing on a GPU may not yet seem optimal, but with rapid development of graphics hardware, it may be an alternative to single CPU-based solutions.

CD-ROM Contents

ON THE CD

On the companion CD-ROM, you find binaries and the shader source code in HLSL and GLSL for the ray tracer. An NVidia GeForce 6 is required to run both ray tracers.

References

[Amanatides87] Amanatides, John, Andrew Woo. "A Fast Voxel Traversal Algorithm for Ray Tracing," 1987.

[Arvo89] Avro, J., and D. Kirk. "A survey of ray tracing acceleration techniques," *An Introduction to Ray Tracing*, edited by A. Glassner, Academic Press, 1989: pp. 201–262.

[Möller97] Möller, Tomas, and Ben Trumbore, "Fast, minimum storage ray-triangle intersection," *Journal of Graphics Tools*, 2(1), 1997: pp. 21–28.

[Purcell02] Purcell, Timothy J., Ian Buck, William R. Mark, and Pat Hanrahan, "Ray Tracing on Programmable Graphics Hardware" ACM Transactions on Graphics. 21 (3), (Proceedings of ACM SIGGRAPH 2002): pp. 703–712.

[Smits96] Smits, Brian, "Efficiency issues for ray tracing," *Journal of Graphics Tools* 3, 1998.

[Wald04] Wald, Ingo, "Realtime Ray Tracing and Interactive Global Illumination," Available online at *http://graphics.stanford.edu/papers/egSTAR03/star03.pdf*. January 2004.

[Whitted80] Whitted, Turner, "An Improved Illumination Model for Shaded Display," Available online at *http://www.cs.virginia.edu/~gfx/Courses/2003/ImageSynthesis/papers/General%20Rendering%20Stuff/An%20Improved%20Illumination%20Model%20for%20Shaded%20Display.pdf*, June 1980.

6.4

GPU-Powered Pathfinding Using Preprocessed Navigation Mesh Approach

Renaldas Zioma

Introduction

Challenging AI can dramatically improve a game experience and increase the player's immersion rate. However, it is not uncommon for modern games to sacrifice the quality of high-level AI in favor of the unavoidable low-level AI tasks like pathfinding. Such low-level AI tasks require a high amount of memory and CPU power. The main focus of this article is to improve the pathfinding process by using the benefits available in a modern GPU in order to reduce the need for CPU processing power for more challenging high-level AI behavior. The navigation mesh—a popular environment's spatial representation suitable for navigations in 3D computer games—was chosen as a target for implementation. The approach to a fast preprocess step of a navigation mesh using GPU implementation and its usage for fast specific path search is discussed here.

The navigation mesh is a structure containing spatial connectivity, which is widely used for pathfinding in modern games. By leveraging the power of modern programmable graphics hardware with VS2.0/PS2.0 shaders, the rapid precomputation of navigation mesh can be implemented, reducing the overall cost of pathfinding.

Overview of Pathfinding

There are three main parts that can be identified in path-finding solutions:

- Search space representation
- Traversal cost heuristics
- Search algorithm

Search Space Representation

The game environment needs to be split into a set of primitives in order to create data that can be used for searching. [Stout00] describes many possible partitioning techniques: rectangular grids, quad-tree, convex polygons, point of visibility, and generalized cylinders. The aim of these techniques is to split continuous game environment space into a discrete space, which is required for search algorithms.

Traversal Cost Heuristics

A discrete space can be represented as a graph, in which discrete elements are nodes and edges are paths between pairs of nodes. The trip of the AI agent from one node to another can be evaluated as a scalar value—usually called traversal cost. The simplest algorithm for determining traversal cost between two nodes is to calculate the distance between their centers. More complicated algorithms will take into account moving speed over specific terrain, various hazard possibilities, tactical environment advantages, or any other game-specific parameters.

Search Algorithm

The path search solution is a set of nodes that need to be traversed by AI agents in order to travel between two specified nodes. The goal of the search algorithm is to find the best possible path with minimal traversal cost. The traversal cost of the path is a sum of traversal costs between consecutive nodes that form that path.

Preprocessed Navigation

A real-time search for a route in a complex 3D environment is usually an expensive task and can be prohibitive for most real-time applications—especially for games with a large number of entities simultaneously traveling around the game world. Various approaches and optimized data structures have been developed in order to achieve near optimal discrete representations of the 3D environment containing as few nodes as possible [Tozour02]. However, even after employing different optimization approaches, the search space representing complex environments of the modern games can contain thousands of nodes for searching.

Search algorithms often visit a large number of nodes, so a significant amount of memory is required to store temporary information about these visited nodes. Optimized data structures and specific memory management are used to speed up the search task. In some cases, the path search is omitted in favor of less time-consuming navigational methods [Rabin00].

The alternative solution to a runtime search algorithm is to preprocess navigation information before the actual search takes place. The idea behind a preprocessed navigation is to create a lookup table of all possible path solutions needed for later navigation. A preprocessed solution table significantly reduces the order of complexity of a runtime search between any two nodes to O(1) [Surasmith02]. The problem for creating a solution for the lowest-cost path between every two nodes in the search space is called an *all-pairs shortest path* problem [Aho83].

Navigation Mesh

A navigation mesh is a common search space representation suitable for path search algorithms in 3D environments. A navigation mesh, sometimes called a NavMesh, is a mesh that consists of convex polygons. Each polygon represents a spatial "walkable" region of the 3D environment. Convex polygons guarantee that an AI agent can move in a straight line inside the walkable region without colliding with any obstacle. The AI agent can also move between pairs of polygons that share edges. External edges of the navigation mesh represent an impassable space and cannot be crossed without colliding with other obstacles.

In other words, all surfaces of the game environment that can be used by the AI agent for traveling will be simplified and split into convex regions—convex polygons of the navigation mesh. Walls and other obstacles are represented as external edges of the navigation mesh (see Figure 6.4.1).

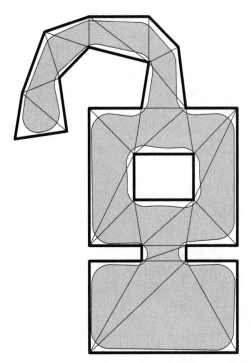

FIGURE 6.4.1   *A sample navigation mesh. The AI agent can freely move inside polygons; however, external edges of navigation mesh are impassable.*

[Snook00] describes the concept of navigation mesh along with suitable movement and pathfinding techniques. [Tozour02] proposes techniques for constructing efficient navigation mesh for the pathfinding system.

Graph Representation for Navigation Mesh

Navigation mesh splits a continuous 3D environment into a set of discrete elements; therefore, it can be represented as a graph. Nodes of the graph will represent a navigation mesh polygon, while edges represent connectivity information between polygons. Traversal costs for each pair of navigation mesh polygons are assigned to graph edges connecting their representing nodes. An infinitely large cost of traversal is assigned to the edge-connecting pair of nodes with no possible route between them (see Figure 6.4.2). Navigation mesh is addressed further in the article as a graph.

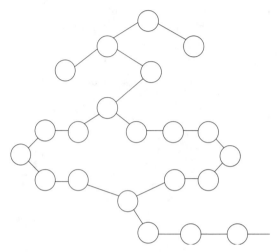

FIGURE 6.4.2   *A graph representation of sample navigation mesh.*

Precomputed Navigation Mesh

Full solution for all-pairs shortest paths can be preprocessed for static navigation mesh. All-pairs shortest paths are stored in a lookup table known as a solution table. Preprocessing the full solution minimizes the cost of path search at runtime. Instead of an expensive runtime algorithm, the process is reduced to a number of value lookups in the solution table. The speed of such an approach is gained at the expense of required memory to store the solution table.

The Solution Table

The solution table requires N^2 number of entries to store preprocessed all-pairs shortest path information for a graph with N nodes. Columns of the solution table represent starting nodes and rows—the destination node of the navigation mesh. Each entry in the solution table represents the next node in the solution path leading to the destination node. An example of the solution table is shown in Figure 6.4.3.

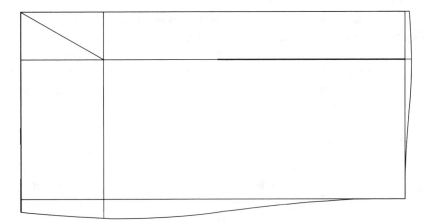

FIGURE 6.4.3   *The solution table for a sample navigation mesh.*

Generating the Solution Table

Search results of the shortest paths between two nodes in the navigation mesh are stored into the solution table. In graph theory, finding the shortest paths between all node pairs in the graph is called all-pairs shortest path problem [Skiena90].

At the heart of all-pairs shortest path solution for navigation mesh lays Dijkstra's algorithm. Dijkstra's algorithm solves the single-source shortest path problem for a directed graph with nonnegative edge weights; in other words, it finds the shortest paths from specified source nodes to all other nodes in the graph.

In order to solve all-pairs shortest path, multiple iterations of Dijkstra's algorithm need to be executed. The number of iterations required to complete the solution table is equal to a number of nodes in the navigation mesh.

Using the Solution Table

As soon as the solution table processing finishes, its results can be used to determine specific paths by AI agents.

Use of the solution table to find a shortest path between any two nodes simple. The columns of the solution table are start nodes, and rows are destination nodes of the desired path. The value in the table represents the next node along the shortest path to the destination node.

The AI agents repeatedly look up next value from the solution table using its current location as a starting node (column) and then travel to the specified node until the desired destination is reached.

It is important to note that there is no need to implement any additional logic for AI agents in order to handle dynamic changes in the environment. Once dynamic change occurs and the solution table is updated, the AI agent automatically changes its route if necessary. That happens even if the AI agent is in the middle of its path between its original starting location and destination without any additional computational cost.

Proposed Approach

The preprocess step for large navigation mesh is a very CPU intensive task, because all paths should be searched. As you can see, such a preprocess is viable only for static environments. Adding dynamic events such as doors, destroyable walls, or other changes in traversal costs between nodes will potentially lead to propagation of the change throughout the entire solution table. Fast implementation of such an algorithm is not a trivial task. As a result, the static nature of preprocessed navigation mesh usually hinders usage of complex reasoning AI because no information about traversal cost can be added at runtime.

To speed up the full solution search for navigation mesh and dramatically reduce CPU and system memory workload, this article proposes the GPU-based implementation. A modern programmable GPU can be used for a rapid full solution search for navigation mesh. Utilizing speed, fast video memory, and the parallel nature of GPU lookup table computations for navigation mesh can be offloaded from the CPU, saving precious cycles and memory bandwidth for more complex AI behaviors. The solution table computation process can be implemented solely on the GPU, while the CPU is required only as a director, issuing `DrawIndexedPrimitive` and `SetRenderTarget` commands for DirectX API.

Comparison with Common CPU Pathfinding

If the solution table is generated only once for specific navigation mesh, why should one care about the performance of the algorithm? There are at least two important cases when the performance of the solution table computation is very important:

- The solution table must be recalculated once the navigation mesh is changed. The fast solution table generation algorithm in this case is the key for navigation in a dynamic environment.
- The solution table for a full navigation mesh of the modern game environment requires a prohibitive amount of storage memory. Only necessary parts of the solution table can be generated at a specific moment—the shortest paths for a pair in a subset of the navigation mesh [Dickheister04] [Sterren04].

The solution table recalculation can greatly benefit from the CPU and GPU running in parallel.

As discussed earlier, the solution table approach has a very convenient property— AI agents don't stall on their current paths while the solution table is recalculated. The solution table update process can be executed as soon as the navigation mesh is modified or a request for the path exceeding current solution table is predicted.

The changes in the underlying environment are not visible for AI agents until the update is finished. However. longer latency in the navigational data updates allows you to reach an otherwise impossible goal—the result of the specific path search is known to the AI agent almost instantly. In comparison, nonprecomputing pathfinding approaches such as A* are performing heavy computations for each specific path request, thus stalling the AI agent until the final result is obtained. Additional care is usually required to increase the responsiveness, such as dividing the path search into several steps [Higgins02]. However, such a solution cannot guarantee an instant path result and is not robust, requiring additional hand tuning for specific cases.

In other words, the proposed approach will do the bulk of the navigational data processing task on the GPU as early as possible, while freeing more CPU power and reducing the specific path search for the AI agent to a simple memory lookup operation.

Pathfinding with the Solution Table Generated on the GPU

The following steps outline the pathfinding process using a GPU preprocessed navigation mesh:

1. The navigation mesh (in its spatial representation) is preprocessed to compute node-to-node traversal costs. The output of this step is a graph, stored in a form of a large node-to-node traversal cost matrix, which resides in GPU memory. The traversal cost data can be either computed on CPU in explicit matrix form or extracted and processed using specific vertex and pixel shaders during uploading to the GPU.
2. The navigation mesh lookup matrix is calculated using Dijkstra's graph shortest-path algorithm implemented on GPU. Since each shortest-path calculation for each goal node is completely separate, the algorithm benefits from parallel computations.
3. The lookup matrix is used for specific route searches.

Once the computational process of the navigation mesh is complete and the solution table is constructed, several scenarios can take place:

1. The solution table can be read back to the CPU main memory by locking the texture surface containing the solution table. Since the all-pair shortest path in the graph solution is computationally expensive, read-back time can be neglected.
2. The specific destination node-representing row can be copied to 1D texture. Only 1D texture is locked and read back to the CPU main memory. Several requests can be batched together to compensate for surface lock overhead.

3. The DirectX API query mechanism can be used to read a specific solution table entry value. The solution table entry value must be converted into a format that can be retrieved using the query mechanism. Texel entry of solution table is represented as a variable-length line.

Dijkstra's Algorithm

Dijkstra's algorithm finds the lowest cost path between two nodes by repeatedly spanning along the adjacent nodes with the lowest summed cost until the destination node is found. It first sets the start node as the current node with the traversal cost of zero. It marks the current node as traversed. Then, from the current node, it lists all adjacent nodes that have not been traversed. Each node on the list contains the sum of the cost since the start node and the previous node along the path. From the list, it chooses the node with the lowest cost, sets it as the current node, and continues checking the new current node's list of adjacent nodes. The algorithm terminates when the destination node is reached [Surasmith02].

Let's examine a commonly used CPU implementation for Dijkstra's algorithm. Dijkstra's algorithm operates on the following variables:

- **d**   Array of best estimates of path with lowest traversal cost to each node
- **pi** Array of predecessors for each node
- **Q**   Nodes to be processed

Pseudocode for Dijkstra's algorithm:

```
Q := all graph nodes
while not empty( Q )
    u := find_cheapest_node( Q )
    remove u from Q
    for each node v in graph
        relax( u, v, traversal_cost_matrix )
end
relax( node u, node v, costs[][] )
    if( v.d > u.d + costs[u][v] then
        v.d = u.d + costs[u][v]
        v.pi = u
    end
end
```

All-Pair Shortest Path Solution Using Dijkstra's Algorithm on GPU

The algorithm used to create the solution table iterates overall possible source nodes in the graph applying Dijkstra's algorithm, finding single-source shortest paths to all destination nodes.

In CPU implementation, the single-source node is chosen and Dijkstra's algorithm is run to find the shortest paths to other nodes. Then, the next source node is taken, and Dijkstra's algorithm is applied to it. This process is repeated for each node in the graph.

In contrast, the GPU-friendly implementation takes advantage of parallelism and calculates the shortest paths for all nodes simultaneously—all source nodes are processed by multiple instances of Dijkstra's algorithm running simultaneously.

The proposed GPU implementation of Dijkstra's algorithm performs the following steps:

1. GPU resources representing data structures required by the algorithm are allocated.
2. Data structures are initialized to default values on the GPU.
3. Node-to-node traversal cost matrix is uploaded to the GPU.
4. Search routines for the "cheapest" nodes are executed in parallel on the GPU.
5. The shortest-path information is updated for all source nodes on the GPU.
6. Ping-pong buffers are swapped.
7. If there are more nodes to process, repeat from step 4.

Details of the GPU implementation are discussed further in the article.

Allocation of GPU Resources

Dijkstra's algorithm implementation operates on large two- and one-dimensional matrices. These matrices are represented on the GPU as textures with render target capabilities. The navigation mesh nodes are indexed. Indexes are used in order to reference nodes in the solution and temporary matrices.

Following, square two-dimensional matrices are defined, where N is the number of nodes in the navigation mesh:

- **traversal_costs:**   A $N \times N$ element matrix containing node-to-node traversal costs
- **pi:**   A NxN element matrix containing indices to predecessors of the node along the shortest path, the so-called solution table
- **d, d_temp:**   A pair of $N \times N$ element matrices storing accumulated path costs
- **d_masked:**   An $N \times N$ element matrix containing accumulated path costs for remaining to be processed nodes. Processed nodes are marked with negative values
- **Q:**   A boolean $N \times N$ matrix containing information about nodes not yet processed by the algorithm

The following nonsquare matrices are defined:

- **dmin, dmin_temp:**   pair of $(N/16) \times N$ element matrices storing minimal costs during the iteration
- **u:**   one-dimensional N elements matrix containing indices to "cheapest" nodes with minimal cost during the iteration

Each instance of the algorithm is solving the single-source shortest-path problem for different source nodes of the navigation mesh. Each row in matrices, except

traversal_costs matrix, is used by separate instances of simultaneously running Dijkstra's algorithms, thus all matrices has a number of rows equal to number of nodes in the navigation mesh.

Since the same texture cannot be used both as a source and destination in computations, the so-called ping-pong approach is taken. A pair of textures is created, and one texture is used as a source while another is used as a destination. Paired textures are swapped after single computational iteration [Owens05].

The solution table is represented as (**pi**) matrix and contains the result of the algorithm solving the all-pairs shortest path problem.

Initialization of GPU Data Structures

Temporary and result matrices are initialized on the GPU side with the following values:

- For (**pi**) matrix, all node predecessors are set to itself.
- Accumulated path costs in (**d**) matrix on the main diagonal are set to zero, while the rest are set to infinity.
- All values of the (**Q**) matrix are set to true, since no nodes were processed yet.

Traversal Cost Matrix Generation

Connectivity information of the navigation mesh must be converted into the form suitable for Dijkstra's algorithm. The graph adjacency matrix suits the requirements. An adjacency matrix is a square two-dimensional matrix in which columns and rows represent graph nodes, and entries hold the values assigned to edges between graph nodes.

The adjacency matrix for the navigation mesh case stores the traversal cost for each pair of navigation mesh nodes, thus called the node-to-node traversal cost matrix. If there is no possible route between two nodes, the infinity is stored. The main diagonal of the traversal cost matrix holds 0 values, since there is no cost associated for moving inside the node.

The traversal cost matrix can be generated solely on the CPU and uploaded to the GPU as a texture. However, for large navigation meshes with a relatively small number of possible routes between nodes, the traversal cost matrix is a sparse matrix. The sparse matrix can be stored in compact form on the CPU and extracted to matrix form while uploading to the GPU. The pair of indices and assigned traversal costs are stored in the vertex stream and are passed to the vertex shader. A polygon covering only a single texel of the traversal cost matrix is constructed from a pair of indices in the vertex shader, and the traversal cost is passed to the pixel shader. The pixel shader outputs the traversal cost value, storing it in the destination matrix.

The traversal cost generation can be fully implemented on the GPU if the cost is affected only by distance and connectivity between navigation mesh polygons. The node-specific information, such as center position, is uploaded to the GPU in the form of constants. The navigation mesh in spatial form is passed to the GPU as a vertex stream. A simple ray-casting algorithm is implemented in the vertex shader to test if the ray between the pair of nodes is intersecting with the external edges of the navigation mesh. The distance between the pair of nodes, or infinity if the ray hits the external edge, is stored in the destination matrix.

Minimum Value Search on the GPU

The following GPU-friendly approach is taken to implement a minimum value search in a one-dimensional array:

1. The source array is read in buckets of 16 values.
2. The minimum value for each bucket is found and is stored in a temporary array.
3. The source and temporary arrays are swapped.
4. The operation is repeated from step 1 until a single minimum value is found.

A search for a minimum value in an array of 256 elements will require 17 iterations.

The read buckets consist of 16 sequential values in the source array. The 16 values are read from the source array using offset texture coordinates for eight samplers, and dependent texture reads are used for the remaining eight samplers. The minimum value for the bucket is found and is returned as the result of the pixel shader.

Queue Implementation on the GPU

Dijkstra's algorithm processes each node only once. The cheapest node is found, processed, and removed from the queue during iteration of the algorithm. The GPU implementation uses an additional (**Q**) boolean matrix to mark elements that are in the queue and still need to be processed. The cheapest node search is operating only on the nodes that are marked as remaining in queue.

Cheapest Node Search on GPU

The `find_cheapest_node` function implements the search routine for the cheapest node and uses the previously described algorithm for finding the minimum value. The search is performed for all rows of the source (**d**) matrices simultaneously. The index to the cheapest node in each row is stored in the (**u**) matrix.

1. The mask (**d**) matrix using (**Q**) matrix and store values of the nodes to be processed.
2. For each row, find the minimal value in (**d_masked**) matrix and store it in (**dmin**) matrix.
3. For each row, find the index of the node with the minimum value and store its index in (**u**).
4. Update (**Q**) to remove (**u**) from further processing; store **Q[u]=false**.

Shortest Path Construction on GPU

The relax function implements the update of the shortest-path information. This information is updated for each row in the same manner as it would be done in CPU implementation of Dijkstra's algorithm. The following code is applied to all nodes in all rows:

```
if dmin + traversal_cost_matrix[u][i] < d[i][j]
    d[i][j]  = dmin + traversal_cost_matrix[u][i]
    pi[i][j] = u
end
```

where **u** is the index to the node returned as a result of the find_cheapest_node function, and dmin is the cost of the shortest path.

The accumulated costs matrix (**d**) is updated and the predecessor node index is stored in the solution table (**pi**).

Specific Path Search Using GPU Preprocessed Navigation Mesh

The solution table provides information about all possible paths for the given navigation mesh. Since the solution table resides in the GPU memory data, it should be accessed from the CPU to find the specific path for AI agents.

The texture containing the solution table can be read back to the CPU main memory; however, this will cause the GPU to stall and will require sending a large amount of data back through the bus. Because an operation like this is expensive, it should be avoided if possible.

You can use the following techniques instead:

* Partial transfer of the solution table data
* DirectX API Query for accessing the solution table data

Partial Transfer of the Solution Table Data

To reduce the amount of data sent back from the GPU, only the required parts of the solution table can be transferred. A specific search is interested only in the path for the given destination.

A single row of the solution table provides all the information necessary to find a path from any node in the navigation mesh to the given destination. Thus, only one specific row assigned to the destination node needs to be transferred at a time. A specific row is copied from the solution table texture into the temporary one-dimensional texture. Only data from the temporary texture is read back to the CPU. A simple caching algorithm can be implemented on the CPU to avoid reading the same information twice.

Query Mechanism

Texture read-back can be avoided completely by using the Query mechanism provided by DirectX API. Instead of asking for information about the whole path, the CPU can retrieve information about the next node in the path.

To form the request for the next node in the path, the pair of current and destination node indices is stored in the vertex stream. The DirectX Query is issued when returning the index of the next node to the CPU. DirectX Query operation helps the GPU to avoid stalls and read-backs at the expense of relatively small latency.

Results

The described algorithm is implemented using DirectX9 HLSL and compiled for VS2.0/PS2.0 target.

GPU Implementation Summary

The most important difference between the GPU and the CPU implementation are simultaneously running instances of Dijkstra's algorithm to generate the solution table for the given navigation mesh. The minimum value search necessary for Dijkstra's algorithm is implemented in the GPU in respect to parallel computations as well.

Performance Comparison

The all-pairs shortest path solution for CPU and GPU implementation performance comparison is shown in Table 6.4.1. The following hardware was used for performance testing:

- **CPU:** Pentium 4 (HyperThread) 2.6GHz
- **RAM:** 1GB, 400 DDR, Dual Channel
- **GPU:** Radeon 9500

Table 6.4.1 All-Pairs Shortest Path Solution CPU and GPU Implementation Performance Comparison

	1024 nodes NavMesh	512 nodes NavMesh	256 nodes NavMesh	128 nodes NavMesh	64 nodes NavMesh
CPU	90.934 s	12.242 s	3.650 s	0.875 s	0.066 s
GPU	29.507 s	3.873 s	0.529 s	0.320 s	0.069 s
CPU/GPU ratio	3.08	3.16	6.89	2.73	0.95

Performance observations show that a navigation mesh consisting of 256 nodes is most optimal in the current implementation because it provides the best-processed data to render-target switch ratio.

Conclusion

This article presented an approach for the navigation in large environments that can be represented using navigation mesh data structure. The article proposed GPU-based implementation of fast preprocess of the navigation mesh data into a resulting solution table, which is used for a specific path search. The article discussed tips that can be used to reduce CPU-side memory consumption and the amount of data transferred.

The presented approach can be helpful when offloading CPU pathfinding related computations to the GPU at the expense of latency in an underlying environment. On the other hand, the presented approach minimizes the latency time for a specific path search, thus providing a better sense of interactivity.

References

[Aho83] Aho, A. V., J. E, Hopcroft, and J., Ullman, *Data Structures and Algorithms*, Addison Wesley, 1983.

[Dickheister04] Dickheister, M., "Inexpensive Precomputed Pathfinding Using a Navigation Set Hierarchy."

[Higgins02] Higgins, D., "How to Achieve Lightning Fast A*," *AI Game Programming Wisdom*, Charles River Media, 2002.

[Owens05] Owens, J. D., D. Luebke, N. Govindaraju, M. Harris, J. Krüger, A. E. Lefohn, and T. J. Purcell, "A Survey of General-Purpose Computation on Graphics Hardware," Eurographics Proceedings, 2005.

[Rabin00] Rabin, S., "A* Speed Optimizations," *Game Programming Gems*, Charles River Media, 2000.

[Skiena90] Skiena, S., "All Pairs Shortest Paths," *Implementing Discrete Mathematics: Combinatorics and Graph Theory with Mathematica*, Addison Wesley, 1990.

[Snook00] Snook, G., "Simplified 3D Movement and Pathfinding Using Navigation Meshes," *Game Programming Gems*, Charles River Media, 2000.

[Sterren04] Sterren, W., "Path Look-Up Tables—Small Is Beautiful."

[Stout00] Stout, W. B., "The Basics of A* for Path Planning," Game *Programming Gems*, Charles River Media, 2000.

[Surasmith02] Surasmith, S., "Preprocessed Solution for Open Terrain Environments," *AI Game Programming Wisdom*, Charles River Media, 2002.

[Tozour02] Tozour, P., "Building a Near-Optimal Navigation Mesh," *AI Game Programming Wisdom*, Charles River Media, 2002.

ENVIRONMENTAL EFFECTS

Introduction

Matthias Wloka

The next generation of game consoles is just around the corner, and the current buzz in the game business is all about how expensive it is to generate content for these new machines: after all, producing dazzling next-generation environments are very labor intensive. These environments also take up significant storage space, which is a concern when memory capacity is at a premium, as is the case for consoles, and low-end PCs that represent the minimum spec for PC entertainment.

As a result, procedural techniques have high appeal. They promise to automate content creation and reduce labor cost. And they typically generate renderable data on the fly from implicit and thus highly compact data, which alleviates memory requirements.

This section of the book introduces several new procedural techniques. First, Bryan Dudash shows in Article 7.1 how to generate a "Winter Wonderland" procedurally and in real time from an existing scene. Bryan describes the algorithm in detail, and provides valuable insight into common failure cases, how to recognize them, and how to fix them.

The next article, "Render Snow Cover," by Gilberto Rosado focuses on techniques for shading snow so that it actually looks like, well, snow—a nontrivial task, as snow is surprisingly difficult to render convincingly.

Carsten Dachsbacher and Marc Stamminger introduce a new procedural-based terrain rendering technique in Article 7.3, "Cached Procedural Textures for Terrain Rendering." They show how to efficiently render terrain from a compact representation without sacrificing image quality or real-time requirements.

And to conclude, "Realistic and Interactive Ocean Animation" presents a brand-new approach that can be used to render animation of ocean water in an efficient way.

ON THE CD

The book's CD-ROM includes source code for all of these articles, and I invite readers to run those code samples to fully appreciate the presented work.

7.1

Winter Wonderland

Bryan Dudash

Introduction

Modern games require more and more time to produce art. Any method that produces good-looking results and saves art production time is a schedule win. This article introduces a technique to procedurally render snow accumulation.

The technique calculates a snow coverage value for a scene taking sky exposure as well as surface orientation into account. Snow thus accumulates less on partially occluded or slanted surfaces. If Shader Model 3 (SM3) hardware is available, offsetting vertices based on snow accumulation value enhances the effect. Figure 7.1.1 demonstrates the results of this technique.

The algorithm builds on concepts found in [Ohlson04] and [Everitt02].

FIGURE 7.1.1 *Screenshot of the technique in action.*

How It Works

At its heart, this method calculates the snow coverage of a scene, and then uses this information to procedurally modify the scene's geometry, normal, and shading information to simulate snow accumulation.

To calculate the snow coverage, the technique first renders a scene from the viewpoint of the sky in an orthographic projection. Similar to shadow map rendering [Everitt02], it only stores the distance to the closest point in the scene in a frame buffer that we call a snow map. The vector parallel to this orthographic projection is the snowfall direction.

Then, in a second pass, we render the scene from the viewpoint of the camera. In this pass, we compute the level of snow accumulation for each pixel. In addition to computing the usual pixel attributes to render the scene, we transform each pixel's position into the previous orthographic projection. We compare this projected point with the value stored in the snow map: If the distance to one another is small, then the point is exposed to snow. If the distance is large, it is snow-free. For snow-exposed points, we project their normal onto the snowfall direction to determine a level of accumulation (see Equations 7.1.1, 7.1.2, and 7.1.3).

$$F_e = \frac{\left(\sum_{sample} texturedepth - actualdepth \geq threshold \right)}{\# samples} \tag{7.1.1}$$

$$F_a = \overline{N} \bullet \overline{V}_{snowfalldirection} \tag{7.1.2}$$

$$F = F_e + F_a \tag{7.1.3}$$

We then use this level of accumulation to color pixels. Pixels with high accumulation values become snow-colored; pixels with no or little snow accumulation values remain mostly unchanged.

Discussion of the Exposure Coefficient (F_e)

As previously mentioned, the exposure coefficient F_e approximates how much a given surface point is exposed to snow. The first rendering pass determines and stores all surface points that are closest to the sky in the snow map: all of these points are maximally exposed to snow. Note that the snow map only stores a surface point's distance to the sky.

The subsequent render pass again computes the distance of the current surface point to the sky. This distance computation is an orthographic projection of each surface point onto the snowfall direction. Because the projection is orthographic, it varies linearly across a triangle. We can therefore compute sky distance per vertex and simply let the rasterizer interpolate this distance for all pixels, and thus save computation cycles.

If the difference between a surface point's sky distance and the corresponding distance stored in the snow map is close to zero, the current surface point is one of the points closest to the sky, and it is thus fully exposed to snow, that is, F_e is 1. If the difference exceeds a small threshold, the current surface point is not exposed to snow, that is, F_e is 0.

In this current formulation, the exposure coefficient F_e is binary, causing hard exposure boundaries, and hence aliasing. To minimize such artifacts we compute multiple exposure coefficients for a given surface point. Instead of sampling only at the surface point, we sample in a local neighborhood of the surface point and average the resulting exposure coefficients. For reference, the code on the accompanying CD-ROM implements this technique.

ON THE CD

Discussion of the Incline Angle Coefficient (F$_a$)

The incline angle coefficient F_a represents steep slopes accumulating less snow than flat ground. While real snow follows complicated rules for such accumulation, we instead simply approximate accumulation by applying Perlin noise [Perlin85] to the dot product of the surface normal and the snowfall direction. The code on the accompanying CD-ROM shows our F_a computation in a pixel shader.

ON THE CD

Implementation Details

While the previous sections explain the general algorithm in sufficient detail to implement our technique, this section discusses pitfalls one discovers along the way. It also points out further quality enhancements. Finally, the next aticle in this book [Rosado05] describes further enhancements for rendering snow.

Depth Precision Issues

Shadow mapping and our snow-rendering technique are similar in that they both use an additional intermediate render target to calculate and store distance values. These distance values have only limited precision and are thus prone to artifacts [Everitt02]. Figure 7.1.2 displays a typical artifact resulting from this problem.

The solution for shadow mapping is to offset surface samples in the light direction. The same solution applies to snow rendering: offset surface samples in the direction of snowfall. Unlike shadow mapping, our snow-rendering technique is less sensitive to the magnitude of the offset; even substantial offsets produce acceptable snow exposure results.

Even though depth precision is less of an issue for this technique as compared to shadow mapping, depth aliasing is still problematic on steep slopes. Increasing the bias amount or increasing the precision of the snow map (for example, by using an fp32 render target) avoids these artifacts.

FIGURE 7.1.2   *Aliasing due to depth precision issues on a steep slope. Biasing the depth values in the direction of snowfall addresses this problem.*

Edge Aliasing

The snow map of our technique has only finite resolution. Choosing a low resolution causes aliasing because the rendered scene quantizes into that render target. Figure 7.1.3 illustrates the resulting artifacts. The lower the render target resolution, the more pronounced these artifacts become.

Conversely, increasing the render target resolution reduces these aliasing artifacts. However, it also consumes more video memory, increases the amount of time it takes to render the first pass (since more pixels are rasterized and evaluated), and increases the amount of time it takes to render the second pass (since the snow map is larger and hence consumes more memory bandwidth).

An alternative to increasing resolution in trying to reduce aliasing artifacts is to sample the snow map multiple times for each surface pixel when computing F_e, as pointed out in the section "Discussion of the Exposure Coefficient (F_e)." Edges look progressively smoother with more samples. In addition, varying the sample distance from the surface point controls the blurriness of the resulting edges. More samples, however, add instructions and increase the texture bandwidth requirements of the shader. If shader instructions are a performance bottleneck, then adding samples hurts performance.

FIGURE 7.1.3 *Aliasing resulting from using a low-resolution snow map and no multi-sampling for computing* F_e.

Per-Vertex Snow Accumulation and Displacement

With SM3 hardware it becomes possible to also access the snow map in the vertex shader and hence to compute a level of snow accumulation per vertex. The accumulation level of a vertex can thus directly displace it along the snowfall direction. The result is a more compelling depiction of snow coverage. Figure 7.1.4 compares the results of using vertex shader displacement versus not displacing vertices. More subtle effects, such as the more curvy look of the ground, are hard to demonstrate with a screenshot; we encourage the reader to run the demo included on the CD-ROM in the article 7.1 folder to gain a better understanding of the differences.

These vertex displacements, however, are prone to aliasing if a scene contains large triangles. In that case, displacing a vertex of a large triangle affects a large area, that is, a single snow accumulation value displaces many pixels. Additionally, if the mesh contains vertices with multiple different vertex normals per face, for example, a cube, offsetting the vertices creates visible cracks between triangles.

Solutions include tessellating all geometry in a scene to roughly similar-sized, small triangles and multi-sampling the accumulation level in the vertex shader. Multi-sampling the accumulation level attempts to average the offset values to better represent the area of the triangle affected. The sample code for article 7.1 is on the companion CD-ROM and it loads four samples from the snow map for every vertex.

Offsetting vertex position in this manner changes the geometry of a scene. As a result, per-vertex normals no longer match the displaced geometry; they are wrong. In practice, this error is minor as long as vertex displacements are relatively small. If,

FIGURE 7.1.4   *Displacing vertices based on snow accumulation (left) versus not displacing vertices (right). For illustrative purposes, we exaggerate the displacement amount, resulting in obvious image differences; for example, in the tree branches.*

however, the difference between the original mesh and the offset snow mesh is large, then lighting becomes incorrect and needs adjustment. This error also applies to other types of lighting, such as shadowing and light maps.

Conclusion

This article introduced a technique to procedurally simulate snow accumulation based on shadow mapping concepts. It is thus useful in transforming existing scenes into a winter wonderland with minimal art staff intervention, saving valuable resources. Finally, our technique is fast; it computes snow accumulation levels and renders the snow on the original geometry for the scene depicted in Figure 7.1.1 at 65 Hz on a GeForce 6800 Ultra running in 1280 × 1024 full-screen resolution. It is therefore useful as part of an interactive tool that lets artists tweak various parameters of our algorithm to quickly achieve a desired look. Alternatively, it could simulate snow accumulation in a game in real time.

References

[Everitt02] Everitt, Cass, Ashu Rege, and Cem Cebenoyan, "Hardware Shadow Mapping," available online at *http://developer.nvidia.com/object/hwshadowmap_paper.html*, 2002.

[Ohlson04] Ohlsson, Per, and Stefan Seipel, "Real-Time Rendering of Accumulated Snow," in SIGRAD 2004 Conference Proceedings, 2004.

[Perlin85] Perlin, Ken, "An Image Synthesizer," Computer Graphics, vol. 19, no. 3 (SIGGRAPH 85), pp. 287–296.

[Rosado05] Rosado, Gilberto, "Rendering Snow Cover," in *ShaderX⁴*, edited by Wolfgang Engel, Charles River Media, 2005.

7.2

Rendering Snow Cover

Gilberto Rosado

Introduction

A common technique to add variety in games is to base levels on different climate types. A game might have a sunny beach level, a fiery hot lava level, and an icy cold snow level. Some games may even depict the changing of seasons during game play: as players progress through a game, they may return to a familiar location and find it newly covered with snow. Being able to add snow to an existing environment with minimal changes in art assets is thus desirable [Dudash05].

While the previous article [Dudash05] focuses on classifying what areas are and are not covered in snow, this article concentrates on how to shade the snowy areas. The shading techniques simply rely on a snowy/not snowy classification, irrespective of how this classification is derived, for example, whether through automatic [Dudash05] or manual methods. Furthermore, other than the snowy classification, this technique requires no additional per-object art assets.

We discuss multiple aspects of snow shading. We start with equations that describe how to light snow, show how to add detail with the help of normal maps, describe how to generate texture coordinates fit for texturing snow attributes from, and finally outline how to make the snow sparkle. The conclusions contemplate possible further extensions. See Figure 7.2.1 for a screenshot resulting from our work.

FIGURE 7.2.1 *Rendering of a sample scene covered in snow.*

Lighting Snow

When computing diffuse lighting, we convert the diffuse term from the −1 to 1 range to the 0 to 1 range, which results in a softer look. The diffuse calculation thus becomes:

```
float diffuseCoeff = saturate((1+dot(N, L)) * 0.5f);
```

We then use this diffuse coefficient to blend between white and a light blue color to tint the snow. Following is the resulting pixel shader code:

```
float3 MinSnowColor = float3(0.1f,0.1f,0.4f); // light blue
float3 MaxSnowColor = float3(1.0f,1.0f,1.0f); // white

float3 diffuseColor = lerp(MinSnowColor, MaxSnowColor,
                           diffuseCoeff);
```

Using Normal Maps to Add Detail

ON THE CD

We use normal maps to add detail to a snow surface. A good approach is to blend multiple normal maps; for example, blend a procedural noise normal map and a detail normal map together to get both high- and low-frequency detail. (See the code on the enclosed CD-ROM for details.)

Generating Texture Coordinates

To map the previous normal maps onto the models we are rendering, we require proper texture coordinates. Using existing texture coordinates is likely insufficient: they are authored to map regular color and material textures onto a model. Instead, we dynamically and procedurally generate texture coordinates for the snow normal maps in the vertex shader: we set a projection matrix to project the normal maps from the direction of the falling snow onto the surface to render. (See [Fernando03] for a thorough explanation of projective texture mapping.)

Generating texture coordinates procedurally in the vertex shader, however, may result in incorrect vertex tangent and binormal vectors. To correct this problem, computing these additional tangent and binormal vectors is possible. If a model is static, we can compute these texture coordinates ahead of time on the CPU and store them with each vertex in memory. [Fernando03] shows how to compute the tangent and binormal vectors of a model.

Making Snow Sparkle

Snow consists of many tiny particles that bounce light in many directions, causing snow to sparkle. We simulate this effect by altering the normal used to compute specular lighting: instead of using just the surface normal, we blend it with a random per-pixel vector and use the result of that blend as input for the specular lighting calculations. To limit the amount of sparkles, we subsequently apply a threshold to the resulting specular value; the following code illustrates this technique.

```
// compute a random vector
float3 rndVector = float3(
                         noise(objectPos.xyz),
                         noise(objectPos.yzx),
                         noise(objectPos.zxy)
                 );

// blend the random vector with the surface normal
float3 sparkleNormal = lerp(normal, rndVector, .8));
sparkleNormal = normalize(sparkleNormal);

// compute specular lighting using the sparkle normal
float sparkle = saturate(dot(sparkleNormal, H));
sparkle = pow(sparkle, Shininess);

// constrain the sparkle to specular values above
// a certain threshold
float minSparkleValue = .6;
sparkle = step(minSparkleValue, sparkle) * SnowColor;
```

Conclusion

This article discussed ways to render snow on arbitrary 3D geometry using vertex and pixel shaders. The main concept of the technique was to adjust the diffuse and specular lighting equations to simulate the look of snow.

Combining our technique with other special effects was possible and desirable. For example, HDR blooming emphasized the snow sparkles we generated. Similarly, a particle effect of falling snowflakes complemented our technique nicely.

Acknowledgments

Thanks to our fellow programmers on the DigiPen project "Kisses." Thanks in particular to Lewis Mohr and Ryan Juckett for the snow shader discussions and for helping to implement the initial snow effect.

References

[Dudash05] Dudash, Bryan, "Winter Wonderland," *ShaderX⁴*, edited by Wolfgang Engel, Charles River Media, 2005.

[Fernando03] Fernando, Randima, and Mark J. Kilgard, "The Cg Tutorial," Addison Wesley, 2003.

7.3

Cached Procedural Textures for Terrain Rendering

Carsten Dachsbacher and Marc Stamminger

Introduction

High-quality texturing of real-time rendered terrain is a challenging task. Previous solution approaches range from simple to complex: precomputing texture maps and combining them with detail and bump maps is insufficient due to visible repetition. Using unique high-resolution texture maps consumes impractical amounts of memory. Wang tiles can solve this problem, but require a set of precomputed texture tiles and do not account for varying terrain features, like steep slopes and plains.

Texture splatting [Bloom00] combines different input textures (for example, rock, sand, and grass) depending on terrain elevation using alpha blending. More recent approaches apply a fragment shader in screen space during terrain rendering and determine a color value depending on height and slope. This approach, however, suffers from high computational overhead (that is, computing a color for each screen pixel in each frame) and aliasing.

This article presents a new method for real-time procedural texturing of terrain that avoids these problems. The method generates terrain textures on the fly and caches them using a quad-tree-like data structure. Each frame it then only updates a few or even no textures in the cache.

Overview

Our technique takes a heightmap (stored as a texture) and a tree of surface-layer descriptions as input. A surface layer consists of a color value, a height-displacement function, and constraints that define where on the terrain the color and height offsets apply. For example, a snow layer has a white color and only appears where terrain slope is small. Generally, multiple surface layers apply to a given terrain; a tree stores these multiple layers and defines the order in which we evaluate and apply the layers: the last layer evaluates its constraints after all other layers are applied to the terrain.

In the simplest case, the algorithm works as follows. We want to compute a color texture for the entire terrain; with a higher resolution than the input data. A base color initializes this terrain texture. We evaluate and apply only one surface layer at a time: for each texel of the terrain heightmap we evaluate the layer's constraints. If met, apply the surface layer's color and height offset to the terrain. If the constraint is unmet, do nothing. The next surface layer operates on the output color and elevation data of the previous step.

After applying all layers, the final heightmap determines the terrain's surface normals for use in lighting the terrain. Our technique thus produces modified elevation data through displacements, a corresponding normal map, and a color texture that represents the final, lit terrain color.

Because terrain closer to the viewer requires higher texture resolutions than terrain farther away, the algorithm operates on texture tiles: small textures representing square terrain subregions stored in a common texture atlas [Wloka05]. Tiles may become invalid as the current view changes or as the current view requires them to be of different resolution.

Surface Layer Storage

This section describes the underlying model that we use to determine a terrain's surface color and its material parameters.

The distribution of different surface types depends on terrain height and slope constraints, but may also rely on additional constraints evaluating information like distribution of erosion or rainfall stored in an input texture. Each surface layer consists of an RGB color value, a noise function, and height/slope constraints (see Table 7.3.1). If a constraint is unsatisfied, that surface layer does not contribute to the surface color at that location. A hierarchical tree structure of surface layers specifies the appearance of terrain (see Figure 7.3.1). We evaluate layers in depth-first order, and layers whose parents fail to satisfy their constraints cannot contribute.

We denote the contribution of a surface layer and thus the maximum contribution of one of its children as coverage. Each surface location, that is, each texel in the output texture, and each level of the hierarchy tracks its own coverage—which is only needed for intermediate render passes.

Table 7.3.1   Surface Attributes Stored in a Surface Layer When Texturing Terrain

Surface Attribute	Description
Surface color	RGB color of surface material.
Bumpiness/Roughness	Wherever this surface layer contributes, a noise function displaces the elevation data.
Noise function	Noise values in the range $[0 \ldots 1]$ that multiplicatively modify the result of constraint computations.
Bias and scale noise	Scalar values that bias and scale noise values before constraint modification.
Minimum/maximum altitude constraint	Defines elevation bounds for where this layer applies. Bounds may be fuzzy to avoid sharp borders.
Minimum/maximum slope constraint	Defines a slope constraint. The minimum or maximum slope bounds may be fuzzy to avoid sharp borders.

FIGURE 7.3.1 *A terrain textured with our technique. The surface-layer hierarchy consists of rock, grass, and sand layers.*

Surface Layer Evaluation

We use pixel shaders to evaluate surface layers. Instead of evaluating the entire terrain at once at a fixed resolution, we split the terrain into multiple square areas and compute texture tiles for each. Each tile guarantees constant sampling of the input height field, as the input is upsampled isotropically and uniformly.

Texture tiles and intermediate data for evaluating surface layers are off-screen render targets. We describe how to manage these various render targets efficiently in the section "Caching Terrain Textures." Figure 7.3.2 shows the inputs and outputs of rendering a surface layer.

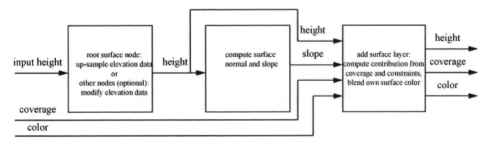

FIGURE 7.3.2 *Applying a surface layer includes modification of the elevation data, normal/slope computations, and the determination of the new surface color and height value.*

Our application evaluates all surface layers in depth first order. The root node is special in that it has no constraints (that is, the base material of the terrain is present everywhere). The input to the root node is the original terrain elevation data.

Because a surface layer may modify height values, the height output of one surface layer feeds back as the input for the next surface layer. Coverage, on the other hand, only feeds back to a layer's children; Figure 7.3.3 illustrates an example traversal of a simple surface-layer hierarchy.

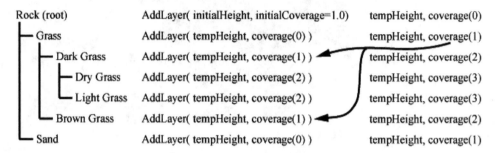

FIGURE 7.3.3   *Traversal of a surface-layer hierarchy. Height data always passes to the layer that is evaluated next, but coverage only feeds back to a layer's children.*

In general, the render-target texture resolution is much higher than the resolution of the original elevation data. Thus, height values are typically interpolated. Because we compute normals and shading from the elevation data, simple linear interpolation of the elevation data results in piecewise linear patches and thus causes undesirable artifacts.

To avoid these artifacts we use cubic B-spline interpolation instead. While this type of interpolation is costly, we only require it when processing the root node. All subsequent surface layers operate at the same texture resolution as the root node's output heightmap. Equations 7.3.1 and 7.3.2 compute the interpolated height at a location (x,y) given a heightmap function H(x,y) (see also Figure 7.3.4).

$$H(x,y) = \sum_{i=-1}^{2} \sum_{j=-1}^{2} H(\lfloor x \rfloor + i, \lfloor y \rfloor + j) R(i - frac(x)) R(j - frac(y)) \qquad (7.3.1)$$

$$R(x) = \frac{1}{6} \left[P(x+2)^3 - 4P(x+1)^3 - 4P(x-1)^3 \right] \text{with } P(x) = \max(0, x) \qquad (7.3.2)$$

Evaluating these equations in the pixel shader directly is expensive; fortunately, we can precompute and store the weighting term $R(i - frac(x))R(j - frac(y))$ of the sum in a texture. We thus require four textures ($j = -1..2$) storing four components each ($i = -1..2$) on the domain of $[0;1) \times [0;1)$ for $frac(x)$ and $frac(y)$. The textures' resolution depends on the maximum upscaling of the terrain—we use 128×128 resolution textures in the demo on the CD-ROM accompanying this book. Finally, to ensure sufficient precision, the texture format needs to be 16-bit integer or floating point.

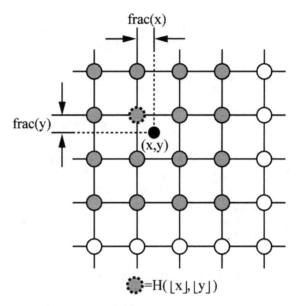

FIGURE 7.3.4   *Bicubic interpolation uses a 4×4 grid of height values.*

We can speed up the shader further by reducing the number of texture lookups. Instead of storing a single height value in every texel of the heightmap, each texel stores the original height value and the height value of its right neighbor. This trick doubles the heightmap's memory requirements, but halves the number of texture reads. Following is the resulting shader:

```
float4    h04, h15, h26, h37;

h04 = float4( tex2D( H, texC0 ).xy, tex2D( H, texC4 ).xy );
h15 = float4( tex2D( H, texC1 ).xy, tex2D( H, texC5 ).xy );
h26 = float4( tex2D( H, texC2 ).xy, tex2D( H, texC6 ).xy );
h37 = float4( tex2D( H, texC3 ).xy, tex2D( H, texC7 ).xy );

// fraction of height map texture coordinate
float2 tc = frac( texC0.xy * heightMapSize );

float h;
// weighted sum to obtain height value
h  = dot( h04, tex2D( bicubicWeight03, tc ) );
```

```
h += dot( h15, tex2D( bicubicWeight47, tc ) );
h += dot( h26, tex2D( bicubicWeight8B, tc ) );
h += dot( h37, tex2D( bicubicWeightCF, tc ) );
```

A Pixel Shader 2.0-capable GPU is thus able to compute cubic B-spline interpolation in real time in a single pass.

After a surface layer modifies the elevation data, it needs to store it in a render-target texture. Elevation data requires at least 16-bit precision for storage; otherwise terraces become apparent when computing normals via local differences. Our implementation thus stores height across three components of 8 bits each for a total of 24-bit precision. A single instruction dot product suffices to decode height stored in this manner:

```
h = dot( height24.xyz, float3( 1, 1/255, 1/(255*255) );
```

Finally, after we evaluate all layers for a render target texture, a final pass computes the terrain's surface lighting. This final pass first computes surface normals via differencing the local height values. Then, using the normals and final surface colors from intermediate render targets, we compute lighting and store the result in the texture atlas. If lighting is dynamic, the final pass instead stores surface normals and colors separately in the atlas; we then compute lighting during rendering of the terrain.

Evaluating Constraints and Computing Height and Color

As Table 7.3.1 shows, surface-layer constraints mostly derive from a terrain's height and slope. Terrain height is available directly either via the upsampled original elevation data or from the intermediate off-screen render-target textures. Slope computes as the difference between neighboring height values. Hat functions represent both height and slope constraints; that is, they are the minimum of two linear functions clamped to the range [0, 1] (see also Figure 7.3.5).

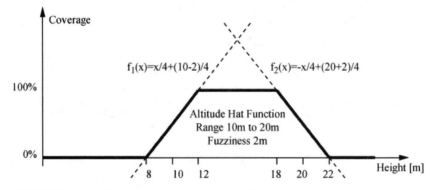

FIGURE 7.3.5 *A hat function evaluates a surface layer's constraint.*

```
// left side
slopeL_A = +1.0 / ( 2.0 * AltitudeFuzziness );
biasL_A  = -slopeL * ( AltitudeMin - AltitudeFuzziness );

// right side
slopeR_A = -1.0 / ( 2.0 * AltitudeFuzziness );
biasR_A  = -slopeR * ( AltitudeMax + AltitudeFuzziness );
```

A pixel shader's vector instructions thus evaluate multiple constraints in parallel:

```
hatFuncAlt   = saturate( min( height*slopeR_A+biasR_A,
                              height*slopeL_A+biasL_A ) );
hatFuncSlope = saturate( min( slope*slopeR_S+biasR_S,
                              slope*slopeL_S+biasL_S ) );
```

To diversify surface layer distribution, we allow per-pixel noise values to modify constraint results. A precomputed texture stores noise values in the [−1, 1] range that each surface layer then scales and biases based on its attributes (see Table 7.3.1):

```
noiseValue = noiseScale*tex2d(texNoise,coord) – noiseBias;
```

The coverage of a surface layer is the product of its constraints, the noise value, and its parent's coverage:

```
srfCoverage = saturate(   hatFuncSlope * hatFuncAlt
                                 * noiseValue );
coverage    = saturate( parentCoverage * srfCoverage );
```

Finally, a surface layer's output color and height are:

```
outputColor  = lerp( inputColor, surfaceColor, coverage );
outputHeight =   inputHeight
                 + coverage * bumpiness * texDisplacement;
```

Caching Terrain Textures

To account for varying (geometric and texture) resolution, terrain divides into square subdomains for processing and texturing. Creating a unique texture for each of these subdomains causes many render-target changes during the computation of the textures and many texture switches during rendering. To avoid these state changes, we pack textures into a few large texture atlases [Wloka05]. While our current implementation only stores terrain color in atlases, using atlases to store normal maps, for example, to enable dynamic lighting, is possible. To ensure tight and easy packing of textures, we restrict our render target texture dimensions to powers of two. The example terrain in Figure 7.3.1 uses the generated texture atlas shown in Figure 7.3.6.

All other textures—for example, storing per-pixel coverage (see the section "Surface Layer Storage")—are only needed during computation of the terrain textures and have the same resolution as a texture of the atlas.

FIGURE 7.3.6   *Texture atlas used in the terrain rendering shown in Figure 7.3.1.*

Managing the Texture Atlas

We render the terrain using a Chunk-LOD [Ulrich02] approach: a quad-tree divides the heightmap into a hierarchy of subdomains. A given view then selects an appropriate subdomain such that:

- The geometric error is below a user-defined threshold.
- The required texture resolution for the subdomain is reasonable (medium-sized textures of approximately 128×128 texels work well in our experience).

If the viewer is close to the ground, the second criterion is impossible to satisfy, even for the finest geometry representation (that is, the smallest world size subdomains). In that case, we permit higher texture resolutions.

The CPU keeps track of whether a given subdomain already exists on the GPU, and if so, where it is, or whether we need to create and evaluate a new subdomain texture. We use a simple heuristics that places newly allocated regions in already densely occupied parts of the texture: Because we are more likely to be able to allocate a few non-maximum-size textures, we split our texture atlas into several 512^2 or 1024^2 textures, although 2048^2 render-to-textures would be possible on contemporary GPUs. Fragmentation of the texture atlas is not a problem. Because we have multiple atlas textures anyway, we preferably place tiles of equal size into the same atlas texture.

Using an atlas texture introduces several potential image quality problems, most notably when using bilinear filtering [Wloka05]. We are able to sidestep these problems—partly because we do not need a mipmap chain for our textures because texture tiles automatically regenerate whenever their resolution requirements change, and partly because we only ever access the upper mipmap levels when rendering terrain.

To provide seamless texturing of the terrain that is correctly bilinearly filtered, however, texture tiles adjacent on the terrain partially overlap. Hence, each texture tile in the atlas has an inner region representing the covered terrain subdomain of the size $(2x - 2 \cdot \text{border})^2$, and a border used for overlapping regions. In our implementation we use a 4-pixel-wide border for all generated tiles. This border size is only feasible if we assume a minimum tile size of 16^2 texels. Note that the heightmap resampling density is not a power-of-two of the original sampling density when using tile borders.

Rendering the Texture Tiles

When rendering a new frame, we first traverse the terrain quad-tree to determine all visible and appropriately tessellated subdomains. During this traversal, each subdomain computes its required texture resolution. If the texture atlas does not contain an up-to-date texture tile of adequate resolution representing that subdomain, then we create this new texture tile and mark it as out of date. Each subdomain stores the part of the terrain it represents, and the texture tile stores its elevation data and its color data.

Atlas textures track which of its tiles need updating. After traversal of the terrain quad-tree completes, we update all atlas textures with a nonempty tile update list. For each surface-layer texturing step, we render all required tiles as appropriately positioned screen-aligned quadrilaterals, thus reducing render-target changes.

After performing the final lighting computation for the surface-texture tiles, we use the texture atlases to render the final image. Due to temporal coherence when moving the camera, we generally only update few or even no textures in the cache. Together with the preference for medium-sized texture tiles, the terrain texturing runs without stalling.

Discussion

In our current implementation, procedural height data only influences the final color of the rendered terrain; that is, it does not change the actual terrain geometry. Adding surface-layer-driven, procedural geometric deformation is desirable when the input height fields are of limited resolution.

Because our algorithm stores intermediate height samples in world space texture atlases, we evaluate the various surface layers in world space as well. This observation is crucial, because filtering height or slope constraints in, say, screen space suffers from severe sampling problems. When filtering in screen space, a slight change in camera parameters may result in a slightly different height value. Slope calculations then amplify these differences to the point where it causes a slope constraint to fail, thus disabling an entire surface layer and resulting in a vastly different color. Filtering in world space avoids these problems. Enough precision for the cubic B-spline interpolation during upsampling of the elevation data, however, is crucial to avoid the same problem: a lack of precision causes noise within the height values and consequently wrong slopes, and thus wrong texturing.

Conclusion

When using level-of-detail methods with geomorphing, it is insufficient to only rely on the computed geometric error for selecting terrain chunks for rendering. Texture tile resolution is equally important. Thus, texture resolution errors also influence selection of geometric resolution. We therefore suggest obtaining the geomorph factor by multiplying the geometric and texture errors.

Using slope and height constraints for procedural texturing of terrains is a widely used technique. By employing texture atlases and caching of texture tiles, it is possible to render highly detailed terrain and generate procedurally enriched elevation data on contemporary GPUs.

References

[Bloom00] Bloom, Charles, "Terrain Texture Compositing by Blending in the Frame-Buffer," available online at *http://www.cbloom.com/3d/techdocs/splatting.txt*, 2000.

[Ebert02] Ebert, David S. et al, "Texturing & Modeling: A Procedural Approach," Morgan Kaufman, 2002.

[Ulrich02] Ulrich, Thatcher, "Rendering Massive Terrains Using Chunked Level of Detail Control," available online at *http://www.tulrich.com/geekstuff/chunklod.html*, June 2005.

[Wloka05] Wloka, Matthias, "Improved Batching via Texture Atlases," *Shader X³: Advanced Rendering with DirectX and OpenGL*, edited by Wolfgang Engel, Charles River Media, 2005: pp. 155–167.

7.4

True-to-Life Real-Time Animation of Shallow Water on Today's GPUs

Yung-Feng Chi

Introduction

Interactive modeling and visualization of today's oceanic scenes has become more important, especially for games. Although modeling and rendering of animated water surfaces has been studied extensively and the underlying physical models and optical properties are well understood, the complexity of the numerical solution method in general prohibits real-time visual simulation [Premoze01]. With the advancement of programmable graphics hardware, many algorithms limited to offline processing have become available for real-time usage. This article presents efficient algorithms for real-time lifelike rendering of ocean scenes on today's GPUs. It differs from previous work in three aspects:

- A screen-space-based surface tessellation scheme that allows users to interactively fly over an unbounded animated ocean, as our scheme does not require the ocean surface mesh to be predetermined. It also offers a novel way of level-of-detail (LOD) control.
- The interactive spume effect for breaking waves when water meets shore.
- The sophisticated optical behaviors such as sunlight glare, sky light reflection and refraction, and water color effects for both calm and modestly stormy waves.

Ocean Water Simulation

There are three aspects of the ocean water simulation: the surface mesh, the wave models that describe the shape of the ocean surface, and the optical properties that describe the shading of the ocean water. The water surface for the ocean is virtually unbounded, and the wave animation is continuous. Interactive ocean animation needs an efficient tessellation scheme to determine points where the height field should be sampled. In previous works, the LOD control is done in object space. A denser mesh is typically used for closer areas of the ocean, while a coarser mesh is used for distant areas. For example, [Kryachko05] used a concentric circular pattern. However, its vertex efficiency (the amount of tessellated vertices that ends up within the view frustum) is about 25%. [Hu04] used view-dependent wave geometry. Two conic curves are used to decide regions that cover all ocean waves with visible height variation for all viewing heights and directions. An extra binary tree is embedded to determine the refinement level based on the height of the viewport. In this work, we use a screen-space approach instead. It tessellates the visible region of the water surface and also achieves a continuous LOD control for any viewpoint.

In general, water waves are represented as a height field, where each grid point stores the height of the water. The height field offers several advantages such as easy rendering and low memory consumption. But the height field restricts the wave model to convex shape, that is, no breaking waves; therefore, extra modeling for breaking waves is needed. We apply a texture-based method for rendering of foam when the water meets the shore.

A water surface exhibits complex interaction with light from the surrounding environment, such as direct sunlight and sky light scattered by the atmosphere. Modeling these optical properties is crucial for producing the look of water. Unlike the wave model, which can be computed per vertex, the optical simulation on the water surface often requires complex terms to be evaluated per pixel. The optical behavior is well simulated in real time in [Hu04]. However, their method is limited to the rendering of calm ocean water waves only, due to the use of planar mirrors for local reflection and refraction.

Water Surface Representation

A predefined grid is a straightforward way to represent the water surface, but it suffers from static resolution. So, we apply a view-dependent tessellation scheme [Belyaev03] [Hinsinger02] [Johanson04] to tessellate the visible region of the water surface according to the current viewpoint. The basic idea of our method is to generate the mesh for the ocean surface by projecting a regular grid onto the water surface (see Figure 7.4.1).

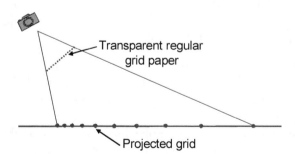

FIGURE 7.4.1   *The regular grid projected on the water surface. The resulting grid on the water surface has more detail on the near-end side.*

First, we determine a rectangle of the water surface that is big enough to cover the maximum height variations in waves according to the current viewpoint (see Figure 7.4.2). Then, this minimum visible region of the water surface is discretized in screen space to a regular grid with a set of coordinates that span across the $[0,1] \times [0,1]$ range in the homogeneous coordinate in the same fashion as interpolating texture coordinates. Finally, we project these screen-space grid points to object space, and the resulting grid points provide the positions where the height field of waves are evaluated. Figure 7.4.3 shows the visible area in screen space for a view point. Compared to previous work such as [Hu04] where an extra LOD representation is included in the tessellation process, our screen-space-based tessellation automatically controls the mesh resolution of the water surface depending on the current view.

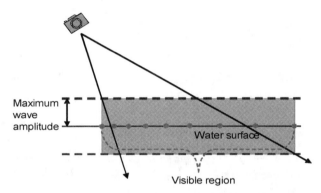

FIGURE 7.4.2   *The minimum visible region of the water surface.*

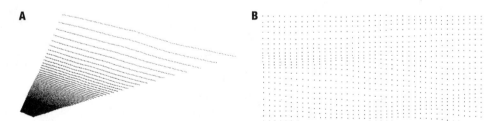

FIGURE 7.4.3   *(a) The visible grid points in object space for the current view. (b) The corresponding screen-space rectangular region with tessellation grid and the height of the ocean wave.*

The amount of tessellated vertices that end up within the frustum (vertex efficiency) is about 95% for a calm wave. However, this approach works fine in most cases except when the resulting visible region includes the backward region of the viewer, that is, the corner's point with negative w-value as shown in Figure 7.4.4. We cannot directly discretize this bounding region because it spans into infinity on both sides. To avoid this exception, we create an auxiliary viewpoint for tessellation purposes, when the viewer is under the upper-bound of the wave and is aiming away from the water surface. This auxiliary viewpoint is above the upper-bound of the water wave and looking toward the water surface. Using the auxiliary viewpoint for tessellation causes the overall ocean surface to expand beyond the view frustum slightly, thus reducing the vertex efficiency.

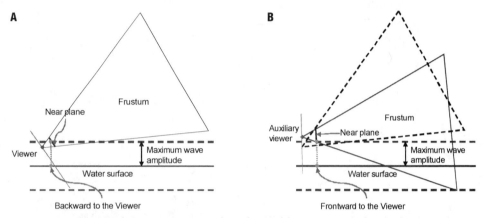

FIGURE 7.4.4   *(a) The exception case when the visible region includes the backward region of the viewer. (b) The auxiliary viewpoint is above the upper-bound of the water wave and looking toward the water surface to exclude the backward region.*

Waves Modeling

For ocean water animation, the wave model is what makes the water move, change shape, and interact with the environment. We apply a spectral approach to generate wave shapes and dynamics. The spectral-like waves as described in [Jensen01] [Tessendorf04] are suitable for the creation of a height field that spans over a large area. It is tiled in both space and time, and can be stored to textures. These textures are height maps where each value represents the evaluation of the corresponding point above the horizontal plane.

Specifically, we use the following formula to generate a height map representing the ocean wave over a rectangular region.

$$h(x,t) = \sum_k \bar{h}(k,t)e^{ik\cdot x}$$

$$\bar{h}(k,t) = \bar{h}_0(k)e^{i\omega(k)t} + \bar{h}_0^*(-k)e^{-i\omega(k)t}$$

$$\bar{h}^*(k,t) = \bar{h}(-k,t) \tag{7.4.1}$$

where $h(x,t)$ is the height field for a point $x = (nL_x/N, mL_z/M)$ at the time t, (M,N) is the grid resolution, (L_x, L_z) is the scale parameter, and $\tilde{h}_0(k)$ defines the Fourier amplitudes of ocean waves at initial time t_0. More detail of this method is in [Tessendorf04]. After generating a height map, we can span this height map over an unbounded water surface by performing texture wrapping.

As described in the section "Water Surface Representation," the resulting grid points of the visible water surface provide the positions where the height field of the wave is evaluated. So, we subsequently sample a set of height maps at a different scale to get a different spatial resolution of waves as follows:

$$H_w = \sum_{i=0}^{n} tex2D(wave_i, Vpos.xz \mathbin{/} scale_i) \qquad (7.4.2)$$

where $tex2D()$ is an intrinsic sampling function of GPUs, V_{pos} is the grid point of the water surface, and $scale_i$ controls the filtering that is done during sampling.

Although the tessellation changes in each frame, we always use the object-space position of suitable scale from the resulting grid points to sample the height field of the waves. In this manner, we avoid flickering artifacts across successive frames.

Wave Breaking

Whenever the wave is strong enough and collides with obstacles such as the shore, we could see spume and spray resulting from the breaking waves. We focus on the interactive visualization of breaking waves when the water meets the shore. Because the spume always lies on the water surface, we can apply a texture-based method for rendering it. Spume is rendered by blending the precomputed animating spume textures on the top of the water surface. Therefore we need to calculate the reproduction and expansion of the spume itself and the blending factor for each pixel of the water surface. The blending factor for the spume texture is:

$$C_{foam}.\alpha = 1 - exp(-(H_w - H_t)) \qquad (7.4.3)$$

where H_t is the height of terrain and H_w is the height of water wave (see Figure 7.4.5).

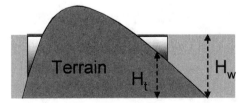

FIGURE 7.4.5   *The black lines mark the region for spume generation.*

Optical Properties

Here, we discuss the illumination model for the water surface. A water surface exhibits complex interaction with the light from the environment, such as direct sunlight and sky light scattered by the atmosphere. Modeling these optical properties is crucial for producing the look and feel of water. Unlike the wave model, which can be computed per vertex, the optical simulation on the water surface requires complex terms to be evaluated per pixel. We decompose the optical properties into a reflection component and a refraction component, modulated by a Fresnel function as follows:

$$C_{result} = F(\theta)^*C_{reflect} + (1 - F(\theta))^*C_{refract} \qquad (7.4.4)$$

where C_{result} is the resulting color of the water surface, $C_{reflect}$ is the color coming from the above-water environment along the reflection vector, $C_{refract}$ is the color coming from the underwater scene along the refraction vector, $F(\theta)$ is the Fresnel term, and θ is the angle of the viewer to the water surface.

Reflection

The reflection color caused by the environment can be further divided into three parts: sky reflection, sunlight, and local reflection.

$$C_{reflect} = C_{skylight} + C_{sunlight} + C_{localreflect} \qquad (7.4.5)$$

Sky reflection can be simply based on environment mapping or Preetham's spectral radiance model [Preetham99] to approximate full-spectrum daylight for various atmospheric conditions instead. The equations for Preetham's model are parametric fits to data from simulations of scatters in the atmosphere. We implement those equations to calculate the sky color on a per-vertex basis. The inputs for this model are the sun position and the view direction on the sky dome for the sky rendering. For skylight reflection on the water surface, we apply the reflection of the view vector for the water surface normal and the sun position instead. This effect greatly enhances the realism of the water surface with a minimal performance hit. We also apply an environment map storing the cloud's thickness in the alpha channel for sky rendering.

$$C_{cloud} = texEnv(T_{cloudmap}, V_{reflect}) \qquad (7.4.6)$$

$$C_{skylight} = C_{skycolor}^*(1 - C_{cloud}.a) + C_{cloud}.rgb^*C_{cloud}.a \qquad (7.4.7)$$

where $C_{skycolor}$ is Preetham's spectral radiance.

Water is an excellent specular reflector at grazing angles. It is usually better to use the typical per-pixel Phong lighting model with a large specular exponent to calculate the specular highlight term for sunlight instead of putting it into an environment map. We also multiply the depth value to the shininess term to adjust the shape of sunlight on the water surface.

$$C_{sunlight} = C_{suncolor} * (V_{reflect}, \cdot V_{sun})^{Shininess*VhPos.2)} \qquad (7.4.8)$$

While the environment mapping is ideal for reflecting the environment in the distance, it is not suitable for local reflection (for example, a boat floating on the water) as described in [Belyaev03] [Jensen01]. The reflection color caused by the local environment can be generated as follows: the water surface is regarded as a mirror and all objects above the water surface are rendered into a reflection map. Implementing a mirror is relatively easy: mirror the camera as shown in Figure 7.4.6 and then render the scene from this reflected camera. This method works well for a calm water surface. For oscillating water, Figure 7.4.7(a) shows the artifacts resulting from using static height (for example, the plane $y = 0$) to clip those objects across the water surface. To avoid this, we take into account the per-pixel height of ocean waves to clip those objects across the water surface accurately as shown in Figure 7.4.7(b). We use the object's x-z coordinates to look up height fields to skip those pixels that are under the water, as shown in the following:

```
height = lookup_heightfield(worldpos.xz);
        diffy = worldpos.y − height;
        if (diffy > 0.0) calc_reflection();
        else discard this pixel;
```

where `lookup_heightfield()` is the lookup function for the height field of ocean waves and *worldpos* is the world coordinate of objects.

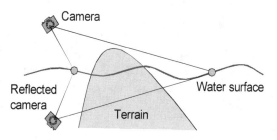

FIGURE 7.4.6   *The camera is reflected to generate the local reflection map.*

To simulate high-frequency waves, the local reflection map is sampled by projective texture computations with perturbed texture coordinates from the bump map. We also divide the distortion with the post-perspective z-coordinate to make the distortion

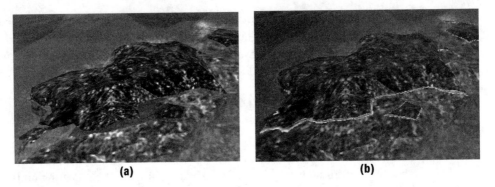

(a)   **(b)**

FIGURE 7.4.7   *Artifacts caused by using static height y=0 to clip objects (a). Per-pixel height of ocean waves to clip those objects accurately (b).*

distance-dependant and to make its post-perspective space magnitude lessen with distance.

$$C_{localreflect} = tex2D(T_{reflmap}, V_{scr} \cdot xy + \xi * V_{nor} \cdot xz / V_{scr} \cdot z) \qquad (7.4.9)$$

where $T_{reflmap}$ is the local refection map. V_{nor} is the texel fetched from the bump map, V_{scr} is the screen coordinates of the water surface, and *strength* is the user-defined scale factor for the perturbed texture coordinate.

Refraction

We repeat the same consideration as described in the section "Reflection" for the refraction map generation with two differences— all objects under the water surface are rendered into a refraction map (see Figure 7.4.8). Perceptually, the refraction distorts the image of all objects under water, so those objects under water are all scaled by 1/1.33 along the y-axis to conform to Snell's law. This can be used to remove the artifacts of texture miss for projective texture mappings as shown in Figure 7.4.9. The refraction color is decided by the scattering object color ($C_{objectcolor}$) inside the water and the color of the water ($C_{watercolor}$), where that was influenced by scattering and absorption effects of water molecules and suspensions. So, the refraction color can be approximated with the following equation:

$$C_{refract} = (e^{-attenuation*distance}) * C_{objectcolor} + (1 - e^{-attenuation*distance}) * C_{watercolor} \qquad (7.4.10)$$

where *distance* is the distance from the water surface to the object and *attenuation* is the attenuation coefficient of water.

In reality, water contains a varying amount of impurities, mostly in the form of small dirt particles floating in suspension. These particles and the water molecules alter the optical properties by scattering and absorbing part of the transmitted light.

FIGURE 7.4.8 *Per-pixel clipping for reflection and refraction maps generation. The refraction map is the image of all objects under water plus spume effect on the water surface around rocks (a). The reflection map (b).*

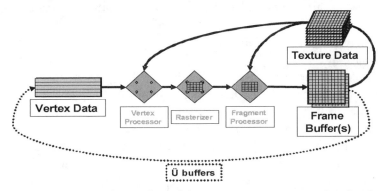

FIGURE 7.4.9 *The pipeline of the current-generation graphics hardware.*

This is the reason why shallow water seems more transparent than deep water does [Belyaev04]. The greater the distance light travels through the water, the higher the probability that it is scattered or absorbed by a particle or molecule. The light scattering and absorption are also dependent on wavelength. This is why ocean water exhibits the commonly perceived blue and green tones. Our refracted water color is based on the experiment performed in [Anthoni05]. For example, from the light extinction diagram for 1 meter of water, the average coastal water gives 70% loss in red light per meter, and the remaining (transmission) is 30%. Over 2 meters, the remaining red light is 30% × 30% = 9%. The remaining green light is 73% and the remaining blue light is 63%. So the color at depth y for average coastal water can be calculated as follows:

$$C_{watercolor}.r = 0.30^{\,kd^*y}$$
$$C_{watercolor}.g = 0.73^{\,kd^*y}$$
$$C_{watercolor}.b = 0.63^{\,kd^*y} \qquad (7.4.11)$$

We also add spume effects resulting from the breaking of waves colliding with obstacles such as the shore. Since the spume always lies on the water surface, we use Equation 7.4.1 to calculate the transparency factor for each pixel of the water surface to blend a precomputed animating spume textures or a single white color with the water color.

$$C_{watercolor} = C_{watercolor}*C_{foam}.a + C_{foam}.rgb\ (1 - C_{foam}.a) \qquad (7.4.12)$$

Implementation

Modern graphics hardware is a fully programmable floating-point pipeline as shown in Figure 7.4.9. It provides a mechanism for communicating pixel data to the vertex pipeline, and a number of useful features (dynamic branches, multiple render targets, render-to-texture, and so on) that can be used to aid the rendering of realistic water effects. Our water simulation system is divided into four stages: wave generation, surface tessellation, optical simulation, and water surface rendering. Except for the first stage (wave generation), they are all implemented as shader programs in graphics hardware.

In the first stage, we use Equation 7.4.1 to generate the height field of waves in a 16-bit integer format with mipmaps. Two different frequencies and amplitudes of FFTs with the size of 128×128 are applied to the water surface geometry generation as shown in Figure 7.4.10.

In the second stage, we input the four corner points of the visible region for the current view and a quad into the vertex shader. After rasterization, we project each grid point from screen space to object space by dividing by its w-component in the pixel shader. Then we use Equation 7.4.2 to sample the height field tri-linearly by the horizontal position (that is, X and Z components) for the displacement map generation. Figure 7.4.11 shows the resulting displacement maps. We apply Equation 7.4.2 again to generate the bump map with the size of 512×512 by different spatial scale for height field sampling. The shader programs for displacement and bump maps generation are listed as follows:

```
// Water surface tessellation
void vsWaterSurfaceTessellation( float2 tuvIn : TEXCOORD0,
                 out float4 hposOut : POSITION,
             out float2 tuvOut :TEXCOORD0)
{
  hposOut = float4(2*tuvIn.x-1, 1-2*tuvIn.y, 0.0, 1.0);
  tuvOut = tuvIn;
}

void psWaterSurfaceTessellation( float2 tuvIn : TEXCOORD0,
        out float4 worldPosOut : COLOR0,
        out float4 normalOut : COLOR1)
{
  float4 hPos;
  float3 worldPos;
```

```
// Position generation
// water surface tessellation, Coners[4] are the screen-space
// corner points of the visible region for the current view
 hPos = lerp(lerp(Corners[0], Corners[2], tuvIn.y), lerp(Corners[1],
Corners[3], tuvIn.y), tuvIn.x);

// back project to world space by multiplying (1/w)
worldPos = hPos.xyz / hPos.w;

// Lookup height field to generate the wave shapes
  worldPos.y = lookup_heightfield(worldPos.xz);
worldPosOut = float4(worldPos,1.0);

    // Normal generation
  …
}
```

FIGURE 7.4.10   *The multiple octaves of FFT waves to generate ocean waves.*

FIGURE 7.4.11   *The water surface displacement map along with the grid normals. On the left is the position map; on the right is the normal map.*

In the third stage, we focus on local reflection and refraction maps generation. The following lists part of the shader code for refraction map generation:

```
float4 vsCalcRefraction( )
{
```

```
                     // objects under water are all scaled by 1/1.33 along the y-axis
              foat4 hPos = mul(float4(i.Pos.x, 0.75*i.Pos.y, i.Pos.z, 1), mView-
          Proj);
              ...

          }


          float4 psCalcRefraction( float4 ObjectColor, float3 wPos,
          float3 eyePos )
          {
                   height = lookup_heightfield(worldPos.xz);
                   depth = max((height - wPos.y), 0);
              float hscale = 7.5;

          WaterColor.r = pow(0.30, depth * hscale);
             WaterColor.g = pow(0.73, depth * hscale);
             WaterColor.b = pow(0.63, depth * hscale);

                                 // distance = depth/dot(eye_vec, float3(0,1,0))
              float3 eye_vec = normalize(wPos - eyePos);
              float distance = depth /eye_vec.y;

          WaterColor = lerp(WaterColor, ObjectColor, exp(-distance *0.0005));

              ...


              return WaterColor;

          }
```

The spume color for each pixel of the water surface is also blended into the refraction map and the amount of spume is calculated as follows:

```
          // add foam around rocks
             waveHeight = lookup_heightfield(worldPos.xz);
          float absDiffy = abs(waveHeight - wodelPos.y);

             if ( absDiffy < threshold )
          {
             WaterColor.rgb = lerp(WaterColor.rgb, float3(1, 1, 1),
          absDiffy*1000 );
          }
```

In the last stage, we render the water surface by fetching the displacement maps
(position and normal) for wave animation and color computation, respectively. In the
pixel shader, the reflection and refraction maps are looked up with perturbed texture
coordinates from the bump map.

```
          // look up local reflection map
          float3 texCoord = hScrPosIn.xyz/hScrPosIn.w;
          texCoord.xy = 0.5 + 0.5*texCoord.xy*float2(1,-1);

          // disturb the texture coordinate by bump map
          texCoord.z = reflrefr_offset/texCoord.z;
          float4 localrefl = tex2D(reflmap, texCoord.xy-texCoord.z*N.xz);
```

The viewpoint position and the sunlight direction are input to the pixel shader for sunlight calculation by using Equation 7.4.8. We use the reflection vector of the view direction for both Preetham's sky color computation and the cloud texture lookup by using Equations 7.4.6 and 7.4.7. After the sky reflection, sunlight, and local reflection computations, we put it all together to generate the reflection color.

```
// calculate sun light specular
sunlight = sun_strength*pow(saturate(dot(normalize(IN.v),
IN.sun)),sun_shininess/depth)*sun_color.rgb

float3 R = normalize(reflect(normalize(p, eye), N));
float cloud_alpha = texCUBE(cloud_alpha_map, R).w;

// calculate sky color using Preetham model
float4 preetham_color = preethamModel(R, sun_vec) * (1- cloud_alpha);

// Put it all together to generate the reflection color
float4 skyreflection = preetham_color + float4(1,1,1,1) * cloud_alpha
+ sunlight;
```

Finally, we use Equation 7.4.4 to compose the reflection and the refraction to produce the final pixel color. Figure 7.4.12 demonstrates the sunlight specular and sky light illumination, how the color changes with depth, and the local reflection and refraction and underwater scattering effects.

FIGURE 7.4.12   *The results captured from our real-time rendering system: The sunlight specular and sky light illumination (a); the local reflection and refraction (b); the color of water changes with depth and spume around rocks (c); the underwater scattering effect (d).*

Conclusion

In this article, we proposed a system for real-time ocean water simulation with novel effects, such as the phenomenon of spume for breaking waves and optical behaviors with the environment. We also proposed screen-space-based tessellation of the ocean surface that offers a more intuitive level-of-detail control. As shown in the results, our method made extensive use of cutting-edge graphics hardware features to reach a new level of realism in real-time ocean rendering.

References

[Belyaev03]Belyaev, V., "Real-time simulation of water surface," GraphiCon'2003, Conference Proceedings, pp. 131–138.

[Belyaev04] Belyaev, V., "Real-time rendering of shallow water," GraphiCon'2004, Conference Proceedings.

[Hinsinger02] Hinsinger, D., F. Neyret, and M. Cani, "Interactive animation of ocean waves," Symposium on Computer Animation, July 2002.

[Hu4] Hu, Y., L.Velho, X. Tong, B. Guo, and H. Shum, "Realistic, real-time rendering of ocean waves," Computer Animation and Virtual Worlds.

[Johanson04] Johanson, C., "Real-time water rendering," Master of science thesis, Lund University, March 2004.

[Jesen01] Jensen, L.S. and R. Goliá_, "Deep-water animation and rendering," Gamasutra article on real-time water, Sept. 2001, *http://www.gamasutra.com/gdce/jensen/jensen_01.htm*

[Kryachko05] Kryachko, Y., "Using vertex texture displacement for realistic water rendering," GPU Gems 2, Chapter 18, 2005.

[Premoze01] Premoze, S. and M. Ashikhmin, "Rendering natural waters," 2001 Computer Graphics Forum 20, 4, pp. 189-200.

[Preetham99] Preetham, A. J., P. Shirley, B. Smits : "A practical analytic model for daylight," Proc. of ACM SIGGRAPH 1999, August 1999, pp.91-100.

[Seafriends] Seafriends marine conservation and education centre, "Under water photography: water and light," *http://www.seafriends.org.nz/phgraph/water.htm*

[Tessendorf04] Tessendorf, J., "Simulating ocean water," ACM SIGGRAPH 2004 course notes, *http://home1.get.net/tssndrf/*

TOOLS, TIPS, AND TRICKS

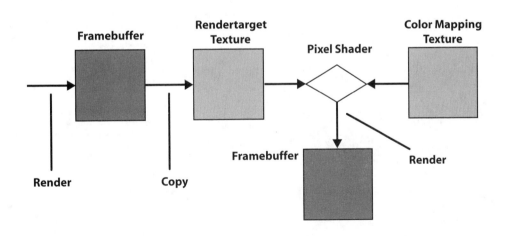

Introduction

Wolfgang Engel

Morgan McGuire's article "The SuperShader" covers a super shader that uses hand-coded shader fragments and then uses GLSL preprocessor macros to remove unused features at shader compilation time. On the application side, a C++ class hides the large number of shaders. It maintains a cache of shaders to minimize recompilation at load time and state changes at runtime. This keeps the SuperShader fast and abstracts its complexity from the rest of the rendering engine.

The article "Implementing Radiosity for a Light Map Precomputation Tool" by Florian Born covers the implementation of a light map precomputation tool that can store radiosity light maps.

Kurt Pelzer's article, "Indicator Materials," describes a system that uses the render pipeline for displaying different kinds of information about the scene and its visible objects. This helps to debug and optimize an application.

The article "Dynamic Branching on Non-PS3.0 Hardware" by Emil Persson describes a way to emulate dynamic branches on hardware that does not support it by using the stencil buffer.

Damian Trebilco describes in his article, "GLSL Shader Debugging with GLIntercept," a tool that enables users to see exactly what shaders are used, and in which parts of the scene those shaders are being used. In addition, this tool allows you to modify or recompile shaders while the application is running to debug shader problems.

The article "GPU Performance of DirectX 9 Per-Fragment Operations Revisited" by Mike Eissele updates the performance article in ShaderX³ and adds a few new test cases. It helps to estimate the performance characteristics of modern graphics cards.

Have fun,

8.1

The SuperShader

Morgan McGuire

Introduction

SuperShader renders surfaces with many of the effects used in next-generation game engines, and allows arbitrary combinations of those effects to be applied simultaneously. These effects are:

- Parallax mapping
- Percentage-closer shadow maps
- Environment lighting
- Emissive lighting
- Phong lighting
- Colored transparency
- Reflection
- Refraction
- Separate RGB control of all constants

ON THE CD

Figure 8.1.1 shows a screenshot of the demo accompanying this article on the companion CD-ROM. In the image, every surface is rendered by the SuperShader even though the material properties of the objects vary significantly.

SuperShader gives artists control over per-pixel and per-color channels over physical material properties. Most important for games, it is also able to execute efficiently at runtime despite the flexibility and combinatorial explosion of the number of possible effect combinations.

SuperShader requires Pixel Shader 2.0. The GLSL version of SuperShader first shipped with version 6.05 of the G3D 3D Engine. Because it relies only on preprocessor macros in the shading language, shader can easily be ported to the DirectX HLSL and Cg shader languages.

SuperShader is inspired by the classic offline Ueberlight [Barzel97] [Pellacini04] shader that uses a single, flexible shader to model all kinds of lights, and by FarCry and other real-time renderers that contain hundreds of precompiled shaders describing every possible material and lighting combination. The SuperShader combines techniques used in next-generation game engines, including soft shadows, light bloom, and parallax mapping.

The shader addresses three goals: image quality, artistic control, and performance. The quality goal is to make a real-time renderer that produces physically realistic images. The strategy employed is to throw away traditional real-time rendering and

FIGURE 8.1.1   *Screenshot of the SuperShader demo.*

rederive the illumination strategy using ideas from off-line renderers like ray tracers. By the end of this article, we introduce approximations that are variations on classic real-time techniques, but with some subtle differences that improve image quality. One of the differences is the use of tone mapping to fix both gamma correction and the limited dynamic range of computer displays.

To add artist control, every component of the underlying illumination model is directly exposed. These components are generalized to the product of a texture and a color so that both global and local control are present. By processing red, green, and blue color channels separately, phenomena like colored reflections in metals can be modeled.

The key implementation idea is to hand-code the most general fragment shader and then use GLSL preprocessor macros to remove unused features at shader compilation time. On the application side, a C++ class hides the large number of shaders. It maintains a cache of shaders to minimize recompilation at load time and state changes at runtime. This keeps the SuperShader fast and abstracts its complexity from the rest of the rendering engine.

Our tour of the shader begins with the mathematics behind it. These form an illumination algorithm. SuperShader separates this into artist-controllable components and a schedule of rendering passes. With the algorithm in place, the remainder of the article dives into the code and performance optimization details.

The images in this article are rendered by a demo that also applies tone mapping and bloom effects as a post-process. The SuperShader source code, including the C++ framework and ToneMap post-processor, is available on the companion CD-ROM and for download with the G3D library.

ON THE CD

From Ray Tracing to Real Time

Let's put performance on hold for a moment and consider the image that we would actually like to render if we had all the time in the world. With real time out of consideration, a good goal is to produce the same image as a ray tracer that uses a global illumination solver like photon mapping or radiosity. Such a program computes a physically correct solution that should be indistinguishable from a real photograph if we give it a good enough model of the scene.

A camera produces an image because it captures light reflected off the scene. Those reflected photons (which we'll call "bounced photons" to distinguish them from mirror reflections) can follow a convoluted path from the light source that emitted them through the scene into the eye. The job of a global illumination solver is to consider all possible bounce paths into each pixel and count the number of photons at each wavelength that follow those paths.

We begin by building a mathematical model of the amount of light reflected off a single point x to the eye at location e, and then extend that model backward to consider the path the photons originally took to reach x. The resulting "Rendering Equation" and way of looking at rendering was introduced by [Kajiya86]. He shows how ray tracing, radiosity, Phong illumination, and other lighting methods are all different approximations of the same equation. Readers already familiar with the Rendering Equation may want to skip ahead to the end of this section, where we bring back performance considerations and present the approximation that SuperShader uses to approximate the equation on modern graphics hardware in real time.

The total light intensity $I(x, e)$ to the eye from a point x in the scene is the sum of the light emitted at x (if it is a light source) and the light "bounced" off x in the direction of the eye:

$$I(x, e) = I_{emit}(x, e) + I_{bounce}(x, e) \tag{8.1.1}$$

Because light that bounces off x can come from any other point in the scene, the bounce term expands to an integral of light bounced from every other point:

$$I(x, e) = I_{emit}(x, e) + \int_{scene} RF(y, x, N_x, e) * I(y, x)\, dy \tag{8.1.2}$$

The expanded bounce term contains two parts inside the integral. The reflectance function RF describes the amount of light that bounces from y to e at x as a function of the bounce angle and surface normal N_x at x. One familiar BRDF is the Phong reflectance model, under which the (diffuse) reflectance coefficient the product of a small constant and the cosine of the angle of incidence, unless the angle of incidence is near the angle of refraction. In that (specular) case, the reflectance coefficient is large. The second part of the integrand is the actual amount of light from y to x that is modulated by *RF*. $I(y, x)$ is computed in the same way as $I(x, e)$, so it in turn expands into an emit and bounce term, and the bounce term expands into an integral. It is the nature of the recursive integral equation that this expansion is endless. This means that in the long run, light may leave a source and bounce off every surface in the scene before eventually entering the eye. If we correctly computed every possible light path, the image rendered would be perfect.

To approximate the perfect rendering equation in real time, we cut off the recursive expansion of the integral and replace it with the most significant illumination effects. Bounced light is fairly dim in most cases—for example, the illumination at a tree trunk primarily comes from the sun and not from the grass. A special case is bounced light from a light source, which is very bright. A reasonable approximation is to only compute the diffuse and specular Phong bounces for light sources. Mirror reflective surfaces are another special case—even if the scene around them is not bright, these surfaces have such high reflectance coefficients in the mirror (incidence = reflectance) direction that we cannot ignore mirror-reflected light. Likewise, highly transparent surfaces transmit significant light from behind them.

The remaining light has made more than two bounces since leaving the source and is not bounced in a special direction like the mirror case, so it is likely to be very dim. However, if we ignore that light entirely, the image will be too dark and have unrealistic harsh transitions from fully lit to fully dark. Therefore we approximate the remaining bounces with an "ambient illumination" term. The ambient term models all other light as bouncing off a sphere with two colors. The top of the sphere is bright and blue like the sky, and the bottom is a dark earth tone, like the ground. It is also possible to use a slightly more sophisticated model [Hargreaves03] that uses a texture map to reflect changing local ground color at the expense of an extra texture lookup.

The illumination equation now resembles the familiar ray-tracer terms (with global illumination approximated by ambient):

$$I = I_{emit} + I_{reflect} + I_{transmit} + I_{ambient} + \int_{lights} (shadowing)(I_{diffuse} + I_{specular})\, dy \quad (8.1.3)$$

The diffuse and specular terms in the integral are modulated by shadowing information. If a light source point y cannot see a surface point x, then x is in shadow and receives no illumination from y. We use shadow maps to compute the visibility because they offer nice filtering to fake penumbrae (soft shadows). Shadow volumes are a good alternative for cases where high-resolution hard shadows are visually preferable.

Each of the illumination terms can be rendered in real time: emissive, diffuse, and specular terms are part of the traditional real-time Phong illumination model; two-tone ambient environment lighting acts like additional light sources above and below each object; shadow visibility is implemented with shadow maps (or volumes); reflectance is easily accommodated by a cube-map reflection; and transmission can be handled through alpha blending where there is no refraction or cube maps where refraction is desired.

Rendering Passes

When rendering on hardware, we must break the illumination model from Equation 8.1.3 into a series of rendering passes through the graphics processor:

1. Nonshadowed, combines:
   a. Environment lighting (ambient)
   b. Contribution from nonshadowed lights
   c. Reflection
2. One pass per shadowed light
   a. Use additive blending, `glBlendFunc(GL_ONE, GL_ONE)`
3. Transparents
   a. Break each object into convex pieces
   b. Sort all pieces in back-to-front order
   c. For each piece, render all back faces before front face
   d. For each set of faces, render:
      i. Transmissive color with `glBlendFunc(GL_ZERO, GL_SRC_COLOR)`
      ii. Nonshadowed with `glBlendFunc(GL_ONE, GL_ONE)`
      iii. One pass per shadowed light with `glBlendFunc(GL_ONE, GL_ONE)`
4. Post-process, for example:
   a. Tone map
   b. Depth of field
   c. Film grain

The transparent pass is the trickiest. It is actually divided into three passes for the front of each convex piece of the scene and three for the back. These three passes are the modulation of the background by the transmissive color and then the regular illumination contributions from nonshadowed and shadowed sources. Note that transparent objects can receive shadows in this model, and that the final color is the modulation of the background and not an interpolation between background and transmissive color. These important effects are an advance over most current rendering systems and fall naturally out of looking at the problem from the perspective of the rendering equation.

The modulation of the background can also be replaced with a refraction approximation that instead disables alpha blending and modulates with the environment (read through the refraction vector) by the transmission color. Games like *Half-Life 2* use this trick and use the current frame buffer image as an approximation of the dynamic environment. Other games use the reflection cube map of the static environment.

The sorting of transparent pieces provides nearly correct rendering, but it is imperfect because some objects may overlap in depth (or even interpenetrate). The pieces don't have to be exactly convex, but the more convex, the less likely for an object to overlap itself and cause a problem. There's a long history of algorithms that break transparent objects apart to solve the perfect sorting problem, but the conclusion is that for games with mostly opaque objects it isn't worth trying to fix the final artifacts. In fact, many games don't sort transparent objects at all. However, going to that extreme can lead to very strange artifacts where transparents overlap. Given the speed of the C library qsort for small arrays, there's no reason not to sort transparents at least back to front.

Components

To allow artists to control the material properties of a surface, we must break out the individual coefficients as components. SuperShader approximates the rendering equation with Equation 8.1.3. In terms of components, this is:

$$
\begin{aligned}
I = \\
&k_e + & \textit{Emissive} \\
&V[k_d\,C_{\text{light}}\max(N \cdot L, 0) + k_s\,C\,\text{pow}(\max(R \cdot L, 0), k_h)] + & \textit{Phong \& shadowing} \\
&\text{lerp}(C_{\text{ground}}, C_{\text{sky}}, N_y) + & \textit{Environment lighting} \\
&k_r\,\text{Environment color}(N) + & \textit{Reflection} \\
&k_t\,\text{Refracted color}(N, E) & \textit{Refraction}
\end{aligned}
$$

$$(8.1.4)$$

V = visibility from light source (0 if shadowed, 1 if unshadowed)
E = eye vector, normalize(viewerPos − x)
$\quad C$ = lighting environment colors
$\quad N$ = surface normal in world space
$\quad L$ = vector to the light (lightPos − x)
$\quad R$ = reflection vector (V rotated about N)

The k values are the material property components. Each component may be zero, an RGBA constant, a texture map, or the product of a texture map and an RGBA constant. Concretely, we need a series of variables:

- Emissive
- Diffuse
- Specular
- Shiny (Phong exponent)
- Transmissive
- Index of refraction
- Reflection
- Normal + bump map

that are instances of a C++ class component:

```
class Component {
public:
    /** Color that is constant over the entire surface. */
    Color3              constant;

    /** Color that varies over position.  NULL means white.*/
    TextureRef          map;

    inline Component() : constant(0, 0, 0), map(NULL) {}
    inline Component(const Color3& c) : constant(c), map(NULL) {}
    inline Component(double c) : constant(c, c, c), map(NULL) {}
    inline Component(TextureRef t) : constant(1, 1, 1), map(t) {}
    inline Component(const Color3& c, TextureRef t) : constant(c),
            map(t) {}

    inline bool isBlack() const {
        return constant == Color3::black();
    }

    inline bool isWhite() const {
        return (constant == Color3::white()) && map.isNull();
    }

    /** Returns true if both components will produce similar
        non-zero terms in a lighting equation.  Black and white are
        only similar to themselves. */
    inline bool similarTo(const Component& other) const{
        // Black and white are only similar to themselves
        if (isBlack())return other.isBlack();
        else if (other.isBlack()) return false;

        if (isWhite()) return other.isWhite();
        else if (other.isWhite()) return false;

        // Two components are similar if they both have/do not
        // have texture maps.
        return map.isNull() == other.map.isNull();
    }
};
```

This code sample is written to the G3D abstraction of OpenGL textures and colors to simplify the logic. Each component has a color and a texture, where the texture is considered all white if unspecified. The methods are used to optimize the rendering in the next section of this article; they identify cases where a component is trivially black or white, and where two components produce the same nonzero terms in Equation 8.1.4.

The normal map is stored in the same format as other components, but with a slightly different interpretation. The map stores tangent-space (Nx, Ny, Nz, height) values in the RGB components. The y-axis is the normal, x-axis is the tangent, and the z-axis is the binormal. The constant component encodes the multiplier for height. Increasing it increases the perceived height of the rendered bumps.

To create alpha cutouts—for example, for tree leaves—the "matte" is the product of all alpha channels. Note that the alpha channel is *not* used to create translucency effects—that is handled through the multi-pass rendering strategy that allows correct colored transparency.

To demonstrate how the maps interact, Figure 8.1.2 shows component maps for a model of the globe (color version in color plate section). Texture map (a) is the diffuse texture. It is the base color for surfaces. The map is blue where there is water, white for ice, and green and brown for land. Map (b) is the specular map. It controls how shiny each surface appears. The land is black so that it will not have highlights and the water and ice are white. Although the map is monochrome, it could be colored. For example, to model a brass fitting, set the reflective and specular maps to yellow to color the reflections seen in its surface. Map (c) is the emissive map. It specifies locations that should glow regardless of the illumination environment. For the globe, these locations are cities. Note the concentration of cities in the eastern parts of the United States.

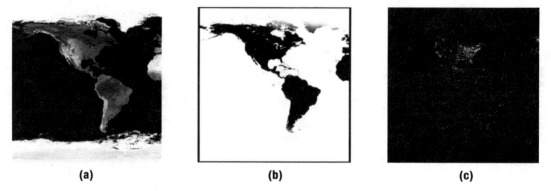

   (a)   **(b)**   **(c)**

FIGURE 8.1.2   *Diffuse, specular, and emissive maps for the Earth.*

Each map can also be modulated by its constant color. If the specular highlights appeared too bright, we could either dim map (b) to gray or leave it unchanged and set the constant color to (0.5, 0.5, 0.5).

Optimization Strategy

We've derived a real-time realistic rendering equation from the theoretical ideal and have seen how to implement it as a series of rendering passes. Because those rendering passes are in hardware, the rendering will be much faster than the ray tracer on which we based the equation. However, for real-time rendering we need the fastest possible rendering. The ways to speed up the rendering are to not compute the terms of the equation that will be zero, and to compute the nonzero terms using the fewest possible operations. In terms of writing a shader, this means that we need a separate shader for each material. For example, where the reflection coefficient is zero, no code corresponding to reflection should appear in the shader. Where the diffuse color is a constant instead of a texture map, no texture read operations should appear in the shader.

Writing every material's shader by hand is prohibitive, and managing the resources for all of the different shaders presents a major bookkeeping problem. The Super-Shader solution to hand-coding is to maintain a single shader that implements every rendering effect and specializes that template using macros. Management of the large number of shaders generated is handled through a C++ class that caches compiled shaders and binds arguments on the fly.

GLSL Shader Template

The shader source is GLSL code stored in a C++ string described in this section. The same string is used for every shader instance. It is specialized by prepending another string as described in the next section.

ON THE CD

The shader string is given here without quotation marks for ease of presentation. It is also broken up into sections for discussion. See the `.glsl` files on the CD-ROM for the complete shader template.

The string is a template because it contains code branches that will later be specialized before use. These branches are encoded using GLSL `#ifdef` statements. Using the preprocessor guarantees compile-time optimization so that there is no cost for generality when actually rendering. The preprocessor is used instead of building the string with conditional C++ code because macros allow all of the code to appear together and in a single language for easy maintenance. It is the difference between generated code and C++ templates.

The shader template begins by conditionally defining the uniforms that are the material properties. For example, the diffuse constant and texture map:

```
#if defined(DIFFUSECONSTANT)
    uniform vec3        diffuseConstant;
#endif

#ifdef DIFFUSEMAP
    uniform sampler2D   diffuseMap;
#endif
```

We use the same structure for each component. Inside the body of main, the component is reduced to a per-fragment color that combines the texture and constant. Of course, we don't need the color at all if the component is always black, and if the texture or constant is white we can eliminate that term from the computation. The preprocessor instructions to generate the optimal per-pixel component code are:

```
#   if (defined(DIFFUSECONSTANT) || defined(DIFFUSEMAP))
        vec4 diffuseColor =
#       ifdef DIFFUSECONSTANT
            diffuseConstant
#           ifdef DIFFUSEMAP
                * texture2D(diffuseMap, offsetTexCoord)
#           endif
#       else
            texture2D(diffuseMap, offsetTexCoord)
#       endif
        ;
#   endif
```

In addition to the preceding code for each component, we compute the visibility using percentage-closer shadow filtering. The filtering is texture-space blurring of the shadow map test result that low-pass filters the jagged shadow boundaries. It produces a visible phenomenon that is similar to the penumbra of a "soft shadow" cast by an area light. We use a five-tap filter for sampling the shadow map. NVIDIA hardware automatically performs a four-tap filter for each of our taps as well, producing a superior blurring with a net total of 20 taps. The GLSL shadow code for this filtering is:

```
// Compute projected shadow coord.
vec4 projShadowCoord = shadowCoord / shadowCoord.w;

const float s = 0.5 / shadowMapSize;
vec3 shadow =
 (shadow2D(shadowMap, projShadowCoord.xyz).xyz +
  shadow2D(shadowMap, projShadowCoord.xyz + vec3( s,  s, 0.0)).xyz +
  shadow2D(shadowMap, projShadowCoord.xyz + vec3( s, -s, 0.0)).xyz +
  shadow2D(shadowMap, projShadowCoord.xyz + vec3(-s,  s, 0.0)).xyz +
  shadow2D(shadowMap, projShadowCoord.xyz + vec3(-s, -s, 0.0)).xyz) /
  5.0;
```

Surface normals for shading are defined by the interpolated vertex normal or by parallax mapping. Parallax mapping is the most sophisticated form of bump mapping in use in games today. In addition to defining the surface normal by a tangent-space normal map, it also offsets the current texture coordinate according to the bump map to simulate self-occlusion and parallax. See [Welsh04] for a derivation of the algorithm. In SuperShader, normal mapping is enabled by the normalBumpMap component and implemented as:

```
#   ifdef NORMALBUMPMAP
        // Push the texture coordinate along the projected eye vector
        // proportional to the height of the bump map
        float bump = (texture2D(normalBumpMap, texCoord).w - 0.5) *
                        bumpMapScale;
        vec3 tsE = normalize(_tsE);
        vec2 offsetTexCoord = texCoord.xy + vec2(tsE.x, -tsE.y) * bump;
          mat4 tangentToWorld = mat4(tan_X, tan_Y, tan_Z, tan_W);
        vec3 tsN = ((texture2D(normalBumpMap, offsetTexCoord).xyz -
                vec3(0.5, 0.5, 0.5)) * 2.0);
```

```
        // Take the normal to world space
        vec3 wsN = (tangentToWorld * vec4(tsN, 0.0)).xyz * backside;
#   else
        vec2 offsetTexCoord = texCoord;
        vec3 wsN = tan_Z.xyz * backside;
#   endif
```

The `backside` variable is used when rendering two-sided surfaces. OpenGL has a built-in Boolean for communicating which normal to use in the pixel shader, but it is not actually supported by any driver. We must therefore emulate this built-in by rendering every (two-sided) surface twice, once with back-face culling and once with front-face culling, and setting the uniform variable `backside` explicitly. When rendering with back-face culling `backside = 1`; when rendering with front face culling `backside = -1;`.

The `#else` clause in the parallax segment avoids the texture reads and uses the interpolated per-vertex normal when there is no bump map component.

Shading is computed from the surface normal, shadowing, and lighting components. We implement the rendering equation approximation from Equation 8.1.4 by combining each of the nonzero terms into the final fragment color. The GLSL code that combines terms is:

```
    gl_FragColor.rgb =
        lightColor * shadow * (
#   if defined(DIFFUSECONSTANT) || defined(DIFFUSEMAP)
        max(dot(wsL, wsN), 0.0)
        * diffuseColor.rgb
#   endif
#   if defined(SPECULARCONSTANT) || defined(SPECULARMAP)
        + pow(vec3(max(dot(wsL, wsR), 0.0)),
            specularExponentColor.rgb) * specularColor.rgb
#   endif
        );
```

Finally, the alpha channel is the product of the alpha channels of each component for which there is a texture map. The alpha channel is used only for alpha test cutouts and not for blending, so a simple product is sufficient to combine the alpha values. The final GLSL code is:

```
    gl_FragColor.a = 1.0
#       if defined(DIFFUSECONSTANT) || defined(DIFFUSEMAP)
            * diffuseColor.a
#       endif
#       if defined(SPECULARCONSTANT) || defined(SPECULARMAP)
            * specularColor.a
#       endif
#       if defined(SPECULAREXPONENTCONSTANT) || defined(SPECULAREXPONENTMAP)
            * specularExponentColor.a
#       endif
        ;
```

All of the code in this section is from the shadow-casting light rendering pass. The ambient rendering pass has similar structure, but it removes the Phong terms and instead uses the emissive and environment lighting. The full details of the code are available on the companion CD-ROM.

ON THE CD

Instantiating from C++

The shader template is stored as GLSL source code in a C++ string called body. To specialize, we build a second string called defines that contains GLSL preprocessor macros. These macros selectively enable parts of the templated code. There is one macro for each component that is nonzero. The logic that decides which macros to enable is in C++. Following is the C++ code that decides which macros to define in GLSL for the diffuse component:

```
if (material.diffuse.constant != Color3::black()) {
    if (material.diffuse.map.notNull()) {
        defines += "#define DIFFUSEMAP\n";

        // If the color is white, don't multiply by it
        if (material.diffuse.constant != Color3::white()) {
            defines += "#define DIFFUSECONSTANT\n";
        }
    } else {
        defines += "#define DIFFUSECONSTANT\n";
    }
}
```

In the code listing, a black constant color for the diffuse component completely knocks out all diffuse terms. That is because if the constant color is black, any texture and lighting will be modulated to black. When the constant color is not black, there are three cases. If there is no texture map, only the constant term is needed. When there is a texture map, either the texture term or both the texture and constant will be needed depending on whether the constant was white.

This process is repeated for each component. The final GLSL shader is created on the fly from the concatenated string defines + body. Of course, the shader is only instantiated the first time it is used.

When binding the shader for rendering, we only want to configure the arguments (components) that are used. The logic for determining which arguments to configure is identical to that for creating defines. The following code example assumes the use of a shader runtime for setting arguments. Here it is the Open Source G3D:Shader class, but any similar shader runtime manager can be used.

```
if (! material.diffuse.isBlack() && material.diffuse.map.notNull()) {
    if (material.diffuse.constant != Color3::white())
        args.set("diffuseConstant", material.diffuse.constant);
    args.set("diffuseMap", material.diffuse.map);
} else if (material.diffuse.constant != Color3::black()) {
    args.set("diffuseConstant", material.diffuse.constant);
}
```

This code is also repeated for each of the shading components.

Shader Cache

Creating a separate shader for every single surface in a scene would be too expensive. Shaders occupy video memory, so creating many shaders takes away memory that could be better spent on geometry and textures. More critically, changing shaders can slow rendering by causing cache misses and pipeline stalls. Fortunately, we don't need a different shader for every surface. Many surfaces can use "similar" shaders. Sorting the scene to render surfaces with these similar shaders reduces state changes and speeds rendering.

What does it mean for two shaders to be similar? Our goal is to avoid respecializing and recompiling the shader template, so similar shaders should have exactly the same specialization. Looking back at the branches that are specialized, it means that two materials use the same shader if and only if they have the same nonzero illumination terms (that is, the same #defines). Now we see the motivation for the Component::similarTo method presented at the beginning of the article. It implements the logic that determines when two materials differ only in terms of the *values* of their components, but have precisely the same nonzero terms.

The decision to use a previously compiled shader or construct a new one is embodied in the Shader Cache. This is a C++ hash table that maps material (sets of components) keys to compiled shader values. Instead of strict component equality, the hash table uses Component::similarTo to determine when two keys are equivalent. For console development, where the hardware and drivers are fixed, this table need not be created at runtime. The shaders can be precompiled and stored on the distribution disk. For PC development, hardware and drivers can change and even the game content can change through downloaded patches and upgrades. Here, there is potential for better rendering performance by building the table at runtime. That allows us to compile the shaders with the newest driver, which knows how to best optimize high-level shaders for the actual hardware available.

Conclusion

To recap, the key ideas behind the SuperShader are:

- Approximate the rendering equation
- Generate material-tailored shader code at runtime
- Use GLSL preprocessor macros to templatize shaders
  - Efficiently compiles statically decidable branches
- Manage the generated shaders with a cache
  - Two shaders are identical if their materials have the same nonzero terms

These form an effective strategy for providing high-quality, general, and controllable shading effects while maintaining high performance.

ON THE CD

This article opened with Figure 8.1.1, which is a screenshot from the demo on the CD-ROM. Every object in the demo uses SuperShader. The spaceship and Earth models in the foreground have specular, emissive, and diffuse maps. The yellow ball demonstrates correctly colored transparency of the objects behind it. The ground plane receives soft shadows and is parallax mapped. Other objects in the scene (less visible in the figure) are a reflective teapot and a stained glass window with parallax mapping.

Looking forward, the template shader technique is likely to become increasingly important. The number of different effects that artists demand and that graphics cards can simultaneously support continues to increase. Ideally, the shading language itself should support on-the-fly optimization. Perhaps a future version of GLSL or HLSL will be backed by drivers that automatically detect zero-components at the object level and remove them from processing at the pixel level without any additional work by the programmer. Until then, the SuperShader framework presented in this article is a natural way to create efficient "one size fits all" shaders.

Acknowledgments

Thanks to Max Shelekhov for permission to use the spaceship model from 3DRT.com and Terry Welsh for permission to use his stone bump and texture map from Infiniscape.

References

[Barzel97] Barzel, Ronen, Lighting Controls for Computer Cinematography, *Journal of Graphics Tools*, vol. 2, no. 1, pp. 1–20, 1997. *http://www.acm.org/jgt/papers/Barzel97*

[Hargreaves03] Hargreaves, Shawn, "Hemisphere Lighting With Radiosity Maps," Gamasutra, August 13, 2003. Available online at *http://www.gamasutra.com/features/20030813/hargreaves_01.shtml*.

[Kajiya86] Kajiya, James T., "The Rendering Equation," *SIGGRAPH '86: Proceedings of the 13th annual conference on computer graphics and interactive techniques*, pp. 143–150, ACM Press, 1986. Available online at *http://doi.acm.org/10.1145/15922.15902*.

[Pellacini04] Pellacini, Fabio, and Kiril Vidimce, "Cinematic Lighting, Randima Fernanco, *GPU Gems*, pp. 167–183, Addison Wesley, 2004.

[Welsh04] Welsh, Terry, Parallax Mapping with Offset Limiting: A Per-Pixel Approximation of Uneven Surfaces. *Infiscape Corporation*, Technical Report, 2004. Available online at *http://www.infiscape.com/doc/parallax_mapping.pdf*.

8.2

Implementing Radiosity for a Light Map Precomputation Tool

Florian Born

Introduction

Static light mapping is a very common technique to simulate the global diffuse lighting contribution in a real-time scene. Because the light map textures are computed in a pre-processing step, rather sophisticated algorithms can be used to physically simulate the static lights.

A trivial approach for light map computation just sums up the direct light contribution of each light source by testing occlusion with ray tracing between the world space texel position and the light's position. This basic approach, however, does not consider any light reflected by surfaces (radiosity) or "sky lighting" caused by atmospherical effects such as Rayleigh scattering. As a result, the scene lighting is missing important visual cues and looks unnatural. Compare the images in Figure 8.2.1.

FIGURE 8.2.1 *Scene lighting using ambient color, and the same scene lighting using radiosity.*

The first part of this article describes a robust way to generate light maps in a light map generation tool. The second part introduces a technique that contributes for radiosity; that is, the inter-surface light reflection and sky lighting.

The Theory Behind Radiosity

In a closed environment there is a *radiative equilibrium*, which means the overall amount of emitted light equals the amount of absorbed light. The visual effect can be observed in a dark room with only one spot light enabled. Although only a small part of the room is directly exposed to the light, the whole room gets illuminated by the indirect lighting of the bouncing light.

Mathematically, the amount of radiation emitted by a sample i, is often formalized by the following radiosity equation [Nerheim-Wolfe93]:

$$B_i = E_i + \rho_i \cdot \sum_j B_j F_{i,j} \qquad (8.2.1)$$

where B_i is the overall amount of energy received by sample *i*. E_i and ρ_i are material properties of sample *i*, namely E_i: the amount of inherent energy emitted by sample i, for example, when it is a light source and ρ_i the reflectivity percentage. $F_{i,j}$ is the so-called Form Factor that describes a physical relationship between sample *i* and *j*, namely the fraction of energy emitted by sample *j* and received by sample *i*.

The Form Factor $F_{i,j}$ evaluates to:

$$F\left(dA_i, dA_j\right) = V_{i,j} \cdot \frac{\cos\phi_i \cdot \cos\phi_j}{\pi \cdot |r|^2} \qquad (8.2.2)$$

where $V_{i,j}$ is a visibility indicator that evaluates to 1 or 0 depending on whether sample *j* is visible of sample *i* or not.

The radiosity formula (8.2.1) can thus be stated as an equation system with the unknowns $F_{i,j}$. Unfortunately, this can become a huge matrix to solve; any naïve implementation, such as splitting the scene into geometry patches of texel size and solving the equation system, proves to be impractical for larger scenes.

However, there are many approaches to solve the equation system and keeping the computation time respectable and the memory overhead low. The method described in this article is rather a progressive approach that can involve an arbitrary number of iterations, where the result after each iteration gets closer to the exact result. It turns out that two or three iterations are sufficient to drastically increase the realism of static lighting in a scene.

Writing a Robust Light Map Generation Tool

This article provides some implementation details for developing a light map generation tool. It is limited to the basic ideas, but a tool that works for real scenarios, however, has to handle a lot of special cases.

So let's assume that we have a scene that consists of occluders and light receivers; that is, geometry that needs a light map. Both occluders and receivers are lists of triangles (tool input). The following preprocessing steps can be used to generate light maps for the scene (tool output).

Generate Charts

In the first computation step, the relevant receiver geometry has to be unfolded and uniquely mapped onto the light map pages. This algorithm involves some tweakables and some heuristics to avoid light map split artifacts later in the scene.

In the scope of this article, batches of triangles that are adjacent on the light map texture are called charts. Figure 8.2.2 shows the chart of a single cube mesh.

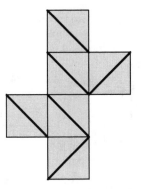

FIGURE 8.2.2 *Example of unfolding the mesh of a cube.*

The main issue of a charting algorithm is to split up the charts in a way that geometry that needs a smooth light map transition remains connected in light map space; for example, large polygons that have been tessellated, or smooth-curved geometry. Hard edges in the scene, on the other hand, can be used to split up a chart. A chart, however, has to be split in case it self-intersects (see Figure 8.2.3).

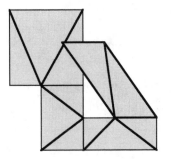 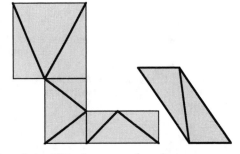

FIGURE 8.2.3 *(a) Example of self-intersecting chart. This chart must be split into two charts (b).*

Distribute Charts

After all charts have been generated, they are distributed over the light map texture pages using an algorithm that can be compared to "playing Tetris." For each chart, find the position on a light map texture where it wastes the least amount of texels (see Figure 8.2.4).

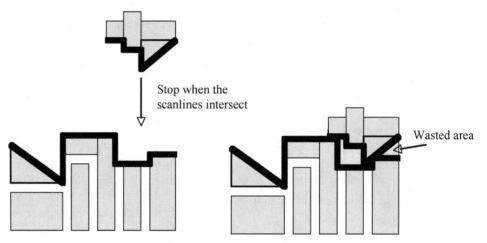

FIGURE 8.2.4   *Dropping charts in the "Tetris" algorithm. Try to keep the amount of wasted area low.*

The pseudocode for this might look as follows, where the function `DropChartAt-Column` tries to insert the chart on the light map page by "dropping" it until it intersects with the current height values as shown in Figure 8.2.4:

```
// put all charts into light map pages
for (int i=0;i<iChartCount;i++)
{
  bool bFound = false;
  float fMinWastedArea = LARGE_NUMBER;
  // find best fit of chart i in all pages
  for (int j=0;j<iPageCount;j++)
  {
    // find best position of chart i on page j
    for (int k=0;k<Page[j].Width - Chart[i].Width; k++)
    {
      fWastedArea = Page[j].DropChartAtColumn(Chart[i], k);
      if (fWastedArea<fMinWastedArea)
      {
        fMinWastedArea = fWastedArea;
        bFound = true;
        iBestPage = j;
        iBestColumn = k;
      }
```

```
      }
    }
    if (bFound)
      Page[iBestPage].DropChartAtColumn(Chart[i], iBestColumn);
    else
    {
      // fits nowhere, so create a new page and put the chart into it
      Page[iPageCount] = CreateNewPage();
      Page[iPageCount].DropChartAtColumn(Chart[i], 0);
      iPageCount++;
    }
  }
```

In case a chart doesn't fit on any of the pages, start a new page. If a chart doesn't even fit on an empty page, increase the page size or restart the chart generation with a more aggressive chart splitting.

After this step, the layout of the light map pages has been determined and the lighting result can be computed.

Generate Index Maps

Before performing the actual color determination, an index map of each light map page is generated. An index map is a two-dimensional array of 32-bit integers where the dimension of the index map matches the size of the light map page, so that each integer corresponds to a texel on the light map. Now all charted triangles are rendered into the index map using their triangle array index. Any texel that is not referenced should have an index of -1 in the map.

To avoid writing your own software rasterizer for rendering the triangles into the index map, the GPU can be used for rendering triangles in solid 32-bit colors and reading back the result from the frame buffer.

Now we can iterate through all light map pages and evaluate the light colors in world space. All we need is a function that generates a world space position and normal from a light map position. Because we know from the index map which triangle we have at light map position (u,v) and we also know the triangle's vertex positions on the light map, we can write a function that maps a light map (u,v) position to world space position and normal.

The code for evaluating the light maps might look as follows:

```
for (int i=0;i<iPageCount;i++)
{
  for (int v=0;v<Page[i].Height;v++)
    for (int u=0;u<Page[i].Width;u++)
    {
      int iTriIndex = Page[i].IndexMap(u,v);
      if (iTriIndex<0) // this texel isn't referenced on the light
map page
        continue;
```

```
        // determine the world space position and normal of the trian-
gle that corresponds to the (u/v) position on the light map
        Vector vWorldSpacePos, vNormal;
        Triangle[iTriIndex].BackProject(u,v, vWorldSpacePos, vNormal);

        // now we have a valid world space position and normal of the
texel to be lit
        Color result = EvaluateColor(vWorldSpacePos, vNormal);
        Page[i].SetColor(x,y, result);
    }
}
```

The following code can be used to evaluate the light contribution color caused by direct light exposure:

```
Color EvaluateColor(const Vector &vWorldSpacePos, const Vector &vNormal)
{
  Color result(0,0,0);
  for (int i=0;i<iStaticLightCount;i++)
  {
    Vector d = StaticLight[i].Position - vWorldSpacePos;
    float fIntensity = StaticLight[i].Intensity / (d*d); // I/r^2
attenuation
    d.Normalize();
    float fDot = d*vNormal;
    if (fDot<=0.f) // texel backface
      continue;
    if (OccluderList.TraceIntersection(vWorldSpacePos,
StaticLight[i].Position))
      continue; // something is in the way
    result += StaticLight[i].LightColor * fIntensity * fDot;
  }
  return result;
}
```

This algorithm is used to determine the local illumination, which in contrast to global illumination does not consider any inter-surface light reflections. The next sections discuss possibilities to extend the algorithm to take global illumination—that is, radiosity—into account.

Implement Global Illumation (First Approach)

Sky Light

Sky lighting simulates the sunlight that is scattered by the atmosphere (Rayleigh scattering). A common way to model this in a precomputation tool is to determine the percentage of the sky hemisphere that is visible for a specific light receiver position in the scene (see Figure 8.2.5).

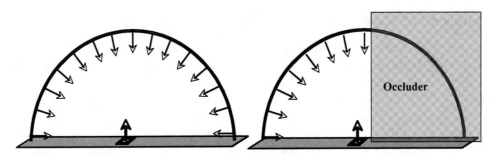

FIGURE 8.2.5   *(a) The texel is lit by the full hemisphere. (b) Only half of the hemisphere contributes to the lighting.*

In our first approach to adding global illumination to the lighting tool, we used a *Monte Carlo* method: the tracer was used to trace a bunch of randomly generated rays for each texel to the hemisphere and sum up the results weighted by the dot product of the normal vector:

$$C_{result} = C_{Sky} \cdot \frac{1}{n} \cdot \sum_{i=1}^{n} \left(\vec{N}_{Texel} \cdot \vec{N}_{Ray[i]} \right) \cdot I_{Ray[i]}$$

where n is the number of ray samples, C_{Sky} is the constant color of the sky (for example, light blue), $\vec{N}_{Texel}$ is the normal vector of the texel, $\vec{N}_{Ray[i]}$ is the unit length ray direction of sample i, and $I_{Ray[i]}$ is an indicator function that evaluates to 0 if there is an intersection with occluder geometry between the texel and the hemisphere in the directionof the ray *i*. It evaluates to 1 if there is no intersection.

The disadvantage of this technique is that we need a large amount of samples—a few hundred per texel—to avoid stochastical sampling artifacts on the result light map. Now imagine we have a few light maps each of size 1024 × 1024 to process. We easily get into a magnitude of a billion trace line tests. This takes a couple of hours even with highly optimised trace line tests.

Furthermore, a still managable amount of ray samples is by far not enough to perform color lookups on an HDRI sky dome texture.

Radiosity

To implement radiosity for the tool—that is, considering the inter-reflections of light between surfaces—we again started with a *Monte Carlo* approach: we traced a bunch of rays for each texel and looked up the diffuse lighting at the hit point. With this color information the incoming light for any texel can be estimated. Again, it turns out that far too many traces are necessary to get decent results. We then implement tracing over an adaptively subdivided hemicube to get higher tracing details in direction of high lighting variance. But this also failed to provide satisfactory results because there were far too many—even very simple—cases that caused severe artifacts.

Implement Global Illumination (Second Approach)

When we discovered that the *Monte Carlo* approach only works for fixed color sky lighting and not for radiosity in general, we decided to test a different approach based on rendering the scene with the graphics hardware and analyzing the frame buffer.

A real-time graphics engine allows rendering the scene from the texel's point of view. When using a large camera field of view (FOV) and an appropriate rendering setup, the image result can be an indication for the amount of radiation that influences the texel. When the incoming radiation for all receivers in the scene is collected, it does not solve the radiosity Equation 8.2.1, but it is a first iteration for progressively getting closer to the result. After the first iteration over the whole scene, the lighting result can be saved and used as an input for the next iteration. In the next iteration, everything already appears brighter because the light maps emit the light they received in the first iteration. The pseudocode of the iteration loop can be stated as follows:

```
EvaluateDirectLight();
SaveSceneLightmaps(); // save the light maps with only direct lighting

For (j=0;j<iNumIterations;j++)
{
  ReloadSceneLightmaps(); // use light maps from previous iteration
  foreach (sample in allLightmaps)
  {
    RenderScene(sample.Position, sample.Normal);
    sample.newColor = sample.directLight + ReadbackColor();
  }
  SaveSceneLightmaps(); // save the new light maps
}
```

It is important that the new color result in the inner loop does not influence the light map color of the sample immediately, but only after the scene light maps have been saved and reloaded again.

We can now look again at Equation 8.2.2 that determines the amount of incoming radiation and see in detail how we can contribute to all components in the formula.

$$F\left(dA_i, dA_j\right) = V_{i,j} \cdot \frac{\cos\phi_i \cdot \cos\phi_j}{\pi \cdot |r|^2}$$

The right-hand side of the formula can be split into the following components:

- Occlusion term $V_{i,j}$,
- Angle dependency terms $\cos\phi_i$ and $\cos\phi_j$ and
- Distance dependency term $|r^2|$

So, how can these dependencies be put into the scene rendering?

Occlusion

We get occlusion because of the z-buffer: when rendering from the receiver's point of view, the rendered image exactly shows the fraction of each emitter surface that influences the receiver.

Angle between Emitter and Direction, ϕ_i

Since the scene is rendered in the direction of the receiver's normal, the direction vector of emitter/receiver position matches the vertex position vector in eye space (eye vector).

When rendering the occluder geometry, we use a simple shader that calculates the dot product between the fragment and the eye vector, which is $\cos\phi$. The corresponding vertex resp. fragment shader program looks as follows (for readability reasons it is written as GLSL code, but the shader is simple enough to be implemented with old assembly-style programs as well):

```
// vertex shader
varying vec4 vEyeVec;
varying vec4 vNormal;

void main(void)
{
  gl_Position  = ftransform();

  vEyeVec = -(gl_ModelViewMatrix * gl_Vertex);
  vNormal =  gl_ModelViewMatrix * vec4(gl_Normal,0);
}


// fragment shader
varying vec4 vEyeVec;
varying vec4 vNormal;

void main(void)
{
  vec3 vNorm = normalize(vNormal.xyz);
  vec3 vEye = normalize(vEyeVec.xyz);
  // simply use dot of eye vector and texel normal as luminance output
  float fIntensity = dot(vNorm, vEye);
  gl_FragColor = vec4(fIntensity,fIntensity,fIntensity,1);
}
```

The output of the fragment shader is a luminance value that indicates the amount of radiation that reaches the camera position from the rendered fragment. This intensity can be used to be modulated with the diffuse scene brightness of the same texel; that is, the base texture times light map result. Thus, for performance reasons, the shader should be combined with all combinations of scene render states involved in the scene, where each scene render state combines its final color result with the luminance calculated the way mentioned previously. Alternatively, the luminance shader can be rendered on top of the scene geometry using multiplicative blending and depth test set to "equal."

Angle between Receiver and Direction ϕ_i

To get the angle between receiver normal and direction vector, we can again exploit the fact that the scene is rendered from the receiver texel's point of view using its normal as a camera direction. In this case, the angle is always the same for a specific screen position. This means that we can precompute the dot product of the screen position rays with the camera direction, put the result into a float array, and multiply the color readback values with it when reading back from the frame buffer. Unfortunately, it is not only the dot product that has to be put into this array. Because we need an even distribution of angles, we have to compensate for the fact that the screen plane has evenly subdivided pixels rather than angles that cause the angles in the center to be larger than in the screen corner. This gets worse when a large FOV is used as seen in Figure 8.2.6.

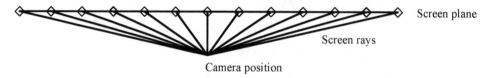

FIGURE 8.2.6   *For large FOVs, the angles between the rays are larger in the screen center.*

This situation means a larger number of samples would be required in the middle of the screen. The weighting factor can compensate for it if we multiply each screen position weighting factor by the opening angle of the camera/screen texel frustum. Figure 8.2.7 shows how this angle is calculated.

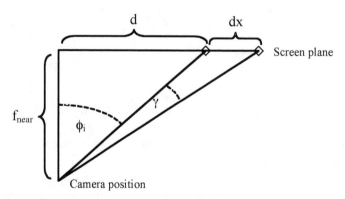

FIGURE 8.2.7   *Calculation of γ, the opening angle of the screen texel frustum.*

From $\tan\phi_i = \frac{d}{f_{near}}$ and $\tan(\phi_i + \gamma) = \frac{d + dx}{f_{near}}$ we get

$$\gamma = \tan^{-1}\left(\frac{d + dx}{f_{near}}\right) - \tan^{-1}\left(\frac{d}{f_{near}}\right)$$

where f_{near} is the distance to the screen plane, d is the distance to screen center, dx is the size of a texel on the screen plane, and γ is the angle we are looking for. With this correction, the screen-weighting factor $w[x, y]$ for each screen position is set to the product of γ and the dot product between ray and camera direction, which is naturally the z-component of the normalized screen ray:

$$w[x, y] := \gamma \cdot \cos\phi_i = \gamma \cdot ray.z$$

We can use degree or radians since the array of weightings should be normalized anyway.

As mentioned before, the weighting array needs to be calculated only once at initialization time.

The multiplication with the screen weightings is done on the CPU after reading back the pixels from the frame buffer after each rendered frame. As an alternative, the weighting factors can be put into a luminance texture and rendered as a multiplicatively blended full-screen quad after the scene has been rendered. The luminance texture generated by the previous weighting equation looks like Figure 8.2.8.

FIGURE 8.2.8 *Screen modulation mask to contribute for the angle between receiver normal and direction.*

The screen modulation mask shows that we get the most lighting contribution for surfaces that are rendered in the middle of the screen. This is the geometry that the receiver's normal vector points at.

Doing the multiplication operation on the GPU via the blended quad is, of course, faster, but has the drawback of losing important accuracy especially in the corners of the screen—at least when 8-bits-per-color channels are used. This is why we prefer the software multiplication after the readback.

Consider the Distance?

The texel's distance is already considered by the rendering: the emissive surfaces get smaller when they are further away. Please notice that the distance law in Equation 8.2.2 applies for infinitesimal areas, so no distance-based modifications must be applied to the readback result.

Sky Lighting in the Rendering Approach

One big advantage of the rendering approach is that we get sky lighting absolutely for free. For a sky with a constant color we just need to use the sky color as the rendering clear color. The readback of the rendered image will then find the sky color at all pixels that are not occluded. For a textured sky, the sky cube just needs to be rendered as usual in the engine. Because any normal of samples on the hemisphere points toward the receiver texel, no shader has to be applied to the sky—in contrast to all other light-emitting surfaces.

Optimizations

The radiosity approach described here requires quite a lot of scene renderings. The overall number of renderings equals the number of iterations times the number of receiver samples on the light maps. This is usually more than a million times. Therefore, it is important to look at possible optimizations.

Size of the Readback Window

The resolution of the readback window can be quite small; for example, 128×128 pixels. For small windows, GPU fill rate is not an issue at all and the readback is much faster. In fact, we could not recognize any quality differences between a resolution of 128 and 256. A small size also helps for the next optimization.

Avoid Synchronization

Every readback forces a synchronization. This can be quite significant for the overall processing time. One method to reduce the number of synchronizations is to split the screen buffer into tiles, render a scene into each tile, and read back the result for all at the same time.

Reduce the Number of Renderings

For tracing the direct light it is important to trace every referenced texel on the light map, because direct lighting can cause hard shadow edges within single triangles. The radiosity contribution, on the other hand, does not have a too large variation over a single triangle. Thus, inside a triangle it is sufficient to use a lower light map resolution and perform the rendering for 2 × 2 blocks (see Figure 8.2.9).

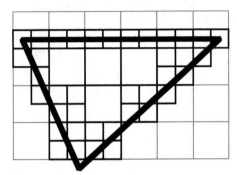

FIGURE 8.2.9 *Optimization: span the blocks inside a triangle.*

Clearly, this optimization only applies for blocks that are completely inside a triangle because adjacent triangles might differ too much in their normal.

Optimize the Rendering Speed

For the readback view, no high-quality output is needed, so everything should be set to lowest rendering details:

- Only render the occluder geometry
- Use lowest LOD settings for rendering objects
- Use low-quality texture mipmap bias, no anisotropic filtering, or FSAA

Light Grid

The described method for evaluating radiosity for light maps also applies for generating a light grid. Because a cell of a light grid is a light receiver and not an emitter, a single iteration is sufficient, unless static objects in the scene are lit with the light grid.

Conclusion

This article provided a good starting point for developing a robust light map generation tool. It described how geometry can be efficiently charted on the light map textures and how light calculation is then performed by processing the light map pages.

Furthermore, this article described an idea of how to contribute to global illumination. Rather than solving huge equation systems, the described technique used an adaptive algorithm that measured the incoming amount of radiation for any sample position. It turns out that a real-time rendering engine can be configured in a way that the rendered image can be used directly as an indication for the incoming light. Using the readback of a rendered image also has some nice advantages; for example, sky lighting can be added with no additional performance overhead and special shaders in the scene can be used to get radiosity from light-emitting surfaces.

Finally, the main drawback of this technique—rendering performance for millions of images—can be improved by applying the optimizations mentioned in this article.

References

[Ashdown94] Ashdown, Ian, *Radiosity—A Programmer's Perspective*, Iley & Sons Inc., 1994.

[Nerheim-Wolfe93] Nerheim-Wolfe, Rosalee, Toby Howard, and Stephen Spencer, 1993 SIGGRAPH Educator's Slide Set, ACM SIGGRAPH, 1993. Available online at *http://www.siggraph.org/education/materials/HyperGraph/radiosity/overview_1.htm*.

8.3

Indicator Materials

Kurt Pelzer

Before launching into a new software project, every good programmer gets some tools ready to generate additional feedback from a running application. The usual way to handle this feedback is standard text output to display different kinds of messages, warnings, errors, statistics, and so on. We need this additional output to keep a log of all critical events that happen. And, it is a good practice to examine this log, even when some problems with your new program occur. But, there are many situations where you want more information from running applications. Especially, when your new software is used to render complex scenes, it is helpful to get some visible feedback directly on the objects or pixels in the scene.

This article describes a uniform system that allows us to use the render pipeline for displaying different kinds of information about the scene and its visible objects. Additionally, we take a closer look at how to use this feedback to detect malfunctions in our software and analyze the content that comes from our artists and level designers. In this article, the complete system, including the collection of examples, is named *indicator materials*.

Goals and Scope

As just mentioned, many situations exist where you want more information from running applications. Ideally, we would like to be able to detect problems and malfunctions directly on each object in the scene. For example, missing resources like textures, shaders, or materials should be visualized by special error colors. Furthermore, every developer who creates real-time applications that use 3D graphics is concerned about performance optimization. Therefore we will need several indicator materials that help us to find critical sections or objects in the scene. Here are some examples: we want to find areas with higher overdraw and bad occlusion culling, objects with expensive materials or shaders must be able to warn us, and each material should show us if it's solid, alpha-tested, or alpha-blended.

Looking ahead again, we see that we will want to be able to use a uniform system for all indicator materials. For this to work, we must use a two-step technique. The first step is different for all indicator materials and generates a unique output for each one. This output will be used by the second step, which is the same for all materials. Once we have done this work, it is easy to add new indicator materials. But how do we implement this system? The next section, "Uniform System," discusses the second step of our technique. A list of useful indicator materials and their unique first steps is presented later (see the sections "Simple Applications" and "Advanced Applications").

Uniform System

In this section, we create a uniform system that is able to handle all indicator materials in the same way. To achieve this behavior, our technique uses a prepared content of the frame buffer that is filled by the active indicator material (first step of our technique). The trick is to make it possible for a special pixel shader to map the color in the frame buffer to a new color. To realize that, we either copy the frame buffer into a render-target texture or render the scene directly into a render-target texture. However, if we have this information it is easy to run the next step. Again, once we have this special texture, we present it with mapped colors on the screen (see Figure 8.3.1 for the complete process).

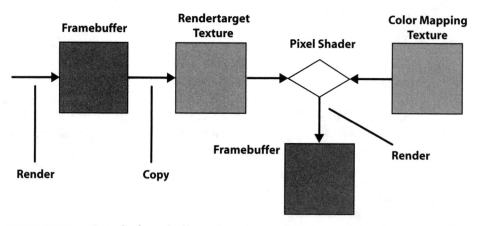

FIGURE 8.3.1   *Copy the frame buffer and use the copy for color mapping via post-processing.*

Copy the Frame Buffer

Because switching the render target adds additional cost to each frame, we prefer to copy the content of the frame buffer. Our code calls `IDirect3DDevice9::StretchRect` to copy the device frame buffer (that is, typically the back buffer) to a texture surface so that the pixel shader in the second step can use it to fetch the final colors.

Following is the code of the copy process based on DirectX9.0c:

```
// Get the current render-target surface (the framebuffer)
IDirect3DSurface9* pFrameBufferSurface;
m_pD3DDevice->GetRenderTarget( 0, &pFrameBufferSurface );

// Get the texture surface of our render-target texture
IDirect3DSurface9* pTextureSurface;
m_pRTTexture->GetSurfaceLevel( 0, &pRTTextureSurface )

// Copy the contents of the source rectangle (the
```

```
// framebufffer) to the destination rectangle (the render-
// target texture)
m_pD3DDevice->StretchRect( pFrameBufferSurface, NULL,
                    pRTTextureSurface, NULL, D3DTEXF_POINT );

// Decrease the internal reference count of both surfaces
pFrameBufferSurface->Release();
pRTTextureSurface->Release();
```

Color Mapping via Pixel Shader

Finally, we ensure that the screen presents the wanted color results. So, to continue with the next step, we render a quad that fills the complete frame buffer. Additionally, we activate a pixel shader that is able to map the colors of our frame buffer copy to the final colors. For this, the shader takes the fetched red channel value of the render-target texture and uses this value as texture coordinate U when sampling a special color-mapping texture (see Figure 8.3.2).

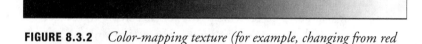

FIGURE 8.3.2 *Color-mapping texture (for example, changing from red [left] to yellow to green to white [right]) See insert for color version.*

Following is the code of the pixel shader based on Effect/HLSL:

```
// Define the samplers for the render-target texture and
// the color mapping texture
sampler2D RTTexture : register( ps, s0 );
sampler2D CMTexture : register( ps, s1 );

// Simple input structure
struct PS_INPUT
{
    float4 vTex0 : TEXCOORD0;
};

// Pixel shader using the red color channel of the
// RTTexture to fetch the CMTexture colors
float4 PS( const PS_INPUT input ) : COLOR
{
    float4 fNewTexCoord = tex2D( RTTexture, input.vTex0 );
    float4 OutputColor  = tex2D( CMTexture,
                            float2( fNewTexCoord.x, 0 ) );
    return OutputColor;
}
```

```
// The effect technique (high level abstraction)
technique T0
{
    pass P0
    {
        AddressU[0] = Clamp;    // Clamp the RTTexture
        AddressV[0] = Clamp;
        AddressU[1] = Clamp;    // Clamp the CRTexture
        AddressV[1] = Clamp;

        PixelShader = compile ps_2_0 PS();
    }
}
```

Each indicator material uses its own method to fill the frame buffer before the preceding code is passed. The following sections, "Simple Applications" and "Advanced Applications," present a list of useful examples and discuss how to fill the frame buffer.

Simple Applications

Let's think for a moment about where we are trying to go. At this point, we have a way of using the frame buffer content as a source for a fix color mapping. But first, we fill the frame buffer with the wanted values. We want to be able to generate values that allow us to use the color mapping for displaying the objects or pixels of the visible scene with the colors indicating the wanted information.

Given our uniform system (see the section "Uniform System"), it is not hard to implement several useful applications. The rest of this section explains some easy-to-implement indicator materials that display the following information:

- Material quality or costs
- Alpha-blending versus alpha-testing versus full opacity
- Shader version
- Level of detail (material/mesh)
- Missing resources (materials, textures, or shaders)

Now, let us see how to handle these indicator materials. The idea here is that each application needs its own special values in the red channel of the frame-buffer colors. Aside from that, the basic technique is almost the same. All indicator materials presented in this section are using the same simple process to visualize their information. However, rendering the visible objects will fill the frame buffer with the values that force the color mapping via pixel shader to find the final colors. For example, a color-mapping texture like the one presented in Figure 8.3.2 (using the following areas: Red 0.0–0.25, Yellow 0.25–0.5, Green 0.5–0.75 and 0.75–1.0) would lead us to map a red channel value equal to 0.3 in the frame buffer to a yellow color, because 0.3 interpreted as a texture coordinate U points into the yellow area.

Material Quality or Cost

Suppose, for example, that the materials our application uses to render the surfaces of all scene objects are able to deactivate normal maps or switch to lower shader versions. This would enable us to classify different material quality levels. The idea, therefore, is to display each of these levels with its own color. Red could be used to indicate the highest level via 0.0 in the red channel of the frame-buffer color, and each of the next lower levels must use a greater value (for example, +0.1). Moreover, if we further have the possibility to estimate the costs of each material, we are able to take this technique to present the current cost using the color range from green to red (via texture coordinates from 0.7 to 0.0).

Alpha-Blending versus Alpha-Testing versus Full Opacity

Often, it is useful to see which objects are rendered with enabled alpha-blending. Because the rest is rendered with full opacity, we should combine this information with the alpha-testing state. For example, we can use these colors: red (value 0.0) for pure alpha-blending, yellow (value 0.35) for alpha-blending combined with alpha-testing, green (value 0.65) for full opacity, and white (value 1.0) to indicate solid rendering combined with alpha-testing.

Shader Version

Assuming that we can obtain the version numbers of our shaders, then this information would also be a candidate for our visualization. We could use the colors white, green, yellow, and red to differentiate simple multi-texturing from Pixel Shader version 1.1–1.4, 2.0, and 3.0.

Level of Detail

Because the idea of showing the current LOD of meshes or materials fits well with the previous material quality example, we can build an indicator material to handle this similarly. The highest level could be indicated by the color red (using the value 0.0), and all lower levels use higher values in the red channel of the frame buffer to force the mapping to other final colors.

Missing Resources

As usual, it is important to make sure that nothing goes wrong when loading the resources. But, if our running application can't find resources or needs some time to load them into the cache, we want to see which objects are concerned by these. Textures, shaders, or materials are resources that can make problems, so we use our color white (value 1.0) to indicate objects without problems, and red, yellow, and green to display objects with missing resources.

All examples presented in this section can be implemented without running the color-mapping mechanism, because they are able to write the final color directly into the frame buffer. In the next section, "Advanced Applications," we see how to handle indicator materials that really make a profit from using an explicit color-mapping pass.

Advanced Applications

Now that we've defined some indicator materials that can be easily implemented, let's make a swing to the more advanced applications that can't do their work without the color-mapping mechanism. All examples presented here must run some complex calculations. Their blending of the source and destination colors changes the frame-buffer values many times. Finally, a scene that is rendered completely has an associated frame buffer that holds the final results and that can be used to find the colors that indicate the wanted information.

The rest of this section discusses these indicator materials:

- Overdraw visualization (software render pipeline and frame-buffer content)
- Occlusion culling test
- Overdraw + material costs visualization

Overdraw Visualization

Writing pixels multiple times while rendering a scene is called overdraw. Objects that are using alpha-blending to combine their colors with the already existing content of the frame buffer explicitly need this overdraw (for example, semitransparent polygons in a particle effect). On the other hand, there can be pixels in the scene that are rendered without blending. Their calculations unnecessarily cost additional performance because their colors are written multiple times without an accumulating effect. We distinguish two different types of overdraw. First, there is the overdraw that actually happens in the frame buffer (our render target). Second, there is a potential overdraw forced by our software rendering pipeline through draw calls, but some parts of this overdraw may be detected by the depth testing of the hardware and don't cause a real overdraw in the frame buffer. Let's call the first one *per-pixel overdraw* and the second *object overdraw*.

A concrete implementation of our overdraw indicator materials can be done this way: first, fill the frame buffer with 1.0 in the red channel of all pixels; next, render the scene as always, but use a red color value of, for example, 0.8 for each object and activate a multiplicative blending (DestinationColor * SourceColor + 0 * DestinationColor) by calling `IDirect3DDevice9::SetRenderState( D3DRS_SRCBLEND, D3DBLEND_DESTCOLOR )` and `IDirect3DDevice9::SetRenderState( D3DRS_DESTBLEND, D3DBLEND_ZERO )`. Thus, the red channel values of each pixel in the frame buffer are initialized to 1.0, and rendering objects that write pixels will decrease this values. For example, pixels that are written five times will result to hold a value equal to $0.32768 =$

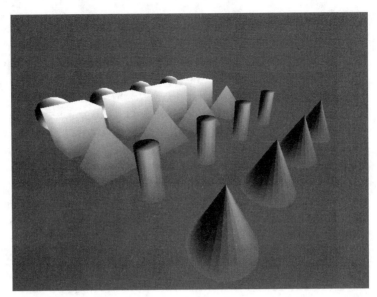

FIGURE 8.3.3 *Simple scene with several geometric bodies.*

1.0 * 0.8 * 0.8 * 0.8 * 0.8 * 0.8. Our results will never fall below 0.0 because all factors are positive. We need to implement two different overdraw indicator materials, handling the two types of overdraw introduced earlier (per-pixel and object-based). Both materials have their special depth testing state: per-pixel overdraw detection must use standard depth testing via IDirect3DDevice9::SetRenderState(D3DRS_ZFUNC, D3DCMP_ LESSEQUAL), and object overdraw needs a disabled depth testing using D3DCMP_ALWAYS, since we don't want to see any culling done by the hardware. Finally, after running the color-mapping pass, we will get an output that looks like what is shown in Figure 8.3.4 for a scene presented in Figure 8.3.3.

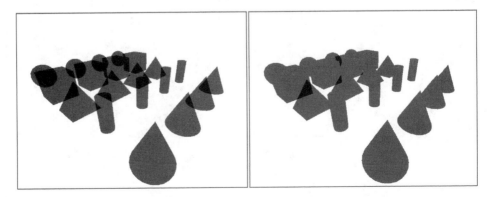

FIGURE 8.3.4 *Object overdraw (left), and per-pixel overdraw (right).*

Occlusion Culling Test

Once we have the two overdraw indicator materials discussed earlier (object and per-pixel version), it's easy to implement a test to detect the effectiveness of the occlusion culling techniques our rendering pipeline uses. We simply have to calculate the difference between both overdraw tests, where the per-pixel overdraw must be rendered with enabled z-testing and all nonblended objects sorted from back to front to make use of the z-culling implemented in the hardware. Each pixel that results in a difference equal to 0 indicates an optimal occlusion culling. In addition, each difference greater than 0 shows us areas with an overdraw that is higher than necessary.

We can build up a concrete implementation of our occlusion-culling test as follows: first, the frame buffer must be filled with 1.0 in the red channel. The next step would be to subtract the results of the per-pixel overdraw red-channel values P (without color mapping). Finally, we have to add the results of the object overdraw red channel values O (without color mapping). This will result in $1 - P + O = 1 - (P - O) = 1 - over$-$draw \ difference$, the value we need to start the color-mapping pass. Areas without a difference between P and O are displayed in white because 1.0 points to the white texels of the color-mapping texture. All other pixels are rendered with colors that indicate the extent of unnecessary overdraw: the results are less than 1.0, pointing to green, yellow, and red colors. Figure 8.3.5 shows an example of that final output of our special indicator material.

FIGURE 8.3.5   *Occlusion test (see Figure 8.3.3 and 8.3.4).*

Overdraw + Material Costs Visualization

The overdraw visualization we discussed previously can be modified to display more meaningful information. Actually, we want to know how expensive each pixel of a rendered scene is. The pure count of overdraw passes is only one parameter we need to calculate that cost. Indeed, each pass has its own expense, because different materials and shaders can be used. If we are able to detect the cost for each draw call, we can accumulate the overall costs in the frame buffer.

Now let's look at how we implement this cost accumulation. Instead of rendering each object with a constant red channel value, we vary this value dependent on the cost of the activated material or shader. Given this new indicator material, we can see that areas in the frame buffer with low overdraw count but expensive materials can be more critical than areas with much higher overdraw count but lower material costs. For example, we can use a value of 0.8 for standard materials and 0.5 for very expensive pixel shaders. Again, we use multiplicative blending (source color * destination color). This generates an output that is more helpful to find performance-critical sections in your scenes than the simple overdraw indicator material.

Conclusion

This article explored a feature each of us wants to use in the software development process. We figured out how to build a uniform system that is able to display different kinds of additional feedback from a running application using its render pipeline. Additionally, we saw how to use this system, including a collection of examples to simplify the detection of malfunctions in our software (for example, engine, render pipeline, resource management) and to discover problems with the content made by our artists.

8.4

Dynamic Branching on Non-PS3.0 Hardware

Emil Persson

Introduction

One of the cool features in recent hardware is the addition of dynamic branching in the fragment pipeline. While many things that can be done on ps3.0 hardware could also be done in ps2.0, dynamic branching opens up a range of new possibilities, some that can be realized on older hardware as well, but in particular many that are much more convenient using dynamic branching. However, old hardware still hangs around, and the ps2.0 installed user base is, as of this writing, much larger than ps3.0 by far. While the use of dynamic branching is the way to go for the future, it's still too early to let go of the previous generation. At the same time, dynamic branching is such a useful feature that it feels bad to leave it alone for now. Many optimization tricks that can be applied with dynamic branching—such as skipping past large chunks of fragment shader code or even early-outing—would be great for older cards as well. In fact, the previous generation cards need it much more than the current ones do. This article aims at providing such a replacement for dynamic branching that will run on previous-generation hardware as well.

Early-Out

Okay, so you got your game or application running with all the eye-candy your graphics card could possibly produce. Just one problem—it's slow. It costs to be on the top, right? You have a good engine that takes good responsibility and cuts down the amount of work passed to the graphics card. Perhaps not dogmatically down to the last triangle, but on a higher level, so you can keep a high polygon count and also work efficiently on the CPU. But that fragment processing kills the performance. You figure that you're wasting lots of shading processing parts of the scene that essentially are left untouched. You render a light, but much of the scene is in shadow, or back-facing the light, or too far away from the light to get any noticeable light contribution. So, what do you do?

If your graphics card supports dynamic branching in the fragment shader, there's an easy solution: you early-out from the fragment shader. For example, beyond a certain distance from the light, you decide that enough is enough. Either you use an attenuation function that falls to zero at that distance, or you assume that below a certain threshold, the contribution is so low that it's not visible. After a quick check in the beginning of your fragment shader, you might skip most parts of it by jumping its end. Easy enough, except your customers don't have that new shiny hardware.

Early-outing is one of those common cases that apply to a wide range of games and applications. It's very useful and simple in concept. We'll start from here and go on to more general dynamic branching problems later. Essentially, what we want to do is be able to kill fragments that we find are either useless and not contributing in a meaningful way, or perhaps even harmful and can't be allowed to write to any buffers. So, we have a number of options: the discard keyword in GLSL (KIL in ARB_fragment_program, TEXKILL in ps2.0), the alpha test, the depth test, and the stencil test. Explicitly discarding fragments with discard may sound like the solution at first, but it turns out that this doesn't interrupt the shader execution on any of the hardware we're trying to help. It will kill the fragment after the entire shader is evaluated. The alpha test is by its semantics directly unable to kill any fragments prior to finishing its execution, unlike discard that is just limited by the currently available implementations. The depth test is obviously something we wouldn't want to fuss around with from the shader, and if we did, it would kill HyperZ and similar optimization technologies and would likely actually slow us down. The stencil test, however, turns out to be a good candidate. Not only can it logically kill fragments before they are even shaded, but the cards actually do this, and not just do it, they do it fast, very much like the early depth-rejection schemes. So, given a stencil mask available in the stencil buffer we can reject pixels even faster than any dynamic branching shader can do. We need to create this mask, however, so no reason to sing hallelujah just yet. It will turn out that the shader work needed for this technique will, in theory, be pretty much equal to the equivalent dynamic branching implementation in most situations; however, in practice there will, of course, be some differences.

To create this stencil mask, we use a shader that basically evaluates the early-out branching condition. This means we do two passes. First, we run a condition shader to create the mask, and then in a second pass we run the remaining parts of the shader and use the stencil test to kill any part of the scene where the condition shader is tagged for early-out. As we can't write stencil from the shader, we need to use another fragment-killing means to only update parts of the stencil buffer. Either discard or the alpha test will do. Personally, we like the alpha test, as it sometimes allows you to move the condition evaluation outside the shader and thus slightly increase the speed. So, what we do is simply set the stencil test to GL_ALWAYS and set it to write 1 everywhere. In the shader, we write the condition to alpha. The alpha test then kills fragments that the condition shader tags as not being early-outers, so that 1 is only written to the stencil buffer where we wish to run the full shader in the second pass. In the second pass, we then check for stencil equals 1 and draw the lighting as usual. The hardware will early-reject any pixels that fail the stencil test, and no shading is done on them. This means that the total shading cost is one condition for all pixels, and lighting for the pixels where the condition is true; that is, exactly the same as with real dynamic branching. Of course, in practice, there will most likely be performance differences.

Sound complicated? It's actually very simple and is illustrated with this code:

```
glColorMask(GL_FALSE, GL_FALSE, GL_FALSE, GL_FALSE);
glDepthMask(GL_FALSE);

glEnable(GL_ALPHA_TEST);
glAlphaFunc(GL_NOTEQUAL, 0);

glEnable(GL_STENCIL_TEST);
glStencilOp(GL_KEEP, GL_KEEP, GL_REPLACE);
glStencilFunc(GL_ALWAYS, 1, ~0);

DrawCondition();

glDisable(GL_ALPHA_TEST);
glColorMask(GL_TRUE, GL_TRUE, GL_TRUE, GL_TRUE);
glStencilFunc(GL_EQUAL, 1, ~0);

DrawLighting();

glDisable(GL_STENCIL_TEST);
```

Here, the condition shader is assumed to output a Boolean value, so that nonzero values will write 1 to stencil. In the case of range-limited lights, however, we could, for example, output dot(lightVec, lightVec) to alpha instead (assuming that the light vector is divided by the light radius in the vertex shader) and compare this result to values less than 1.0 instead. This moves the actual condition check outside the shader and cuts the workload down to a single operation. It doesn't get better than that. So, the shader would look something like this:

```
[Vertex shader]

uniform vec3 lightPos;
uniform float invRadius;
varying vec3 lightVec;

void main(){
    gl_Position = ftransform();
    lightVec = invRadius * (lightPos - gl_Vertex.xyz);
}

[Fragment shader]

varying vec3 lightVec;
void main(){
    gl_FragColor = vec4(0.0, 0.0, 0.0, dot(lightVec, lightVec));
}
```

We left out two things in the preceding code. First, it's assumed that prior to rendering this code, a so-called pre-Z pass has been executed; that is, the scene's depth should be available in the depth buffer already, either through a separate depth-only pass or combined with, for example, ambient lighting or something else. "Oh, more passes to add," you may think. Well, if your lighting is expensive enough for you to consider using this technique, then you're most likely doing this already anyway—or at least you should. A pre-Z pass is not a burden; it's usually a performance gain, unless your lighting is trivial. Besides, for many rendering techniques, such as, for example, stencil shadows, this is required anyway.

The reason we need this is that stencil tags pixels, not fragments. So, without a proper depth pass, the same stencil value could be written to several times due to over-draw. This means a hidden surface could tag parts of the scene as the condition being true, then a surface drawn over it has the condition being false and thus gets its fragments killed, incorrectly leaving a value of true in the stencil buffer. For a case where you just remove noncontributing fragments from a lighting computation, this is only a performance loss as parts of the scene are needlessly shaded, but in other cases it could cause incorrect rendering because it's basically executing the wrong path of the branch. With a depth pass first, you ensure that only the front-most pixels are processed. After the depth pass we can leave depth mask to GL_FALSE for the rest of the frame. To get maximum efficiency of HyperZ, you should remember to use GL_LEQUAL as your depth test as opposed to GL_EQUAL.

Another thing is that we need to clear the stencil buffer if we wish to use this technique for another pass—either something completely different or just processing another light. There are two ways to go ahead with that. The most obvious is to simply clear the stencil buffer with glClear(GL_STENCIL_BUFFER_BIT). The other option is to zero it as we go. This can be done with glStencilOp(GL_KEEP, GL_KEEP, GL_ZERO). Because only one fragment per pixel survives the depth test, this is safe to do. It's important that we use GL_KEEP on stencil fail and depth fail, and to not prematurely zero the stencil or zero it where it's already zero. An important thing to note here is that different hardware fares differently with these techniques. On ATI cards, zeroing it as we go is faster—as one would expect—because we don't need the clear. Using a clear is not slow, it's just not as fast as not clearing. On NVIDIA cards, however, zeroing as we go seems to disable early-stencil rejection. This, of course, eradicates any performance benefit we expect to see. So, we're forced to do a full clear and keep to strict GL_KEEP for our stencil ops. It's only two lines of code that differ, however, so it's simple enough to support both paths.

The General Case

So far, we have been looking at a special case, although a very important one, but there are, of course, more general cases to consider.

The Else-Clause

The early-out case is basically an if-statement where the bulk part of the code is enclosed in the then-clause. The next logical step to study is the addition of an else-clause. As you may have guessed, it's trivial. Basically, all we need to do is draw another pass with the else-clause's shader, but with the stencil test inverted. So first, we draw the then-clause checking for stencil equaling 1, and then we draw the else-clause checking stencil for 0. Although this adds another pass, the total fragment shading cost still equals that of real dynamic branching. The code for this would look like the code listed previously, except the last few lines would look like this:

```
glStencilFunc(GL_EQUAL, 1, ~0);
DrawThenClause();

glStencilFunc(GL_EQUAL, 0, ~0);
DrawElseClause();

glDisable(GL_STENCIL_TEST);
```

Multiple If-Statements

What if we don't have a simple if-statement? Perhaps part of the shader code is not encapsulated in either the then- or else-clause. Or maybe we have more than one if-statement? Or even nested ifs? It turns out the general case is fully possible to implement. The first thing we do is change the ~0 in the preceding code to 0x1. We only need one bit of stencil for the if-statement. In the general case, each stencil bit corresponds to a condition, having that bit set if the condition is true. So, we can have as many conditions as we have stencil bits; typically, the maximum is eight. This is more than enough in the vast majority of cases. Each stencil bit needs to be evaluated individually, so each condition adds another condition shader rendering pass. We utilize the stencil write mask to update individual bits.

Let's also talk about paths through the shader. Assume we have a shader that has some common code, then an if-statement with a then- and else-clause. It would seem this code has three parts—the common code, and the two branches of the if-statement—so at first it would seem that we need three passes. However, there are only two paths through this shader, depending on the outcome of the condition. Either we execute the common code plus the then-clause, or we execute the common code plus the else-clause. So, we only need two shaders and two passes, one for each path. In fact, not only do we "only need" two shaders, it's actually required in the general case that we do it this way because there's no general way to concatenate two shader fragments without storing intermittent results in one or more render targets. Again, given early-stencil rejection, the actual fragment shading work is still equal to that of real dynamic branching. The number of passes are quite a few more, though. As mentioned, we need one pass for each condition. In addition, we need one pass for each possible path through the shader. We talk more about this pass explosion in the "Performance Considerations" section later in the article.

So given a stencil mask with the relevant stencil bits set to their respective condition Boolean values, we use the stencil reference mask to select what bits are relevant for each shading path. Then, we draw where those bits match a bit-mask indicating what bits needs to be 1 and what bits need to be 0. Consider the following pseudo-shader:

```
void main(){
    if (c0){
        shaderCode_0();
        if (c1){
            shaderCode_0_1();
        } else {
            shaderCode_0_not1();
        }
    } else {
        shaderCode_not0();
    }
    shaderCodeCommon();
}
```

Here we have two conditions and three possible paths through the shader, which gives us five passes. The first two passes evaluate c0 and c1 and store those to stencil bit 0 and 1 in the way we discussed. For the other three passes, we split the shader into these paths through the shader:

```
void main(){          // c0 && c1
    shaderCode_0();
    shaderCode_0_1();
    shaderCodeCommon();
}

void main(){          // c0 && !c1
    shaderCode_0();
    shaderCode_0_not1();
    shaderCodeCommon();
}

void main(){          // !c0
    shaderCode_not0();
    shaderCodeCommon();
}
```

For the first pass, we care about bits 0 and 1, so the stencil reference mask will be 0x3. We want both c0 and c1 to be true, so the stencil reference value should also be 0x3. In the second pass, we care about the same bits, so it's 0x3 for the reference mask here, too, but we want c1 to be false, so the reference value is 0x1. In the third pass, we only care about c0 and it's supposed to be false, so it's 0x1 for the mask and 0x0 for the value. The code for this looks very similar to the first code with just a few changes:

```
glColorMask(GL_FALSE, GL_FALSE, GL_FALSE, GL_FALSE);
glDepthMask(GL_FALSE);

glEnable(GL_ALPHA_TEST);
glAlphaFunc(GL_NOTEQUAL, 0);

glEnable(GL_STENCIL_TEST);
glStencilOp(GL_KEEP, GL_KEEP, GL_REPLACE);
```

```
glStencilMask(0x1);
glStencilFunc(GL_ALWAYS, 0x1, ~0);
DrawCondition0();

glStencilMask(0x2);
glStencilFunc(GL_ALWAYS, 0x2, ~0);
DrawCondition1();

glDisable(GL_ALPHA_TEST);
glColorMask(GL_TRUE, GL_TRUE, GL_TRUE, GL_TRUE);

glStencilFunc(GL_EQUAL, 0x3, 0x3);
DrawShader0();

glStencilFunc(GL_EQUAL, 0x3, 0x1);
DrawShader1();

glStencilFunc(GL_EQUAL, 0x1, 0x0);
DrawShader2();

glDisable(GL_STENCIL_TEST);
```

That sums up the general-case if-statement.

The Big Stencil Clash

"This is all nice and cool," you may say, "but I really need stencil for shadows, so I'm afraid I can't use this technique." Well, actually, in many cases you can. You seldom need all those 8 bits for stencil shadows. The stencil isn't likely to be increased or decreased more than 127 times in a row (if at all) at any place in the scene under normal circumstances. If you use double-sided stencil, the probability of this happening is even smaller because it won't run all increases and decreases together like the regular two-pass implementation does. Something like 5 or 6 bits should be more than enough cover for you. So, that leaves us with at least a couple of bits for dynamic branching. In some sense, stencil shadows can be considered a form of dynamic branching, too. Anyway, what we need to do to combine stencil shadows with this dynamic branching technique is to move our conditions to the upper bits instead. This is because stencil shadows require the increase and decrease of operations, which, of course, applies mainly to the lower bits.

The idea here isn't all too different from what we've discussed so far. The stencil shadows have their bits and the conditions has theirs. For the stencil shadow, you set a stencil write mask that allows writes to only the bits allocated for the mask, and similarly with the conditions. The stencil shadow works as a condition in itself. There's one tricky bit, though, because the stencil shadow's bits don't return a specific value, but instead indicate that you're in light if you get a value above or equal to what you cleared the stencil buffer to. We need to use GL_LESS as our stencil function for the stencil. But this doesn't always mix very well with the desire to filter out a particular condition code in the upper bits. What we really want to do is do GL_LESS on the lower bits and GL_EQUAL on the upper bits. Unfortunately, there's no such stencil function. However, some combinations work out anyway and can be sorted out by putting the conditions in the upper bits in such an order that they would work with GL_LESS and the lower bits. If you're doing stencil shadows, you're most likely doing lighting, and it wouldn't be a too wild guess to assume that something like early-out is what you're looking for with this technique. In that case, it works out pretty well. Bit 7 will then indicate, for example, whether the pixel is within the light radius, and the rest of the bits are for stencil shadows. You are then in light if both the condition and stencil test hold true; that is, if you cleared stencil to 0x40 and the lower bits are above or equal to that and if the early-out condition is true (0x80), then we're in light and need to execute our lighting shader. So, our reference stencil value is 0x80 | 0x40 and we're in light if that's less than what we have in the stencil buffer.

Loops

What about loops, then? If we know an upper bound on the number of loops that can be executed, it works out pretty well. It's worth noting that even with real dynamic branching, there's an upper limit of 255 loops, at least in ps3.0.

```
for (int i = 0; i < 3; i++){
    if (condition) break;
    ShaderCode();
}
```

This can be rewritten into this equivalent code:

```
if (!condition(0)){
    ShaderCode();
    if (!condition(1)){
        ShaderCode();
        if (!condition(2)){
            ShaderCode();
        }
    }
}
```

This maps directly to the if-statements as discussed earlier and can be implemented as such. There is, however, a risk that the condition in later loops depend heavily on the work performed in ShaderCode(), which would reduce the effectiveness of this technique versus real dynamic branching. Depending on the situation, it could limit the usefulness of this technique. It may only be worth it to early-out on the first or the first few conditions and let the rest be sorted out in the shader by executing all loops and selecting the right result in the end.

There's an important special case, though, where the results from the loops are simply accumulated or otherwise possible to combine with a simple blending, such as looping over a bunch of lights in a lighting computation. In that case, we can simply move the loop outside the shader and perform a condition pass and a shader pass for each loop. When a fragment survives the condition pass, we increase stencil, and then in the shader pass we check whether stencil is equal to loops counter plus one. Any pixel that ever fails any test will thus be left behind and never updated again. We can even let the stencil test early-out on the condition pass by checking stencil to be equal to the loop counter. In an implementation like this, we'll be able to have up to 255 loops with 8 bits of stencil, just like in ps3.0. If the maximum number of loops is high, it can also be beneficial to use an occlusion query to check whether any fragments survived at all.

Performance Considerations

So, when is it beneficial to use this technique to increase performance and when is it not? The most obvious case when it's not is when you're not limited by fragment shading work, but rather CPU, vertex fetch, or transform. In that case, you'll either not see any difference or see a slowdown by using this technique. Other cases when it's not so useful are when the shader stubs that you try to skip are quite short or when the condition computation is a significant part of the shader. It is worth noting that in many cases, the same can be said about real dynamic branching. In some cases, it may simply be faster to evaluate both paths of the shader and select the right one.

The largest problem with this technique, though, is that the number of passes often grows quite a bit if the branching is complex—which can significantly increase the vertex shader burden. So, it's possible that this technique won't give you much on a highly detailed character that doesn't cover much of the screen, while it may provide a huge boost on floors and walls that have less geometric detail and typically make up a significant part of the scene.

If you've decided to implement this technique, there are some important optimizations. It can prove to be a healthy boost to carefully order the condition passes so that you can early-out even on the conditions. For example, if c_0 can only be true when c_1 is true, then it's best to evaluate c_1 first, and then check stencil equal to 0x2 when drawing the c_0 condition. This idea also works when combining stencil shadows with early-out. You can draw the early-out condition based on light radius in the first pass, and then let it cull the parts of the stencil shadow volume in the second pass that the condition already tagged as unlit. Or the other way around—whichever is faster in your case.

Finally, it's important to remember that dynamic branching didn't necessarily make old optimization tricks go out of fashion. Scissor rectangles and clip planes can still provide huge performance boosts. The best performance is achieved when you properly use all tools in your toolbox.

Conclusion

We discussed a way to implement dynamic branching on non-ps3.0 hardware. This, of course, doesn't mean ps3.0 is useless technology, nor does this technique try to eliminate the need for it. It won't be able to implement everything that you can do with ps3.0 with this technique, but it's feasible to implement many of the most important cases of dynamic branching. In particular, various kinds of early-out situations are probably where this technique is most interesting. It should in many cases work fine as a carry-over technology until ps3.0-capable hardware is the norm in the marketplace, at which point we're probably already discussing ways to implement ps4.0 level effects on ps3.0 hardware.

8.5

GLSL Shader Debugging with GLIntercept

Damian Trebilco

Introduction

The advent of programmable shaders has delivered a new age of flexible graphics programming and exciting visual effects. However, programmers are finding the task of debugging shader-intensive applications increasingly difficult. To aid this process, a plug-in for the OpenGL tool GLIntercept was created. This tool enables a user to see exactly what shaders are used and in which parts of the scene those shaders are being used. In addition, shaders may be modified and recompiled while the application is running to debug shader problems.

How GLIntercept works

GLIntercept is an OpenGL function call interceptor providing a replacement wrapper (opengl32.dll) that exports all OpenGL entry points. When an OpenGL call is made, the GLIntercept wrapper processes it before passing the call onto the real OpenGL system (see Figure 8.5.1). While many tools provide similar functionality, mostly for logging purposes, GLIntercept provides an extensible plug-in interface to allow custom logging or manipulation of the OpenGL state. There are currently many useful debugging plug-ins like "free-camera" and "extension override"; however, this article focuses on the shader editor plug-in. (Information on GLIntercept's other plug-ins can be found in the GLIntercept documentation.)

Setting up GLIntercept

ON THE CD

After installing GLIntercept from the CD-ROM (or from the Web site at *http://glintercept. nutty.org*), navigate to the install folder (typically C:\Program Files\GLIntercept_ x_xx). Located here is the opengl32.dll wrapper and a listing of gliConfig.ini files.

GLIntercept was designed to be highly configurable such that different debugging options can be tuned to what an application does. The gliConfig.ini file contains these options and must be copied with the wrapper opengl32.dll into the target exe's directory. Figure 8.5.2 shows GLIntercept in use with an application.

GLIntercept's design allows a user to place the wrapper OpenGL32.dll in the output debug directory during development so that if an error or graphics artifact appears, GLIntercept can be invoked to debug the problem while the program is still

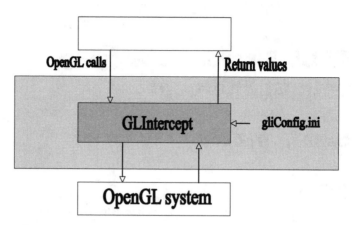

FIGURE 8.5.1   *How GLIntercept interacts with an application and the OpenGL system.*

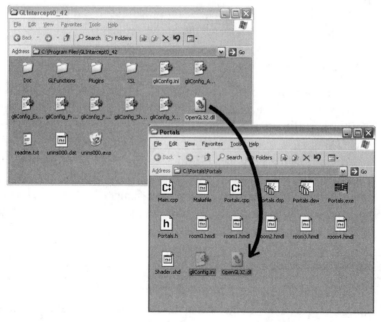

FIGURE 8.5.2   *Using GLIntercept with an application.*

running. While GLIntercept does have some CPU overhead, provided continuous logging is not enabled, the impact is minimal.

By viewing the gliConfig.ini file you see a list of configuration options and comments explaining what each option does. While reading these options can be useful for a full understanding of GLIntercept, this article presents tutorials that use the pre-built configuration files supplied with a GLIntercept install.

Tutorial 1: OpenGL Error Detection

Before using the shader editor, it is usually a good idea to remove all OpenGL errors from the application. Fortunately, GLIntercept has built-in functionality for tracking down such errors.

Step 1

Copy the wrapper OpenGL32.dll and the config file gliConfig_FullDebug.ini file to the directory of the target exe. Note that this must be the directory containing the exe, which may be different from the working directory.

Applications that use Java/Python or some other scripting language may not have a "real" exe. To use GLIntercept on these applications, put the wrapper dll in the directory of the system that loads OpenGL (that is, for Java this is the directory with javaw.exe; for Python it is python.exe/pythonw.exe).

Step 2

Rename the copied gliConfig_FullDebug.ini configuration file to gliConfig.ini and start the application. Stop the application when a good section of the OpenGL rendering has occurred.

The "Full_Debug" profile performs many additional checks and continuously logs all OpenGL calls. Because of this, your application will run significantly slower when using this profile.

Step 3

If interception is successful, a glInterceptLog.txt and gliLog.txt file are generated in the exe's directory. The glInterceptLog.txt file contains a listing of all OpenGL calls made while the gliLog.txt contains any OpenGL errors/abnormal states/memory leaks. Ensure no OpenGL errors are detected before attempting to run the more advanced debuggers like the shader editor.

If you run your application from a debugger IDE, the gliLog.txt is mirrored to the output debug window. In addition, a programmer debug breakpoint is thrown on any OpenGL error to allow stepping into the code causing the error.

Tutorial 2: Starting the Shader Editor

Once an OpenGL application is clean of OpenGL errors, the shader debugger can be invoked to resolve shader-based errors. This is accomplished by visualizing what shaders are used on what rendered objects with the ability to edit and fix shader problems at runtime.

Step 1

As in Tutorial 1, copy the OpenGL32.dll and gliConfig_ShaderEdit.ini files into the target exe's directory. Then, rename the gliConfig_ShaderEdit.ini file to gliConfig.ini.

Step 2

Start your application, and when there are some shaders active, press Ctrl-Shift-S to start the shader editor (press and hold the keys if your application has a low frame rate). Full screen applications may have to be changed to start in windowed mode to make shader editing easier.

The CTRL-SHIFT-S key combination can be changed if it conflicts with your program. See the GLIntercept documentation for details.

The shader editor needs continual contact with the OpenGL application. For applications that do not continually render (for example, OpenGL user interface components), the following line needs to be added to the gliConfig.ini file in the "Plugins" section:

```
PingPlugin = ("GLFramePing/GLFramePing.dll")
```

This plug-in attempts to force a continual redraw of the OpenGL application.

Step 3

A code view and shader listing should now be displayed (see Figure 8.5.3). The shader editor runs as a separate process and can be closed and reopened as necessary. Usage of the shader editor is discussed in the next section.

Shader Editor Usage

The shader editor displays two main windows: the editor window displays the shader source for editing, and the shader list window lists all currently loaded shaders in the program.

Shader List Window

The list window displays a list view of properties about the currently loaded shaders:

Shader UID: Shader unique identifier. This is a number assigned by GLIntercept to uniquely identify each shader as it is loaded (note that OpenGL IDs can be duplicated across different contexts).

OpenGL ID: The identifier assigned to the shader by OpenGL.

Type: The type of shader. This can be GLSL or other assembly-type shaders like ARB/NV vertex program/fragment program.

Frame Num: The last frame number that the shader used (at the time the shader editor was opened). By default, the shaders are sorted in descending order according to this number.

The following command buttons are shown on the dialog:

Open: Opens the selected shader in the shader editor window. You can also open a shader by double-clicking it in the list view.

Revert: Reverts the selected shader. This undoes all changes to the selected shader. It will also close the shader in the shader editor if open.

Refresh: Refreshes the shader list. This resyncs the current list of active shaders to match the current state of the OpenGL application. It also updates the frame number of all existing shaders.

Show Shader Usage: When enabled, this makes the objects using the currently selected shader "flash" in the render window. This is useful in large programs for finding which shader is being used on what object.

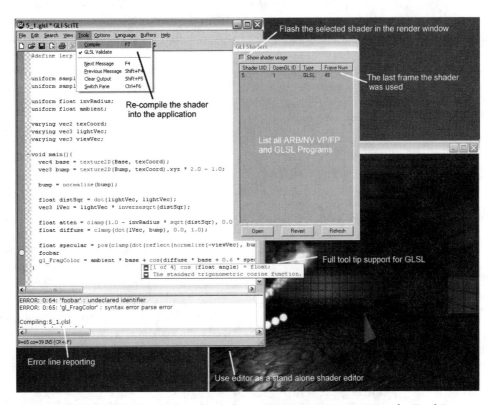

FIGURE 8.5.3 *Using the shader editor plug-in in GLIntercept.—Demo by Emil Persson (a.k.a. Humus). Used with permission.*

Shader Editor Window

Once a shader has been selected and opened, it is available to be edited and recompiled. The editor window itself is a modified version of SciTE with full syntax highlighting and tool tips. This editor supports all the usual features (cut, copy, past, find, replace, and so on) and should be instantly useable by most programmers.

It should be noted that the debugger does not currently support breakpoints and variable inspection. Debugging usually consists of outputting a variable as a color to "see" it, which can be done quickly with shader edits at runtime.

To compile an edited shader back into the application, click Tools->Compile in the menu (shortcut F7). Any errors that occur are reported in the output window. Double-click the error to jump to the error line.

By default, the 3DLabs shader validator is run on all GLSL code before being sent to the driver for compilation. This helps catch nonstandard code features from accidentally being used. This feature can be turned off with the Tools->GLSL Validate option in the menu.

It is also possible to use the shader editor and validator in an offline mode (i.e., without debugging an application). Offline mode can be useful when initially writing the shaders. Simply run `<install dir>\Plugins\GLShaderEdit\GLISciTE.exe`.

Here are some useful shortcuts when using the shader editor:

- Ctrl-F—Find
- F3—Find next
- F4—Next error
- F7—Compile
- Ctrl + Space—Listing of all GLSL API commands
- Ctrl + Shift + Space—Tool tip for the current function

Tutorial 3: XML Frame Grabbing

While using the shader debugger is useful for debugging problems in the shader source, shader state setup can also cause problems (for example, textures bound and uniforms passed, and so on). To debug such problems, GLIntercept has an XML frame grab option to grab all OpenGL calls, shaders, textures, and frame buffer changes in the targeted frame. This information is saved to an XML file that can be viewed using a Web browser. See Figure 8.5.4 for an example of what the XML frame should look like.

```
glTexCoordPointer(3,GL_FLOAT,56,0xa82740);
glEnableClientState(GL_TEXTURE_COORD_ARRAY);
glClientActiveTextureARB(GL_TEXTURE3);
glTexCoordPointer(3,GL_FLOAT,56,0xa8274c);
glEnableClientState(GL_TEXTURE_COORD_ARRAY);

glDrawElements(GL_TRIANGLES,42,GL_UNSIGNED_SHORT,0xa82db8); Shaders=(GLSL1) Tex=(0,2   ) (1,3   ) Color(       )
```

FIGURE 8.5.4   *Example render call with textures, shaders, and color buffer icon links from the XML frame log.*

Step 1

As in Tutorial 1, copy the OpenGL32.dll and gliConfig_XMLFrame.ini files into the target exe's directory. Rename the gliConfig_XMLFrame.ini file to be gliConfig.ini.

Step 2

Start your application. When the scene you want to grab is shown, press Ctrl-Shift-F. This operation may take some time and will make the application unresponsive during the frame grab.

Step 3

A directory in the exe's path should now exist with the name "Frame_<FrameNumber>," where FrameNumber is the number of the grabbed frame. Inside this directory, the file gliInterceptLog.xml can be opened in a modern Web browser to present a view similar to Figure 8.5.4.

Step 4

Each render call in the XML log file has the prepost contents of the color buffer (as well as a "diff" image) so you can track down the exact render call where the problem occurs (click on the icons to reveal the full image). Once you find the problem render call, examine the textures and shader bound as well as the preceding OpenGL state calls to find your error.

Conclusion

This article demonstrated how GLIntercept can be a powerful asset in debugging modern OpenGL shader-based applications. Through the use of the shader debugger and XML logger, most shader-based errors can be tracked and resolved quickly. GLIntercept is still in active development to take advantage of the latest changes in OpenGL and will soon be ported to other systems.

References

[Humus] OpenGL demos. Available online at *www.humus.ca*.

[SciTE/Scintilla] Available online at *www.scintilla.org*.

[Trebilco05] Trebilco, Damian, "GLIntercept," available online at *glintercept.nutty.org*, 2005.

8.6

GPU Performance of DirectX 9 Per-Fragment Operations Revisited

Mike Eiβele

Introduction

Currently, the third generation of GPUs that allow complex programmable shading programs is about to be introduced. This means that today, programmable pixel and vertex units are widespread in typical consumer-level hardware. Also, an increasing number of graphics software and interactive titles now make usage of these functions and first commercial programs, which use more complex shaders with several dozen instructions. This is likely to grow even further with even more complex and longer shader programs in next-generation game engines like Unreal Engine 3 [Epic04]. Good performance and a wide knowledge of performance issues both on high- and low-level shader programming on a great variety of hardware platforms will become even more crucial than before. This is also true for a new trend to use GPUs in so-called GPGPU (General Purpose GPU) applications. Good knowledge of instruction scheduling, instruction out-sourcing, and what type of instructions to use can make a tremendous performance difference.

This article is a follow-up of the previously published one in *ShaderX³* [Diepstraten04] and takes a look at changes that can be seen between this and last year. It looks at the new shader versions introduced in the meantime, like the extended Pixel Shader version 2.x and Pixel Shader version 3.0, and tests some of the more "exotic" GPUs that sometimes are installed in consumer hardware. In addition, some subjects that could not have been addressed in the previous article, like multiple render targets, multi-pass rendering, and per-fragment frame-buffer operations, are examined.

Measurement Methods: The Benchmark Tool

Many changes have occurred since last year. For example, the DirectX 9 Software Development Kit now includes a tool called PIX. PIX is a great tool for analyzing applications that use Microsoft Direct3D. It can be used to gather and analyze statistics that are useful to understand why some frames render more slowly than others and helps to identify inefficient usage of the API and system resources. But PIX is designed to get an overall performance overview of an application instead of concentrating on a single aspect of the rendering pipeline, as desired in this article.

Following the guidelines from the previous article [Diepstraten04], a self-written benchmark program (which is available on the CD-ROM accompanying this book) is used to test the performance of different shading instructions, combinations of shader instructions, different texture formats, render target formats, and per-fragment frame-buffer operations. The benchmark program was completely rewritten from the previous one. It now makes use of the common Direct3D Effect File interface, which should make it easier for developers to plug in their production code with less effort than before. Using the effect file interface has some additional benefits. For example, it allows using high-level shading pixel code and even multi-pass rendering. Additionally, it is possible to test several, currently nonprogrammable render states like alpha blending, stencil test, alpha test, and other less frequently used rendering states. However, the core of the benchmark is still the same as the previous one and its outline is as follows: we draw 1500 quads—all vertices of which are pretransformed. This means they do not go through the vertex transformation stage, and each of these quads has a size of 512 × 512 pixels. By disabling depth tests and depth writes, we get a massive amount of over-draw, which is required to reach the rasterization bound of a graphics card. Note that effect files may overwrite the depth test and depth write modes, but they will not take effect because these state changes are hard-coded through API calls inside the rendering loop. All 255 possible shader constants are set with random numbers but can be over-written in the pixel shader code itself. Boolean and integer registers are not set at all. The 1500 quads are rendered 15 times with the same pixel shader, textures, and the neces-sary shader constants. Before each `BeginEffect` call and after each `EndEffect` call—if the query that follows the `EndEffect` returns OK—the timer values of the window's high-precision multimedia timer are stored. The difference between both timings is computed and written to a protocol file. Afterward, the worst three timings are removed and from the remaining the average value is taken. Therefore, all measurements shown in the diagrams show the time in seconds for rendering 1500 quads—where each has a size of 512 × 512—with the tested shader. For multi-pass rendering, if desired, besides the recording of the total elapsed time, the elapsed time for each individual pass can be recorded as well. This is done by rendering the same test again but recording the time after each pass. This way, the measuring of the overall time is not influenced.

All performance measuring presented in this article is based on the latest officially available drivers from the Web site of the corresponding GPU vendor and the latest DirectX release running in nondebug mode. Several systems were used for the perfor-mance evaluation, but systems with equal GPU installed showed exactly the same per-formance. Even 32-bit and 64-bit machines showed the same result, which indicates that the benchmark tool is for the most part independent of the host CPU.

Arithmetic and Texture Performance on Modern GPUs

This section provides a direct update to the topics addressed in the previous *ShaderX³* volume [Diepstraten04]. In addition, some other basic fragment operations are examined. It is shown how newer cards behave on arithmetic and texture instructions that are supported by Pixel Shader 2.0. Because today most graphic cards—including mainstream cards—support this instruction set, it can be seen as the biggest common denominator and therefore be used for comparing the performance of the GPUs. Not all measurements that were taken can be presented here. Results presented in the previous article are revisited using newer graphic cards, but are only shown if new conclusions can be drawn out of them. Therefore, only the most relevant results are discussed in the article, but for completeness, all measurement diagrams are contained on the accompanying CD-ROM.

ON THE CD

Arithmetic Performance

The performance of the arithmetic instructions—all instructions that do not perform texture operations—increased with the availability of newer GPUs. The ATI X800-class hardware shows a very similar performance pattern for the different instructions when compared to its predecessor, the ATI 9x00 series. Nevertheless, most instructions got a boost in performance of roughly a factor of two, when comparing, for example, an X800XT PE with a 9700PRO. The similar behavior in performance confirms that the hardware designs of the two generations are—at least to some extent—quite similar. A slightly different story can be seen on NVIDIA GPUs. The new generation GPUs—the 6x00 series—seem to implement a partially different hardware design, as the performance characteristics of the NVIDIA 5x00 class cards can no longer be recognized.

Figure 8.6.1 shows the performance of the Pixel Shader 2.0 *add* instruction on different graphic cards. Already for this single instruction, huge differences between

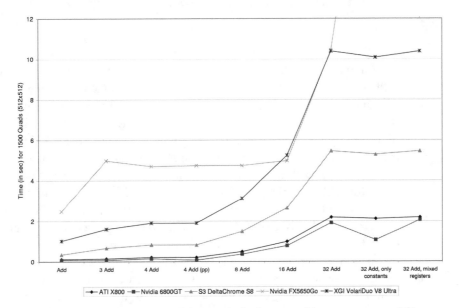

FIGURE 8.6.1 *Performance of the Pixel Shader 2.0 add instruction on different GPUs.*

graphic processors can be seen. It is interesting that only the recent NVIDIA GPUs take advantage of the partial precision modifier _pp in combination with an *add* command, while on the other hand the FX 5800Ultra suffers a very slight performance decrease. The results for the remaining instructions and register read modifier are summarized in Figure 8.6.2.

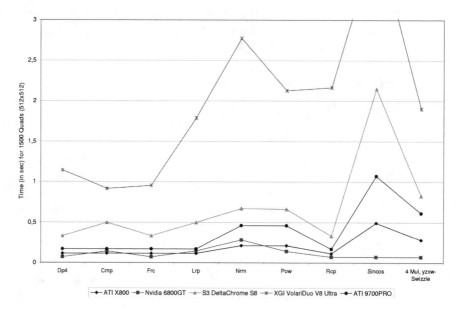

FIGURE 8.6.2 *Performance characteristics of arithmetic instructions on different GPUs.*

On the one hand, it can be seen that the total performance increased with the new GPU generation, while on the other hand, NVIDIA GPUs no longer suffer any performance loss when using swizzles or write masks. The throughput of the XGI VolariDuo V8 Ultra card is clearly below an ATI 9700PRO card, but is still acceptable. The S3 DeltaChrome S8 behaves quite well, and is in the range of an ATI 9700PRO. However, some commands—for example—*sincos*, are still almost two times slower.

If multiple arithmetic instructions are executed for all four components of a vector, most GPUs simply execute one instruction after another. But if the instructions are targeted for different components of a vector, the instructions may be co-issued by the hardware; that is, two different instructions are processed in parallel. The newer 6x00 from NVIDIA can schedule two instructions where each has a 2D vector instruction for parallel execution [NVIDIA05]. This type of co-issue is also supported by the S3 DeltaChrome S8 and the XGI VolariDuo. Combining a 3D vector instruction with a 1D scalar, where the scalar operation takes place in the *w*-component operation, is supported by all tested GPUs [Riguer02] except for the FX5x00 cards.

An instruction that might become more important is *texkill*. One might think it can be used to speed up the shader execution by discarding fragments, but this strongly depends on its implementation within the GPU. Up to now, the *texkill* instruction has a high potential to deactivate any early-Z optimizations on the GPU and therefore it is seldom used. In addition, the *texkill* instruction is not able to speed up a shader program in most situations, even on the most modern GPUs such as ATI X800XT PE or the NVIDIA 6800Ultra. More crucial, there are cases where discarding a fragment slows the shader execution. So, even today it still seems to be true that the hardware cannot efficiently skip instructions, and, therefore, the final result is just discarded after the full shader program execution. As the new Pixel Shader model 3.0 supports up to 32,768 instruction slots and the finally executed number of instructions might even be higher due to loop instructions, an efficient implementation of the *texkill* command might become important.

The results shown in Figure 8.6.3 strongly depend on the instructions—amount and complexity—that are skipped after the *texkill* command. The reference measurement taken for each shader represents the execution time of the shader with just the *texkill* command removed. ATI graphic processors experience a slight performance increase if the skipped instructions amortize the cost of the *texkill* command. In contrast, for NVIDIA GPUs we were unable to produce shader codes that could be accelerated via a *texkill* command. This behavior is even more surprising as the NVIDIA 6800 series supports the Pixel Shader 3.0 specification where dynamic loops are specified, which can potentially be terminated in an arbitrary iteration.

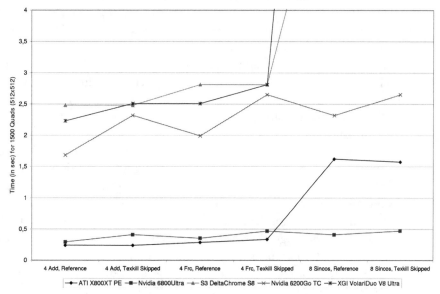

FIGURE 8.6.3   *Efficiency of the* texkill *instruction on different graphic cards.*

The S3 card executed the shaders in exactly the same time as the reference shaders where only the *texkill* instruction was removed. Therefore, the S3 implementation lies in the middle of ATI and NVIDIA—no performance loss and no performance gain.

The XGI Volari card showed the same performance behavior as the NVIDIA cards: the *texkill* command needs additional execution time.

Texture Performance

The overall performance of the texture stages also increased with the new GPU generation. The ATI X800XT PE has in most cases an increased texture performance of about 100% compared to its ancestor. But there are also scenarios where it can still be expensive, especially when fetching textures from eight different samplers. The NVIDIA 6800Ultra received an even higher performance upgrade of about 100% to 150%. The other tested cards are clearly behind the actual ATI and NVIDIA models. For various situations, the XGI card has a texture lookup time that is 20 times higher, whereas the S3 DeltaChrome's lookup time is 10 times more. Most mysterious performance discrepancies of the different texture formats—for example, as it has been for 8- and 16-bit luminance textures on NVIDIA hardware—are gone and therefore the texture performance directly depends on the total bit depth of the texture format. On textures with four 8-bit components, there is basically no performance impact up to a texture size of 256×256. If textures are larger or have more precision—for example, four 16-bit components—the texture lookup times start to increase.

Dependent texture lookups into medium-sized textures—that is, up to 256×256—are as fast as nondependent ones except for the S3 card, which seems to handle indirections less efficiently in those cases and therefore the performance falls behind the XGI VolariDuo card. If larger textures, in size or precision, are used, dependent texture lookups start to be less efficient. Switching from point sampling to linear sampling does not have a performance impact on any GPU for nondependent texture lookups. But—as for the previous GPU generation—linear sampling of dependent lookups is still much more expensive than using point-sampled dependent lookups. Already at a texture size of 128×128 a slowdown can be recognized. This dramatic performance impact can be reproduced on all measured hardware. The impact was estimated to be about 400% on an ATI X800XT PE, about 450% on a NVIDIA 6800Ultra, the XGI card undergoes a loss of 750%, and the S3 DeltaChrome S8 is only 380% slower. It is our opinion that this behavior is caused by the texture cache, which is in some situations too small to hold the needed data for a fast texture lookup. Therefore, textures for dependent lookups should be, if possible, point filtered and as small as possible. Figure 8.6.4 summarizes the texture lookup times for diverse GPUs showing two formats using point or linear filtering.

An adequate method to minimize the needed texture memory is to use non-power-of-two textures. Compared to power-of-two textures, the performance of non-power-of-two textures is only marginally less on all GPUs we examined. If dependent lookups into non-power-of-two textures are considered, the results differ. On ATI

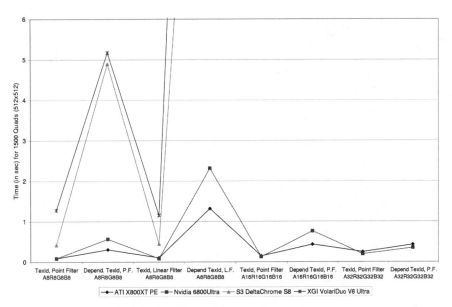

FIGURE 8.6.4 *Texture lookup throughput on diverse GPUs.*

9700PRO class cards, only a slight speed penalty could be measured. On the more recent cards, such as the X800 series, no remarkable difference in the performance of non-power-of-two versus power-of-two texture can be noticed—at least up to a size of roughly 256 × 256. In contrast, NVIDIA cannot efficiently handle dependent lookups into non-power-of-two textures on the older FX5x00 cards. Already in our previous article we found out that the FX cards suffer a performance drop of about 200% in these scenarios. This disadvantage is partially cured on the 6800 series, but still dependent lookups into non-power-of-two textures are up to 30% slower than for power-of-two textures.

In the same way as the texture performance, the demand of it has also increased, because in applications—primarily in games—high dynamic range (HDR) images start appearing more frequently. Therefore, textures with a higher dynamic range— for example, 16-bit float textures—become more important. When it comes down to filtering, some GPUs only support nearest-neighbor filtering of HDR textures. To overcome this limitation, the filtering has to be implemented manually using a pixel shader program. A performance comparison of linear texture filtering on HDR textures is shown in Figure 8.6.5.

Most measurements were taken by using a manually implemented linear filter marked as *(ps)* for an assembler optimized version and *(ps, HLSL)* for a simple high-level shading language version. The texture-filtering performance on NVIDIA 6800 class GPUs was measured using the hardware functionality *(hw)* and the pixel shader *(ps)*. The texture format used for the measurement was a four-component 16-bit float

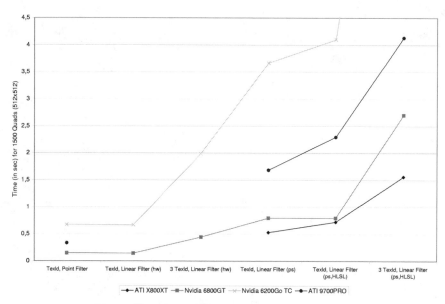

FIGURE 8.6.5   *Linear filtering on HDR textures.*

texture. As a reference value the timing for a point-filtered texture lookup is also included. For the 6800 GPUs, linear filtering of 16-bit float textures behaves equally to 8-bit textures: linear filtering is free, as long as the lookups do not have dependent accesses.

The performance of 16-bit-precise liner texture filtering is much faster if dedicated hardware capabilities to filter the texture lookup are available. Figure 8.6.5 shows that a NVIDIA 6800GT card can perform three filtered 16-bit lookups in the same amount of time an ATI X800XT PE takes for only a single filtered lookup. The S3 DeltaChrome S8 and the XGI VolariDuo V8 Ultra card cannot be measured, because neither GPU supports four-component 16-bit float textures.

The counterpart to HDR textures is a high-precision frame buffer. A more general concept of a frame buffer is the so-called render target that is discussed in the following section.

Scheduling of Texture and Arithmetic Instructions

As indicated in the first paragraph, it is important to schedule scalar, 2D, 3D, and 4D operations properly to maximize the shader performance by utilizing the co-issue and dual-issue possibilities of the GPUs. Scheduling texture and arithmetic instructions adequately is for some scenarios even more severe. An optimal scheduling of texture and arithmetic instructions strongly depends on the pipeline architecture of the underlying GPU. Therefore, a rescheduling of instructions should be performed by vendor-specific GPU drivers, as they potentially have all the knowledge of the GPU architecture.

This kind of optimization is already implemented by the drivers, but a driver can only modify the arrangement of the instructions, it cannot change the algorithm itself. Some calculations—for example, normalization, reflection vector, fresnel factor, and so on—can be performed alternatively by arithmetic or texture lookup instructions, thus it is still worth it to look at the balance of texture versus arithmetic instruction. To decide which technique is the optimal implementation to maximize the overall performance of a shader, one has to consider the entire shader code and balance out the ratio of texture versus arithmetic (ALU) instructions. Figure 8.6.6 illustrates the performance of shader programs with different numbers of ALU instructions.

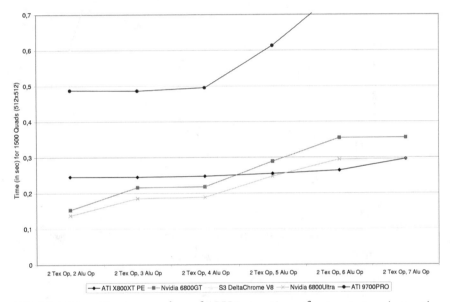

FIGURE 8.6.6 *Varying numbers of ALU instructions after two texture instructions.*

The performance of the ATI card is limited by the texture lookup time in this scenario, because additional arithmetic instructions do not increase the execution time on the first four tested shaders. Even more important is the fact that during the time a texture lookup is performed, the ATI hardware can already execute further ALU instructions if and only if they are independent of the lookup result. The diagrams in Figures 8.6.6 and 8.6.7 show that roughly four to six ALU instructions can be performed in the time of two texture lookups. On the previous generations of ATI GPUs—the 9700PRO—already three to four ALU instructions are slower than two texture lookups.

On NVIDIA GPUs, a different situation is seen. Figures 8.6.6 and 8.6.7 indicate that the performance depends on the sum of arithmetic and texture instructions. The hardware architecture of the 6x00 series allows it to perform—for most instruction sequences—two ALU, or one texture and one ALU instruction per cycle [Kilgar-iff05]. Therefore, the performance does not always decrease if instructions are added. In contrast, for the NVIDIA FX5800Ultra—besides the lower overall performance—the measurements show a nearly constant delay added for each additional texture or arithmetic instruction.

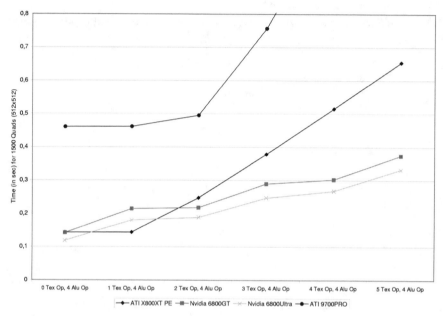

FIGURE 8.6.7   *Four ALU instructions after a varying number of texture instructions.*

The S3 Delta Chrome card shows also a constant increase in execution time for every ALU instruction added. In general, the S3 card is slightly faster than the FX5800Ultra if two texture instructions are executed, but still both cards are roughly five to 10 times slower than an ATI X800XT PE or a NVIDIA 6800Ultra. If the number of texture instructions is increased from zero to three in combination with four arithmetic instructions, the DeltaChrome GPU shows the same performance for all combinations. The Volari card did not produce comparable measurements in this test, as the values show a performance of only about 40% of the S3 DeltaChrome V8. However, the measurements indicate a similar behavior as the NVIDIA 5800Ultra: both a texture and an arithmetic instruction add a constant delay.

Efficiency of Single- and Multiple-Render Targets

In general, the output of a rendering pass is stored in the frame buffer. To further process the result in a subsequent render pass, the frame buffer values are often transferred to a texture that is read by following shader programs in later passes. To speed up this data transfer, DirectX offers the possibility to redirect the output of a rendering pass into a texture. This so-called render target can thereby support arbitrary, as well as high dynamic range, formats, dependent on the GPU. Furthermore, DirectX specifies multiple simultaneous render targets to which a shader program can independently write its data. These are called multiple render targets (MRTs).

Estimating the performance of MRTs is very hard, because it depends on at least the following factors: number of components per target, type of components (integer or float), number of bits per component, and number of targets. On an ATI 9700PRO, four render targets where each has two 32-bit float components are almost 40% faster than two render targets configured with four 32-bit float components, although the precision and the number of values that are finally stored are exactly the same. This is no longer true for the X800 series, but other things could be noticed: rendering to two targets each with one 16-bit float component is as fast as rendering to two targets each with two 16-bit float components. Another example is that a setup with four two-component 16-bit integer render targets is nearly twice as fast as two targets with four 16-bit float components. But overall, it can be said that using more targets is in most cases slower than packing the values into fewer targets. A more interesting fact is that since the 9x00 class, ATI hardware already somehow seems to implement a write cache—at least the measured results indicate such a technology. Figure 8.6.8 shows the performance for two different render-target (RT) formats—A8R8G8B and A16B16G16R16.

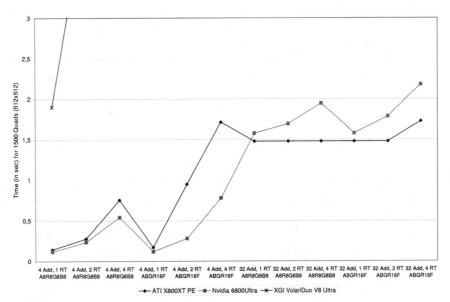

FIGURE 8.6.8   *Execution time for shaders using multiple render targets.*

When using render targets to write a huge amount of data per fragment, bandwidth memory for the shader can easily become limited because the data cannot be written to the graphics memory fast enough. In this situation, the performance of the GPU cannot fully be utilized because the fragment processor is stalled until the data is written to the graphic memory. Optimizing shaders that experience this behavior by reducing instructions is no cure, only a reduction of the amount of data written out can increase the speed of such shaders. This might happen only if small, fast shaders are executed; in contrast, when using large shaders the performance is limited by the arithmetic and texture units of the GPU plus an additional delay for storing the shader result to the render target. For this case, ATI implemented a cache to temporarily store the shader result and start working on the remaining fragments that need to be processed. While processing further fragments, the results of previous fragments can be stored to the render target. Therewith, slow shaders with much data output are limited by exactly their execution time; no further delay is added due to storing the data. The highest performance of the GPU can be achieved whenever the execution time of the shader program nearly reaches the limit of the memory bandwidth. On the tested X800XT PE, a shader that writes to four targets, each with four 8-bit components, can roughly use 16 instructions without a performance penalty. If a program fills four targets with 16-bit, four-component values, then shaders with up to 32 instructions are still memory limited. Notice that the number of instructions mentioned only provides a rough estimation. The exact number of instructions to match the memory bandwidth might differ because modern GPUs interleave instructions and execute different instructions for the value components in parallel.

Based on our measurements, we found no evidence that any NVIDIA graphic processor has a similar caching strategy—at least it is less noticeable. This fact is verified by the measurements shown in Figure 8.6.8. The used shader executes the same amount of instructions independently of the number of render targets by writing the final result in the render target 0. Therefore, the total time spent to evaluate the shader program through the arithmetic units should be the same. We think that the reason why a shader with a higher amount of data output is delayed comes from the fact that the memory write operation is not efficiently cached. A related problem is that—at least on the tested driver—the GPUs from NVIDIA statically divide the available memory bandwidth for each render target by the number of active render targets. Therefore, multi-pass algorithms where different numbers of render targets are used per pass must deactivate the unused render target in order to utilize the entire memory bandwidth. Because of the unbuffered memory writes, shaders cannot reach the memory bandwidth limit as on ATI hardware. So, optimizing shaders on NVIDIA hardware is easy: reduce the number of instructions and reduce the amount of data output—both directly result in a speedup of the shader.

The measurements on the XGI VolariDuo V8 Ultra card indicate that the shader outputs are buffered to a certain amount. Therefore, only a small delay is added to the total arithmetic execution time of the shaders. XGI supports only a maximum of 32 bits—divided in up to four components—to be written out per target. The performance on this card can easily be predicted by the number of render targets used; that is, writing out four 16-bit float values to four targets is as fast as writing four 32-bit values to four targets. Shaders with approximately eight instructions are still memory limited if two targets are used. When using four targets, shaders with up to 32 instructions are no longer limited by the memory bandwidth.

The S3 DeltaChrome S8 hardware does not support multiple render targets and—as in the Volari card—can only write a maximum of 32-bit values to the output. For each possible format—four components, 8-bit; two component, 16-bit; or one component, 32-bit—the performance is exactly the same.

Performance Beyond Pixel Shader 2.0

When measuring the performance of fragment processing units capable of more than Pixel Shader 2.0—that is, Pixel Shader 2.x and 3.0—many new aspects came into play: more arithmetic instructions (derivative, and so on), dynamic branching, loops, position register, face register, and predicate register. Most of these are a required feature for Pixel Shader 3.0. All features—number of instructions, available registers, and so on—of the Pixel Shader 2.0 standard are fixed. Some features of Pixel Shader 2.x and 3.0 are given by the capability bits of a device. Therefore, some devices support different "versions" of Pixel Shader 2.x. To handle this discrepancy in the High Level Shading Language (HLSL) two additional profiles were introduced: 2.a and 2.b. These are directly configured for the capabilities of the X800 series (profile 2.b) and the FX5x00 series (profile 2.a). When looking into the details, 2.b basically just increases the number of temporary registers up to 32 and the total number of instructions up to 512 for the fragment shader unit. Several tests with very large shaders using many registers showed no extra delay due to extra features used on ATI processors. On the other side, the 2.a profile extends Pixel Shader 2.0 only up to 22 registers and 512 instructions, but additional functionality, like evaluating derivatives and arbitrary swizzles, is supported. The measurements for NVIDIA FX5800Ultra are included in Figure 8.6.9. As on ATI, the number of instructions or number of registers did not show any obscure performance. The additional swizzles come in handy when programming shaders and are supported at the same speed as the Pixel Shader 2.0 swizzlse.

Graphic cards that support Pixel Shader model 3.0—for example, the NVIDIA 6800 series—also fully support the specified Pixel Shader 2.x features. This includes instructions for calling subroutines, loops, branching, and texture lookups with user-provided gradients. To evaluate the throughput of these commands, a reference program executing 16 *add* instructions was rewritten and retested multiple times using several methods to generate the same result. A shader with a loop that already executes 16 *add* instructions within the loop was terminated after the first iteration to measure the efficiency of the *break* command and its variants. The static and dynamic *if* instructions were tested using an if-else construct, where also 16 *add* commands were executed either in the true clause—shaders marked with (true)—or in the false clause—shaders marked with (false). The not measured clause was filled with a rather expensive program to see if the hardware can efficiently skip these instructions when evaluating the other clause. The performance of the Pixel Shader 2.x instruction set on several NVIDIA GPUs is illustrated in Figure 8.6.9.

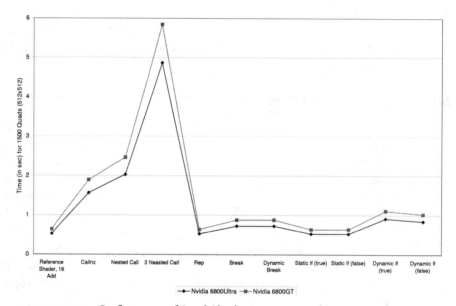

FIGURE 8.6.9   *Performance of Pixel Shader 2.x commands.*

The diagram points out that nested calls—calls within calls—can get rather expensive because each call adds an extra delay to the total execution time. Looping instructions via a *rep* command are as efficient as the rolled-out reference program. Static conditionals also seem to be free in execution time. In contrast, dynamic conditionals slightly decrease the performance; mysteriously, the 16 *add* shader executed faster when running in the false clause.

As all features of 2.x are included in Pixel Shader version 3.0, all measurements presented before were revisited but showed exactly the same performance. A new feature of the 3.0 version is a loop instruction with an additional loop counter and the possibility to index into input registers with this loop counter. We examined the *loop* instruction in the same way as the *rep* instruction of Pixel Shader version 2.x and found no differences in its performance. The relative addressing of the input registers is compared to a nonrelative addressing to figure out the additional costs. The measurements showed that accessing input registers via indexing is about half as fast as a direct access. However, an instruction sequence that simulates an indexing into input registers via compare instructions is much more expensive. The results for Pixel Shader 3.0 are summarized in Figure 8.6.10.

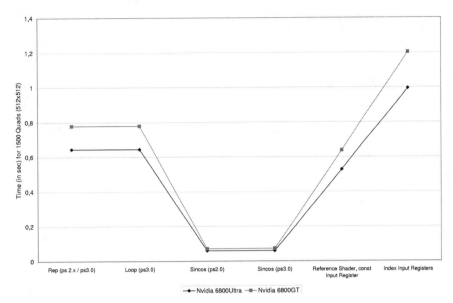

FIGURE 8.6.10 *Performance of Pixel Shader 3.0 instructions.*

Loops, Multiple Render Targets, and Multi-Pass Rendering

Multi-pass rendering—rendering the same geometry multiple times—can get very expensive for scenes with complex geometry. With the steady increasing power of the fragment units, it is often possible to convert multi-pass rendering algorithms to single-pass techniques. Loops in pixel shader programs increase the total instruction count dramatically: the NVIDIA 6800 GPU supports up to 65,535 instructions to be executed within a shader program. On the other hand, multiple render targets (MRTs) increase the amount of data that can be written out by a shader up to four times four 32-bit float values.

Using these features does not come for free as examined in the previous section. It basically depends on the algorithm. In contrast, multi-pass rendering has also some additional costs: the data generated in a previous pass has to be reloaded via a texture fetch, and after the execution the result has to be written in the GPU memory to be used in subsequent passes. In some cases, the texture lookup to read back previous calculated data can be replaced by an alpha-blending setup, so the costs of these multi-pass techniques are less. All three alternatives are used to execute a code with 375 mixed instructions; (for the measurements the number of quads rendered was reduced to 300) the results are shown in Figure 8.6.11.

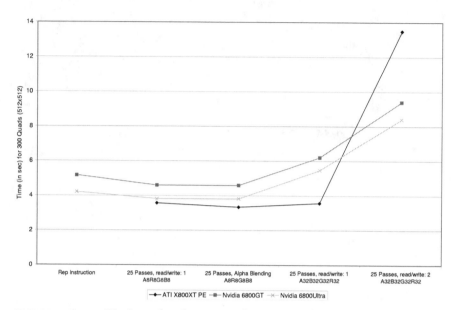

FIGURE 8.6.11   *Timings of multi-pass rendering versus loop instruction.*

Notice that the results are only valid if the geometry is very limited—two triangles in this case—and the data that has to be transferred is no more than four 32-bit values.

A similar comparison was set up for evaluating the advantage of multiple render targets versus multiple rendering passes. If multi-pass rendering is applied to replace multiple render targets, the performance strongly depends on the amount of calculations that have to be redone for each pass.

Based on our measurements for the NVIDIA 6800 hardware, we come to the conclusion that multi-pass techniques that need to recalculate more than about six instructions are already slower than algorithms that utilize multiple render targets. In contrast, ATI hardware of the X800 class seems to be faster using multiple render targets independently of the number of instructions that need to be redone within each pass.

Performance of Per-Fragment Frame-Buffer Operations

Programming a GPU is often used synonymously for programming a vertex or pixel shader. But, in fact, graphic processors also have other possibilities that influence the final result of a pixel in the frame buffer. Alpha blending, alpha test, and stencil test are the most significant operations in this part of the graphics pipeline. We call these operations per-fragment frame-buffer operations because they are executed on a per-fragment basis, and often data originating from the frame buffer is involved in the calculations. Often, these functions are crucial for implementing algorithms on GPUs.

Therefore, when talking about performance on the fragment level, it is also important to consider the throughput after the fragment shader unit; that is, where operations like alpha blending, alpha test, or stencil test take place.

The measurements indicate that only for some GPUs the performance of alpha blending depends on its setup configuration. These are either the GPUs that are equipped with a slow memory interface or use a shared memory technology; for example, the NVIDIA 6200Go TC. Some configurations are faster than others: the basic rule seems to be that whenever the alpha values—or more severe the color value—of the destination are needed to evaluate the blending equation, the setup tends to be a little slower. Notice that nearly every useful blending setup needs the alpha and/or color value of the destination in some sense. Figure 8.6.12 presents the measurements for some alpha-blending configurations.

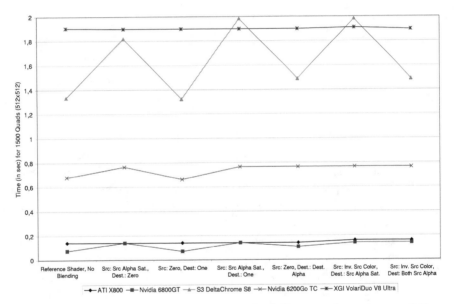

FIGURE 8.6.12   *Alpha-blending throughput for different configurations on different graphic cards.*

For testing the alpha blending, a standard 8-bit RGBA frame-buffer configuration was used. For more advanced effects—especially for high dynamic range renderings—a higher precision for the blending is required. The NVIDIA 6800 series supports alpha blending in 16-bit precision. The performance of the 6800GT GPU in contrast to 8-bit blending is shown in Figure 8.6.13.

It can be seen that blending on 16-bit precision is clearly slower than on 8-bit targets. When 16-bit values are blended, NVIDIA GPUs also receive some speed penalties for extreme blending modes; for example, when source color and destination color are used as blend weights.

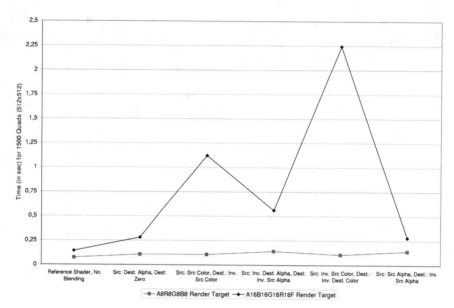

FIGURE 8.6.13 *Alpha blending with 8- and 16-bit precision on the NVIDIA 6800GT hardware.*

Besides blending, alpha values can also be used as a comparison function to discard or accept fragments. The performance of this so-called alpha test was evaluated for all available alpha-test comparison functions by setting up the alpha-test parameters and applying a shader that writes out a constant alpha of 0.5. Each configuration was measured when it evaluates to true and again with a setup where it evaluates to false. The measurements show that there is practically no speed impact when enabling the alpha test, although we were able to identify very slight performance increases if the alpha test discarded the fragments.

Finally, the performance of different stencil-buffer configurations was examined. The test is divided into two categories: performance of stencil value modifiers—that is, replace stencil, increment stencil, zero stencil, and so on—and expenses of the different stencil functions; for example, greater, equal, or not equal. For the first part, a very simple pixel shader that just copies the texture coordinate to the final color was executed while the stencil function was set to *always*. This way, every fragment that is rendered triggers the stencil operation to modify the stencil buffer value. The timings for different modifiers are illustrated in Figure 8.6.14. Additionally, the execution time for the used shader with a deactivated stencil test was taken to serve as reverence time.

In the measurements, most GPUs did not show any noticeable speed impact. However, for stencil modifiers that result in a memory read, modify, write sequence—for example, increment or invert—the NVIDIA 6200Go TurboCache card has some disadvantages that possibly originate form the nonlocal video memory of this graphic processor.

For the second part of the stencil test, one shader is always used to write a specific stencil value in the stencil buffer, and afterwards, in a second pass, a shader uses dif-

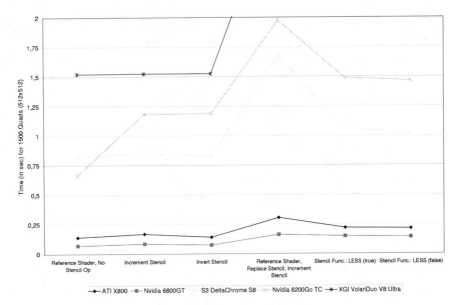

FIGURE 8.6.14 *Stencil-buffer modifiers on various graphic processors.*

ferent stencil functions to process the stencil value written in the first pass. Every setup was tested twice: first, the setup was chosen to evaluate the stencil function to true; second; with a setup where the stencil function evaluates to false and discards the fragments. All tested graphic cards processed all functions without any measurable performance difference. Only marginal speed improvements can be noticed whenever the fragments are discarded, except for the FX5800Ultra, where all functions took exactly the same amount of time.

Conclusion

The measurements illustrated that the power of fragment shaders—concerning functionality and performance—increased dramatically with each new GPU generation. In combination with the results presented in *ShaderX³*—where exclusively arithmetic and texture performance were examined—this article presented an evaluation on the entire fragment-processing performance within graphic processors. This includes fragment shaders, render targets, alpha blending, alpha test, and stencil test.

Our previous article closed with the statement that shaders were optimized whenever arithmetic calculations can be replaced by a single texture lookup. This statement is now only partially correct, as can be verified via, for example, looking at the *sincos* command on NVIDIA hardware. If multiple arithmetic instructions are replaced by a texture access, most shaders end up faster, but lookups also can get expensive when using large textures with a high precision. GPUs have an enormous memory bandwidth to efficiently handle textures, but it is still easy to reach the limit with a shader program. Therefore, one has to think of the available memory bandwidth—especially on graphic processors with a limited memory interface—and find an optimal mixture of arithmetic and texture instructions in order to get the highest possible performance. In some cases, the scheduling of the different instruction types can be further improved if algorithms are redesigned to utilize texture instructions instead of arithmetic instructions or vice versa.

Another situation where the memory bandwidth can be the limiting factor are render targets or even multiple render targets with high precision values. On today's GPUs, shaders can generate an output of up to 512 bits per fragment. Fast shaders that generate huge amounts of data even surpass the throughput of fast memory interfaces as, for example, implemented on an ATI X800XT PE. This results in memory bandwidth-limited shaders that can only be optimized by restricting the output data. For many multi-pass algorithms, there is another way to overcome memory bandwidth restriction that might occur between passes as seen in, for example, [Stegmaier05] Pixel Shader 2.x/3.0 loop instructions allow to compact multiple rendering passes into a single-pass algorithm.

Processing units executed after the pixel shader—alpha blending, alpha test, or stencil test—are in most cases practically for free, except for 16-bit alpha blending. Most GPUs even receive a slight speedup if fragments are discarded by these so-called post-pixel shader operations.

Overall, we believe that for efficient pixel shader codes, one has to balance the workload of arithmetic units and memory bandwidth. We expect that this ratio will further drift to the favor of arithmetic instructions on upcoming graphic processing units.

References

[Diepstraten04] Diepstraten, Joachim, and Mike Eißele, "In-Depth Performance Analyses of DirectX 9 Shading Hardware Concerning Pixel Shader and Texture Performance," *ShaderX³—Advanced Rendering with DirectX and OpenGL*, edited by Wolfgang Engel, Charles River Media, 2004: pp. 523–545.

[Epic04] Epic Games Inc., "Unreal Engine 3," available online at *http://www.unreal-technology.com/*, Unreal Technology, 2004.

[Kilgariff05] Kilgariff, E., and R. Fernando, "The GeForce 6 Series GPU Architecture," *GPU Gems 2—Programming Techniques for High-Performance Graphics and General-Purpose Computation*, edited by Matt Pharr, Addison Wesley, 2005: pp. 471–491.

[NVIDIA05] NVIDIA Corporation, "NVIDIA GPU Programming Guide," Revision: 2.3.0, NVIDIA Corporation, 2005.

[Riguer02] Riguer, Guennadi, "Performance Optimization Techniques for ATI Graphics Hard-ware with DirectX 9.0", whitepaper, available online at *http://www.ati.com/developer/*, ATI Technologies, 2002.

[Stegmaier05] Stegmaier, Simon, Magnus Strengert, Thomas Klein, Thomas Ertl, "A Simple and Flexible Volume Rendering Framework for Graphics-Hardware-based Raycasting," in *Proceedings of the International Workshop on Volume Graphics*, The Eurographics Association, 2005: pp. 187–195.

About the CD-ROM

The CD-ROM contains the example programs and source that accompanies the various articles, along with demos where applicable. The directory structure closely follows the book structure by using the chapter number as the name of the subdirectory. To use the files, you need to have (or download) the DirectX 9 June 2005 update SDK.

General System Requirements

To use all of the files on the CD-ROM, you will need:

- The DirectX 9 June 2005 update SDK
- OpenGL 1.5-compatible graphics card
- A DirectX 8, 8.1, or 9.0-compatible graphics card
- Windows XP with the latest service pack
- Visual C++ .NET 2003
- Some require Visual Studio C/C++ 6.0
- 512 MB RAM
- 500 MB of free space on your hard drive
- Pentium IV/ATHLON with more than 1.5 GHz
- The latest graphics card drivers

Updates

Updates of the example programs will be available on *www.shaderx4.com* and on *www.charlesriver.com*.

Comments, Suggestions?

Please send any comments or suggestions to *wolf@shaderx.com*.

INDEX